Bent Wood and Metal Furniture: 1850–1946

Bent Wood and Metal Furniture: 1850–1946

EDITED BY DEREK E. OSTERGARD

TEXT BY ALESSANDRO ALVERÀ / GRAHAM DRY / ROBERT KEIL /
DEREK E. OSTERGARD / CHRISTOPHER WILK / CHRISTIAN WITT-DÖRRING

The University of Washington Press
The American Federation of Arts

The American Federation of Arts wishes to acknowledge the important contribution of Alexander von Vegesack who initially proposed the concept of an exhibition of this material and provided continuous support throughout its development. We are particularly grateful to him for his assistance in Europe in locating key loans, assuming diverse administrative responsibilities, contributing to the fund-raising effort, and generously lending to the exhibition.

This book has been published in conjunction with the exhibition Bent Wood and Metal Furniture: 1850–1946, which was organized by the American Federation of Arts and curated by Derek E. Ostergard. The exhibition and publication have been supported by the National Endowment for the Arts, the Mabel Pew Myrin Trust, the National Patrons of the AFA, Lufthansa German Airlines, and the Foreign Office of the Federal Republic of Germany and the Institute for Foreign Cultural Relations, Stuttgart, West Germany. The publication has been additionally supported by The J. M. Kaplan Fund and the DeWitt Wallace Fund through the American Federation of Arts's Revolving Fund for Publications.

The American Federation of Arts is a national nonprofit educational organization, founded in 1909 to broaden the knowledge and appreciation of the arts of the past and present. Its primary activities are the organization of exhibitions which travel throughout the United States and abroad and the fostering of a better understanding among nations by the international exchange of art.

Design by Betty Binns Graphics/
Betty Binns and David Skolkin
Composition by
U.S. Lithograph, typographers
Manufactured by South Sea International
Press Ltd., Hong Kong

Participating institutions

IBM GALLERY OF SCIENCE AND ART,
NEW YORK, NEW YORK

THE NELSON-ATKINS MUSEUM OF ART,
KANSAS CITY, MISSOURI

MILWAUKEE ART MUSEUM,
MILWAUKEE, WISCONSIN

TAMPA MUSEUM OF ART,
TAMPA, FLORIDA

THE BALTIMORE MUSEUM OF ART,
BALTIMORE, MARYLAND

INDIANAPOLIS MUSEUM OF ART,
INDIANAPOLIS, INDIANA

FLINT INSTITUTE OF ART,
FLINT, MICHIGAN

CENTER FOR THE FINE ARTS,
MIAMI, FLORIDA

THE CLEVELAND MUSEUM OF ART,
CLEVELAND, OHIO

© 1987 The American Federation of Arts

Published by The American Federation of Arts
41 East 65th Street, New York, New York 10021

LCC 36-0716773 ISBN: 0–295–96409–x

AFA Exhibition 85-50

Circulated September 1986–October 1988

Clothbound edition published by the University of Washington Press in association with the American Federation of Arts.

Contents

Foreword

AS is so often the case, the original concept for an exhibition undergoes myriad changes as it develops. The idea for a bent-wood and bent-metal furniture exhibition was first proposed to the American Federation of Arts in 1982 by Alexander von Vegesack, a knowledgeable collector and exhibition organizer on this subject. During his many years of personal research and collecting, he has acquired a wealth of information on the subject and established many contacts with public and private collectors and institutions throughout Europe and the United States. Concurrent with the AFA project he was involved with numerous exhibitions of this material and was instrumental in the formation of several public collections, most importantly the Museum der Stadt in Boppard am Rhein, West Germany, the birthplace of pioneer craftsman and designer Michael Thonet.

Christopher Wilk, assistant curator of decorative arts at the Brooklyn Museum, was next to join the project. He participated in several organizational meetings with Mr. von Vegesack and the AFA and was to act as the exhibition's guest curator. However, Mr. Wilk's commitments and obligations at the museum forced his reconsideration of the position, and he suggested we invite Derek E. Ostergard, Adjunct Professor for the Parsons School of Design/Cooper-Hewitt Museum Masters Program in the History of the Decorative Arts, to take on the curatorial responsibilities of the exhibition and publication. Mr. Wilk remained as consultant to the exhibition and contributed an essay to this publication.

It is primarily to these three individuals that we owe our special gratitude. Mr. von Vegesack remained fully committed to the project and generously assisted on many of its aspects. Acting as European coordinator, he was instrumental in locating key loans and following through on difficult negotiations, which many times consumed major portions of his busy personal schedule. He was always at our service, no matter what the request, and we are particularly appreciative of his work in securing a generous subvention from the Cultural Affairs Office of the West German Government and Lufthansa German Airlines. His "hands-on" assistance with this as well as with other aspects proved invaluable.

We are indebted to Mr. Wilk not only for his foresight in recommending Mr. Ostergard, but for his continued support and professional guidance. Mr. Wilk's overall knowledge of the material and established curatorial expertise and background provided a secure foundation during many of the early stages of the project and throughout its frequent, seemingly endless review processes.

To Mr. Ostergard, guest curator, we are specially grateful. His enthusiasm, determination, unrelenting attention to detail, and pursuit of accuracy expanded the original concept of the exhibition into a project that will for the first time focus on the entire body of work and its collective impact on and contributions to the history of furniture. In addition to selecting and negotiating loans for the exhibition, Mr. Ostergard acted as curatorial editor for the publication, contributed an essay, and wrote the catalogue entries. His task was not an easy one and, to his credit, he remained enthusiastic and, most of all, resilient through the many arduous tasks and unforeseen setbacks.

There are many other individuals to whom we extend our sincere thanks for their contributions to this publication, beginning with the distinguished group of authors who, in addition to Mr. Ostergard and Mr. Wilk, provided essays: Alessandro Alverà, a practicing architect from Vienna; Graham Dry, an art historian working in Munich; Robert Keil, a social historian from Vienna; and Christian Witt-Dörring, Assistant Director, the Austrian Museum of Applied Arts in Vienna. Special consideration is due Mr. Wilk and Dr. Dry for their assistance in Europe, and for the encouragement, cooperation, and expert advice afforded both the AFA and Mr. Ostergard during the planning, editing, and production of this book.

We wish to thank Irene Gordon for her initial editorial work on this assignment. The major task of editing could not have been completed without Barbara Einzig who helped to shape Dr. Alverà's and Dr. Witt-Dörring's essays and Martina D'Alton who not only edited Dr. Keil's essay and the catalogue entries, but undertook the responsibility of finalizing the editorial project and worked closely with the designer through the production schedule.

Many persons provided English translations of source material, and we wish to thank Matt Ward, Eliot Mitchell, Vera Pitcher, Pavel Filip, among others. In particular, we wish to recognize the contributions of Martha Humphreys, Camilo Antonio, and Franz Prüller for their translations of three of the main chapters.

We would also like to acknowledge Dana Levy and Letitia O'Connor of Perpetua Press; Donald Ellegood of the University of Washington Press; and Victoria Scott, Berenice Hoffman, and Joan Agranoff for their support and contributions. To Betty Binns and David Skolkin we are deeply appreciative for undertaking the major task of designing and producing this book and for providing such a thorough and handsome document of this project. We owe thanks to Sophie-Renate Gnamm, Richard P. Goodbody, and countless other photographers whose services we engaged throughout Europe and the United States.

If one were to compare the production of this publication with that of a full-length feature film, several individuals would certainly have walked away from the award ceremonies with trophies. The diligent and patient assistance of Marianne Lamonaca Loggia and Nina Stritzler was unparalleled by others with similar supporting roles. Their interest and enthusiasm, along with a strong work ethic and absolute commitment to the project, were unmatched. Together with Ruth Mayberry, who helped to shape and direct an exhausting design schedule, they functioned as a team without which this publication might not have been completed.

At the American Federation of Arts, we wish to express our particular appreciation to Jeffery J. Pavelka, Director, Exhibition Program, for overseeing the very complex organizational and administrative aspects of the project. Other current and former AFA staff to whom we are grateful for valuable contributions include: Jane S. Tai, Associate Director; Amy McEwen, Exhibition Coordinator and Schedulor; Albina De Meio, Registrar; Guillermo Alonso, Associate Registrar; Sandra Gilbert, Public Relations Director; and Teri Roiger and Konrad G. Kuchel, Exhibition Assistant and Loans Coordinator respectively. For their varied skills and support we are grateful to Mary Ann Monet, Michaelyn Bush, Laura Nierenberg, Dagmar Huguenin, and Jennifer Dalsimer.

No exhibition of this scope and importance is possible without substantial financial support. We are deeply indebted to the initial generous grants from the National Endowment for the Arts and the Mabel Pew Myrin Trust. Additional support was provided by the Foreign Office of the Federal Republic of Germany and the Institute for Foreign Cultural Relations, Stuttgart, West Germany; Lufthansa German Airlines; Goethe House, New York, and its branch institutes across the United States; and the National Patrons of the American Federation of Arts. We also wish to express our appreciation to The J. M. Kaplan Fund and the DeWitt Wallace Fund for their support of the American Federation of Arts's Revolving Fund for Publications.

Finally, we are extremely grateful to all the lenders, institutional and private, foreign and domestic, whose generosity has so enriched the exhibition and publication.

WILDER GREEN
Director
The American Federation of Arts

Introduction

THIS catalogue and its accompanying exhibition comprise the first comprehensive examination of furnishings made from materials that have been bent. Historically, the process of bending not only enhanced the structural stability of a design but also allowed for the most economical use of materials and manpower. Commercially, the reductivist nature of the process lowered the cost of construction and gave bent wood and metal furnishings a competitive edge over designs made by more conventional, laborious means—with elements that had been cut, carved, or cast, and then joined. The ultimate success of the bending process occurred after the middle of the nineteenth century, when through mass production bent-wood furnishings flooded the market. Durable, inexpensive, and often aesthetically distinctive, these furnishings became leitmotifs of the industrial age. Eventually, their enormous popularity made

them ubiquitous, even anonymous fixtures within society. As a result, they have been resurrected in surveys in recent years merely as minor appendages to larger historic periods, when in fact they possess their own rich traditions, setting them apart from other kinds of furnishings. This catalogue explores these traditions and relates them to the fabric of a rapidly changing society, dating from the mid-nineteenth to the mid-twentieth century.

Despite the revolutionary changes that the bending process underwent through mechanization, the innovation itself is deeply rooted in the past. "Before Industrialization: Bent Wood and Metal in the Hands of the Craftsman," the first essay in the catalogue, examines the breadth of craft traditions and the bending process, prior to its industrialization in the mid-nineteenth century. Unsubstantiated evidence suggests that as early as dynastic Egypt (ca. 2500 B.C.), some furnishings may have been fabricated from this imaginative process. Nearly two thousand years later, the classic Greek Klismos chair was introduced as a furniture form; some scholars believe that the graceful form of the chair's sabre legs was achieved through the bending process.

In addition, the bending of metal, specifically iron, when forged into a designated form, is a technique that has been deeply ingrained into society for millenia. The freestanding pieces of wrought-iron furniture as well as the wrought-iron mounts of case pieces dating from the Middle Ages must be viewed as vital components of this extended tradition. The case pieces in particular would not have survived decades of atmospheric changes and considerable use had they not been secured with bent-metal mounts.

In the eighteenth century, the employment of the bending process expanded dramatically in terms of sophisticated methodologies and widespread societal use. The Windsor chair displayed the most expressive use of bent-wood elements during this time. The other expressions of bent-wood methods were more discreet in appearance than the Windsor chair—an indication that their makers were more concerned with the economical replication of mainstream aesthetics than the bold display of an innovative means of production. The bending process, used as a gesture of economy, satisfied the needs of certain craftsmen until their efforts were eclipsed by the machine.

The greater portion of the catalogue is devoted to those designs that evolved after the industrialization of the bending process. The simplification of form permitted by the bending process fostered an increased use of standardized elements that revolutionized principles of furniture construction. This new approach to furniture making was most successfully developed by German-born Michael Thonet, a craftsman by training. Dissatisfied with traditional principles of construction and the limitations of the shop environment, Thonet introduced the bending process into the sector of the factory and translated shop production into mass production. In "Michael Thonet and the Development of Bent-Wood Furniture: From Workshop to Factory Production," Alessandro Alverà traces Thonet's unraveling of the complicated technical properties of wood, his ex-

ploration of the limits of its flexibility, and his development of a new body of design whose appeal extended beyond mere novelty. The primary importance of Thonet's contribution to the history of bent-wood furnishings is evident in his minimalist approach to the technical components of a design. That his often irreducible designs evolved from the production process reveals an integration of design and production rarely achieved by his peers.

Essential to an understanding of Thonet's genius is his development of the Model Number 14 chair, the most popular design manufactured in the nineteenth century. Through an examination of five different versions of this model, Dr. Alverà illustrates the subtle technical and aesthetic changes introduced in the original design to simplify the manufacturing process—a primary technical and commercial consideration. The phenomenal success of the bent-wood furniture industry rests in part on the abstracts of these experiments.

By the last quarter of the nineteenth century, the bent-wood furniture industry was dominated by two enormous firms—Gebrüder Thonet and Jacob & Josef Kohn. The unassailed primacy of these two companies has obscured the many small, contemporary firms also engaged in the production of bent-wood furniture. In "The Development of the Bent-Wood Furniture Industry," Graham Dry takes a strong revisionist approach to the history of the industry that emerged overnight once Thonet's patent for the bending of wood had expired in 1869. With the end of the patent came the end of Thonet's monopoly in this highly lucrative market.

By concentrating on the history of firms outside the Thonet and Kohn sphere, Dr. Dry has re-established the extent of the creative and economic forces within this industry. His examination of the small, little-known firms focuses on their histories, their participation in national and international design exhibitions, and the exchange of aesthetic and technical concepts, frequently no more than undisguised theft. In his discussion of early twentieth-century circumstances within the industry, Dr. Dry also broadens former perceptions of this period by including the work of notable German architect-designers who were not of the dominant Viennese school, but who also worked in bent wood. Peter Behrens,

Richard Riemerschmid, and Hans Reinstein are among those who must now be included in future studies. Finally Dr. Dry reattributes several design icons of the period, making a valuable contribution to the field, and, in the appendix, has compiled a list of bent-wood furniture firms prior to World War I.

In "Bent Wood Production and the Viennese Avant-Garde: Thonet Brothers and J. & J. Kohn, 1899–1914," Christian Witt-Dörring examines the vital regeneration of the Viennese design community at the turn of the century. This revitalization was almost immediately exploited by the bent-wood furniture industry, particularly by J. & J. Kohn, a firm invested with an innate understanding of consumer needs. Many individuals who produced furniture designs for Kohn have been overlooked in the light of the achievements of such luminaries as Josef Hoffmann and Otto Wagner. Gustav Siegal and Marcel Kammerer now emerge as figures worthy of further consideration.

More important, however, is Dr. Witt-Dörring's interpretation of the currently perceived value of these designs in relation to their original worth. He diffuses the considerable emphasis on bent-wood furnishings known as "Secessionist," an appellation they did not bear at the turn of the century. The canonization of these designs in recent years by historians has obscured the way in which they were originally perceived. By determining responsibility for that circumstance, Dr. Witt-Dörring charts the critical and commercial motivations of recent years for making this transformation. By examining many of the attitudes and perspectives of early twentieth-century Vienna, instead of those of the present era, he offers an analysis of the rapid intellectualization and aesthetic development of bent-wood furnishings. He provides new insights into this body of designs, enabling them to be more clearly understood as the continuance of a nineteenth-century tradition.

Christopher Wilk's essay, "Furnishing the Future: Bent-Wood and Metal Furniture: 1925–1946," charts the development of innovative furniture design after World War I. At that time, a general stagnation plagued the bent-wood furniture industry through a widespread reliance upon outmoded technologies and materials. Mr. Wilk explores the revolution that occurred in furniture design and production after the bending process was transferred from wood to tubular steel. Suddenly, seemingly overnight, previously unattainable forms and concepts in furniture design became realities. Mr. Wilk focuses on the role that architecture and architects played in the development of new furniture. With their increasing concern for social goals rather than individual expressive statements, architects thrust bent wood and metal furniture design into the vanguard of societal reform. Mr. Wilk examines the ideological postures bestowed on progressive furniture at that time as well as the impact that art movements, and design schools, exhibitions, and publications had upon design.

By the early 1930s, wood, denigrated by many progressive architects and designers as archaic and inappropriate to the needs of the new concrete and steel architecture of the late 1920s, reemerged as a materials alternative. This reinstatement of wood was due, in part, to technological innovations in the production of laminated wood. Increased stability and strength in this material permitted innovations in furniture design —most importantly, the cantilevered form, which had been unattainable in bent, solid wood, and the curved, sweeping sheets of plywood that dispensed with the need for upholstered seats and backs, a restatement of the earlier reductivist principles of Michael Thonet.

The broader impact of bent wood and metal furniture upon the consumer is the subject of Robert Keil's essay, "The Social and Cultural Context of Bent Wood and Metal Furniture." These mass-produced furnishings were turned out in vast quantities and at remarkably low prices. They were readily incorporated into society at a dramatic rate, even though they had no substantial antecedents in Western Europe before the mid-nineteenth century. Yet despite their low cost and wide availability, it remains a source of debate whether such furnishings ever made their way into the homes of the poor, at least as new purchases.

Through an examination of housing statistics compiled by various urban governments, Dr. Keil has established that circumstances of the growing urban poor could not have accommodated the new furnishings for numerous reasons, and these furnishings appear to have remained outside the realm of the poor until well into the twentieth century. They were more often found in cafés—those large public environments that were a by-product of the Industrial Revolution and the increased affluence and leisure time it created for the privileged—or in the private homes of the financially and later intellectually advantaged. While bent wood and metal furniture had an impact upon society, the needs of society were correspondingly engineered into the designs. This is evidenced by such sales catalogue offerings as rocking chaises, walking sticks, fancifully contorted chairs, and music and magazine racks or other accoutrements for leisure-time activities.

While the essays deal with the broader issues of bent wood and metal furniture, the catalogue entries examine the historical, aesthetic, and, wherever possible, technological components of the individual pieces selected for the exhibition. Many of the entries also discuss connoisseurship, a subject rarely dealt with in the field of mass-produced furnishings dating from after the middle of the nineteenth century. Connoisseurship proved to be an essential consideration when selecting many of these objects, which were produced over an extended period of time by many manufacturers. Modifications were often introduced into these designs in order to accommodate either the manufacturing process or the taste of the marketplace. In many such instances, the alterations were inaugurated without the control or approval of the original designer, thereby making the earlier production models closer to the designer's original concept. The pursuit of these earlier examples has been of the utmost importance to the scope of this exhibition; these objects should be considered barometers of quality, to be used by institutions and individuals endeavoring to collect in this area.

In presenting such a comprehensive history for the first time, the authors consulted primary sources whenever possible in order to avoid the misconceptions and myths that have plagued this field since its emergence nearly twenty years ago. However, even when consulting primary sources, contradictions have arisen, and editorially they have been preserved in this catalogue and footnoted when necessary. All sources have been gathered in the bibliography but are cited in the reference notes at the end of each essay. These notes use a short-

ened form of citation with the full reference given in the bibliography. (For a further explanation of the arrangement of source material and the keying of reference notes, see page one of the bibliography.)

The term *bentwood*, a closed compound adjective, is relatively new but has come into common usage. However, because there is no equivalent adjective designating metal that has been bent, we have chosen to adopt the old usage. "Bent wood" and "bent metal" are the noun forms; hyphenated versions are used as compound adjectives—"bent-wood" and "bent-metal"—except when the two are combined into a single adjective, in which case they become "bent wood and metal" as in the title of this book. We apologize for any initial confusion this may cause the reader, but we do feel that ultimately this is a more accurate use of terminology.

The illustrations in the essays are numbered according to chapter. In the catalogue section, the main photograph of the piece carries the same number as the exhibition and catalogue entry. Auxiliary figures are assigned figure numbers amended with A, B, and so on.

In both the essays and the catalogue section, certain figures have been repeated to illustrate points made in the text by the different authors. This was done to spare the reader the many cross references that would otherwise have been necessary. Where such a repeat figure is of an actual piece in the exhibition, the caption includes a reference to the piece and the reader is referred to that catalogue entry for further information.

In the assembly of such a large catalogue and exhibition, many people have made important contributions and should be thanked for their efforts. Two individuals in particular have been intimately associated with the project from start to finish: in Europe, Alexander von Vegesack, and in the United States, Christopher Wilk. Mr. von Vegesack presented the original idea for an exhibition of bent wood and metal furniture, was persistent in his search for European funding, and assisted with research and the securing of loans. Mr. Wilk, after passing the position of chief curator and general editor on to me, provided patient and loyal support and continued to place his considerable expertise and advice at my disposal throughout the project.

At the American Federation of Arts, Jeffery Pavelka, as the exhibition coordinator, provided all the numerous support systems which finally helped the project to materialize. His calm demeanor and substantial experience were absolutely essential to the final success of *Bent Wood and Metal Furniture*.

Late to the project, but no less important, Ruth Mayberry organized the enormous body of details that went into the making of this book. Her stewardship through its most pressured moments and meticulous attention to detail were responsible for its completion, and her loyalty has been most appreciated

Marianne Lamonaca Loggia and Nina Stritzler are responsible for the catalogue's final accuracy. From the earliest days, Ms. Loggia was the consummate curatorial assistant; her pursuit of accuracy and cohesiveness are assets that have been made tangible in the published work. She also served as a proofreader and more importantly as photography editor, supervising the location of hundreds of illustrations and securing publishing rights. Ms. Stritzler's research and work on the bibliography and glossary have helped to make the catalogue all the more substantial. Her own knowledge of twentieth-century design made her an invaluable proofreader as well.

Also at the AFA, Amy McEwen played a particularly important role; her kind persistence and belief in this project were responsible for placing the exhibition in so many museums of high caliber throughout the United States. Albina De Meio, with the able assistance of Guillermo Alonso, assembled the exhibition material from the United States and Europe and undertook the preparation and care of these objects. Numerous other individuals at the AFA provided considerable help: Wilder Green, Jane Tai, Sandra Gilbert, Mary Ann Monet, and Charles Springman.

A catalogue of this scope and complexity requires much editorial help. I am grateful to Irene Gordon for her assistance in the early stages of the project. Martina D'Alton shepherded the catalogue from manuscript to press, keeping it on schedule and providing a focus. Her cheerful demeanor and professional standards have made this a pleasant project. Barbara Einzig edited two of the essays with considerable sensitivity and insight into the authors' concepts, working from translations from the German. The translations of original texts were made by Camilo Antonio, Franz Prüller, and Martha Humphreys.

Richard P. Goodbody and Sophie-Renate Gnamm made careful photographs of the pieces in the exhibition for this catalogue. Betty Binns and David Skolkin conceived of and executed a book design flexible enough to accommodate a wide range of images.

There have been many others who have helped with the project, and to them all I am most grateful. In the United States, those associated with museums and collections are: Milo M. Naeve, Lynn Springer Roberts, Art Institute of Chicago; Brenda Richardson, Baltimore Museum of Art; Ann Curtis, Caroline Mortimer, The Brooklyn Museum; Emmy Dana, Busch-Reisinger Museum, Harvard University; Henry H. Hawley, Cleveland Museum of Art; Margaret Luchars, Katherine Martinez, Kenneth Peters, Sarah A. Seggerman, Cooper-Hewitt Museum, Smithsonian Institution; Gillian Wilson, Carolyn Gay Nieda, J. Paul Getty Museum; Rudolph Colban, Charles Little, The Metropolitan Museum of Art; Christopher Monkhouse, Museum of Art, Rhode Island School of Design; Edward S. Cooke, Jr., Janice Sorkow, Jeffrey H. Munger, Museum of Fine Arts, Boston; Robert Coates, Arthur Drexler, Thomas Grischkowsky, J. Stewart Johnson, Cara McCarty, Richard L. Tooke, The Museum of Modern Art, New York; Deborah Emont Scott, The Nelson-Atkins Museum of Art; Rodris Roth, Smithsonian Institution; John D. Kilbourne, Society of the Cincinnati; Richard Nylander, Society for the Preservation of New England Antiquities; Karol Schmiegel, Dr. Frank H. Sommer, Neville Thompson, The Henry Francis duPont Winterthur Museum; Carol Alper, Michael Bleichfeld, Mitchell Wolfson, Jr., Mitchell Wolfson, Jr. Collection of Decorative and Propaganda Arts; William Cuffe, Janine Skerry, Patricia E. Kane, Yale University Art Gallery.

There were also many private individuals and people associated with galleries or commercial firms in the United States: Anna Ramsey, Atelier International; Sarah B. Sherrill, The Magazine Antiques; Tina Barney; Joan Burgasser, Joan Burgasser Design/Marketing Associates; Dean Failey, Ellen Jenkins, Peter Krueger, Marion Parry, Lisa Wilson, Christie Manson Woods, New York; Martha Deese; Anthony DeLorenzo, DeLorenzo Gallery; R. H. Hensleigh; Barbara DeSilva, The Mediators; Michael

Meeks, William Doyle Gallery, Inc.; Ralph Cutler, Mark Isaacson, and Mark McDonald, Fifty-50; Thomas Frank; Barry Friedman, Stuart Friedman, Jonathan Hallam, Debra Pesci, Barry Friedman, Ltd.; Karen Goldman, Paul R. Goldman, Plycraft Inc.; William Gruenbaum; David A. Hanks, Caroline Stern, Jennifer Toher, David A. Hanks & Associates; June Hargrove, University of Maryland; Paul H. Hazlett; Merle Gordon, IBM Gallery of Science and Art; Roland Kuchel; John Loggia; Miles Lourie; Wit McKay; Melissa Moreno; Patricia Riley; Scott Defrin, Barbara Deisroth, Sarah Hill, Caroline Holmes, Elaine Whitmire, Sotheby Parke Bernet, New York; Edward J. Stanek and Douglas K. True; Suzanne Tise.

In Europe, my thanks go to the individuals at museums and collections who gave of their time and expertise: Dr. Rosemarie Stratmann-Dohler, Dr. Irmela Franzke, Badisches Landesmuseum, Karlsruhe; Dr. Magdalena Droste, Dr. Peter Han, Bauhaus-Archiv, Berlin; Vibeke Woldbye, Danske Kunstindustrimuseum, Copenhagen; Mrs. Evelyne Trehin, Marielore LeBouche, Fondation Le Corbusier; Marjan Boot, Dr. Th. van Velzen, Dr. Abraham Westers, Haags Gemeentemuseum; Dr. Phil Carl Benno Heller, Hessisches Landesmuseum, Darmstadt; Dr. Franz-Adrian Dreier, Dr. Barbara Mundt, Kunstgewerbemuseum, Berlin; Dr. Reinhold Baumstark, Leichtenstein collection; Marc Bascou, Musée d'Orsay; Marianne Aav, Kristian Gullichsen, Jarno Peltonen, Museum of Applied Arts, Helsinki; Dr. Günther Keinheckel, Museum für Kunsthandwerk, Dresden; Dr. Annaliese Ohm, Museum für Kunsthandwerk, Frankfurt; Dr. Georg Himmelheber, Neue Pinakothek; Carl Thomas Edam, Nordic Council of Ministers, Copenhagen; Dr. Elisabeth Schüttermaier, Österreichisches Museum für angewandte Kunst; Dkfm. Kurt Nösslinger, Norbert Pichler, Österreichische Postsparkasse; Mr. Glachs, Purkersdorf Sanitarium; F. Liefkas, Rijksmuseum, Amsterdam; Dr. Hennig, Schloss Köpenick, East Berlin; Dr. Klaus-Peter Arnold, Dr. Herman Jedding, Dr. Axel von Saldern, Staatliche Kunstsammlungen, Museum für Kunst und Gewerbe, Dresden; Dr. Gutta Hörning, Dr. Gerhard Rudolf, Staatliche Kunstsammlungen, Weimer; Dr. Lutz Tittel, Städtisches Bodensee-Museum; Reyer J. Kras, Stedlijk Museum; Otakar Máčel, Technische Hogeschool Delft; Dr. Dagmar Héjdova, Dr. Olga Herbenová, Dr. Jana Horneková, Uméleckoprùmyslove Muzeum, Prague; Dr.

Geoffrey Beard, Simon Jervis, John H. Morley, Maurice Tomlin, James York, Victoria & Albert Museum, London; Dr. Georg Opitz, Wissenschaftlich-Kulturelles Zentrum Bauhaus, Dessau; Dr. Heike Schröder, Württembergisches Landesmuseum, Stuttgart.

Many firms and private individuals in Europe were very helpful: Elissa Aalto; Dr. Paul Asenbaum; Maria de Beyrie, Galerie Maria de Beyrie, Paris; Mr. & Mrs. Bokelberg, Hamburg; Dr. Beate Dry-von Zezschwitz; Dr. Penelope Eames; Jan van Geest; Hanno von Gustedt, Gebrüder Thonet, Frankenberg; Mr. and Mrs. Georg Heinrichs, Berlin; Igor Herler; Mr. and Mrs. Johannes Hintze; Mr. and Mrs. von Kalnein; Erik Krogh; Martin Levy, H. Blairman & Sons, London; Dr. Karl Mang; Egidio Marzona; Monika Meier, Antiquitäten & Thonetmöbel, Berlin; Baron Hippolyt von Poschinger, Oberfrauenau; Jessica Rutherford, Royal Pavilion, Brighton; Manfred A. Sauter, Zeppelin-Metallwerke GmbH; Rudolph Schmutz, Austria; Peyton Skipworth, Fine Arts Society, Ltd., London; Michel Souillac, Paris; Theo Stachels, Munich; Mrs. Thea Mejstrik-Thonet, Gebrüder Thonet, Vienna; Andreas Wilkes; Franz Wittmann, Franz Wittmann, K.G. Inge Zerunian, Vienna.

I have been truly fortunate in having had such fine contributing authors as colleagues. The high degree of cooperation between these scholars has been unusual. I am particularly grateful to Dr. Christian Witt-Dörring for his kind advice, considerable knowledge, and truly expansive perspective that has helped everyone involved with the project. Dr. Graham Dry's diligence and encyclopedic knowledge of the subject and his generous help with research and with many of the details that went into this catalogue were most appreciated. Dr. Robert Keil's enthusiastic engagement of his subject and pursuit of truth provided a substantial addition to the catalogue. Dr. Alessandro Alverà's hard work at unlocking the secrets of Michael Thonet's innovations and his supervision of splendid drawings that illustrate parts of this catalogue are much appreciated.

Finally, my deepest thanks go to my wife Lillian whose patience and good advice have seen me through a long and wonderful project.

DEREK E. OSTERGARD
Guest Curator
Bentwood and Metal
Furniture: 1850–1946

Bent Wood and Metal Furniture: 1850–1946

1
Before industrialization: Bent wood and bent metal in the hands of the craftsman

DEREK E. OSTERGARD

IF the years 1850 to 1950 represent the mature stage in the industrial exploitation of the process of bending wood and metal for the manufacture of furniture, then the preceding century and a quarter must be viewed as the fledgling period of that technology as it developed in the workshops of England, Western Europe, and the eastern seaboard of the United States. The richest period of invention in the realm of craftsman-produced work began in the early eighteenth century in England with the appearance of the Windsor chair and ended by the middle of the following century with John Henry Belter's work in New York City—just as Michael Thonet was beginning to translate the craft of bending wood for the creation of furniture from workshop production to industrial manufacture in the forests of Moravia. It was just then, however, that the craftsman who saved labor, material, and time by his use of the bending process was overwhelmed by the

flood of mass-produced furnishings that began to enter the market. The craftsman could not compete with the machine, and the impetus for his innovative technology disappeared.

Unlike the lucid development presented by the body of mass-produced designs, the history of the work produced in the workshop is characterized by anonymous craftsmen, widely diverging aesthetics, and technological innovations separated by time and geographic distance. It is the seemingly sporadic nature of these accomplishments that has prevented this avowedly small but highly diversified group of works from being perceived as a cohesive entity. Nevertheless, these hand-crafted designs are united by two essential factors: the nature of the profession responsible for their production and the innovative means of their construction. Indeed, it is the departure from conventional joinery and use of materials that aligns

Figure 1–1
Bowyer, facsimile of wall painting in the Tomb of Amenemhat, Beni-Hasan. Egyptian, Twelfth Dynasty, ca. 1971–1928 B.C. (From Newberry, pl. XI).

these earlier craft-produced pieces with the works later manufactured by industrial systems.

Unlike the mass-produced designs of the mature period, the examples that constitute the early history of bent-wood and bent-metal furniture do not always diverge from the aesthetics of conventionally produced furniture. The tastemakers who determined the aesthetics of eighteenth- and early-nineteenth-century furniture were basically unconcerned with technological innovation, and their designs were intended to be constructed by traditional joinery. The progressive craftsman, not trained to be his own designer, was in most cases forced to respond to an aesthetic determined by people ignorant of method. As a result, he subjugated technique to prescribed aesthetics and frequently produced work in which distinctions between innovation and tradition are barely discernible. This discreet deployment of innovation contrasts vividly with the later mass-produced designs, which boldly expose their symbiosis of material, process, and aesthetic. The premium placed on this unity by twentieth-century critics has indirectly minimized the achievements of the earlier craftsmen.

An additional reason for the diversity of design and individuality of technical achievement during this earlier period lies in the transformation of the Western world by the Industrial Revolution. The circle of craftsmen employing innovative technology from 1725 to 1850 was remarkably small, but it lacked the intimacy that characterized the considerably larger design community of subsequent years. From the mid-nineteenth century onward, exposure to design concepts was considerably expanded by the growing ease of travel, the proliferation of publications, the organization of vast international expositions, and—that leitmotif of the industrial age—sophisticated marketing techniques. During the second half of the nineteenth century, the transmission and absorption of aesthetic and technological innovations proceeded rapidly. After the first international exposition, the Exhibition of the Works of Industry of All Nations held in 1851 at London in the Crystal Palace, individual or national concepts of design immediately entered the international marketplace, and nearly identical furnishings could be designed, produced, and sold throughout most of the world.

The craftsman prior to this time had none of these advantages. The opportunity to exchange technological concepts was practically non-existent outside a specific body of work, such as those Windsor chairs or American card tables that used bent-wood elements. Confined by the limitations of location and era, individual creativity blossomed in relative intellectual and creative isolation.

Bent-wood furniture in the ancient world

Although the methodology of bending wood and iron can be certifiably documented to several hundred years before the eighteenth century, there is evidence that hints at an even earlier development of this technique. However, much of this material exists in supposition only, indicated by references that allude to the use of bent wood in the ancient world but do not necessarily substantiate it.

The extensive reliefs and paintings that adorn Egyptian tombs, which are so rich in their representations of all phases of daily life in ancient Egypt, would seem to indicate that a bent wood process was already known in the Old Kingdom. The reliefs in the tomb of the scribe Hesire at Saqqara, dated circa 2800 B.C., contain representations of furniture, among them a chair whose seat has been described as "strengthened by bent wood supports, in hard- and soft-woods" and a stool "with bent wood reinforcements."[1] More immediate evidence that the process of bending wood was known to the Egyptians is provided by the paintings in the Middle Kingdom tomb of Amenemhat at Beni-Hasan, circa 1971–1928 B.C., which contain among extensive representations of various occupations an illustration of a bowmaker (figure 1–1) who holds a rod over a receptacle (of hot water?), while straight rods and completed bows are displayed nearby.[2] It has been noted that the furniture found in the New Kingdom tomb of Tutankhamen (ca. 1334–1325 B.C.) "differs from earlier work in its predilection for the curve rather than the uncompromising right-angle" and that various beds,

thrones, and stools among the tomb's contents have "frames and stretchers deeply curved by some process of bending the wood, or by cutting it on a curve, or by the use of specially grown timber."[3]

The largest surviving body of ancient Egyptian furniture that suggests the Egyptians' use of bent wood is formed by the primitive three-legged stool. According to testimony provided by paintings and reliefs, this type appeared with increasing frequency during the New Kingdom.[4] A three-legged stool with a dished seat (figure 1–2) dated to the eighteenth dynasty (ca. 1570–1305 B.C.) has legs that "seem to have been bent to shape, as it is possible to distinguish parts of the grain flowing around the curve."[5] This correspondence of the grain of the wood with the form of the leg could have been achieved through the selection of timber grown into this curvature. And it hardly seems probable that a sophisticated bending process would have been undertaken in the fabrication of a stool in which the most rudimentary mortise and tenon joinery methods were employed and which has legs that measure only ten inches from floor to seat.[6]

The classic Greek chair known as the klismos, which emerged in the fifth century B.C., is familiar from its frequent representations in vase paintings and reliefs (figure 1–3). However, unlike the circumstances in Egypt, neither the climate of Greece nor ancient Greek funerary practices were conducive to the preservation of wood, and thus no original specimens have come down to us. The dramatic, concave sweep of its distinctive "saber" legs has led to the conclusion that the form was probably achieved by steam bending.[7] The hypothesis cannot be tested by direct examination, but what is certain is that the process of bending wood was known to the ancient Greeks. This is indicated in the discussion by the Greek philosopher and scientist Theophrastus (ca. 372–287 B.C.) of woods best suited for the carpenter: "In general the woods which are tough are easy to bend. The mulberry and the wild fig

Figure 1–2
Three-legged stool. Egyptian, Eighteenth Dynasty, ca. 1567–1320 B.C. Wood. British Museum, London.

Figure 1–3
Wine jug. Greek, ca. 350 B.C. The Metropolitan Museum of Art, New York (Fletcher Fund, 1925).

Figure 1–4
Thomas Chippendale the Younger, attributed to. Klismos chair. English, ca. 1820. Simulated rosewood (upholstery modern). Whereabouts unknown.

Figure 1–5
Side chair. American, ca. 1800–1815. Mahogany and ash. The Metropolitan Museum of Art, New York (Rogers Fund, 1926).

Figure 1–6
Nicolai Abraham Abildgaard. Klismos chair. Danish, ca. 1800–1809. Mahogany with painted decoration by Abildgaard. Danske Kunstindustrimuseum, Copenhagen.

Figure 1–7
T. H. Robsjohn-Gibbings. Klismos chair. Made by Saridis Furniture Manufacturers, Athens, ca. 1970. Cooper-Hewitt Museum, The Smithsonian Institution's National Museum of Design (Gift of Saridis Furniture Manufacturer).

seem to be specially so, wherefore they make of these theatre-seats, the hoops of garlands, and, in general, things for ornament."[8] This statement has led to the observation that "there seems, therefore, no reason for supposing that the Greeks took recourse to the alternative method—more wasteful and more laborious—of cutting the curving parts of the klismos out of blocks of wood."[9]

However, later examples of the klismos chair indicate that alternative methods could have been used which would not have wasted wood. Most interpretations of the klismos chair produced in early-nineteenth-century Europe (figure 1–4) and the United States (figure 1–5) under the aegis of Neoclassicism reveals the near-exclusive use of cut elements. However, curved legs could also be achieved by employing wood from trees that either had grown naturally into an approximation of the necessary curvature or were artificially trained to do so. After the

stock was taken from the tree, it was reduced by carving to the appropriate form. In this manner, the natural alignment of the wood grain was in concert with the final shape of the leg, which produced a form with a minimal number of liabilities. The outstanding example of this procedure is provided by a number of chairs designed by the Danish architect Nicolai Abraham Abildgaard (1748–1809) some time between 1800 and 1809 based on ancient Greek and Roman representations. Documentation indicates that the curved, splayed legs of the klismos chair included in the group (figure 1–6) were executed from specially selected pieces of timber which had grown into the conformation necessary to produce the saber legs.[10]

After World War II, an analysis of the Greek klismos form was conducted by British-born designer Terrance Robsjohn-Gibbings. The result of this research was a line of furniture based as closely as possible on ancient prototypes, completely crafted by hand.[11] An examination of the grain of a chair from this line (figure 1–7) reveals that the deep concave curve of the saber leg was fashioned from a tangential cut of timber and not bent.

In point of fact, it would have been difficult to execute the robust proportions and dynamic curvature of the ancient klismos leg in bent wood except under the most sophisticated woodworking conditions. Finally, had the legs of the ancient chairs been made of bent wood, it is likely that they would eventually have relaxed at different rates, making them unbalanced on level floors. This liability alone would have excluded them from the popularity they enjoyed over an extensive time, lasting through Classical and Hellenistic Greece well into the Roman Empire.

Bent-metal furniture: 1176–1725

The next period under consideration, which proceeds from Early Gothic to the Late Baroque,[12] is dominated by developments in furniture production that were determined by the use of wrought iron. The natural structure of the metal, forged by hand and hammer, is altered by heat and pressure and can be bent by the ironworker into shapes suitable for the production of furniture. One of the earliest examples, which can be dated with authority, is a freestanding armoire (figure 1–8) in the Abbey Church of Saint-Etienne at Obazine in south central France. The armoire, which dates from the final quarter of the twelfth century,[13] is constructed of oak planks. Wrought-iron straps bind the individual boards that comprise the doors and also attach these doors to the case of the armoire. Bent only in one plane, as seen in the fleur-de-lis configuration of the hardware, the flat iron elements are integral components in the construction of this piece.

In the thirteenth century greater technical and artistic virtuosity was achieved in the manipulation of bent-metal elements, as can be seen in the group of low chests employing boarded or clamped construction (figures 1–9, 10, 11). The nails in boarded construction and the mortise and tenon joints of clamped construction secure the

Figure 1-8
Freestanding armoire. French, ca. 1176. Oak and wrought iron. Abbey Church of Saint-Etienne, Obazine (Corrèze), France.

Figure 1-9
Chest. English, ca. 1280–1300. Oak and wrought iron. Library, Merton College, Oxford.

wooden elements of these chests in a manner that prevents the wood from easily expanding and contracting in response to changes of temperature and humidity. Even when well-seasoned, these boards have a tendency to shrink and eventually split with age. The use of wrought iron with these chests evolved as an essential structural component, for these metal strips compensated for the rudimentary methods of joinery by holding the chair together when the wooden elements failed. The particularly fine and early example of a clamped-front chest[14] in the Musée Municipale de la Ville de Paris (figures 1–10 and 1–11), reputed to have come from the Abbaye Royale de Saint-Denis, displays a remarkable unity between the functional virtues of the iron bands and their aesthetic potential, which relieves the austere rectilinear mass of the chest. Although here the iron is bent in two planes as it rounds the corners of the chest, this again was primarily a constructional consideration, but enhanced by the decorative treatment of the iron.

Figure 1–10
Chest. French, ca. 1250–70. Oak and wrought iron. Musée Municipale de la Ville de Paris, France.

Ironwork was employed more extensively in a group of wooden chests that date from the following century and later, which were completely encased in flat bands of iron woven in a simple pattern. A barrel-lidded chest in the Gruuthuse Museum in Bruges (figure 1–12)[15] is completely enveloped in sheets of bent iron and bound with iron straps as well. More secure than all-wood chests, or those in which combinations of wood and iron strapwork were combined, these ironclad cases provided maximum security at the time.

The nomadic existence pursued by many individuals during the Middle Ages prompted the use of smaller receptacles, known as caskets, which could be easily transported. A group of these diminutive chests made in France and elsewhere, known as *à mailles* or *à la manière d'Espagne*, were often embellished with sheets of iron that were laminated together and bent (figure 1–13).[16] By staggering an identical pierce-work design on each sheet of metal, the craftsman gave an illusion of depth to the decorative patterns used on these small caskets.

Figure 1–11
Detail of figure 1–10.

Case pieces—armoires, chests, caskets, desks—were not the only type of furniture in which wrought iron was employed during this period. An outstanding armchair based on a curule form (figure 1–14) and a freestanding brazier (figure 1–15), both dating from the fifteenth cen-

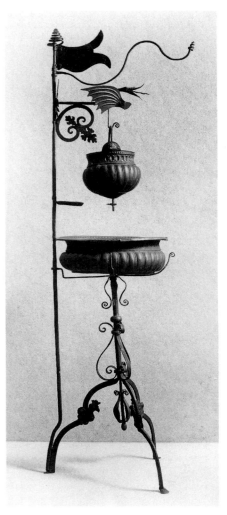

Figure 1-14
Curule chair (below).
Gothic, 15th century.
Wrought iron, wood,
and textile. The Cleveland
Museum of Art (Purchase
from the John L.
Severance Fund).

Figure 1-12
Chest. Low Countries, ca. 1450–1500. Wood
encased in wrought iron. Gruuthuse Museum, Bruges.

Figure 1-13
Coffret. European, 15th–16th centuries.
Wrought iron. The Metropolitan Museum
of Art, New York, The Cloisters Collection.

Figure 1-15
Tripod brazier (above). Italian, 15th
century. Wrought iron and copper. The
Cleveland Museum of Art (Purchased from
the Dudley P. Allen Fund).

Figure 1-16
Table. Spanish, 17th century. Walnut and wrought iron. The Metropolitan Museum of Art, New York (Bequest of George Blumenthal, 1941).

Figure 1-17
Firescreen. English, ca. 1675. Wrought iron with silver mounts (panel of later date). Ham House, Petersham (Richmond, Surrey), England.

tury,[17] demonstrate a virtuosic use of forged metal. Here the material has not only been manipulated to add decorative embellishment, it has also been used to execute the load-bearing structure of each piece. Although these particular objects are catalogued as having been executed in Tuscany, both types were part of the standard repertory of forms executed in wrought iron for the next several centuries in most major urban centers of Western and Central Europe.

After the Middle Ages, as society became more secure and less nomadic, wrought iron was used with growing frequency for interior and exterior architectural detailing, particularly in the seventeenth century. The pliable nature of iron made it an eminently suitable material for the execution of the voluptuous curves characteristic of the Baroque, then the determinant of high-style taste. In Spain and Portugal during this period numerous tables, called *pie de puente*, were produced (figure 1-16) in which extensive wrought iron stretchers were employed that combine both functional and aesthetic merits. The wrought-iron elements not only provide a dynamic sweep that relieves the planar qualities of these tables but also offer the added advantage of creating a piece that can be easily disassembled and transported. Freestanding *torchères* in wrought iron also appeared throughout Western and Central Europe at this time. Patinated and sometimes partially gilded, these pieces replicated much of the appearance of carved wooden examples, which were gessoed and gilded. Other standing forms in wrought iron include music stands and pole screens for fireplaces. The 1679 inventory for Ham House,[18] the country residence of the Duke and Duchess of Lauderdale outside London, includes a firescreen (figure 1-17) made of wrought iron whose scrolling legs are evidence of fashionable Baroque taste in England in the latter portion of the seventeenth century.

What differentiates the work of this period from that of the next is its overwhelming reliance on the malleability of metal for both functional and aesthetic purposes. Wood technology dominates the next period, with the occasional metal pieces usually responding to an aesthetic lead determined by innovations in bent-wood furniture design.

The eighteenth century

The Windsor chair

It was not until the beginning of the second quarter of the eighteenth century that the "Windsor" chair appeared. The origin of the appellation is obscure, but the elements of the chair's construction are clear. A succinct definition characterizes it as possessing "an all-wooden single-block seat in which the bow and spindles of the back and the legs are dowelled into the seat."[19] The Windsor chair does not always incorporate bent members; however, those chairs that do have this feature constitute the largest, the most aesthetically diversified, and, in terms of time, the most persistent body of craftsman-produced chairs created by the process of bending materials.

Although the use of the term *Windsor* can be dated to 1708,[20] in, curiously, an American document, the chair itself in the recognizable form that defines it today does not appear in England, its birthplace, until nearly twenty years later. In the quarter of a century that follows its emergence, the evolution of the Windsor chair is characterized by measured growth in terms of aesthetic development and considerable influence as a form. However, beyond its spread from England to the eastern seaboard of Colonial America by the middle of the eighteenth century, the chair does not appear to have developed elsewhere. With the exception of minor concessions to contemporary fashionable taste, these chairs present a remarkably stable body of work executed over centuries, which remained essentially unchanged in the face of major aesthetic and technological innovations and apparently had little influence on other designs employing the bending process, with the exception of the mass-produced Windsor chairs manufactured by Thonet (figure 4-1).

Although the Windsor chair appears somewhat suddenly in documents of the early eighteenth century, it had been in a developmental stage for some time before that. Several of the technical components that define the chair were already part of the vocabulary of English seating forms long before the eighteenth century. More important, however, the Windsor chair evolved in response to the needs of a society that had been in a state of transformation since the dissolution of the Commonwealth in 1660. In that year, following an eighteen-year exile on the Continent, the Stuart dynasty had returned to the English throne, bringing with it many of the sophisticated social and cultural nuances it had acquired abroad, particularly at the French court of Louis XIV. Much of this exposure would result in the replacement of an antiquated Tudor aesthetic legacy by a much more fashionable Continental Baroque taste. The economic and cultural stagnation that had plagued England during the years of the Commonwealth was over. The fashionable dwelling would be irrevocably altered within twenty-five years of the return of the Stuarts, and the garden would undergo a similar transformation.

The garden had been in an early state of development in England under the late Tudor and early Stuart monarchies, but it emerged as a far more important component of English Restoration society following the Stuart reinstatement. As guests of the Bourbon family in the 1650s, members of the Stuart family were exposed to the numerous royal châteaus in the Île-de-France, where the garden already was a vital sector of the court environment. The English garden received a further infusion of French taste when William of Orange and his wife, Princess Mary, assumed the English throne in 1689, bringing with them from Holland political Francophobia but cultural Francomania. Evidence of this is seen in their employment of the French-educated designer Daniel Marot,[21] who served as arbiter of taste for the English court in the late seventeenth and early eighteenth centuries. Sir Peter Lely's paintings of the powerful and fashionable members of Restoration society,[22] as well as several portraits he painted during the Commonwealth, depict many of these individuals in a garden setting, unlike most earlier portraits of the English aristocracy, which show their sitters indoors, often against abstract backgrounds. A Lely portrait of

ca. 1679 displays the Duke and Duchess of Lauderdale, the fashionable and influential owners of Ham House, in a garden environment, seated on a stone settee.[23] By the middle of the seventeenth century, the garden was clearly an accepted domain of Restoration society.

Although stone seats were common garden fixtures at this time at the grander establishments, less imposing properties were outfitted with simpler furnishings, and it is likely that many of the earliest pieces were of stick construction.[24] Inexpensive and easy to produce, tables and chairs constructed by this method were ideal furnishings for the open spaces of the garden and for the semi-enclosed pavilions situated along the garden walks for shelter. Primitive in its essential formulation, stick construction had been aesthetically enhanced during the medieval period in Europe and England through the addition of turned members, which could be shaped or scored for decorative purposes.[25] English turned chairs were common throughout medieval and post-medieval Europe; in England they were the staple seating form, "the standard cottage/farmhouse chair in eighteenth and early nineteenth century England."[26] It is from the technical and aesthetic repertory of these stick pieces that the Windsor chair evolved in Georgian society during the early decades of the eighteenth century.

The members of the London Company of Turners, which received its charter in June 1604,[27] presumably enjoyed a great boost in business after the Great Fire of 1666. The massive reconstruction of the city that followed the disaster generated a need for inexpensive furnishings that could be produced quickly. Consumer demand, abetted by fashion, prolonged the interest in turned furniture in urban, if not sophisticated, circles until well into the early years of the eighteenth century. By that time, however, as noted by Nancy Evans,[28] the fashion for this manner of furniture, particularly chairs, may have been on the wane: "Members of the turned chairmaker's craft may have recognized the need for a new design that could stimulate the chair market and achieve the same general popularity that cane seating [a type of turned chair] had held."[29]

Economic survival of a trade may well have provided the incentive that led to the creation of the Windsor chair,

Figure 1-18
Lipp-work chair. Welsh, early 19th century. Bent ash frame, woven straw, leather. Welsh Folk Museum, Saint Fagans. National Museum of Wales.

but unfortunately, none of the early references to Windsor seating note the use of turned elements. One such mention, in a 1718 treatise on rural gardening, refers to "a large Seat, call'd a Windsor Seat," whose salient feature was a device that enabled it to "turn round any way, either for the Advantage of the Prospect, or to avoid the Inconveniences of Wind, the Sun, & c."[30] Although this account refers to this revolving chair as a *Windsor*, Evans discounts this particular type of chair as a true Windsor precursor by associating it with another revolving chair, described by Daniel Defoe seven years later, which possessed "a high Back, and Cover for the Head, which turns so easily, the whole being fix'd on a Pin of Iron."[31] By linking these two chairs on the basis of their construction—"the mechanical aspect of the seat"—and the boxlike structure indicated by Defoe and presumed for the earlier example, Evans removes both pieces from the repository of Windsor antecedents. Such boxlike—i.e., board—construction, she adds, would have been the product of a joiner or carpenter, whereas "the 'stick' oriented Windsor almost certainly emerged from the craft of turnery."[32]

It is undeniable that the substantial planklike construction of a box is the antithesis of the delicate open forms attained by a turner. It should therefore be noted that another craftsman may have been able to produce a partially enclosed seating form, namely, the weaver. Woven basketwork construction had been used for centuries in England for the production of baskets, beehives, floor coverings, and even cradles, stools, and chairs.[33] Lipp-work chairs (figure 1–18),[34] which were often constructed

Figure 1-19
Jacques Rigaud. *Stowe Garden, Buckinghamshire* (detail). Engraving, ca. 1739. The Metropolitan Museum of Art, New York (Harris Brisbane Dick Fund, 1942).

on bent-willow or bent-ash frames, may be considered appropriate candidates for the enclosed chairs described in the aforementioned accounts. Lighter in weight than an object made of solid planks of wood assembled with boarded construction, and able to provide the enclosure described by Defoe, a lipp-work seat would have pivoted more easily on a rotating mechanism. Such a chair would also have been inexpensive to produce and was dispensable in the garden environment if damaged or decayed. Certainly, the bent inner frames of this type of construction provide an additional and appropriate antecedent for the later bent frames used for many Windsor chairs.

The thesis deriving the Windsor chair from a wheeled conveyance is further strengthened by an account written in 1724 by Lord Perceval describing a visit to the gardens of Hall Barn in Buckinghamshire: "The narrow winding walks and paths cut in [the garden] are innumerable; a woman in full health cannot walk them all, for which reason my wife was carry'd in a Windsor chair like those at Versailles."[35] An image of a sedan chair comes to mind, for it is known that these were used at Versailles. But if one interprets the word "carry'd" to mean "conveyed," one of the three possible interpretations suggested by Evans,[36] it then becomes probable that Lord Perceval's wife was taken about the garden on a wheeled platform.

This possiblility of a seating element on a stand as a precursor to the Windsor chair is heightened by an engraving attributed to Jacques Rigaud dating from the 1730s (figure 1–19), depicting a view in the garden at Stowe.[37] A man and a woman are shown seated in fully developed Windsor chairs set on wheeled platforms, which grant these chairs several of the same advantages accruing to the chair described by Daniel Defoe a decade earlier. A common chair with a value equal to that of the crude platform was needed for these vehicles, and it is possible that prior to the development of the Windsor chair, a turned or woven chair was used. Certainly, the lightness of the latter type would have permitted easy movement of the wheeled platform. Again, the spoke construction of the wheels of these carts, produced by wheelwrights, may have provided the turners with a mode that was then translated into the constuction of the back of the

Windsor chair. By the late eighteenth century this association between the Windsor chair and spoke construction culminated in a special body of designs offered by English chairmakers. Trade cards of craftsmen depict Windsor chairs with wheel elements fully integrated into a single structure (figure 1B),[38] which may have been used as either mobile garden seats or invalid chairs.

By the 1730s and 1740s, estate and sale inventories indicate an increasing use of the Windsor chair, which was frequently referred to as a garden seat. The simple form of the Windsor—single-plank seat with staked leg and back construction—could be inexpensively produced. In addition, it was ideally suited to repetitive craft production, a methodology that must be viewed as a precursor to the techniques of mechanized mass production in the following century. From published accounts it is known that Windsor chairs were inexpensive in comparison with chairs assembled by means of traditional joinery or cabinetmaking. It was this factor, perhaps more than any other, that made the Windsor chair such a common fixture in the eighteenth century.

However, these early chairs do not appear to have been made by a bending technique. Spindles set into the seat support a comb that is sometimes slightly bent. The arm rails were not bent, but seem to have been constructed from three contiguous pieces of cut wood, secured with lap joints in the characteristic C-shaped configuration. Eventually, as the production of Windsor chairs progressed, more sophisticated means of construction came into use, such as the single section curved and bent arm rail and the sweeping hoop back, apparently used from approximately 1750 onward. Through this innovation, the stiles and crest rail of side chairs were incorporated into one piece, thereby introducing further aspects of constructional stability, reduction of material, and aesthetic cohesiveness. The C-shaped hoop back, often mirrored by the shape of the arm rail, which in turn followed the configuration of the plank seat (figure 1–20), was further enhanced by the introduction of stretchers employing the same form. These supports, known as "cow-horn" stretchers, enforced the overall unity of the design. A century later this simplification of elements would be developed to its fullest in the No. 14 chair by Michael Thonet (figure 1–21).[39]

Figure 1–20
Hoop-back Windsor armchair. American, ca. 1780. Chestnut and bent ash. Private collection, New York. CAT. NO. 1.

According to one authority, the bent elements of Windsor chairs were achieved by the use of steam,[40] which loosened the resin in the wood grain by introducing additional moisture, thus permitting the fibers of the grain to be realigned more easily under the pressure of bending. During the bending process, the compression of the grain on the inner face of the curvature causes the wood to buckle, while on the outer face, the grain, which is being stretched, has a tendency to tear apart. It has been assumed that the eighteenth-century craftsman counteracted this danger by retaining the bark on the outer face of the wood in order to stabilize the grain under tension; once shaped, the bent element was cooled in a clamp. The rapport of craftsman, materials, and design is evident in the types of wood chosen for these chairs. Itinerant turners, known as "bodgers," would frequently set themselves up where there was a supply of favorable wood, a practice quite unlike that of the joiner or cabinetmaker, who had a permanent shop and ordered wood from wholesalers. In the production of Windsor chairs, woods were used with great care, matching properties of the material to structural requirements: straight-grained beech for the legs, tough elm for the seats, pliant yew for the hoops.

By the mid-eighteenth century, a central vertical splat with pierced motifs had been introduced to the Windsor design. This element served a twofold purpose, practical as well as ornamental. The splat strengthened the hoop back, and the pierced motifs, adapted from expensive, high-style furniture that was illustrated in the numerous design books published in England during the second

Figure 1–21
Side chair, Thonet Model No. 14, ca. 1855. Bent solid and laminated beech and cane. Collection Alessandro Alverà, Vienna. CAT. NO. 15.

Figure 1-22
Gothic-back Windsor armchair. English, ca. 1770. Yew. Private collection.

half of the eighteenth century, provided the chair with fashionable associations. "Wheelbacks," "Gothick" tracery (figure 1–22), and "Prince of Wales" plumes were only a few of the decorative devices incorporated into these more elaborate manifestations of the Windsor chair. In many examples produced during this period, the turned decoration of the legs was replaced or augmented with discreetly carved decoration, or by cabriole legs, a hallmark of high-style design during the middle of the eighteenth century.

The Windsor chair originated in England and apparently was produced only in that country and in regions under her dominion. Trade in furniture between England and her American colonies was well established in the eighteenth century. Evidence of the rapid transmission of taste in this particular aspect of furniture design is provided by an advertisement placed in the *Pennsylvania Gazette* of August 1748 by David Chambers of Philadelphia advising that he was engaged in the production of Windsor chairs[41] —no later than twenty-five years after the design seems to have appeared in England. By the third quarter of the century, numerous craftsmen along the eastern seaboard were engaged in making this chair.

Nevertheless, production of the Windsor chair at this time appears to have been confined to a fairly small region of the Western Hemisphere.[42] It also remained somewhat restricted in status in Georgian, Regency, and Victorian society. It was most often used in taverns, in kitchens, in secondary rooms of upper-middle-class interiors, in servants halls, and as garden seats. Occasionally, the Windsor chair was executed in mahogany,[43] or Japanned, but such chairs can at best be described as high-style Windsors, not as high-style furniture. Rarely are they found in the ultrafashionable interior of the eighteenth century, nor do they ever serve as an integral component of a cohesively designed environment where all the furnishings respond to an aesthetic common denominator, as in the interiors of a Robert Adam or a William Kent.

Case pieces

A different manner of exploiting the possibilities of bent wood is presented in high-style furniture produced in

England during the eighteenth century. The use of veneers for carcass furniture (case pieces) in particular had already reached a high stage of development in the late seventeenth century. Employment of these thin sheets of wood had evolved as an economy measure, whereby a supply of exotic woods, often imported at great expense, could be extended by applying them to a base wood of lesser quality. In the same period that the Windsor chair became an established fixture in the garden setting, tables embellished with decorative, pierced galleries appeared in the fashionable interior (figure 1–23). Pliable laminates were employed by the furniture-making trades for the first time in post-Renaissance Europe in the execution of these fretwork galleries. Cabinetmakers discovered not only that it was easier to execute these decorative elements from long strips of veneers glued together than from a solid board, but also that laminate stock was stronger than solid wood and thus less likely to split under the vigorous action of the fret-saw that carved pierced patterns. In addition, the curved galleries that often appear on more elaborate examples were certainly technically difficult, and probably artistically impossible, to achieve with a solid board, which had first to be cut in a curvilinear shape and then pierced.

A pair of candlestands whose circular tops have pierced galleries (figure 1–24) are two of the earliest pieces in which the laminate method was employed, yet they display the technique at its most virtuosic. Stylistic analysis dates them to 1730. Although the laminate technique practiced during this period usually employs three layers of veneer,[44] these particular stands are made of a five-ply laminate. It is possible that an early plywood was used here, since the different layers of wood form a distinct light-dark-light-dark-light pattern when the gallery is viewed from above. Plywood is considerably stronger than the basic laminate, for it is constructed so that the grain of each sheet of veneer runs at a right angle to the adjacent sheet, in contrast to all sheets running in the same direction as in the standard laminate method. This alternate-grain process counteracts the stress incurred in the wood when it is bent. Thus plywood is eminently suitable for use on a circular gallery, since the stress created, though equally distributed throughout the closed form, is considerable.[45]

Figure 1-23
Tea table. English, ca. 1760. Mahogany and mahogany laminate. The Metropolitan Museum of Art, New York (Bequest of Marion E. Cohn, 1966).

Figure 1-24
Pair of candlestands. English, ca. 1730. Mahogany and mahogany laminate. The Metropolitan Museum of Art, New York (Gift of Mrs. Ernest G. Vietor, 1962).

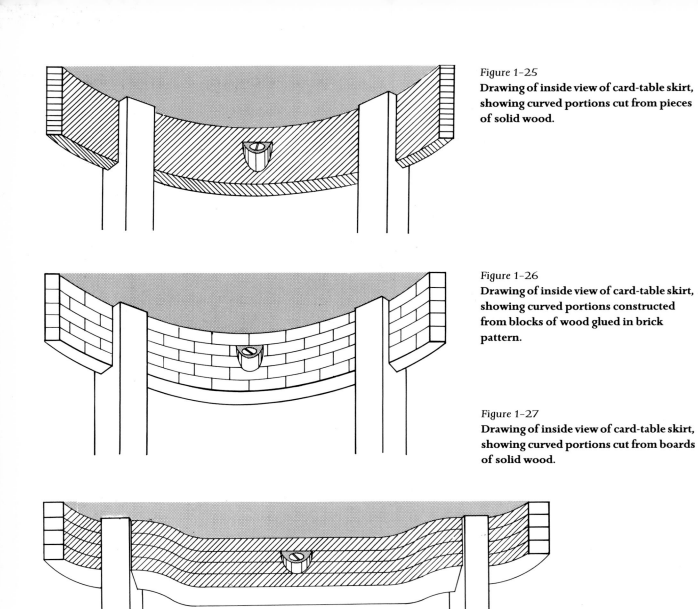

Figure 1-25
Drawing of inside view of card-table skirt, showing curved portions cut from pieces of solid wood.

Figure 1-26
Drawing of inside view of card-table skirt, showing curved portions constructed from blocks of wood glued in brick pattern.

Figure 1-27
Drawing of inside view of card-table skirt, showing curved portions cut from boards of solid wood.

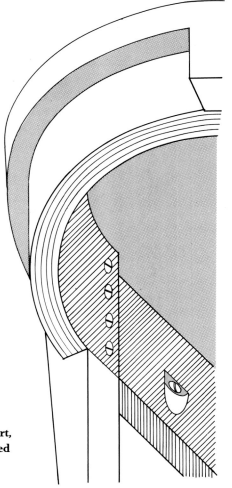

Figure 1-28
Drawing of underside of card-table skirt, showing vertical alignment of laminated veneers.

The application of the bending process to table construction evolved in a far more dynamic manner in the United States. An examination of card tables produced along the upper eastern seaboard during the late eighteenth and early nineteenth cenury reveals a varied and daring exploitation of bent laminates as well as bent solid boards.[46] There were several traditional methods for achieving the curved forms of eighteenth-century case pieces. In one system, pieces of solid wood were cut into shapes that were then combined to form the curve (figure 1–25), but this was a difficult procedure, with the added disadvantage of wasting much wood. In an alternative method, small blocks of wood were glued in a bricklike arrangement to form a curve (figure 1–26) and shaped to achieve the desired curvature. Because it permitted the use of small scraps of wood, this procedure had the advantage of conserving precious materials. In yet another system, long blocks of wood were sawn into identical shapes, stacked in horizontal layers, and glued to replicate the plan of the required curve (figure 1–27).

Two different, and more innovative, methods were devised in New England for the execution of these curved forms. In the first procedure, a number of long, thin sheets of veneer were vertically aligned (figure 1–28), glued, and then bent and bound into the desired shape (figure 1–29). This technique may have been devised by craftsmen familiar with the methodology employed by those engaged in the production of fretwork galleries. The second innovative technique wasted the least amount of wood and was theoretically the easiest to execute. By selecting a long board of tightly grained secondary wood and by cutting a series of deep, vertical kerf marks into it (figure 1–30), the craftsman introduced a degree of pliability to the board. By filling these slits with glue and binding them with cloth, he then bent and clamped the board

Figure 1-29
Hepplewhite-style card table. American, 1812–16. Mahogany, white pine, tulip, and maple. Skirt constructed of vertically aligned laminated veneers. Yale University Art Gallery, New Haven (Mabel Brady Garven Collection).

Figure 1-30
Drawing of underside of card-table skirt, showing curved portion constructed from solid board cut with kerf marks.

Figure 1-31
William Leverett, attributed to. Card table. American, ca. 1800. Mahogany and white pine. Curved portions of skirt constructed of solid wood cut with kerf marks. Yale University Art Gallery, New Haven (Gift of Benjamin A. Hewitt).

Figure 1-33
Table. American, 1725–50. Maple. The Henry Francis du Pont Winterthur Museum, Winterthur, Delaware.

Figure 1-32
Card table. English, late 18th century. Satinwood, tulipwood, and holly. Curved portions of skirt constructed from traditional methodology. The Metropolitan Museum of Art, New York (Rogers Fund, 1912).

into the desired curvature (figure 1–31). Each of these innovative techniques achieved the same aesthetic effect that resulted from traditional methodology (figure 1–32) once the tables were veneered with primary woods.

In a gesture of economy, the same ingenious concept of removing wood in order to facilitate the bending process was used on more commonplace tables as well (figure 1–33).[47] In order to form the legs, a wedge-shaped block of wood was extracted just above the foot; then, by bending the foot upward, the gap was closed and the foot was brought out of its vertical alignment with the leg. By this method an effect was achieved similar to that of a cabriole leg, without expending precious wood, time, and skilled labor. Apparently this technique was used only on table legs,[48] which were subject to less stress than the legs of a chair. Unlike Windsor chairs, these tables do not constitute a body of designs whose appearance was dependent on the method of their production. It is precisely for this reason that these sophisticated production techniques remained unrecognized until fairly recently.

The nineteenth century

Jean-Joseph Chapuis and Samuel Gragg

Although classicism dominated progressive thought during the last quarter of the eighteenth century, by the end of that period a dramatic transformation had occurred. Interest in archaeological accuracy became predominant, overshadowing the interpretive trend that had prevailed. In the furniture-making trades of the Western world during the last quarter of the eighteenth century and the first quarter of the nineteenth, reliance on ancient prototypes had become the ideal (figures 1–34 and 1–35). It is therefore not coincidental that two craftsmen—one Belgian, the other American—expressed their innovative technology in the archaeological language of their day.

Despite his long life, very little is known about the general production of *menuisier* (chairmaker) Jean-Joseph Chapuis (1765–1864) and even less about his use of bent laminates,[49] which must be viewed as the most advanced

Figure 1–34
Sarcophagus of a physician (portion). Roman, first quarter of 4th century A.D. **Marble. The Metropolitan Museum of Art, New York (Gift of Ernest and Beata M. Brummer in memory of Joseph Brummer).**

Figure 1–35
Drawing-room taboret. Plate 26 in *Repository of the Arts* (detail). London: R. Ackermann, 1809.

of its kind until the appearance of Michael Thonet's work of the 1830s. In fact, it is solely on the basis of one design, an armchair (figure 1–36) whose lower portion derives from an ancient Roman *sella curulis* with S-curved legs (figure 1–34), that Chapuis comes into consideration. Almost the entire frame of this chair—the continuous stile and side seat rail, as well as the paired legs—is fashioned from bent laminated wood.[50] A series of four solid wooden rods, each a quarter of an inch thick, were glued together, bent, bound in a caul (mold), dried, and then shaped to the appropriate form with a rasp. Whether Chapuis used steam to bend these sections is not known. The front and back seat rails, and perhaps the crest rail as well, were fashioned from sections of cut solid wood. According to one account, this particular model, with its lateral arrangement of the curule form, was installed at the Chateau Royal at Laeken in 1806.[51] However, it is not known whether those chairs were executed by means of innovative technology or from cut and traditionally joined sections of wood, as were similar examples by other joiners of the time (figure 1–37). The models used at Laeken, unlike those in the Anderson House Museum (cat. no. 2), are painted white,[52] an indication that the technique was less significant than the decoration. In the second quarter of the eighteenth century painted furnishings had become an important component of the high-style interior, and chairs such as these by Chapuis would have been very much in the vanguard of progressive thought in the early nineteenth century.

The painted, or fancy, chair fashioned after classical examples was also the type Samuel Gragg (1772–1855?) executed by means of a bent wood technique. Little is known of Gragg's early training and where he might have been schooled in the methods of bending wood.[53] However, some knowledge of Gragg's boyhood in New Hampshire permits one to speculate that his family had provided him with some exposure to the bent wood process. Before taking up farming, his father had been trained as a wheelwright, which would have brought him into contact with coachmakers, who had been using a bent wood technology for decades in the construction of enclosed cabs for carriages. In order to bend the thin wooden panels used for these cabs, part of the panel would be submerged in a vat of heated sand, which caused partial evaporation of the moisture in the wood while forcing the panel to contract in controlled curves.[54] For centuries, cabinet-makers, too, had been immersing pieces of wood used for pictorial marquetry in baths of hot sand in order to achieve artistic shading.

During the second half of the eighteenth century and into the first quarter of the nineteenth, several noteworthy experiments and patented inventions involving bent wood were published in England and Continental Europe.[55] Yet, with the exception of *The Drawing Book* (1793–94) by Thomas Sheraton, which mentions the use of bent wood in conjunction with furniture design and manufacture, and a brief notation in *The London Chair-Makers' and Carvers' Book of Prices, for Workmanship* (1807), which gives the rate for bending banisters of chairs, none of these investigations are concerned with the making of furniture. Also, they evolved in circles geographically and culturally too distant for Gragg to have been aware of them. Further, the publication of both Sheraton's book and the price guide may well have been too close in time to Gragg's own work to have had any influence upon him.

It is likely, however, that Gragg's environment included examples of Windsor chairs, which, by the late eighteenth century, were becoming increasingly important components of the middle-class interior in the Colonies. An example of a Windsor armchair made by Gragg and dated some time in the first quarter of the nineteenth century (figure 1–38) indicates that he was engaged in the production of these generic seating forms at some point in his career. The use of turned spindles in the back of this chair not only reminds one of wheel spokes and his father's earlier profession, but also recalls the hypothesis proposed above that relates the spoke backs of early-eighteenth-century Windsor chairs with the spokes of the wheels used on the early garden carts of Bourbon France and Georgian England. The reinvention of the Windsor may indeed have occurred in Gragg's experience and provided him with an intimate understanding of the nature of wood, which the mere rote replication of Windsor forms might not have granted him. Despite the late date of Gragg's Windsor chair and the fact that it does not have any bent elements, its very existence

Figure 1-37
Duncan Phyfe. Armchair. American, ca. 1810. Mahogany, cane, and removable cushion (modern). The Metropolitan Museum of Art, New York (Gift of C. Ruxton Love, 1960).

Figure 1-38
Samuel Gragg. Armchair. American, ca. 1808–25. Painted wood. Old Sturbridge Village, Massachusetts.

Figure 1-39
Samuel Gragg. Side chair. American, 1805–15. Bent ash and hickory (painted). Museum of Fine Arts, Boston (Gift of Mrs. Ralph Lowell, in memory of her godmother Mrs. Arthur L. Williston [Mary DeForest Denny]). CAT. NO. 3.

suggests a conjunction between earlier Windsor forms and Gragg's own revolutionary chairs, whose bent elements were patented in the first decade of the nineteenth century.

Gragg had moved to Boston around 1800 and almost immediately established a furniture-making firm with his future brother-in-law. Several years later, on August 30, 1808, and by now a sole proprietor, Gragg received a United States patent for a bent-wood chair. In the following year an advertisement in the *Columbian Centinel* (May 10, 1809) announced that Gragg had for sale "Patent CHAIRS and SETTEES, with elastic backs and bottoms, made in a new, elegant and superior style, of the best materials."[56] The word *elastic* is particulary revealing, for it is just this characteristic, it would seem, that Gragg is emphasizing to a clientele interested in comfort.

Gragg produced several types of chairs and settees constructed of bent elements; among them are two that demonstrate especially well his evolution as a designer and manufacturer. The earlier of the two is probably the side chair painted white and embellished with painted decorations (figure 1–39). This chair is fabricated in part of two long strips of oak that have been bent to create a continuous stile and side rail, similar to the construction of Chapuis's chair (figure 1–36). These strips define the frame of the chair and enclose five additional bent members that comprise the slats of the back and the ribs of the seat. Dovetailed into the crest rail, these flat oak strips, which mirror the lines of the stiles, are secured to the rear seat rail with lap joints and then continue on to form the seat, ending in another series of single dovetails cut into the front rail. The legs were executed separately by turning and attached with a mortise and tenon.

This earlier chair lacks the aesthetic and technological sophistication of the second example (figure 1–40), which exhibits a more masterful manipulation of bent wood. Here one continuous piece of bent ash extends from the crest rail, down the stiles, along the seat rail, and over the front rail to create the front leg. The single-piece, continuous back and seat splats are treated exactly as in the previous chair. Similar designs were used by numerous known and anonymous craftsmen of the early nineteenth century, who employed traditional joinery in the creation of their designs (figure 1–41).

Gragg's specific methodology for bending wood remains unknown, since patent papers awarded before 1836 were destroyed in a fire. It is nevertheless possible to speculate that bending by heat alone would not have been sufficient to produce the ambitious, load-bearing curves employed in both designs. It is more likely that steam was used, as this would have kept the fibers more pliable under the tension of bending than dry heat could. What remains remarkable about Gragg's work is his confident use of bent solid wood—a goal not attained by German-born Michael Thonet, despite repeated experiments, until nearly fifty years later. The process of preparing and then bending laminates would eventually be eliminated from Thonet's manufacturing process as both structurally unstable and time-consuming, and therefore economically inadvisable.

Figure 1-40
Samuel Gragg. Side chair. American, ca. 1815. Bent ash and hickory. Museum of Fine Arts, Boston (Charles Hitchcock Tyler Residuary Fund).

Michael Thonet

In the eighteenth century, German-born cabinetmakers had distinguished themselves at many of the courts of Europe, most notably at Versailles, and in Paris. By the 1780s, artisans with German names dominated the cabinet-making trades in France, and certain individuals, such as David Roentgen, were experiencing strong sales of their work as far east as Saint Petersburg at the court of Catherine the Great. The technical perfection of German work and its contribution to advanced taste had established a solid reputation by the end of the century. But this did not survive the Napoleonic wars intact. The political repression and economic depression that occurred in Germany and Austria following the abdication of Napoleon contributed to the restriction of the German cabinetmakers' geographic sphere of influence.

Thus, by the end of the first quarter of the nineteenth century, these cabinetmakers had turned their attention to the home markets, which were primarily composed of a middle-class clientele with limited budgets. Aware of the decrease in the number of princely patrons, many cabinetmakers sought innovations that would enable them to survive within their financially restricted markets.[57] Inexpensive stamped metal mounts instead of cast ones, pressed ornaments made from sawdust, and advances

Figure 1-41
Joshua Holden, attributed to. Side chair. American, ca. 1810. Painted wood (upholstery modern). Courtesy Robert E. Kinnaman, Long Island, New York.

Figure 1–42

Michael Thonet. Armchair. Germany, ca. 1836. Bent laminated wood, solid wood, veneer (walnut?), cane. Collection Rudolf Schöneberger, Boppard am Rhein, West Germany. CAT. NO. 4.

made with the processing of wood characterize the basic tenor of the trade at this time. The battle for economic survival incited a degree of innovation, in both technique and aesthetics.

It was the improved techniques for cutting veneers that helped make Michael Thonet's achievements in bent wood a possibility. With sophisticated machinery that reduced waste and costs, logs could be transformed into seemingly endless sheets of veneer. Economics also dictated that indigenous trees that had formerly been considered inappropriate for veneer production be brought into use, further reducing costs. It is more than likely that it was this increased availability of material at lower costs that permitted Michael Thonet to take his early financial risks in pursuit of his experiments.

Born in the small river town of Boppard am Rhein in 1796, Thonet began his experiments with bent wood in the 1830s with the intent of replicating the effects of established Biedermeier aesthetics at a lower cost than furniture assembled by conventional techniques. Although entering a period of debased design by the time Thonet undertook his investigations, Biedermeier classicism was still the prevalent mode of expression in fashionable circles. Little is known of Thonet's early work, which was produced with traditional joinery, a practice he must have followed at least until the mid-1830s when his experiments with strips of bent laminates produced the so-called Boppard chair (figure 1–42).

In this laminate process, which took advantage of the increased availability of veneers, Thonet cut his wood sheets into strips, bound them together in layers of varying thickness, and soaked them in a vat of heated glue. It is not clear how long these bundles were left to soak, but when they were removed from the bath, they were immediately bound into forms that were probably made of cast iron.[58] Once dry, these elements were assembled with carved pieces of solid wood to produce chair frames that were then veneered with more expensive wood that fully obscured the innovative construction. Although it subscribes to a Biedermeier aesthetic, the undulant form of these chairs was rarely attained by chairs of the same period executed from solid wood by means of traditional joinery.[59]

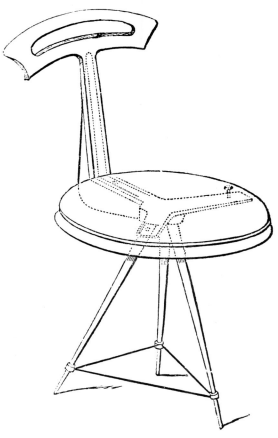

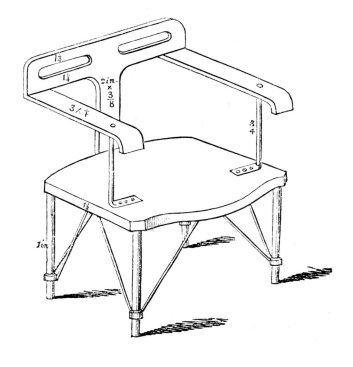

Figure 1-43
John Claudius Loudon. Project for a revolving desk chair. English, ca. 1833. Figure 651 in *Encyclopaedia of Cottage, Farm and Villa Architecture*.

Figure 1-44
John Claudius Loudon. Project for a cottage armchair. English, ca. 1833. Figure 650 in *Encyclopaedia of Cottage, Farm and Villa Architecture*.

John Claudius Loudon

During the previous decade, John Claudius Loudon (1783–1843), the prominent English landscape gardener and critic whose publications would have a decisive effect on architectural thought in pre–Civil War America, had published his *Encyclopaedia of Cottage, Farm and Villa Architecture and Furniture*, which was directed to a simpler taste than that catered to by cabinetmakers engaged in the production of high-style, traditionally joined furniture. In his chapter on furnishings for cottage dwellings, Loudon discusses Windsor chairs,[60] which had persisted as a staple item of rural furnishings into the nineteenth century, and follows this immediately with two cottage chairs that include the use of bent members (figures 1–43 and 1–44). In the design for a revolving desk chair, gas tubing is used for the three-legged support system of the chair, which is also constructed from cast and wrought iron. Gas tubing

is also proposed for the execution of the arms of the other chair, although it is not apparent how these sections were bent. These austere designs, mechanistic in their construction and composition, may be interpreted as isolated precursors to much of the architect-designed furniture of the 1920s and 1930s. These suggestions by Loudon do not appear to have been executed, as no known examples exist.[61]

John Henry Belter

It would not be until the middle of the nineteenth century, and in the United States, that furniture constructed from bent laminates would emerge as fully acceptable elements of the high-style interior. That one major designer and maker of these furnishings, John Henry Belter (1804–1863), freely advertised their innovative construction, as Gragg had done, indicates that a premium was placed on these

Figure 1-45
J. and J. W. Meeks, attributed to. Side chair (left). American, ca. 1855. Carved rosewood, upholstery (modern). The Brooklyn Museum, New York (Gift of Mrs. Alfred T. Zoébisch).

Figure 1-46
John Henry Belter. Side chair (right). American, ca. 1855. Bent rosewood plywood, solid rosewood, upholstery (modern). The Manney Collection.

designs that extended beyond mere aesthetics. Perhaps no single body of craftsman-produced work was so comprehensive as Belter's in its application of bent wood to almost every type of furniture used in the home. Beyond a wide variety of seating forms, his repertory included tables, étagères, beds, and even case pieces. It is fitting that this individual, the culminating figure in this century and a quarter of craftsman-produced work, should also be one of the most accomplished designers involved with the development of bent wood technology in the furniture-making trades. And, if one is to believe the published accounts of the period, Belter also made the transition from craftsman to businessman and "factory" owner.

Although it is known that Belter was born in Ulm, Germany, there is no evidence that he received his early training in that city before emigrating to the United States sometime around 1840. It is informative to trace Belter's professional and geographic advancement through the New York City directories dating from the 1840s until his death in 1863. He appears for the first time in 1844, listed as a cabinetmaker. Not until a decade later, when he appears at his fourth address in the city, is he listed as John Henry Belter and Company. Three years afterward, the directories list him with a factory operation at Third Avenue and Seventy-sixth Street.[62] On the basis of the surviving examples of Belter's work, as well as its far-flung geographic disposition, it is safe to assume that he produced a considerable amount of furniture. However, it must be kept in mind that this work, although frequently imperial in scale and elaborate in terms of decoration, was primarily destined for the luxury trade, which in the nineteenth century, despite the dramatic growth of the plutocracy, must have been somewhat limited in size. It is unlikely that Belter's furniture was made under actual factory conditions with a standardized, assembly-line procedure. The methodology of repetitive craft production was probably used for his designs, which required meticulous attention to detail. Ultimately, it is the union of aesthetics and technology in Belter's work that remains the most fascinating aspect of his accomplishment.

By the early 1820s the all-embracing classicism that had dominated artistic thought in the earlier years of the century was supplanted by an increasing interest in historicism.

This interpretive manipulation of the past fostered a taste for historicist revivals that remained constant throughout the century. During the 1830s and 1840s in Europe, and the 1840s and 1850s in the United States, the dominant revival style in furniture was undoubtedly the Rococo (figure 1–45). A romanticized evocation of the epoch of the ancien régime, this lavish torrent of curves provided a reassuring image of the past to the emerging plutocracy, the primary beneficiaries of the Industrial Revolution. Belter's Germanic background infused his work in this mode with a vigorous expression of line well suited to the scale of his designs, which are considerably larger than their eighteenth-century predecessors.

The suitability of conventional joinery for the execution of his furniture and the low salary of skilled labor in the mid-nineteenth century lead one to ponder Belter's need to devise and then apply his technically complicated methodology to this type of luxury work. First, in the use of plywood—a laminate whose sheets of veneer are laid so that the wood grain of each sheet runs at right angles to the adjacent layer—Belter produced a chair that was lighter in weight than one made from sections of solid wood cut and then joined. This reduced weight was important in furniture of imposing scale. Second, the need for strength was especially essential in the laminate construction of Belter's chair backs (figure 1–46), which were frequently pierced with extravagant openwork carving (figure 1–47) that has a weakening effect no conventionally

Figure 1–47
John Henry Belter. Crest, detail of armchair. American, ca. 1855–63. The Manney Collection. CAT. NO. **21.**

constructed chair could withstand. In addition, the pli-ability of a laminate allowed for fewer constructional components in the fabrication of a design. Belter fused the traditional system of rails, stiles, and subsidiary supports into a single sheet of bent laminated wood, a procedure also employed in the hoop back of Windsor chairs (see cat. no. 1). This reductivist approach was most brilliantly realized in Belter's career in his patented process for the construction of a bed (figure 1–48). The laminate used in this design permitted Belter to construct a bed frame (figure 1–49) from two major elements, in contrast to the traditional methodology that used four sections of wood for headboard, footboard, and pair of side rails. A board produced by sheets of veneer glued together is in fact stronger than a solid wood board of similar size and thickness.

The construction of Belter's furniture, particularly his seating forms, displays an ingenious expansion of the potential of innovative woodworking over conventional construction. Cauls had been used for centuries to apply pressure during the application of protective decorative veneers to cheaper secondary wood in the production of case pieces. According to the patent awarded Belter by the U.S. Patent Office in 1858 (figure 1–50), he used several cauls simultaneously. Eschewing the traditional aim of these cauls—to apply a decorative skin—Belter used them to glue as many as sixteen layers of veneer. After placing the layers around an inner caul that had been heated (figure 1–50, number 14), he encased this with outer cauls that repeated the curvature (figure 1–50, numbers 15 and 17). By clamping this assemblage and allowing it to dry for twenty-four hours, he effectively "cast" eight chair backs simultaneously in a procedure that saved time and money, and presaged mass production.

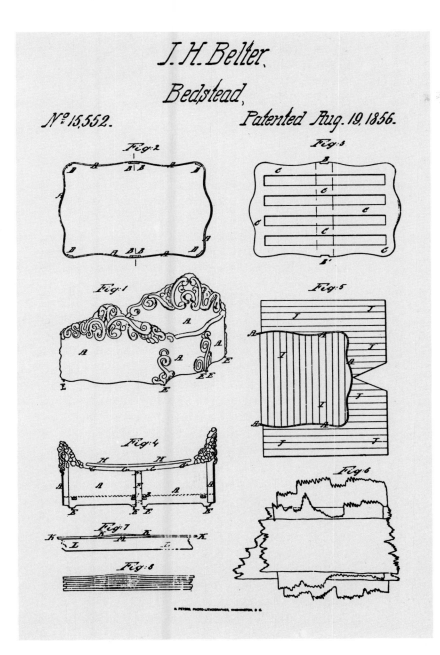

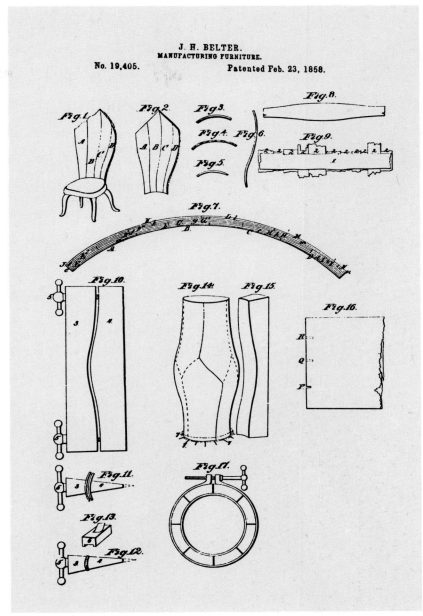

Figure 1–49
John Henry Belter. Diagrams indicating manufacture of bed frame. Letters Patent, No. 15,552, August 19, 1856. U.S. Department of Commerce, Patent and Trademark Office, Washington, D.C.

Figure 1–50
John Henry Belter. Diagrams indicating manufacture of laminated chair backs. Letters Patent, No. 19,405, February 23, 1858. U.S. Department of Commerce, Patent and Trademark Office, Washington, D.C.

Figure 1–51
John Henry Belter. Side chair. American, ca. 1850. Molded rosewood plywood, solid rosewood, upholstery (modern). Collection Dr. and Mrs. Milton L. Brindley, Augusta, Kentucky.

Between the appearance of Belter's earliest designs in the 1840s and the time of his final patent in 1860, the forms of his furniture grew more and more intricate. This was perhaps as much a reflection of changing taste as it was an indication of Belter's increasing mastery of his process and materials. The backs of his chairs in particular display a development from a simple cylindrical shape to a conical one to the most complicated of all: the spherical, or dished, form (figure 1–51). This last type of back remains Belter's most substantial contribution to the use of laminates for the production of furniture. In Belter's method, plywood was bent in a complex curve similar to that found on a segment of a sphere. The difficulty of stabilizing sheets of wood that are forced to bend in opposing directions under stressful conditions is such that it was not until the early 1930s that this form appeared again—in the work of Alvar Aalto (cat. no. 101).[63] The advantage of this compound curve is that it introduces a degree of comfort to a chair back that is not available in cylindrical or conical curves. In the twentieth century this form would also eliminate the need for upholstery, a circumstance inconceivable to Belter's clientele. The century-long interlude between the accomplishments of the American John Henry Belter and the achievements of the Finnish Alvar Aalto is one more example of the sporadic rhythm and far-flung distances that accompany the earlier body of work with bent woods and bent metals, obscuring its connections with twentieth-century developments.

Notes

1. Aldred, p. 697, fig. 498. Aldred sees this bent-wood construction as a transitional stage in a development from rush work "to a plainer, less organic type, depending for its appeal on clean lines and good proportions."

2. Newberry, p. 31 and pl. XI; Killen, p. 1.

3. Aldred, p. 701.

4. Killen, p. 44.

5. Ibid., p. 45, No. 17, where the stool is published for the first time.

6. Killen does not mention the condition of the stool, namely, its stability, which might contribute further evidence. Were these legs bent, there would have been considerable variation in the relaxing of these three members when the stool was transferred from the hot, arid climate of Egypt to the more humid, temperate environment of England.

7. Richter, p. 125.

8. *Hist. Plant.* 5.6.2 and 5.7.3,4; quoted in Richter, p. 125.

9. Ibid.

10. London 1972, p. 741, entry by William Reider.

11. Produced by Saridis Furniture Manufacturers, Athens, the line was introduced to the luxury trade in 1962.

12. The date of 1176 for the inception of this period and the selection of many of the objects cited in this discussion are based on the research of Dr. Penelope Eames, who has published the most comprehensive work of its kind on the aesthetic, historical, social and technical aspects of medieval furniture.

13. Eames, p. 23.

14. One of the most superb Gothic chests to remain essentially intact, this piece has been dated as early as 1100 (Viaux, pp. 35–36) and as late as 1250–70 (Eames, pp. 175–77).

15. Although displaying an archaic, dug-out form with its barrel lid, this particular chest is nevertheless dated by Eames (pp. 175–77) as late as the second half of the fifteenth century.

16. Frank, pp. 148, 150.

17. See Cleveland 1971, Nos. 81 and 82.

18. Macquoid and Edwards, vol. 3, p. 72, fig. 12; for a more detailed analysis, see Thornton and Tomlin, p. 60 and fig. 69.

19. Macquoid and Edwards, vol. 1, p. 319, entry by Margaret Jourdain.

20. Chinnery, p. 533, cites this earliest mention of Windsor chairs, which appears in the inventory of the estate of a Philadelphia merchant named John Jones. It records three chairs by this name, but provides no information as to their appearance or manner of construction, making it impossible at this point to conclude precisely what sort of chairs these were.

21. Daniel Marot (ca. 1663–1752) was a French-born Huguenot who fled France in 1685 at the revocation of the Edict of Nantes and emigrated to Holland. He soon entered the service of William of Orange, who ascended the throne of England in 1689 as William III. As architect to the royal couple, Marot was responsible for many of the interior schemes of several of their residences in both Holland and England. Marot helped foster the growth of late Baroque design in England during this period, bringing with him many of the concepts he had acquired while living in France.

22. For a review of these portraits, see Baker.

23. Thornton and Tomlin, fig. 107; Hardy, p. 119.

24. Stick construction depends on a simple wedged joint: the legs of a stool or chair are rammed through holes bored into the seat board and then secured by wedges; see Chinnery, p. 75.

25. Turnery "consists essentially of shaping a piece of wood with chisels while it revolves around an axis between the jaws of a lathe"; ibid., p. 83.

26. Ibid., p. 87.

27. Ibid., p. 85.

28. Although the discussion presented here does not follow Evans's conclusions in all their particulars, it should be noted that her study of the English Windsor chair is the most comprehensive, scholarly examination yet published.

29. Evans, p. 31.

30. Ibid., p. 27, quoting Switzer, vol. 3, p. 125.

31. Ibid., p. 27, quoting Defoe, vol. 1, p. 304.

32. Ibid., p. 28.

33. For a detailed discussion of this type of construction, see Chinnery, pp. 65–69.

34. Lipp-work construction consists of an inner support system (generally poles) of a pliable wood such as ash, which acts as a frame for the woven straw shell.

35. Evans, p. 31, quoting Amherst, pp. 240–42; also Macquoid and Edwards, vol. 1, p. 319, entry written by Margaret Jourdain, who first published it circa 1924.

36. Evans, pp. 31–32.

37. Ibid, p. 35.

38. See also Hardy, fig. 4.

39. For an extensive discussion of this design and its popularity in terms of numbers produced in the nineteenth century, see the essays in this volume by Alessandro Alverà and Graham Dry, and cat. nos. 14–18.

40. Hughes, p. 1242, describes the process that may have been used and discusses the types of wood employed.

41. Goyne, p. 229.

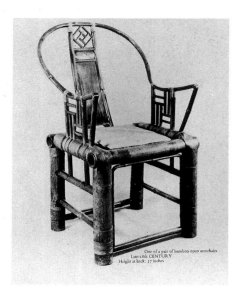

One of a pair of bamboo open armchairs
Late-18th CENTURY
Height at back: 37 inches

Figure 1–52
Armchair. China (?), late 18th century. Bamboo. Whereabouts unknown.

42. Although unsubstantiated by current scholarship, a Chinese garden seat made of bent bamboo (a grass, not a wood) was sold as a late-eighteenth-century chair at John Sparks, Ltd., London, in 1974. The continuous arm rail of the chair (figure 1–52) shows a mastery of form that rivals the accomplishments of the English or Colonial craftsmen.

43. Thornton and Tomlin, p. 149, figs. 168 and 169.

44. "The pierced galleries on small tables were generally constructed of three thicknesses of mahogany veneer glued together"; Macquoid and Edwards, vol. 2, p. 239. See also Symonds, p. 174: "When original, these frets are invariably of a 3-ply construction, the two outer layers of wood having the grain running along the length, the middle layer with the grain across the width. This built-up construction provided strength and prevented warping or twisting. The top edge of the gallery is covered by a capping, sometimes decorated with a checker inlay."

45. The maker of these candlestands may have deviated from the customary three-ply method in favor of a five-ply process specifically because of the circular form of the fretwork's base. Three-ply veneers may have been more frequent for tables with straight or serpentine-shaped galleries, which distribute far less stress throughout their forms than the closed circle.

46. For the most extensive survey of the remarkable body of designs using bent wood methodology, see New Haven 1982. The author expresses his thanks to Edward Cooke for bringing this valuable catalogue to his attention.

47. Kirk, pp. 152–53, 158.

48. It is not yet certain whether this methodology was used for furnishings other than occasional tables.

49. For details regarding Chapuis, see Ledoux-Lebard, pp. 118–21.

50. Verification of these details was generously communicated by Christopher Monkhouse of the Museum of Art, Rhode Island School of Design, Providence, and verified in subsequent examination by the author. In addition to his knowledge of the pair of Chapuis armchairs in his own institution's collection, Mr. Monkhouse has also examined an unpainted pair in the collection of the Victoria & Albert Museum, London. He also brought to the author's attention the set of seven Chapuis armchairs in the collection of the Anderson House Museum, Washington, D.C., which has graciously lent one to this exhibition (cat. no. 2).

51. Ledoux-Lebard, p. 119.

52. Ypersele de Strihou, p. 278.

53. For an extensive article on Gragg, see Kane.

54. For the techniques employed by coachmakers, see Roubo, pp. 491–95.

55. See Kane, pp. 27–31.

56. Deutsch, p. 939. Gragg's further characterization of these chairs—"very strong, light and airy . . . in their form and construction . . . combining fancy with convenience and strength"—anticipates the descriptions that would accompany notices of mass-produced bent-wood chairs later in the century.

57. For a detailed discussion of these innovations, see Himmelheber, pp. 39–41.

58. In suggesting cast-iron molds, the author differs from Alessandro Alverà (see the essay in this volume) and Wilk 1980a, p. 7, who refer to wooden molds. It would seem that casting a bundle of glue-saturated strips of wood in a wooden mold would result in having the two components adhere.

59. For the patents Thonet sought in France, England, and Belgium to protect his inventions, see the essays in this volume by Alessandro Alverà and Graham Dry.

60. Loudon, pp. 320–21.

61. Nearly ten years after the publication of Loudon's work an individual in France by the name of Gandillot employed a new method for welding gas tubing, which enabled him to produce a side chair whose delicate members, painted to resemble wood, anticipated the Anglo-Japanesque taste of nearly a quarter of a century later. See Giedion, p. 489, fig. 312, where the chair is illustrated, dated 1844, and located in the Musée des Arts Décoratifs, Paris, but not otherwise documented.

62. The criterion for defining a factory in the third quarter of the nineteenth century is ambiguous. In an era when civic pride was extensive, financial worth of a company listed with Dun and Bradstreet does not necessarily provide an accurate indication of a company's standing. Descriptions of a firm's operation may well reflect self-congratulatory inflation and must be interpreted with care.

63. Aalto's experimental chair, which employed this same type of compound curvature, was apparently in limited production for only a brief period, circa 1932–34. It would not be until 1946, with the designs of Charles and Ray Eames, that this type of curvature would be used successfully in mass-produced furniture.

2
Michael Thonet and the development of bent-wood furniture: from workshop to factory production

ALESSANDRO ALVERÀ

FROM the outset of his career, Michael Thonet strove for maximum efficiency, not only in his selection of woods on the basis of their particular structural potential, but also in the progressive development of his method. This same goal characterized the designs of his chairs, in which simplicity of form was never overwhelmed by the technical problems of production. From the first Thonet-made chairs of the mid-1830s to the opening of the factory at Koritschan some twenty years later, each new technical solution may be seen to have spurred Thonet on to an immediate demonstration of its possibilities by the virtuoso creation of intertwined forms. It was during this period that the critical problems of mass-producing bent-wood furniture were solved. A detailed examination of these early chairs from a technical standpoint reveals an interplay between design and production that ultimately led to Thonet's

creation of the immensely popular chair known as Number 14. This chair, which journeyed from the Biedermeier era into the modern world, exemplifies the transformation of workshop traditions into factory production.

Beginnings

The Thonet family, originally from Andernach-am-Rhein, moved to Boppard am Rhein (Prussia) ten years prior to Michael's birth on July 2, 1796. His father operated a tannery, but arranged for young Michael to study cabinet-making.[1] At the time that Michael Thonet was learning his craft, the Napoleonic era was drawing to a close, and in reaction to Empire, the Biedermeier style was developing in Germany and Austria. It reflected the economic status and special demands of the bourgeoisie; excluded from political participation by the consequences of the Congress of Vienna (1814–15), bourgeois families retreated to the domestic sphere, providing an impetus for the creation of furniture that was practical, inexpensive, and refined.

Political conditions were favorable for Thonet's career. Prince Clemens von Metternich, the chancellor of Austria, had established a police state, but his mistrust of all experimentation did not extend to the realms of trade, industry, or applied arts. Such repression of economic and technological progress would have resulted in fiscal setbacks to the state and in social discontent among the bourgeoisie. It was therefore considered politically expedient to encourage the citizenry to direct their creative energies toward this kind of progress, and the industrialization of the state was one of Metternich's priorities.

Industrial fairs had long been frequent in the area: as early as 1791 one was held in Prague for the entire Austro-Hungarian Empire. In 1807 Emperor Francis I of Austria founded the Kaiserlichen Königlichen Fabrika-Produkten-Kabinett, a collection of art, arts and crafts, and commercial products, in an attempt to foster a national artistic con-

sciousness.[2] Following in the footsteps of the French industrial fairs that had been held in the Louvre since 1798, the first German exhibition of art and industry took place in 1812 in Stuttgart, followed by further presentations in 1815 in Munich and in 1816 in Düsseldorf and Leipzig. These exhibitions, in which entries were judged and awards granted, were held with increasing frequency and were instrumental in stimulating a consciousness of style distinct from French influence. Throughout his career, Michael Thonet was to use such competitions to bring his productions to the attention of the public.

Under Metternich, Austria sought to assure the effectiveness of technical fields of endeavor through an increased emphasis on education; much attention was given to the advanced training of master craftsmen. In urban centers, polytechnical institutes were founded to disseminate information about machines, tools, materials, and foreign production methods. At that time the apprenticeship period lasted two to four years, after which one could work as a journeyman before taking the examination to qualify as a master. This required the design and construction of a piece of furniture within four weeks.

While undergoing his training, Thonet must have been struck by the trade's frequent use of unsuitable wood and by a general disregard for its natural structure. When a curved shape was required for use as a chair leg, arm, or back, for example, it was cut from a flat board, resulting in the waste of the remaining pieces. Yet in Austria there were furniture-manufacturing methods that were designed to conserve solid hardwoods, and these processes must also have fascinated Thonet. One such method was the use of veneer. Expensive, fine hardwood veneers, primarily made from indigenous woods, served as an important design element in furniture making. Veneer was used over a less expensive softwood ground. The direction of the grain of each veneer was kept consistent so as to encase the piece of furniture, which was often finished with carved and turned parts of solid wood (figure 2–1). To counteract the expansion and contraction of the softwood ground, face veneers were glued on both sides of the substrate with their grain at right angles to it. This process of layering the veneers most likely inspired Thonet to dispense with the substrate.

There were also attempts to economize on the produc-

Figure 2–1
Michael Thonet. Sofa, ca. 1836–40.

tion of decorative "carvings" through the development of a technique for pouring and pressing a mixture of sawdust and additives into molds. This technique, first used in Berlin in 1816[3] and a year later in England by Peter Hamelin, exemplifies the economy of process that attracted Michael Thonet.

Advances in such processes were simultaneously felt in the tool industry: from England came several innovations initially intended for manual use, such as "glasspaper" (sandpaper) and an improved planer. In 1817 the brothers Alois and Martin Mundig patented a circular saw, or "buzz saw," based on English models. Although intended for veneer production, its disadvantage was the thickness of its blade, which caused half the lumber to be wasted. Significant economy resulted from Alois Mundig's patent in 1821 for a veneer-cutting machine that cut rather than sawed the wood.[4]

The era was not without precedents for bent-wood experimentation. Apart from the basket-weaving practice of exploiting the elasticity of fresh, moist willow shoots, wood was bent for use in shipbuilding and bridge construction, as well as in the making of kegs and walking sticks. For these purposes, however, the wood was bent prior to being structurally incorporated and either was curved within the limits of its elasticity[5] or, in the case of very resistant hardwood, was repeatedly heated to remove its natural moisture until the desired degree of curve was obtained. In Austria in 1821 the wagonmaker Melchior Fink obtained a patent for his process of bending wheel rims from one piece of wood,[6] but the invention was not exploited. Around the same time an Englishman, Isaak Sargent, developed a method of bending wood by softening it in hot water, pressing it into curved molds, and drying it in the shade, a significant technological advance used in the making of wagon wheels.[7]

Thonet's first workshop: Boppard

Having acquired both practical experience and innovative ideas, Michael Thonet established his own workshop in Boppard am Rhein in 1819. He began by working in a traditional manner while steadily developing his ideas for lighter, more stable furniture than had previously been possible. By the 1830s he had begun to experiment with bent and laminated veneers, producing furniture parts such as the head- and footboards of beds and sofas. By 1836 he was also producing bent and laminated parts for chairs (figure 2–2; cat. no. 4). (This innovative use of structural veneers is to be distinguished from the aforementioned decorative use, which Thonet did continue in all of his chairs of this period.) Business was good: the furniture was relatively inexpensive and extremely popular in Boppard and nearby Rhineland towns.[8] A staff of twenty to twenty-five people was employed in Thonet's workshop.[9]

In 1841 Thonet exhibited at the Koblenz fair and came to the attention of Prince Metternich, a fellow Rhinelander, who immediately recognized Thonet's ideas as according with his own intentions of promoting Austria's industrialization. He invited Thonet to his castle, Johannisberg-am-Rhein, to learn more about these new inventions. Thonet brought with him a selection of chairs and canes, a wagon wheel, and several other pieces as demonstrations of his ideas. Metternich, greatly enthusiastic, urged him to relocate in Vienna, saying: "In Boppard you will always remain a poor man. Go to Vienna, I shall recommend you there at court."[10] In the spring of 1842 Thonet decided to take the chancellor's advice, for with Metternich's support he hoped to secure patents in Austria. Acting on behalf of Metternich, the Baron Karl Hügel showed several examples of Thonet's furniture to the kaiser in Vienna; the response was most favorable. On July 16, 1842, the Austrian court granted Michael Thonet the right "to bend any type of wood, even the most brittle, into the desired forms and curves by chemical and mechanical means."[11] Meanwhile, however, during Thonet's absence from Boppard his creditors, who had advanced him money the year before for the purpose of acquiring patents in France, England, and Belgium, confiscated all of his belongings. His success at court and subsequent difficulties in Boppard prompted Thonet to move his family to Vienna in the fall of that same year.

Vienna

Shortly after his arrival in Vienna in 1842, Thonet was able to produce inexpensive bent-wood chairs at the workshop of Franz List, a furniture manufacturer; extant documents

Figure 2–2
Michael Thonet. Side chair, ca. 1836–40. Bent laminated wood, solid wood, veneer, cane. Alexander von Vegesack, Düsseldorf.

give no indication of what these chairs looked like. List, who was about to retire, recommended Thonet to the English architect P. H. Desvignes, who was then renovating and furnishing Liechtenstein's estate in Vienna. Desvignes was immediately receptive to Thonet's work and asked him to execute designs for a parquet floor in the Liechtenstein Palace. The architect was very pleased with the results and would have given Thonet other projects for the palace, but Carl Leistler had already been engaged to produce all the necessary woodwork.[12] Instead Desvignes mediated a compromise, whereby Thonet and Leistler drew up a contract stipulating that for a fixed remuneration Thonet and his sons could produce all of the bent-wood work and would be given work space in the Leistler factory.[13] There Thonet produced parquet flooring, various ornaments, and fretwork, and, during this period of collaborative work, became familiar with the most recent stylistic trends, particularly the rococo revival.

At the same time Thonet continued to explore new bent-wood production techniques. Vienna was an environment that fostered such experimentation. It was a city just beginning to undergo industrial expansion, and there was a growing need for inexpensive, mass-produced items. Thonet sought to meet this demand by progressively reducing his designs to as few pieces as possible; by the late 1850s he was to succeed in producing the back legs and backrest of a chair as a single unit.

After completing the pieces for the Liechtenstein Palace, Thonet suggested to Leistler that they open a workshop together. Thonet was willing to share his patent in return for work space and the use of Leistler's machines. However, Leistler rejected the offer, and in May 1849 Thonet and his sons Franz, Michael, August, and Joseph, opened the family's first workshop in the second floor of a house in the Viennese suburb of Gumpendorf.

The process of industrialization that had already encouraged Thonet's creativity was now intensifying, the general mood of the era being one of change and a fresh start. After the stormy events of March 1848 Metternich resigned his office and fled to Great Britain. Kaiser Franz I abdicated in October, and Franz Josef I became kaiser of Austria. The parliament in Vienna abolished every form of rural subservience, and Austria further evolved from a feudal agrarian country into a modern industrialized nation. This atmosphere continued to motivate Michael Thonet to adapt his developing bent-wood technology for industrial production.

In late 1849 Desvignes returned to England, where he had expected to receive a large government commission. He intended to engage the Thonet family for this project and bring them to England, but the plan did not materialize. Despite this, for the first two years of Thonet's new workshop, Desvignes supported the craftsman's family with regular payments, enabling Thonet to concentrate on the development of furniture for mass production.

Technological development of the early chairs

The Thonet workshop was eventually to evolve into Gebrüder Thonet, an international business force. But before examining this expansion, a detailed review of the Thonet chairs from the days of the first Boppard workshop of 1819 to the founding of the Koritschan factory in 1856 will serve to demonstrate Thonet's elegant solutions to the critical problems of producing bent-wood furniture.

The Boppard period

Thonet's earliest chair designs incorporated his innovative use of bent laminates but retained the forms characteristic of the Biedermeier period. The model illustrated in figure 2–3, although still quite stiff and made of many components, nonetheless represents the first step in a development leading to a chair made entirely of bent wood.[14] The chair consists of two side components of bent and glued laminates in which the back leg (extending to the backrest) forms one continuous element with the front legs. These components were produced as follows: using a rectangular cross section of a large piece of wood, long strips of thickly cut veneers (hereafter referred to as bundles), were cut in the direction of the grain. Immediately after being softened in a bath of boiling glue thinned with water, these were bent around a wooden mold.[15]

Figure 2–3
**Michael Thonet. Armchair and side chair,
ca. 1836–40.**

Figure 2–4
**Michael Thonet. Side chair, ca. 1840–42.
Bent laminated wood, solid wood, veneer,
upholstery (modern). Collection Georg
Thonet, Frankenberg, West Germany.**

This process had to be completed very quickly in order to take advantage of the wood's increased flexibility, and its application was limited insofar as parts could only be bent in a single plane. In this chair the bent-wood process was therefore restricted to the lower portion of the chair, as well as to the armrests of the armchair model. The sides are connected by crest rail and splat (the two horizontal backrest components), seat frame, and stretchers. The crest rail and splat are again composed of bent and glued laminates, but here the curve has been achieved by pressing them into heated wooden molds.[16] In keeping with the prevailing style, the splat was also carved. The

seat frame is of traditional construction—softwood covered on top with fine veneer.

The next step in the development of Thonet's method was the chair seen in figures 2–4 and 2–5[a] (available only without arms). Here the front and back legs repeat the technique of the first chair, but the backrest represents a significant technological advance. A single element, it is once again formed of bent and glued laminates. Unlike the Boppard chair in which the crest rail and splat are inserted as independent elements, the splat of this chair is structurally integrated into the one-piece construction of the stiles and crest rail. The layers of the laminate have

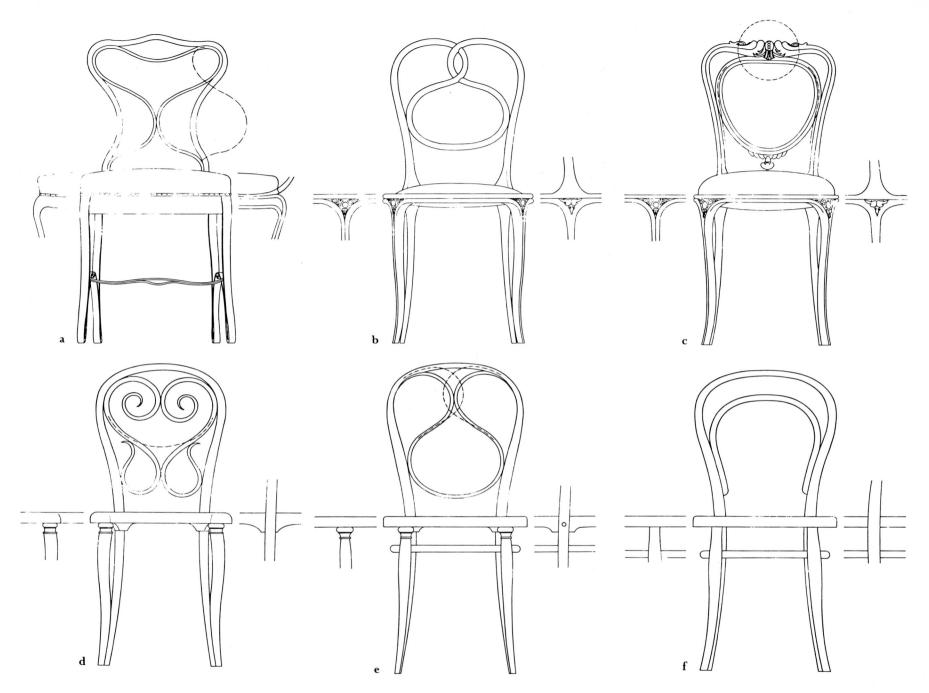

Figure 2–5
Drawings of side chairs designed by Michael Thonet. *From left*: a, side chair, ca. 1840–42; b, side chair, ca. 1843; c, side chair, ca. 1844–45; d, side chair, Model No. 4, ca. 1848; e, side chair, Model No. 1, ca. 1850; f, side chair, Model No. 14, ca. 1855.

Figure 2-6

Figure 2-7

Figure 2-8

been pulled inward and downward from the back element and secured together. The rectangular cross section of the backrest has been rounded off with a rasp.[17] The backrest has been glued and screwed onto the seat frame, a solution that is less than satisfactory aesthetically. Thonet compensated for this by providing thick upholstery (the upholstery in figure 2–4 is a replacement).

The Liechtenstein chairs

The first model Michael Thonet designed for the Liechtenstein Palace was gilded (figures 2–5[b] and 2–6; cat. nos. 5 and 6). It reveals both stylistic and technical distinctions when compared to an armchair by Carl Leistler (figure 2–7). Leistler's chair is made of solid wood, decorated with carving, and executed in keeping with traditional practices of craftsmanship, while the Thonet

chair, which was probably based on a design by Desvignes, is innovative in form and construction. Pieces of solid wood were layered between strips of thickly cut veneers, composing a rectangular cross-section, which was then rounded off with a rasp. These segments were cut into appropriate curves, joined together, and coated with white grounding in preparation for the gilt finish. Where the legs and back connect to the seat frame, a triangular carved element has been inserted. Thonet's goal of assembling a chair from separate components is evident, in contrast to Leistler's more conventional idea of a chair as an individual and unified product.

Other chairs for the Liechtenstein Palace are similar in structure (figures 2–5[c] and 2–8). The seat rails, however, slightly differ in shape, and the back splat has been replaced by an upholstered element, reflecting Thonet's progress toward prefabricated, interchangeable components.

Café Daum

Shortly after Michael Thonet opened his own workshop in Vienna in 1849, he produced the side chair that was subsequently known in the sales catalogue as model No. 4 (figures 2–5[d] and 2–9; cat. no. 7). The chair has a back insert and woven cane seat. The bending technique used in making this chair was one that had already been tested; the seat frame was bent from four laminates, and eight thinner laminates were used for the back insert. Supports were placed beneath the seat frame at the points where the backrest was screwed into the seat. The technological advance that this chair represents may be found in the method of connecting the seat frame to the front legs. The sturdy front legs have been dowelled directly into the seat frame. At this crucial intersection, Thonet integrated a turned capital at the top of the leg, broadening the contact between these two elements and thus reducing the stress. This solution enabled Thonet to attain his goal: a chair assembled entirely from prefabricated components, some of which were interchangeable. In 1850 the chair was exhibited at the Lower Austrian Crafts Association, along with parquet flooring patterned with various types of bent woods. The exhibition, well received in Vienna, attracted the attention of the proprietress of the Café Daum, a fashionable coffeehouse located at the Kohlmarket in Vienna. She commissioned Thonet to produce bent-wood chairs for the café. For this order, his first major commission since opening his own workshop, Thonet executed a model in mahogany laminates, and a short time thereafter supplied the Hotel Zur Königin von England, in Budapest, with four hundred chairs of the same model in ash laminates.

The Crystal Palace exhibition

At the suggestion of the English architect Desvignes, who was still subsidizing the Thonet family at this time, Thonet sent luxury furniture to the first world's fair—the Great Exhibition of 1851—which took place at the Crystal Palace in London. The selection (figure 2–10) represented Thonet's work since 1850 and included two armchairs, six side chairs, a settee of bent palisander laminates, and

three tables. The latter's surfaces, inlaid with tortoise shell, brass, and mother-of-pearl, testify to Thonet's virtuoso mastery of bent-wood techniques. The display was greatly admired, received a bronze medal, and was purchased in its entirety by Desvignes for his country house.[18]

The side chair, model No. 9 (figure 2–11), displays the solutions to two problems that Thonet was facing. He wanted to eliminate the use of carving, whether decorative or structural, and did so by replacing the triangular carved element that he had used in the Liechtenstein chairs with a small loop of bent laminates. Thus he succeeded in creating visual separation while gaining greater stability than in earlier chairs. He also wanted to enhance seating comfort; to do so, he sought to produce compound curves in the back insert and in the rear element comprising the legs, stiles, and crest rail. Because his earlier technique of bent laminated veneers (as specified in the 1842 patent) was limited in application to one plane, producing only a simple curve, Thonet began to experiment with a new technique of bending wood. Using bundles that were already bent and glued, he recut them, perpendicular to the glue lines, into thin strips. He then reglued them into a new bundle and bent them. The result was a compound curve. However, the method was arduous and time-consuming and Thonet soon abandoned it.[19]

Chair Number 14

Michael Thonet's most famous chair, which came to be known as model No. 14, was systematically developed during the 1850s. This chair may be seen as the last logical extension of the Biedermeier quest for complete and natural simplicity. Minimal in its design and economical in its use of material, it anticipates classical modernism. Five variations of this design reveal its gradual evolution as Thonet sought to improve seating quality and to simplify production methods (figures 2–5[f] and 2–12; cat. nos. 14–18). All five models are made of beechwood, with each slightly curved front leg from one piece of solid wood. The back is bolted to the seat in all versions except the first. Aside from these general features in common, each chair is characterized by differences in the methods of construction of the backrest and seat frame. Following

Figure 2-9
Michael Thonet. Side chair, Model No. 4, ca. 1848. Bent solid beechwood, bent laminated beechwood, solid beechwood, cane. Alexander von Vegesack, Düsseldorf. See CAT. NO. 7.

MÖBEL

AUSGESTELLT AUF DER WELTAUSSTELLUNG LONDON 1851.

TAFEL II.

Figure 2–10

Michael Thonet and sons. Furniture, shown at the Exhibition of the Industry of All Nations, Crystal Palace, London, 1851.

Figure 2–11

Michael Thonet. Side chair, Model No. 9, ca. 1860. Bent solid wood, bent laminated wood, cane. Manufactured by Gebrüder Thonet, Vienna. Alexander von Vegesack, Düsseldorf.

the development from the earliest to latest example, there was a progressive reduction in the amount of laminated wood used, as Thonet developed a new technique for the bending of solid wood through the use of steam. The final model includes the minimum number of necessary components, and is suitable for mass production. Thonet's shift from predominately manual to industrial production occurred with his move in the spring of 1853 to a larger work space in Gumpendorf, a mill formerly owned by the painter Amerling. Thus the production model, which appeared in the late 1850s, spans and embodies the transition from workshop to factory production.

Decisive for the creation of the No. 14 chair was the development of the backrest, the basis for which was the back insert seen in previous chairs. Thonet tried dispensing with the caning he had used in the Crystal Palace chair, but the back was then uncomfortable. So once again he developed a back insert from loops of bent wood. But he now bent the wood in a single arch (similar to the upper portion of the former back insert). In figure 2–12[a] the back legs and backrest, although appearing to be a single component, are actually separate: the one-piece element of the backrest, fabricated from a laminate, has been spliced by insertion into a V-shaped receptacle in the solid wood

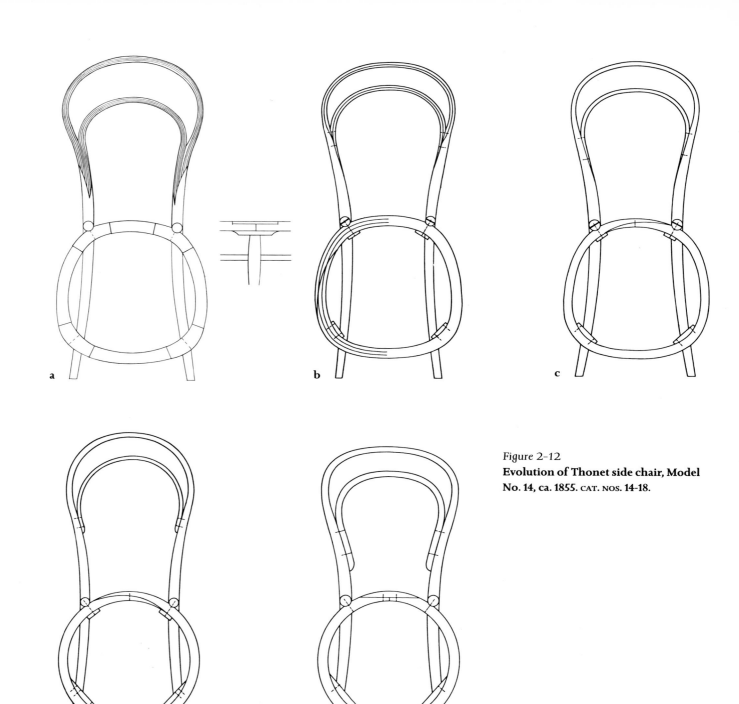

Figure 2-12
Evolution of Thonet side chair, Model No. 14, ca. 1855. CAT. NOS. 14-18.

a

b

c

d

e

portion of the stile, just above the seat rail. Initially, this solution was not particularly successful: the curves of the crest rail and splat required additional, labor-intensive work in order to achieve a round cross-section, thereby increasing production expenses. In addition, the laminates, as previously mentioned, could only be bent in a single plane, so that both the crest rail and splat were stiff rather than contoured. The stirrup-shaped seat frame of this first model is composed of four segments of solid wood, glued together in a manner similar to that used in bonding bricks. The back is attached by two screws inside the seat frame, thereby creating invisible joints. In contrast, the stretcher has been bent from a single piece of solid wood, a technique that in later examples will be applied to the circular seat frames. Thonet's ability to employ it here is due to the thinness of the cross section of the stretcher, which approximates that of a thick veneer.

In the next version of the No. 14 chair (figures 2–12 [b] and 2–13; cat. no. 15), for the first time Thonet tried to bend the element comprising the back legs and stiles from a single piece of solid wood. Experience had taught him that wood's ability to bend is limited by its thickness. Therefore, even before bending the piece, he had to reduce it at the place where it would form the crest rail. At the point where the curve was most dramatic, he flattened the cross section into an elliptical form; where the wood was only slightly curved the cross section was relatively round and thick. To stabilize the crest rail a very thin, curved strip of wood was glued to the inner curvature. The splat was made from two equally strong laminates that were spliced to the inner sides of the stiles and secured with countersunk screws that were concealed with putty.[20] The frame of the seat is again stirrup-shaped but is now composed of three strips of half-inch veneer, which have been vertically laminated and bent. In an attempt to reduce the number of parts of the chair, the stretcher has been eliminated. Support is instead provided by a turned capital, broadening the contact area between the top of the leg and the underside of the seat frame.

The third chair (figure 2–12 [c]; cat. no. 16) manifests a number of successes in Thonet's continuing simplification of the production process. The crest rail is now composed of a single, unreinforced piece. The splat is made from

Figure 2-13
Michael Thonet. Side chair, Model No. 14, ca. 1855 (back view). Bent laminated beechwood, bent solid beechwood, solid beechwood, cane, painted. Manufactured by Gebrüder Thonet, Vienna. CAT. NO. 15.

one piece of wood, which is again spliced into the stiles, and the seat frame has been bent from one piece of solid wood and secured into its stirrup configuration by a scarf joint. As in the first No. 14 chair, support is provided by a solid stretcher.

The fourth chair (figure 2–12[d]; cat. no. 17) solves two more problems: the splat, no longer spliced into the stile as in the former models, has been screwed onto the inner side of the stile in a simple butt-joint, and the seat frame, which has again been bent from a solid piece of wood, is now in a circular shape, distributing the stress of the curve in a more even manner.

There was a flaw, however, to this version. The front

legs are inadequately secured: there is neither a stretcher nor a capital. This absence of support, mitigated only by a strengthening of the seat frame along the inner side of the front legs with corner blocks, appears to reflect Thonet's continuing reductionism and his concern for aesthetics sometimes at the expense of function.

The final model of chair No. 14 (figures 2–5[f] and 2–12[e]; cat. no. 18) repeats many features of the previous one. Again the bent solid seat frame is reinforced with corner blocks, but the stretcher returns as an unavoidable necessary element. In both the fourth and fifth chairs the holes for the cane seat were bored vertically rather than diagonally toward the inside, as in earlier models. This change yielded advantages in the hole-boring process, since boring must be done in only one direction. The final model is distinguished by complete economy of process. Suitable for mass production, it represents a high point in Michael Thonet's creativity.

Mass production

Gebrüder Thonet

On July 28, 1852, Michael Thonet received a patent in the name of his five sons for his method of "giving wood various curves and forms by cutting and regluing." Around the same time, he opened a retail shop in the Strauchgasse, a central location in Vienna. His business was thriving. As he shifted from manual to industrial production in his workshop, several machines were acquired: in late 1853, he purchased his first steam engine, of four horsepower. His staff had grown to include forty-two workers: nine cabinetmakers, one lathe-turner, eight veneer-cutters (manual operation), two gluers, eight sanders, two stainers, ten finishers, and two assemblers.[21] (The caning was contracted out.) The composition of this list is a clear indication of the high-volume emphasis in the production plan at that time. Technological developments would later reduce the need for certain specialized workers, such as veneer-cutters.

Austrian guilds were not abolished until 1867, and there were already expressions of envy. Thonet held the patent for bending wood but did not belong to the cabinetmakers' guild, which created difficulties for him concerning the filling of an order for a parquet floor in the Offener Schloss in Budapest.[22] Only the intervention of a ministerial councillor made it possible for him to continue the work.

On November 1, 1853, Michael Thonet, age fifty-seven, signed over the business to his five sons, who became the co-owners of Gebrüder Thonet (Thonet Brothers). Michael Thonet remained in charge of management and procurement and also represented the interest of his son Jakob, who was still a minor. In 1854 Gebrüder Thonet exhibited in Munich, and in 1855 their products were featured at the Paris Exposition Universelle. For the first time they displayed inexpensive mass-produced items, which had already been successful in Vienna. The chairs were ideal for export, consisting of few components that could easily be packed and then assembled at their destination. The designs were greatly admired by experts and the public. In Munich the company received a bronze medal, in Paris a silver medal and a significant increase in foreign orders, including several orders from South America.

Thonet's new bending technique

These successes compelled Thonet to expand his operation. At the same time, the problems involved in shipping laminated chairs to South America were to have a profound effect on bent wood production. Glue dissolved in high humidity, both at sea during transport and in the tropics upon arrival. It was clear that the problems of mass production for an international market could only be solved by bending solid wood. Fortunately, this was a period of technical breakthroughs: on July 10, 1856, the Thonet firm was granted a nonrenewable thirteen-year patent "for manufacturing chairs and table legs of bent wood, the curvature of which is effected through the agency of steam or boiling liquids." In order to achieve the goal of mass production, the new technology was combined with Thonet's unique idea of bending the wood with the assistance of a metal strip.

Through the application of moisture and heat, the bending capability of wood can be increased. When exposed to steam, the wood's oil and resin partially dissolve, loosening the matrix of the grain, which may then be shifted in the bending process. When bending wooden rods, three different zones are created within the grain.

The structure of the grain remains unchanged in the middle of the rod, the neutral layer. Along the inner curvature of the rod, the grain changes by accumulating, causing the wood to buckle, while along the convex surface it stretches, causing the wood to split. Thonet solved the problem of splitting by securing a flat metal strip along the straight length of wood with screw clamps (figure 2–14). As the wood was bent, the metal strip was snug against the convex surface, keeping it from stretching. The neutral layer was pushed toward the convex surface and all of the grain below the strip accumulated, causing the rod to thicken in the area of the curve. As a result, the strain on the wood was equalized during the bending process.

In order to apply this technique to his furniture, Thonet needed to find a suitable wood. Many qualities pointed to beechwood—its structure, thickness, specific weight, hardness, strength, and, above all, elasticity. The wood of the common beech, a hardwood, has numerous finely structured pith rays;[23] the thickness of the thick-walled cells remains fairly constant during spring and fall growth. Thus the wood is fine and evenly textured. As its moisture content averages 35 percent, it lends itself well to staining and polishing. Another advantage of beech is that it grows straight, with few branches.

With problems of technique and material basically solved, it was possible for Thonet to bend even the strongest wood, and all prerequisites for mass production had been satisfied. Protected by patent, Gebrüder Thonet was to be the only firm in the Austro-Hungarian Empire for more than a decade that could legally produce bentwood furniture.

The Koritschan factory

In the spring of 1856, Michael Thonet founded a new factory in Koritschan, a small border town along the western slopes of the Moravian mountains. This site was selected because of the abundant forests of common beech, the good train connections, and the cheap labor provided by the new rural proletariat, a result of the 1848 revolution. Thonet contracted with Hermann Wittgenstein, the owner of the Herrschaft Koritschan, for the long-term delivery of wood and then traveled to Koritschan, leaving his sons behind to run the workshop in Vienna.

Thonet drew up the construction plans and supervised the building and equipping of the factory.[24] He personally designed and built the machinery, initially for reasons of economy and later for the purpose of secrecy. His machines, which were in many instances simple but functional, were primarily designed to his particular production specifications.[25] After his bad experiences with creditors in Boppard, he wanted to avoid outside financing, and as much as possible he restricted his capital to that generated by the factory. (This policy proved especially advantageous when in 1873 the Vienna stock market crashed in the wake of the Paris stock market collapse.)

Toward the end of 1856, Thonet was joined in Koritschan by his sons August and Michael, and in 1857 the factory started operation. From the beginning, there was a true division of labor: work that could be performed by unskilled workers was kept separate; heavy work, such as cutting, turning, steaming, and bending, was done by men, while women, who constituted half the work force, performed the sanding, polishing, caning, and packing operations. At a later date, the caning process became a cottage industry. Bending machines that had been designed and built in the firm's own special workshop were first used in 1862. Because labor was still very cheap, the use of these machines was limited to the manufacture of seats, stretchers, corner braces, and table legs.

Initially, the Koritschan factory suffered a shortage of skilled workers to train the newly hired unskilled employees, and the quality of the products from the new factory was less than satisfactory. To maintain standards, Thonet had the pieces completed and assembled in Vienna. Only in late 1857 were models entirely produced in the Koritschan factory ready for shipment. At this point, the Vienna workshop was closed down, and the warehouse was moved to Leopoldstadt (now district two of Vienna). The retail shop in the Strauchgasse was also shifted shortly thereafter.

The work sequence: from felling the tree to the finished product

After the tree, usually the common beech, was felled, its wood had to be used within six months to avoid the loss of natural resins and oils essential to the bending process.

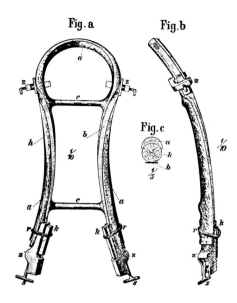

Figure 2–14

Drawing of iron-mold to form the back of Thonet side chair, Model No. 14. (Exner, p. 6).

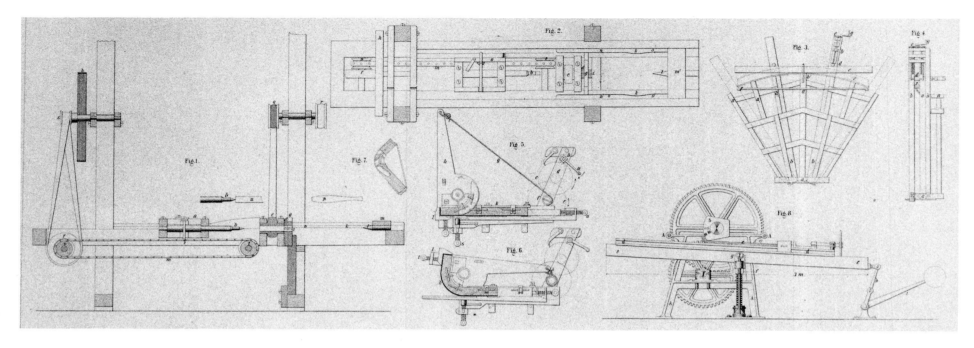

Figure 2–15
Michael Thonet. Turning lathe developed for the wood-bending process. (Exner, pl. 4).

The trunk, stripped of branches, was sawed into straight boards, their various lengths corresponding to the furniture components.[26] Square rods of suitable longitudinal strength were then cut from these boards. During a later period, steam-driven sawmills were set up in the forests to handle these phases of production. This was much more efficient, since only the wood suitable for manufacturing—approximately 40 percent of the trunk—was brought to the factory, thereby reducing transportation expenses.[27]

The rods were turned on a lathe developed by Thonet, according to the furniture part being produced (figure 2–15). After being cut to the proper length, the rods were placed in a steam chamber and, depending upon their moisture level and cross section, subjected to steam at a steady temperature of approximately 100° centigrade (212° F.) for from six to twenty-four hours.

After the rods were removed, they had to be bent imme-diately and quickly, in order to exploit their flexibility. Because bending machines were used initially in a limited capacity only, manual bending continued to be important. This work was performed by two men, who first attached a strip of veneer to the component (figure 2–16) to act as a buffer between it and the metal strip that was also clamped to it. The unit was bent, placed in a cast-iron form, and secured firmly with screws and clamps. The filled forms

Figure 2–16
Production of bent-wood furniture, at the factory of Gebrüder Thonet, Koritschan, Moravia, late 1850s.

were dried at 40° centigrade (approximately 102° F.) in a ventilated drying room for at least one day before the bent components were removed from them. Stretchers had to be attached, and the parts were then either sanded manually or by a sanding machine designed and built by Thonet.

The next process was staining—several shades of water-soluble stain were used to achieve a variety of finishes.[28] The component was sanded again after staining. There were two alternative finishing treatments: varnishing, which was simpler and cheaper, and polishing, which was labor-intensive. The pre-bored frame was now provided with woven cane, and the components were either assembled with special bevel-headed screws designed specifically for this purpose, or were packed for shipping. When packed, the separate components of three dozen chairs fit in a carton of approximately thirty-six cubic feet; they were assembled with screws at their destination.

Expansion

Michael Thonet's versatility extended to the realm of management. Recognizing the vast market that existed for his bent-wood furniture, he took full advantage of the monopoly that Gebrüder Thonet temporarily enjoyed. The extraordinary success of the firm may be seen in the production record of the No. 14 chair. Mass production of this chair began in Koritschan in 1859. In 1860, it cost three gulden, a sum sufficient at that time for the purchase of three dozen eggs or three-quarters of a bottle of wine. By 1891, 7.3 million No. 14 chairs had been sold, and by 1914 this figure had reached 40 million. Of course, the firm expanded accordingly; in 1862 there were 300 employees producing 200 pieces of furniture daily, and by 1904 there were 25,000 employees in 60 factories and 52 offices, producing approximately 4,000 pieces of furniture daily. The variety of models steadily increased, as the basic components were designed for interchangeability, constantly yielding new versions of old models that could easily be adapted to current fashions. The range of items broadened to include furniture for work and leisure, for public and private use. In 1859, the year of the firm's first sales catalogue, 25 items were offered. By 1873, there were 80; by 1884, 110; and by 1911, there were 1,400 items (figure 2–17). Geared to export, Gebrüder Thonet became a highly

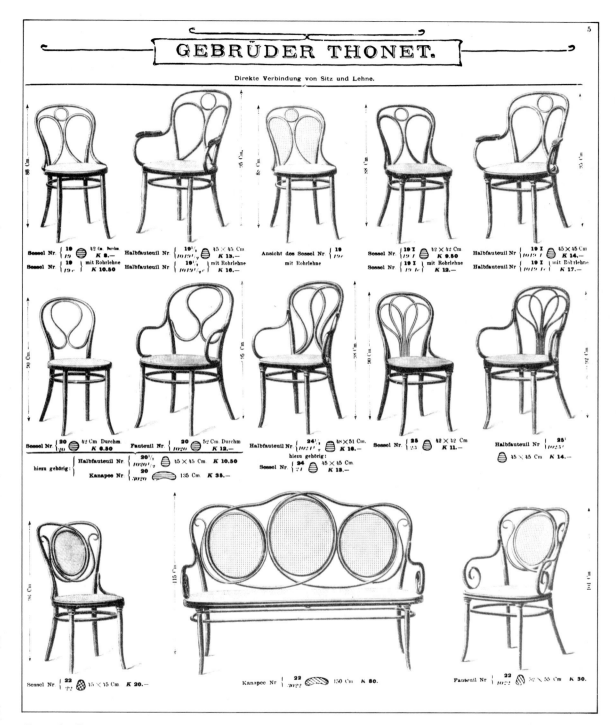

Figure 2-17

Page from Gebrüder Thonet sales catalogue, 1904. (Wilk 1980b, p. 5).

THE INTERNATIONAL EXHIBITION.

FURNITURE AND PARQUETERIE FLOORING BY THONET BROTHERS, OF LONDON AND VIENNA.—SEE NEXT PAGE.

Figure 2–18
Bent-wood furniture and parquet floor-ing exhibited by Gebrüder Thonet at the International Exhibition, London, 1862. (From *The Illustrated London News*, November 1, 1862, p. 472).

visible international presence, entering countless industrial fairs and opening branches throughout Europe in the decade of the 1860s.

In the 1862 International Exhibition in London, a group of Thonet's designs intended specifically for the popularly priced market was awarded a bronze medal (figure 2–18). Even before the exhibition opened, the products were offered for sale in Gebrüder Thonet's new London shop. The exhibition sales were the greatest in the history of the company, even though there were already imitators of Thonet's designs. Such infringements were kept in check through secrecy concerning bent-wood techniques and through the patents held by Thonet.

In 1862, the firm marketed a type of chair fairly unfamiliar in continental Europe—the rocking chair, which ap-peared in the sales catalogue as model No. 1 (figure 2–19; cat. no. 29). Its basic design is similar to the early Boppard chairs in that the seat and the backrest connect two side components that are sharply curved in a single plane.

There was a great demand for Thonet products, and

production could no longer keep pace with it, especially when beset by problems of wood shortage. To solve such problems, a new factory was built in 1862 in Bistritz am Hostein, a wooded site fifty kilometers (thirty-one miles) from Koritschan.[29] Once again the machines used were to a large extent built by the Thonets themselves. This time, however, the training of new, unskilled workers was significantly easier, as there were now experienced workers from Koritschan to oversee training in Bistritz. Just three years later the Thonet firm purchased an area of woodland in Gross-Ugrócz, Hungary, where, starting in 1866, a sawmill and an adjacent machine shop for lathing supplied half-finished products to the Moravian factories. Soon the sawmill itself was enlarged into a factory where products were completed and shipped. As the Hungarian site ceased delivering raw material to the Moravian factories, it became necessary to contract anew for the delivery of wood. This was done in Saybusch, Galicia, in 1867 and in Wsetin in 1868, towns where transportation was facilitated by an expanding train system.

Interest in new technical challenges continued. In the late 1860s August Thonet attempted to produce a chair from a single eight-meter (twenty-two-foot) beech rod. He aimed at the elimination of all joints and extraneous material such as woven cane. The resulting chair, illustrated in figure 2–20, is a bravura display of bent-wood technique. It was displayed at the 1867 Paris Exposition Universelle and at many subsequent fairs.

On December 10, 1869, the patent granted the Thonet firm thirteen years earlier expired. Competing firms, notably that of Jacob & Josef Kohn in Vienna, had al-ready been producing copies of Thonet designs, partic-ularly the No. 14 chair, even before this date. The Thonets' response was to concentrate on satisfying consumer pref-erence so as to maintain their edge in the increasingly competitive market.

Michael Thonet's death on March 3, 1871, may have marked the end of an era, but it did not stop the Thonet company from continuing research and experimentation, leading to new offerings. The No. 18 chair (figure 2–21) was launched in 1876, one of a group of chairs whose back inserts consisted of curves and loops of bentwood. With the insert reduced to this single loop, the chair is

Figure 2-19

Figure 2-19
Rocking chair, Model No. 1, after ca. 1888. Bent solid beechwood, solid beechwood, cane. Manufactured by Gebrüder Thonet, Vienna. Alexander von Vegesack, Düsseldorf. See CAT. NO. 29.

Figure 2-20
Gebrüder Thonet. Experimental chair, ca. 1867. Solid bent wood. Manufactured by Gebrüder Thonet, Vienna. Technisches Museum, Vienna.

Figure 2-21
Gebrüder Thonet. Side chair, Model No. 18, ca. 1876. Bent solid wood, cane. Manufactured by Gebrüder Thonet, Vienna. Collection Georg Thonet, Frankenberg, West Germany.

Figure 2-20

Figure 2-21

From workshop to factory 49

Figure 2-22

Gebrüder Thonet. Experimental chair, ca. 1880. Bent laminated wood. Manufactured by Gebrüder Thonet, Vienna. Technisches Museum, Vienna.

Figure 2-23

Gebrüder Thonet. Side chair, Model No. 56, ca. 1886. Bent solid wood, cane. Manufactured by Gebrüder Thonet, Vienna. Collection Georg Thonet, Frankenberg, West Germany.

more comfortable than No. 14, since it provides support for the back without touching the spine. It also has greater stability. This model became very important as an export item; quantities were shipped to South America, especially to Brazil.

Around the same time the Thonet firm further explored the range of possibilities of laminated veneers. Around 1880 another experimental chair was designed, probably by August Thonet (figure 2-22). It was cut from boards of laminated veneers (a form of plywood), bent into shape, and then cut out in decorative patterns. The same technique was employed on a child's rocking chair. Both of these chairs were exhibited worldwide but never mass-produced, due to the exceptionally high manufacturing costs.

During this period of research Gebrüder Thonet sought to invent a substitute for the cane seat, which required frequent replacement. They produced a seat from three layers of glued and molded veneer. The inner layer was of birch, while the surface layers were of acorn and later of beech. Such plywood seating surfaces were being produced at this time by the Gardner firm in New York, but a legal dispute in 1880 concerning the patent was won by Gebrüder Thonet whose long-standing use of the technique could be proved.

The Thonets sought optimal exploitation of the increasingly scarce raw material, common beech. New models had few bent components, or alternatively had bent components that were made of shorter segments of wood as in Model No. 56 (figure 2-23), the least expensive chair in the entire line. This chair was offered in 1885 in an attempt to economize on wood. The back legs and stile were no longer bent from a single piece of wood. Instead, the backrest component was subdivided, using shorter rods. Since the components in this model were

bent in only one plane, they could be bent by machine, further reducing manufacturing cost. The sales program was expanded to include other products that made more efficient use of wood, such as chests with panels of pressed plywood, available in a choice of stained finishes, and cupboards with structural parts of solid oak and panels of pressed oak veneers.

The company introduced the "tip-up" theater chair in 1888 (cat. no. 45). Designed for the new Deutsche Volkstheater in Vienna,[30] the chair made possible a significantly more efficient use of space. Its impact was revolutionary, and it was soon being ordered by theaters throughout Europe. It was comprised of three main components —the sides (with or without arms), the backrest, and foldable seat. For an extra charge, the folding mechanism was equipped with a spring and a counterweight that automatically raised the seat. The first theater chairs were delivered in groups of four which were joined together and bolted to the floor by means of a rod. Later they were available singly, making possible a better adaptation to any desired curve within the row.

The plywood technique was also used in the new contoured seat, which made a range of new seat-shapes possible. One might select a round, oval, trapezoid, heart-, or stirrup-shaped seat, and beginning with the 1895 catalogue one could choose the surface type as well. The traditional woven cane or upholstered seats were available, as were many styles of the new plywood seat. The latter could be perforated or decorated with designs etched into the heated sheets of plywood in engraved, woven, or intarsia patterns (figure 2-24). Seats and other chair parts could be ordered separately, allowing for easy repair.

The sales catalogue of 1904 serves as a measure of how far the Thonet enterprise had come. It featured a vast number of chairs for as many uses—swivel chairs, desk chairs, recliners, rocking chairs, nurse's chairs, prayer benches, barber's chairs, piano stools, theater chairs. There were combination sets of various chairs and settees, nesting tables, coffee tables, salon and game tables, and flower stands, desks, washstands, and commodes. There were specialized items such as walking sticks, folding furniture, children's and doll's furniture scaled down from the adult versions, and hospital furniture such as stretchers and sedan chairs. The range of sports equipment included skis, sleds, tennis rackets, gymnastic rings, hoops, and automobile steering wheels.

The story of Michael Thonet is one of transformation: the cabinetmaker of the Biedermeier era becoming an international businessman in the pioneer years of industrialization. This development reveals his ability to grasp accurately and to influence the trends of his changing times. Thonet's rhythm of work was unremitting, and he freed himself gradually, logically, and steadily from any obstacles encountered, using all data available to him with extreme discipline and economy. The breadth of his talents allowed him to discern the correct approach as he developed and improved the Thonet products, fac-

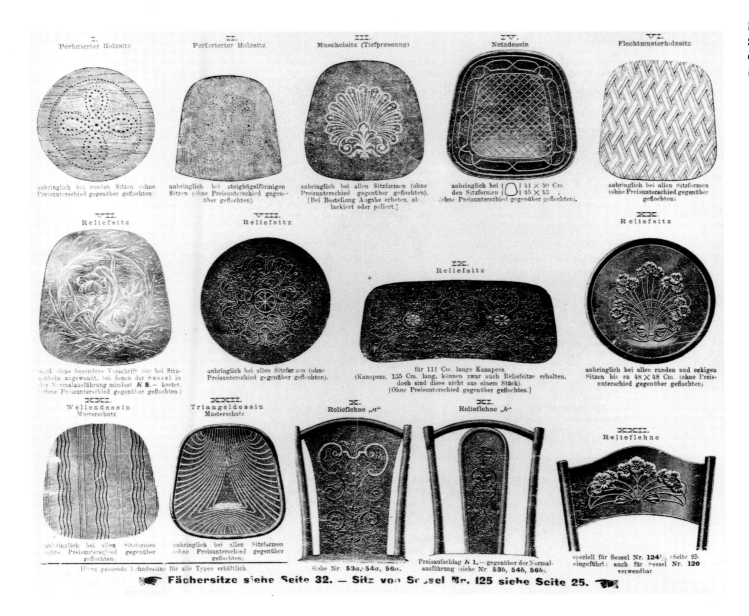

Figure 2-24

Selection of seats and backs. Page in Gebrüder Thonet sales catalogue, 1904. (Wilk 1980b, p. 36).

tories, and methods of procuring raw materials. Despite his tremendous success, he never stopped working in his factories himself. He was also an enlightened employer; his responsibility toward his employees was reflected in the various social benefits that he established for them, such as medical and accident insurance, housing, kindergartens, and schools. Although Michael Thonet was very much a representative of his generation, his major designs have survived that era, and today are considered classics, inimitable and contemporary.

Notes

1. Heller.

2. London 1979, p. 24.

3. The name of the inventor was Menke, a former model-maker with the Berliner Porzellanmanufaktur (Himmelheber, p. 26).

4. Himmelheber, p. 69.

5. Exner 1876, p. 4.

6. *See* note 11.

7. *Polytechnisches Journal* vol. 21, p. 29, cited in Exner 1876, p. 6.

8. Exner 1876, p. 6; Thonet 1896, p. 9.

9. Thonet, p. 14.

10. Thonet, pp. 1–11.

11. Such rights were known as privileges and were granted through the k. k. *[kaiserlich koniglich] allgemeine Hofkammer*, the Ministry of Finance with a department for trade and industry. The system of privileges was superceded by the patent law on January 11, 1897. However, the privilege law covered the rights granted to Thonet in 1842, 1852, and 1856, but for the ease of the contemporary reader all three rights have been referred to in this essay as patents.

12. Carl Leistler's work on the Liechtenstein Palace project lasted from 1842 to 1846 and was decisive in freeing design from the classical strictures of the Biedermeier style in favor of the playful forms of the rococo revival.

13. Thonet, p. 15.

14. Another armchair from Thonet's Boppard period, now in the collection of the Neue Sammlung in Munich, reveals a variation in construction: the bundle of laminates was bent to comprise the stile, side rail, and front leg. By incorporating the stile into the bent-wood element, the construction offered a potentially more stable design than in the model discussed in this essay [Ed. note].

15. The glue referred to throughout this essay is hide glue, similar to a type in limited use today.

16. Ostergard, in the essay in this volume, disputes the use of wooden molds on the assumption that the glue-saturated wood would have bonded itself to the mold [Ed. note].

17. The author here refers to another version of this model which he believes is in the collection of the Palais Liechtenstein [Ed. note].

The model illustrated in figure 2-4 (collection of Georg Thonet, Frankenberg, West Germany), examined by Derek Ostergard, was not rounded with a rasp.

18. This group was acquired by the Thonet family after the architect's death in 1883 (Thonet, p. 20).

19. The procedure probably led Thonet to the next experiment in simplification: gluing together thin rods with a rectangular cross section and bending them in a compound curve.

20. Thonet had used this method of construction in the Schwarzenberg Palace chair, designed in 1850, but a different back insert was used (figure 2-5e; cat. no. 12).

21. Thonet, p. 21.

22. Ibid., p. 21.

23. Andés, p. 31.

24. Thonet, pp. 25–29.

25. Ibid., p. 27.

26. The lengths were of 1.5 m. (59$\frac{1}{16}$ ins.), 1.8 m. (70$\frac{7}{8}$ ins.), 2.25 m. (88$\frac{1}{16}$ ins.), and 3.6 m. (142 ins.); Exner 1876, p. 24.

27. Certain parallels may be drawn between Thonet's bent-wood chairs and the traditions of the English vernacular chair, the Windsor chair, which from the early eighteenth to the early twentieth century was made by hand almost completely in England's beechwood forests. At times a kind of mass production could be found: specialized craftsmen at different locations produced components from the most suitable woods, such as beech, yew, and elm, for assembly at a later time. A conservative approach to forestry dictated that forests be thinned only. Saplings, highly bendable by nature, were cultivated, and all waste wood was used. Since the English vernacular chair was inexpensive, it was originally found in middle-class homes and later in the homes of the poorer classes. Production rates were remarkably high; between the 1790s and 1877, almost 100 manufacturers in High Wycombe were ultimately producing 4,700 chairs a day (Sparkes, p. 24).

28. All furniture was available in "natural" as well as a variety of finishes, including simulated walnut, palisander, mahogany, ebony, matte walnut, matte black.

29. The death of Michael Thonet's wife Anna in 1862 was a severe blow to the family, and Thonet focused all his energies on building the new factory in Bistritz am Hostein.

30. This theater was built in 1888–89 by architects Fellner and Helmer.

3
The development of the bent-wood furniture industry 1869–1914

GRAHAM DRY

THE patent held by Thonet Brothers for the manufacture of bent-wood furniture expired on December 10, 1869. On that day the way was finally opened to competitors, and new bent wood companies were quickly established in the Austro-Hungarian Empire, as well as in other parts of Europe. Over the years, as the names of the many European bent wood firms active from the early 1870s up to the outbreak of World War I were gradually forgotten, the name "Thonet" became synonymous with "bent-wood furniture." Research into the bent wood industry of these years as represented both by Thonet Brothers and its competitors has not until recently been the subject of any extensive consideration. Whereas the technical development and the range of products of certain Thonet competitors in Bohemia is now clearer,[1] important aspects of the industry have still to be examined. These include the relationship of the individual companies to each other, as well as the role of the designer. Serious problems still surround the attribution of bent-wood furniture produced by Jacob & Josef Kohn during the 1900–1914 period. Much bent-wood furniture of obvious quality bears no maker's label or other distinguishing mark, and the factories that made such pieces have still to be identified. In the case of bent-wood furniture clearly inspired by architect-designed furniture made by J. & J. Kohn and Thonet Brothers but of anonymous manufacture, the names of individual designers have yet to be discovered.

As long ago as 1893 Georg Lauboeck published a list of bent-wood furniture companies known to him in his edition of W. F. Exner's *Das Biegen des Holzes*.[2] The assessment of the bent wood industry in Europe presented here therefore includes a revised version of Lauboeck's list—the only such list ever to have been published

Figure 3-1

Michael Thonet. Armchair and side chair, ca. 1850. Bent laminated wood. Exhibited at The Exhibition of the Industry of All Nations, Crystal Palace, London, 1851. (From Heller).

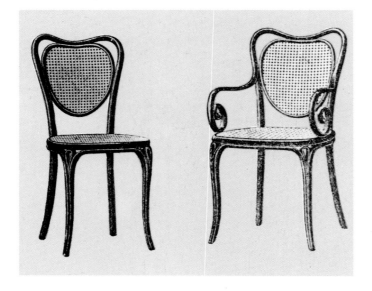

—together with the names of additional companies that either were unknown to Lauboeck or were established after 1893. In addition, this study hopes to suggest that the enormous extent of the bent wood industry as a whole in the late nineteenth and early twentieth centuries is a remarkable tribute in itself to Michael Thonet and his invention, and that the industry reached a hitherto unsuspected diversity and level of achievement during those years.

Austria

Thonet Brothers, Vienna

Michael Thonet's early technique of bending layers of flat wood for the purposes of manufacturing furniture had been protected since July 16, 1842, when the Imperial and Royal General Court Chamber in Vienna granted Thonet the sole privilege (No. 28877/1158) of "bending even the most brittle types of wood by chemico-mechanical means into any shapes and curves desired."[3] Ten years later, on July 28, 1852, shortly before the firm of Gebrüder Thonet (Thonet Brothers) was established, Michael Thonet (1796 –1871) received a patent in the names of his sons Franz, Michael, August, Josef, and Jacob, for his invention

of "giving wood any curvature and form in any desired direction by means of cutting lengths of wood and gluing them together."[4] During the first half of the 1850s, Michael Thonet and his sons gradually perfected the technique of bending rods of solid wood, and on July 10, 1856, the firm of Thonet Brothers was accorded the sole privilege of "manufacturing chairs and table legs made of bent wood, the curvature of which is effected through the agency of steam or boiling liquids."[5] During this same year, in order to exploit the new technique, which was less expensive, less time-consuming, and produced more reliable results than the obsolescent method employing laminated veneers, Thonet Brothers built a factory at Koritschan in Moravia, where production began in the following year.

Although the methods, techniques, and scale of production had changed enormously since Michael Thonet's first experiments with glued and curved veneers in the early 1830s, the aim of the firm—to produce solid, elegant, lightweight, and relatively inexpensive furniture—had remained unaltered. When Michael Thonet exhibited his laminated mahogany furniture at the *Allgemeine deutsche Industrie-Ausstellung* (German Industrial Exhibition) in Mainz in 1842, the exhibition report observed that the advantages of Thonet's furniture lay in its "exceptional lightness allied with perfect durability and elegance." In addition, the report continued, "A pleasant resilience of the back- and armrests is another advantage of his method, to which the exhibitor draws attention; and, he further points out, the work involved in the manufacture of his chairs proceeds at a brisker rate and entails the use of less wood than chairs of conventional make."[6] In 1851, Thonet was awarded a Prize Medal at the Great Exhibition in London for his "curious" chairs (figure 3-1).[7]

In the following decades, the firm took every opportunity to show bent-wood furniture at national and international exhibitions. Critical comment was consistent in its praise of the practical virtues of the bent-wood chairs, tables, and sofas, which might at first have seemed uncomfortably without precedent to an age accustomed to carved, heavily upholstered, joined, gilded, and ornamentally embellished furniture. The jury's report of the 1854 *Allgemeine deutsche Industrie-Ausstellung* in Munich pointed out that a normal Thonet chair consisted of four pieces of wood screwed together; the seats were pleasantly shaped and comfortable to sit on; the chairs themselves were extremely light and were more impervious to damage than solid chairs made by cabinetmakers. Furthermore, they could be mass produced and easily dispatched, as their construction allowed them to be taken apart and reassembled with the greatest facility.[8] A photograph of the exhibition taken by the Munich court photographer Edgar Hanfstaengl—surely the first photograph showing bent-wood furniture—includes a view of the Thonet display (figure 3-2). In contrast to the furniture he showed at the 1851 Great Exhibition in London, which included consciously artistic pieces of a neo-Baroque type clearly in emulation of the Viennese cabinetmaker Carl Leistler (figure 2-7), here Thonet's display is marked by an increased simplicity and light elegance, which must have stood out well among the surrounding works of decorative art.

At the 1855 Paris Exposition Universelle (Universal Exhibition), where Thonet Brothers was awarded a Silver Medal, one German critic was "filled with amazement" at the stability and lightness of bent-wood furniture, and its inexpensiveness as well. Moved by a childlike wonder that such furniture was possible at all, the critic reported that a bent-wood chair "hurled a good twenty paces with considerable force, did not exhibit the slightest sign of damage and stood up remarkably well to the rocking motions to which it was subsequently subjected by a person of portly frame."[9]

The No. 14 chair (cat. nos. 14–18), made of six pieces of bent wood, ten screws, and two washers and produced

Figure 3-2
Gebrüder Thonet display (lower left), *Allgemeine deutsche Industrie-Ausstellung*, Munich, 1854. Photograph by Edgar Hanfstaengl. Fotomuseum, Stadtmuseum, Munich.

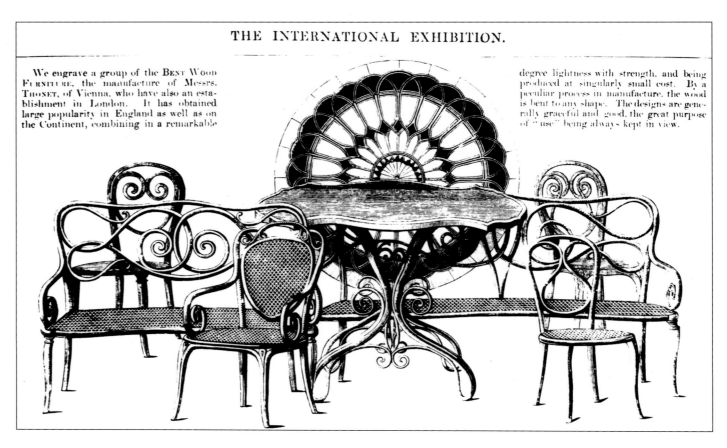

THE INTERNATIONAL EXHIBITION.

We engrave a group of the BENT WOOD FURNITURE, the manufacture of Messrs. THONET, of Vienna, who have also an establishment in London. It has obtained large popularity in England as well as on the Continent, combining in a remarkable

degree lightness with strength, and being produced at singularly small cost. By a peculiar process in manufacture, the wood is bent to any shape. The designs are generally graceful and good, the great purpose of "use" being always kept in view.

Figure 3–3
Bent-wood furniture exhibited by Gebrüder Thonet at the International Exhibition, London, 1862. (From *The Art-Journal Illustrated Catalogue*, 1862, p. 291).

from 1859 onward in the Koritschan factory, was exhibited for the first time internationally at the 1862 London International Exhibition.[10] This exhibition was the first at which Thonet displayed his newly developed solid bent-wood furniture, the first in which inexpensive objects of everyday use (*Consumwaare*) were shown,[11] and the first to demonstrate that bent-wood furniture had reached a degree of perfection that made it eminently suitable for export purposes.[12] The *Art-Journal Illustrated Catalogue* reproduced a number of examples of bent-wood furniture by the Thonet Brothers, which had just opened a branch in London, describing them as "combining in a remarkable degree lightness with strength and being produced at singularly small cost [figure 3–3]."[13]

By 1862, the two Thonet factories, in Koritschan and Bistritz (built in 1862), were employing eight hundred workers and producibout 70,000 chairs a year, of which

about 45,000 were for export.[14] The success of bent-wood furniture at international, as well as regional, exhibitions engendered a steady increase of orders during these years, and a third factory was built at Gross-Ugrócz in Hungary, which began production in 1867, the year of the Paris Exposition Universelle. The selection of bent-wood furniture shown by Thonet in 1867 won the Gold Medal for the firm and was chiefly remarkable for a sinuous chair whose front and back legs, seat, and back were formed from two continuous pieces of bent wood.[15] This chair must surely have caught the fancy of the general public and—by this display of technical mastery—made it even more aware of the virtues of bent-wood furniture. As a provocative symbol of the achievements of Michael Thonet and Thonet Brothers, this bent-wood capriccio must also have been a reminder to a growing group of prospective competitors, eagerly waiting for the Thonet monopoly to expire, that standards of inventiveness and perfection had been reached which they would find hard to surpass, or even emulate.

By the end of 1869, Thonet Brothers had demonstrated at national and international levels that bent-wood furniture was elegant, light, sturdy, cheap, and ideally suited for both production on a large scale and export. Its production simply required technical dexterity and could thus employ a labor force that needed no particular training. A profound knowledge of historical ornamental styles and a close concern with the changing fashions of the carved and gilded furniture that populated nineteenth-century drawing rooms were not necessary prerequisites for the production of this novel type of furniture. The general availability of illustrated broadsheet catalogues issued by Thonet Brothers from 1859 onward[16] usefully displayed to all would-be imitators the scope of inventiveness that had helped shape Thonet's work over the years. By the end of 1869—when the Thonet Brothers patent expired—these catalogues also provided an immediate guide to the various formal and technical capabilities of bent-wood furniture. Imitators would be spared costly experimentation, and original designs were for the most part superfluous.

The main, and purely commercial, concern of the Austro-Hungarian firms that began to produce bent-wood furniture after December 10, 1869, was to gain a foothold in the steadily expanding market that Thonet had created. They attempted to do this by producing as rapidly as possible a series of models that were closely based on well-established Thonet designs. The first major competitors were Jacob & Josef Kohn and D. G. Fischel Söhne, but the continuing cheapness of the raw material—beechwood—enabled even small firms to produce Thonet-style furniture.

Indeed, by 1873 the annual production of bent-wood furniture by the various factories in Hungary, Bohemia, and Moravia reached a total of 530,000 pieces, of which Thonet Brothers alone accounted for 450,000.[17] A large proportion of the 80,000 pieces produced by Thonet's competitors in Austria-Hungary was certainly contributed by the four other firms that exhibited bent-wood furniture at the 1873 Wiener Weltausstellung (Vienna World Exhi-

bition). These were the K.-privilegierte Möbelfabrikation aus massiv gebogenem Holze (Imperial and Royal Privileged Solid Bent-Wood Furniture Factory) Jacob & Josef Kohn; the cabinetmaker Josef Neyger in Hernals near Vienna; Teibler & Seemann, Fabrik Massiv Gebogener Möbel (Solid Bent-Wood Furniture Factory) in Oberleutensdorf, Bohemia; and D. G. Fischel Söhne, Erste Böhmische Fabrik von Möbeln aus Massiv Gebogenem Holz (D. G. Fischel Sons, First Bohemian Solid Bent-Wood Furniture Factory), Niemes, Bohemia.[18]

Jacob & Josef Kohn, Vienna

The Kohn family firm was originally founded in 1850, probably in Wsetin, Moravia, as a producer of lumber.[19] In September 1867, Jacob Kohn (1814–1884) went into partnership with his son Josef, and they founded the firm of Jacob & Josef Kohn.[20] The company built its first factories in Wsetin and Litsch toward the end of 1869, and production commenced in the following year. By 1873, the year of the Vienna World Exhibition, further large factories had been erected in Teschen (1871), Cracow, and Gross-Poremba, while smaller works were operating in Ratibor and Keltsch in Moravia, and Wagstadt, Skotschau, and Jablunkau in Silesia.[21] The firm already employed 2,800 workers. Three years later, J. & J. Kohn exhibited at the 1876 Philadelphia International Exhibition. They reported that their factories were enlarged each year and that as a rule production went on by day and by night, without interruption, "except on Sundays and holidays." The work force varied between 3,000 and 4,000 men, and the factories produced about 500,000 pieces of furniture from 30,000 cubic meters of timber a year, about eighty-five percent of which was for export, to "almost all known countries of the earth."[22]

By 1882, Kohn had opened important branches in Berlin, London, Hamburg, and Paris. Large factories were built in Nowo-Radomsk (1884) and Holleschau (1890), and by 1904 the total number of employees had grown to 6,300, who were producing 5,500 pieces of furniture a day. The firm's 1904 catalogue contains 407 different models, many of which are copies of well-established nineteenth-century Thonet pieces, as well as a large selection of historicist and Secessionist designs.[23] The following years saw further expansion, and by 1916, the year in which the final European catalogue bearing the name of J. & J. Kohn appeared, over 1,000 models were being produced and sold in the firm's own branches in Vienna, Budapest, Berlin, Cologne, Munich, Hamburg, Danzig, Brussels, Antwerp, Basel, Warsaw, New York, and Chicago,[24] not to mention countless general retail furniture stores in Germany and elsewhere, such as Heidebroek & Bode in Hannover, who were Kohn agents.[25]

On August 20, 1914, J. & J. Kohn merged with the Mundus company.[26] In 1922, that group joined forces with the Thonet company, and the new combine was called Thonet-Mundus-J. & J. Kohn. In 1932, the name of Kohn disappeared from the company's title in Germany.

It is still extremely difficult to trace the development of this important and attractive firm. Contemporary magazines such as *The Studio*, *Moderne Bauformen*, *Das Interieur*, *Die Kunst*, and *Ver Sacrum* occasionally illustrated furniture designed for Kohn by such leading Viennese architects

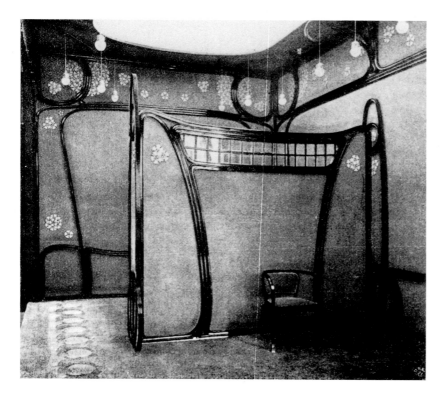

Figure 3–4
Gustav Siegel. Interior with applied bent-wood wall decoration and chair of bent solid wood, Jacob & Josef Kohn display at the Exposition Universelle, Paris, 1900. (From Kraemer, *Das XIX, Jahrhundert*, vol. 4, p. 239). See CAT. NO. 38.

and artists as Josef Hoffmann, Koloman Moser, Otto Wagner, Marcel Kammerer, Josef Urban, and Leopold Bauer. The lack of all source material, however, such as drawings and correspondence, seriously impedes a proper study of J. & J. Kohn's history.[27] No European catalogue of the years 1909–15 has yet come to light, which means that it is not possible at present to give a complete account of the interesting years after 1900, when the sinuous possibilities of the bent-wood line became an increasingly serious consideration and object of experimentation for avant-garde Viennese designers. The pioneering role played by J. & J. Kohn at the very end of the nineteenth century in the development of architect-designed bent-wood furniture has recently been underlined, however, in connection with the now-famous chair designed by Adolf Loos in 1899 for the billiard room of the Café Museum in Vienna.[28] It has been regularly stated up to now that this chair was manufactured by Thonet Brothers,[29] and it has always seemed natural that the credit for this first example of an architect-designed bent-wood chair should be due to the firm that had the longest history of technical innovation and initiative. Recent research has shown, however, that the Loos chair was produced by J. & J. Kohn.[30] It must therefore be regarded now as the firm's first step in a long development that would allow the design of bent-wood furniture to reflect contemporary trends in the fields of architecture and the applied arts.

The appointment of the nineteen-year-old Gustav Siegel (1880–1970) as head of J. & J. Kohn's design department in 1899 guaranteed that explicitly modern Viennese furniture would become an important feature of Kohn's production in the following years. The son of a cabinet-maker, Siegel was born in Vienna. At the age of seventeen, after a three-year apprenticeship and study at an advanced school for cabinetmakers in Vienna, Siegel enrolled in the Wiener Kunstgewerbeschule (Vienna School of Applied Arts), where he was registered in the General Department. In 1899, before being engaged by Felix Kohn, president of J. & J. Kohn, Siegel had qualified for admission to Josef Hoffmann's architectural class.[31]

Siegel's immediate contribution to the development of bent-wood furniture was brilliantly demonstrated by a room shown by J. & J. Kohn (figure 3–4) at the 1900 Paris

Exposition Universelle, in which the walls were divided into vertical and horizontal sections by a superimposed Art Nouveau pattern made up of sweeping lines of applied bent-wood decoration.[32] During the last quarter of the nineteenth century, J. & J. Kohn had made great strides in the development of the technique of bending wood and had constructed, among other improvements, a machine for making circular seat frames.[33] The firm had recently introduced a new method of bending thick pieces of wood at an angle of almost ninety degrees, which allowed even the corners of rooms to be filled by juxtaposed, flowing lines of bent wood. As no glue was used in this novel type of applied wall decoration, no deterioration in quality through damp could occur, and the design was therefore indefinitely durable. Commenting on the J. & J. Kohn installation at the Paris Exposition, which consisted of a modern bedroom (figure 3–5) and drawing room, an observer reported: "There can be no doubt that Jacob & Josef Kohn's exhibits have raised the bent-wood furniture industry as a whole to a new technical and artistic level. For the first time, complete schemes of interior decoration can be carried out exclusively in bent wood, without recourse to any other expedient. Design and execution of these rooms are immaculate and completely original."[34]

The rooms had been carried out after designs by Gustav Siegel, who, with Koloman Moser and Otto Wagner, appears to have been solely responsible for the early Art Nouveau phase of Kohn bent-wood furniture. This phase is characterized by an uninterrupted linearity of outline, construction, and detail—elements that are well illustrated in the three designs for a bedroom offered by J. & J. Kohn that appeared in the German magazine *Innen-Dekoration* in 1901,[35] one of which bears the monogram GS. The decorative talent of these drawings and the slightly trembling hand of the draftsman reappear in the following years in several of Kohn's unsigned posters and other graphic work, and it seems likely that Siegel himself, rather than any outside artist, was responsible for the Kohn advertisements that were published in the Vienna Secession exhibition catalogues between 1904 and 1908.[36]

A further problem concerning J. & J. Kohn's activity after 1900 is the vexing question of to what extent Gustav Siegel was responsible for the development of a second

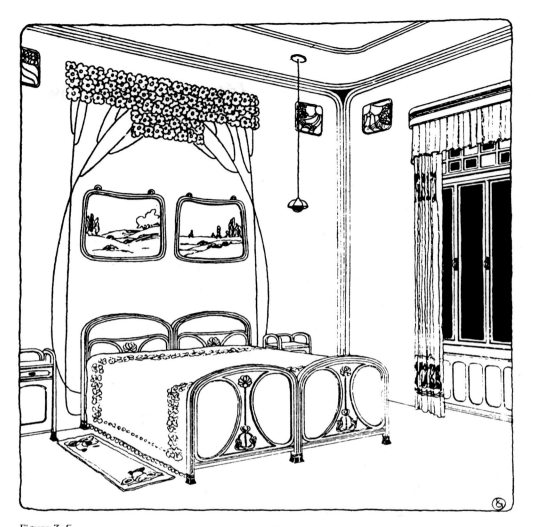

Figure 3-5
Gustav Siegel. Design of a bedroom with furniture and paneling of bent solid wood by Jacob & Josef Kohn, Vienna, 1900–1901. Designer's monogram at lower right. (From *Innen-Dekoration*, 1901, p. 102).

geometric style of furniture. This can best be illustrated by the well-known chair, Kohn Model No. 728, designed around 1907, which was selected by Josef Hoffmann in 1907 for use in the Cabaret Fledermaus in Vienna (figure 3–6).[37] Hoffmann was responsible for the overall conception of this cabaret, whose details included decorative tiles by the Wiener Keramik (Berthold Löffler and Michael Powolny). Chair No. 728, the simplest element of a suite (figure 3–7) that also includes an armchair (No. 728/F) and a settee (No. 728/C), is generally regarded as having been designed by Hoffmann on the basis of an illustration that appeared in a Darmstadt magazine in 1908, which shows the chairs in the Theater of the Cabaret Fledermaus (figure 55A).[38] The characteristic use in this chair of spheres of wood set at the juncture of the seat rail and chair legs

has in consequence come to be regarded as a sure sign that any Kohn furniture that embodies this decorative and constructive element is certain to have been designed by Hoffmann,[39] especially as it forms a salient feature of such a well-known Kohn chair as the model used in the Purkersdorf Sanatorium of 1904, a building designed by Hoffmann.[40]

The ramifications and pitfalls besetting the attributions of Kohn furniture are beyond the scope of this discussion, but it is worth noting that Karl Mang, who spoke to Siegel in 1968,[41] has attributed the Kohn tub chair No. 728/F—and therefore also the smaller chair No. 728 used in the Cabaret Fledermaus, as well as the settee No. 728/C—to Gustav Siegel.[42] Furthermore, A. S. Levetus, writing in Vienna for the 1908 *Studio Year Book of Decorative Art*, stated—stressing the role of Kohn's art director—that it was "Gustav Siegel who is devoting all his energy to the solving of the bent-wood problem, ably supported by Messrs. J. & J. Kohn." The caption of the illustration accompanying her article, "Bent Wood Furniture Designed by Arch. Gustav Siegel, Executed by J. & J. Kohn" (figure 3–8),[43] underlines the emphasis she places on the designer. This rare contemporary example of credit given to the designer of bent-wood furniture rather than the factory that produced it is particularly important, because the chairs (No. 415/F), the settee (No. 415/2), and a plant stand (No. 1015; figure 3–9) all employ the element of the wooden sphere as used in the Cabaret Fledermaus.[44] Moreover, chair No. 415,[45] which is not illustrated in the *Studio Year Book*, has the double spherical braces found at the juncture of the legs and seat rail that are a characteristic feature of the Kohn Purkersdorf chair—a chair generally considered by many historians to have been designed by Hoffmann.[46]

Siegel's contribution to Kohn's bent wood production after 1899 has been blurred by legitimate attempts to comb through Kohn furniture in search of work attributable to historically more spectacular figures, such as Josef Hoffmann, Koloman Moser, and Otto Wagner. The evidence, in spite of Werner Schweiger's reservations,[47] is that Siegel was responsible for a far greater proportion of the Kohn production up to 1914 than historians and dealers have so far supposed. The quality of his bent-wood wall decorations and furniture at the 1900 Paris Exposition was

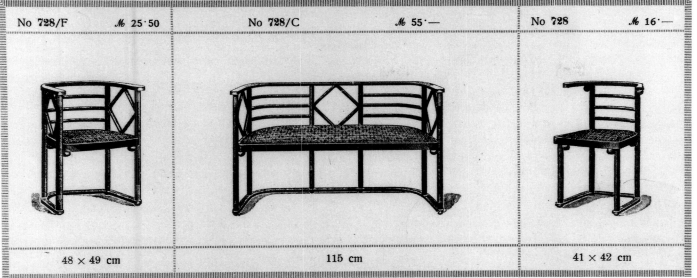

No 728/F M 25·50	No 728/C M 55·—	No 728 M 16·—
48 × 49 cm	115 cm	41 × 42 cm

Figure 3-7

Figure 3-7
Armchair, settee, and side chair, Suite No. 728. Sales catalogue of Jacob & Josef Kohn, Vienna, 1916.

Figure 3-8
Gustav Siegel. Armchair, settee, and side chair, Suite No. 415, 1907. Manufactured by Jacob & Josef Kohn, Vienna. (From *Studio Year Book*, 1908, pl. A19).

Figure 3-9
Gustav Siegel. Plant stand, ca. 1901. Bent solid wood. Manufactured by Jacob & Josef Kohn, Vienna. Exhibited at the *Winterausstellung*, Österreichisches Museum für Kunst und Industrie, Vienna, 1901/2. (From *Kunstgewerbeblatt*, 1902, p. 211, erroneously titled "L. Siegel").

Figure 3-8

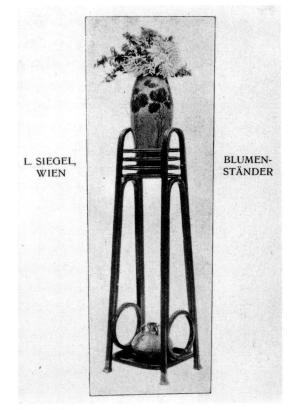

L. SIEGEL, WIEN   BLUMEN-STÄNDER

Figure 3-9

immediately apparent to contemporary critics, who by general consent judged J. & J. Kohn to have overtaken Thonet Brothers in the ability to adapt the technical capabilities of bent wood to the linear nature of the modern decorative style, Art Nouveau.[48]

In light of Siegel's brilliant designs for Kohn shown in Paris in 1900, it can be assumed that Siegel himself designed a large majority of the various progressive models in the geometric style that were produced from about 1902 onward, although dealers—above all—have been understandably quick to ascribe these to Josef Hoffmann. There is no reason, however, to suppose that Siegel's designing skill failed for some unaccountable reason at the very moment that contemporary developments in the field of Viennese furniture made the introduction of a geometric style of bent-wood furniture both possible and necessary. There is good reason, of course, to suppose that Siegel and Hoffmann employed the same tested details in their bent-wood furniture designs, borrowing from each other as colleagues and regarding certain constructive and decorative elements as part of a standard repertoire that could be employed whenever a new design could usefully incorporate them. It is probably safe to imagine that the relationship between Siegel and Hoffmann, at least in the early years of Siegel's activity at J. & J. Kohn, continued to reflect something of the natural respect of an assistant toward his professor. Unless there is documentary evidence to the contrary, it should be logical as a general rule to ascribe the design of all Kohn bent-wood furniture after 1900 to Siegel. If this approach to the question of the authorship of Kohn bent-wood furniture is adopted, Gustav Siegel must then be regarded as one of the great, and most imaginative, furniture designers of the twentieth century.

The history of no other important bent wood company is complicated to such a degree by the problem of individual contributions of outside artists and architects. Research is further hampered by the lack of source material and by the fact that J. & J. Kohn's catalogues[49] do not disclose the identity of the designers of the individual pieces. As no other bent wood company founded after 1869 ever had the good fortune to have a man of Siegel's caliber in charge of design, the problems that attend the Kohn production do not apply to other firms. With other Austro-Hungarian companies, we are on much safer ground.

D. G. Fischel Söhne, Vienna

D. G. Fischel Sons was founded in Niemes (Mimoň, Northern Bohemia) in January 1870 by the brothers Alexander and Gustav Fischel. Building of the new factory began in July 1870 and production commenced in March 1871 (figures 3–10 and 3–11). The company gradually grew to become one of the main competitors of Thonet Brothers. By 1873 the firm had representatives in Berlin, Cologne, Hamburg, Pest, Prague, and Rotterdam. At the Vienna World Exhibition of that year, this imaginative firm displayed, among other furniture, a bent-wood peacock house, which one critic found "bizarre rather than beautiful," a "practical armchair-bed," and a novel and comfortable upholstered armchair (as yet unpriced), which Fischel, claiming it to be indestructible, had named "The Invulnerable."[50]

Since Fischel did not exhibit at the international exhibitions in Philadelphia (1876), Paris (1889 and 1900), or Saint Louis (1904), it is difficult to gain a clear idea of the firm's history and development during this time, or, indeed, even at a later period. It is known that by 1893 the company had built four branch factories,[51] and that by 1904 the Fischel family had severed its connection with the company. On September 1 of that year, Ernst Hirsch of Vienna was officially registered in Vienna as the firm's proprietor, and on July 1, 1912, D. G. Fischel Sons became an unlimited mercantile partnership, the partners being Ernst and Fritz Hirsch. On November 5, 1929, the Vienna branch became independent. On August 12, 1938, the Jewish partners were dispossessed, and the company was entrusted provisionally to the engineer Roland Ambrosius. In 1940, after the German occupation of France, the Fischel factory in Weissenburg (Wissembourg), Alsace, which had been built in 1920, was handed over to August Meder, proprietor and manager of the Erste Acherner Stuhl-Fabrik August Klar (First Achern Chair Factory August Klar), in Achern, Baden. The Fischel factory was absorbed into the Achern company, and the combined undertaking was known during the war years as August Meder Stuhl-Fabriken, vormals August Klar (August Meder Chair Factories, formerly August Klar), Achern-Baden und Weissenburg-Elsass, which August Meder supervised until 1945. The name of D. G. Fischel Sons was officially deleted from the Company Register in Vienna on March 20, 1952.

Figure 3-10
**Factory of D. G. Fischel Söhne, Niemes
(Mimoň, Czechoslovakia), ca. 1924–30.**

The earliest documents relating to D. G. Fischel Sons[52] that have so far been traced are catalogues published by the company in the 1890s. According to Jaromíra Šimon-íková, who has recently researched the company's history, these catalogues show a rich variety of original designs, many with decorative, turned elements, as well as a selection of models copied from Thonet Brothers's production.[53] In 1893, Fischel introduced schoolbenches that rested on bent-wood supports, and these were awarded medals at various exhibitions in the following years. In 1914, Fischel issued a 180-page catalogue in which such novelties as furniture with variously colored cane seats and backs and tables with removable tops were illustrated.

As far as can be ascertained at present, Fischel did not produce original architect-designed bent-wood furniture between 1900 and 1914, the golden age of the Austro-Hungarian industry, but was content to follow the contemporary activity of Thonet Brothers and J. & J. Kohn. There are, for instance, Fischel variations of Otto Wagner's Thonet armchair, designed in 1906 for the Board Room of the Postsparkasse (Imperial Austrian Postal Savings Bank) in Vienna,[54] although the Fischel chair was offered with protective metal casings for the sabots (feet) as an optional extra, whereas Wagner's chair was provided with distinctive aluminum fittings on the armrests and legs as well as the feet (cat. no. 46). The Fischel settee No. 254, illustrated in the 1914 catalogue, is an exact copy of Gustav Siegel's design for J. & J. Kohn (No. 715/C), which dates from 1900.[55] Fischel's adjustable armchair No. 503, also illustrated in the 1914 catalogue, is a close copy of the original model designed by Josef Hoffmann for J. & J. Kohn (No. 669)

Figure 3-11
**Interior view, factory of D. G. Fischel
Söhne, Niemes (Mimoň, Czechoslovakia),
ca. 1910.**

and exhibited at the Vienna *Kunstschau* in 1908.[56] The Fischel version incorporates a crossbar between the leg elements. The geometric cutout pattern of the side panels, consisting of four rows of squares and oblong rectangles, is a conscious variation on the five rows of the Hoffmann design for Kohn. Fischel also manufactured a copy of an interesting two-tiered oval table with supporting spheres, which had originally been produced by Kohn (No. 960/2).[57] In addition, there is a Fischel table supported by flat bent-wood straps (figure 3–12), which corresponds to the Thonet model No. 8042 of about 1907.[58]

No large Fischel catalogue has yet emerged in either Germany or Austria, and the only source material known here is a broadsheet catalogue (19½ x 27¼ inches) issued in October 1928 by Fischel for Julius Fürfang, Werkstätten für Sitzmöbel und Tischfabrikation (Workshops for the Manufacture of Chairs and Tables), Munich,[59] which illustrates forty-four stock items of anonymous late-nineteenth and conventional early-twentieth-century design, not unsimilar to the Thonet production of these years.[60]

Fischel's true capacities in the late 1920s are best demonstrated by a remarkable armchair with cantilever backrest (figure 3–13), which was probably designed in 1929 in response to the Thonet-Mundus international competition for the design of chairs and other small pieces of bent-wood furniture.[61] Its design clearly shows the influence of tubular-steel furniture and is a reminder that bent-wood furniture companies had to face a challenge at this time from the new and fast-developing type of furniture that Marcel Breuer had created at the Bauhaus in 1925.[62] This chair may, however, have been an exception. As indicated by Šimoníková, Fischel catalogues issued in the 1920s and 1930s show that an increasing proportion of the company's production was devoted to gilt furniture with applied carved details, as well as to seating for theaters, hospitals, offices, and cafés. Another publication of these years is the booklet issued by Fischel in celebration of the company's sixtieth anniversary. It is uninformative, but reveals at least that a third Fischel factory, apart from those at Niemes and Weissenburg (Wissembourg), existed in Valisoara, Romania. It also proudly advertised that the firm had just provided the furnishings of the Hotel Terminus in Monte Carlo (figure 3–14).[63]

Mundus and the small bent wood firms of the Austro-Hungarian Empire

Besides the large firms of Thonet Brothers, J. & J. Kohn, and D. G. Fischel Sons, two smaller firms showed bent-wood furniture at the 1873 Vienna World Exhibition. These were Teibler & Seemann, Oberleutensdorf (Bohemia), and Josef Neyger, Hernals near Vienna.

Teibler & Seemann, Fabrik Massiv Gebogener Möbel (Solid Bent-Wood Furniture Factory), which had agents in London and Hamburg, exhibited two sofas, five chairs, a dressing table, a tea trolley, a rocking chair, and an easy

Figure 3–13
Armchair, ca. 1929. Bent solid wood. Manufactured by D. G. Fischel Söhne, Niemes (Mimoň, Czechoslovakia). Private collection, Munich. CAT. NO. 95.

chair.[64] One critic, Justus Brinckmann, remarked that "one virtue of the firm's products is said to be their cheapness," which may have been intended as an ironic comment on their quality.[65]

The firm of Josef Neyger showed side chairs, armchairs, a sofa, a table, an easy chair, a folding chair, a revolving chair, and a smoker's chair.[66] The astonishing thing about Neyger's work was that the furniture was not of bent solid wood, but was made by the laminated-and-glued-veneer method developed by Michael Thonet in the 1830s, which further advances in bent wood technique had made anachronistic. Examples of Neyger's work have yet to be identified, and if any have survived at all, they are no doubt mistaken for early work by Michael Thonet. In 1873, Neyger's furniture was selling at prices comparable with bent-wood furniture made by the modern and more rational methods.[67] Interestingly enough, one German critic, who had little else to say in favor of Thonet Brothers "imitators," specifically singled out Neyger for the "novelty" of its producing bent-wood furniture from glued veneers.[68]

After 1873, small Austro-Hungarian bent-wood furniture factories do not appear to have exhibited with any great frequency in national or international exhibitions until 1900. It can only be assumed that these firms were not ambitious either technically or artistically and were generally quite content to find a niche in the European bent wood market by reproducing Thonet and Kohn models at a cheaper price than the originals.

Although cooperation between the leading bent wood firms and smaller companies was not customary, it was not impossible. The official exhibition catalogues make no mention of it, but the two leading firms, Thonet Brothers and J. & J. Kohn, had in fact joined forces for the purposes of the 1900 Paris Exposition and, under the aegis of the Verband der Österreichisch-Ungarischen Fabriken für Möbel aus gebogenem Holz (Association of Austro-Hungarian Bent-Wood Furniture Factories), showed together with an unnamed, smaller Hungarian factory, which can be identified with some degree of certainty as the Ungvárer Möbelfabrik (Ungvár Furniture Company).[69] This, however, was an isolated instance of collaboration. Individually, the smaller factories could not hope to compete indefinitely with the combined force of Thonet

Hotel Terminus, MONTE-CARLO (furnished by "FISCHEL" / installé par "FISCHEL")

Figure 3-14
Bent-wood dining chairs, Hotel Terminus, Monte Carlo, 1930. Manufactured by D. G. Fischel Söhne, Niemes (Mimoň, Czechoslovakia). (From *Fischel 1870–1930,* **pl. 16).**

Brothers, J. & J. Kohn, and D. G. Fischel Sons, whose sheer volume of production ensured a low level of prices that was almost impossible to match.

By the late 1890s and early 1900s, small bent-wood furniture companies were beginning to feel the effect of the domination of Thonet Brothers and J. & J. Kohn. The optimistic picture of the bent-wood furniture industry presented by F. Wiisa's emblematic design *Möbel aus massiv gebogenem Holze* (Solid Bent-Wood Furniture) of about 1890 (figure 3–15), reflects the economic state of only the largest firms.[70] It suggests the atmosphere of a carefree medieval workshop, old-fashioned qualities of handicraft skills, the romance of world trade, and filled order books at home. Cane seating supplies the decorative background to the title of the design. The double-headed eagle, surmounted by the Imperial Crown, places the industry in the Austro-Hungarian Empire. The roundel at the left, containing a representation of the sun with a naturalistic branch, suggests the growth of the forests, on which the industry depended. The right-hand roundel, containing the seated figure of Justice and the owl, the symbol of wisdom, suggests the balance, symmetry, and judgment required by the bent wood technique. The Latin motto SI•FRACTUS•ILLABATUR•ORBIS •IMPAVIDUM•FERIENT•RUINAE, which is a quotation from Horace, can be roughly translated in this context as, "Even if the curve breaks and splits, the fragments strike those who are nonetheless undismayed"—a literary rendering of the Thonet family motto, "Biegen oder Grechen" ("Bend or break").

In the years of general economic recession between 1901 and 1906, the smaller Austro-Hungarian companies began a murderous campaign of undercutting both each other and factories abroad in an attempt to survive.[71] Sixteen of these smaller firms eventually decided to form a wholesaling association, and in 1907 Mundus, Aktiengesellschaft der vereinigten Österreichischen Bugholzmöbel-Fabriken (Joint-Stock Company of the United Austrian Bent-Wood Furniture Factories) was founded, with headquarters in Vienna. The merger was financed by the Wiener Credit-Anstalt, the largest bank in Central Europe and the bank of Thonet Brothers, J. & J. Kohn, and other bent wood factories.The individual firms comprising Mundus appear to have avoided innovation, content to follow in the wake of the industry's leaders.

By 1910, Mundus had branches in Amsterdam, Basel, Berlin, Breslau, Brussels, Düsseldorf, Hamburg, London, New York, and Paris. The factories in Austria were situated in Heinzendorf, Teschen, Buczkowice, Drholetz, Niemes, and Mährisch-Weisskirchen; those in Hungary were in Beszterczebánya (Neusohl), Ungvár, Warasdin, and Borosjenö.[72] The names of all the individual factories have not yet been identified. Among them was Florijan Bobič in Warasdin; the fourth largest was Rudolf Weill & Co.;[73] the Joseph Jaworek factory in Teschen[74] was surely a member, for Jaworek was a director of Mundus.[75] J. Sommer in Mährisch-Weisskirchen, founded in 1886, was almost certainly a member of the Mundus group, since it is likely that the firm is identical to the bent wood wholesalers J. Sommer & Co. of Düsseldorf and Mannheim, for whom Mundus published a seventeen-page catalogue in 1913. Other companies may be identified by the known situation of Mundus factories: Beszterczebánya, Ungvár, and Borosjenö are known to have been the locations, in that order, of the bent wood manufacturers Harnisch & Komp., Ungvárer Möbelfabriks-Aktiengesellschaft, and Holzindustrie-Aktiengesellschaft, and it is therefore likely that they, too, were members of the Mundus group.[76]

The outbreak of World War I, the conscription of a large part of the bent wood factories' labor force, and the growing threat to the Austro-Hungarian Empire all contributed to the decision of Mundus and J. & J. Kohn to pool their resources for the sake of survival. The merger took place on August 16, 1914. This must have been particularly bitter for J. & J. Kohn, which was exhibiting at the 1914 Deutsche Werkbund exhibition in Cologne and must have hoped, with the advantage of a well-established branch store in Cologne, to capture an even larger share of the German bent wood market. In their Austrian House pavilion the firm was exhibiting interesting new drawing-room bent-wood furniture designed by Hoffmann (figure

Figure 3-15

F. Wiisa. *Bent Solid Wood Furniture*, ca. 1890. Lithograph, 6¼ x 9″. (From *Grafische Musterblätter*, Supplement to *Die Freien Künste*, ca. 1890).

Figure 3-16
Josef Hoffmann. Furniture display in the Austrian Pavilion, *Deutsche Werkbund-Ausstellung*, Cologne, 1914. Manufactured by Jacob & Josef Kohn, Vienna. (From *Jahrbuch des Deutschen Werkbundes 1915*, pl. 62).

3–16),[77] as well as a fascinating group of chairs designed by members of the Hoffmann class at the Wiener Kunstgewerbeschule.[78] In 1918, Kohn-Mundus moved from Vienna to Zurich, and in 1922 it merged with the Thonet firm, to form the Thonet-Mundus-J. & J. Kohn company.[79] In the coming years, the group was to move into new fields of architect-designed bent-wood and tubular-steel furniture. On June 22, 1928, Mundus was dissolved. On December 28 of the same year, the name of the firm was deleted from the Vienna Company Register.[80]

Germany

In the Austro-Hungarian Empire, prospective competitors, such as J. & J. Kohn, were certainly making plans for the production of bent-wood furniture long before December 10, 1869, the date the Thonet Brothers patent expired. Although work may have begun during 1869 on the building of factories for bent-wood furniture production, there is no evidence that any new firm was actually producing such furniture before the day the Thonet patent terminated.

German furniture factories, on the other hand, seem not to have been legally bound by Austro-Hungarian patents and were the first to produce bent-wood furniture outside Austria-Hungary.

Thonet's success at the 1851 Great Exhibition in London apparently evoked the interest of furniture manufacturers more rapidly than has hitherto been considered possible. There is indeed evidence that bent-wood furniture was being made in Germany well before 1854. Eberhard Jonák, in his report on the 1854 *Allgemeine deutsche Industrie-Ausstellung* (German Industrial Exhibition) in Munich, specifically mentions Thonet's bent-wood furniture as being "superior in lightness and elegance to German furniture of the same type."[81] The official catalogue of the Munich exhibition does not record bent-wood furniture among the furniture displayed by any other German exhibitor; however, if Jonák's remark can be interpreted as implying that comparable German bent-wood furniture was in fact shown at the Munich exhibition, the manufacturer may possibly be identified as F. C. Deig & Co. of Lauterberg, Sankt Andreasberg, and Oderfeld. This company exhibited a variety of chairs and tables in Munich in 1854, and another report on the exhibition, by Dr. von Steinbeis, mentions F. C. Deig & Co., in the same breath as Thonet Brothers, as being a rapidly expanding firm engaged in the manufacture of good and cheap furniture for export.[82] The Oderfeld factory, one of Deig's establishments, is known to have exhibited bent-wood furniture at the 1870 *Allgemeine Industrie-Ausstellung* (Exhibition of Industry) in Kassel.[83] It is also possible that the Austrian report on the 1862 London International Exhibition was referring to F. C. Deig's factories when it stated that "Thonet's furniture has already been imitated in the *Zollverein* [German Customs' Union]."[84]

The Hamburg chair-maker J.H.C. Wipper was making bent-wood furniture as early as 1857 and exhibited it in that year in Hamburg's "Patriotische Gesellschaft" (Patriotic Society). Another German manufacturer of bent-wood furniture was H. N. Koste, who established his business in Hamburg in 1859. According to the *Official Catalogue of the Industrial Department* of the 1862 London International exhibition, H. N. Koste & Co. exhibited chairs, a sofa, a table, and a piano stool in curved wood.[85] The company was awarded an Honourable Mention "for

excellence of workmanship," much to the gratification of one observer, who found it quite correct that Thonet Brothers should be awarded the Prize Medal and that an imitator should console himself with a lesser award.[86] H. N. Koste later exhibited at the 1869 *Industrie- und Gewerbe-Ausstellung* (Industry and Trade Exhibition) in Hamburg. Hamburg's pioneering role in the establishment of a German bent wood industry was certainly due in part to its significance as a port, and the possibilities of rapid export[87] no doubt made up for the disadvantages of its location far from extensive beech forests.

Bent-wood furniture produced in Germany was made of laminated veneers until well into the 1860s.[88] By 1867 at the latest, solid bent-wood furniture was being manufactured in Germany by Andrecht & Krüger in Kassel. In 1869 one of the partners, Carl Andrecht, formed a new partnership with Adolf Bingel and exhibited "tables and chairs of solid bent-wood furniture" at the 1870 Kassel Exhibition of Industry. Other bent wood exhibitors in Kassel were Thonet Brothers, which was awarded a Gold Medal, and F. C. Deig's Oderfelder Fabrik (Oderfeld Furniture Factory). The furniture of both the Kassel and Oderfeld firms was described by one reporter as "pure imitations of Thonet furniture."[89]

In Southern Germany, a bent wood industry began to thrive in the late 1860s. At the 1869 Munich *Lokal-Industrie-Ausstellung* (Exhibition of Local Industry), the Munich furniture company Gebrüder Seitz showed "various cane-seated chairs made of walnut, acacia, beech, and mahogany, a beechwood armchair, and a small table with an engraved top." Surprisingly, in the words of the exhibition catalogue, "All the chairs and the tables are made of solid bent wood, and the peculiar method of the construction guarantees exceptional durability."[90] Otto Seitz, whose firm had been founded in 1834 by his father, Nikolaus, a cabinetmaker, was probably the first of a number of Bavarian manufacturers to turn his attention to the production of bent-wood furniture. His ambitions were doubtless fired by the success of the Thonet Brothers display at the 1854 Munich German Industrial Exhibition.[91] Thonet Brothers was represented in Munich at this time by the upholsterer Max Pfeiffer, Jr., who is mentioned in a Thonet advertisement of 1865.[92] Otto Seitz, with the advantage of a local factory and local knowledge, clearly hoped to become a serious rival to Thonet Brothers as far as the fast-expanding Munich market was concerned.

Since the 1869 Munich exhibition opened on July 15, Seitz's bent-wood furniture, like that of Andrecht & Bingel and the Hamburg pioneers, had been manufactured before the expiration of Thonet's patent. Seitz's furniture had probably been made in the firm's factory in the Geierstrasse 11½, which had been built in 1864.[93] In 1871, Seitz and the Munich businessman Friedrich Schwab became partners and founded a new firm, Otto Seitz & Cie, Möbel- & Sessel-Fabrik (Furniture and Chair Factory), probably with the intention of producing bent-wood furniture on an even larger scale. A new factory was opened in 1871 at the Theresienwiese No. 2,[94] and in 1872, with no fewer than 105 employees, the firm began production and exhibited chairs, sofas, and other bent-wood articles at the 1873 Vienna World Exhibition.[95] One visitor to the exhibition noted that the Seitz furniture was characterized by "several very pleasant forms" and commended the Munich firm on having had the courage to exhibit this type of furniture in Vienna—in the lion's den, so to speak. "Want of courage," he added, "seems to have prevented numerous German workshops from participating."[96] This may have been veiled criticism of the Oderfeld Furniture Factory, which, though it participated in the exhibition,[97] had apparently not dared to submit its bent-wood furniture to the critical gaze of the experts, although the firm had shown such furniture three years earlier at the 1870 Kassel exhibition.[98] The firm may even have had good reasons for its restraint: a Swiss exhibitor of Thonet-style furniture, Heinrich Robmann of Turbenthal, Zurich, was taken severely to task by one writer for the imperfection of his work, who noted that "even the symmetry of his curves leaves much to be desired."[99] The industry was in a buoyant state outside the Austro-Hungarian Empire, but the newly founded firms obviously had not had time to gain the experience that the bent wood technique demanded.

The casual mention quoted above of "numerous" German manufacturers who were already making bent-wood furniture by 1873 is surprising. Relatively few have so far been identified, and even the names of "important chair factories of this kind" situated in the Bavarian Forest, according to a nineteenth-century German historian of furniture, are lost in oblivion.[100] Only two other German bent wood firms exhibited at the 1873 Vienna exhibition. One of them, Bieler & Co. of Leipzig, had been established in 1870 and showed chairs, a sofa, tables, felloes (circular rims of wheels), and wagon shafts.[101] The other firm, the Sächsische Holzindustrie-Gesellschaft, of Rabenau near Dresden in Saxony, was commended for the "most notable achievements among all the firms producing bent-wood furniture in Germany."[102] The firm was to become one of the more important German bent wood factories, and Dresden itself was to become a major producer of bent-wood furniture and to remain so until the early 1930s.

Saxony

SÄCHSISCHE HOLZINDUSTRIE-GESELLSCHAFT, RABENAU

The Sächsische Holzindustrie-Gesellschaft was founded in Rabenau near Dresden in 1869, probably for the express purpose of producing bent-wood furniture. By 1871 the company had 639 employees, 150 of whom worked outside the factory making cane seats, and was producing chairs for the home market and for export to the value of 300,000 reichsmarks. In 1873 the firm's production comprised "solid bent-wood furniture, felloes, wagon shafts, etc.," which were made with the assistance of a forty-horsepower boiler. In addition to these articles, the company showed a sofa, a table, and sled runners at the 1873 Vienna exhibition. The company had already exhibited successfully in Dresden (1871), Paris, Lyons, and Moscow (1872); in the following years, it took part in exhibitions in Dresden (1877), Leipzig (1979), Sydney (1879), Melbourne (1880), London (1891), and Leipzig (1897).[103]

About 1900, the company issued a forty-two-page catalogue of bent-wood furniture in English, French, Italian, Spanish, and German, illustrating 293 items, several of which were original models that had not been copied from Thonet Brothers. Some of the furniture illustrated had the relatively new perforated and patterned three-ply veneer seating that had been developed both in the interests of greater durability and as a measure of avoiding damage to women's dresses often inflicted by cane seating. The catalogue describes this kind of seating, which was the same price as cane seating, as "genuine American veneer seats,"[104] and these were indeed a welcome con-

Figure 3-17
Side chair, copy of Thonet Model No. 4, after 1875. Bent solid wood and cane. Manufactured by Sächsische Holzindustrie-Gesellschaft, Rabenau, Germany. Collection Dr. Klaus-Peter Arnold, Dresden.

Figure 3-18
Armchair, Model No. 11, ca. 1880. Bent solid wood and cane. Manufactured by Sächsische Holzindustrie-Gesellschaft, Rabenau, Germany. Museum für Kunst und Kulturgeschichte der Hansestadt Lübeck.

Figure 3-19
Detail of figure 3-18: Manufacturer's label.

tribution to European bent wood design in the nineteenth century. Further development eventually led to the use of burned-in and relief patterns in historicist, Jugendstil, and geometric styles, thereby enabling otherwise anonymous standard bent-wood models of purely technical finesse to move with the times and to assert a supplementary modernity by means of surface ornament.[105]

Two elegant chairs dating from the early period of the company's production have been identified. One, model No. 4 (figure 3–17), is an interpretation of Thonet's Café Daum chair (see cat. no. 7).[106] The other, model No. 11 (figure 3–18)[107] also an imitation of a Thonet production,[108] still has the Rabenau firm's printed label attached to the inner surface of the seat's frame (figure 3–19).

Little is known at present of the firm's activities after 1900. The company exhibited only garden furniture at the 1906 III. *Deutsche Kunstgewerbeausstellung* (Third German Applied Arts Exhibition) in Dresden but was still making bent-wood furniture as well.[109] At the 1913 *Internationale Baufach Ausstellung* (International Exhibition of Architecture) in Leipzig, the firm showed only leather furniture, which suggests that the production of bent-wood furniture may by then have been discontinued.[110]

DRESDNER FABRIK FÜR MÖBEL AUS GEBOGENEM HOLZ
A. TÜRPE, JR.

One reason for this decline may have been the increasing importance of the Dresdner Fabrik für Möbel aus gebogenem Holz, A. Türpe, Jr., which by 1906 had representatives in Amsterdam, Alexandria, Barmen, Berlin, Cairo, Frankfurt, Hamburg, Königsberg, Leipzig, Lübeck, Paris, Posen, and Seville. A. Türpe, Sr., had been one of the leading nineteenth-century German cabinetmakers and Purveyor to the Prussian Court.[111] His son established his factory in 1867, probably with the sole intention of manufacturing bent-wood furniture. The firm existed in Dresden until 1934, when it moved to Alsfeld in Hesse, and produced a diversified program of chairs, armchairs, rocking chairs, and the usual sundry items illustrated in the firm's catalogues (figures 3–20, 21, 22).[112]

The orders of bent-wood chairs for the Stadt Dresden restaurant in Freiberg, Saxony, in 1875, for 1,200 chairs for the main bar of the Pschorr brewery company in Munich in 1912, and for 6,000 chairs for Berlin's "largest room," the Neue Welt restaurant, in 1903 demonstrate the capabilities and ambitions of a firm that in 1906 was calling itself, probably correctly, "The Largest German Bent-

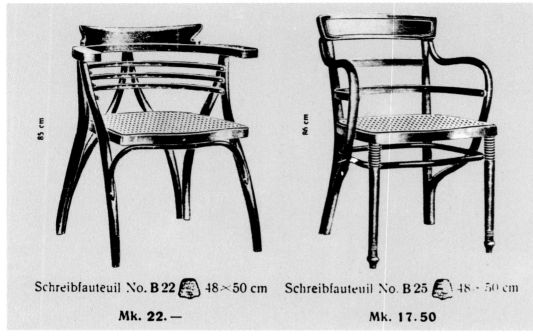

Schreibfauteuil No. B 22 ⬡ 48×50 cm Schreibfauteuil No. B 25 ⬡ 48 - 50 cm

Mk. 22. — **Mk. 17.50**

Figure 3-20

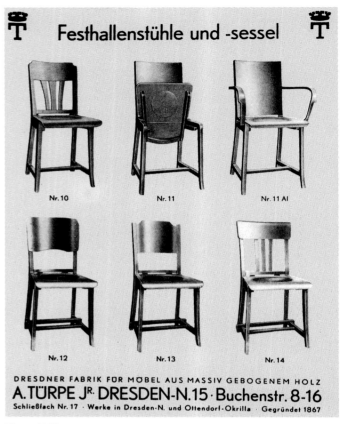

Figure 3-22

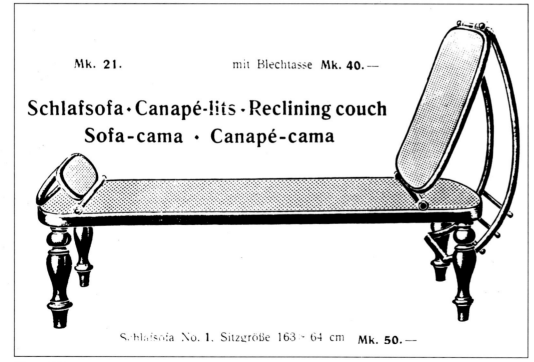

Mk. 21. mit Blechtasse **Mk. 40. —**

Schlafsofa · Canapé-lits · Reclining couch
Sofa-cama · Canapé-cama

Schlafsofa No. 1. Sitzgröße 163 - 64 cm **Mk. 50. —**

Figure 3-21

Figure 3-20
Desk chairs, Model Nos. B22 and B25. Sales catalogue of Dresdner Fabrik für Möbel aus massiv gebogenem Holz, A. Türpe, Jr., Dresden, ca. 1906.

Figure 3-21
Chaise, Model No. 1. Sales catalogue of Dresdner Fabrik für Möbel aus massiv gebogenem Holz, A. Türpe, Jr., Dresden, ca. 1906.

Figure 3-22
Theater seating, advertisement of Dresdner Fabrik für Möbel aus massiv gebogenem Holz, A. Türpe, Jr., Dresden, 1932.

Wood Furniture Company."[113] The firms' trademark, often found on labels on bent-wood chairs, was a crowned *T* (see Appendix).

Hesse

ALSFELDER MÖBELFABRIK, ALSFELD

On December 2, 1893, the bankrupt Hammonia Möbel-fabrik (Furniture Factory) in Alsfeld, which had been making bent-wood furniture, was bought at auction for 118,000 reichsmarks by Jacob Koch X of Alsfeld.[114] He at once formed a limited company with nine other partners, and the Alsfelder Möbelfabrik G.m.b.H. was registered March 17, 1894. The newly formed company was an immediate success, and a branch factory was built in Angenrod in 1904–5.

In 1894, the first year of production, 21,803 pieces of bent-wood furniture were produced with a total value of 79,397 reichsmarks. Production in the two factories reached a peak in 1907, when 87,868 pieces were produced with a total value of 349,604 reichsmarks. A comparable result was achieved only once again, in 1913 before the outbreak of World War I. Production decreased steadily during the war years and when, in 1916, the rubber shortage made it impossible for bicycle manufacturers to obtain the raw material they needed for tires, the Alsfeld company revived a traditional technique of bending wood and produced wooden rods as substitutes for tires. Between 1916 and 1918 they sold these for a total of 103,989 reichsmarks.

The factory's models were, naturally, copied to a large extent from Thonet Brothers, and this may explain the firm's reluctance to exhibit its products in competitions. However, a variety of bent-wood furniture was shown in Alsfeld itself in 1895 on the occasion of the *Oberhess-ische Industrie- und Gewerbe-Ausstellung* (Upper Hessian Industry and Trade Exhibition),[115] and filing cabinets, a typewriter table, a conference table, chairs, benches, and armchairs "in the Viennese style" were shown at the 1908 *Hessische Landesausstellung für freie und angewandte Kunst* (Hesse State Exhibition of Fine and Applied Art) in Darmstadt.[116]

This contact with Darmstadt, whose artists' colony,

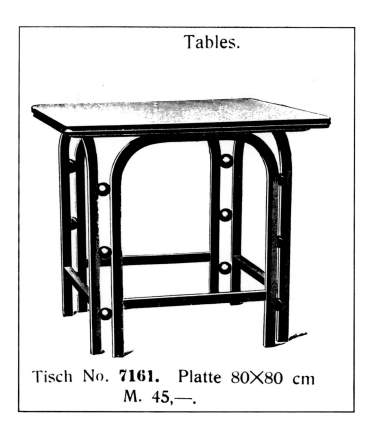

Tables.

Tisch No. **7161.** Platte 80×80 cm M. 45,—.

Figure 3-23
Table, Model No. 7161. Sales catalogue of Alsfelder Möbelfabrik, Alsfeld, Germany, ca. 1908.

directed first by Joseph Olbrich and then by Albin Müller, made it one of the most important artistic centers in Germany, may have prompted the Alsfeld company to introduce a modern element into its bent-wood furniture production. The reference in 1908 to furniture "in the Viennese style" may not simply be a general term for bent wood alone, but may rather refer to furniture in the style of the architect-designed pieces made, for example, by J. & J. Kohn in Vienna. As one of the Alsfeld company's catalogues shows, bent-wood furniture in the modern Viennese style was certainly in production around 1908.[117] Table No. 7161 (figure 3–23) is clearly derived from the idea of the Kohn side chair with seven spheres between two elliptical arches of bent wood forming the back (cat. no. 54) shown at the 1908 Vienna *Kunstschau*,[118] as well as from Otto Wagner's stool (cat. no. 48) for the Main Banking Room of the Postsparkasse (Imperial Austrian Postal Savings Bank), designed in 1906.[119] Other "Viennese

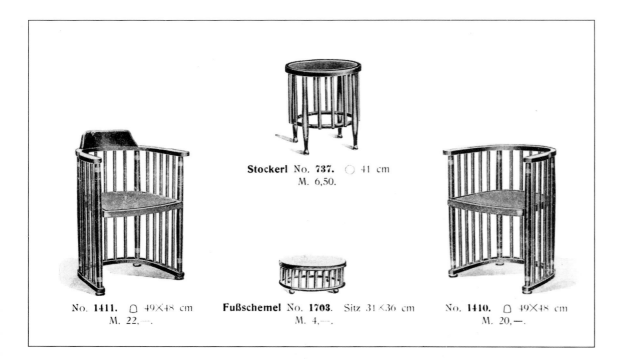

Stockerl No. **737.** ○ 41 cm
M. 6,50.

No. **1411.** ⬜ 49×48 cm
M. 22,—.

Fußschemel No. **1703.** Sitz 31×36 cm
M. 4,—.

No. **1410.** ⬜ 49×48 cm
M. 20,—.

Figure 3-24
**Armchairs, Model Nos. 1411 and 1410;
stool, Model No. 737; footstool, Model No.
1703. Sales catalogue of Alsfelder Möbelfabrik, Alsfeld, Germany, ca. 1908.**

style" furniture produced by the firm is even less original:
one armchair, model No. 1410 (figure 3-24, right), is a
version of Kohn armchair No. 729/F (figure 59A), while
another, model No. 1411, with the applied crest rail (figure
3-24, left), is a variation of Kohn armchair No. 729/2F
(figure 3-25).[120] However, both Alsfeld chairs dispense
with the characteristic Kohn spherical wooden braces at
the juncture of seat and legs. Both the Alsfeld stool, model
No. 737, and footstool, model No. 1703 (figure 3-24,
center), are original designs, yet their construction, which
is determined by vertical lines of wood, reflects contemporary Viennese style. It is interesting to note, in view
of the Alsfeld firm's ambition to compete, even if modestly,
with contemporary bent-wood furniture of Viennese
make, that the stool is not listed under the German word
Hocker, as one might expect, but under the Austrian word
Stockerl. It is reasonable to suppose that the Alsfeld company made other such "Viennese" furniture, but it is not
at the moment possible to identify individual models, for
the firm did not begin to label or brand its products until
the 1930s.

In 1930, Thonet-Mundus opened negotiations with the
Alsfeld firm with a view to taking it over and turning it
into a sales depot for its own products in the western
portion of Germany, but the plan came to nothing. In
1934, the Dresdner Fabrik für Möbel aus gebogenem Holz,
A. Türpe, Jr., under its general manager, Otto Schumann,
moved to Alsfeld to merge with the Alsfelder Möbelfabrik
under Schumann's management. The move had become
necessary because the freight charges for wood imported
from Czechoslovakia to Dresden had become so high
that the company's existence was threatened. The company
still exists in Alsfeld as the Stuhlfabrik Alsfeld-Türpe, but
no longer manufactures bent-wood furniture.

Baden

ALBERT STOLL, WALDSHUT

One of the German bent wood firms that might easily
have dared to exhibit at the 1873 Vienna World Exhibition
was Albert Stoll of Waldshut. The firm was founded in
1870 specifically for the production of bent-wood furniture.[121] Stoll was a native of Cannstatt near Stuttgart, where
his parents owned a small engineering firm: the first boiler
for the new Waldshut factory was probably made by the
Cannstatt family firm. In the same year, branch factories
were erected in Koblenz and Klingnau,[122] both across the
border in Switzerland, and Thonet-style furniture was
produced. An interesting commission that came to the
firm before 1914 was for richly decorated bent-wood
seating for the carriages of the Brünig Railway, which linked
the Vierwaldstätter See (Lake of Lucerne) with the upper
Aare valley above the Lake of Brienz.[123]

Albert Stoll ceased production of bent-wood furniture
in 1918.

ERSTE ACHERNER STUHL-FABRIK AUGUST KLAR, ACHERN

The Erste Acherner Stuhl-Fabrik August Klar in Achern
produced large quantities of bent-wood furniture of the
café and beer-hall type from the late nineteenth century
until the factory's destruction by bombing in 1945.[124]

The firm's founder, Josef Aegidius Klar, set up as a turner
in Achern in 1795. Bent-wood furniture was first made by

the founder's grandson August, who in 1909 introduced *Klar's Fortschritt* (Klar's Progress), a chair incorporating bent-wood elements that he curiously advertised in leaflets as being cheaper than the Thonet-style furniture he also manufactured. He also claimed that his "invention"—by which the four legs were joined by horizontal bars of wood instead of being connected by an inner bent-wood ring—was, in fact, much more stable than bent-wood chairs and was, thus, the perfect substitute for them.[125]

August Klar's unremarkable furniture is no more than a footnote in the history of bent-wood furniture, but the firm has a certain historical significance. August Meder, the founder's great-grandson and proprietor of the firm in 1939, became managing director of the D. G. Fischel factory in Weissenburg (Wissembourg) after that firm was appropriated from its Czechoslovakian Jewish owners in 1938 and carried on production there until the end of the war.

Bavaria

GEORG BENEDIKT VON POSCHINGER, OBERFRAUENAU

Georg Benedikt von Poschinger was one of the seven German bent-wood furniture factories listed in the first survey made of the growth of the industry after 1869.[126] In the field of the applied arts, the name of Poschinger is known today only in connection with the glass industry of the Bavarian Forest.[127] The fact that a member of the family also devoted himself to the manufacture of bent-wood furniture has long been forgotten.

Georg Benedikt von Poschinger (1845–1900) inherited the Oberfrauenau family estate in 1864. Woodworking factories are mentioned in a list of the Poschinger possessions drawn up in January 1873,[128] and Poschinger's decision to manufacture bent-wood furniture in Oberfrauenau was possibly made during that year. In 1875, a first workshop was set up in a former agricultural building on the Oberfrauenau estate. Bent-wood furniture was made there for about ten years, until a boiler explosion in 1885 severely damaged the building. A new and much larger factory was erected on the estate and production was resumed in 1886. Shortly after Poschinger's death in 1900,

No 729/2 F   ℳ 27·50

48 × 49 cm

Figure 3-25
Armchair, Model No. 729/2F. Sales catalogue of Jacob & Josef Kohn, Vienna, 1916.

Figure 3-26
**Side chair, ca. 1890. Bent solid wood and
cane. Manufactured by Georg Benedikt
von Poschinger, Oberfrauenau, Germany.
Private collection.**

the manufacture of bent-wood furniture and other wooden
articles was discontinued.

There are no surviving records of the volume or even
appearance of Poschinger bent-wood furniture, and the
firm exhibited at none of the frequent industry and trade
exhibitions that took place between 1875 and 1900. Nevertheless, several bent-wood pieces can be identified as
having been made in Oberfrauenau: a chair (figure 3–26)
modeled after Thonet No. 18, and an armchair (figure
3–27) that is a mixture of Thonet No. 1 and No. 20.[129] In
the absence of any printed source material such as a trade
catalogue, the best image of the Poschinger production
can be gained from a very curious staircase (figure 3–28)
in a worker's house on the Oberfrauenau estate, which is
probably unique in Germany. The banisters appear to
be composed of a disparate assortment of rocking-chair
elements, headboards of beds, and various chairs—all,
perhaps, odd bits and pieces left over when production
ceased in 1900. This staircase has great attraction as a cu-
riosity, but can make no claims to any beauty. Indeed,
it serves as a sad reminder that bent-wood furniture was
never given a real opportunity in the nineteenth century
to tackle the wonderful task of staircase and banister design,
to which it is so obviously suited. The beautiful bent-wood
spiral staircase installed in the Thonet factory in Bistritz
am Hostein in 1875 gives a good idea of bent wood possibilities in this respect,[130] and it must be considered a

Figure 3-27
**Armchair, ca. 1890. Bent solid wood. Man-
ufactured by Georg Benedikt von Poschinger, Oberfrauenau, Germany. Private
collection.**

matter of deep regret that Art Nouveau and Jugendstil
designers apparently never had an opportunity to exercise
their boundless imagination on similar exercises.

Bent-wood furniture designed by German architects

Vienna, capital of the Austro-Hungarian Empire and
headquarters of the international bent-wood furniture
industry, was also an important center of avant-garde
European art. Leading designers could scarcely avoid
becoming interested in the development of a type of
chair that was synonymous with the beloved Viennese
café. The quality of Viennese bent-wood furniture and
the ability of Viennese designers to adapt bent wood
quickly and brilliantly to every decorative style may well
have discouraged German architects from devoting very
much attention to this type of chair. Few of the German
firms could afford a director of design such as Gustav
Siegel, for the limited volume of production, unlike that
of Thonet and Kohn, scarcely allowed regular experiments
in the field of artistic furniture. Certain investments were
required, the results were unlikely to be cheaper than
architect-designed Viennese bent-wood furniture, and new
models were liable to become quickly passé.

Both the Sächsische Holzindustrie-Gesellschaft in Rabenau (1906) and Albert Stoll in Waldshut (1914) advertised
that they would carry out designs submitted to them by
outside designers,[131] but the interest taken by German
designers in bent-wood furniture during the 1900–1914
period is disproportionately small when compared to
their other activities in furniture design. There is no indication that Germany was ever a worthwhile market
for architect-designed bent-wood furniture. Here such
furniture remained in almost all instances a type of anonymous object, public furniture devoid of all prestige,
designed for use in vast numbers in beer halls, restaurants, and cafés, and having no place in households. One
German author, Heinrich Pudor, advocating optimistically
in 1913 that people should really be making their own
furniture, thought it incredible that "furniture purchased
at a furniture store or an exhibition, intended for the
purchaser's personal individual life . . . could ever signify

anything more to the owner than mere restaurant tables and café chairs."[132] Pudor's disdain for bent-wood furniture suggests that a concern for it was not one of the likely pursuits of a self-respecting German designer. There were, nevertheless, exceptions to this general neglect that German architects and designers showed toward the humble bent-wood chair.

RICHARD RIEMERSCHMID

The interior of the Schauspielhaus in Munich's Maximilianstrasse has been rightly described as the "most beautiful Jugendstil interior to have survived in Germany."[133] The theater was built between 1900 and 1901 by Heilmann & Littmann, Munich's leading construction firm, and the interior decoration (figure 3–29) was carried out by Richard Riemerschmid (1868–1957), a young Munich painter and designer. The theater seating designed by Riemerschmid was manufactured by the German branch of Thonet Brothers in Frankenberg, which also made the various single chairs standing in other parts of the theater;[134] whether these were designed by Riemerschmid is not known.

Riemerschmid's automatic tip-up seating for the Schauspielhaus is interesting for historical and iconological reasons. It was the first occasion, although this was not considered significant at the time, that a German designer turned his attention to bent-wood furniture. Ignoring the precedent of Thonet Brothers's normal theater seating, which consisted fundamentally of rows of single, juxtaposed chairs,[135] Riemerschmid attempted to give each row of chairs an appearance of unity by the use of a single, uninterrupted plywood backrest. He also gave the backrest an undulating outline, not only for the sake of employing a popular Jugendstil motif, but also to enhance the impression of a submarine world by means of a stylized wave motif.

Riemerschmid's guiding idea behind the decorative scheme of the Schauspielhaus was derived, above all, from the work of August Endell, whose notorious Atelier Elvira, built in Munich 1896–97, was filled with decorative details based on seaweed-like forms and had a facade decorated with a spiky sea monster of uncertain pedigree. The walls and ceilings of Riemerschmid's Schauspielhaus are full of

Figure 3–28
Staircase, Oberfrauenau, ca. 1900. Bent solid wood elements manufactured by Georg Benedikt von Poschinger, Oberfrauenau, Germany.

Figure 3–29
Richard Riemerschmid. Interior, Schauspielhaus, Munich, 1900–1901. Seating of bent solid wood. Manufactured by Gebrüder Thonet, Frankenberg, Germany. (From *Kunst und Handwerk*, 1901, p. 288).

allusions to underwater plant life.[136] Riemerschmid's bent-wood seating must therefore be seen as a supplementary element in an overall architectural fantasy, in which even the audience assumes the role of indistinct sea dwellers in the dim half-light—a fantasy that reflects the humorous world of the Munich magazine *Jugend* and reveals a light-hearted, imaginative solution to the serious problems of theater design.

Christopher Wilk has suggested that chairs designed by Riemerschmid around 1898–1900 influenced certain Viennese bent-wood furniture designs, such as Thonet chair No. 511.[137] However, these seats for the Schauspielhaus, an early example of architect-designed bent-wood furniture that appeared less than a year after Adolf Loos's chairs for the Café Museum in Vienna were produced by J. & J. Kohn, have been overlooked until now.

Although Riemerschmid probably had no further

dealings with Thonet Brothers after 1901, there is evidence that some years later he designed furniture for the Munich firm of Hans Kadeder, which provided the bent-wood seating in various restaurants and beer halls at the exhibition *München 1908* (figure 3–30).[138] This exhibition was, in the words of the official catalogue, "a military parade of Munich's achievements . . . [an exhibition] that contains nothing foreign, unless Munich design or execution is involved."[139]

A photograph of a section of the side room of the main restaurant (figure 3–31) shows that two models of bent-wood chairs were used. One, seen in the foreground, is the Viennese-style chair that is a variation of Otto Wagner's armchair of 1906 for the Board Room of the Postsparkasse (Imperial Austrian Postal Savings Bank) (Kohn Model No. 715/F; see cat. no. 46). The other model, seen in the background, has a back with a distinctive double-fan shape, which is closely related to a chair that Riemerschmid had designed in 1900 for J. Fleischauers Söhne in Nürnberg (figure 3–32).[141] The evidence would appear to indicate that the Kadeder bent-wood chair seen in the background is an original design by Riemerschmid. Unfortunately, no example has yet been traced. The model eventually found the approval of Thonet Brothers; in 1911, possibly delighted to be able to profit at last from one of its competitors, the firm produced its own version of the design.[142]

EMANUEL VON SEIDL

Emanuel von Seidl (1856–1919) studied at the Technische Hochschule (Technical University), Munich, and practiced as an interior decorator before becoming an architect. At the 1898 *Jahres-Ausstellung* (Annual Exhibition) at the Glaspalast (Glass Palace) in Munich he exhibited a Roman Living Room,[143] inspired by the furniture and interiors of the Villa Stuck in Munich, the residence of Franz Stuck (1863–1928), a leading Munich painter and sculptor who had built it after his own designs in 1897–98.[144] Seidl later became the leading country-house architect in Southern Germany and also numbered several important Munich breweries among his clients, for whom he designed bar-rooms.

The Banquet Hall of the main restaurant at the *München 1908* exhibition (figure 3–33) was designed by Seidl. The

Figure 3-31

Figure 3-32

Figure 3-33

Figure 3-31
Side room of the main restaurant at the exhibition *München 1908*, Munich. Bentwood furniture manufactured by Hans Kadeder, Munich. (From *Die Kunst*, 1908, p. 465).

Figure 3-32
Richard Riemerschmid. Living room, 1900. Manufactured by J. Fleischauers Söhne, Nürnberg. (From *Die Kunst*, 1901, p. 347).

Figure 3-33
Emanuel von Seidl. Banquet Hall at the exhibition *München 1908*, Munich. (From *Die Kunst*, 1908, p. 462).

Figure 3-34

Letterhead of Hans Kadeder, Munich, ca. 1910, with illustrations of chairs by Emanuel von Seidl (left) and Richard Riemerschmid (right). Private collection, Munich.

chairs in this hall are less exciting than the bent-wood chairs at the same exhibition that have been ascribed here to Riemerschmid. The model is, of course, in the tradition of café or beer-hall bent-wood furniture. The only characteristic feature, easily overlooked, is the diamond-shaped vertical piece of plywood at the center of the back. This very modest chair was nevertheless designed by Seidl for H. Kadeder and is even illustrated as his in a letterhead of the firm about 1910 (figure 3-34).[145] It was later copied by Thonet Brothers and appeared for the first time in the 1911 catalogue as Model No. 615 (figure 3-35).[146]

In a section of the side room of the main restaurant at the *München 1908* exhibition (apart from the area that contained the "Riemerschmid" Kadeder chairs), there were high-backed bent-wood chairs in a historicist, neo-Baroque style that were also probably designed by Seidl for H. Kadeder (figure 3-36).[147] Lack of documentary evidence makes it impossible to ascertain whether this small but enterprising firm produced architect-designed bent-wood furniture other than that designed by Emanuel von Seidl and, as suggested here, Richard Riemerschmid. As H. Kadeder was sold by the Kadeder family in 1909 and the firm became wholesalers and retailers only, the bent-wood furniture exhibited in 1908 was certainly the last of this kind.

At the 1910 Brussels Exposition Internationale (World Exhibition), Emanuel von Seidl once again used his bent-

Figure 3-35

Emanuel von Seidl. Chair, designed 1908 for Hans Kadeder, Munich. Manufactured by Gebrüder Thonet, Vienna, ca. 1911. Private collection, Munich.

wood chair in his Wine Restaurant and in his Munich House, which also contained the German beer restaurant. Here, the diamond motif of the chair's back is repeated in the balustrade of the balcony that served as a musician's gallery.[148]

HANS GÜNTHER REINSTEIN

The overall concept of the interior of the café at the *Darmstädter Künstlerkolonie Ausstellung* (Darmstadt Artists' Colony Exhibition) of 1914 (figure 3-37) was the creation of the Viennese architect and colony member Emanuel Josef Margold (1889–1962). The café chairs (figure 3-38) were made of bent wood that incorporated a U-shaped section of corrugated and strengthened paper composition, not unlike papier-mâché, which formed the sides and back of the chairs. The central leg of the tables was similarly constructed, a vertical oval section of this molded composition resting on a wooden base and supporting the oval table top.[149]

At first glance, there would appear to be no good reason for thinking that Margold was not the designer of this bent-wood furniture, which is among the most attractive ever designed. The furniture's black-and-white color scheme was often used by Viennese artists in furniture design, ceramics, glass, and wall decoration. The café chairs are perfectly subordinated to Margold's overall interior design, which is based on black-and-white geometrical forms. Furthermore, the chairs are reminiscent of Josef Hoffmann's Kohn armchair No. 720/F, designed about 1902, whose arms, legs, and back consist of an uninterrupted piece of bent wood framing a single U-shaped length of plywood to which the seat is attached by rivets.[150]

All the evidence points to a Viennese designer and a Viennese factory, but the chairs were, in fact, produced by the Vereinigte Möbelfabriken Germania in Bad Lauterberg, Germany,[151] and they were designed by the German architect Hans Günther Reinstein (1880–?).[152] In 1902, after training to be a painter in Cologne, Reinstein moved to Darmstadt, where he became a pupil of Peter Behrens and co-founder of a group called the Vereinte Kunstgewerbler Darmstadt (United Applied Art Workers of Darmstadt) together with the architect Alfred Koch, the sculptor C. F. Meier, and the needleworker Marie Elisabeth

Figure 3-36
Emanuel von Seidl (?). Bent-wood chairs designed for the exhibition *München 1908*, Munich. Manufactured by Hans Kadeder, Munich. (From *Die Kunst*, 1908, p. 464).

Figure 3-37
Hans Günther Reinstein. Tables and chairs, in café designed by Emanuel Josef Margold, *Darmstädter Künstlerkolonie Ausstellung*, Darmstadt, 1914. See CAT. NOS. 62 and 63.

Figure 3-38
Hans Günther Reinstein. Armchair, ca. 1909. Manufactured by Vereinigte Möbelfabriken Germania, Bad Lauterberg, Germany. See CAT. NOS. 62 and 63. Private collection, Bad Lauterberg, West Germany.

Figure 3-39
Hans Günther Reinstein. Armchair, in Garden Hall designed by Robert Oerley, *Wiener Frühjahrsausstellung*, Vienna, 1912–13. Manufactured by Press-Stoff-Möbel Gesellschaft, Vienna. (From *Deutsche Kunst und Dekoration*, November 1912, p. 180). See CAT. NO. 62.

Kleinsteuber,[153] all of whom were Behrens's pupils. Reinstein moved to Hannover in 1905 and in the course of 1908 developed his new method of combining bent wood and paperboard. He received a patent for his invention in November of that year, which granted him the sole right to produce "furniture made of cardboard, characterized by the employment of corrugated, or similarly profiled and strengthened, cardboard as an autonomous, self-supporting structural material."[154]

Although this furniture must have been well known in Germany[155] and was used, as mentioned above, in an important Darmstadt exhibition, it enjoyed even greater popularity in Austria, where it was enthusiastically and unsuspectingly accepted as full-blooded Viennese. Robert Oerley used these chairs, painted black, in his Garden Hall at the 1912–13 *Wiener Frühjahrsausstellung* (Vienna Spring Exhibition), where their vertical lines corresponded perfectly with the lines of the stucco coffers of the walls (figure 3–39).[156]

The furniture used by Oerley would not have been made in Bad Lauterberg by the Germania firm, but had

certainly been produced by the Press-Stoff-Möbel-Gesellschaft G.m.b.H., a company that had been established in Vienna in March 1911, after Reinstein had secured an Austrian patent in September 1910.[157] The Vienna company had the right to manufacture and distribute furniture incorporating Reinstein's invention of corrugated and strengthened paper and continued to do so until 1929, when the company was dissolved.

The Germania itself was an association of Bad Lauterberg chair factories that was formed in October 1908, shortly before Reinstein's patent was granted, probably for the same economic reasons that had dictated the foundation of the Austro-Hungarian Mundus group in 1907. The Germania was eventually disbanded in 1915. One of the original members in the association was the firm of A. H. Hillegeist & Co., later known as Karl Hillegeist & Co., a bent-wood furniture manufacturer. The Hillegeist armchair No. 170 (figure 3–40),[158] is a variation with an upswept back of the Kohn armchair No. 423/F[159]—a further exam-

Figure 3-40
Armchair, Model No. 170, ca. 1912. Sales catalogue of Karl Hillegeist & Co., Bad Lauterberg, Germany, ca. 1912.

ple of the close attention that the German bent wood manufacturers paid to contemporaneous developments in Viennese furniture.

RUDOLF AND FIA WILLE

Rudolf (1873–?) and Fia Wille (1868–1920), Berlin designers and interior decorators, designed a mahogany dining chair with woven leather seat in 1904, which, although there is no documentary evidence, would seem to incorporate an arch-shaped piece of bent palisander in the back (figure 3–41).[160] This was manufactured by the W. Kümmel Möbelfabrik, Berlin, a firm not otherwise known to have made bent-wood furniture. The incorporation of pieces of bent wood into industrially produced furniture of conventional construction had occurred in Germany since the 1870s, and this simple example refutes the pessimistic prophecy of a critic at the 1878 Paris Exposition Universelle, who declared that experiments in this direction "have led to no acceptable results and probably never will."[161]

LUDWIG PAFFENDORF

The Cologne architect and designer Ludwig Paffendorf (1872–ca. 1936) designed a bent-wood chair in 1906 that was an elegant version of a conventional bent-wood café chair (figure 3–42). The turned decoration of the front legs was repeated on a writing table of Paffendorf's design made for the Monopol-Hotel in Cologne in 1906, and the chair itself was used in the hotel restaurant in the cellar. It also appeared in the Prince's Room of the *Deutsche Kunstausstellung* (German Art Exhibition) held in Cologne in the same year.[162] The name of the firm that produced this furniture is unrecorded, but may well have been J. & J. Kohn, which had an important branch in the Hohenstaufenring 27 in Cologne.

Figure 3–42
Ludwig Paffendorf. Writing table and chairs, Monopol-Hotel, Cologne, 1906. (From *Innen-Dekoration*, 1907, p. 266).

Figure 3–41
Rudolf and Fia Wille. Dining chairs, 1904. Manufactured by W. Kümmel Möbelfabrik, Berlin. (From *Berliner Architekturwelt*, 1905, p. 36).

Figure 3-43
Bruno Paul. Chairs, Café Kerkau, Berlin, 1910. Manufactured or supplied by the Vereinigte Werkstätten für Kunst im Handwerk, Munich. (From *Innen-Dekoration*, 1910, p. 370).

BRUNO PAUL

The Café Kerkau in Berlin designed by Bruno Paul (1874–1968) in 1910 contained chairs that appear to be of bent wood, which were certainly designed by Paul himself and were used only in this café (figure 3–43).[163] Made of mahogany, with a higher back than the normal café chair and comfortably upholstered seats and backs, the chairs had been made or supplied by the Vereinigte Werkstätten für Kunst im Handwerk in Munich, of which Paul had been a founder-member in 1897. The elegant solidity of these chairs sets them apart from the usual type of bent-wood café furniture and corresponds well with the representative element that began to appear in Paul's work around 1910, after a period of restrained and even puritanical simplicity. The Music Room of the Café Kerkau also contained bent-wood chairs, which corresponded, with variant leg braces, to Kohn chair No. 369/5.[164]

PETER BEHRENS

The bent-wood armchair used by Peter Behrens (1868–1940) in the Tonhaus (Concert Hall), which he built in the Flora park on the occasion of the 1906 *Deutsche Kunstausstellung* (German Art Exhibition) in Cologne, was the J. &. J. Kohn chair No. 728/F.[165] Until 1906, Behrens had apparently not concerned himself with bent wood furniture design. In 1910, when the need arose for cheap and durable seating for the AEG (Allgemeine Elektrizitäts-Gesellschaft) shop in the Königgrätzer Strasse 4 in Berlin, bent-wood chairs were installed which had a distinctive back consisting of three horizontal and slightly concave slats (figure 3–44).[166] As the overall design for this shop was in Peter Behrens's hands, there is no reason to doubt that the design of this chair was not also by Behrens, especially as he had designed all the other furniture in the shop.[167]

These same chairs were used in the club room of the Elektra Boathouse, also designed by Behrens in 1910, which served as a clubhouse for officials of the AEG and BEW (Berliner Elektrizitätswerke) who had founded the rowing association Elektra.[168] The firm that made these chairs has not been identified.

The monumental Festhalle (Banquet Hall) designed by Behrens for the *Deutsche Werkbund-Ausstellung* (German

The German bent-wood furniture industry in 1914

In 1897, the Austrian writer Jacob von Falke was of the decided opinion that bent-wood chairs had no place in the home: "Our bent-wood chairs may admittedly be recommended for their extreme lightness and can be used in certain cases to great advantage in cafés, for example. However, they can find no place in an artistically decorated apartment, for they confront us with transparent cane seating and thin rods, whereas our gaze prefers to fall upon some substantial object that is distinguished by form and color. Bent-wood chairs are also too insignificant for a second purpose, namely, colored decoration, which, even more than form, enables chairs to contribute to the general harmony and artistic effect of a room."[172]

Writing in 1897 as a protagonist of a monumental neo-

Figure 3-44
Peter Behrens. Chairs, AEG shop, König-grätzer Strasse 4, Berlin, 1910. (From Meyer-Schönbrunn, *Peter Behrens*, p. 53).

Werkbund Exhibition) held in Cologne in 1914 contained bent-wood chairs of unknown manufacture whose design can reasonably be ascribed to Behrens (figure 3–45). They are related to the bent-wood chair for the AEG shop in that both have the same gently angled back slats: here, there are only two, both of concave, not convex, form.[169] The Hall contained fifteen hundred of these chairs,[170] which were also used in Bruno Paul's Wine Restaurant at the same exhibition.[171] A large firm such as Thonet Brothers or J. &. J. Kohn is likely to have made them.

Figure 3-45
Peter Behrens (?). Chairs, in Banquet Hall, *Deutsche Werkbund Ausstellung*, Cologne, 1914. (From *Jahrbuch des Deutschen Werkbundes 1915*, p. 157).

Baroque style of interior decoration associated with the name of the Austrian painter Hans Makart (1840–1884), Falke was repeating an opinion he had already expressed in an earlier edition of his widely read book.[173] This opinion was to have greater influence on designers outside the Austro-Hungarian Empire. For German designers, certainly, the field of bent-wood furniture, with the few exceptions mentioned, was of only sporadic interest, while the factories themselves were more interested in mass-produced stock designs that offered financial security than in artistic designs that were liable to sell poorly and for a limited time.

The concentration in Germany (and probably elsewhere) during the nineteenth century on the production of a limited number of stock models, such as Thonet Brothers No. 14 chair, and for the most part during the early years of the twentieth century on the production of artistically unexciting models meant that German firms were in competition with the Austro-Hungarian companies only insofar as the bent-wood café chair was concerned. The production figures of Thonet Brothers do not suggest that competition gave serious cause for alarm before 1900. In 1869, the year the Thonet patent expired, Thonet factories produced 386,668 pieces of furniture, a figure that dropped minimally to 385,604 in 1870,[174] which might indicate that Thonet's position was beginning to falter. This very first fall in production was more than compensated for, however, by the 1871 production figure of 472,641 pieces. Slight decreases in the steadily increasing rate of production were recorded in 1874, 1886, and 1890, but in 1900 more than 1,090,000 pieces of furniture were produced in Thonet factories,[175] 20,000 of which were rocking chairs.[176] From 1901 to 1913, Thonet's production, based on the number of pieces made, increased by a further seventy percent: in 1913 the firm manufactured 1,810,000 pieces of bent-wood furniture—a figure that does not even include furniture made in the Frankenberg factory in Germany.[177]

Although no comparable figures are known for the total quantity of bent-wood furniture produced in the factories of Thonet's competitors, some idea of the extent of this competition can be gauged from figures issued in the late nineteenth century, which refer to the famous Thonet No. 14 chair. Thonet Brothers itself had produced a total of 8,466,926 such chairs between 1859—the year the chair appeared in its first catalogue—and 1886.[178] In 1896, by comparison, the total number of No. 14 chairs produced since 1859 by *all* bent-wood furniture factories in the Austro-Hungarian Empire and elsewhere was estimated to amount to about forty million.[179] This figure not only indicates the popularity of this particular chair, but also suggests the dependence of Thonet's competitors on one best-selling model—a dependence that allowed a certain degree of success and confidence in the future, but was no serious threat to Thonet's position as the leader in this branch of the furniture industry. One result of competition, however, may have been the continuously low prices of bent-wood furniture. In 1884, for example, a No. 14 chair cost three Austrian florins, the same price as when it was first produced in 1859.[180]

With the exception of the A. Türpe firm in Dresden, German bent-wood furniture companies mainly supplied the home market and were content to leave the international market to Thonet Brothers, J. & J. Kohn, and D. G. Fischel Sons. A degree of relative harmony between the leading Austro-Hungarian manufacturers and firms elsewhere may be assumed for the period leading up to the turn of the century. After 1900, the situation changed. Between 1901 and 1906, which were years of general economic decline, Austro-Hungarian firms attempted to recoup their losses at home by becoming increasingly active in the German market. Labor and raw-material costs were much cheaper in the Austro-Hungarian Empire than in Germany, which greatly facilitated exports. The import into Germany of Austro-Hungarian bent-wood furniture benefited further by the low rate of German customs duty, which amounted to ten marks for every one hundred kilograms of wood. In 1901, the German bent wood factories attempted to remedy matters by petitioning the government to raise the duty on imported bent-wood furniture. After almost five years of negotiations, a bill raising the import duty to nineteen and one half marks was introduced, but in subsequent negotiations between the German and Austro-Hungarian representatives, the German delegation relented; in 1906, when new trade tariffs between the two nations were drawn up, the old rate of ten marks was retained.

Since this rate was set for a term of eleven years, direct negotiations between the German and Austro-Hungarian bent-wood furniture factories began, with the object of coming to an agreement on fixed prices. In November 1912, an accord was finally reached when representatives of Thonet Brothers, J. & J. Kohn, D. G. Fischel Sons, Mundus, Alsfelder Möbelfabrik, Albert Stoll, and Germania in Bad Lauterberg met in Munich and put an end to years of ruinous undercutting. This sketch of the relationship between the German and Austro-Hungarian bent-wood furniture factories from 1901 to 1912[181] suggests that the German bent wood industry had now become important and that it was in the interests of the Austro-Hungarian firms to come to an agreement rather than compete at all costs.

Lack of documentary evidence, such as the invaluable catalogues of individual firms, makes it impossible at present to determine how far the competition created by Italian, Spanish, Belgian, as well as German bent-wood furniture manufacturers was also due to excellence in design. A dispassionate review of some of the more remarkable bent-wood furniture produced after 1900 shows that much interesting work bears neither a manufacturer's label nor any other distinguishing mark that could identify it as the product of a particular factory. Thonet Brothers, J. & J. Kohn, D. G. Fischel Sons, and Mundus appear to have taken particular care to label or stamp their work, and it is safe to assume that unmarked bent-wood furniture is the product of one of the minor but active firms listed in the Appendix. Though these companies were small in comparison to Thonet, Kohn, Fischel, and Mundus, they were nevertheless capable of original and imaginative designs. A striking example of such a possibility is the case of the well-known rocking chair (figure 3–46) that is generally identified by historians and dealers alike as having been designed by Josef Hoffmann and manufactured by J. & J. Kohn—the highest accolade that post-1900 bent-wood furniture can receive.[182] However, this model, with its characteristic oval side elements, does not appear in any known Kohn catalogue, and no example has yet been found that bears a Kohn label or the mark of any other manufacturer.[183] The chair was, in fact, produced about 1922 by the Società Anonima "Antonio Volpe" in Udine,

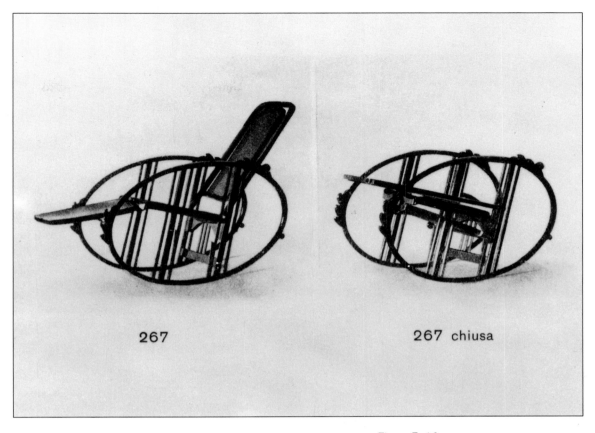

267   267 chiusa

Figure 3–46
Rocking chaise, Model No. 267. Sales catalogue of Società Anonima "Antonio Volpe," Udine, Italy, ca. 1922.

Italy, and is illustrated as No. 267 in a catalogue issued by that firm about 1922.[184] Antonio Volpe began to produce bent-wood furniture in 1884, and, not surprisingly, its first chair (No. 1) was a copy of Thonet Brothers best-selling No. 14. In the following years, Volpe's bent-wood furniture became increasingly independent of models already produced by the major Austro-Hungarian companies, and its post-1900 bent wood, judging only by the small proportion of the work illustrated in the catalogue, was witty, idiosyncratic, and highly original. Indeed, "originality" was the company's foremost concern. The catalogue's introduction states specifically that "the ability to 'create' is a particular sign of a serious attention to industrial values." For this reason, the text continues, the company had always produced and would continue to make "models of its own invention, not derived from the products of other manufacturers, but challenging them to compete with fairness and honesty. Other manufacturers . . . base their activities on the comfortable system of reproducing the work of others as badly as they possibly can, whereas the Volpe company is creative."[185]

The Volpe rocking chair, the work of an as-yet-unidentified Italian designer, is an excellent illustration of the high standards of innovation that the small Udine company set itself. It also serves as a reminder of the heights to which even a minor representative of the bent-wood furniture industry could rise. Further research into the production of other Italian firms, as well as Belgian, French, Russian, Polish, Romanian, Spanish, and even Austro-Hungarian companies, will surely reveal evidence that J. & J. Kohn and Thonet Brothers did not have a monopoly of either the good designers or the good design that helped shape bent-wood furniture in Europe from 1900 onward.

Notes

1. Šimoníková.

2. Exner and Lauboeck 1893.

3. Thonet 1896, p. 12; Heller, p. 13.

4. Lauboeck 1900, p. 2 n. 1. This patent, which protected the technique of Thonet's early bent-wood chairs, such as those supplied in 1849 to the Café Daum in Vienna (see cat. nos. 7–9 and Wilk 1980a, fig. 19), remained in force until July 28, 1864 (Lauboeck 1900, p. 2).

5. Ibid, n. 2. In the author's opinion, the nature of each of the three patents may be distinguished as: 1842, applying only to veneers, i.e., of Boppard-type chairs; 1852, applying to bent-wood type of glued and rounded thick rods; 1856, applying to bent solid wood furniture.

6. Mainz 1842, p. 113.

7. London 1851b, Class 26, pp. 120l, 1212.

8. Munich 1854b, pp. 84–85. Thonet Brothers showed "tables inlaid with brass, etc; a sofa with two armchairs; upholstered chairs; chairs with cane seats, armchairs, and sofas; a whatnot with brass inlay"; see Munich 1854a, p. 124. The firm was awarded a Medal of Honor for "the quaint construction of the bent-wood chairs made in this important establishment, which are characterized by lightness and strength"; Munich 1854b, p. 85.

9. Paris 1855, p. 627.

10. London 1862c, Austria, Class 30, p. 246, No. 1221.

11. London 1862d, pp. 39–40.

12. Heller, p. 37.

13. London 1862a, p. 291.

14. London 1862d, pp. 39–40.

15. Wilk 1980a, fig. 44.

16. Ibid., figs. 35 and 42 illustrate respectively the l859 and 1866 broadsheets.

17. Vienna 1873c, p. 270.

18. Ibid., pp. 277–81.

19. Wilk 1980a, p. 40.

20. Behal, p. 61. Wilk 1980a, p. 40, gives a slightly different account of the firm's beginnings.

21. Vienna 1873c, No. 108, p. 278. J. & J. Kohn received a Medal of Merit.

22. Philadelphia 1876a, pp. 41–42. Thonet Brothers, by comparison, employed 4,500 workers and produced about 730,000 pieces of furniture a year; ibid., pp. 42–43.

23. Candilis, p. 61.

24. Dry 1980, p. 1.

25. The firm advertised Kohn furniture in the Exhibition Newspaper published regularly during the course of the Hannover Industrial Exhibition of 1878; see Hannover 1878a, p. 47, No. 8.

26. Wilk 1980a, pp. 77 and 138 n. 71.

27. Eva Schmertzing-Thonet has suggested that all such J. & J. Kohn material was destroyed in the 1930s; letter to the author, Vienna, February 8, 1980.

28. Schölermann 1900, p. 168, pl. 293; Vienna 1979, pl. 21.

29. As, for instance, Dry 1980, p. 2, and Wilk 1980a, pp. 60–61 and 137 n. 51, who assumed, on the evidence of Mang 1969, n.p., that the Loos chair had been produced by Thonet.

30. Rukschcio and Schachel, pp. 418–19, quote Hevesi 1899, who firmly states that the bent-wood furniture of the billiard room, which included the tables, had been made by J. & J. Kohn. Mang 1982, p. 102, states incorrectly that the billiard tables were surrounded by "Thonet chairs" and, adding confusion, that the Loos chair "was produced in 1898 by Thonet and was similar to the chairs used by Loos in the Café Museum, which according to contemporary reports were made by J. & J. Kohn" (p. 103). There is, however, no reason to doubt that Loos designed this chair for J. & J. Kohn in 1899.

31. The author is indebted to Werner Schweiger for these details of Siegel's youth, which are published here for the first time. For Schweiger's biography of Gustav Siegel, see Vienna 1979, n.p.

32. *Das Interieur* 1900, p. 156; Vienna 1979, pl. 25.

33. Exner and Lauboeck 1893, pp. 25–26; Andés 1925, pp. 97–102.

34. "Österreichische Möbel aus gebogenem Holz," in Malkowsky, p. 417.

35. ["*Die verschiedenen*"], p. 102.

36. For illustrations of these, see Dry 1980, inside of front cover; Vienna 1979, pl. 65, illustration of advertisement in 1908 Secession catalogue (as "Kolo Moser").

37. *Deutsche Kunst und Dekoration* 1908, pp. 158–59; Vienna 1979, pl. 74.

38. Vienna 1979, p. 158. Müller, pl. 82, regards this chair as a Hoffmann design.

39. See Vienna 1979, pls. 67, 75, 80–82, 84, 85, 87, 88.

40. Holme, pl. C10; Vienna 1979, pl. 72.

41. Mang 1969, n.p., thanks Gustav Siegel for information on Thonet chronology; Mang 1982, p. 104, mentions a 1968 visit to Siegel in a home for the aged in Vienna, two years before Siegel's death in 1970.

42. Mang 1969, fig. 73. To complicate matters still further, Mang 1982, p. 107, states unequivocally that the chair used in the Cabaret Fledermaus was designed by Hoffmann!

43. Levetus, p. xlvi and pl. A19.

44. Dry 1980, pp. 46 and 100.

45. Ibid., p. 46.

46. See n. 40.

47. Schweiger begins his short but vigorous essay on Siegel (Vienna 1979, n.p.): "Furniture dealers quote the name of Gustav Siegel as a designer with the same arrogance with which they talk about Louis Seize, as if Siegel alone were responsible for half a century of furniture production. I have never come across anyone with the slightest knowledge of Siegel. Only a few pieces of furniture designed by him are illustrated or discussed in contemporary publications. All other attempts at interpretation are nothing less than special pleading, to be continued for as long as it is necessary for a Siegel to materialize from nowhere."

48. As expressed, for example, by Julius Leisching, director of the Moravian Crafts Museum at Brno (Leisching, p. 143).

49. Wilk 1980a, pp. 140–41, publishes a list of these catalogues, to which may be added: an Italian catalogue of 1906, comprising two sections, the first with plates numbered I–LII, the second with plates numbered 1–108 (published in Massobrio and Portoghesi 1980, pp. 345–411); an undated catalogue of circa 1908, 40 pp., with an unsigned cover probably designed by Gustav Siegel (Private collection, Diessen, Germany); a broadsheet catalogue printed in blue illustrating twenty-one "stock chairs" (*Lagersorten*) issued for the Cologne branch, Hohenstaufenring 27, dated August 1911, with a price list for these dated February 15, 1912 (Private collection, Munich).

50. Vienna 1873e, p. 496. Brinckmann's designation of the armchair-bed as a *fauteuil-lit* and Fischel's naming the novel armchair *L'Invulnérable* seem to suggest that Fischel had a particular interest at this time in the French market.

51. Exner and Lauboeck 1893, p. 30.

52. Handelsgericht Wien, Handelsregister (Court of Trade, Vienna, Company Register), Section A, No. 24/52; Section B, No. 38/225. For information on the Fischel factory in Weissenburg (Wissembourg), I am grateful to August Meder, Achern.

53. Furniture from Fischel catalogues is reproduced by Šimoníková in her pioneering article. I have drawn on this article for several facts concerning the firm's history, and I am grateful to both Henry Hawley, Cleveland, for bringing this article to my attention, and Dr. Pavel Filip, Munich, for his help with the translation.

54. Asenbaum, pp. 210–15, figs. 267, 273, 275, 279; Dry 1980, p. 41, No. 718/F.

55. Šimoníková, p. 249, fig. 10; Dry 1980, p. 40.

56. Vienna 1908a, p. 370; Dry 1980, p. 68; Vienna 1979, No. 78.

57. Dry 1980, p. 69.

58. Wilk 1980b, p. 143. Massobrio and Portoghesi 1976, p. 60, illustrate an elegant Fischel armchair with adjustable backrest, of circa 1880. For information on Fischel furniture in Viennese private collections, I am indebted to Wolfgang Bauer, Vienna.

59. The Fürfang family had been making furniture in Munich since about 1843. In 1928, Julius Fürfang II, grandson of the firm's founder, Mathias, owned a factory in Dreimühlenstrasse 55. He was an agent for Fischel and later for the Achern furniture manufacturer August Klar. Anton Fürfang, great-grandson of Mathias, kindly provided me with information about his family's history.

60. Wilk 1980a, p. 94, fig. 117.

61. Ibid, p. 94.

62. Ibid, p. 99.

63. *Fischel* 1870–1930. Album in English, French, German, and Spanish, 16 pp. A copy in a Munich private collection bears the rubber stamp of the Brussels furniture store A. Micheau, 129, rue Berkendael. For an account of the Fischel catalogues of the 1920s and 1930s, see Šimoníková.

64. Vienna 1873c, p. 281, No. 214.

65. Vienna 1873d, p. 496.

66. Vienna 1873c, p. 279, No. 148.

67. Vienna 1873d, p. 497.

68. Vienna 1873a, p. 353.

69. "Österreichische Möbel aus gebogenem Holz," in Malkowsky pp. 417–18. The anonymous author of this article does not specify the name of the Hungarian factory, but it is likely to have been the Ungvárer Möbelfabriks-Aktien-Gesellschaft (Ungvár Furniture Company) in Ungvár. This firm was represented in France in 1900 by the Paris furniture

Figure 3–47

Factory of Gebrüder Seitz, Munich, 1866. (From *Adressbuch von München*, 1867, p. 59).

store A. Quittner, 62, rue du Faubourg Saint-Antoine. The company issued a 77-page catalogue in French, probably in anticipation of the 1900 Paris Exhibition; see Dry 1983.

70. Wiisa's design, printed in three colors, was one of a series of "examples of graphic design" (*Grafische Musterblätter*) that appeared as supplements in the magazine *Die freien Künste*, published in Vienna and Leipzig. It was probably not offered as an advertisement for bent-wood furniture, but intended as an illustration of the possibilities of color lithography in the service of commerce.

71. Revealed in a report on the Alsfelder firm that traces its history from 1893/94 through 1918; see "Alsfelder Möbelfabrik," p. 6

72. As indicated on the title page of an undated Mundus catalogue, circa 1908, illustrated in Massobrio and Portoghesi 1976, p. 79.

73. Bang, p.111; Wilk 1980a, p. 78. Wilk's invaluable account of the formation of Mundus was the first to throw light on a hitherto unsolved bent wood mystery.

74. Exner and Lauboeck 1893, p. 30.

75. Court of Trade, Vienna, Company Register, Section B, No. 1/190, Aktien-Gesellschaft der Vereinigten Österreicheschen Bugholzmöbel-Fabriken, p. 190, column 8.

76. Exner and Lauboeck 1893, pp. 30–31.

77. Cologne 1914a, pl.66.

78. Dry 1980, p. xii. Christian Witt-Dörring kindly identified these chairs for me.

79. Wilk 1980a, p. 78 and fig. 97. For the history of the firm after 1922, see ibid., pp. 112–19.

80. See note 75, above, p. 194.

81. Munich 1854c, p. 160: ". . . die Möbel von gebogenem Holze von Gebr. Thonet, welche die deutschen durch Leichtigkeit und Eleganz übertreffen."

82. Munich 1854d, p. 85.

83. Kassel 1870a, p. 250.

84. Markert, in London 1862e, p. 592.

85. London 1862c, Hamburg Section, No. 94; on J.H.C. Wipper, Hamburg, see Meier-Oberist, p. 104.

86. Markert, in London 1862e, p. 592.

87. Meier-Oberist, p. 104. See also Hamburg 1977, p. 64.

88. Markert, in London 1862e, p. 592.

89. An entry in the *Adressbuch von Cassel* for the years 1868 and 1869 reads: "Andrecht, Carl, Fabrikant, Firma: Andrecht u. Krüger, Fabrik von Möbeln und Holzwaren aus massiv gebogenem Holz." On the 1870 Kassel exhibition, see Kassel 1870b, No. 114; "Thonet Brothers, Vienna and Berlin, chairs etc. made from bent wood"; and No. 607, "Andrecht & Bingel." Thonet Brothers had a half-page illustrated advertisement in this guide. The Oderfeld firm is listed in neither the official catalogue of the Kassel exhibition (Kassel 1870b), nor in the condensed version (Kassel 1970c).

90. Otto Seitz exhibited at the Munich exhibition in 1869 as the Seitz Stuhlfabrik; see Munich 1869, p. 62, No. 482.

91. Thonet Brothers were listed in the 1854 Munich exhibition under No. 3731; see Munich 1854a, p. 154.

92. The Thonet Brothers advertisement, which lists Max Pfeiffer, Jr., as their Munich agent, appeared in the *Illustrirtes Familien-Journal* (1865), p. 176. Pfeiffer opened his shop in the Salvatorstrasse in 1859 and retired in 1886. Eight years earlier, in 1878, he had been granted the title of Royal Bavarian Court Purveyor and Court Purveyor to His Royal Highness Prince Leopold and Her Imperial Royal Highness Princess Gisela of Bavaria. In the same year, Thonet Brothers opened its own store in the Theatinerstrasse 11, not far from the Munich Residenz.

93. An advertisement for the Seitz Brothers factory illustrating the three-story establishment (Fig. 3–47) appeared in the 1867 Munich city directory; see *Adressbuch von München*, 1867, p. 59. In 1869 new premises were taken in the Kapuzinerstrasse 1.

94. *Adressbuch von München*, 1972.

95. Vienna 1873b, p. 347, No. 73; Vienna 1873d, p. 519.

96. Vienna 1873a, p. 369.

97. Vienna 1873d, p. 347, No. 72. The firm showed "Furniture," but it is not mentioned as an exhibitor of bent-wood furniture in any of the otherwise very complete reports.

98. Kassel 1870a, p. 250.

99. Vienna 1873e, p. 479.

100. Thurneyssen, p. 48 n. 1.

101. Vienna 1873b, p. 347, No. 75.

102. Ibid., p. 347, No. 74.

103. The exhibitions are listed in part on the front cover of the company's trade catalogue *Möbel aus massiv gebogenem Holz, 2. Theil,* of circa 1900. At the Melbourne World Exhibition (1880) the company exhibited seventeen pieces of bent-wood furniture, entered as *Krummholzmöbel* (crooked furniture) in the official list of German exhibitors; see Melbourne 1880, No. 389. At the 1897 *Sächsisch-Thuringische Industrie- und Gewerbe-Ausstellung* in Leipzig, a collection of "bent and curved chairs and luxury furniture" was shown; see Leipzig 1897, p. 102, No. 1176.

104. Sachsische (bibl., section 4), p. 42. Perforated and laminated seats were invented in 1868 by John K. Mayo; see Lehnert, vol. 2, p. 454, and Hanks, p. 47. According to Schuldt, p. 44, the American patent was held by Gardner and Company, New York, which developed a double-sided press (caul) in which the glued veneers were steamed under pressure and then dried. This type of early plywood seating had first attracted attention in Europe through its use on the benches of horsedrawn carriages imported from America. After the expiration of the American patent, German chair manufacturers at once began their own production; however, the advertisements of German agents of the American companies insisted that successful plywood seating could only be guaranteed if the "world-famous Peter Cooper glue" were used. German glue was soon found to be a more-than-adequate substitute.

At the industrial exhibition held in Vienna in 1880, Johann Heydner, Parkring 4, Vienna, exhibited Gardner and Company's chairs with their patented continuous seats and backs made from a single piece of three-ply walnut and birch veneers nailed to the seat frame. The chairs were intended for use in offices, waiting rooms, and cafés, etc. "It is reported that European attempts to imitate these glued veneers have all failed," one report noted, "and it is therefore advisable to consider only products bearing the original American trademark, or to purchase such chairs only from Heydner"; see Vienna 1880, p. 76.

The first German factory to develop the American laminated seating technique and to be granted patents for improved methods of production was that of Carl Wittkowsky, in Charlottenburg, Berlin. Wittkowsky's experiments began in the early 1870s, and his factory for the manufacture of "thermoplastic wood productions" was built in 1884; see "Die thermoplastischen."

Around 1900, Karl Fätsch, in Kandel (Palatinate), was an important wholesale supplier of ornamental seats to the German chair industry. The seats, decorated with perforations or in relief, were delivered to the factories in squares measuring roughly 15¾ by 15¾ inches and then shaped for insertion into the individual frames; see Fätsch.

Thonet Brothers, using Wittkowsky's discoveries, began to manufacture laminated seating in 1877 in its Gross-Ugrócz factory, but was careful at first to supply it only when specifically requested, in order not to jeopardize the cane-seating home industry on which many families depended for their livelihood; see Schuldt, p. 43. Mang 1982, p. 70, gives a different version of this development, stating that Thonet and Gardner invented the laminated seat "almost at the same time" and that Gardner's patent had to be annulled since Thonet was able to prove priority of invention.

105. In the "burned-in" (*Flachbrand*) method, the pattern was applied to the veneer by means of a heated printing plate which caused the patterned surface to rise and turn white, in contrast to the dark-brown background. The veneer was then flattened under great pressure. The result was an imitation of marquetry. "Pressed-relief" refers to the application of a heated molded plate to the veneer, imparting a relief pattern of one color (*Hochrelief*); the term "deep relief" (*Tiefrelief*) denoted a surface imitating embossed leather. The various processes are described in brief in Fätsch.

Thonet Brothers began the production of pressed-relief seating in 1888, and by 1914, sixty percent of its chair production had such seats; see Andés 1903, p. 115; Exner and Lauboeck, 4th ed., p. 43; Andés 1925, pp. 142–48.

106. See Thonet's broadsheet catalogue of 1866, No. 4, illustrated in Wilk 1980a, p. 38. Dr. Klaus-Peter Arnold, Museum für Kunsthandwerk, Schloss Pillnitz, Dresden, kindly drew my attention to the Rabenau chair and supplied the photograph reproduced here.

107. Museum für Kunst und Kulturgeschichte, Lübeck, Inv. no. 7071; Hamburg 1977, No. 46.

108. Thonet's broadsheet catalogue of 1866, No. 11, illustrated in Wilk 1980a, p. 38.

109. Dresden 1906, p. 199. The firm has an advertisement for bent-wood furniture in the advertising section.

110. Leipzig 1913, p. 228: "Public Reading Room of the *Dresdner Anzeiger*".

111. Vienna 1873a, p. 361.

112. Two catalogues are known: a 60-page catalogue of about 1904, in which chair No. 279 is the highest catalogue number; and a 43-page catalogue of about 1906, in which the numbering has reached chair No. 342½.

113. Ibid, title pages. Various leaflets of the firm dating from about 1930 are in a private collection in Munich.

114. For various details of this factory I have drawn liberally from the typescript "Alsfelder Möbelfabrik, Gesellschaft mit beschränkter Haftung, 1894/95 bis einschliesslich 1918." This short history of the firm was probably written by Peter Heinrich Gustav Ramspeck II, one of the original partners and one of the two managing directors of the factory in 1918.

115. Alsfeld 1895, p. 37, No. 78. I am grateful to Dr. Herbert Jäkel, director of the Alsfeld Regional Museum, for drawing my attention to this exhibition and its catalogue.

116. Darmstadt 1908, p. 50: "Room 51. Office Designed by J. Krug, Darmstadt, exhibited by Heinrich Lantz, Stationers, Darmstadt."

117. Undated; incomplete catalogue in the possession of Stuhlfabrik Alsfeld-Türpe, Alsfeld. Kurt Reichel, the managing director, kindly allowed me to photograph this document and took much time and trouble to answer many questions about his company's history.

118. In Vienna 1908a, p. 368, the top of the settee variation may be seen projecting above the parapet wall of the porch of the small country house designed by Hoffmann for the Kohn display. The armchair with the same back, No. 371/F (figure 54B), is illustrated in a J. & J. Kohn catalogue of about 1908, p. 19 (Private collection, Diessen).

119. Asenbaum, pp. 210–15, figs. 267, 273, 275, 279.

120. Dry 1980, p. 38.

121. Martin Stoll, the founder's grandson, and Dr. Schluchter, managing director, Christof Stoll GmbH & Co. KG, Waldshut, kindly provided me with information concerning the firm's history and generously placed photographs at my disposal.

122. The Klingnau branch was soon taken over by one of Stoll's employees and exists today as the Tutsch Aktien-gesellschaft, Klingnau.

123. Shortly before 1914, Albert Stoll's son made a study tour of furniture factories in the United States and brought back the idea of the "Record" chair. (The first machines for these were also purchased in the United States.) The chair, Stoll Model No. 8000, does not strictly belong to the bent-wood furniture family, but the use of bent-wood braces where the seat meets the stiles on this attractive country-style chair (figure 3-48) is an interesting example of the way in which bent wood was used to give added stability cheaply to all types of furniture. Stoll's *Record-Stühl Catalogue* of 1914 contains illustrations of some twenty inexpensive chairs and stools, as well as seats.

Figure 3–48
Stoll's Record-Stühle, sales catalogue of **Albert Stoll, Waldshut, Baden, 1914.**

124. See *Meder Sitzmöbel* (Erste Acherner, bibl., section 4). August Meder, Achern, a descendant of Josef Aegidius Klar, kindly supplied me with information on the firm's history.

125. Leaflets in a private collection, Munich.

126. Exner and Lauboeck 1893, p. 31.

127. The name became well known around 1900 when the Buchenau Glass Works under Ferdinand Karl Benedikt von Poschinger (1856–1921) began to make vases and other glass objects in the style of L. C. Tiffany. At the same time, Benedikt Ferdinand von Poschinger (1856–1918) was in charge of the Oberzwieselau Crystal Glass Factory, which produced table glass after designs by such leading German artists as Peter Behrens and Richard Riemerschmid. A third important glass works in the Bavarian Forest, the Theresienthal Crystal Glass Factory near Zwiesel, under the direction of Johann Michael von Poschinger III (1834–1908), was also widely known for its products.

128. Poschinger, n.p. I am particularly grateful to Baron Hyppolit von Poschinger and to Benigna Countess Keyserlingk for their generous assistance in matters concerning the Oberfrauenau bent-wood furniture production.

129. Wilk 1980b, p. 4, and pp. 1 and 5. These Poschinger chairs are in a private collection, Oberfrauenau.

130. The staircase is probably identical to the one exhibited by Thonet Brothers in Vienna in 1873, which Charles Rossigneux described in a report on the furniture as "a very beautiful staircase whose airy lightness in no way precludes an adequate solidity and . . . bears remarkable witness to the perfection of M. Thonet's techniques"; Vienna 1873f, p. 420. For an illustration of the staircase, see Candilis, p. 167.

131. For the Sächsische Holzindustrie Gesellschaft, see Dresden 1906, p. 84. Among the introductory remarks in Stoll's *Record-Stühle Catalogue* is the statement, "I manufacture . . . chairs of my own design and after designs submitted to me."

132. Pudor, pp. 129–30.

133. Munich 1982b, p. 388.

134. *Das Münchener Schauspielhaus*, p. 24. The Schauspielhaus was badly damaged during World War II and none of the 727 seats survived. (The number of seats is noted in "Das Münchener Schauspielhaus," p. 188.) When the theater was restored after the war, under the supervision of Riemerschmid's great-nephew Reinhard Riemerschmid, Thonet seating was not installed.

135. Gebrüder Thonet, Verkaufskatalog 1895; see Wilk 1980a, pp. 111–12. The first theater in the world to be fitted with tip-up seating was the Deutsche Volkstheater in Vienna in 1888; see Gebrüder Thonet, Verkaufskatalog 1904, reprinted in Wilk 1980b, p. 110.

136. For the stucco ceiling in the side corridor on the first floor with the motif of intersecting concentric circles as formed by objects thrown into water and *seen from below*, the motif of rising bubbles surrounding the cloakroom mirror in the side gallery, and the embroidered theater curtain designed by Margarethe von Brauchitsch, see *Die Kunst* 1901, vol. 4, pp. 365–69. Gerhard P. Woeckel, in an unpublished lecture held in the Zentralinstitut für Kunstgeschichte, Munich, March 1971, was the first to point out this use of submarine motifs in the Schauspielhaus. He kindly made his manuscript available to me.

137. Wilk 1980a, p. 68.

138. Noted in the firm's advertisement (figure 3–30) the following year in the catalogue of the *Deutsche Brauerei-Ausstellung* (German Brewery Exhibition); see Munich 1909, p. 155.

139. Munich 1908a, p. 17.

140. Munich 1908b, p. 465 ill.; see also *Funfundzwanzig Jahre Postsparkasse*, p. 9 ill., and Dry 1980, p. 41, No. 718/F. The legs of the Kadeder chair appear to thicken to a pad-foot, whereas the feet of the Wagner chair have rectangular metal casings.

141. *Die Kunst* 1901, vol. 4, p. 347; Munich 1982b, color plate p. 125 and pp. 154–55, No. 84c.

142. Thonet Brothers Catalogue 1911; see Candilis, p. 182, "Gebrüder Thonet," bottom row, second chair from left.

143. Munich 1898, p. 190: "Römischer Wohnraum"; Rosner, pp. 201–15, ills. 154–161.

144. See Munich 1982a.

145. For a variant Kadeder letterhead of this period which also illustrated the Seidl bent-wood chair, together with a chair designed by Riemerschmid, see Munich 1982b, p. 246, No. 209.

146. Candilis, p. 182, "Thonet Irmaos," center row, chair at right.

147. *Die Kunst* 1908, p. 464.

148. Brussels 1910b, p. 75; Brussels 1910a, color plate p. 10.

149. Darmstadt 1914a, pp. 257, 259; Darmstadt 1976, vol. 5, p. 157, pl. 3.

150. Dry 1980, p. 50; Vienna 1979, pl. 44.

151. Darmstadt 1914b, p. 29: "Caféhalle".

152. For a full account of H. G. Reinstein and his "cardboard furniture," see Dry 1982.

153. The full name of the group was "Vereinte Kunstgewerbler Darmstadt, Atelier für angewandte Kunst, Architektur, Malerei, Bildhauerei."

154. Deutscher Reichspatent (DRP) No. 214284. The patent was published on October 7, 1909; see Dry 1982, p. 133.

155. Various articles of furniture—tables, chairs, mirrors, benches, writing desks—are still in use in homes in Bad Lauterberg. The Germania is not known to have labeled, or otherwise marked, its products.

156. Vienna 1912a, p. 61; Vienna 1912b, p. 180.

157. Dry 1982, p. 135; Behal, p. 66.

158. A copy of the firm's catalogue is in a private collection, Göttingen.

159. Dry 1980, p. 39.

160. Brüning, p. 36, pl. 54 and p. 103, pl. 155; *Spemanns Goldenes Buch*, p. 53.

161. Paris 1878a, p. 100.

162. Schölermann 1907, ills. pp. 266, 268, 270–72, 278.

163. Westheim, pp. 370–72.

164. Dry 1980, p. 33.

165. Ibid., p. 38; *Die Rheinlande* 12 (1906), pp. 129 and 131. Anna-Christa Funk-Jones, M.A. Hagen, to whom I owe the *Rheinlande* reference, informs me that one of these Tonhaus chairs is in the Karl-Ernst-Osthaus-Museum in Hagen.

166. Meyer-Schönbrunn, p. 53.

167. Buddensieg, pp. D134–37, pls. P4–P6.

168. Hoeber, pp. 152–55 and fig. 181; Buddensieg, pp. D108–110, pl. A179. Henning Rogge, in Buddensieg, dates the Boathouse as of 1912, from the date of the formal opening; Hoeber, writing in 1913, dates it 1910, which is surely correct.

169. Cologne 1914a, p. 157.

170. Cologne 1914b, p. 248: "Die Festhalle."

171. Cologne 1914a, pp. 155–58; *Die Kunst* 1914, pp. 553–55.

172. Falke, 6th ed., p. 297.

173. Ibid., 5th ed., pp. 322–23.

174. "Nachruf Josef Thonet."

175. Exner and Lauboeck, 4th ed., p. 42.

176. Lauboeck, p. 4.

177. Exner and Lauboeck, 4th ed., p. 42.

178. "Nachruf Josef Thonet." Exner and Lauboeck 1893, p. 28, gives a different figure, stating that 7,276,100 Thonet No. 14 chairs had been produced by 1891. "One would hardly go wrong," the report continues, "in estimating that all national and foreign factories currently making bent-wood furniture are producing between six and seven thousand No. 14 chairs a day."

179. Thonet 1896, p. 30. Heller, p. 29, gives a lower figure, estimating that a total of thirty million No. 14 chairs had been produced by all factories up to 1926.

180. "Kleine Nachrichten."

181. Derived from "Alsfelder Möbelfabrik," pp. 6–8 (bibl., section 4, Alsfelder).

182. In 1983, a leading Austrian furniture company, Franz Wittman KG in Etsdorf, Austria, reproduced this chair and marketed it as a design by Josef Hoffmann for J. & J. Kohn. It is exhibited as such in the design museum Die Neue Sammlung in Munich; see Wichmann, p. 197: "Josef Hoffmann, Schaukelstuhl, um 1905," with illustration.

183. Ketterer, No. 307. The example illustrated in Vienna 1979, which is listed as made by Kohn, does not bear a maker's label.

184. Volpe, p. 14. I am extremely grateful to Dr. Tiziana Ribezzi, keeper of the Civici Musei e Gallerie di Storia e Arte in Udine, for her generous assistance in matters concerning the Volpe company.

185. Volpe (bibl., section 4, Volpe), Introduction, n.p.

4
Bent-wood production and the Viennese avant-garde: The Thonet and Kohn firms
1899–1914

CHRISTIAN WITT-DÖRRING

The primary task is twofold: to give form to knowledge
and grace to function.
JOHN RUSKIN

The transformation of Viennese bent-wood furniture

The bent-wood furniture that was produced by the Thonet Brothers and by Jacob & Josef Kohn in the years spanning the turn of the century and the outbreak of the First World War displays a particularly distinctive and recognizable style. The progressive designs of this period are easily distinguished from others in the history of these two firms, as well as from the general production of other bent-wood manufacturers prior to the turn of the century.[1] Although most of these furnishings were originally published without credit to specific designers,[2] they bear the inimitable signature of Viennese architects trained in the same modernist spirit and seeking the same goal: unity of function, material, and technical methods of production.[3] During this period of extraordiny collaboration between designers and industry, Gustav Siegel, Josef Hoffmann, and Koloman Moser were employed by the Kohn firm, while the second Kunstfrühling (Sacred Spring) generation —Marcel Kammerer, Otto Prutscher, Leopold Bauer, and Josef Urban—designed for Thonet. Otto Wagner was never employed by either firm, but both executed his designs.[4]

The increased interest during the past fifteen years in the products of these designers, many of whom have achieved "name" status, has brought about an ironic situation within the commercial marketplace. Required by pressure of demand to supply the "genuine article," numerous questionable attributions have arisen. Those responsible for this development are, in the end, the consumers, whose general attitude is characterized by a lack of knowledge and failure of sensitivity. As is true with respect to many "prestige" items, the name of the designer has become synonymous with value, guaranteeing the acceptability and worth of the purchase. The consumer is freed of any independent value judgment, and at the same time the supplier frequently yields to the temptation of offering artifacts of unsubstantiated or even false attribution. Thus the law of supply and demand has created not only a substitute for the very idea of aesthetic value, but also an ersatz product that represents a new form of historicism.

In studying the Thonet and Kohn production lines of the early 1890s, a clear picture emerges of the various styles of furniture and interior decoration then prevalent in Austria. The Thonet catalogue of 1895 displays both the original collection from the early years of the firm and a noticeably wider range of furniture from the second half of the nineteenth century. The latter includes a multiplicity of styles (though the Zweites Rokoko—rococo revival—is not in evidence), with the inventory enlarged to address the needs of new consumer groups. Although the firms took pride in their economically priced, attractive furniture that was designed for institutions and commercial establishments, they also tentatively began to explore the untapped market of the domestic consumer and to adapt to its particular requirements. The interior decoration of the home had long been associated with the social status of the owner. For this reason, the taste of the petty bourgeoisie concentrated upon the decoration of those rooms that were accessible to visitors, where such status, whether actual or imagined, could be evoked. It was thus possible to obtain an accurate idea of a person's class through an analysis of home furnishings. In contrast to the situation today, little attention was paid to such strictly private areas as the bedroom or bath.

The earliest mass-produced Thonet chairs of the 1850s and 1860s had achieved success through their elegant and versatile utility and their low price, which was reduced during the 1850s when new, more economical production methods were introduced. However, the consumer sought more from bent-wood furniture than practical function, and new models were tailored to meet demand, featuring a large assortment of simulated surfaces, such as a faux palisander finish as well as a lathe-turned "bamboo" treatment. The originally austere structure could be augmented with interchangeable ornaments or upholstery. The result was that an originally unpretentious and efficient product was changed into one that suggested more than it actually could deliver. A brochure published at the 1876 Philadelphia International Exhibition praised in unequivocal terms the "new purposes" of bent-wood furniture, drawing attention to "its suitability for the salon . . . the extension of this branch of industry into the most sophisticated living rooms of the middle and upper classes."[5] The short history of J. & J. Kohn that was included in the catalogue of the 1878 Paris Exposition Universelle (Universal Exhibition) further elaborates on this theme, promising to reconcile values that by nature conflict: "Furniture has just been produced featuring sculpted ornaments, carvings, and inlay, in such a way that great elegance and perfection of style complement the excellent qualities for which this furniture has been well-regarded—durability, economy, and utility."[6]

The production of historicist bent-wood designs that conformed to the middle-class taste for ornament changed Michael Thonet's original working principle of organic form, destroying the elegance of revealed construction. This situation was countered in the late 1890s by the initiation of the Kunstreform (Art Reform) in Vienna, a movement that sought to create new forms expressive of such values as honesty and functionality, thereby facilitating the aesthetic renewal of society.[7] The change in aesthetics which the Kunstreform fostered serves as the context for this examination of the concurrent stylistic transformation of the Thonet and Kohn furniture lines. Was this stylistic reorientation, particularly notable in the production of the Kohn firm, an attempt to satisfy contemporary market demand, a fostering of *Jugendstil* and the modern because they were merely fashionable? Or did the initiative come from young avant-garde architects who saw the use of bent wood as a unique opportunity to realize their ideals in product design? In order to clarify this complex issue, it is necessary to analyze the first manifestations of the new style, which may be traced to 1899, a time of experimental attempts to create a modern Viennese furniture.[8]

At the Österreichisches Museum für Kunst und Industrie (Austrian Museum for Art and Industry) Winterausstellung (Winter Exhibition) of 1899–1900, the Thonet firm exhibited two armchairs—a corner chair and a desk chair. These models are almost certainly the same reproductions of English eighteenth-century armchairs that were listed in Thonet's catalogue of 1904 under the heading "Moderne Fauteuils" (figure 4–1).[9] They maintain a continuity with older traditions; the classic Windsor chair is both retained and reinterpreted through the application of industrial bent-wood technology. Since the exhibition catalogue refers to these Thonet chairs as being "after English originals,"[10] it is tempting to regard them as "in the English style," an indiscriminate phrase that might be used to describe a wide range of products. However, Thonet's participation in this exhibition was specific and significant, demonstrating the collaboration of the bent-wood industry in the new ideas of reform. The Winterausstellung was exclusively dedicated to products from England or inspired (in a more than superficial sense) by English design. The third exhibition of its kind at this museum, it represented a serious attempt on the part of the museum's new director, Arthur von Scala, to present outstanding achievements in English design that might serve as a catalyst for a regenerated vitality in the applied arts of Austria. Such a presentation of simple yet superbly crafted articles for everyday use was a novelty for the Viennese public, which was accustomed to finding only deluxe objects or those with pretensions to luxury in the museum's exhibitions. Von Scala's exhibition also overturned the old concept of decorating one room with a matching suite of furniture. Instead, new ideas of simplicity and interchangeability were stressed; many single items could be selected and variously arranged to suit changing living requirements.[11]

At the 1900 Paris Exposition Universelle, the award-winning J. & J. Kohn display was comprised of rooms in which an extensive program of bent wood furnishings was complemented by wall partitions and panels made from the flowing lines of bent wood (figure 4–2). Contemporary literature concerning this exhibition makes

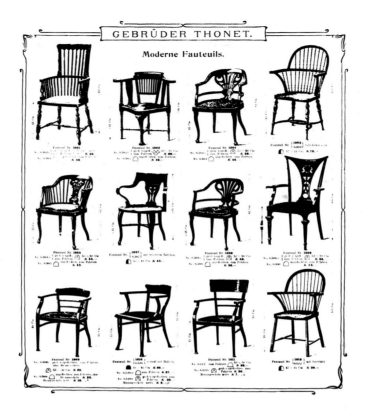

Figure 4–1

Armchairs, Model Nos. 1001–1012. Sales catalogue of Gebrüder Thonet, Vienna, 1904.

Figure 4–2

Sales catalogue of Jacob & Josef Kohn, Vienna, 1904. Interiors designed by Gustav Siegel, Jacob & Josef Kohn display at the Exposition Universelle, Paris, 1900.

Figure 4–3, 4, 5, 6

Gustav Siegel. Designs for furniture and applied bent solid wood wall decoration by Jacob & Josef Kohn, Vienna, 1900–1901. (From *Innen-Dekoration* 1901, pp. 102–103).

Figure 4–3

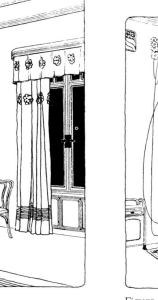

Figure 4–5

Figure 4–4

Figure 4–6

occasional reference to Gustav Siegel in general terms as one of the designers; no documents exist crediting him with specific models. However, evidence appears in an article from 1901 that discusses the modernity of the furniture of the Kohn firm.[12] Here suggestions for interior decoration are illustrated by drawings (figures 4–3, 4, 5, 6). The bent-wood furniture illustrated, clearly conceived in the modernist spirit, is identical with that of the Paris display. Many of the furnishings are made of square wooden rods, with brass sabots sheathing the feet. The drawing in figure 4–5 is signed "GS," which must stand for Gustav Siegel, establishing his identity as the designer of this important Paris Exposition furniture. All of the bent wood furniture from the Paris Exposition published in *Das Interieur* in 1900—a double-door cupboard, bed, chaise longue, armchair, rocking chair, and plant stand—can be confirmed as being of Siegel's design.[13] The plant stand was also published two years later under the name of Siegel, although the initial erroneously was given as "L" (figure 4–7).[14]

The armchair designed by Gustav Siegel for the Paris display (figure 4–2, bottom; cat. no. 38) is made from three major pieces of bent wood, the longest of which comprises the front legs, armrests, and crest rail. A smaller piece forms the back legs, stiles, and inner crest rail, while the third and shortest piece constitutes the seat frame. This simple construction is very stable and is based on the Thonet Model No. 47 chair, in which the sweeping unified curve of the front legs, armrests, and crest rail originated. The form of Siegel's design was eventually borrowed by Otto Wagner for armchairs in several variations used throughout the Österreichische Postsparkasse (Imperial Austrian Postal Savings Bank; cat. no. 46).

The very early date of Siegel's armchair—perhaps 1899—is close to that of the Christmas Exhibition of the Niederösterreichische Gewerbeverein (Lower Austrian Trade Association), at which J. & J. Kohn displayed their latest products. A contemporary critic praised the "outstanding adaptability of the manufactured product to the modern style" and enthusiastically predicted commercial success.[15] One would normally be forced to receive this opinion with considerable reservation, as much of what was advertised as "modern" had not been inwardly con-

ceived as such and would have been more properly classified as fashionable ephemera. Yet the products displayed at the Niederösterreichischen Gewerbeverein must have been those destined for the 1900 Paris Exposition Universelle, following their first test of public reaction in Siegel's home environment.

Gustav Siegel's extraordinary abilities may be apprized by comparing his scheme for bent-wood wall partitions installed at the 1900 Paris Exposition Universelle (figure 4–2) with a design by Carl Bamberger from the same period (figure 4–8). Bamberger's seating ensemble of purple-stained cherrywood has been constructed by means of traditional cabinetmaking techniques to which the *Jugendstil* line of the vitrine bears no relation, appearing

Figure 4–7
Gustav Siegel. Plant stand. Manufactured by Jacob & Josef Kohn, Vienna. (From *Kunstgewerbeblatt* 1902, p. 211; erroneously credited L. Siegel).

Figure 4–8
Carl Bamberger. Ladies' drawing room, 1900. (From *Das Interieur* 1900, p. 76).

obligatory and forced, an attempt to conform to a fashion. In contrast, the sweeping bent-wood lines of Siegel's wall design are logically integral to the material, the natural solution to the task at hand.

Viennese architect and social polemicist Adolf Loos was also preoccupied with bent-wood furniture as early as 1899. Loos believed that the architect's function was not to pursue formal innovations per se but rather to recognize established, successful design and to adapt such design to specific new purposes. With this conviction, he designed one of the most beautiful chairs produced by J. & J. Kohn (cat. no. 37). Made for the Café Museum in Vienna (figure 4–9), this design was never incorporated into the firm's general production line.[16] Loos's inspiration for it came from the early, unadorned classic bent-wood chairs; their basic structure was retained but the diameter of the bent-wood rod was varied relative to the stress born by each component.[17] He paid equal attention to the finishing work. The beechwood was stained a vibrant red and then polished to a brilliant sheen, resulting in a finish that contrasted with the Café Museum's mahogany

Figure 4–9
Adolf Loos. Café Museum, Vienna, 1899.
See CAT. NO. **37.**

interior.[18] The great structural stability of the original Thonet chairs was maintained, and their elegance and lightness enhanced. Just as Loos revitalized the tradition of the Viennese café in his treatment of the Café Museum interior, so he brought new life to the classic bent-wood chair. When viewed alongside Thonet's "consumer chairs"[19] of the 1850s with their light proportions as yet unburdened by the ridigities of mass production, this chair by Adolf Loos stands as a self-sufficient creation in the same pioneering spirit.

The transformation of established Viennese bent-wood furniture can thus be traced to the young creative forces in Vienna—artists, architects, and artisans—who were able to implement the visionary principles of Otto Wagner, the father of the Austrian art revival. The works of Adolf Loos and Gustav Siegel marked the beginning of an immensely productive collaboration between designers and industry. The firm of J. & J. Kohn stands out as a pioneer in such ventures. Aware of the myriad possibilities presented through the combination of the "New Style" and bent-wood manufacturing processes, J. & J. Kohn nevertheless did not initially yield to the temptation of using bent wood for purely decorative purposes. On the contrary, the firm fully explored the constructive possibilities inherent in this new material and technology.[20] An article written by Viennese architect Robert Oerley in 1900, entitled "The Creation of a Modern Piece of Furniture,"[21] outlines the same problems of constructing a cupboard that were enumerated by J. & J. Kohn in a brochure from the 1876 Centennial Exhibition in Philadelphia nearly a quarter of a century earlier. Oerley discusses the construction problem faced in making an inexpensive cupboard—shrinkage of the doors and sides of the cupboard, which allows the easy penetration of dirt and dust to the inside. His solution to the problem (figure 4–10) was to construct the frame from softwood and the doors and sides from light-colored cardboard panels, varnished to make them washable. The cupboard described by J. & J. Kohn in 1876 deals with the same problem in a different way: "The cupboard bears no trace of cracked miters or gaping fissures, since the cornices, friezes, and door and drawer frames are made of bent wood, while the other components are of split, rather than sawn, wood . . . .

Figure 4–10
Robert Oerley. Wardrobe, ca. 1900. (From
***Das Interieur* 1900, p. 185).**

Ideas of the Kunstreform

Taking the lead among its competitors, the firm of J. & J. Kohn recognized a creative and economic potential in the emerging Viennese avant-garde of design. As the art critic Ludwig Hevesi stated, "Even mass-produced goods wish to bear a respectable signature."[23] By associating a manufactured item with a particular designer or style of design it was possible to lift it from anonymity and bestow upon it the individuality and exclusivity of a luxury item. The priority that J. & J. Kohn gave to its furniture designed in the Kunstfrühling spirit was made clear in the preface to the 1904 French edition of the firm's catalogue, in which the suites of rooms presented at the 1900 Paris Exposition Universelle were claimed as the height of the firm's production. Around 1910, in the American edition of its catalogue, the firm saw itself on the brink of a whole new enterprise, stating with even greater confidence, "Among the artistic designs shown in this catalogue, the modern style is represented in many varieties, for the very reason that among all other furniture, ours alone, by the uniformity and indestructibility of the bent parts, is able to cope with the requirements of the modern style in point of durability and construction. In fact, the adoption of the modern style by us at its early stages has opened up to our branch of manufacturing entirely new and wider fields undreamed of until now."[24] These "artistic designs" were coming out of both the Wiener Kunstgewerbeschule (Vienna School of Applied Arts) and the Wiener Akademie der bildenden Kunste (Vienna Academy of Fine Arts), where Otto Wagner had been teaching since 1894. At the Kunstgewerbeschule the children of Viennese industrialists, merchants, and craftsmen were being educated by such leading exponents of the Austrian reform movement as Josef Hoffmann and Koloman Moser. This fortuitous situation facilitated a lively and intense discourse concerning new ideas in the arts, new values in the media, and new developments in the manufacturing sector. The

Surfaces are of plywood joined under high pressure and therefore waterproof, and have been further treated so that the cupboard can be easily and quickly cleaned with a wet rag."[22] Thus it is possible to solve the same problem by means of different solutions, each arrived at through the determination of function, material, and the process of production—a practical demonstration of the modernist credo that had its roots in the first half of the nineteenth century.

ERSTE ÖSTERR. ACTIEN-GESELL-
SCHAFT ZUR ERZEUGUNG V. MÖBELN
AUS GEBOGENEM HOLZE
JACOB & JOSEF KOHN
WIEN, I. BURGRING 3

GRAND PRIX | PARIS 1900

o SCHLAFZIMMER, SPEISEZIMMER o
SALONMÖBEL IN MODERNEM STILE

Figure 4–11

Figure 4–13

SALON-GARNITUREN
POLSTER- UND
PHANTASIE-MÖBEL

Figure 4–12

Figure 4–14

Figure 4–15

Figure 4–11
Advertisement of Jacob & Josef Kohn, in the catalogue of the XV Ausstellung der Vereinigung bildender Künstler Österreichs Sezession (Fifteenth Exhibition of the Fine Arts Association of the Vienna Secession), Vienna, 1902.

Figure 4–12
Title page in sales catalogue of Jacob & Josef Kohn, Vienna, ca. 1909.

Figure 4–13
Showroom of Jacob & Josef Kohn, Berlin, 1906. (From *Berliner Architekturwelt* 1906, fig. 462).

Figure 4–14
Page in sales catalogue of Jacob & Josef Kohn, Vienna, 1904, showing the firm's showroom at No. 109 Faubourg Saint-Antoine, Paris.

Figure 4–15
Josef Hoffmann and Koloman Moser. Storefront of the Jacob & Josef Kohn building, Berlin. (From *Berliner Architekturwelt* 1906, fig. 461).

effort to implement the goals of the reform movement found solid ground in the coalescence of business interests, a ready market, and a pool of progressive and creative designers ready to apply themselves to the task. Joseph August Lux, a critic and leading cultural commentator, regarded this group of architects and artists as "that invaluable economic commodity: TALENT." In a series of articles published in *Hohe Warte*, a magazine known for its remarkable sense of mission, Lux advanced his thesis of an "economy of talents" that would enable Austrian production to attain international recognition for its standard of quality.[25]

The influence of the Viennese Kunstfrühling movement was felt throughout the publications of this period in their advertisements for mass-produced goods that had attained improved standards of quality, in part due to the long struggle to reintroduce craftsmanship in production. Newspaper advertisements, company catalogues, and the showrooms and storefronts of business establishments all bore the imprint of the young Viennese avant-garde (figures 4–11, 12, 13, 14, 15). Firms attracted to this type of philosophy and image collaborated closely with the teaching staff and the students of the Kunstgewerbeschule. As may be seen in advertisements for Prag-Rudniker (figures 4–16 and 4–17), the firm produced baskets and wicker furniture designed by Hans Vollmer and Wilhelm Schmidt, both pupils of Josef Hoffmann; the textile manufacturer Backhausen drew on the new "talent" for the design of upholstery fabrics and carpets for its own line as well as for the interior decoration of the Wiener Werkstätte (Vienna Workshop); and the manufacturers Josef Böck and E. Bakalowits Söhne extended the new style into the industrial production of ceramics and glass, respectively (figure 4–17). Through the enterprise of highly committed firms who also anticipated tremendous economic opportunities, nearly all aspects of life experienced some "reshaping."[26]

Such attempts to unite the artistic and utilitarian drew on the ideas of John Ruskin and William Morris, leaders of the English Arts and Crafts movement who brought a social dimension to the new aesthetic.[27] Morris advocated a return to handicraft production and the guild system. He felt that the division of the fine and decorative arts had led to an acceptance of ugliness as part of daily life,

and contrasted this situation to the ideal he found in the Middle Ages, when artistic expression was considered not a prerogative of the fine arts but a quality integral to everyday life.[28] Art was not to be regarded as a luxury but as a right.[29]

A change in the common aesthetic

Although such visionary reforms did not come to pass, partly due to the exclusive aspect of handicraft production methods, through the collaboration of designers and industry the currents of change did influence the primary contemporary aesthetic. The Wiener Werkstätte mediated between crafts and industrial production, while clearly distinguishing between them. The artistic directors of the Werkstätte saw their task as a struggle against the domination of the profit motive in mass production at the expense of workmanship. The mass-produced object could be

Figure 4–16

Advertisement of Prag-Rudniker Korbwaren-Fabrikation, in the catalogue of the XV Ausstellung der Vereinigung bildender Küntsler Österreichs Sezession, Vienna, 1902.

Figure 4–17

Page with advertisements of E. Bakalowits Söhne, Prag-Rudniker, and Josef Böck, Vienna. (From *Hohe Warte*, 1905, vol. 1, no. 6).

Figure 4-18

Josef Hoffmann. Dining room, Purkersdorf Sanitorium, near Vienna, ca. 1904. Furniture manufactured by Jacob & Josef Kohn, Vienna. See CAT. NO. 43.

given a quality of its own through a sensitivity to appropriate technology, that is, through bringing high standards to the mass-produced article. In the 1903 *arbeitsprogramm* (work program) for the Wiener Werkstätte, Josef Hoffmann wrote, "We too are aware that, under certain circumstances, an acceptable article can be made by mechanical means, provided that it bears the stamp of manufacture. . . ."[30] Commissions for the furnishing of various institutions and commercial establishments were instrumental in this regard. The Wiener Werkstätte commissioned J. & J. Kohn to produce tables and chairs, according to Hoffmann's design, for the dining room of the Purkersdorf Sanitorium (1904–5; figure 4–18 and cat. no. 43). Chairs and tables by Hoffmann were also commissioned from Kohn for the theater room and bar room of the Cabaret Fledermaus in Vienna (1907; figures 4–19, 4–20 and cat. no. 55).[31] Otto Wagner also appreciated the aesthetic and functional possibilities of bent wood for the furnishing of some of the public buildings he was commissioned to design, such as the Depeschenbüro (news dispatch bureau) of *Die*

Figure 4-19
Josef Hoffmann. Theater room of Cabaret Fledermaus, Vienna, 1907. (From *Deutsche Kunst und Dekoration* December 1908, p. 158). See CAT. NO. 55.

Figure 4-20
Josef Hoffmann. Bar room of Cabaret Fledermaus, Vienna, 1907. (From *Deutsche Kunst und Dekoration* December 1908, p. 159). See CAT. NO. 55.

Figure 4–19

Figure 4–20

Figure 4–21
**Otto Wagner. Board room, Österreich-
ische Postsparkasse (Austrian Postal Savings Bank), Vienna, 1904–1906. See** CAT.
NO. **46.**

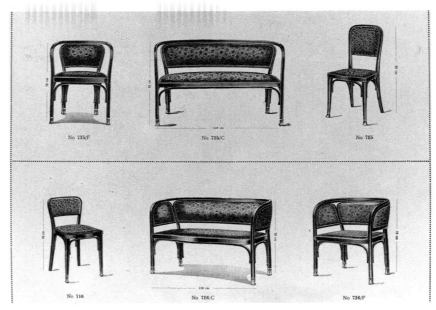

Figure 4–22
**Suites of drawing room
furniture. Sales catalogue
of Jacob & Josef Kohn,
Vienna, 1909?**

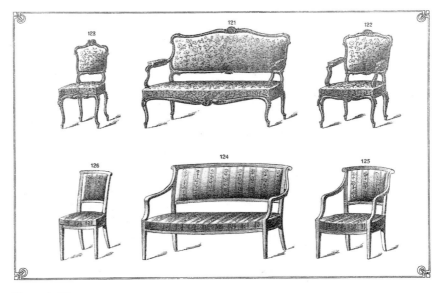

Figure 4–23
**Suites of drawing room furniture. Sales
catalogue of Wiener Tischler Genossenschaft (Viennese Cabinetmakers' Association), Vienna, ca. 1907.**

Zeit built in 1902 and the Österreichische Postsparkasse
(figure 4–21) built between 1904 and 1906. Through such
projects the Viennese public was exposed to the new,
unusual furniture within an everyday context. Some of
the chairs and benches designed for these buildings were
also retailed to the general public by the firms that manufactured them and were occasionally plagiarized, although
in altered form, by competing firms. Thus the furniture
commissioned for specific projects had a positive influence
on designs produced for the general market and when
part of a production line was price-competitive.

The bent-wood furniture produced by Kohn from
designs by architects, regarded today as jewels of industrial
design, did not carry "prestige" price tags and was not
regarded as prestigious. This may be demonstrated by
comparing sets of drawing-room furniture offered by Kohn
with sets in the line of the Wiener Tischler Genossenschaft
(Viennese Cabinetmakers' Association) around 1907 (figures 4–22 and 4–23). Relative to labor-intensiveness prices

Figure 4–24
Advertisement of Jacob & Josef Kohn, Vienna. (From *Hohe Warte* 1905/06, nos. 23 and 24, supplement, p. 2).

were comparable; in fact, Kohn's were somewhat lower. Another indication that the bent-wood furniture under discussion was not presented as a prestige item is the fact that at the 1908 Kunstschau in Vienna a model country house was filled with furnishings designed by Hoffmann and fabricated by J. & J. Kohn, whereas the following year at the International Kunstschau in Vienna the same house was furnished with pieces manufactured by the Deutsche Werkstätten für Handwerkskunst (German Workshops for Handicrafts), an association, located in the Dresden suburb of Hellerau and known for inexpensive furniture intended for the lower and middle classes.[32] The German architect Hermann Muthesius, a founder of the Deutsche Werkbund (German Werkbund), used an advertisement for J. & J. Kohn's latest line of case pieces (figure 4–24) to illustrate his article on machine-made furniture. Such inclusion indicated that he considered Kohn's products to correspond with his own ideal of creating a range of high-quality utilitarian products that would be standardized (typiserung) so as to increase volume to a level of affordability.[33] Both Kohn and Thonet belonged to the Österreichisches Werkbund (Austrian Werkbund) and fully supported the ideas of Muthesius.[34]

Invention and imitation

A product that has proven itself commercially and become synonymous with a certain style attracts not only buyers but also competitors in business. A manufacturer may embark on a product-adaptation program of prototypes as a cheap, quick formula for profit making, without taking into account the purpose of the designer and the ideological aspects of the original product. What ensues is a generation of plagiarisms and lifeless imitations. The history of bent-wood and tubular-steel furniture is a case in point.

When Michael Thonet's patent expired in 1869,[35] his firm became the primary source of bent-wood prototypes for all other European bent-wood manufacturers, most notably J. & J. Kohn. Yet by the turn of the century it was the Kohn firm that was taking the initiative in bent-wood design by recognizing the capabilities of the Kunstfrühling in Vienna. The differences in design approach on the part of these two firms become obvious even when comparing

the appearances of their catalogues. Thonet's catalogue of 1906 employs a rectangular format, with floral and curvilinear motifs framing a gothic typeface, while the Kohn catalogue of 1904 (figure 4–25) is designed in the new square format and decorated with a pattern of black and white squares surrounding a sans-serif typeface.

Kohn's advanced sense of product design had a great impact on competitors. All bent-wood manufacturers were by this time well aware of the phenomenon of plagiarism and tried to protect themselves through prompt registry of designs. But plagiarism was facilitated through the practice of ascribing designs exclusively to the manufacturer rather than the designer,[36] and the problem of patents could be evaded through slight adaption of successful products, such as minor changes in details of construction, measure, or form. Thonet, forced to consider Kohn as a serious competitor, joined the ranks of manufacturers engaged in such practices. This move was dictated by the market demand for contemporary styling, and the new forms were merely spread as secessionist drapery over

Figure 4–25
Cover of sales catalogue of Jacob & Josef Kohn, Vienna, 1904.

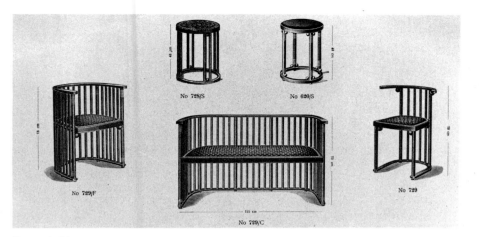

Figure 4–26

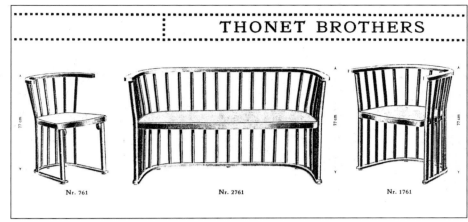

Figure 4–27

the Thonet products.[37] In 1906, Kohn began producing Josef Hoffmann's Cabaret Fledermaus chair and variations, followed four years later by Thonet with their own series of variations on this design (figures 4–26, 4–27, and cat. no. 55).[38] In one of Thonet's variations, Hoffmann's straight line of rear legs and backrest has been angled out above the level of the seat frame, and the shape of his spherical reinforcement (at the juncture of leg and seat rail) has been changed to an ovoid form. (It was not until 1922, when the two firms merged, that the ovoid shape was abandoned and the spherical form came to dominate the market.)

It is ironic that a style of such integrity and purpose generated so many fashionable imitations. These borrowed forms could, however, be easily detected, precisely because they lacked the requisite quality of inner dimension.[39] Such questionable business practices provide a background to our present difficulties of design attributions. Today's market, which trades in these bent-wood furnishings as costly icons of the modern movement, is frequently dependent upon attributions so unsubstantiated as to be nothing more than wishful thinking.[40] A system of attribution can only operate properly through reference to and profound knowledge of the literature. Yet even then the task is complex, as primary sources often carry conflicting information. The history of bent-wood furniture production is characterized by a lack of definitive supporting archival documents and sketches. An awareness of the associations between designers and manufacturers is helpful in determining attributions, as are the clues within period catalogues provided by rare references to designers. Contemporary reports and photographic documentation may also be used, but only with great caution, for experience has shown that in respect to Viennese art at the turn of the century, comparisons of syle and form can lead to incorrect attributions. An example of the unreliability of contemporary sources may be seen in an armchair published the 1907 *Studio Yearbook of Decorative Art* and described as having been designed by Leopold Bauer and made by Thonet Brothers (figure 4–28). The same armchair appears three years later in a different publication and is referred to as having been produced and designed by Thonet Brothers.[42] An illustration in the *Studio Yearbook* of 1914 identifies some wicker chairs with the name of Josef Hoffmann, yet we know from other sources that these chairs were designed by Josef Zotti and Wilhelm Schmidt.[43] Even identifications provided by the same publication are contradictory. For example, the 1910 *Das Interieur* distinguishes between one piece of furniture "designed and fabricated by the Thonet Brothers" and another "designed by Marcel Kammerer." This apparently meaningful distinction is rendered suspect by the same publication's presentation of the veranda furniture illustrated in figure 4–26 as being "designed and fabricated by the Thonet Brothers"[44] while the Thonet catalogue attributes these pieces to Kammerer.

Figure 4–28
Leopold Bauer. Armchairs and table. Manufactured by Gebrüder Thonet, Vienna. (From *Studio Yearbook of Decorative Art 1907*, p. 217).

Design attribution

Despite these uncertainties, we may draw some conclusions in regard to the works of Gustav Siegel, Josef Hoffmann, Otto Wagner, Marcel Kammerer, Josef Urban, and Otto Prutscher. There is, however, a particular problem of contradictory source material as regards the work of Koloman Moser; not a single piece of bent-wood furniture can be documented as his, despite recent attributions.[45]

Gustav Siegel appears to have been the first designer of the Viennese reform movement to be employed by the bent-wood furniture industry, and he became so identified with it that he was called "the man of bent wood."[46] Following an apprenticeship as a cabinetmaker, Siegel studied under Hoffmann at the Wiener Kunstgewerbeschule. His training provided him with a profound grasp of the unity of form and function and appears to have predestined him for his new responsibilities, undertaken around 1899, as designer for the firm of J. & J. Kohn. Werner J. Schweiger contends that Siegel's importance

for Kohn is overestimated and cites a lack of documentation.[47] Yet the bent-wood production of the Kohn firm in the early twentieth century is a clear reflection of Siegel's crucial and prominent role as the firm's designer. The earliest documented work by Siegel for the Kohn firm is his previously discussed installation at the Paris Exposition Universelle of 1900 (figure 4–2). Encouraged by the success of this exhibition, J. & J. Kohn presented some of the same pieces by Siegel in a new suite of rooms—bedroom (figure 4–29), drawing room (figure 4–30), and dining room (figure 4–31)—at the Winterausstellung of the Österreichisches Museum für Kunst und Industrie, 1901/02. An argument often repeated in secondary literature that the dining room furniture (Kohn Model No. 719) was designed by Koloman Moser is not supported by any documentary evidence, and it is mostly likely a variation of work previously designed by Siegel. At this Winterausstellung a new system of case pieces was used in the bedroom, the authorship of which can no longer be ascribed to Siegel but instead must be tentatively considered the work of Josef Hoffmann, as will be detailed and illustrated below. The drawing room furnishings (figure 4–30) are characterized by certain features typical of Siegel's work: the rectangular cross section of the wooden rods, the feet encased in brass sabots, and the gradual curves of the upper portion of the frames. One of these pieces is identical to that identified as Model No. 412 in the Kohn catalogue of 1904 (this bench has been attributed to Wagner in secondary sources without documentation from any primary sources).[48] Although there is very little documentary material on Siegel's work after 1902, the *Studio Year Book* of 1908 presents furniture for the living room (Model No. 415 in the 1909 Kohn catalogue) under Siegel's name, and it is interesting to note that this model shows the spherical reinforcement that is commonly interpreted today as the signature of Josef Hoffmann. This same source provides further evidence of Siegel's continued activity by claiming that it is "Gustav Siegel who is devoting all his energy to the solving of the bent-wood problem, ably supported by Messrs. J. & J. Kohn."[49]

In assembling a catalogue raisonné of bent-wood furniture by Josef Hoffmann, one must rely exclusively on literature from this period, as Hoffmann himself kept no

Figure 4–29

Figure 4–31

Figure 4–30

Figure 4–29
Bedroom, Jacob & Josef Kohn display at the Winterausstellung (Winter exhibition), Österreichisches Museum für Kunst und Industrie (Austrian Museum for Art and Industry), Vienna, 1901/02.

Figure 4–30
Drawing room, Jacob & Josef Kohn display at the Winterausstellung, Österreichisches Museum für Kunst und Industrie, Vienna, 1901/02.

Figure 4–31
Dining room, Jacob & Josef Kohn display at the Winterausstellung, Österreichisches Museum für Kunst und Industrie, Vienna, 1901/02.

SALONECKE

Installation und Möbel aus gebogenem Holze, scharfkantige Biegungen nach dem neuen System-Entwurf
Professor JOSEPH HOFFMANNS

Erste österreichische Aktiengesellschaft
zur Erzeugung von Möbeln aus gebogenem Holze

JAKOB & JOSEF KOHN

Wien, I. Elisabethstrasse Nr. 24.

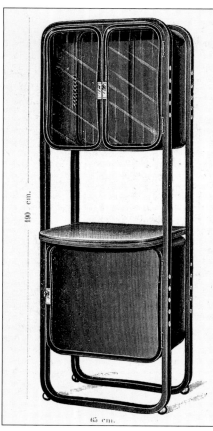

190 cm.

65 cm.

Figure 4–32

Advertisement of Jacob & Josef Kohn, Vienna. Installation and case pieces in a new system of construction designed by Josef Hoffmann. (From *Hohe Warte* 1905/06, 2nd annual volume, nos. 19 and 20, supplement, p. 2).

known record of his works. As mentioned above, the bedroom (figure 4–29) presented by J. & J. Kohn at the Österreichisches Museum für Kunst und Industrie Winterausstellung of 1901–02 included a new system of case pieces in which bent-wood frames were enclosed within bent-wood frames. Such a use of square-sectioned curves is publicized under the name of Josef Hoffmann in a J. & J. Kohn advertisement published in 1905 in *Hohe Warte* (figure 4–32), the earliest bent-wood furniture to be published in association with Hoffmann.[50] Thus the new system of case pieces included in the Winterausstellung may be tentatively ascribed to Hoffmann. Yet this same advertisement reveals an additional complication, for the vitrine seen in the foreground had already been published as one designed by Koloman Moser for this same Winterausstellung (figure 4–33).[51] The question thus arises as to whether this "new system," comprised of chairs and case pieces of enclosed bent-wood frames, with the runners so typical of Hoffmann, was in fact designed by Hoffmann and simply used by Moser as a convenient framework for one of his own designs. The system might also represent a collaboration between the two designers; it has been confirmed that both worked together closely in designing the storefront of the J. & J. Kohn showroom in Berlin (figure 4–15). It is in fact often difficult to distinguish Hoffmann's work from that which has recently been ascribed to Moser, a problem aggravated by conflicting reports from contemporary sources. Other furniture in the style of this "new system" was published under Hoffmann's name in the special 1906 issue of the *Studio Yearbook* (figures 4–34 and 4–35).[52] Considering the

Figure 4–33

Koloman Moser. Vitrine. Sales catalogue of Jacob & Josef Kohn, Vienna, 1904.

unreliability of design credits provided by this publication, one may assume that these rooms may represent the collaborative work of Hoffmann and Moser.

In 1906, the *Studio Yearbook* reported that Hoffmann had "given much care to the solving of bent-wood and wicker problems in furniture, in which he has been ably supported by Messrs J. & J. Kohn and the Prag-Rudniker Korbwaren Fabrikation, Vienna."[53] As previously men-

Figure 4–34

Josef Hoffmann. Bedroom furniture. Manufactured by Jacob & Josef Kohn, Vienna. (From Holme, *Art Revival in Austria*, pl. C17).

tioned, Hoffmann's designs for the Cabaret Fledermaus in 1907 were followed by a major project for the 1908 Kunstschau in Vienna, a model country house for which he designed bent-wood furnishings fabricated by J. & J. Kohn (figures 4–36, 37, 38, 39, 40; cat. no. 54). The country house was well documented in contemporary sources and therefore plays a crucial role in identifying Hoffmann's

Figure 4–35
Josef Hoffmann. Dining room furniture. Manufactured by Jacob & Josef Kohn, Vienna. (From Holme, *Art Revival in Austria,* **pl. C14).**

Figure 4–36
Josef Hoffmann. Drawing room of small country house, Jacob & Josef Kohn display at the Kunstschau, Vienna, 1908. (From *Moderne Bauformen* **1908, p. 374).**

Figure 4–37
Josef Hoffmann. Children's room of small country house, Jacob & Josef Kohn display at the Kunstschau, Vienna, 1908. (From *Moderne Bauformen* **1908, p. 373).**

Figure 4–38

Figure 4–40

Figure 4–39

Figure 4–38
Josef Hoffmann. Dining room of small country house, Jacob & Josef Kohn display at the Kunstschau, Vienna, 1908. (From *Moderne Bauformen* 1908, p. 375).

Figure 4–39
Josef Hoffmann. Smoking room of small country house, Jacob & Josef Kohn display at the Kunstschau, Vienna, 1908. (From *Moderne Bauformen* 1908, p. 371).

Figure 4–40
Josef Hoffmann. Bedroom of small country house, Jacob & Josef Kohn display at the Kunstschau, Vienna, 1908. (From *Moderne Bauformen* 1908, p. 372).

bent-wood oeuvre.[54] Both the drawing room (figure 4–36) and the children's room (figure 4–37) included chairs that were adaptations of the Fledermaus chair. The so-called Sitzmaschine (Kohn Model No. 670; cat. no. 56) and the Kohn Model No. 421 drawing room furnishings were presented here for the first time (figure 4–36; cat. no. 59). The project reveals the Kohn firm's responsiveness to the stylistic trends that had begun to make themselves felt around 1906. All of the new pieces retain the Kunstfrühling spirit, but are now imbued with a distilled classicism. The turn of the century had been characterized by a search for values lost in the Industrial Revolution, and rediscovered values of the Biedermeier era contributed to authentic innovation in design. Yet within the space of less than a decade, the Biedermeier influence had been reduced to a mechanical generation of preconceived designs. The Sitzmaschine is a bent-wood adaptation of the famous Morris chair but is so dominated by aesthetic formalism that it has nothing but function in common with its English forebear.[55] The Model No. 421 furnishings adapt the formal qualities of classicist chairs to the medium of bent wood. The furnishings for the dining room (figure 4–38), smoking room (figure 4–39), and bedroom (figure 4–40) are all harbingers of the classical revivalist trend that was to dominate Austrian designs during the next decade as the search for functional types gave way to a concern with aesthetic solutions.

One of Hoffmann's last projects for J. & J. Kohn prior to the First World War was a ladies' drawing room presented at the Winterausstellung of the Österreichisches Museum für Kunst und Industrie in 1913–14 (figure 4–41).[56] All the furnishings demonstrate this return to classical ideals and detailing, and the types of furniture and their arrangement clearly reveal Biedermeier origins. Bent wood as a material is no longer formally respected but has been reduced to being merely another technology concealed beneath a facade. The same furniture was included in the Kohn showroom at the 1914 Deutsche Werkbund Exhibition in Cologne (figure 4–42).[57] The row of chairs along the wall consists of models distinguishable from each other only through variations in the backrest components, a further reminder of the Biedermeier era.[58]

Figure 4–41
Josef Hoffmann. Ladies' drawing room, Jacob & Josef Kohn display at the Winterausstellung, Österreichisches Museum für Kunst und Industrie, Vienna, 1913/14.

Figure 4–42
Josef Hoffmann. Furniture, Jacob & Josef Kohn display at the Deutsche Werkbundausstellung (German Werkbund exhibition), Cologne, 1914. (From Eisler, Österreichisches Werkkultur 1916, p. 30).

The armchairs designed by Otto Wagner for the Depeschenbüro of *Die Zeit* and for the boardroom of the Postsparkasse in Vienna (figures 4–21, 4–43, and 4–44; cat. no. 46) are structurally simplified versions of the armchair that Gustav Siegel designed for the 1900 Paris Exposition Universelle (figures 4–2, 4–45; cat. no. 38).[59] The Wagner armchairs represent the first use of aluminum as a furniture component in Austria; aluminum sabots sheathe the feet, and flat strips protect the sides of the chair. The chairs vary in the shape of the sabots, the method of fitting the strips to the armrests, the struttings of the backrest, and the shape of the apron. Wagner's Depeschenbüro stool (figure 4–46) also derives from two models most likely designed by Siegel:[60] a bench for the drawing room at the Winter Exhibition of 1901–2 of the Österreichisches Museum für Kunst und Industrie (figure 4–30), and a bench in the ladies' drawing room at the Esposizione internazionale d'arte decorativa moderna in Turin in 1902 (figure 4–47).[61] These stools and benches are the forerunners of the Postsparkasse étagère (cat. no. 47) in their use of closed bent-wood frames as strutting structural elements. For the étagère Wagner used aluminum caps to conceal the screws that connect the structural components, thereby formally emphasizing the stress points. Wagner's stool for the main banking room of the Österreichische Postsparkasse (cat. no. 48), in which five closed bent-wood frames are joined with screws, is his consummate work

Figure 4–45
Gustav Siegel. Armchair, 1899/1900. Bent solid wood, brass. Manufactured by Jacob & Josef Kohn, Vienna. Collection Dr. Paul Asenbaum, Vienna. See CAT. NO. 38.

Figure 4–44
Otto Wagner. Armchair, for the board room of the Österreichische Postsparkasse, Vienna, 1906. Bent solid wood, upholstery, aluminum. Manufactured by Jacob & Josef Kohn, Vienna. Österreichische Postsparkasse, Vienna, See CAT. NO. 46.

in its unification of material, function, and design. This stool and the side chair designed by Loos for the Café Museum represent the peak of modern Viennese furniture.

Economic considerations played a decisive role in the commissioning of bent-wood furniture for the Österreichische Postsparkasse, and the Kohn and Thonet firms both submitted bids for the project and consequently manufactured furnishings for it.[62] The Postsparkasse side chair used by the banking clerks entered mass production, in several variations, in both the Kohn and Thonet lines, while versions of the Postsparkasse armchair (cat. no.

Figure 4-46
Otto Wagner. Stool, for the telegraph office of *Die Zeit*, Vienna, 1902. Manufactured by Jacob & Josef Kohn, Vienna. (From *Das Interieur* 1903, p. 76).

Figure 4-47
Ladies' drawing room, Jacob & Josef Kohn display, Esposizione internazionale d'arte decorativa moderna (International Exhibition of Modern Decorative Art), Turin, 1902.

46), stool (cat. no. 48), and desk all became part of the Thonet catalogue. A simplified version of the armchair from *Die Zeit*'s Depeschenbüro was produced commercially by Kohn. The aluminum strips on the armrests were discarded, and the sabots were made of brass, apparently a concession to the popular taste, which had not yet accepted the application of aluminum to furniture.

The association between Thonet and Wagner in connection with the estimates for the Postsparkasse interiors provided Thonet Brothers with an opportunity for increased contact with the ideas of the Viennese avant-garde. By 1905 this new dialogue had resulted in the establishment of a collaborative relationship with Marcel Kammerer, a student and colleague of Wagner. Kammerer's first known designs for Thonet are variations of the Postsparkasse furnishings (figure 4–48). A three-seater bench and the corresponding armchair use an adaptation of Wagner's strapping system to attach the cushions of seat and backrest. In the Postsparkasse Wagner used this system in the design of the marble bench that was positioned at the foot of the staircase to the director's office (figure 4–49). Kammerer's work also copies Wagner's use of bolts and

Figure 4–48

Figure 4–50

Figure 4–51

Figure 4–48
Marcel Kammerer. Furniture, ca. 1904. Manufactured by Gebrüder Thonet, Vienna. (From *Das Interieur* 1905, p. 82).

Figure 4–49
Otto Wagner. Marble bench, for the Österreichische Postsparkasse, Vienna, ca. 1906.

Figure 4–49

Figure 4–50
Marcel Kammerer. Reading room, Gebrüder Thonet display at the Austrian Exhibition, London, 1905. (From *Das Interieur* 1906, p. 139).

Figure 4–51
Leopold Bauer. Armchairs and tables. Manufactured by Gebrüder Thonet, Vienna. (From *Studio Yearbook of Decorative Art* 1907, p. 217).

metal strips as decorative accents. Only the small table and flower stand (figure 4–48, upper right and lower left) are innovative in construction; square-sectioned wooden rods comprise U-shaped components opening in alternate directions, which are joined to each other with screws. Somewhat simplified models of both of these pieces entered the Thonet production line.

In 1905, at the Austrian Exhibition in London, Thonet displayed a room decorated by Kammerer in the latest Viennese fashion (figure 4–50). One of the armchairs is an adaptation of a Leopold Bauer design (figure 4–51).[63] The new surface use of riveted plates, derived from Wagner, blends with Kammerer's interior design. Metal work also appears in another armchair designed by Kammerer (figure 4–52), although unfortunately it is used for decorative rather than functional purposes. By 1910, Thonet's line included many of Kammerer's designs,[64] although only one was truly original—an armchair used by Wagner in his villa in Hütteldorf (figure 4–53).[65] During the same period, six new suites of veranda furniture by Kammerer entered production, two of which have been previously mentioned as plagiarisms of Hoffmann's chair for the

Cabaret Fledermaus. During this same period, Viennese architect Josef Urban also designed a model for Thonet Brothers: an upholstered side chair with a high backrest, rising in a dramatic line (figure 4–54).[66]

According to contemporary sources, it seems that Otto Prutscher, one of Hoffmann's students, replaced Kammerer as Thonet's designer around 1910. The interior design and furniture of the Viennese branch of Thonet's firm came from Prutscher.[67] Prutscher's designs, presented at the Internationale Baufachausstellung (International Building Exhibition) in Leipzig in 1913 (figure 4–55) and at the Deutsche Werkbund Exhibition in Cologne in 1914, are wholly dominated by Hoffmann's stylistic influence, although they fall short of achieving his natural elegance and grace. Such derivative designs are symptomatic of the general state of artistic creation in Vienna around 1910 (figure 4–56). The efforts made by the Kunstreform movement to transform the immediate environment had created a new public consciousness of the design of everyday objects. But the Kunstreform could not be accepted by the majority of consumers in its initial radical ideological form. Ultimately, the deeply held convictions of the Viennese avant-garde became less influential, yielding to a combination of forces: the weakening of their own fighting spirits; industry aiming at quick profits; and consumers wishing to satisfy an appetite for the superficial and becoming frightened of an apparently radical ideology. Bent wood, as a unique combination of material and production values, had lost its supporters in Austria on the eve of the First World War and was now treated merely as raw material, like any other. After the war Austria began to face the challenge of changing social structures, and new creative forces abroad were boldly realizing their new ideas in the design of furniture made out of a new material: tubular steel.

Figure 4–52

Marcel Kammerer. Armchair. Manufactured by Gebrüder Thonet and Franz X. Schenzel, Vienna. (From *Das Interieur* 1909, p. 24).

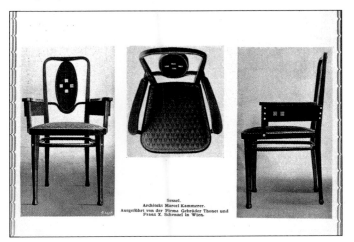

Figure 4–53

Marcel Kammerer. Armchairs, in the hall of the second Villa Wagner, Hütteldorf, Austria. Manufactured by Gebrüder Thonet, Vienna.

Figure 4–54

Otto Prutscher - Gebrüder Thonet — Industriemöbel.

Figure 4–56

Empfangsraum des öst. Pavillons auf der Internat. Baufachausstellung in Leipzig

Entwurf: Architekt Professor Otto Prutscher.   Ausführung: Gebrüder Thonet. Wien

Figure 4–55

Figure 4–54
Josef Urban. Side chairs, in the Restaurant Paul Hofer, Vienna, ca. 1906. (From *Das Interieur*, 1906, p. 21).

Figure 4–55
Otto Prutscher. Reception room of the Austrian Pavilion, Internationale Baufachausstellung (International Building Exhibition), Leipzig, 1913. (From *Das Interieur* 1913, pl. 184).

Figure 4–56
Otto Prutscher. Dining room furniture. Manufactured by Gebrüder Thonet, Vienna. (From Eisler, *Österreichisches Werkkultur* 1916, p. 31).

Notes

1. For a consideration of the number and range of bent-wood manufacturers, see Graham Dry's essay in this catalogue [Ed. note].

2. In addition to the "name" designers considered in this essay, both Thonet and Kohn employed designers whose works were either adaptations or models designed to complement a particular suite of furniture.

3. E.g., Josef Hoffmann: "We want to avoid technical problems. The straight fibers of the wood have not been respected; curves are made on top of curves, which rarely can be joined to the necessary straight surfaces of furniture. We forget that for every curved component we would have to go into the forest to look for the correctly curved branch, like the peasant who builds his plow or sled. Bent wood, of course, is another matter—the fiber is artificially bent, and the curve is therefore justified" ("Simple Furniture," *Das Interieur* 2 [1901], cited in Sekler, p. 484).

4. Asenbaum, p. 210.

5. Brochure of the Philadelphia International Exhibition of 1876, cited in *Die Groszindustrie Österreichs*, vol. 3, p. 321.

6. Paris 1878, p. 86.

7. For a more extensive discussion of the reform movement, see Robert Keil's essay in this volume [Ed. note].

8. Such experiments featured the *Brettlstil*, or plank-style, a form of revealed construction that united structure and decoration. For a more detailed analysis see Vienna 1985, pp. 40–48.

9. Reprinted in Massobrio and Portoghesi 1976, p. 232.

10. Vienna 1899, p. 85, cat. nos. 630–53.

11. Loos 1899a; and Loos 1899b.

12. *Innen-Dekoration* 12 (1901), pp. 102–3.

13. *Das Interieur* 1, no. 10 (1900), pp. 156, 167–68.

14. *Kunstgewerbeblatt: Zeitschrift für bildende Kunst*, vol. 13 (1902), Neue Folge, p. 211.

15. The Christmas Exhibition was held from December 1, 1899 to January 6, 1900; Vienna 1900, p. 63.

16. Loos was not employed by the Kohn firm, but simply had this model fabricated by them. The same model was used in a restaurant on the Kärntnerstrasse in Vienna that was renovated by Hans Mayr (*Das Interieur* 3 [1902]: 125).

17. *Kunst und Kunsthandwerk* (1899), pp. 196ff; *Dekorative Kunst* (1899), pp. 173–74.

18. The original finish of this chair survives in only a few examples; the rest have been treated with a uniform mahogany-colored stain that obliterates the contours and vitality of this refined chair. In general, restored turn-of-the-century bent-wood furniture is marred by commercial stains that obscure the wood behind a deadening layer. Thus the material is violated and the object's integrity destroyed.

19. Thonet's early chairs were described as "consumer chairs" in the Thonet catalogues.

20. "Three rooms need to be mentioned as being distinctively Viennese. They are furnished exclusively with bent wood by the firm of Jacob & Josef Kohn. Bent wood, in which Hoffmann's school has a particular interest, has gained much through modern methods of treatment. The flexibility of beechwood corresponds well to the modern way of dealing with curves; even structural problems of such furniture, particularly of chairs, have seen new solutions lately. . . . Bent wood, a material originally restricted to seating furniture, is now used for everything [such as case pieces]. One could hardly say this was done without force, as without force it is simply not possible to achieve bending" (Hevesi 1902, pp. 12–13).

21. See Oerley.

22. Brochure of the Philadelphia Centennial Exhibition of 1876, cited in *Die Groszindustrie Österreichs*, vol. 3, p. 321.

23. Hevesi 1902, p. 4.

24. American edition of Kohn catalogue, 1910.

25. Lux 1904–05, pp. 73ff.

26. Efforts to achieve a constructive unity of material, decoration, and function can be traced to the "architects of Napoleon," Charles Percier (1764–1838) and Pierre François Leonard Fontaine (1762–1853); see *Recueil de décorations intérieures*, 1801. The English designer and architect A.W.N. Pugin (1812–52) was also dedicated to such goals; see *The True Principles of Pointed or Christian Architecture*, 1841.

27. The works of Ruskin and Morris were published in *Ver Sacrum* (from 1899), *Hohe Warte* (from 1904), and Secession exhibition catalogues (from 1901).

28. Morris 1893, p. vii.

29. Morris 1901, pp. 41ff.

30. In *Hohe Warte* 1, no. 15 (1904–05), p. 268.

31. Hevesi, in a report on the Cabaret Fledermaus, stated, "This [the decoration of the theater room] is another way to do it and it is wonderful—the proportions, the light atmosphere, cheerful flowing lines, elegant lighting fixtures, comfortable chairs of new shape and, finally, the whole tasteful ensemble. Genuine Hoffmann (Hevesi 1909, p. 243). (Readers will note the disagreement here with Graham Dry, who in his essay in this volume attributes the Kohn tub chair No. 728/F—and therefore also the smaller chair No. 728 used in the Cabaret Fledermaus, as well as the settee No. 728/C—to Gustav Siegel [Ed. note]).

32. Vienna 1908b and 1909.

33. Muthesius, p. 2, supplement to issues 19/20, 21/22, and 23/24.

34. Eisler, pp. 251, 260, also notes that during the 1914 Werkbund exhibition in Cologne, Muthesius reiterated his concerns and caused a heated confrontation with the architect Henry van der Velde. The latter had been an advocate of machine production, but took objection to the level of standardization that Muthesius was suggesting.

35. On July 10, 1856, the Thonet firm was granted a patent "for the production of chairs and table legs of bent wood, the bending of

which is achieved by the use of steam and boiling liquids." The patent extended for a period of thirteen years and was not renewable [Ed. note].

36. In Vienna 1899 and Paris 1900b the products of Kohn, Thonet, and Prag-Rudniker are presented with credits given solely to the manufacturers; no reference is made to the designers.

37. "The possibility of bent wood being used for cheap articles of furniture was first recognized by the firm of Messrs. Thonet Brothers in Vienna, but, curiously enough, it was long before they saw that it could be developed on artistic lines" (*Studio Year Book* [1907], p. 211).

38. In the Thonet Brothers' newsletter, *Zentralanzeiger der Firma Gebrüder Thonet*, No. 27 (15 July 1910), pp. 16ff., the seating group No. 761-64 illustrated in figure 4-27 was offered for sale for the first time.

39. Literature dealing with the problem of plagiarism was common in the early years of the twentieth century, e.g., "Eine Entgegnung zum Jahresbericht der Niederösterreichischen Handels- und Gewerbekammer," in *Hohe Warte* 1, no. 4 (1904), pp. 73ff.; and "Das künstlerische Plagiat" in *Hohe Warte* 1, no. 10 (1904-05), pp. 187-88.

40. "*Zugeschrieben* ('attributed to') when used in this catalogue indicates that the furniture was designed by the person named, but there is no reference to the design in the contemporary literature" (Dorotheum Auction House, November 15, 1983, p. 15).

41. *Studio Year Book* (1907), p. 217.

42. Von Preissecker, p. 100.

43. *Studio Year Book* (1914), p. 227.

44. *Das Interieur* 12 (1910), p. 99, pl. 61.

45. For such recent attributions of bent-wood furniture to Koloman Moser see Oberuber and Hummel, p. 176, where cat. nos. 191 and 192 (Kohn Nos. 413S and 413T, respectively) are attributed to Moser; also see Venice 1984, p. 295; and Fenz, p. 161, fig. 67, where a buffet is attributed to Moser. Fenz indicates that all of his attributions are based on stylistics, and that he has uncovered no evidence that Moser ever designed an entire program of furniture for Kohn. Müller, color plate 1; p. 68, fig. 44; p. 127, fig. 105.

46. Hevesi 1906, p. 336.

47. Schweiger in Vienna 1979, the biographical section. [Schweiger, while underestimating Siegel's importance for Kohn, nevertheless indicates that Siegel was Kohn's chief designer. However, the author believes that the exact role of Gustav Siegel in Kohn's design department remains unclear—Ed. note.]

48. Venice 1984, p. 246, fig. 1.

49. *Studio Year Book* (1908), p. 46.

50. *Hohe Warte* 2, nos. 19, 20 (1905/6), supplement, p. 2.

51. *Kunst und Kunsthandwerk* (1902), p. 4.

52. Holme, figs. C14 and C17. The dining room illustrated in figure 4-35 was also illustrated in *Hohe Warte*, nos. 23 and 24, supplement, p. 2, n.d.

53. Holme, p. 505.

54. "The firm of Jakob & Josef Kohn provides the market once again with bent-wood furniture after designs by Josef Hoffmann which meet the highest standards of good taste and elegance" (Vienna 1908c, p. 52); see also *Moderne Bauformen* 7 (1908), pp. 368-75; *Studio Year Book* (1910), p. 223; and *Hohe Warte* (1906), p. 53.

55. In *Hohe Warte* (1906), p. 53, a journal with which Hoffmann was involved, a Morris chair in the mission style was published. This first publication in Austria of the Morris chair associated its adjustable backrest with the impact of American practicality.

56. No. 604b of the photographic pattern collection of the Österreichisches Museum für angewandte Kunst.

57. Eisler, p. 30.

58. One of the first chairs to display this Biedermeier influence was J. & J. Kohn's no. 371, an adaptation of the Purkersdorf dining room chair. It was presented at the entrance to the model country house at the 1908 Kunstschau and thus may be identified as Hoffmann's (*Deutsche Kunst und Dekoration* 23 [1908/9], p. 37).

59. *Das Interieur* 4 (1903), pp. 76-77.

60. For further discussion of the origins and attributions of the *Depeschenbüro* stool, see Asenbaum et al., pp. 85-89.

61. Christopher Wilk (Wilk 1980a, p. 61, fig. 69) previously identified this photograph as the 1900 Paris Exposition Universelle. However, the author's archival research at the Österreichisches Museum für angewandte Kunst confirms the photograph as the Esposizione internazionale d'arte decorativa moderna in Turin, and Mr. Wilk is now in agreement.

62. Asenbaum et al., pp. 205-10.

63. *Studio Year Book* (1907), p. 217.

64. Von Preissecker, pp. 97-104.

65. Ibid., p. 97.

66. Holme, fig. C61; *Das Interieur* 7 (1906), pl. 21.

67. Eisler, pp. 47, 129.

5
Furnishing the future:
Bent wood and metal furniture
1925–1946

CHRISTOPHER WILK

THE 1920s ushered in a period of crucial change in the design and production of furniture employing bent elements. During these years, Germany rather than Austria was the source of the most important designs. Austrian furniture, in fact, turned in a decidedly conservative direction and was virtually ignored in avant-garde circles. Although French, Dutch, Russian, and Eastern European designers produced aesthetically advanced furniture during these years, none matched the seminal role played by their German counterparts.[1] This was also a time of crucial change in the choice of materials. Bent, solid beechwood, the chief means of expression during the nineteenth century, gave way during the 1920s and early 1930s to metal, which became decisively more important than wood, at least in the context of progressive work. By the mid-1930s and into the 1940s, plywood was the material of choice for most avant-garde designers.

Another critical distinction between the bent-wood and metal furniture dating from the nineteenth century and that produced during the early years of the twentieth lies in their points of origin. Whereas the work of Michael Thonet and his successors was initially the achievement of a determined, innovative craftsman and subsequently the remarkable realization of an increasingly sophisticated community of businessmen and manufacturers, the furniture created during the early years of the twentieth century had its genesis with neither the craftsman nor the businessman—although both still had their roles—but arose within the context of early-twentieth-century artistic movements: Cubism, Futurism, Expressionism, De Stijl, Constructivism, and the early phase of Neue Sachlichkeit (New Objectivity). The furniture that emerged during these years was part of the architectural trend known at the time by a wide variety of names—International Architecture, Neues Bauen, New Architecture, International Style—which today is broadly identified by the term *modernism*.

While the bent-wood and bent-metal furniture produced between 1925 and 1946 differs significantly from that manufactured formerly, it nevertheless shares much with Viennese furniture of the years 1899–1914, for during both periods the most important designs derived from architects. However, unlike the nineteenth-century furniture of the Thonet, Kohn, and other companies, many of the avant-garde designs of the twentieth century were fated to inhabit the environments of a clientele that belonged to the economic elite. This is not to deny that during the early decades of the twentieth century much bent-wood furniture was specifically designed for such public places as cafés, stores, and hotels, and for working-class housing projects. Commercial and institutional sales were the bread and butter of the bent-wood and bent-metal furniture industry, and furnishings for the working classes were the object of considerable attention of an avant-garde frequently intent on creating a new physical world to accommodate a new social order. But the origin of these radically new furniture designs is firmly located in the rarefied world of progressive art and architecture; only eventually would these avant-garde objects filter down to the general marketplace.

Rather than offer a comprehensive survey of the seemingly limitless range of bent-wood and metal furniture designed between 1925 and 1946, the discussion that follows focuses on the major themes, objects, and figures of the period. The lack of significant bent furniture dating from the late thirties is evidence of the oncoming war and the displacement of so many European designers. The post-war culture of the 1940s had little in common with that of the 1920s; by the time the work of Charles and Ray Eames emerged, the formal, structural, and artistic statements of furniture were no longer as intimately connected to painting, sculpture, and architectural design as they had been during the twenties. The furniture world of the 1940s was less ideological, more pragmatic, increasingly populated by industrial designers rather than practicing architects. The profound changes caused by World War II, and the seminal influence of the Eameses, moved the center of progressive development from Europe to America.

This transfer was accompanied by a corresponding change in emphasis from the self-consciously artistic to the practical: with the notable exception of the endlessly inventive Eameses, the design studio as atelier was replaced by the studio as adjunct to the factory. In many ways this represented a realization of the dreams of the 1920s; rhetoric was replaced by the reality of industrial production. But this shift was predicated on a loss of the utopian, grand worldview that had motivated the cultural radicals of the twenties. With a few notable exceptions—such as Alvar Aalto and the Eameses—furniture no longer seemed to be the universal and demanding issue it once had been; formal invention became less common, and intellectual concerns were of decreasing interest.

Bent wood

The rediscovery of bent wood

Central to the story of bent-wood and metal furniture between the two world wars was the renewed popularity of traditional nineteenth-century bent-wood furniture that began in the 1920s and its effect on new wood and metal designs. For bent-wood furniture entered the world of 1920s modernism not in the form of startlingly new avant-garde designs—relatively few modernist bent-wood chairs were designed before the end of the twenties—but in its most common and ubiquitous form: the simple nineteenth-century bent-wood café chair.

As noted by the Frankfurt architect Ferdinand Kramer in 1929, the popularity of bent wood in the modern interior did not represent a continuation of earlier progressive twentieth-century taste. Writing specifically about the Thonet firm (which was producing several of his own designs), Kramer cited the popularity of bent wood as a recent phenomena:

Only today does Thonet reap its reward. Chairs that were regarded as suitable for nothing but cafés and bars as recently as ten years ago—as unthinkable for the home—are seen today as the ultimate realization of this kind of industrial-economic thinking.[2]

It is not surprising that during the economically depressed years following World War I inexpensive bentwood furniture was very much in demand. While economic instability limited the extent of recovery in some countries, tables and chairs were nevertheless basic necessities required by both businesses and individuals in shattered Germany and Middle Europe, as well as in rapidly expanding Holland and France. By 1925, the recently formed bent wood conglomerate Thonet-Kohn-Mundus was manufacturing as much furniture as Thonet itself had produced during the boom years of 1906–13.[3]

This renewed interest in nineteenth-century bent wood occurred not only in the general marketplace, but also among avant-garde designers; the best-known example of the use of bent wood in early modern interiors was that of Le Corbusier (figure 5-1). In 1925, describing his choice of furniture for his exhibition building, the Pavillon de L'Esprit Nouveau at the Paris Exposition Internationale des Arts Décoratifs et Industriels Moderne (figure 5-2), he wrote what are perhaps the most quoted lines in the history of bent-wood furniture:

We have introduced in the Pavillon de l'Esprit Nouveau, as we have in our mansions and in our modest working-class homes, the humble, bent-wood Thonet chair—surely the most common and least expensive of chairs. And we believe that this chair, millions of which serve our continent and the two Americas, is a noble thing, for its simplicity is a distillation of forms that harmonize with the human body.[4]

The citing of Le Corbusier is neither arbitrary nor due to his later fame. As examples of the newly developing modernist architecture emerging in the post-war years, Le Corbusier's buildings were among the very first built, photographed, and published. From the early twenties it was Le Corbusier's work that was widely known and admired within progressive circles. While many of his peers also used bent wood, their buildings were not built as early as his, nor were they ever as well known. Before 1927, and especially before 1925, Le Corbusier's interiors provided the most apparent examples of the bent wood revival within the field of progressive architecture.[5]

Just as Le Corbusier had chosen bent wood for his important and polemical exhibition house at the Paris Exposition, so did other European architects, especially

Figure 5-1
Le Corbusier and Pierre Janneret. Living room, Albert Jeanneret House, La Roche-Jeanneret Houses, Paris, 1923. (From *L'Architecture Vivante*, Autumn 1927, pl. 11).

Figure 5-2
Le Corbusier and Pierre Jeanneret. Living room, Pavillon de L'Esprit Nouveau, Exposition Internationale des Arts Décoratifs, Paris, 1925.

Figure 5-3
Mart Stam. Living room, Mart Stam House, Deutsche Werkbund exhibition *Die Wohnung* **at Weissenhofsiedlung, Stuttgart, 1927. (From Gräff,** *Innenräume,* **fig. 98).**

the exhibition-minded Germans, use bent-wood furniture extensively in the model rooms, houses, and exposition spaces they designed for exhibitions in Berlin, Breslau, Vienna, Basel and, above all, Stuttgart (figure 5–3). During the mid-twenties bent-wood furniture became as readily identified with avant-garde interiors as it was with cafés and restaurants.

The appeal of bent wood

The primary appeal of nineteenth-century bent-wood furniture to modernist designers was based, above all, on aesthetics. The tendency of the avant-garde to put all its likes and dislikes, prejudices and biases into pseudoscientific jargon—"technical efficiency . . . standardization . . . maximum utility"—notwithstanding, the curvilinear shapes, pure form, and lack of applied decoration characteristic of the best-known bent-wood designs attracted the modernist sensibility. Beyond the immediate sensory response evoked by the furniture, there was a long list of qualities inherent in or attributable to bent wood which could be cited in the argument for its unique suitability to the modern interior and, hence, to modern life. Not surprisingly, these characteristics reflected the modernists' dreams for their architecture and furnishings. To most, bent wood stood as the shining example of what could be achieved through design.

To modernist eyes, the appearance of a typical bent-wood chair (cat. no. 18) in no way referred to furniture of the past; despite its true age, it was regarded as ahistorical and styleless. Its form both expressed and symbolized the manufacturing process that lay behind it.[6] Technically, its simplicity and success remained unmatched. It was the embodiment of the principles of mass production: it could be manufactured inexpensively at the lowest possible price and transported in large quantities throughout the world; it was made with a small number of parts that could be used in dozens, if not hundreds, of different designs; it was strong and stood up to constant use. A bent-wood chair was lightweight, important not only for shipping, but also for the mobility required in modern interiors. Its thin, linear quality resulted in a chair that was virtually transparent, unencumbering to interior space.

On many levels, bent-wood furniture also fit the social and moral agenda laid down by the modernists, especially the Germans. Not only was it "modern" in appearance, it was also inexpensive, hence available to society as a whole, not only the elite. It fit neatly into, and may even have helped inspire, the idea of *Typenmöbel* (standardized furniture).[7] German, as well as Dutch and Swiss, designers were seeking such standardized types in order to eliminate the need for suites of furniture designed as specific groupings for each interior. A limited number of models within each type would result in reduced production costs and, therefore, in cheaper furniture and a greater coherence of design. Standardization of types would result in large-scale assembly-line production (presumably modeled on that of the bent wood firms). Advocates of *Typenmöbel* wanted each individual piece of furniture to be "a typical expression of its nature," an honest, functional statement uncluttered with references to any specific style. In 1928 the German architect Willi Lotz could identify the Thonet chair and the iron bedstead as "the only standard designs to come from industry."[8] And Ferdinand Kramer could maintain that bent wood, and the Thonet firm in particular, "gives very interesting pointers for the further development of rationalization in the furniture industry."[9]

The rejection of bent wood

Only after a solution to the question "How do we furnish the new interior?" had been found was one nagging problem of bent-wood furniture addressed by the modernists. While it was mass-produced, not decorative in form, truly the product of industry, inexpensive, "transparent," lightweight and therefore mobile, bent-wood furniture was still made of wood, a traditional material that was an awkward reminder of the despised past. Further, it did not sufficiently express its machine origins visually. In 1928, three years after Marcel Breuer had found the vaunted "new solution" employing tubular steel (cat. no. 67), Le Corbusier renounced his "humble" and "noble" bent-wood chairs, later stating that "wood, being a traditional material, limited the scope of the designer's initiative."[10] In place of wood, there was only one appropriate material, a material Charlotte Perriand cleverly linked to the some-what idealized "technological" basis of modern design in her emphatic statement, "Metal plays the same part in furniture as cement has done in architecture."[11]

Thus, following Marcel Breuer's first modern tubular steel designs of 1925, most avant-garde designers—especially those who designed chairs—elected tubular steel as the material proper for their time. In terms of sales or production numbers, the figures of tubular-steel furnishings never approached those of traditional bent wood, and many of the same architects who designed metal furniture specified bent wood, especially for low-budget institutional or commerical projects, as well as for government and privately sponsored housing. Nonetheless, beginning in 1925 tubular steel represented the leading edge of modern design for nearly a decade.

Tubular steel: Marcel Breuer

It is surprising that Marcel Breuer, a young Bauhaus student-turned-teacher, rarely used, or discussed, traditional bent-wood furniture, which he surely knew well. The products of his student years (1919–24) in Weimar were numerous De Stijl–influenced furniture designs (figure 5–4) that matched the emphatic aestheticism and seriousness of purpose of Gerrit Rietveld's furniture.[12] Breuer's lack of interest in bent wood may have been a sign of his youth and of a student's determination to transform the domestic environment rather than rely on even officially sanctioned "modern" forms of the past.

Because of his youth, Breuer was one of the few architect-designers of the period who was educated and trained only in the modernist world; in his quest for a new approach to design he was encumbered by neither traditional education nor experience. In 1924, at the age of twenty-two, Breuer completed his studies at the Weimar Bauhaus and left for Paris. The next year, after it was certain that the Bauhaus would relocate in Dessau, Walter Gropius invited

Figure 5–4
"Bauhaus film, five years long...." (From *Bauhaus* [magazine], July 1926).

1921
1921¹/₂
1924
1925
19??

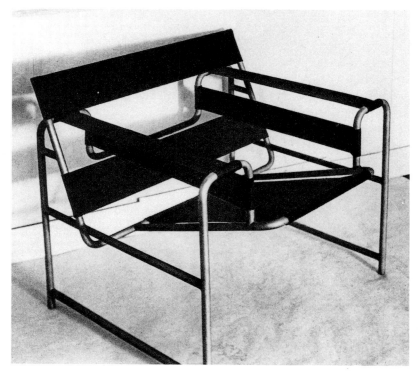

Figure 5-5
Marcel Breuer. Club chair ("Wassily"), prototype, 1925. Welded and bent tubular steel. (From *Das Werk*, July 1926, p. 210). See CAT. NO.67.

Breuer to join the faculty as Master of the carpentry workshop, and Breuer returned to Germany. His precocity as a student was matched by his first-known design as a teacher (figure 5-5): a large club chair with an intricate frame of bent and welded metal and a contrasting support system of tautly strung pieces of fabric—a thoroughly unexpected design from a carpentry master.

Six decades later, this first modern tubular-metal chair is apt to be rejected with a casualness that is inappropriate to its startling novelty. Though Breuer's club chair still manifested the designer's strong indebtedness to De Stijl (figure 5-6) . . . it was a bold and revolutionary design that caught the imagination of architects and designers throughout Europe. Breuer became a major form-giver of his time, and his furniture was imitated on a scale not matched until the full effect of the early work of Charles and Ray Eames was felt in the 1950s.

The genesis of Breuer's first tubular-steel chair has achieved the status of modernist legend. It tells of how the designer was inspired by the strength, lightness, and utility of the bicycle he was riding; of how he approached the bicycle company with his idea of furniture made of bicycle tubes and of the company's predictable rejection of the novel idea; of how at first he purchased lengths of tubular aluminum (an unsuccessful experiment) and then "precision steel tube," which he worked into a crudely constructed chair with the help of a plumber.[13]

The construction of the new Bauhaus buildings in Dessau provided Breuer with the perfect opportunity to produce additional tubular-steel furniture and, perhaps more importantly, to break out of the De Stijl mode within which he had been working for some three years. It was, in reality, the corpus of the four Bauhaus tubular-steel designs that date 1925–26—the club chair (the so-called Wassily) and three subsequent designs—which served as models and inspiration to those designers who quickly took up the challenge of designing in tubular steel. These four designs also demonstrated that the first chair had not been an isolated, chance event, but was the beginning of an ongoing design process.

In these first tubular steel designs Breuer tackled each of several furniture types: the club chair (figure 5–5), the

Figure 5-6
Gerrit Rietveld. Armchair, 1917–18. Painted plywood. The Brooklyn Museum, New York.

Figure 5-7
Marcel Breuer. Side chair, 1925–26, in dining room of the Moholy-Nagy House, Dessau, 1926, designed by Walter Gropius and Marcel Breuer. (From *Das Werk*, January 1928, p. 9, photo by Lucia Moholy).

Figure 5-8
Marcel Breuer. Stools, 1925–26, in Bauhaus canteen, Dessau. See CAT. NO. 68.

side chair (figure 5–7), the stool (figure 5–8), and multiple auditorium seating (figure 5–9).[14] Installed in the Bauhaus interiors they seemed more than the perfect complement to the building (figure 5–10); they completed, even expanded on, the ideas presented in this early and forceful example of the New Architecture. The geometric design and skeletal, transparent structure of the furniture, as well as the machine imagery of shiny metal, emphasized the modernity of the interiors and the factory aesthetic embodied by the "curtain wall" of glass and metal that serves as the exterior of the building.

Breuer's first tubular steel designs not only show a wide range of design ideas, but also reveal the speed with which his handling of the material progressed. The complex De Stijl formula of the club chair was quickly abandoned to the remarkable minimalist stool and the structurally daring auditorium seating. The stool was the first tubular steel design to provide the illusion of an object made from a single, continuous frame. This idea was to become one of the most persistent and pursued notions in tubular steel and many subsequent modern furniture designs. Both the stool with its minimal support structure and the auditorium chair with its cantilevered seat were testaments to the strength of bent tubular steel. The auditorium seating, though based on similar bent-wood forms of the nineteenth century, allowed for no structural support of the seat beyond resistance from the rear frame.

With his first series of tubular steel designs, Breuer established the formal basis for modern tubular-steel furniture. While he went on to create numerous other important and successful furniture designs—some, such as his B19 table for Thonet (cat. no. 77), are unsurpassed for their dynamic planar qualities—it was left for two architects, the Dutch Mart Stam and the German Ludwig Mies van der Rohe, to take the next step by designing the first freestanding cantilevered tubular-steel chairs.

Sitting on air: cantilevered chairs

A cantilevered chair may be defined as one in which the seat is supported only at one end, unlike traditionally conceived chairs, which are supported at both front and

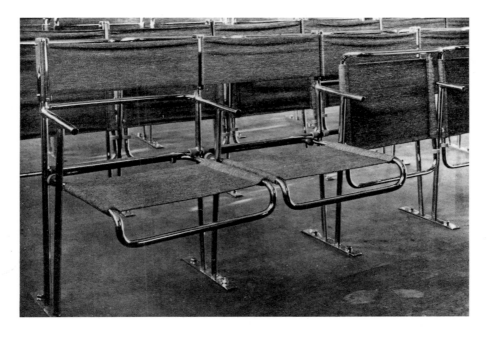

Figure 5-9
Marcel Breuer. Theater seating, 1925–26, in Bauhaus auditorium, Dessau. (From *Der Baumeister*, October 1928, p. B202).

Figure 5-10
Walter Gropius. Bauhaus, Dessau, 1925–26.

Figure 5–11

Mart Stam. Side chair and table, 1926–27. Manufactured by L. & C. Arnold GmbH, Schorndorf, Germany. (From Gräff, *Innenräume*, fig. 51).

back. Although often described as controversial or unresolved, the facts concerning the design of the first such modern chairs seem quite clear.[15] In 1926 the Dutch architect Mart Stam designed and built a cantilevered side chair made from pipes and pipe fittings; no photographs of the chair survive. During that same year, on November 22, at a meeting held in Stuttgart in preparation for the massive Deutsche Werkbund exhibition of modern architecture, *Die Wohnung* (The Dwelling), scheduled to open the next summer at the Weissenhofsiedlung, Stam made a drawing of his chair for, among others, architects Mies van der Rohe and Heinz Rasch.[16] By the time the exhibition opened in July 1927, Stam had contracted with the L. & C. Arnold Company of Schorndorf, Germany, to manufacture his cantilevered side chair (figure 5–11) as well as a lounge (figure 5–12) that was also exhibited at Weissenhof.[17] According to a court judgment the side chair was made of "lacquered, cast (non-resilient) steel tubing"; also, the interiors of the tubes were reinforced with solid rods. Thus, although cantilevered, the chair was not resilient.[18]

Inspired by Stam's drawing, Mies van der Rohe designed a cantilevered chair that was also exhibited at Weissenhof (figure 5–13).[19] Mies van der Rohe's chair, however, was made from thin, resilient, precision-steel tubing and was a design of such grace, elegance, and comfort that it eclipsed Stam's original, and remarkable, invention.

There are many other candidates for the title of originator of the modern tubular-steel cantilevered chair. Although Breuer himself did not produce a cantilevered chair until 1927 or 1928, he maintained that he was working on the idea in 1926 and had even discussed it at the time with Stam.[20] In a lawsuit brought in 1937 and revived in 1950, the Mauser Company of Waldeck claimed that Gerhard Stüttgen, a teacher at the Kölner Kunstgewerbeschule

Figure 5–12

Mart Stam. Lounge chair. 1927. (From Gräff, *Innenräume*, fig. 52).

(Cologne School of Arts and Crafts), had designed a chair in 1923 similar to Stam's; no original example of the chair existed to prove its date of origin, and the claim was disallowed.[21] Finally, the French designer Felix Del Marle declared in 1927 that he had been working on a series of cantilevered chairs—clearly derived from Mies van der Rohe's 1927 designs—since 1926; he did, however, feel uneasy enough about his claim to observe that he had worked "parallel" to Mies van der Rohe, Breuer, and Stam and that the similarities were attributable not to "plagiarism," but to the fact that all their work represented "a collective art."[22] The cantilevered chair, like tubular-steel furniture in general, hit a responsive chord so deep among designers, it allowed for apparently guiltless appropriation.[23]

From the moment the Stam and Mies van der Rohe chairs were shown at the Weissenhof exhibition and published in accompanying books, magazines, and newspapers, the question of whose design had come first became irrelevant to most contemporaries. As the Breuer Bauhaus furniture had first sparked a designer such as Stam, for example, to try his hand at tubular steel, so the new chairs exhibited in 1927 opened a wide world of possibilities.[24] The exhibition and publication of the canitilevered chairs so profoundly affected the avant-garde (and beyond) that hundreds of designers immediately took to their drafting boards to plan their own two-legged chairs.[25]

Few notions appealed more to modernist designers than that of the sitter floating in mid-air. It was implicit in the design of Breuer's first metal chair, partly realized in his Bauhaus auditorium seating, and fantasized in his "Bauhaus film, five years long. . . ." where a woman is pictured sitting comfortably upright in mid-air with no visible means

of support (figure 5–4); she demonstates the future when, the caption informs us, "We will sit on resilient air columns." Indeed, many modernist chairs, by Rietveld, Breuer, the Rasch brothers, and Aalto, emphasized a separately articulated, suspended or hung seat and back; but a true cantilevered chair—with its seat extending far beyond its visible structural support—eliminated the need to make the distinction between frame support and seat and back. The entire message was conveyed in the chair's innovative structure.

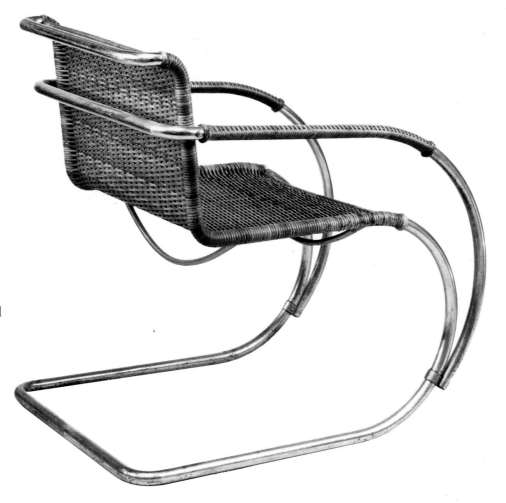

Figure 5–13
Ludwig Mies van der Rohe. Armchair, 1927. Tubular steel and caning. Collection Mr. and Mrs. Al Luckett, Jr., Boulder, Colorado. CAT. NO. **71.**

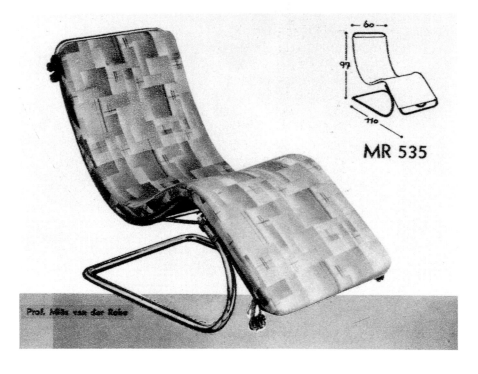

Figure 5-14
Ludwig Mies van der Rohe. Lounge chair, 1931. Model No. 535 in Thonet sales catalogue 3209, 1932.

MR 535

Figure 5-15
Ludwig Mies van der Rohe. Tugendhat chair, 1929–30. Chrome-plated steel bars and pigskin. The Museum of Modern Art, New York (Gift of Herbert Tugendhat, Caracas, and Knoll International).

The urge to appropriate whatever modern technology could offer as liberation from the traditional conventions of structure was a powerful one during the 1920s. The cantilevered chair boldly proclaimed the designer's triumph over a basic and age-old form: the four-legged chair. With a seat that seems to hang in mid-air, lacking all traditional means of support, the new chair flaunted the virtuosity of both designer and material, almost daring the spectator to sit.

For innovative modernist designers, however, the cantilever alone was not sufficient; it became essential that the new cantilevered chair also be resilient (the very point at which a designer such as Mies van der Rohe superseded the innovation of Mart Stam). A resilient seat—one that noticeably flexes under the weight of the sitter—was truly unprecedented in domestic seating.[26] Resiliency was entirely appropriate to the more informal way of life advocated during the twenties, and it fulfilled a practical requirement: since most modernist furniture had stripped away layers of upholstery to reveal pure structure, a resilient frame became a comfort-giving substitute for the cushions and springs of traditional upholstery.

Although the cantilevered chair was an expression of the designer's elimination of a traditional structure through the exploitation of the technical possibilities of a material only recently considered suitable for the production of furniture, it was also a powerful symbolic and aesthetic statement. Like tubular-steel furniture itself, the cantilevered chair stood as a symbol of the new architectural order, a sign of the revolutionary intent of the new design. It reordered the conventions of furniture design and interior space while conveying a visual image—of floating or suspended structure—as powerful, but more immediate and accessible, than that provided by the few extant modernist buildings.

Varieties of form

The range of expression within the category of cantilevered chairs was wide and varied. Stam's simple, rectilinear side chair (figure 5–11) spawned Mies van der Rohe's seemingly effortless exercises in curvilinear form (figure 5–13), the first of which were shown at the Weissenhof exhibition.

Figure 5-16
**Ludwig Mies van der Rohe. Brno chair,
1929–30. Stainless steel bars and leather.
Collection Mr. and Mrs. Al Luckett,
Jr., Boulder, Colorado.** CAT. NO. **84.**

These were just the beginning for Mies van der Rohe.
During the course of the next seven years (1927–34), he
designed at least two dozen cantilevered chairs in metal
and wood, eight of which were produced. They ranged
from mass-produced chairs eventually manufactured by
Thonet—including the structurally daring MR 535 (figure
5–14)—to custom-made (and expensive) designs such as
the cantilevered Tugendhat and Brno chairs (figures 5–15
and 5–16) made of flat bars of heavy steel. Actually, the
chairs of Mies van der Rohe, whose graceful and pure
designs bespoke the Platonic objectivity of form he
claimed for his work, stood apart from most bent-metal
furniture of the period, cantilevered or not. While his
chairs were, in fact, no more "objective" than any other
designer's work, his sensitive and refined attention to
form, proportion, and geometry—qualities that did not
carry over to his many unexecuted bent-wood designs
(figures 5–60 and 5–61)— resulted in chairs that were, as
formal statements, concise, direct, and unsurpassed for
pure beauty.

Certain designers carried the idea of the cantilever
beyond the seat and into more complex forms, at times
to new levels of invention, occasionally to decorative
excess. Breuer's so-called Cesca side chair (Thonet model
B32; figure 5–17) represented a symbolic and literal marriage of the tradition of bent wood with the new bent-
metal furniture. His first metal furniture (figures 5–5, 7, 8,
9) had referred to bent wood through the round section
of the material as well as the bending process used for

Figure 5-17
**Marcel Breuer. Side chair ("Cesca"), 1928.
Tubular steel, wood, and cane. Model No.
B32 in Thonet sales catalogue, ca. 1930. See**
CAT. NO. **72.**

B 64
Thonet

Figure 5-18
Marcel Breuer. Armchair, 1928. Model No. B64 in Thonet sales catalogue, ca. 1930.

B 55
Thonet

Figure 5-19
Marcel Breuer. Side chair, 1928. Model No. B55 in Thonet sales catalogue, ca. 1930.

manufacture. In the B32 chair Breuer became the first designer to use wood and cane in a bent tubular-steel chair. The kinship with bent wood was proclaimed in a sophisticated, thoroughly realized chair that would come closer to fulfilling Breuer's dream of "styleless" furniture than any other design.

The Cesca transformed the vocabulary of modern tubular steel by introducing a non-continuous frame on a cantilevered chair, a back support curved or bent on the vertical plane, as well as the soft curves and warm color and feel of wood. In model B64, the armchair version (figure 5–18), Breuer worked out one of the more difficult problems in modern furniture: how to join horizontal arms to a vertical frame in a continuous design. Rather than merely join the arms to the stiles with welds or screws, as Mies van der Rohe would later do in his Tugendhat chairs (figure 5–15), Breuer made them a continuation of the frame; the transition from back to arm, from horizontal to vertical plane, is carried out with great assuredness and control. The result was a design in which the cantilever was doubly emphasized by the repeated parallels of arms and seat.

As Breuer continued to work on this concept—whose resolution eluded many other designers—he arrived at various possibilities. The uncharacteristic but exuberant curve employed in the B55 chair (figure 5–19) required the addition of a separate, rectangular back unit. The cantilevered planes were emphasized, but the new note of the curve, a half-circle attached to the back of the chair, became a distinctive element in its own right, perhaps one reason why the chair was not a particularly popular one in modernist interiors.

The B35 lounge chair (figure 5–20), one of Breuer's most under-appreciated but satisfying designs, represented a mature solution to the problem of designing a comfortable, low club armchair. Breuer's first response had been his complicated Wassily chair, which appears almost naïve,

or hopelessly aesthetic, when compared with the B35, whose beauty was matched by few chairs of this period. Whereas the occupant of the chair might focus on the long lines of the horizontal arms and see them as an echo of the lines of the seat, to the observer the most remarkable aspect of the design is the opposition of the two cantilevers: the seat coming from the front of the chair, the arms emerging from the rear. The horizontals of the arms parallel the lines of the seat that rises between them, which in photographs often creates the illusion that they are, perhaps, attached at the intersection.

Occasionally the cantilever became the basis for daringly simplified attempts. The frame of Hans and Wassili Luckhardt's side chair of 1931 (figure 5–21) is, in side elevation, reduced to a sweeping diagonal line that curves to join the horizontal base. The top of the frame represents a cantilevered form from which the delicately shaped and molded plywood seat is tenuously suspended—another example of a cantilever within a cantilever. This unusual chair represented an attempt to escape from the conventional geometry, whether rectilinear or curvilinear, of the best-known "first-generation" chairs of Breuer, Stam, and Mies van der Rohe. Other such attempts were not as successful.

A category of tubular-steel chairs, labeled "steel macaroni monsters" by Mart Stam, was produced by such well-known designers as Erich Dieckmann (figure 5–22), André Lurçat, Jean Burkhalter, and the brothers Heinz and Bodo Rasch, as well as legions of anonymous company designers throughout Europe, especially in Holland (figure 5–23).[27] Rather than search for a way to minimize chair structure, these designers concentrated on finding novel ways of working with tubular steel as well as expressing the cantilever. The results were nervous exercises in overcomplication, completely at odds with the intent of the first-generation designers.

From one end of Europe to the other, designers experimented with cantilevered forms. In Finland, Alvar Aalto began his search for an appropriately modern furniture by combining metal and wood in cantilevered chairs (figure 5–49), which eventually led to the more satisfactory vocabulary of all-wood cantilevered chairs. In a little-known armchair produced by the Czechoslovakian firm D. G.

Figure 5-20
Marcel Breuer. Lounge chair, 1928–29. Tubular steel, wood, *Eisengarn*. Model No. B35 in Thonet sales catalogue, ca. 1930. Barry Freidman Ltd., New York. CAT. NO. 78.

Figure 5-21
Hans and Wassili Luckhardt. Side chair, 1931. Tubular steel and wood. Desta model ST14. Alexander von Vegesack, Düsseldorf. CAT. NO. 85.

Figure 5-22
Erich Dieckmann. Side chair and table, 1931. Manufactured by Carl Beck & Alfred Schulze AG, Ohrdruf, Thuringia, Germany. (From Dieckmann, *Möbelbau*, fig. 104).

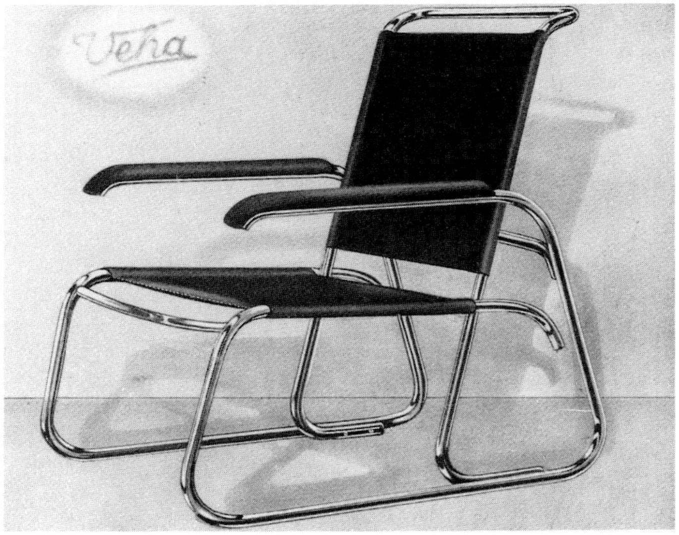

Figure 5-23
Armchair, 1933. Model No. AF2 in J. V. van Heijst & Zonen sales catalogue *Veha Stalen Buis Meubelen*, The Hague, Netherlands.

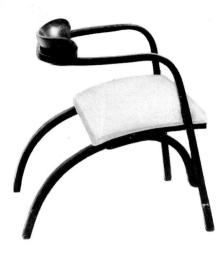

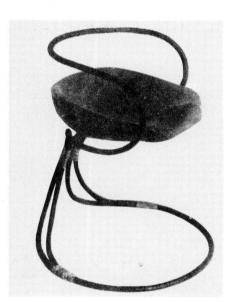

Figure 5-24
Armchair, ca. 1929. Bent solid wood and upholstery. Manufactured by D. G. Fischel Söhne, Vienna. Collection Theo Stachels, Munich. CAT. NO. **95.**

Fischel (figure 5–24), an anonymous designer employed the cantilever principle in the back of a chair but was unable to produce a solid, cantilevered base, for bent wood technology was not sufficiently advanced at that time.[28] This designer, like many Western Europeans, was probably unaware of Vladimir Tatlin's experimental bent-wood cantilevered chair (figure 5–25), described by its designer as a "Viennese bent-wood chair." Its completely curvilinear form was very different from the rectilinear geometry of most first-generation tubular-steel chairs and far closer to traditional bent wood in spirit. Though potentially of importance for the European scene, this chair was apparently not even published in Russia until 1929.[29] Despite the extensive contact between artists in Moscow and Berlin, the chair did not appear in any of the well-known German, French, or Dutch publications of the period and, more to the point, was not included in the many international design exhibitions of the late 1920s and early 1930s.

Figure 5-26
Eileen Gray. Adjustable occasional table, designed 1927. Chrome-plated tubular steel and painted sheet steel. Manufactured 1977. The Museum of Modern Art, New York (Philip Johnson Fund and Aram Designs, Ltd., London).

Finally, there were designs for other types of furniture in which the structural cantilever was used for functional purposes as well as aesthetic reasons. Eileen Gray's adjustable occasional table (figure 5–26), whose design was probably inspired by a hospital table, had a cantilevered top which made it possible to fit it around a chair or bed. Yet the metal-framed glass top supported on only one side was also unmistakably an attempt to create a new aesthetic dimension in a cantilever design.

A necessary apparatus for modern life

Modern tubular-steel furniture occupied a unique place in the history of bent-metal and bent-wood furniture. Rarely in the history of the decorative arts had a type of furniture been as bound up in the closely interrelated aesthetic, social, and political issues of its day. Bent-metal furniture played a role in the design culture of the 1920s and 1930s that was never equaled by traditional bent laminated or the then-contemporary bent solid furniture, or even by the later bent plywood furniture of Alvar Aalto. While it is possible to see the development of modern tubular-steel furniture in terms of technical accomplishment, as the result of improved methods of steel production, metal plating, and welding (figures 5–27, 28, 29, 30), these techniques were crucial factors in the dissemination of the new furniture to a wide market, but not instrumental in the genesis of the first tubular steel designs.[30] Above all, tubular-steel furniture found its roots in the brave new world of modern art and architecture and the modernist preoccupation with the idea and image of the machine.

Figure 5-27

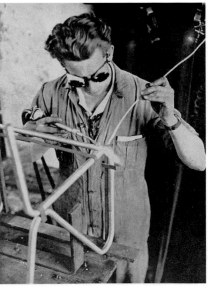

Figure 5-29

Figure 5-28

Figure 5-30

Figure 5-27, 28
Production of tubular-steel furniture, at the factory of Carl Beck & Alfred Schulze AG, Ohrdruf, Thuringia, Germany. (From Dieckmann, *Möbelbau*, figs. 99, 100).

Figure 5-29, 30
Gispen's Fabriek voor Metaalbewerking N.V., Rotterdam. *Above*: Manufacture of armchair, Model 203 (formerly Model No. 3); *near left*: Workers demonstrating strength of tubular steel on table Model No. 515. (From *Metalen Meubels, Gispen Cat. No. 52*, ca. 1933–34).

Figure 5-31.
Aerial veiw of Weissenhofsiedlung, site of the Deutsche Werkbund exhibition *Die Wohnung*, Stuttgart, 1927.

If the new modernist architecture of the twenties (figure 5-31) may be characterized in purely formal terms—as it was in 1932 by Henry Russell-Hitchcock and Philip Johnson—as a skeletal support structure that eliminates the "effect of mass," is covered with the latest, smooth surfacing materials, expresses an "orderliness" (rather than disorderliness) of structure by using similar if not standardized parts that emphasize an underlying regularity, avoids applied decoration of any kind, and allows careful detailing to substitute for decoration, then tubular-steel furniture fits the criteria of the International Style and must be seen as an important and entirely successful aspect of early modern architecture.[31]

Hitchcock and Johnson's delineation was, of course, incomplete. Their own criteria failed to account for all the work shown in both the Museum of Modern Art exhibition and the subsequent book, and they intentionally ignored the important social and political agenda of many of the German and Dutch designers. And, despite their formalist perspective, the two advocate-critics joined with many of the architects they wrote about and glossed

over two points of paramount importance to early modern designers: the contemporary interest in—one might say "obsession" with—pure geometric form and the profound desire to infuse their work with the spirit of the modern machine. These very architects transferred these same concerns to their new chairs and tables.

Tubular-steel furniture embodied the notion of the machine as technical savior and artistic fountainhead. The carnage of World War I and the immediate post-war years of economic inflation, political violence, and disease, led to the search for practical solutions and spiritual salvation.[32] When reconstruction and industrial reorganization actually began in the twenties, the promise of technology seemed to offer the one true hope for the future. Throughout Europe, but in Germany and Russia especially, belief in the anonymous, impersonal machine, symbol of what was often described as a new, collective (rather than individual) impulse, found all manner of artistic expression. Following on the heels of the earlier Futurist example, Léger painted abstractions of machines and machine parts; Moholy-Nagy, through the use of standarized, printed grids, dictated his selection of colors for paintings over the telephone to a wholesale paint supplier, who then arranged for the execution of these "telephone paintings," which did not require the artist's hand; Marcel l'Herbier's film *L'Inhumaine* showed the awesome power, and beauty, of the machine as abstract dynamo; Walter Gropius, director of the Bauhaus, proclaimed the machine to be "our modern medium of design";[33] and Le Corbusier declared, "We must look upon the house as a machine for living in."[34]

For many Europeans, the powerful potentials of the machine were being realized in what was considered the exemplary industrial culture of America, a country highly praised, if not actually visited, by many European architects. The cult of "Americanism" swept Europe. While the Germans turned the autobiography of Henry Ford, who capitalized on the idea of the assembly line, into a bestseller, the French writer Emile Malespine asserted:

The industrial class has just discovered America—
Business, Dollars, Trusts, Taylorization,
Standadrization [sic], Superproduction,
Organization, etc. etc.
The poets have just discovered America—
skyscrapers, 5th Avenue, My Darling Chicago, New
York, Los Angeles, Superfilm, Indian Chief
Cinematography, Browning, Automobile, Telefone . . .[35]

For the poets of structure and space who created the modern interior, an appropriately modern furniture was required that evoked the machine to the same degree as Le Corbusier's architecture or Moholy-Nagy's paintings. Once that furniture was developed, Marcel Breuer could assert with great confidence that "metal furniture is intended to be nothing but a necessary apparatus for contemporary life."[36] At that moment, bent-wood furniture became a relic of an earlier and decidely past industrial age.

To many, tubular-steel furniture, like modern architecture, became the physical realization of a once imagined utopia. This view often set the new furniture into a political context, as it did with much contemporary architecture and design. Radically new and revolutionary, tubular steel was frequently perceived as an element of the left-wing ideology that was such an important part of early modernism in Europe. The new architecture and design, it was hoped, would alter the domestic landscape as profoundly as revolutionary politics would change the contours of the political arena. Thus the aesthetic imagery of gleaming metal merged with dreams of a utopian modernism in which all citizens would be provided with well-designed, affordable, boldly novel furniture. The irony was that tubular steel was by no means the cheapest possible furniture for a classless society of workers. Although arguably offering value in terms of its durability, steel furniture could never supplant low-cost wood furniture, nor could it challenge bent wood as a cheaper, modern alternative.[37] The expensive and elite nature of tubular-steel furniture was noted, perhaps not intentionally, by designer Erich Dieckmann when he referred to it as "an art product."[38]

Many designers working with tubular steel would undoubtedly have characterized the design of the new furniture as purely functional. The idea of functionalism—the design of an object derived wholly from the functions it was intended to fulfill—allowed designers to make grandiose claims for their work and thus become part of the new mythology of the purely functional, styleless art of the building technician, the engineer. Le Corbusier referred to furniture as "equipment," as if it were an element in an anonymous, technical problem: "We must look upon the house as a machine for living in, or as a tool . . . . Henceforth the problem [of house design] is in the hands of the technical expert."[39] Since most designers regarded furniture as simply a part of architectural design, most of their rhetoric was devoted to architecture. But when Mart Stam wrote, "What is important are the functions, and these should dictate the form," he was surely writing about all aspects of design, of furniture as much as of architecture.[40] Le Corbusier repeated his version of the functionalist argument when he asserted, "The scientific study of chairs and tables has, in turn, led to entirely new conceptions of what their form should be: a form which is no longer decorative but purely functional."[41] All the first-generation tubular steel designers claimed, as Mies van der Rohe did, that "Form is not the aim of our work, but only the result."[42] Interest in form—in retrospect an obvious and seminal aspect of the new metal furniture—was steadfastly denied in order to establish a concept of

Figure 5-32.
Le Corbusier and Pierre Jeanneret. Interior, Villa Church, Ville d'Avray, 1929. Furniture by Le Corbusier-Jeanneret-Perriand. *From left:* **Chaise longue B306, 1928 (see CAT. NO. 76); Grand Confort, large version, 1928; Siège à dossier basculant (Armchair with pivoting back) B301, 1928 (see CAT. NO. 75).**

Figure 5-33.
Le Corbusier-Jeanneret-Perriand. Model one-room house, Salon d'Automne, 1929. *Around table:* **Revolving chair B302, 1929;** *center:* ***Siège à dossier basculant* (Armchair with pivoting back) B301, 1928 (see CAT. NO. 75);** *right:* **Grand Confort, small version, 1928.**

an object devoid of the artist's hand, as if the new furniture were truly the product of an anonymous modern-day technician.

The functional aspects of tubular-steel furniture were spelled out in greatest detail by its most important designer and advocate, Marcel Breuer. He described the new metal furniture as being comfortable, lightweight and mobile, sanitary—i.e., easy to clean and not dust-attracting[43]—durable, visually transparent, made from "standardized elementary parts," and mass produced.[44] Above all, it reiterated the formal and structural qualities of the new architecture, thereby becoming the only suitable furniture for the new interior.

Design in France

The emphasis on the social meaning and value of the new modernist furniture was by no means universal. Beyond the atelier of Le Corbusier and a few other individuals, most designers in France who produced furniture of aesthetic merit were interested neither in fomenting revolution nor in dictating what was the only appropriate furniture for modern life. Instead, they designed stylishly modern furniture intended for an elite, fashion-conscious audience unconcerned with questions of ideology. The most important French bent metal designs of the period were, however, created by designers who were vitally interested in establishing which furniture was essential for the modern interior, namely, Le Corbusier, Pierre Jeanneret, and Charlotte Perriand.

Le Corbusier's central position as an architect and as theorist of the modern movement is unquestioned. The breadth of thought and artistic invention he brought to architecture was paralleled only in certain ways by the furniture that he began designing after the young Perriand joined his office in 1927 (figures 5-32 and 5-33). For Le Corbusier and his collaborators, "a chair is in no way a work of art; a chair has no soul; it is a machine for sitting in."[45] Accordingly, the mechanistic imagery of shiny metal and geometric forms predominated. Unlike many of their German, Dutch, and Eastern European counterparts, the French trio did not truly combine an interest in aesthetics with social questions or even with problems of mass production. In his architecture Le Corbusier promoted the idea of mass-produced concrete housing; in furniture he paid only lip service to the notion of inexpensive design. All of the Le Corbusier-Jeanneret-Perriand furniture was extremely costly to produce. Simple bending techniques were eschewed in favor of more complicated constructions that required extensive cutting and welding of tubular steel. Yet, while they did not live up to the designers' rhetoric, the designs were distinguished by artistic inventiveness and formal innovation.[46]

The chair known as the "Grand Confort" (figures 5–32 and 5–33) is a monumental cube raised on a set of short supporting legs that recall the freestanding piers (*pilotis*) of the architect's buildings. Beyond the form of the overall cube, the relationship between frame and cushions was skillfully and cleverly handled. Instead of designing a large club armchair that dispensed with upholstery—as Breuer and subsequent designers had done—the French designers retained all the stuffing, but reversed the traditional relationship between frame and upholstery by placing the frame *over* the cushions. They contrasted the hard, taut, skeletal exterior cube of the frame with the massive but soft, separate elements of its interior.

Reminiscent of Thonet's rocking chaise with an adjustable back (cat. no. 33), the tubular-steel chaise longue B306 by Le Corbusier-Jeanneret-Perriand (cat. no. 76) was probably the most machine-like in appearance of their many designs. Although its configuration suggests that a crank might be necessary to adjust the angle of the tubular-steel frame, this element in fact rests upon a stationary base, unlike the nineteenth-century predecessor, which is a true rocker that moves with each shift of balance. The H-shaped metal stretchers of the B306 base recall the aerodynamic design of an airplane wing. Though perhaps fulfilling the designers' stated desire for machine-like "equipment," the chair combined both art and artifice. Like much subsequent French metal furniture, although it was mechanical in spirit, in reality its elaborate constructional devices were totally unsuited to the truth of the machine: mass production.

The first-generation German tubular-steel furniture of Breuer, Stam, and Mies van der Rohe had been admired by a highly specialized group of architects and wealthy consumers in France. The fact that Le Corbusier, Jeanneret,

and Perriand—France's leading and most controversial modernists—designed metal furniture helped legitimize the material in that country. However, most fashionable Parisian designers, such as René Herbst (cat. no. 79), Louis Sognot (cat. no. 80), and Djo Bourgeois, rejected the cool, austere functionalism of German furniture as well as its intellectual baggage, preferring instead a richer, more decorative approach that resulted in a wide variety of forms, surface effects, and detail.

Equally significant was the post–World War I legacy of intense French nationalism that was combined with distinct anti-German feeling among many Frenchmen. This was responsible not only for the ban on German participation in the Exposition des Arts Décoratifs held in Paris in 1925, but also for the continuation of that prohibition policy until 1930. In that year the Deutsche Werkbund—an association of designers and industrialists devoted to promoting German design—presented a pavilion at the Salon des Artistes Décorateurs in Paris that included the bent-wood and metal furniture of Breuer, Mies van der Rohe, Adolf Schneck, and other designers (figure 5–34). At the same time, Thonet Frères, the French branch of the Thonet firm, expanded its operations, becoming semi-autonomous and commissioning and manufacturing tubular-steel models created by French designers. The result of all this activity was that large numbers of French designers experimented with various types of bent-metal furniture after 1928, although many did not do so until 1930 and later.

Most bent-metal furniture designed in France was designed by French modernists eventually associated with the Unions des Artistes Modernes (Union of Modern Artists), founded in 1929 partially in reaction to the fashionable decorative furniture—now termed Art Deco —exhibited not only at the annual Salon des Artistes Décorateurs or Salon d'Automne, but also in the shops of individual designers and the specialized design departments of the major Paris department stores.[47] In addition to Le Corbusier, Jeanneret, and Perriand, the most prominent figures, there were the designers Pierre Chareau, René Herbst, and Robert Mallet-Stevens (see cat. no. 93). Others who exhibited bent-metal furniture included Djo Bourgeois, Louis Sognot, Jean Prouvé, Jean Burkhalter, and Marcel Gascoin.

Figure 5-34.
Deutsche Werkbund exhibit, Salon des Artistes Décorateurs, Paris, 1930.

Figure 5-35.
Pierre Chareau. Desk, ca. 1930. Bent flat iron, sheet iron, veneered plywood. Sale, Sotheby's, Monaco, March 17, 1985, lot 233.

Certain French designers adopted the vocabulary of first-generation tubular steel: chrome- or nickel-plated steel tubing designed in simple geometric shapes, with minimal upholstery added for support. Pierre Chareau attempted to go beyond these conventions and employed metal in new and different ways.[48] His mechanical-looking desks (figure 5-35), made from bent iron strips and wood and finished in a variety of different materials, were elaborate artistic designs that emphasized the decorative possibilities of construction: functional screws appeared as rivets joining metal to metal or metal to wood; shelves and drawers floated or pivoted in hinged or cantilevered arrangements, often both; and a skeletal structure became the basis for the entire design. The result of the whole was a form as evocative of a machine aesthetic as any other modern German or French furniture of the period.

René Herbst, whose metal furniture was produced by his own firm, designed tubular- and flat-metal furniture of varying types.[49] All his furniture was of complicated construction, requiring substantial welding and upholstery systems (figure 5-36). His more abstract furniture employed tubular-steel frames with seats and backs variously composed of pliant stringing, fabric, or metal sheeting. While Chareau's work in metal always managed to give an industrial appearance to sophisticated forms, Herbst took the industrial aesthetic of tubular steel and created designs that emphasized elegance and decorative possibilities, rather than the structural rationalism of metal.

Despite the acceptance of tubular steel by some segments of the design profession in France, metal furniture never gained as wide an audience there as it did in Germany or Holland. Although rarely expressed directly, many saw tubular steel as a distinctly German phenomenon, hence, as antithetical to the elitist traditions of France. Although the Thonet firm managed to take on a French identity during the period by producing the work of many French designers, and many other French firms were founded,

Figure 5-36.
René Herbst. Armchair, ca. 1928. (From *Art et Décoration,* **June 1928, p. 172).**

there was persistent resistance to a type of furniture that was perceived as violating standards of taste and propriety. These objections were not unique to France; English critics were particularly offended by the use of metal furniture in the home. And when Maurice Dufrène, one of France's leading designers, founder and director of the important design studio of the department store Galeries Lafayette, and editor of many books on French design, criticized metal furniture, he referred not to German furniture, but to the "same chair, mechanical and tubular [that] is to be found in almost every country. . . . It is the anonymous, neutral, universal chair . . . the root cause of the great Dullness."[50]

The demise of tubular steel furniture

Although tubular-steel furniture was designed and produced in ever-increasing numbers through the late thirties, the originality and inventiveness of design had largely ended by the early years of the decade. Once the major figures had turned to other materials—bands of flat steel, aluminum, or plywood—tubular steel became, with very few exceptions, the last refuge of the uninspired.

Unlike the innovative form-givers of the 1920s, the designers of the mid-thirties using tubular steel strove in vain to find or fabricate forms or types that had not already been exploited. Designers and manufacturers with varying motives turned out hundreds, if not thousands, of new designs; some were interested in discovering new ways of handling this thoroughly modern material, most merely sought novelty and the attention of the marketplace. The predictable results were endless versions of certain Breuer and Mies van der Rohe models, tubular-steel barber chairs (figure 5–37), and contorted efforts to expand the range of bent metal designs (figure 5–38). With rare exceptions, the wheel was reinvented again and again.[51] At the same time, tubular-steel furniture was disseminated to a wider world market, with manufacturers and native designers establishing themselves in Scandinavia, England (figure 5–39), the United States, and even Japan. The results, however, were generally derivative and mediocre.

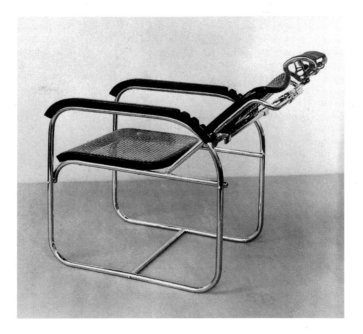

Figure 5–37.
Barber chair, ca. 1932. Thonet Model No. B78.

Figure 5–38.
Vanity, mid-1930s. Manufactured by Fordisk Staalmobel Central, Copenhagen.

Figure 5–39.
Bed. Model No. B4 in *Furniture by PEL*, catalogue of PEL Ltd., London, 1939.

Figure 5-41.
Hans Coray. Armchair, 1938. Aluminum. Manufactured by P. & W. Blattmann, Wädenswil, Switzerland. Victoria & Albert Museum, London.

Figure 5-40.
Marcel Breuer. Armchair and side chairs, 1932-33. Model No. 303 in Wohnbedarf catalogue *Das federnde Aluminium*. See CAT. NO. 90.

The most successful bent-metal furniture of the mid-thirties was created by Marcel Breuer, whose designs for band steel and aluminum (figure 5-40) were to have been produced by manufacturers throughout Europe,[52] although they served more as a conclusion to his work in metal than as the beginning of a new path. A notable molded aluminum chair was produced in 1938 by Swiss designer Hans Coray and manufactured by the firm of P. & W. Blattmann (figure 5-41). The bent and molded perforated aluminum seat carried by a pair of thin, bent legs, splayed to the bottom to allow for stacking,[53] looked forward to the bent plywood shells of Charles Eames and Eero Saarinen. Though an interesting design, it was essentially an example of outdoor furniture with no aspirations toward a domestic setting. Few other designers produced new types of bent-metal furniture of merit until the bent and molded-wire furniture of Harry Bertoia and Eames. Both Mart Stam and Mies van der Rohe patented various bent metal designs, but none were produced.

By the early thirties the design possibilities of bent-metal furniture in Germany seemed to have been exhausted. Accompanying this decline was the emergence of a profoundly reactionary mentality fostered by the rise of the National Socialist (Nazi) Party, which viewed the development of tubular-steel furniture as a parallel to the art, theater, and literature they deemed "degenerate."

While many Europeans struggled to devise new metal designs, the Finnish architect Alvar Aalto was never comfortable with this medium. He experimented with the material, but quickly gave it up. It was the ingenuity of Aalto's designs that signaled the alternative direction to tubular steel: plywood. But these were created when the bent wood industry began to take advantage of the new interest in architect-designed furniture and adopted a new marketing approach to revitalize its business: for the first time in modern history, the names of furniture designers were used to sell the furniture.[54]

Bending wood

The rise of tubular-steel furniture during the 1920s was accompanied by the continued success of bent-wood furniture of various types. In addition to the popular nineteenth-century bent-wood furniture still in production during the twenties and thirties, two other categories of wooden furniture were manufactured that used some type of bending technique. The first, and least innovative in aesthetic terms, was traditionally constructed bent-wood furniture designed by in-house designer-stylists or well-known architects and designers working on a freelance or contract basis. The second and far more fruitful type was furniture made of laminated wood and plywood bent and molded in narrow lengths or large sheets, often a combination of both. The most significant achievements in this field were those of Alvar Aalto and Charles and Ray Eames.

Traditional bent wood

In an effort to revive the bent wood industry, which had been ravaged by the effects of World War I, the conglomerate Thonet-Kohn-Mundus (created in 1922), followed by many smaller bent wood companies, attempted to modernize and update its furniture line to include "modern" versions of traditional bent-wood pieces. Between 1927 and 1930, furniture by such known architects as Ferdinand Kramer, Josef Frank, Josef Hoffmann, and, above all, Adolf Schneck, as well as work by many designers whose names remain unknown, was manufactured in large quantity.[55]

In its attempt to follow the traditional style and production methods of nineteenth-century bent wood, this furniture, mainly chairs, represented a modern, yet conservative and acceptable, mode of design. Some pieces, such as the famous Thonet model A811/1F (figure 5-42), the work of either Josef Frank or Josef Hoffmann, were indeed modern equivalents, not imitations, of nineteenth-century bent wood, which reflect the twentieth-century emphasis on geometric, usually rectilinear, form, tempered only by the curves required for bent-wood production. In the case of the A811/1F the geometry of turn-of-the-century Viennese furniture was also evoked.

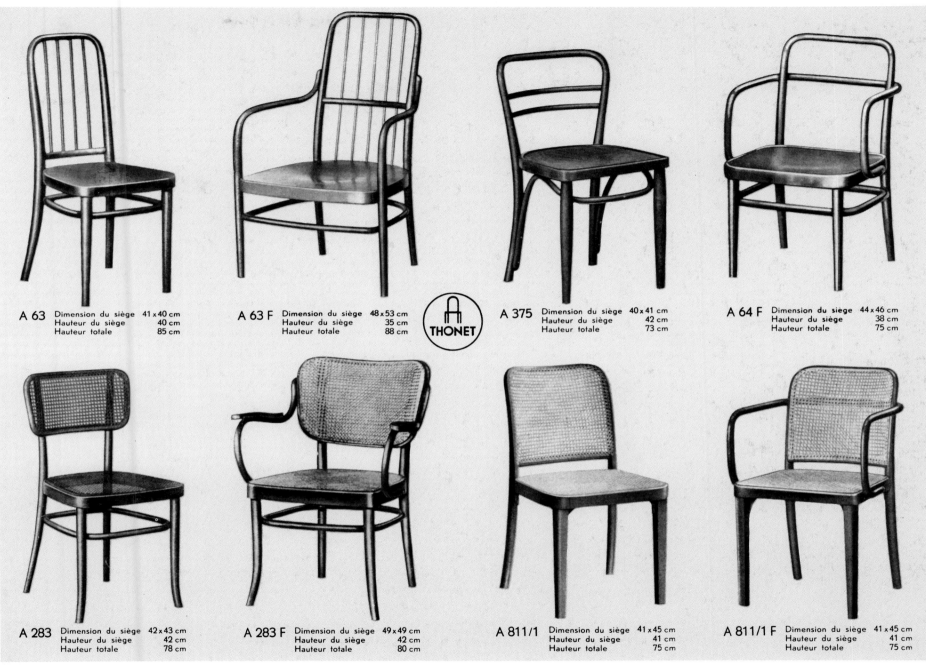

A 63   Dimension du siège   41×40 cm
        Hauteur du siège   40 cm
        Hauteur totale   85 cm

A 63 F   Dimension du siège   48×53 cm
         Hauteur du siège   35 cm
         Hauteur totale   88 cm

THONET

A 375   Dimension du siège   40×41 cm
        Hauteur du siège   42 cm
        Hauteur totale   73 cm

A 64 F   Dimension du siège   44×46 cm
         Hauteur du siège   38 cm
         Hauteur totale   75 cm

A 283   Dimension du siège   42×43 cm
        Hauteur du siège   42 cm
        Hauteur totale   78 cm

A 283 F   Dimension du siège   49×49 cm
         Hauteur du siège   42 cm
         Hauteur totale   80 cm

A 811/1   Dimension du siège   41×45 cm
         Hauteur du siège   41 cm
         Hauteur totale   75 cm

A 811/1 F   Dimension du siège   41×45 cm
         Hauteur du siège   41 cm
         Hauteur totale   75 cm

Figure 5–42.
Architect-designed bent-wood chairs. Page in Thonet catalogue 3308, 1933. See CAT. NO. **96.**

A 781 ³/₄
(39 × 36 cm)

A 780
(41 cm ø)

A 788 ³/₄
(39 × 36 cm)

A 786 ³/₄
(39 × 36 cm)

A 391
(41 × 40 cm)

A 738
(41 × 40 cm)

A 739 L 4.
(41 × 40 cm)

A 64
(41 × 40 cm)

Figure 5–43.
**Company-designed bent-wood chairs.
Composite of two pages in Thonet-
Mundus catalogue, ca. 1928–30.**

The simpler bent wood designs (figure 5–43), often the work of company designers, were closer to true functionalism and admirably fulfilled the modern movement's quest for anonymously designed, inexpensive furniture. Some of these chairs are quite interesting, although most do little more than modify or vaguely update familiar designs of the past. While providing well-made furniture at a low price for a mass market—no small accomplishment—these productions did not break new aesthetic ground.

An indication of the lack of vitality in the designs of traditionally made bent-wood furniture is provided by the competition sponsored by the Thonet-Mundus company in 1930 to celebrate its hundredth anniversary. Despite an extraordinary number of entries—no less than four thousand—the results were an unmitigated disaster. According to the jury, made up of notables in the international architectural community, there was "no outstanding entry," and architect Ferdinand Kramer proclaimed that the "Vienna chair festival was over."[56]

Modern bent plywood before Aalto

Although many types of plywood furniture existed before Alvar Aalto turned to the material around 1929, his designs became so well known and influential that they largely eclipsed other contemporary experiments with laminated wood (as, for example, figures 5–45, 46, 47, 48).[57] Much plywood furniture was produced during the 1920s; though neither as influential nor as aesthetically or technically innovative as Aalto's, it is today unjustifiably little known.

Prior to World War I, plywood was on the whole used for purely economic reasons, as a cheap substitute for solid wood.[58] Its most common applications were as a crating material, especially for tea chests in the United Kingdom, then the largest consumer of plywood in the world. In the furniture industry it was usually employed in parts that are rarely seen, such as drawer interiors or the backs of case pieces. After 1914, plywood was pressed into military service in the construction of airplanes, boats, and eventually airships, which rapidly advanced production techniques and brought plywood to the fore as a structural material in its own right. Nonetheless, plywood was still

Figure 5-44.
Heinz and Bodo Rasch. Side chair, 1927.

perceived as a commercial material and was not commonly available in small European lumberyards.[59]

After the war many avant-garde furniture designers experimented with the material, in both bent and non-bent forms. In addition to its presence in designs of 1900–1914, plywood was used by Gerrit Rietveld in his famous red-and-blue armchair of circa 1918 (figure 5–6) and by Breuer in the hand-crafted case furniture he made at the Bauhaus around 1922–23. Two major exhibitions of the twenties, both held in Stuttgart—the massive *Die Wohnung* (The Dwelling) of 1927 and *Der Stuhl* (The Chair) of the following year, both sponsored by the Deutsche Werkbund—presented many plywood chairs that pre-date Aalto's furniture.[60] Ranging from American and German traditional office furniture to brand-new architects' designs for the home, the pieces shown at these exhibitions indicate the wide variety of types of plywood furniture in existence during the twenties.

Among the furniture shown at both Stuttgart exhibitions were numerous chairs, beds, and case pieces, all employing plywood, designed by the Rasch brothers, Heinz, an architect, and Bodo, a cabinetmaker.[61] Their furniture demonstrated a concerted attempt to attack the technical problems of curved wooden surfaces. A side chair made of both laminated and solid wood (figure 5–44) and lounge chair made of plywood and tubular steel (figure 5–45) are among their most interesting pieces. The form of the side chair could be interpreted as an abstracted diagram of the structural stresses occurring in the chair. While the use of laminated wood was limited to spanning the solid wood supports on the front and back surfaces, the chair's design hints at an unrealized structure of thicker ply. The plywood and tubular-steel lounge chair is a remarkable design. Although the chair would have been covered with large cushions, the design shows an inventive use of a single sheet of plywood for seat and back. The seat is screwed to and visually hangs within the steel frame, while the curve of one echoes, in reverse, the shape of the other.

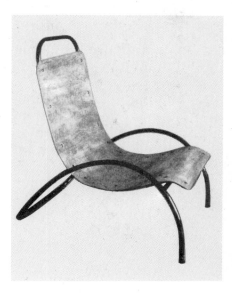

Figure 5-45.
Heinz and Bodo Rasch. Lounge chair, 1927. Manufactured by L. & C. Arnold GmbH, Schorndorf, Germany. (From Gräff, *Innenräume*, fig. 42.).

Figure 5–46
Gerrit Rietveld. Armchair, ca. 1927. Bent plywood and steel rod. CAT. NO. **73. Mr. and Mrs. Al Luckett, Boulder, Colorado.**

In these same years, 1927 or 1928, the Dutch designer Gerrit Rietveld returned to plywood (figure 5–46). Like the Rasch brothers, Rietveld combined a solid steel frame with a single-piece plywood seat and back, which, while somewhat complicated, demonstrates a similar use of the single sheet of plywood seen in the Rasch design. In both the Rasch and Rietveld chairs, however, the plywood seat is secured to the metal frame by a series of screws and bolts, unlike Aalto's later chairs, in which the seating elements are suspended within the frame (cat. nos. 99–101). Accordingly, while the strength and flexibility of plywood was exploited, its resilience was not.[62]

A number of chairs were made at the Bauhaus constructed of bent plywood. The earliest known and technically most interesting is a side chair by Peer Bücking (figure 5–47), with a slightly bent plywood back and curved seat. The design takes advantage of the strength of plywood by introducing a pronounced curve at the front of the seat, thereby presumably offering a certain amount of resilience and comfort to the sitter.[63]

A Bauhaus chair that presaged Aalto, not in its use of a sheet of plywood for its seat, but through its simple frame made from four pieces of ply- or laminated wood, was Josef Albers's armchair of 1929 (figure 5–48).[64] Designed as a "knock-down" chair, it relied on the strength of its laminated legs and arms to support the seat and the weight of the sitter.[65]

Alvar Aalto

Among the thousands of entrants in the Thonet-Mundus competition of 1929 celebrating the Thonet firm's hundredth anniversary[66] was thirty-two-year-old Finnish architect Alvar Aalto.[67] Aalto had only recently abandoned the classicism of his earlier work and was now designing his first modernist—although uniquely Scandinavian—buildings and furniture. He submitted four chair and two table designs, which shared the fate of virtually all the other entries and were deemed by the jury as undeserving of recognition.[68]

Shortly afterward Aalto gave up traditional bent wood and turned instead to laminated wood and plywood made

Figure 5-47
Peer Bücking. Side chair, 1928.

Figure 5-48
**Josef Albers. Armchair, 1929. Laminated
wood, tubular steel, and upholstery.**

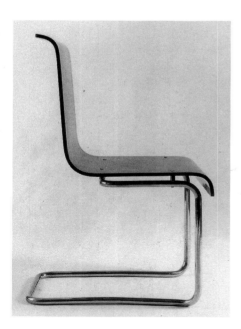

Figure 5-49
Alvar Aalto. Stacking side chair, 1930. Plywood and chrome-plated tubular steel. The Museum of Modern Art, New York (Lord & Taylor Fund).

of Finland's most abundant and popular wood: birch. Although a strong hardwood, birch is easy to cut and work. In its most common appearance it lacks prominent markings, such as grains, pores, or rings, and with its light color is a wood of subtle character. It proved a wise choice, providing Aalto with an ideal material for his new, largely plywood furniture.[69] Between 1929 and 1933, Aalto worked intensively on a number of designs, primarily chairs, which constitute one of the most important series of furniture designs of the modern period. They demonstrate the careful and consistent working-out of what Aalto must have considered the crucial technical, ergonomic, and aesthetic problems in laminated furniture.

Aalto's first widely recognized modernist chair was a combination plywood and tubular-steel cantilevered side chair (figure 5-49). Designed by 1930, it was based on several earlier designs, none of which was manufactured and only one of which (figure 5-50) was photographed.[70] The somewhat awkward design fits very much into the category of second-generation tubular-steel furniture, whose designers, still reeling from the startling originality of the first tubular-steel chairs, often blatantly imitated the work of Breuer, Stam, and Mies van der Rohe. Unsuccessful though it was, the chair proved important as Aalto's first mass-produced design with a single-piece plywood seat and back. It was probably this design that made him decide to give up tubular steel as a frame material and to turn instead to designs made entirely of the much more familiar and acceptable Finnish birch.[71]

It was when Aalto turned to chairs and stools with laminated wood frames and plywood seats and backs that he reached maturity as a furniture designer. Three designs in particular—the so-called Paimio lounge chair of 1931–32 (figure 5-51), the cantilevered armchair of 1931–32 (figure 5-52), and the famous stacking stool of 1933 (figure 5-53)—established Aalto as the major form-giver in the field of plywood furniture. As Michael Thonet's bent solid wood chairs owe much of their form to the bending technique, so Aalto's chairs derive much of their unique character from the undulating shapes and delicate lines provided by the bending and molding process.

The cantilevered armchair—tentatively dated to after

the Paimio chair but surely conceived of before—carried to their most elegant and successful conclusion the ideas first put forth in the tubular-steel and plywood side chair of 1930 (figure 5-49) as well as an experimental armchair version of the following year, in which the combination of tubular steel and plywood had not been satisfactory from an aesthetic point of view. There was nothing structurally wrong with the side chair design; the potential for stacking was both ingenious and surprisingly rare in the modernist design culture that emphasized the use of minimum space for living, but it presented a visually uncomfortable marriage of materials, in which Aalto had, in addition, been forced to fasten the wooden element to the tubular-steel frame by means of unsightly bolts that marred the smooth surface of the wood.

Whether Aalto abandoned the combination of wood and steel on moral and ideological grounds—his later explanation—or, instead, recognized the inharmoniousness of the solution—a more likely immediate reason—he was forced to experiment for some time before arriving at a structurally sound alternative for cantilevered support units to form base, legs, and arms. If it is true that the Paimio lounge chair was designed before the cantilevered chair—it was certainly produced earlier—then the reason for this must lie in the complexity of the construction required for the arm units.[72] Curiously, it was only when Aalto abandoned the cantilever in his Paimio chair that his furniture appeared to lose all reference to the formal precepts of early tubular steel design.[73]

The Paimio lounge chair (figure 5-51) was Aalto's most original and striking design. A continuous frame on each side, highly unconventional in form, carries the intricately shaped, suspended seat and back. The shape of the single-piece seat and back, a simple and uncomplicated curve in the earlier side chairs, is here curled into a form that is at once taut and fixed in a rigid shape while also implying flexibility through the delicate flow of its gently curving line. There is a curious tension between the static form of the chair's non-cantilevered design and the obvious desire for resilience in the open but continuous forms of the narrow frame and suspended, floating seat.

Through its unusual shapes, the Paimio chair became

Figure 5-51

Figure 5-50
Alvar Aalto. Lounge chair and table, ca. 1929–30. (From Hoffmann, *Modern Interiors*, p. 104).

Figure 5-51
Alvar Aalto. Paimio lounge chairs, 1931–32. Manufactured by Oy. Huonekalu- ja Rakennustyötehdas AB, Turku, Finland. Museum of Applied Arts, Helsinki. See CAT. NO. **99.**

Figure 5-52
Alvar Aalto. Armchair, ca. 1931–32. Laminated wood and plywood. Museum of Applied Arts, Helsinki. CAT. NO. **100.**

Aalto's most cogent demonstration (at least in furniture) of the organic curve, a shape derived from the natural characteristics of his beloved birch, i.e., from nature itself. The need to humanize design, to temper the intellectual rigor and so-called rationalism of modernism, was a recurring theme in Aalto's work and writings:

In order to achieve practical goals and valid aesthetic forms in connection with architecture, one cannot always start from a rational and technical standpoint—perhaps even never. Human imagination must have free room in which to unfold. This was usually the case with my experiments in wood.[74]

More than any other design, the Paimio armchair was a tribute to Aalto's free imagination, his concern for human scale and values, and his vision of a curvilinear, organic design aesthetic based in nature.

A key element in the construction of Aalto's Paimio and cantilevered armchairs was his handling of the narrow stack of laminated veneers to form the chairs' frames. In 1933, Aalto, like Michael Thonet a century before, attempted to go beyond the bending of laminated veneers by developing a technique by which to bend a solid piece of birch. By back-sawing into the top of a chair leg and inserting short, individual lengths of veneer, Aalto was able to deal with the problems of tension and compression and arrive at a technical solution that allowed him to bend wood at a ninety-degree angle, albeit rounded at the corner. The result was his so-called bent-knee or L-shaped leg, cited by Aalto himself and later writers as his most important innovation in furniture design.[75] While this claim is open to question—his use of a single sheet of plywood for seat and back was more extensively imitated (see below)—the technique allowed him to produce his simple and ubiquitous three-legged stacking stool (figure 5–53), one of the most unpretentious yet successful examples of modern furniture.

Figure 5-53
Alvar Aalto. Stacking stools, 1933. View at exhibition *Alvar Aalto: Architecture and Furniture,* **The Museum of Modern Art, New York, 1938. See** CAT. NO. **103.**

Aalto and tubular steel

During the 1930s, Aalto's laminated-wood furniture was repeatedly presented as the modernist's alternative to tubular-steel furniture. Lacking the coldness and harshness that so many found uncongenial in tubular steel, Aalto's designs were characterized from the beginning as imbued with the traditional qualities required of domestic furniture. In the half century that has elapsed, most writers and historians have reiterated this opposition. Based mainly on the contrast of materials, it became and still remains a central dialectic in the history of early modernist furniture. Hence, German tubular-steel and Aalto's plywood furniture are characterized as two roughly parallel but unrelated strains in modern furniture, united only by a shared concern for formal values.

These approaches to Aalto's furniture, to the relationship between tubular steel and plywood, have tended to obscure the important and fundamental links that exist between the two materials. In particular, the approach tends to belie Aalto's careful and critical study of first-generation tubular-steel furniture and negates what he learned from Breuer especially, as well as from Stam and Mies van der Rohe. This link is crucial to an understanding of the furniture of the twenties and thirties, as well as of the important relationship between the two most innovative techniques of bent furniture of these years, and thus bears some exploration.

By the time Aalto began designing his modern furniture in 1929, Breuer had designed all of his best-known tubular-steel models. Until recently, it was assumed that Aalto must have known the new tubular-steel furniture either from magazines or from firsthand observation during his trip to C.I.A.M. (Congrès Internationaux d'Architecture Moderne) in Frankfurt in 1929. However, recent research has shown that Aalto had far more immediate knowledge of German tubular-steel furniture. In 1928 he ordered and received a large shipment of Breuer furniture from Thonet-Mundus in Berlin, which he used in his own apartment (figure 5–54) and in a restaurant commission.[76] Included in this substantial shipment were a number of Wassily club chairs B3, cantilevered side chairs B33, and the occasional table B10.

Figure 5-54
Alvar Aalto's apartment, Turku, Finland, 1928. Tubular-steel furniture by Marcel Breuer: table, Thonet Model No. B10; Wassily club chairs, Thonet Model No. B3. (See CAT. NO. **67).**

Figure 5-55
Marcel Breuer. Side chair, 1927-28. Thonet Model No. B33.

That Aalto not only chose Breuer's tubular-steel furniture for a client but also lived with it himself suggests the need for a close comparison of Breuer designs with Aalto's plywood furniture of the following years. For even if, as has recently been suggested, Aalto might not have known or cared who the designer of the furniture was,[77] he was nevertheless impressed enough to use it in his own home —no small tribute from an individual profoundly sensitive to his environment.

The effect of the Breuer furniture is first evident in a comparison of his B33 chair (figure 5-55)—based on Mart Stam's 1927 cantilevered side chair (figure 5-11)—and Aalto's combination plywood and tubular-steel side chair of 1930 (figure 5-49). Aalto's crucial transformation of Breuer's chair lies in his subordination of the role of steel, relegating it to the functional and less visible role of supporting frame. He rejects Breuer's use of the metal frame above the seat, preferring that the sitter come in contact only with wood.[78] In addition, Aalto raises the seat above the metal frame, creating a small gap between them, and articulates legs and seat as two separate, rather than continuous, elements. He further alters the design of the base to allow the chair to be stacked.[79]

Although there seems to be little similarity in appearance, a comparison between Breuer's Wassily chair (figure 5-5) and Aalto's Paimio chairs (figure 5-51) reveals Aalto's artistic reaction to the first modern tubular-steel chair and underlines his transformation of a number of its elements into his own form language. Both chairs are club armchairs, low to the ground, with frames that substitute continuous runners for individual legs. Both suspend the sitter in a resilient structure in which frame and seating element are separately articulated. Above all, both are abstracted notions of the chair form, equally powerful and intensely personal.

Functional requirements are met in both designs, but they play a secondary role to the idea of the chair as a vehicle for artistic expression. In both cases that expression is of a very high order, easily comparable to any form of contemporary art. However, the artistic visions—as opposed to the formal elements—differ profoundly. Breuer's vision is a complex, machine-age, constructivist concept formulated via De Stijl, while Aalto's is a structurally simpler homage to natural, organic materials and the curving forms of nature. One sees the natural world as a dead end for designers, preferring the inspiration of geometric, abstract art and the machine; the other seeks to accept, harmonize, and even glorify the natural world.

A comparison of a drawing of an alternative version of the Paimio chair (figure 5-56) with another Breuer lounge chair, his later B35 (figure 5-20), reveals an astounding affinity of shape that further emphasizes the extent to which Aalto looked to tubular steel. The cantilevering of the arms in Aalto's drawing clearly relies on the Breuer model, as does the treatment of the frame, which begins at one end (the front of the arm or top of the seat) and follows a continuous path to the other. In Aalto's chair there is only one material used; hence, color, surface, and texture are consistent throughout. In Breuer's model there is the contrast of the hard, smooth steel frame to the pliable textured cloth of the seat. While Aalto occasionally contrasted the material by using a burled plywood seat against a natural wood or ebonized frame, a variety of material was unavailable in tubular-steel furniture.

The lack of attention paid to the indisputable influence of tubular steel on Aalto's furniture may be attributed in part to Aalto's own rejection of that material, as well as to his own and his historians' desire to deny the possibility of influence. In several essays and lectures dating from after the design of his all-molded wood furniture, Aalto plainly stated his opinions about tubular steel. In the essay typically entitled "The Humanizing of Architecture" he observed:

The tubular steel chair is surely rational from technical and constructive points of view: It is light, suitable for mass production, and so on. But steel and chromium surfaces are not satisfactory from the human point of view. Steel is too good a conductor of heat. The chromium surface gives too bright reflections of light, and even acoustically is not suitable for a room. The rational methods of creating this furniture style have been on the right track, but the result will be good only if rationalization is exercised in the selection of materials which are most suitable for human use.[80]

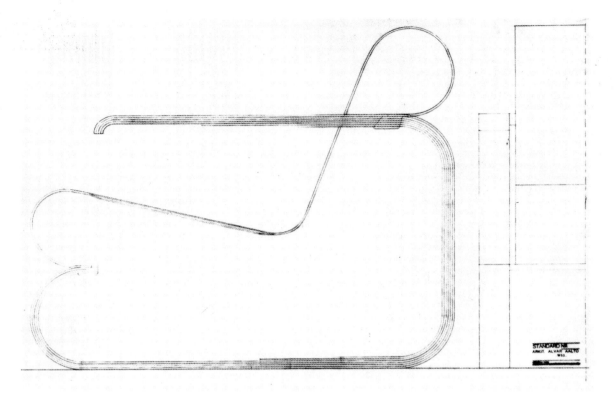

Figure 5-56
Alvar Aalto. Design for alternate version of Paimio chair, 1931–32. Alvar Aalto Architects Ltd., Helsinki.

Aalto's influence

The distribution of Aalto's work to an international market beyond Scandinavia was accomplished by established methods. His furniture was published in architectural journals and appeared in major international exhibitions as well as department store presentations. During the early years it was manufactured and sold by a non-Finnish firm, the Wohnbedarf (Living Necessities) stores of Switzerland.[81] Probably the first modern "design" store, this Zurich-based firm was founded in 1931 by three modernists associated with the Schweizer (Swiss) Werkbund, art historian Sigfried Giedion, architect Werner Moser, and Rudolf Glaber, managing director. In dramatic interiors designed by Marcel Breuer, the stores advanced the cause of modern architecture and design by selling modernist furnishings and arranging exhibitions of all the modern arts. The Wohnbedarf connection was a particularly important one for Aalto, at least as far as sales and promotion of his furniture were concerned. The firm, which began to sell his work in 1933, was a direct link to one of the most design-conscious audiences in Europe by means of the catalogues it mailed to architects and designers throughout Europe (figure 5–57).[82] In fact, Wohnbedarf may have been a model for the Artek company, the firm founded in 1935 by Alvar Aalto, his wife Aino, Marie Gullichsen, and Nils Gustav Hahl to sell Aalto furniture.

Among those individuals whose careers in furniture design are well-documented (Breuer and Mies van der Rohe, for example), the influence of Alvar Aalto's new plywood furniture appears with astonishing consistency.

Figure 5-57
***Das neue Aalto Holzmöbel* (New Wood Furniture by Aalto), sales catalogue of Wohnbedarf, Zurich, 1933, designed by Herbert Bayer.**

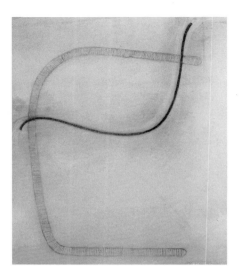

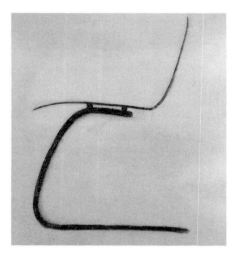

Figure 5-58
**Ludwig Mies van der Rohe. Curvature
study for Brno chair with tubular frame
and molded seat, 1931. Charcoal on paper.
Mies van der Rohe Archive, The Museum
of Modern Art, New York (Gift of the
architect).**

The features of his furniture that most designers adopted
were either his undulating single sheet of plywood for
seat and back or the continuous laminated arms, usually
of C or truncated-S shape, and frequently both.

Although, as is clear, Aalto was by no means the first
designer to use a single sheet of plywood to form the seat
and back of a chair, his mastery of this element made it
his own. Just as Marcel Breuer did not invent tubular-
metal furniture, but nonetheless invested it with its modern
appearance, so it was with Aalto and sheets of plywood.
In fact, although Aalto and many of his chroniclers consider
his so-called bent knee or L-leg (figure 5-53) his most
important contribution to furniture design, it is his use of
the single sheet of plywood that has been the most influential, and most imitated, feature of his work. Apart
from its obvious beauty and its striking visual expression
of the technical possibilities of plywood, this feature seems
to have been imitated for the very reasons that led to the
widespread imitations of Le Corbusier's houses of the
1920s: it caught the spirit of the time and was—or so it
seemed—relatively easy to copy.[83]

One remarkably early example of the use of an Aalto
type of plywood seat is Mies van der Rohe's 1931 study
for a Brno chair with tubular frame and molded seat (figure
5-58).[84] It is possible that this design belongs with a discussion of pre-Aalto plywood, since it could easily have
been inspired by the Rasch brothers' plywood and tubular-
steel chair exhibited at Weissenhof in 1927 (figure 5-45).
Another Mies van der Rohe design of 1931 (figure 5-59)
is quite similar to Aalto's combination wood-and-steel
side chairs (figure 5-49). Between 1933 and 1935, however,
Mies van der Rohe worked on many designs for chairs
with bent and/or molded wood seats, most of which,
while evoking nineteenth-century bent-wood rockers, are

inconceivable without Aalto's elevation of plywood to its
role as an important medium for furniture design. Mies
van der Rohe followed these seminal works of Aalto with
a group of chairs that used bent and laminated wood for
the base, leg, and arm units (figures 5-60 and 5-61). While
interesting from a technical point of view, as well as
allowing a glimpse into the working methods and ideas
of a master architect, none of Mies van der Rohe's bent
or molded wood designs carry the authority of his earlier
metal furniture.

Interestingly, English designers seem to have been better
able than their German, Dutch, or French counterparts
to absorb Aalto's influence in ways that allow for more
complete realization. Following a small but successful
exhibition at London's Fortnum & Mason department
store in 1933 (figure 5-62) arranged by P. Morton Shand,
editor of the *Architectural Review*, Aalto's furniture enjoyed
great popularity and wide influence in England (figure
5-63). English designers seized upon the warm material
and soft, curvilinear shapes of Aalto's furniture as an
alternative to earlier modernist—especially metal—
furniture, which one writer sweepingly characterized as
"so angular and unusual that it was uncomfortable both
to look at and to use."[85]

Among the first chairs to appear in the wake of the
Fortnum & Mason exhibition was the Plan series of furniture by Russian-born architect Serge Chermayeff (figure
5-64).[86] These designs adopted Aalto's laminated Paimio
arms for armchairs and his L-shaped leg for side chairs.
The designs, a generally conservative and workmanlike
response to Aalto's work, while eminently practical, failed
to retain the powerful, organic qualities of the original.

Less well-published at the time was the laminated furniture of Gerald Summers, manufactured by the Makers
of Simple Furniture, Ltd. In addition to manufacturing a
limited number of case pieces, this firm produced several
unusual plywood chairs, the most Aalto-like of which was a
dramatic and technically ingenious armchair made from
a single piece of plywood (figure 5-65).[87] Taking Aalto as
a starting point, Summers dispensed with the separate
frame supports that formed the arms and legs of Aalto's
chairs, and turned the sheet of plywood into a dynamic
form that sprouts arms and legs. The design is distinguished

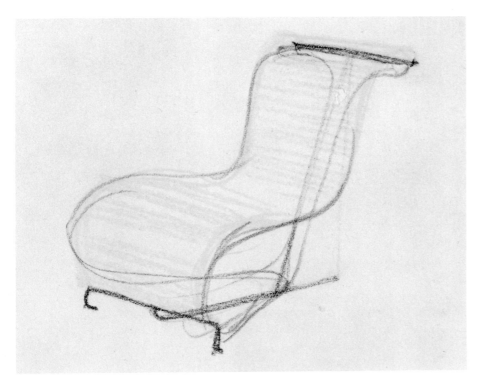

Figure 5-60
Ludwig Mies van der Rohe. Drawing for chair with bent-wood seat and coatrack-type support frame, 1934. Colored pencil on paper. Mies van der Rohe Archive, The Museum of Modern Art, New York (Gift of the architect).

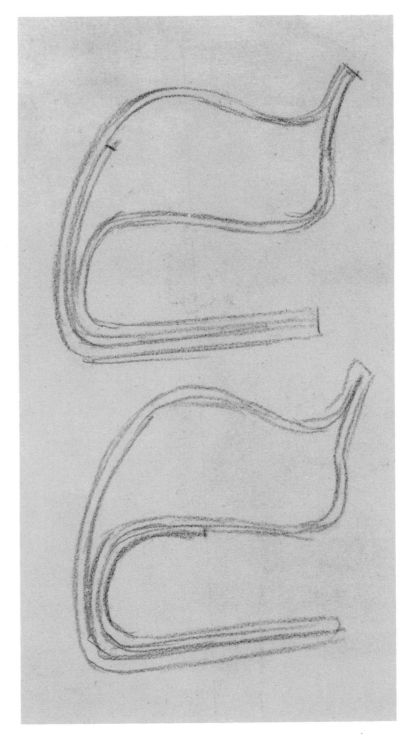

Figure 5-61
Ludwig Mies van der Rohe. Sketch of chairs with split bent-wood frames and steel-rod reinforcement, 1934–35. Colored pencil on paper. Mies van der Rohe Archive, The Museum of Modern Art, New York (Gift of the architect).

Figure 5-62

Figure 5-64

Figure 5-63

Figure 5-65

Figure 5-62
Exhibition of Alvar Aalto furniture, Fortnum & Mason, London, 1933.

Figure 5-63
Osbert Lancaster, "Functional Home," in *Home Sweet Homes*, 1939.

Figure 5-64
Serge Chermayeff. Plan chair, 1933. (From *Architectural Review*, August 1933, fig. 10).

Figure 5-65
Gerald Summers. Lounge chair, 1934. Bent plywood. The Mitchell Wolfson, Jr. Collection of Decorative and Propaganda Arts, Miami, Florida. CAT. NO. 106.

by its grace of line, its very logical interpretation of, and extension beyond, Aalto's work, and its singular attention to the idea of producing a chair from a single piece of material.

Another manifestation of Aalto's influence, which postdates Summers's chair, appears in Marcel Breuer's various plywood designs. By the time Breuer began to design plywood furniture in England, his relationship with Aalto was a symbiotic one. Breuer's armchair for Heal's furniture store (figure 5–66) is unquestionably his fanciful and not wholly satisfactory response to Aalto. It was, like much second-generation tubular-steel furniture, an attempt to put a new twist on a statement that had already been successfully and succinctly made. It was clear testimony to Aalto's position as form-giver of plywood furniture, as were other minor Breuer designs for chairs, desks, and beds.[88] The Isokon long chair, however, was not quite so simple a story.

It could be safely assumed, without any knowledge of Breuer's earlier work, that the Isokon chair (figure 5–67) was an equally direct response to Aalto. Yet we know that this was a translation into plywood of an earlier chair Breuer had designed in bent, flat aluminum and flat steel versions. In fact, it was not even Breuer's idea to manufacture the chair in wood; the suggestion came from Walter Gropius, who had been appointed Controller of Design of the Isokon Furniture Company by its founder, Jack Pritchard.[89] Pritchard had worked for Venesta, a major international manufacturer and distributor of plywood, for ten years, so it was natural enough to turn to that material. Nonetheless, it seems clear that Aalto's work provided the formal vocabulary that allowed Breuer to translate his aluminum chair into the new material. The single sheet of plywood that forms the back and seat, and the thick, supporting laminated arms and legs are the key elements of Aalto's furniture and were adopted entirely by Breuer as the means to re-create his metal design in wood.[90]

By providing a successful alternative to tubular steel, Aalto's work represents the first synthesis, and leading edge, of the modern tradition in plywood. It is probably not an exaggeration to say that his bent and molded experiments focused attention on all methods of plywood con-

Figure 5-66
Marcel Breuer. Armchair, 1936. Designed for Heal's furniture store, London. (From *Form: Svenska Slöjdföreningens Tidskrift*, 1937, p. 36).

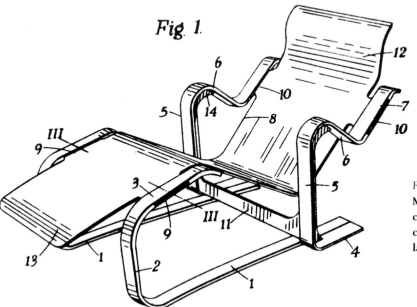

Figure 5-67
Marcel Breuer. Isokon long chair, 1936. Patent drawing for chair made of plywood and laminated wood. See CAT. NO. 109.

struction. Thus, the shift to cutout plywood furniture that began during the mid-thirties and continued into the forties, can also be seen as a reflection of Aalto's influence. Little more than a jigsaw and glue are required to make cutout plywood furniture; even the molds and presses necessary in molded plywood production are not essential. Unfortunately, though cutout plywood seemed to offer a route for great progress, it was not a material that was ever truly successful either artistically or commerically.

The final chapter in the story of bent-wood and bent-metal furniture between the two world wars belongs to the most innovative American designers of the mid-twentieth century and the clear successors to Aalto as form-givers and innovators in the field of plywood furniture: Charles and Ray Eames.

Charles and Ray Eames

Shortly after the furniture of Charles and Ray Eames was put into production, Eero Saarinen sent photographs of the new chairs (figures 5–79 and 5–80) to Alvar Aalto. Aalto's blunt reaction to the three-dimensional molding of the plywood parts, addressed to Saarinen, was that "plastic does not speak the language of wood fibers."[91] Aalto felt that the Eameses' sculptural treatment of sheets of plywood violated the fundamental structure of wood and was, therefore, quite distant from his own work. Aalto was unable to see that the Eamseses' plywood furniture took his own designs as its starting point. Though they went far beyond Aalto in their ability to bend sheets of plywood and in the complexity of their formal and technical solutions, Aalto's influence can be seen as crucial in the genesis of Eames furniture from 1939 through 1946.

In 1938, two years before Eames and Saarinen, colleagues at Cranbrook Academy of Art, began work on their joint entries for the Museum of Modern Art's competition "Organic Design in Home Furnishings" (which they won in 1941), Alvar Aalto's furniture was the subject of a retrospective exhibition at the museum (figure 5–68). At the time, Aalto's furniture had not yet been imported into America, having only recently been manufactured in any quantity by the still fledgling Artek firm. Accordingly,

Figure 5-68
Installation view at exhibition *Alvar Aalto: Architecture and Furniture,* The Museum of Modern Art, New York, 1938.

Figure 5-69
Nathan Lerner. One-piece chair, 1940. (From Moholy-Nagy, *Vision in Motion,* **fig. 94).**

this first showing of Aalto's furniture in America assumes great significance.[92]

There were, to be sure, other Aalto-inspired bent-plywood experiments taking place in the United States. At the Chicago School of Design, transplanted Bauhaus teacher László Moholy-Nagy had his students design a wide range of plywood chairs (figures 5-69 and 5-70).[93] Most of these were characterized by an Aalto-like use of a single-piece plywood seat and back, sometimes combined with laminated or plywood arms. While several students bent plywood in complicated or exaggerated shapes, all followed Aalto's technique of bending the wood on one plane. The most significant innovation of Eames and Saarinen (only later fully realized on an industrial scale by Charles and Ray Eames), it has been said, is that they were the first to bend lengths of plywood on two planes.[94] In contrast to Aalto's bending a flat sheet of plywood into one or more curves, the Eamses were able to mold a single sheet of plywood into different directions, on different planes, at the same time. This claim should be modified to indicate that although Eames and Saarinen were the first to bend plywood on two planes in a manner that eventually permitted large-scale application, there had been previous experiments along these lines. The American John Henry Belter, for example, had been able to perform the same technical feat in the nineteenth century (see cat. no. 21), and a most important earlier twentieth-century example of this procedure was an armchair designed by Alvar Aalto.

Although ignored by all histories of modern furniture and absent even from accounts of Aalto's work, the first manufacturer of Aalto furniture, Oy. Huonekalu- ja Rakennustyötehdas, produced an Aalto design of about 1931–32 which was bent on two planes (figure 5-71). In this truly remarkable armchair Aalto bent the plywood sheet through the seat and lower back in one direction; when it

Figure 5-70
Kenneth Evertsen. Armchair, 1940. Laminated hardwood. (From Moholy-Nagy, *Vision in Motion,* **fig. 95).**

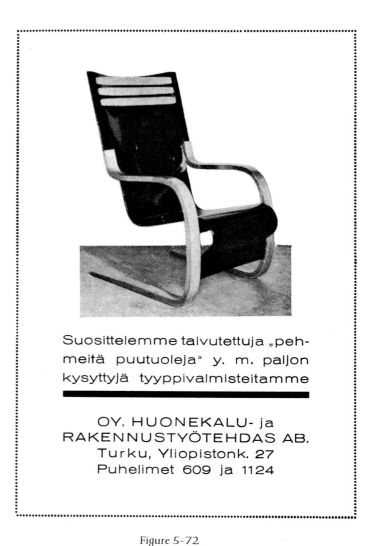

Figure 5-71
Alvar Aalto. Armchair, 1931–32. Plywood and laminated wood. Alexander von Vegesack, Düsseldorf, Germany. CAT. NO. 101.

Figure 5-72
"We recommend 'bent soft-wood chairs' and our other much requested standardized products." Advertisement of Oy. Huonekalu- ja Rakennustyötehdas AB, Turku, Finland, for Alvar Aalto furniture. (From *Domus* [Finland], April 1932).

reached the upper back the plywood was molded into a second plane, creating a shallow depression that cradled the sitter's head. Although advertised for sale (figure 5–72) and exhibited at the Nordic building exhibition in Helsinki of 1932 (see figure 102C), the chair was apparently never produced by Artek, nor, apparently, did it appear in subsequent exhibitions of Aalto's work.[95] Clearly the designer must have been dissatisfied with some aspect of the chair, for the only time he ever returned to a similar form, he covered it with upholstery.[96]

Around 1934 Gerald Summers designed a high-back plywood side chair (figure 5–73) in which the lower rear portion is formed by a cylindrical curve that then rises into a back shaped in a more modified curve.[97]

These experiments may have been unknown to Eames and Saarinen when they worked on their furniture for the Museum of Modern Art competition; and when, about 1942–44, Charles and Ray Eames finally began to mass-produce plywood objects bent in two different directions, these were based entirely on the earlier competition furniture.[98]

The Museum of Modern Art competition entries

As opposed to the early experiments in three-dimensional plywood-molding, the Eames and Saarinen entries, particularly the A3501 drawing (figure 5–74) and the armchair that was actually fabricated and exhibited (figure 5–75), treated the entire upper portion of the chair as a single, sculpted unit; the term *plywood shell* was used to describe the appearance of this unit and to suggest its conceptual basis.[99] Ironically, the profoundly innovative character of these designs has been, for various reasons, insufficiently appreciated. It has been largely due to an acceptance of the innovative *technical* qualities, and on the imprimateur of the Museum of Modern Art, that these designs have been acknowledged as historically important. The use of

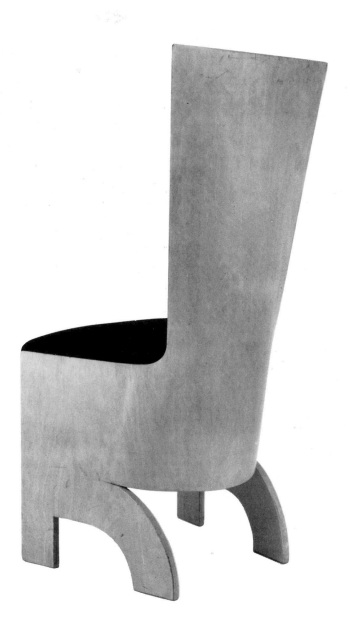

Figure 5–73
Gerald Summers. Side chair, ca. 1934. Plywood. Barry Friedman Ltd., New York.

A3501

RELAXATION

ONE QUARTER FULL SIZE

Figure 5-74
Charles Eames and Eero Saarinen.
Competition drawing, for exhibition
Organic Design in Home Furnishings, The
Museum of Modern Art, New York, 1941.
Colored pencil, wood veneer, and paper
cutouts on white poster board. The
Museum of Modern Art, New York.

Figure 5-75
Charles Eames and Eero Saarinen. Armchair, competition entry in exhibition *Organic Design in Home Furnishings*, The
Museum of Modern Art, New York, 1941.
Molded plywood, foam rubber, padding,
upholstery, solid wood legs.

thick wooden legs in the final version, rather than the intended metal legs, and the difficulty of accepting the aesthetic of the final version have often relegated these designs to the position of a historical footnote, a conceptual preview of things to come: the designs that would be produced and exhibited in 1946. Nevertheless, the Eames and Saarinen competition entries signaled a new direction in modern furniture.[100]

The extensive work and experimentation that went into the Museum of Modern Art competition entries were redirected after it became clear that manufacture of the pieces would be too expensive to reach the lower end of the marketplace, for which they were intended. Charles and his new wife, Ray Kaiser, moved to Los Angeles where, in their spare time, they continued to examine the problems of molding plywood. They were soon helped by a wartime commission from the U.S. Navy to design stretchers, leg splints, and glider shells. In these sculpturally molded designs, the Eameses were able to refine ideas and techniques for molding plywood on more than one plane; the fact that the splints (figure 5–76) and stretchers were actually produced (by the Evans Products Company of Los Angeles) meant that the designers finally had the opportunity to carry their furniture designs through to an equally successful conclusion.[101] Charles was able to give up his job as a set designer at MGM and devote himself full-time to plywood design.

From 1942 to 1944 the Eameses worked on the Navy designs and used what they learned in a series of experimental chairs (figure 5–77). Between 1942 and 1946 they designed their most important and famous furniture, and in 1946, eight years after the Museum of Modern Art had hosted Aalto's one-man exhibition, the Eameses' success was celebrated there by an exhibition of their work (figure 5–78).

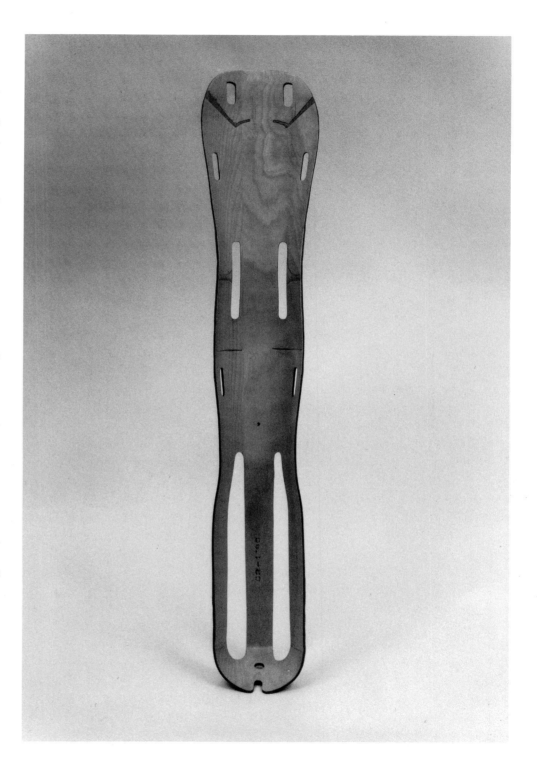

Figure 5–76
Charles and Ray Eames. Leg splint, 1942. Molded plywood. Commissioned by U. S. Navy. Manufactured by Evans Products Company, Los Angeles. CAT. NO. **112. Catherine Kurland, New York.**

Figure 5-77
Charles and Ray Eames. Experimental chairs in plywood and metal, ca. 1944. The Office of Charles and Ray Eames, Venice, California.

Figure 5-78
Installation view at exhibition *New Furniture Designed by Charles Eames*, The Museum of Modern Art, New York, 1946.

The Eames chairs of 1946, best typified by the lounge or dining chairs made with either plywood frames (figure 5–79) or metal (figure 5–80), represent a remarkable achievement. The degree to which they refine and perfect the ideas of the competition entries testifies to the Eameses' determination, intelligence, and skill. Among their many accomplishments was the clear and independent articulation of seat, frame, and back, achieved by the use of ingenious electronically welded rubber shock mounts joining the various parts. This electronic cycle-welding (a process by which wood could be joined to rubber, glass, or metal, which had been reserved for military use during the war years)[102] made possible the resilience and flexibility these chairs possess. The introduction of the shock mounts— a strong contrast to the earlier shell form raised on four separate legs—represented a new level of formal invention in the Eames furniture and a genuine advance beyond Aalto's earlier solution, which had involved the use of bolts to bind the seating element to its support system. Thus, like the cantilevered tubular-steel chairs of the 1920s, the Eames chairs rely on the structural properties of the design to provide comfort, instead of depending on upholstery, as had the competition entries. The mounts allow seat and back to project from the frame. While the seat hovers horizontally, the frame below curves down to meet the rear legs and the back pushes forward and hangs vertically, like a shield, in front of the frame.

This clear visual separation of the frame from seat and back was, in turn, accomplished by the reduction of mass and surface area in the minimal seat and back. The experimental chairs, traditionally dated "circa 1944," show the progressive reduction of the back elements and a simplification of three-dimensional form that gradually brought the frame into greater prominence. Finally, in both its thin metal and bulkier plywood versions, the frame became a contrasting element to the cantilevered sheets of wood that form the seat or back. The frame is, ultimately, the unifying component of these designs through its reference to a living organism with spine, head, pelvis, and four legs. An insistent zoomorphism imbues these chairs with a symbolic aspect that has been frequently overlooked in favor of their structural and technical qualities.

Technology versus aesthetics

In the Eames furniture one again confronts the dialectic between what were often viewed as two different approaches to furniture design: the technical and the formal. However, these approaches cannot exist independently of each other. Aesthetic decisions are routinely made in order to give technical innovations three-dimensional form; and technical solutions must be found to realize formal ideas. Charles Eames's writings and speeches concentrated on technical aspects and his general approach to the design process; rarely were matters of aesthetics addressed.[103] In a rare instance that acknowledged the formative influence of aesthetics, Eero Saarinen described the furniture he had designed with Charles Eames:

New materials and new techniques have given us great opportunities with structural shells of plywood, plastic and metal.... The problem then becomes a sculptural one, not the cubist, constructivist one.[104]

Like the modernist designers of the twenties, Eames denied that the Eameses' furniture represented an individual art; rather, he described their designs as the result of mere technical problem-solving, the quasi-anonymous products through which they were designed and the technology required to produce them.

It is indisputable that the Eameses brought a remarkable degree of technical experimentation and innovation to the process of furniture manufacture. Certainly no previous twentieth-century furniture designers could claim to have revolutionized not only the design but also the manufacturing process to the degree that they had. Designers in tubular steel could claim only minimal achievement in the technical area. Until the accomplishments of Charles and Ray Eames, the technical innovations of Alvar Aalto and Otto Korhonen, technical director of Oy. Huonekalu-ja Rakennustyötehdas, were perhaps the most decisive, yet their furniture was (and still is), despite the use of molds and presses, almost a workshop production. The Eameses, on the other hand, working with various individual and corporate collaborators, introduced new molding and bonding methods to furniture production, which not only allowed them to produce their own designs successfully, but also received broad application in the furniture industry as a whole.

When the Eameses asserted the technological basis of their work they were joining a long line of modernists, the most polemically oriented of whom were the designers in tubular steel of the 1920s. At the same time that Eames adopted his technological position, die-hard modernist Sigfried Giedion completed his *Mechanization Takes Command*, which has since become the classic exposition on mechanization in modern Western history. Although a strident advocate and polemicist for the modern movement, Giedion very clearly saw the non-technical basis of recent bent- and molded-wood furniture. He was able to do so because the tenor of the times had changed so radically. No longer was structural rationalism accepted as an exclusive explanation for the form of furniture. As the rectilinear geometry of the 1920s had finally given way, so had the functionalist argument that all form was based in the logical and rational use of modern materials. In concluding his discussion of modern furniture, Giedion looked to recent wood furniture, including that of the Eameses, and asked:

Was it only the demand for new techniques that gave fresh life to the wooden material and set free its hidden potentialities? The causes go deeper than that; to the trend toward the organic that asserted itself in the early 'thirties and gained strength in following years. We want around us objects that bear the trace of life. Bark, grotesque roots, shells, fossils. Things that have passed through time and tide.[105]

The form that the Eameses gave to their furniture was by no means the result of anonymous technology; it was very much in keeping with the curvilinear, three-dimensional biomorphism that had gained currency among designers since the 1930s and was derived more from the spirit of contemporary painting and sculpture—the work of Arp and Miró, for example—than from contemporary architecture.[106] The rejection of the rectilinear geometry of the twenties was nearly universal by the time the Eameses designed their furniture, and the soft edges and organic forms of Aalto's early furniture were beginning to look geometric by comparison. When the Eameses took large sheets of plywood and overlapped them in configurations that suggested a desire to mold sculptural form

from a soft, pliable material (figure 5-77), it signaled, as had the most sculptural Museum of Modern Art competition entry (figures 5-74 and 5-75), a desire to bend and mold volumetric, enclosing forms. A mere two years later, in 1946, this approach was rejected as unnecessarily contorting wood in a manner that would be suited to more malleable or even liquid materials. The result was the creation of carefully conceived, delicately shaped assemblages of plywood and metal (figures 5-79 and 5-80) unique for their thinness, delicacy, and strength. But the aesthetic that had infused the competition furniture, now artfully refined, remained an integral part of their work.

Ultimately, as Eero Saarinen had suggested to Aalto himself, the Eameses' treatment of plywood differed profoundly from that of Aalto. The continuity of the bent material, an important aspect in Aalto furniture of the early thirties, was intentionally rejected by the Eameses. Separate, independent pieces of plywood were the basis of the Americans' most important designs. In their metal and plywood side chair of 1946, the Eameses were able to combine the two materials in a harmonious and artistic way that had eluded Aalto and other earlier designers.

An additional crucial difference between the furniture of the Eameses and Alvar Aalto, which could be extended to a comparison of the designs of the 1940s and those of the 1920s, is that the relationship between architecture and furniture design is no longer so close and fundamental in the later period. The vital links between Bauhaus architecture and Breuer's tubular-steel chairs, or Aalto's furniture and his buildings, are not analogous to the relationship between the Eameses furniture and contemporary architecture. During the late thirties and the forties, ideas about architectural structure or interior space no longer find their necessary continuation or completion in furniture.

All the Eameses' subsequent furniture—the famous rosewood lounge chair, the molded fiberglass furniture, and the aluminum group—was based on the groundbreaking work of 1940–46. And as these bent- and molded-wood designs have influenced the entire course of the Eameses' work, so have they shaped the course of mid-twentieth-century furniture.

Figure 5-80
Charles and Ray Eames. Side chair, Model No. DCM, 1946. Molded ash plywood, bent steel rod, rubber, metal. Manufactured by the Herman Miller Furniture Company, Grand Rapids, Michigan. Museum of Fine Art, Boston (Gift of Edward J Wormley), CAT. NO. **116.**

Notes

1. The work of the Finnish Alvar Aalto and the Americans Charles and Ray Eames was crucial in the development of bent and molded plywood during the 1930s and 1940s, but their achievements were individual rather than representative of national trends.

2. Kramer, p. 207.

3. Intense competition and price wars had led to the merger of the Mundus and Kohn companies in 1914 and then, in 1922, to their merger with Thonet. The new company, no longer owned by the Thonet family, was the largest furniture conglomerate in history. See the chapter above by Graham Dry; and Wilk 1980a, pp. 77–78. [In Wilk 1980a, p. 78, the date of the Mundus-Kohn merger is given as "1917." This is a typographical error; the correct date, 1914, is given on the preceding page in that publication.]

4. Le Corbusier 1925, p. 145.

5. Although bent-wood furniture was used in the ateliers of such architects as Otto Wagner and J. M. Olbrich (see Mang 1982, pp. 101 and 105), it was not at all common in domestic interiors.

6. Modernist designers pointed to bent wood as proof that "the logic of industrial production methods also leads to good formal solutions with perfect aesthetic proportions": see Kramer, p. 206. It was not enough for modernist designers that an object simply be mass-produced; more important was that it visually convey or symbolize that it was the product of industry.

7. The notion of standardization in design was already hotly debated at the famous meeting of the Deutsche Werkbund in July 1914; see Campbell, pp. 57–68 and passim. It was revived and gained far greater currency during the 1920s; see the many essays in Gräff 1928 and the exhibition catalogue *Typenmöbel* (Basel 1929).

8. Lotz 1928, p. 161; translated in Benton, 1975c, p. 229.

9. Kramer, p. 206.

10. "'Villa Flats' and the 'Pavillon de L'Esprit Nouveau' 1925" (1929), in Le Corbusier 1936, p. 104.

11. Perriand, p. 278.

12. On Breuer's furniture, see New York 1981b.

13. Author's interview with Marcel Breuer, November 30, 1978. The descriptive "precision steel tubing" was essentially a marketing term intended to denote the rigorous standards that governed the construction of this new furniture and to differentiate it from the tubing used in the manufacture of bicycles. It is also an example of the attempt to infuse this furniture with a pseudoscientific/industrial jargon. The term was used in manufacturers' catalogues, and it also appears in the famous court decision regarding the copyright ownership of Thonet B32, Breuer's cantilevered chair; see below; and also New York 1981b, pp. 73–78.

14. During these years, Breuer maintained a stance that advocated the need for only one of each furniture type, an idea belied by his subsequent creation of some seventeen different chair designs.

15. The latest account of the controversy is Máčel. See also New York 1981b, pp. 70–78.

16. Rasch 1960, pp. 1–3.

17. According to an internal Arnold company memo dated October 18, 1934, it was the Deutsche Werkbund—the organization that sponsored the Weissenhof exhibition—that put Stam in touch with the company. This document was generously supplied to the author by Otakar Máčel of Delft, who received it from a Berlin architect who has in his possession certain papers from the personal files of Anton Lorenz, assignee of the Stam patents. These papers have not been made available to the author.

18. From the transcript "Appeal of the Decision of the Tenth Civil Senate of the Supreme Court at Berlin, April 22, 1931, Proclaimed on February 17, 1932, damages set on June 1, 1932"; Breuer Papers, uncatalogued documents. An additional description is included in the memo mentioned in note 17.

19. Described in Rasch 1927, p 101, as "based on Mart Stam."

20. Author's interview with Marcel Breuer, January 19, 1978.

21. Máčel, p. 151 and fig. 115. The same author first wrote about Stüttgen in van Geest and Máčel, p. 26. Although not mentioned, the reason for the suit seems to have been the desire of the Mauser company to manufacture the Stam cantilever side chair, Model B or ST33 (and Anton Lorenz's armchair version, Model B or ST34) without having to pay royalties to Gebrüder Thonet of Germany, which had obtained the rights to the design from Anton Lorenz himself.

22. Del Marle, p. 14; cited in Banham, p. 199.

23. This was especially true outside Germany, in Holland, England, and the United States. The situation bears certain parallels to the widespread imitation of the bent-wood designs of the Thonet firm following the expiration of their exclusive patent in 1869; see the essay above by Graham Dry.

24. It should not be forgotten that other designers, among them Arthur Korn and S. van Ravesteyn, designed non-cantilevered bent-metal furniture, which was exhibited at Weissenhof and was in the first stages of production.

25. This is well documented in the illustrations published in van Geest and Máčel.

26. As Mies van der Rohe learned when he applied for a patent for his cantilevered chair, there were numerous examples of cantilevered seating not intended for use in the home. In fact, he was required to defend his application for a patent against the lawn chair designed by Harry Nolan (U.S. Patent 1,491,918; filed 1922, granted April 29, 1924), as well as an earlier (1904) chaise longue. Giedion (pp. 500–502) illustrates the Nolan chair, as well as two nineteenth-century examples of cantilevered seating: the seat of a reaper and a single-unit table with six chairs, intended for shipboard use. It was never claimed, however, that the German designers would have known of these early designs.

27. Stam 1935, p. 7; cited in van Geest and Máčel, p. 47.

28. Bent solid wood could not be used to form a cantilevered chair

base because it lacked sufficient tensile strength. Only laminated plywood, as Aalto would discover, could provide the strength and flexibility required to support the sitter's weight on only two legs.

29. The chair was published in *Stroitel'stvo Moskvy* (Construction of Moscow), no. 10 (1929). It is dated to 1927 in Lodder, p. 211, and as circa 1927 in Milner, p. 210, while Paris 1979, p. 267, ascribes a date of 1923.

30. There is still a need for an in-depth study of the technology of tubular steel, as well as other materials and processes used in furniture production. John Heskett's essay was a good starting point, but most of his examples and all his illustrations of the use of tubular steel in industry postdate Breuer's furniture of 1925.

31. The comparison with Hitchcock and Johnson was made, with different emphasis, by J. Stewart Johnson in his succinct and provocative essay that serves as the introduction to New York 1981b.

32. Johnson, ch. 1, passim.

33. New York 1938b, p. 27.

34. Le Corbusier 1923, p. 200; 1927, p. 222. Recent considerations of this attitude toward technology may be found in Willett, p. 103 and passim, and in Paris 1982, passim.

35. *Manomètre*, no. 1 (1922); quoted in Paris 1982, p. 149.

36. Breuer, pp. 11–12; translated in London 1968, p. 109.

37. On prices, see Lotz 1930; Seeger; Gräff 1928, pp. 154–63; and Gräff 1933. According to Lotz, the following were retail prices for furniture in 1933, all given in reichmarks. Side chairs: a simple Thonet bent-wood chair, 11.75; a Breuer B5, 32.00; a Mies van der Rohe MR 533, 34.00; "Stam" cantilevered ST12, 39.00. Armchairs: Thonet bentwood B9, 15.00; Thonet bent-wood A811/1F, 27.00; Walter Knoll model KS41, 52.50; Breuer B64, 52.00; Erich Dieckmann 8217, 61.50; Mies van der Rohe MR534, 64.00; Thonet bent-wood Morris chair (sometimes ascribed to Ferdinand Kramer), 80.00; and Mies van der Rohe MR544, 125.00.
  For a complaint about the high prices of modern furniture, out of the question for even a middle-class person—see xy [*sic*], a reviewer who criticized the expense of a group of interiors on view at an exhibition: "The items are simply useless for the kinds of homes we need. [The exhibition] is a display of international luxury . . . a worthless event that takes advantage of a favorable business location and employs a title [International Interior Design Exhibition] that is nothing more than a merchandizing gimmick."

38. Dieckmann, p. 69.

39. Le Corbusier 1923, p. 200; 1927, pp. 222–23.

40. Stam 1926, ABC1, p. 1, translated in Benton and Benton, p. 27.

41. "'Villa Flats' and the 'Pavillon de l'Esprit Nouveau' 1925" (1929), in Le Corbusier 1936, p. 104.

42. Quoted in New York 1947, p. 189.

43. The 1920s concern with hygiene, related to the emphasis on sports and what Breuer called "the healthy-body culture," is a rich topic that has only been summarily treated in writings on the period. See, for example, Willett, pp. 102, 106, and passim; Paris 1982, pp. 161–63; and New York 1981b, pp. 61–62.

44. See New York 1981b, pp. 66–67.

45. Le Corbusier 1923, p. 113; 1927, p. 132. A remarkable statement from one who indeed treated the chair as a work of art. J. Stewart Johnson has commented on the "tentative" and conventional nature of most of the furniture used by Le Corbusier in his interiors prior to the design of his own tubular-steel furniture; see his introduction in New York 1981b, pp. 11–12.

46. Le Corbusier and Jeanneret designed tubular-steel beds for their houses at the Weissenhof exhibition in 1927; see Gräff 1928, pp. 85–86. Other designs may have been in work, but did not arrive in time for the exhibition; see Benton, c. p. 13 (a reference brought to my attention by Nina Stritzler).

47. See Herbst 1956.

48. See Herbst 1954; and Vellay and Frampton.

49. See Boll, pp. 161–70.

50. Dufrène, p. 2.

51. See van Geest and Máčel, passim.

52. Breuer negotiated contracts to produce the furniture all over Europe, but with the exception of those pieces manufactured by the Swiss firm Wohnbedarf, all the other prospects were thwarted, first by delays and then by the impending war; see New York 1981b, pp. 115–16.

53. Little is written about this chair, which, according to catalogue number 49 in London 1970, "was commissioned by Hans Fischli, architect for the *Landi*, Swiss National Exhibition in Zurich."

54. As early as 1927 Standard-Möbel had titled its first catalogue *Breuer Metallmöbel*. Subsequently, some tubular steel firms used the names of designers in their catalogues. No later than January 1929, the Thonet firm began using designers' names in their magazine advertisements; for an example, see New York 1981b, p. 89, fig. 108.

55. See Wilk 1980a, pp. 88–96.

56. See Mang 1982, p. 126. The minutes of the jury's deliberations are in the archives of both Gebrüder Thonet, Frankenberg, West Germany, and the Thonet Company, York, Pennsylvania.

57. One English critic credited Aalto with no less than single-handedly "revitalizing both the form and construction of the arm-chair"; see Dennison, p. 78.

58. According to Logie, p. 77, the term *plywood* was not widely used until after 1919. For descriptions of the use of plywood as a substitute for solid wood, see Logie, p. 76; and in the context of a personal remembrance, Pritchard, p. 53.

59. Author's interviews with Marcel Breuer, October 30, 1980, and Andrew and Eva Weininger, February 17, 1981.

60. See Gräff 1928; and Stuttgart 1928.

61. The Rasch brothers exhibited at least four chairs, as well as beds, tables, and case pieces in the exhibition houses of Peter Behrens and

Mies van der Rohe, as well as in the general furnishings section of *Die Wohnung*; see Gräff 1928, pp. 27, 33, 88; and Marzona, pp. 6–32 and 40. In *Der Stuhl* they were represented by some twelve to fourteen designs.

62. See Brown, p. 172, cat. no. 38; and Baroni, pp. 114–15.

63. See New York 1938b, p. 131; and Wingler, p. 454, fig. c, dated 1928.

64. Wingler, p. 515, dated 1929. It is not clear whether the chair was made of laminated wood or plywood.

65. Other Bauhaus furniture, by Hinrich Bredendieck and "members of the cabinetmaking workshop," is illustrated in Wingler, p. 516.

66. Though Michael Thonet founded Gebrüder Thonet in 1853, his successors always chose to date the firm's origins to 1830, the year of his first experiments with bending wood. This practice has been carried on by the present-day companies in the United States, Germany, and Austria, which, in 1980, celebrated the one-hundred-fiftieth anniversary of the firm.

67. The most comprehensive treatment to date of Aalto's mature furniture is in Schildt 1984.

68. Published in Schildt 1984, p. 73, but not included in the chapter on the competition in Wilk 1980a, pp. 94–95.

69. It is worth reiterating that plywood and laminated wood are not identical. While all plywood is laminated, i.e., made from pieces glued together, all laminated wood is not ply. True plywood must be made from veneers, each of which is laminated with the grain running perpendicular to the grain of the adjacent sheet. Although traditionally referred to as plywood furniture, Aalto's furniture was, in fact, made of both laminated wood and plywood.

70. The starting point for Aalto's new furniture was his use of a single sheet of plywood for the seat and back of a low side chair or lounge chair (1929): one version was produced with four wooden legs (see Schildt 1984, fig. 87b); the other—of which no photographs are known—had what has been described as "a springy tubular frame" (ibid., p. 70).

71. The chair was manufactured by the Wohnbedarf company of Switzerland (see below) after its development by Aalto and his important collaborator in furniture production, Otto Korhonen, technical director of the Oy. Huonekalu-ja Rakennustyötehdas wood-working firm. Although Schildt 1984 (p. 72) emphasizes Aalto's rejection of tubular steel, Aalto returned to the material in a number of later designs: a stackable stool and examination table for the Paimio Sanitorium, as well as a convertible sofa bed eventually produced by Wohnbedarf.

72. The long, curving lengths of birch laminates that form the supports for the cantilevered armchair can be understood as an elaboration of various elements in the designer's contemporary chairs. On the one hand, they can be seen as carrying the arm of the experimental tubular-steel and plywood armchair (Schildt 1984, fig. 101) down to the ground, and, on the other, as allowing the laminated base of the child's chair of 1931 (ibid, fig. 106) to rise up to the back.

73. Aalto returned to cantilevered chairs in his upholstered furniture of 1933–46, but his abandonment of tubular steel is complete by 1930.

74. Statement by Aalto in 1946; quoted in Frampton, p. 198.

75. See Schildt 1984, p. 77.

76. Schildt 1984, p. 69.

77. Schildt 1984 suggests the possibility that Aalto "was not aware of or interested in the designer's name" (p. 69).

78. Aalto used a complete metal frame only once, in a convertible sofa bed; see Schildt 1984, p. 74, fig. 99.

79. Given the contemporary interest in minimum living space, it is surprising to realize that although Breuer designed folding furniture, he never designed any stacking chairs. Stackable furniture is, on the other hand, a recurring theme in Aalto's work.

80. "The Humanizing of Architecture" (1940); reprinted in Schildt 1978, p. 77. A similar attitude is expressed in Aalto's lecture "Rationalism and Man" (1935), portions of which are reprinted ibid., pp. 47–51.

81. See bibliography, section 4, Wohnbedarf.

82. It has been suggested that it was not the actual furniture, but a catalogue that served as a source of inspiration for Mies van der Rohe: "There is . . . no doubt about . . . the source of [his] inspiration; a catalogue of the Alvar Aalto furniture exhibition at the Wohnbedarf store in Zurich, of 1933, was found among his sketches"; New York 1977, p. 16.

83. The compliment of imitation was not extended to Aalto's later Y-shaped or fan-leg designs; their superior craftsmanship and subtlety of design prevented most attempts at borrowing.

84. All the chairs by Mies van der Rohe mentioned here are published in New York 1977.

85. *Studio Year Book* 1932, p. 10.

86. Dennison, p. 72.

87. The Summers chair is noted in *Arts and Decoration* (November 1934), p. 59. It appears in an advertisement for Sanderson wallpapers in *Studio Year Book* 1935, p. AD. 11, and is cited in *The Thirties*, p. 150, cat. no. 477.

88. New York 1981b, figs. 135–41.

89. On Isokon, see New York 1981b, pp. 126–35; and Pritchard, pp. 111–21.

90. Apparently Aalto and his English distributor, Finmar Ltd., felt that Breuer's furniture represented an infringement of Aalto's English patents. Beginning in July 1936, Finmar's director, a Mr. Faulkner, as well as his partner, P. Morton Shand, corresponded at some length with Breuer and Jack Pritchard regarding the matter. The result was a license agreement between Finmar and Isokon that was negotiated but apparently never signed because Pritchard found an illustration of the Aalto chair that had been published before the date of the patent. Various stages of the correspondence are to be found in the Breuer Papers, Box 14, as well as in the Pritchard Archive, uncatalogued.

91. This portion of the letter is from the author's notes taken at the lecture "Aalto's Approach to Design," given by Göran Schildt at a symposium held at the Institute of International Education, New York, October 26, 1984, in conjunction with the Museum of Modern Art

exhibition *Alvar Aalto: Furniture and Glass*. Unfortunately, the complete text of this letter could not be made available to the author.

92. See New York 1938a. Wallace Harrison, Harmon Goldstone, and Laurance Rockefeller were so impressed that they started a firm (New Furniture Inc.) in 1939 to import Aalto furniture to America.

93. See Moholy-Nagy, pp. 88–91.

94. The claim, often repeated, is made in Drexler, p. 10, and in Miller, p. 110.

95. Information concerning the chair's exhibition in 1932, its advertisement in the Finnish magazine *Domus*, no. 4 (1932), and its use in the Women's Hospital, Helsinki, in 1934, was provided by Igor Herler of Helsinki to Alexander von Vegesack, Düsseldorf. It is not mentioned in Schildt 1984, although the subsequent upholstered high-back armchair Artek model 401 appears to be based on the chair under discussion.

96. Pallasmaa, p. 139, fig. 212, Artek armchair 401. The chair was exhibited at the *Esposizione internazionale della Arti decorative ed industriali moderne* (Milan Triennial 1933); see Felice, p. 283.

97. The Summers chair was largely forgotten until illustrated in Ostergard, p. 49.

98. At the time of writing, it was not yet possible to gain access to the papers of Charles and Ray Eames, donated to the Library of Congress in 1982. Much new information will surely emerge when these papers become available for study.

99. The term *shell* was used from the beginning by the designers themselves and may have first appeared in print in New York 1941, p. 11.

100. See Logie, pp. 96–98, writing in 1947 on the novelty of true "moulded" plywood: "As a method it is still expensive, and this may retard its use for furniture until new and cheaper processes have been discovered."

101. Since there is no comprehensive monograph on the Eameses' furniture, and as their papers are still unavailable (see n. 98), much information on this period remains to be gathered. McCoy, p. 134, refers to a "plant jointly owned by Eames and John Entenza."

102. Drexler, p. 12.

103. The same may be said of much contemporary writing on their work, especially texts in which the Eameses themselves or the Herman Miller Company were involved; see Los Angeles 1976, pp. 24–26; and Caplan, pp. 43–60.

104. Saarinen, p. 66; this is not included in the subsequent edition of 1968. Recently quoted in Miller, p. 110.

105. Giedion, p. 508.

106. McCoy, p. 157 n. 4 mentions the parabolic arches in the architecture of Felix Candala as a contemporary instance of such curvilinear forms.

6
The social and cultural context of bent wood and metal furniture

ROBERT KEIL

THEY were the choice of the Kaiser, they graced the stylish coffeehouses of Europe, and eventually they found their way into offices and homes around the world. They were bent-wood chairs, and their development was no less than a revolutionary new design, a merging of art and technology. Furniture styles throughout history have mirrored cultural levels and changes in social attitudes. This is perhaps best seen in the changing form of the ubiquitous chair, that most basic piece of furniture and, as in the case of bent wood, often the first to be rendered in a new style or material.

Chair design is closely linked to customs in seating. Even today, such conventions preserve centuries-old hierarchies of authority, and the chair itself can reflect the status of the sitter. The chair as throne, symbol of authority, survives today in the thronelike chair of many an office executive. At home, the family's seating order around the dining table or the way in which the family gathers around the television set are both old and new rituals.[1] While some of these conventions remain unchanged, the shape of the chair and other furniture has metamorphosed with each new period in history. Some change occurs through consumer demand, spurred on by technological advances; in other cases, new designs are in response to changes from within the social or economic realm. Bent-wood furniture and its offspring, tubular-steel furniture, provide an excellent opportunity to examine both occasions of change.

Innovators and discoverers of any new phenomena think and act within the prevailing social climate; consumer response to the new product is subject to the same influences. Bent-wood construction came into being within the historical context of the nineteenth century in Europe, at a time when both the technology and the market were ready. Since then, the basic technique of making furniture from bent materials has not changed significantly. Such modern materials as tubular steel, layers of material glued together, plywood, and molded plastic are merely variations reflecting recent technological innovations. For today's users, bent-wood furniture is still a splendid innovation that continues to prove itself worldwide.

Defining the market for bent wood is not so easily accomplished. Since the early nineteenth century, when the bent-wood furniture style was first introduced, there have been fundamental social changes, particularly in Europe, that have affected the response of various social groups to design in general and bent-wood and tubular-steel furniture in particular. Through sociological and aesthetic analysis, following the guidelines set down by social research, these responses are made clear.[2]

Early days

The process of bending wood was the invention of Michael Thonet (1796–1871), a Prussian craftsman whose career epitomizes the dawning of the Industrial Revolution. Trained in the high tradition of European craftsmanship, Thonet had an intense personal drive as well as a strong economic sense that enabled him to adjust to economic fluctuations in launching his new designs. He, like the other craftsmen of his era, possessed a solid foundation in his craft and a keen awareness of quality. However, unlike most of his peers, he was willing to experiment, to engage in that intellectual activity most fraught with uncertainty.

Thonet's experiments in bending wood began around 1830, when he fashioned chairs from bent strips of veneer. Until then, the aesthetic demand for curved furniture had to be met by carving designs from solid pieces of wood, a time-consuming process. With the increasing demand for such designs and with the introduction of veneer —thin sheets of high-grade wood used to produce a beautifully refined wood surface—Thonet had both the

impetus and technological basis for his experiments. Inspiration and technique are not always enough for success; luck plays an undeniable role, and for Thonet, luck took the form of a meeting with Prince Clemens von Metternich, the Austrian chancellor. The Viennese statesman, favorably impressed with Thonet's work, was to have a profound influence on the life and career of the craftsman.[3]

Metternich, who became chancellor in 1821, had been the driving force behind the Congress of Vienna (1814–15). An ultraconservative, he had sought not only to restore the order and political power structures that had been destroyed by the Napoleonic Wars, but also to revive absolutism within the Austro-Hungarian Empire. Censors-0ip of the press, a ban on freedom of assembly, enlargement of the secret police, and institution of the practice of denunciation crippled every form of political activity.

On the economic front, however, Metternich pursued a relatively more enlightened policy. He encouraged foreign manufacturers and investors to come to Austria with their new products and processes, among them the German steel producers Krupp and Bleckmann, whose technological expertise laid the foundations for Austrian manufacturing as it exists today.[4] Thonet, like Metternich, was a native Rhinelander, and in 1841, during a visit by the chancellor to his homeland, the two men met. A year later, at Metternich's invitation, Thonet had moved to Vienna and for the first time was submitting furniture made of bent veneer parts to a European industrial exhibition—in Mainz—where the concept of bent-wood furniture was given an enthusiastic reception. The accompanying catalogue discussed the basic advantages of bent-wood construction over traditional production methods, calling Thonet's designs "stable and stylistically elegant; his furniture is pleasingly light in weight and has the features of requiring less wood and permitting more rapid manufacture."[5] In so saying, the writer anticipated later mass production of bent-wood furniture and the reasons for its success.

Thonet's new process was to benefit from Metternich's state-controlled policy of industrialization. New products, such as bent-wood furniture, were intended to increase consumption and result in greater prosperity. Such a consumer society can develop only when needs are created and met; on a broad basis this is accomplished through industrialization. But in Austria as in the rest of Europe, the Industrial Revolution caused extensive social upheaval, making it increasingly difficult to define the target group for certain products, a situation typified by the early years of bent-wood furniture.

Today's research into the identity of the original market for bent-wood furniture is further hampered by the paucity of archival material such as sales orders, business records, and correspondence. Over the years, one way or another, such records were destroyed. However, we can surmise much by studying the social and aesthetic behavior patterns of different social classes during the last century, beginning with the way in which Thonet's early designs were popularized.

Through Metternich, Thonet gained access to the royal court and upper aristocracy of the Austro-Hungarian Empire. His first assignment was to make parquet flooring from designs by Karl Leistler for Prince Alois von Liechtenstein, to be installed in the Palais Lichtenstein in the city of Vienna. By the late 1840s, he had left such work behind and was producing chairs for palaces in Vienna and Bohemia, the homes of other aristocratic trendsetters such as Prince Schwarzenberg, who became chief minister to the newly installed emperor, Franz Josef I.

Initial acceptance by this small group of influential patrons from the upper echelons of society, along with technological developments to this point had assured the popularity of Thonet's bent-wood furniture designs among the aristocracy. These first clients, like many of their modern-day counterparts, responded positively to the new designs not so much out of a desire to improve the standard of living by supporting a new industry, but simply from their pleasure in owning something new and different, something quite exotic; they acted on a certain naïve, playful impulse common to every age.[6] However, while the early purchasers may have been attracted to newness for its own sake, the ultimate success of the first generation of bent-wood furniture must also be attributed to the stability and lightness of the design and the favorable price structure.

With an influential, wealthy clientele practically guaranteeing a steady market for his work, Thonet turned his attention to the production phase of his operation. In his Vienna workshop, he began to streamline production by making a precise division of labor, with different workers performing different tasks—from cutting the wood, bending, glueing, and polishing it, to the final caning or weaving of the seat surface. By 1853, he had a staff of forty-three employees, including nine cabinetmakers, which for the time was a relatively large number of employees.[7]

By comparison, elsewhere in Vienna, in the late 1840s, each independent cabinetmaker hired just two or three workers; in all there were 1,617 such cabinetmakers to meet the needs of the city's 430,000 inhabitants. In no way could these small manual operations compete with Thonet, whose workshop was on the brink of industrialization even though, for the moment, production was still based on manual labor performed by skilled craftsmen. By 1869, the year Thonet's patent ran out, most other cabinetmakers had emulated Thonet and had tripled their work forces. This alone attests to the extremely high level of productivity in the early manufacture of bent-wood furniture.[8]

Outside the nobility, Thonet's work gained the admiration of the proprietess of Vienna's famous Café Daum. In 1849, she commissioned him to make bent-wood side chairs for the café. Through this important assignment, Thonet expanded the market for his still-experimental designs which were steadily gaining popularity among the many visitors to the café, and Thonet obtained his next major commission—an order for four hundred chairs for the Hotel zur Königin von England in Budapest. Such a large order reflects the immediate enthusiasm for Thonet's totally new kind of furniture; it also represents a turning point in the economic and historical development of bent wood.[9]

Mass-produced bent-wood furniture was one of the first new products whose success depended largely on the creation of a need. As a handmade item for the original smallish circle of aristocratic clients, it was certainly successful, but as a mass-produced item, bent-wood furniture owed its phenomenal success to improvements in shipping practices that were the result of the Industrial Revolution. For Thonet, the possibility of reaching a worldwide market was the decisive factor in switching over completely to mass production.[10] And reach it he did, for between 1850 and 1871, Thonet's factories produced more than 4 million pieces of bent-wood furniture, mostly chairs, of which some 2.6 million were exported.[11] The remainder were sold within the Austro-Hungarian Empire; to define this home market it is essential to set it against the backdrop of Europe at mid-century, a time of complex social, economic, and aesthetic change, which saw the disintegration of old feudal, social, and political structures and the evolution of a new class system based on economics. These fundamental changes, combined with the slowly accelerating mobility between social classes, muddy the waters of history until eventually it becomes impossible to isolate the judgments and attitudes toward taste and aesthetics held by any one class.[12]

Stirrings of revolution

The year 1848 was one of political upheaval across Europe. A new nationalistic yearning for liberalism and constitutional government spawned revolutions in France, Italy, England, and Austria. In Vienna, in March of that year, an ill-assorted group of workers and students took to the streets, setting up barricades and storming the imperial palace, momentarily disturbing the foundations of power. Metternich, badly shaken, fled Vienna, traveling undercover to London. Paradoxically, it had been the double-edged sword of his internal policies that had been his downfall. The same industrialization process he had fostered had given the bourgeoisie that he had simultaneously sought to repress just the economic power and impetus to change needed for revolution.

In Austria, the revolution was short-lived. By December 1848, a counterrevolution of conservatives had regained control and installed a new emperor, the eighteen-year-old Franz-Josef. In the wake of the 1848 revolution, a new and more repressive regime was established under Prince Schwarzenberg and his minister of the interior, Alexander Bach. So antiliberal was this regime that it came to be defined as "a standing army of soldiers, a sitting army of officials, a kneeling army of priests, and a creeping army of informers."[13]

Despite the failure of the revolution, it did foster certain lasting changes, notably the abolition of serfdom. Newly liberated from virtual agrarian slavery, an army of workers streamed from Moravia and Bohemia into the already densely populated cities, seeking to improve their lot. While the revolution of 1848 provided the labor, the Industrial Revolution produced the jobs, for in the old city centers had been built new, mechanized factories ready to employ the steadily arriving emigrants from the countryside. However, while they may have found work easily, they also found grinding poverty and a housing shortage, and their new jobs paid little.

In 1840, at the beginning of the Industrial Revolution in Austria, Vienna's population was around 420,000; by 1870, it had swollen to 843,000. At the same time, housing construction had made no attempt to keep pace with this growth. Those with capital to invest were much more eager to put it into more profitable industrial ventures than into housing, and during the 1850s, home-building came to a standstill.[14] Rents were high; apartments, tiny and overcrowded; and their furnishings of little or no concern to their miserable inhabitants. Craftsmen, no longer able to compete with machine-produced wares turned out by their country cousins, were slowly becoming impoverished, and most eventually had to join the ranks of the proletariat and give up their qualitatively better apartments.[15]

Bent-wood furniture and the bourgeoisie

While the Industrial Revolution may have meant poverty to some, to others it spelled opportunity. A new middle class, struggling to emerge from the ranks of the proletariat, gained status through economic means. For them, the Industrial Revolution established a new rhythm of daily life which had a definite impact within the home. Like the various stages of production in the new factories, home and workplace were now separated. No longer did a single skilled craftsman, with one or two assistants working in a small workshop (usually an adjunct to his home), control the entire process of manufacture. Increasingly among the bourgeoisie, the home became the private realm for family living. And, in Austria, under the repressive policies of first Metternich, then Schwarzenberg and Bach, the bourgeoisie, effectively disenfranchised, turned more and more inward, resorting to a family-oriented life style characterized by a quest for privacy and a pursuit of culture. In this early capitalist society, the ideal of privacy and family life constituted the two most important criteria distinguishing the middle classes from the rapidly increasing working class whose restricted living spaces afforded no truly private areas for the family.

Before 1850, the bourgeoisie had popularized the Biedermeier style, so named after a philistine character in the journal *Fliegende Blätter*. The style, an elaborately carved and debased Austrian version of French Empire, was a deliberate attempt by the bourgeoisie to emulate the upper classes and to improve the quality of the home. Ironically, the style may have originated with the bourgeoisie, but it was adopted by the Austrian aristocracy, a transition that, until then, was unprecedented.[16]

As the financially strong bourgeoisie increased, their urge to display their new wealth grew apace. A certain change in furnishing styles was already noticeable by the mid-1840s. The Biedermeier style, no longer seen as a satisfying reflection of status, was replaced by a stylistic borrowing from the Rococo—the Rococo Revival—which in turn gave way to a pluralism of styles now generally designated as historicism.[17] This meant that within a single home, several styles could be used at once—from Baroque for the music room to Italian Renaissance for the dining room.

The upper middle class tended to imitate the past styles and forms associated with the ruling class, and luxury furniture was considered obligatory (figure 6–1). Designed and produced for the individual client (at least in the most affluent social circles), richly adorned and made of the most expensive materials, this furniture was intended to reflect, even raise, the status of the user. The lower middle class had to settle for copies, which were eventually machine-made, crude in comparison to the original, but still intended to be "luxury furniture."

The desire to advertise new status also determined the arrangement of residential spaces. The intimate areas, consisting of master bedroom and children's rooms, were mostly banished to the private, innermost sectors of the

apartment, hidden from the view of strangers. The reception rooms, depending on function, were furnished in any of the various styles borrowed from the past. Walls and ceilings were paneled or covered with heavy wallpaper; windows were hung with thick brocade curtains to keep the sun and natural daylight out and to impart a twilight aura to the space. The impression of gloom was intensified by heavy furniture, especially thickly upholstered settees and easy chairs, that concealed the logical, architectonic structures.[18]

Capturing the mood at mid-century, the catalogue for the Great Exhibition of 1851, held at the Crystal Palace in London, illustrates the range of historical styles considered suitable for homes of the well-to-do. Despite all manner of variations in furniture style, the interiors of the time reveal aesthetic constants: structural elements were con-

Figure 6–1

An upper-middle-class dining room, typical of the era. Am Heumarkt 19, Speisezimmer, Vienna, ca. 1880.

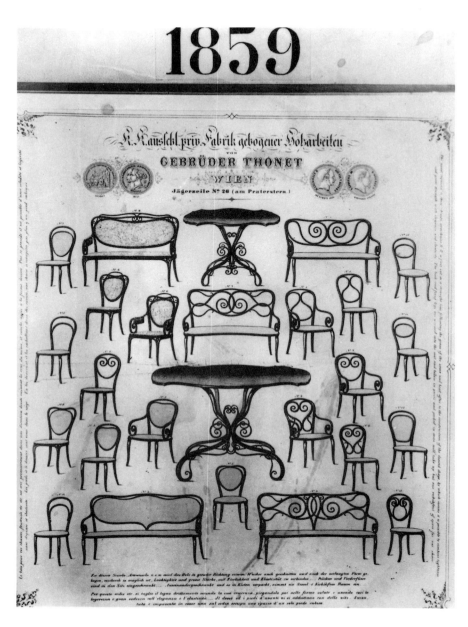

Figure 6–2
Salon furnishings. Sales catalogue of Gebrüder Thonet, 1859.

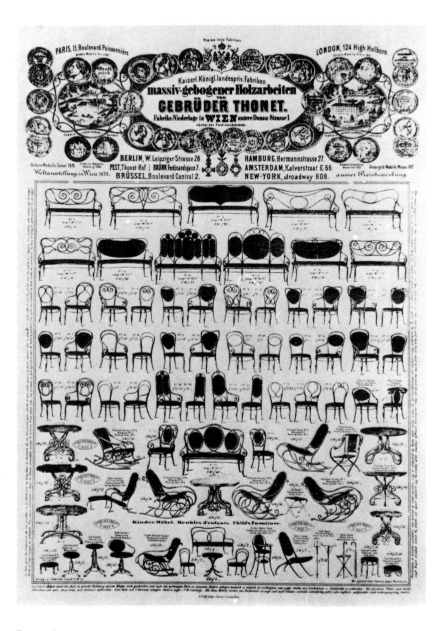

Figure 6–3
Bent-wood furnishings, including walking sticks (*lower right*). Sales catalogue of Gebrüder Thonet, 1873.

cealed; and surfaces were carved or heavily ornamented, never smooth and polished. These design principles were completely at odds with the essence of bent-wood furniture, whose most essential criteria are its revealed structure and smooth, rounded surfaces.[19]

In the context of the room, each object was intended to produce an artistic effect by means of its differentiated surface. The angles, moldings, and columns became blurred in the light filtered through glass windowpanes; the massive structural elements disappeared into colorful nuances. This cult of furnishing ultimately created an illusory world within the apartment, a virtual stage setting for acting out social roles.[20]

The theoretical basis for the primacy of the ornamented surface is spelled out by Gottfried Semper, who considered the curtain the basic element of architecture. Semper derived his theory from the structure of the tent, man's first architectural design, which provided protection from nature by means of the skin—the curtain. Semper's architectural theory was of decisive importance to nineteenth-century historicism. In its application to furniture, it meant that the essential element was the visible surface rather than the actual architectonic structure. Paradoxically, Semper also demanded that "an object must primarily serve its utilitarian purpose. No material employed should be used against its essence or in imitation of another."[21] Only furniture made of bent wood was capable of meeting these criteria, but bent-wood furniture did not belong in the illusory world just described.

While Thonet's first bent-wood chairs had been for aristocratic clients who used them to provide seating at large social functions, by the 1850s Thonet was designing chair and table sets especially for use as salon furnishings (figure 6–2). Throughout society, the salon was the domain of the housewife, and she was not yet ready for the look of bent wood in her social dreams and cultural dramas. In her salon, she stage-directed social occasions in an illusory world. That is was merely an illusion is especially evident in the homes of the lower middle class, where a single room often served several functions—dining room, living room, and salon. Space limitations made it impossible for this room, usually furnished in an imitation Renaissance style that mimicked the furnishings of the

aristocracy, to accommodate any "unnecessary" objects such as a set of bent-wood chairs. In terms of taste the simple and transparent form of lightweight bent-wood furniture seemed meager, a characteristic incompatible with the striving for higher social status.

If the housewife was not yet ready to incorporate bent-wood furniture into her salon's elaborate furniture schemes, she did find a ready place for it in the oriel—that small windowed alcove off the salon, facing the street. Most bourgeois apartments included such a space; it continued the tradition of both oriental balcony and medieval corner tower. Usually only several square feet in area, it was the brightest place in the entire apartment, making it the ideal setting both for plants and for a small set of elegant bent-wood chairs.[22]

Bent-wood furniture also found a ready place in the less-formal country homes of the upper middle classes. Starting in the 1870s, the bourgeoisie began to build country retreats in the outskirts of the historic city centers. There they followed the fashion of spending a vacation relaxing in their own country houses. They sought ideal romantic settings with perfect panoramas—views of unsullied nature, of steep, rocky mountains and deep-blue alpine lakes—as backdrops for their otherworldly feelings. It was nature in sharp contrast to life in the city where light and air were consciously excluded from the home. In the country house, the furnishings could be simpler, and bent-wood furniture, with its unupholstered frames and light, airy structure, coincided with the bourgeois longing for rural simplicity.

Toward the end of the nineteenth century, large hotels and sanatoriums were also built outside the city centers and in alpine regions. They were designed as health-giving retreats for the bourgeoisie from the ills often connected with city life. After all, tuberculosis showed no favorites; it occurred wherever there were unhygienic living conditions, whether among the poorest of the lower classes or the wealthiest of the bourgeoisie. Bent-wood furniture was very much in keeping with the precepts of hygiene. In addition to the already familiar chairs and other furniture, Thonet's 1873 catalogue offered footstools, rocking chairs, and walking sticks that doubled as seating (figure 6–3). All were found in country hotels and homes, and though relatively inexpensive, they could be afforded only by the small, affluent segment of society that had both time and money for relaxation, a life style denied the poorer classes. Even today, elaborate bent-wood furniture is often found in vacation homes.

Starting in 1860, a patented rocking chair was included in the Thonet factory production schedule. It reflects Thonet's practice of creating demand by designing a new product for the European market.[23] While the rocking chair had been popular in the United States, particularly in rural areas, for more than half a century, it was slow to catch on in mid-nineteenth-century Europe. Again, space restrictions in city apartments made it impossible for such a large piece of furniture to attract more than a limited number of buyers. The average apartment consisted of a combination living–dining room and a bedroom, while many simple dwellings had but a single room and a kitchen, sometimes with a tiny extra room that was frequently sublet to help pay the rent.

Another Thonet innovation was a line of children's furniture introduced in the 1873 catalogue. Separate living and play areas for children dated from the Biedermeier era, when middle-class living spaces were first divided into public and private areas. Among the less-affluent bourgeoisie, the child's play area occupied a corner of the adult's living room, until the family moved a step up the social ladder and the child was banished to the kitchen. In the apartments of the upper middle class, the child's room, like the master bedroom, was well out of sight. The children and their nursemaid lived in a separate world that provided the setting for children's rocking chairs, benches, and small tables in imitation of the adult world. During at least the first half of the nineteenth century, the furnishing of separate children's rooms with specially designed children's furniture was a privilege restricted to wealthy families.[24]

The working classes

The identity of Thonet's early high-born clients and the kinds of furniture that Thonet chose to render in bent wood—music stands, footstools, clothing stands, and rocking chairs, for example—clearly refute the oft-held notion that bent-wood furniture was a poor people's furniture, that the "vanguard of change could be mainly under-privileged classes who themselves had nothing to lose."[25] Despite mass production and relatively low prices, bent-wood furniture, in at least its first generation, was meant for the affluent bourgeoisie and aristocracy, whether in their homes, in the fashionable cafés habituated by the intelligentsia, or in the country hotels and sanitoriums. The fashionable addresses of the Thonet showrooms in Vienna, Paris, London, Berlin, New York, and other large cities also suggest an upper-class market for the first generation of bent-wood furniture.

Among the working classes, in Vienna as in every European city at mid-century, poverty, the constant battle for existence, and the severe housing shortage were the overriding concerns. Furniture, beyond the barest necessities, was a luxury few could afford. A profile of Vienna at mid-century, its working classes, and the conditions under which they struggled for survival, will serve to reflect every European industrial center. Vienna had the dubious distinction of leading all other cities at the time in such areas as mortality rate, ratio of illegitimate to legitimate births, overcrowded housing, and high percentage of salary spent on rent.[26]

The housing shortage had been the main problem of the poorer classes since the start of the Industrial Revolution. In Vienna the number of inhabitants in a small apartment consisting of one room and an anteroom rose from an average of three people in 1830 to five in 1857. In the 1860s, housing construction slowly resumed after almost a ten-year hiatus. Even so, it made little headway. In 1857, one-third of the total number of apartments in Vienna were absolutely minimal in size: one room and a kitchen. Sixty years later, in 1917, one-half of all the apartments were that small.[27] The systematic reduction in size of newly constructed apartments was at the expense of the somewhat more generously laid-out middle-class apartments. In reference to apartment size, it was almost as if there was a bipolar social system in which the middle class was systematically squeezed between the two extremes.

The ratio of rent to salary dropped as income and luxury

levels increased. One-quarter of a working-class resident's wages went to pay the rent; for those in the middle class, the percentage was one-sixth, while among the upper middle class, an apartment of eight to ten rooms required only one-tenth of the family income. During the 1880s, an unskilled worker earned approximately three gulden per day, which was the price of the cheapest bent-wood chair (Thonet No. 14; see cat. nos. 14–18). Such a worker was hardly likely to spend a full day's wages on a single piece of furniture.

The majority of laborers arriving in Vienna from rural areas had been small farmers or tradesmen and had lived in extremely modest circumstances. Rural poverty was a far cry from the idyllic country life portrayed by Romantic artists and writers, and however miserable the minimal city apartments of these new urbanites appear to be, they were still an improvement over the former rural housing (figure 6–4). Average working-class housing consisted of a total space of about 133 square feet (40 square meters), with a communal bathroom off the public hallway. Most of the newly arrived rural workers could not afford an apartment of their own, however small. In 1869, just over 55 percent of Vienna's workers had no independent housing: almost 3 percent were housed by their employers, over 13 percent were roomers, and almost 19 percent were so-called bed-subletters, that is, they paid for the use of a bed while the tenant was out working a factory shift. By the 1880s, a housing unit consisting of three rooms (living room/bedroom, kitchen, and tiny one-windowed room) could legally house up to twelve people without having the medical officer declare it overcrowded. This was even at odds with the space requirements governing prisons and hospitals at the same time: there, the minimum space per person was about 13 square feet (4 square meters).[28]

This kind of miserable housing prevailed until the 1920s. Apart from the obviously unhygienic conditions, under the circumstances there could be no private, orderly family life, the highest ideal of the bourgeoisie during the nineteenth century. Instances of adultery and abuse and an increase in illegitimate births were the result of so many people, both family and nonfamily members, sharing a cramped living space.

Figure 6–4

Workers' lodgings. Vienna, 1883. (From *Illustriertes Wiener Extrablatt*, December 21, 1883, p. 1).

While bourgeois apartments were still sufficiently spacious to permit good hygiene, the workers' homes lacked even such basic essentials as adequate light and air. Although housing was in short supply, there was still a great density of buildings in Vienna, meaning that apartments were dark, with narrow patios and poor ventilation. (Construction covered as much as 85 percent of the entire area.)[29] To compound these problems, in winter the windows were sealed with paper to economize on heating fuel. In such an environment, diseases such as tuberculosis, rheumatism, and gout found many victims.

After 1880, the increase in the number of apartments served to reduce at least the ranks of bed-subletters but compelled the family to live in still less space. In addition to the bedroom containing little more than a bed or beds, the apartment included a living area ordinarily consisting of a single room for the entire family, usually furnished with rough, unfinished benches and tables.

The grim picture does not stop there, however, for at

the poorest levels, renters had to change apartments often. This was usually not a matter of choice, but rather the result of eviction if the rent was at all late in being paid. For each tenant lost, another was found ready to take his place. In Vienna in 1900, with a total availability of 370,000 apartments, there were annually about 130,000 moves. Each move meant an added expense, one that most tenants could ill afford. Under such conditions, it is hardly surprising that bent-wood furniture did not make much headway among the working class. The reality of poverty, then as now, leaves little room for such luxuries as style.

Around 1850, socially conscious members of the upper classes began to take up the cause of working-class living conditions. While the Great Exhibition of 1851, held in London at Joseph Paxton's famous Crystal Palace, may have included luxurious examples of Thonet's bent-wood furniture, it also devoted one section to the welfare of the working class. A worker's house, designed by Prince Albert, stood directly beside the entrance to the Crystal Palace.[30] By the time of the Paris Exposition Universelle of 1855, the inclusion of such an exhibition had become a regular feature of large commercial fairs. Congresses addressing the issue of working-class living conditions were held annually in one or another of the capitals of Europe, where new products aimed at the working-class market were displayed.

At the Paris Exposition Universelle of 1867, examples of joinery were exhibited in the tenth and fourteenth classes, and bent-wood designs were singled out for praise by the Prussian newspaper *Der Arbeiterfreund*:

> Worthy of mention is furniture made of bent wood by the brothers Thonet from Moravia. Except for quite small spirals, only two pieces of wood are used in the construction of a bent-wood chair, which consequently is very durable and graceful.
>
> The same exhibitors also display a sample of sturdy wood approximately two feet long by two square inches that is bent into the shape of a snake. Several other pieces of furniture made in Austria should preferably have been left at home. The folding armchairs, though, are comfortable and practical.[31]

Interestingly, no bent-wood furniture was displayed in the ninety-first section of the exposition, where low-priced furniture—*meubles, vêtements, etc., au bon marché*—was shown.[32] Instead, iron furniture was recommended for its durability, ease of shipment, low maintenance, and relative low cost. Of the wood furniture in the section, "the inexpensive Canadian products, not finished but instead merely smoothed over with glasspaper, assumed a conspicuous place. These items are almost entirely machine made and can be disassembled, hence can easily be shipped. It is very probable that this very inexpensive and durable furniture will soon be available in great quantity on the European markets and, along with iron furniture, will fill an important function in apartments of the poorer classes."[33] Again, such an omission suggests that bent-wood furniture was closely associated with the upper classes, no matter what its price structure.

Wicker furniture of French origin was also singled out as appropriate for poorer classes because it was considered both durable and hygienic. In the working-class home "for reasons of cleansing the air, particular consideration is given to uncluttered, lean shapes and easy maintenance. The ease with which wicker furniture can be moved must also be considered a positive factor for interior ventilation. It must always be kept in mind that a worker's dwelling should lend itself to maintenance with the least possible expenditure of labor by the housewife who has no servants."[34] For these reasons, as well as the frequent moves made by the working classes, housing reformers in mid-century began to suggest that workers' apartments be mostly ready-furnished: "A great deal of time and energy gets lost in people's moves if they take along their own old things. In addition, old furnishings may bring dirt and vermin into new apartments."[35] However, it would not be until the 1920s and the Bauhaus that these utopian demands would slowly be turned into reality.

Bent-wood furniture, which shared all the same hygienic and structural advantages as iron or wicker, seems to have fallen roughly midway between so-called luxury furniture and the simple household effects deemed appropriate for the poorer classes. It continued to possess an air of elegance associated with Thonet's early patrons from the upper echelons of society and was not readily recognized as ideal furnishing for working-class homes until tastes and times changed.

Commercial milieus: cafés and offices

Beginning in 1849 with Thonet's first substantial commission—seating for Vienna's Café Daum—the bent-wood chair became an integral part of the design of such public spaces as cafés, restaurants, and hotels. Since then, millions of bent-wood chairs have been in use in recreational spaces around the world—from Cairo to New Orleans to such remote outposts as the Tonga Islands in the Pacific. The simple, ubiquitous design has created an international look, an ambience at once universal and familiar, no longer associated with any one country. That the bent-wood chair has saturated the world market for such seating is reflected in a German trade paper report for the furniture industry: "the 'Viennese chairs' are increasingly excluding seating of German manufacture from the international market. Throughout Germany, cafés and restaurants that were opened since the end of World War I are almost exclusively furnished with bent-wood furniture."[36] Indeed, more than 50 million copies of Thonet's simple No. 14 chair have been produced since the first one was given its final coat of varnish.

This domination of the world market is hardly surprising; the very idea of the "café chair" originated in Austria, specifically in Vienna, the empire's economic and intellectual center. A kind of coffeehouse culture had existed there since the late seventeenth century, reaching a high point during the Industrial Revolution. Soon, cafés could be found throughout the empire; every small provincial town, from Galicia to Trieste, boasted an establishment with a so-called Viennese ambience.

The cafés of Europe have long been a primary meeting place for men of ideas, fulfilling certain basic needs. In Vienna the newspapers, however numerous, could not quench the tremendous thirst for gossip. The café filled this need, offering a place to meet and talk, a forum for ideas, and an informal setting for simple relaxation (figure 6–5). There, the diverse array of offerings, from newspapers and magazines to game rooms for chess and bridge, provided ample distraction from life's problems. Patrons could spend hours over a single cup of coffee, reading, playing cards, or discussing everything from economics and stock reports to the arts and cultural issues.

Figure 6-5
Café scene, *A Night Out* with Charlie Chaplin, 1915.

Figure 6-6
The garden room of the Café Eckel. Vienna, ca. 1900.

Such cafés, however, still maintained the strict boundaries of class (figure 6–6). Basically, the inner-city café was reserved for members of the bourgeoisie. Urbanites below this level of society were not welcome, and workers from the urban ghettos, or from the suburbs, did not penetrate this alien world even on Sundays, their one day off.[37] In the suburbs, inns and dance halls replaced cafés as meeting places, welcome escapes from the harsh realities of life within small, cramped sleeping quarters. These establishments were especially popular during the winter months when people sought to economize on lighting and heating fuel, although economic considerations were always secondary to social ones.

While the bourgeoisie of the city may have frequented cafés, even for them not all social barriers were suspended in this setting. Different cafés catered to different clienteles, and even the choice of bent-wood furniture in the individual locations reflected precise differences in class. The Café Daum is a good example of an establishment serving members of a specific social strata. Situated near the imperial residence, "the Café Daum offered one speciality: it was frequented by representatives of the imperial army regardless of rank. It borrowed from the character of a military casino of the mid-nineteenth century. Its patrons knew it as a setting that offered the greatest opportunity to encounter out-of-town colleagues temporarily on assignment in Vienna."[38] Here upper aristocracy and military elite mingled.

The other basic function of the café was to give the head of the household a place in which to relax alone or with friends. The bourgeois apartment not only lacked coziness, but by day it was the exclusive realm of the wife, the place in which she received her own guests.

There was little opportunity for her husband to relax at home, either in the half light of the heavily draped and furnished mid-nineteenth-century parlor, or in the later simplified but highly stylized world of the modern or Jugendstil apartment. The man gladly gave up his upholstered easy chair at home for the hard, anonymous bent-wood chair and the camaraderie of the café. Social reformers cast a critical eye on this function of the café, noting that drinking was more likely to become a problem for those who had no private realm at home for relaxation (figure 6-7) The solution as they saw it was to raise public funds for use in building inexpensive, simple and clean apartments, and not for investment in speculative transactions.

Whatever the reason for fleeing the everyday world of home and work, the patron of the humblest inn or the most fashionable café was certain to find there the reassuring presence of the bent-wood chair. The design might still have been considered taboo as home furnishing, but its merit as café seating was quickly recognized. Its inclusion in the workplace was also soon assured.

The Industrial Revolution and the shift from an agrarian to an industrial society brought about several fundamental changes in the workplace. The small family-run banks were no longer able to keep up with the demand for investment capital. Before 1848, just five such banks had handled almost the entire capital market in the Austrian Empire. By 1869, there were 3,900 commercial banks and other financial institutions providing this service. New businesses flourished; between 1867 and 1873, about one thousand new companies were founded.[39] As finance and industry grew, so too did its paperwork. No longer could a small home office or one adjacent to the factory floor handle all the sales orders, bookkeeping, payroll, and other clerical demands. Many Austrian companies moved their offices out of the plant altogether and transferred them to Vienna.

Perhaps the largest of the new office industries was a relative newcomer to the world's business arena—the insurance company. Originating in England in the 1800s, specifically as insurers against fire damage, the insurance company expanded its coverage to include factories and factory workers, a logical extension of the Industrial

Figure 6-7
A. Laridelly. *Life in a Suburban Café, Vienna*, ca. 1870. Watercolor, pen and ink on paper.

Revolution's economic boom. Gradually, an army of office employees emerged from the ranks of proletarian workers, and the idea of white-collar and blue-collar worker was born. The division of labor for the purpose of cost-efficiency dominated office work as it had factory work.[40]

Within the new domain of the office, furnishings were simple and sober, and the bent-wood chair became a symbol of the serious work atmosphere nurtured in commerce and at the highest political levels. Emperor Franz Josef I, who called himself the highest "official" of the state, chose a simple bent-wood chair for his study in Schönbrunn (figure 6–8), where in the midst of so much eighteenth-century finery its humble presence strikes an alien note. The room's ambience expresses the contradictory attitude and symbolic language of the late nineteenth century better than any theoretical investigation. Interestingly, in the United States, in the 1890s, President Benjamin Harrison also chose a bent-wood chair for his desk in the Oval Office of the White House.

As the nineteenth century progressed, bent-wood furniture dominated both office and café. Its ubiquitous presence in the public sphere, however welcome, slowed its acceptance in the home.

Figure 6–8
Hans Temple. Portrait of Kaiser Franz Josef I in his study, August 15, 1915.

Transition: new producers, new directions

In 1869, the patent held by Thonet Brothers expired. Competing companies, particularly the firm of Jacob & Josef Kohn, leapt into the field and began producing imitations of Thonet's popular chairs, notably the legendary, low-priced model No. 14. Yet, that same year, in Amsterdam, at the International Exhibition of Objects for the Domestic and Commercial Need of the Working Class, more attention was paid to iron furniture made in England and France than to the widening supply of bent wood designs. No mention at all was made of Thonet's classic, the No. 14 chair. Instead a reviewer cited "bent-wood furniture that was very effectively displayed by August Knoblauch in Vienna—cane-bottom chairs for three Dutch gulden—[and that] attracted appropriate interest, although

it must be said that only more prosperous workers could take advantage of it."[41]

From this point on, the bent-wood furniture industry began to change, both in its production and technology and in its response to shifts in taste as the century came to a close. No longer was it necessary to create a demand for a new product; instead, sound economics dictated that the industry simply accommodate the prevailing taste in order to compete in the home-furniture market. By the late 1870s, new technology enabled bent-wood furniture manufacturers to produce more heavily ornamented designs than the simple chairs of the first generation of bent wood. Entire rooms could now be furnished in bent wood designs, and the new producers took advantage of this development.[42]

The J. & J. Kohn company's promotional brochure of 1898 hinted at the firm's orientation toward a specific purchasing class: "From the outset, the firm of Kohn strove, not by means of greater production, but by means of a new direction, to eliminate the exclusive reliance on the round rod and also to include within the framework of its offerings the manufacture of seating made of angular, bent rods decorated with molding, designs, and sculpture. The efforts resulted in more expensive and elegant bent-wood furniture that was adapted as closely as possible to the most various kinds of styles—Baroque, Renaissance, Gothic."[43] The brochure criticized the Thonet system of bending only round rods, calling it a "characteristic" that slowed progress, for "improvement of this furniture was necessarily limited since it was purchased . . . mainly for coffeehouses and businesses."[44] The goal of J. & J. Kohn's new production and sales policy was to popularize bent-wood furniture for "elegant dwellings and to eliminate the prejudice against the suitability of furniture made of bent wood even in the country of its origin."[45] This meant producing bent wood designs that were translations of earlier styles and conformed to the middle-class taste for ornament.

At the Paris Exposition Universelle of 1878, J. & J. Kohn displayed an elegant bedroom suite and various sets of salon furniture in the Renaissance style; they embodied the new direction in the bent-wood furniture industry. Unfortunately, this new direction meant a debasement of the very principle that had been the main attraction of bent wood design: the lean lines and smooth surfaces of the wood were now disfigured with stylish moldings, and the structure was concealed. Kohn's imitation of earlier styles made its bent-wood furniture simply a surrogate for the heavily ornamented designs favored by the petty bourgeoisie, even though Kohn's intended market was the upper class. This made it possible for the dwellings of the middle class to become smaller, inexpensive copies of the homes of the upper classes. Again, however, the reality was that in middle-class homes, a single room served as salon, dining room, and living room. The originals of the Renaissance, Gothic, or other luxury furniture were handcrafted, traditionally made, and thus of very good quality. Bent-wood furniture was also of high quality, but for exactly the opposite reason: the technology used in

mass production suited it perfectly and more or less eliminated the faulty construction found in so many other machine-made copies of luxury furniture.

Despite a certain technological naïveté and a preoccupation with economic progress, nineteenth-century Europeans were universally fascinated with such nonutilitarian engineering feats as the Crystal Palace (1851) and the Eiffel Tower (1889). Thonet's early bent wood designs reflected the myth of the purest art of engineering: the clear structure and formal perfection of his earliest bent-wood chairs were on the same level as grander architectural achievements. This devotion to the wonders of the industrial age may have been a significant factor in attracting upper-middle-class buyers of bent-wood furniture. They were also drawn to the new designs of J. & J. Kohn and other new producers. The Kohn firm's efforts to prove that ornamented bent-wood furniture was suitable for an entire room—salon or bedroom—overcame the myth that bent-wood furniture was exempt from any specific, class-based taste preference due to its technological and formal qualities.

Even though Kohn and Thonet were both producing pieces of furniture for entire rooms by the 1880s, neither firm took part in the competitions of 1899 and 1910 for designs suitable for workers' apartments, held at the Austrian Museum of Art and Industry (now the Österreiches Museum für angewandte Kunst). Other companies, such as Portois and Fix—which was famous worldwide for luxury furniture and for clients at the imperial court—submitted designs to these competitions. However, the individual pieces of furniture, while presented as though designated for the modest apartments of the workers, were actually purchased by the firms' wealthy clients. The room designed by top prizewinner Sumetzberger was ordered by several members of the nobility for guestrooms in their country houses.[46] The jury competition in 1910 stipulated fixed production costs, and such restrictions could only be met by the least expensive bent-wood furniture offered by Gebrüder Thonet.[47] This furniture had obvious advantages: wood was sparingly used in comparison with slat furniture, the surfaces were smooth and easily cleaned, and it was mass produced, therefore widely available and reasonably priced. Yet the two largest bent-wood furniture manufacturers chose to ignore these competitions, further proof that their intended clientele was not to be found among the lower classes.

By the turn of the century, a basic change in aesthetics had occurred that would affect the bent-wood furniture industry. The pressures of nineteenth-century economic reality had been responsible for the failure of many attempts at social reform, whether from the English Arts and Crafts movement under the leadership of William Morris or the Wiener Werkstätte and the Deutsche Werkbund, whose goals were to reform art fundamentally by raising the standards of craftsmanship. Since the beginning of the Industrial Revolution, craftsmen had been unable to compete with machine production, and the ranks of master craftsmen dwindled accordingly.[48] While nineteenth-century reformers had demanded that it be the worker who adapted to the bourgeois ideal home, modern theoreticians took the opposite, seemingly contradictory approach by suggesting that the bourgeoisie should return to simpler values: "The poorest hut can be richer than the most magnificent palace."

It was time for a re-evaluation, a purification, of bourgeois society. Such reform would follow a "new aesthetic [that] requires that all of us eliminate so-called luxury from our houses and return to honesty and simplicity if we want art to again start at home. Luxury as an attitude has been transmitted to groups completely lacking suitable criteria for the acquisition of luxury items. The attitude was therefore adopted solely in order to create the appearance of elegance and grandiosity."[49]

The ornament—such as the Gothic or Renaissance motif used on certain types of bent-wood chairs—was the visible expression of luxury, whereby "everything was intended to appear as more than it really was and, through the use of a borrowed pretense, to obscure the grotesque plainness and wretchedness of the living quarters."[50] Such conspicuous luxury was replaced by a more subtle, qualitative characteristic, and the critics primarily addressed themselves to the deterioration of quality in machine-made goods. The machine, however, also brought the look of prosperity to the poorer classes by making cheap imitations of luxury furniture available to them.

In fin-de-siècle Vienna, creating designs that were true to the nature of the material used became all-important to artists. This demanded that work possess integrity and not simply imitate styles appropriate to other materials. Adolf Loos, the most vehement opponent of useless ornament, tried in his artistic work to pursue this purism. He considered design that was in keeping with the material to be of the highest ethical and aesthetic quality: "Every material has its own language of form, and no material can lay claim to the forms of another material. For the forms have developed from the suitability and the method of manufacturing used for each material. Forms are determined by the material."[51]

Loos designed the Café Museum (1898–99) and furnished it with Thonet-style bent-wood chairs (cat. no. 37). In doing so, he consciously drew on the stylistic precepts of Biedermeier design: simple, clear architectonic solutions and a simple, discreet furnishing that was subordinated to the user. This unpretentious artistic concept accorded well with the bent-wood chair stripped of useless ornament.

In contrast to Loos, the Vienna Secession artists, particularly Josef Hoffmann, included decorative ornaments on the bent-wood furniture that they designed. The dining hall furnishings for the Purkersdorf Sanatorium (cat. no. 33) and the seating for the Cabaret Fledermaus (cat. no. 55) incorporated lattice-work strutting or spherical elements for aesthetic decoration and functional purposes. While supporting Hoffmann's use of geometry, these spheres provided structural security for the chairs.

In contrast to such furniture, architecture in the early 1900s effectively expressed the new demands for bright, airy, clearly structured spaces. The Purkersdorf Sanitorium, the Café Museum, or the famous Postsparkasse (Imperial Austrian Postal Savings Bank) by Otto Wagner (cat. nos. 46-48), clearly dispensed with the ballast of historicism and its facade effect. The interiors of public spaces, however, continued to be rendered with decoration and ornamental trimmings.

It was in the bourgeois home that basic interior changes occurred. Gone were the surface details, heavy draperies, and concealed structures. In their place, the design of interiors followed the guidelines once so vehemently demanded for the workers by nineteenth-century reformers.[52] The new middle-class apartments were bright, airy places. Conspicuous luxury at last gave way to the leitmotifs of hygiene and simplicity. While the poorer classes at the turn of the century still lived in squalor, their bourgeois counterparts were jettisoning the pomp and eclectic styles of their illusory nineteenth-century world as just so much ballast. In its place, the enlightened few turned their homes into showplaces of a new aesthetic: bright walls, large windows, abundant natural and artificial lighting, smooth unornamented surfaces on furniture, and clearly structured forms in the furnishings. Thonet's earliest bent-wood furniture had actually met these demands, and now new bent-wood designs by famous architects were marketed to a fashion-conscious elite, eager to participate in the new trend in taste. As part of this trend, bent-wood furniture was given new shapes, following an aesthetic revision appreciated only by the enlightened few, and in the process abandoning its convincing form.

The twentieth century: between the wars

World War I wrought tremendous political and social changes across the face of Europe, rivaling those of the Industrial Revolution. In 1916, Emperor Franz Josef, whose reign had begun in the midst of an earlier storm over Europe, died, spelling the end of an era in the Austro-Hungarian Empire. After the war, the empire itself was dissolved into several independent states, and Austria, now a republic, sank into political and economic obscurity. With its large-scale industries located in the newly independent countries of Hungary, Czechoslovakia, and Poland, once part of the far-flung empire, Austria returned to a pre-industrial agrarian level.

The constitutional change from empire to republic was accompanied by a restructuring of political power. The aristocracy, increasingly losing its financial and political power, now lost even its social presence. The loyal members of the bourgeoisie who had invested their financial reserves in Austria's war effort, lost their wealth. During the 1920s, their social position was briefly usurped by a new class of nouveaux riches, risen from the lower middle class and utterly lacking in any sensibility in taste. While this class may have revived the Baroque magnificence of an earlier time, they could not provide a new source of aesthetic inspiration. At the same time, the very poor —the still-disadvantaged workers, petty officials, and craftsmen—were finally to experience a real improvement in their standard of living as the result of state- and community-supported social programs.

The shifting social tide was clearly reflected in new reformed attitudes toward the home. Functionalism, a modern concept dating from the founding of the Deutsche Werkbund in 1907, affected progressive twentieth-century architecture until after the Second World War. In the 1920s, functionalism became the catchword of the decade, synonymous with a particular life style. The creative center of the new trend, however, was neither Vienna nor any other traditional center of European arts. Instead, it was at Weimar, a small town in Germany, where in 1919 Walter Gropius founded the Bauhaus, a design school.

After losing the war, Germany had undergone a more radical social re-orientation than Austria, one that spawned an art community imbued with the ideals of social commitment. While reform movements of the late nineteenth century had been characterized by a kind of dreamy utopian socialism, the Bauhaus group drew upon actual socialist experiences.[53] Viewing furniture, household effects, and the entire living space as strictly utilitarian objects of industrial manufacture, Gropius, Hannes Meyer, and the other members of the Bauhaus demanded that such environmental designs be of standardized construction and form: "The creation of standards for utilitarian objects of daily use is a social necessity. The products reproduced on the basis of Bauhaus models were to attain their moderate price solely by the exploitation of all modern, economical means of standardization and by sales volume."[54] This attitude towards design emerged at the school following its 1923 exhibition (cat. no. 67), and defined the general tenor of the school's doctrine after it relocated to Dessau in 1926.

The furniture designers at the Bauhaus simply carried forward the symbiosis of quality and mechanization that had first been worked out by Thonet some seventy years earlier in the mass production of the bent-wood chair. However, there was an essential difference: unlike Thonet, the Bauhaus artists stressed social commitment and focused their efforts on designs for the worker. The new priority was not to set standards of luxury, but to meet the very basic need for human shelter. New materials that lent themselves to industrial treatment and simple, unornamented forms were intended to demonstrate a total break with the traditions of luxury of an earlier age. The worker was to be provided with greater self-confidence and self-esteem through a new aesthetic of simplified forms, however much this same worker may have longed for a cozy, cluttered home in which to forget his all-too-plain everyday existence.

Like other reformers before them, the Bauhaus artists ignored the workers' own dreams and desires for a comfortable, suitable home. They overruled the concept of comfort, meaning luxury, and attempted instead to create a new working-class culture, stripped of decoration and ornament. From the beginning they were doomed to failure, precisely because the underprivileged classes aspired to achieve the bourgeois life style that had eluded them since the start of the industrial age.

Tubular steel emerged as an important component of these workers' dwellings. Its sleek, uncompromising form and the use of a new material rendered the design anonymous, classless, devoid of any connection to the past. In fact, tubular steel, like earlier materials—cast- or wrought-iron—was often a translation of previous designs into a new medium (cat. nos. 74 and 75). Tubular steel was a substitute for bent wood, a medium thoroughly explored and perfected in the nineteenth century. Many designers considered wood a material overladen with tradition and inappropriate for their "new" society. For them, the traditional comforts of the home or of conspicuous luxury had become negative values. Seating, for example, was not to be considered a status symbol, but rather the simple fulfillment of an elemental need.

Marcel Breuer called his tubular-steel furniture, "in its external appearance as well as in its material expression . . . the most extreme . . . the least artistic, the least homey, the most machinelike. . . . For we no longer have the need, at the expense of reality, to create and to revere imaginative but soon-outdated flourishes of taste or of style."[55]

Mart Stam, the designer of the first tubular-steel cantilever chair, pleaded for social and ethical commitment on the part of designers. He criticized the furnishing styles of designers who, although they had a social conscience, worked only for a small elite group of clients: "Obviously, it is precisely these worthless furnishings that awaken general interest. All these furnishings are more or less for the wealthy and are perceived by the public as the ideal of prosperity. Just as the worker and the minor civil servant long to have miniature villas with miniature salons and dining rooms, they likewise wish to see the ideal of prosperity expressed in their furniture. The consequence is the manufacture of furniture that, although produced in great quantities, creates merely an illusory prosperity. In the present situation, in an era in which each person must struggle for existence and the majority of the population is scarcely able to fill basic needs, what is necessary is the design of a minimal dwelling and of furnishings that, instead of according with the bourgeois ideal of prosperity, satisfy actual needs to the utmost."[56]

Obviously a minimal dwelling is one of the first requirements of those who have nothing. Nonetheless, many progressive architects saw minimal dwellings as the ultimate goal for every modern worker. To be modern meant to simplify one's vision of home and its furnishings. Housekeeping should be reduced to a minimum; furniture, above all, should be practical, functional.

However, the question of beauty was of fundamental importance to the success or failure of the new tubular-steel furniture. What may have been beautiful to the designer was not so to the worker intended to sit in the tubular-steel chair and stare at the clean white wall. Even Le Corbusier dubbed his new work a "machine for living," reflecting their obsession with practicality. Furniture equated with machinery had no appeal at all to the worker who labored all day long, day after day, at a machine. The coldness of steel and other materials was repeatedly criticized, even by the architects of workers' housing who better understood the psyche of the worker. Many architects, however, expected that psyche to change with exposure to modern design. As Breuer commented, "The objection to tubular-steel furniture is that it is cold, that it is suitable for hospitals, and that it reminds people of a chair used in performing surgical operations. These attitudes pale from one day to the next; they are products of custom soon eradicated by a different custom."[57]

Ironically, these complaints were identical to those

Figure 6–9

Figure 6–10

Figure 6-9
**Oswald Haerdtl. Interior of House 40,
Österreichische Werkbund exhibition.
Vienna, 1932.**

Figure 6-10
**Interior of a municipal building, Hohen-
bergerstrasse 16-20. Vienna, ca. 1929.**

Figure 6-11
**Interior of a so-called family shelter,
Adalbert Stifter Strasse. Vienna, 1937.**

Figure 6–11

lodged against the earlier bent wood designs of the nineteenth century, and interestingly, these designers often pointed to the advantages of tubular steel over bent wood. Mart Stam, for example, stressed that

steel, an almost homogeneous material, is far more likely to yield particularly resistant forms than wood, which because of its grain and its property of unevenness is restricted in its mechanical characteristics. A chair frame constructed of high-grade tubular steel and covered where necessary with tautly held fabric yields, in other words, lightweight, springy seating. It offers the comfort of upholstered seating, with the difference that it is far handier and more hygienic, hence far more practical in use. The full consideration of demands in terms of its technological production and manufacture now yielded the social criterion, namely, a price affordable by the broadest spectrum of the public, without which the whole task would not have satisfied me particularly.[58]

Stam's philosophy, however well-stated, simply did not coincide with reality.

Plain tubular-steel furniture was first used to furnish several of the Bauhaus faculty's own apartments in Dessau. The first public exhibition of these objects took place in 1927 at the Weissenhofsiedlung in Stuttgart, Germany, where the International Style was given its first major public showing. Under the leadership of architect Mies van der Rohe, sixteen architects, including Marcel Breuer and Mart Stam, exhibited modern houses and furnishings designed along the guidelines of the new age. They were functional, possessed simplicity, were hygienic and reflected a real break with the past. In addition to the new tubular-steel furniture, more than half of the thirty-three model homes contained the simple, anonymously designed and popular bent wood chairs. These nineteenth-century bent-wood designs fit right into the new surroundings and held their own with the progressive tubular-steel chairs. The bent-wood chair fit the purist attitudes of these avant-garde architects, from which two important conclusions can be drawn: the later bent wood designs by such architects as Josef Hoffmann and Otto Wagner may have been aesthetically successful, but they had not furthered the basic principles of bent wood. The form had been perfected early on, in Thonet's day. The second conclusion is that there is a clear connection, an inner logic, between the simple, functional unornamented bent-

wood chair of the nineteenth century and the tubular-steel furniture of the Bauhaus artists.

The Weissenhofsiedlung was a convincing argument for the construction of decent working-class housing. However, in reality, the apartments and furnishings shown at the Stuttgart exhibition were affordable only by somewhat affluent tenants, not the poorest, underprivileged workers of the post-World War I era.

In 1932, an international group of architects participated in a similar experiment in Vienna, constructing a housing development for the working class. Here again, the workers objected to the "machine-for-living" atmosphere created by "industrial furniture," such as tubular-steel chairs, with which the architects had furnished the model apartments (figure 6–9). Model apartments were also used to reflect the architects' perceptions of the aspirations of the working class for its own long-overdue emancipation; in one such apartment, this was symbolized by a well-filled bookcase (figure 6–10). In reality, when the workers moved into these apartments, they chose older pre-World War I furnishings, with few traces of the architect-envisioned "new" life style (figure 6–11).

The same architects who revealed their social commitment through the Weissenhofsiedlung also designed villas for the very rich and furnished them with steel furniture. Le Corbusier's Villa Savoye (1929) in Poissy near Paris and Mies van der Rohe's Tugendhat house (1928–30) in Brno, Czechoslovakia, pursued the same aesthetic and functional goals as had the designs for the workers. But the tubular-steel furniture destined for the villas was functionally different from the furniture at the Weissenhofsiedlung. The so-called Barcelona chair, for example (cat. no. 83), designed by Mies van der Rohe, was not made of lowly prefabricated industrial-steel tubing but of strip steel, which was more compatible with the laminated seating then being developed. The chair had leather cushions on steel supports, exuding an air of elegance in sharp contrast to the simple tubular-steel furniture intended for workers' apartments.

Starting in 1928, Le Corbusier and his colleagues also began designing steel furniture destined for the elegant, modern "plain" apartment. Charlotte Perriand, one of Le Corbusier's collaborators, justified the use of steel, saying, "The metal plays the same role for the furniture as the

Figure 6–12
Carl Kronfuss. An upper-middle-class salon. Vienna, 1933.

concrete in architecture. It is a revolution. Glowing clarity —integrity—freedom in thinking and acting."[59] Despite the origins of the idea in Bauhaus ideals for workers' housing, Perriand's statement was not only a rush of romanticism but represented the general approach to style that could be taken on any architectural assignment.

In 1930, Gebrüder Thonet began production of tubular-steel furniture, converting a factory formerly used for the production of bent wood. Tubular steel—from night tables to chairs to umbrella stands—rolled off the production lines; entire apartments could now be furnished in the new medium. However, interior designers responded in a predictable way. Like their nineteenth-century counterparts, they first positioned a set of tubular-steel chairs in the oriel, that sunny alcove in which the first bent-wood

chairs had found a home some eighty years earlier (figure 6–12). History was repeating itself. Tubular steel, like the bent wood of an earlier generation, was considered an exotic object and as such was pushed into the realm of luxury furnishing. As early as 1935, Mart Stam warned "against making tubular-steel furniture into a gadget with nickel-plated tubing,"[60] something affordable only by the wealthy. That this did not happen is reflected in the extraordinary proliferation throughout the world of inexpensive bent-metal chairs, especially those based on Marcel Breuer's cantilevered design (cat. no. 72). Since the appearance of the first bent-wood chair in the nineteenth century, bent-wood and bent-metal furniture have proven their resiliency and found their place in history.

Notes

1. Karlsruhe 1982, especially "Vom Thron zum Chefsessel," pp. 84–98; Warnke.

2. Katz, p. 99; Silbermann and Kruger; Kiefer.

3. Vienna 1981, pp. 21–71.

4. Benedikt, p. 25.

5. Heller, p. 14.

6. Kiefer, p. 52.

7. Heller, p. 22.

8. Ehmer, pp. 86–87.

9. The new train line between Vienna and Budapest provided Gebrüder Thonet with cheap transportation and enabled the firm to bid competitively against Hungarian companies.

10. Otto, pp. 20–46.

11. Mang 1982, p. 44.

12. Wilk 1980a, p. 37.

13. Palmer, p. 485.

14. Bobek and Lichtenberger, pp. 51–57.

15. During the 1870s, there were about ten thousand empty apartments due to speculation (Sandgruber).

16. Witt-Dörring, pp. 1–7.

17. Sternberger, p. 151–79; Meier-Oberist, p. 266; see especially Lachmayer, pp. 65–71.

18. Giedion, pp. 364–68.

19. London 1851a, pp. 1040–41.

20. Hirth, p. 94.

21. Semper; Mang 1982, p. 44.

22. See especially Eggert.

23. Heller, p. 32; Giedion, p. 400.

24. Weber-Kellermann.

25. Koschler, p. 12.

26. Sax, p. 9.

27. Bobek and Lichtenberger, p. 57–61.

28. Steiner, pp. 9–14.

29. Sax, p. 69.

30. Günther, p. 23.

31. *Der Arbeiterfreund* 1896, vol. 6, p. 29.

32. Ibid. 1869, vol. 7, p. 110.

33. Ibid., pp. 110–13.

34. Ibid., p. 114.

35. Sax, p. 9.

36. Otto, p. 48.

37. After 1857, the Ringstrasse replaced the medieval city wall and the hierarchical border between suburbs and city. This affected consumer behavior; goods offered in the city were practically unknown to the lower classes living in the suburbs. The Thonet firm, for example, was located in the most expensive part of the business district, opposite the Stephanskirche.

38. Hoffmacher, p. 22; Brandstätter, p. 25.

39. Denscher, p. 70.

40. Kracauer, pp. 207–19.

41. Günther, p. 28; *Der Arbeiterfreund* 1870, vol. 8, p. 14.

42. *Die Groszindustrie Österreiches*, see especially vol. 3, pp. 320–23; *Kunst und Kunsthandwerk* 1902, vol. 5, p. 8; *Das Interieur* 1900, vol 1, p. 167.

43. *Die Groszindustrie Österreiches*, vol. 3, p. 322.

44. Ibid.

45. Ibid., p. 323.

46. For comparisons with the prizewinning interior by Sumetzberger, see *Kunst und Kunsthandwerk* 1900, vol. 3, p. 50; ibid. 1910, vol. 13, pp. 136–39; *Das Interieur* 1900, vol. 1, pp. 65–69.

47. The competition of 1910 was in two parts: design for a small two-room apartment for a family of moderate means, to be furnished with three beds, one child's bed, three nightstands, three cupboards, coat tree, child's chair and mirror, all costing no more that 900 crowns or slightly more than the annual wage of the average craftsman or minor civil servant; design for a worker's apartment for four persons, with one 60-by-80-foot room and a 30-by-40-foot kitchen, to be furnished with two beds, two children's beds, one sofa bed, two nightstands, two cupboards, one table, four chairs, one child's chair, one washstand, one coat tree, one bookcase, and one mirror, all costing no more than 600 crowns, the average annual wage of the worker. In Gebrüder Thonet's sales catalogue of 1912, the average prices were far below those allowed by the jury.

48. Posener 1964; ibid. 1978, p. 18.

49. Lux, p. 24; Rukschcio and Schachel, pp. 38–40.

50. Lux, p. 169.

51. Müller, pp. 90–91.

52. Lux, pp. 17–28.

53. The importance of the Soviet Union to the early phase of the Bauhaus is reflected in the numerous publications issued by the Bauhaus in the Russian language (Staatliches Bauhaus Weimar 1919–23). Several Bauhaus architects including Hinerk Scheper and Hannes Meyer worked in the Soviet Union in the 1930s as city planners (Lang, p. 36– 38).

54. Gropius, p. 8.

55. Van Geest and Máčel, p. 158.

56. Ibid., p. 160.

57. Ibid., p. 161.

58. Gräff 1928, p. 128.

59. Van Geest and Máčel, p. 46.

60. Ibid., p. 40.

Catalogue

TEXT BY DEREK E. OSTERGARD

1

Windsor chair

Bent wood, solid wood, turned wood
36¼ x 25 x 22½ in.
92 x 63.5 x 57 cm

American, ca. 1780–1800
Private collection, New York

THE Windsor chair probably evolved in the sophisticated garden environment of late-seventeenth- and early-eighteenth-century England and not in the lowlier rural circumstances frequently ascribed to it. In their designs for Windsor chairs, craftsmen in England may have responded initially to the wheeled conveyances used by the gentry to tour the extensive gardens of the era in comfort (figure 1A). The original chairs on these platforms may have been simple joined stools, rush-bottomed chairs, or lipp-work (woven-rush) chairs, all of which were lightweight and inexpensive to produce, making them suitable to the open-air environment of the garden. In order to reduce the bulk of these movable seats while retaining their structural stability, craftsmen most likely translated the spokelike construction of the carts' wheels into the backs of these chairs. Stubbs, a late-eighteenth-century London craftsman, illustrated on his trade card (figure 1B) what appears to be just such a chair with wheels that have been integrated into its structure. The earliest known examples of Windsor chairs, dating from the second quarter of the eighteenth century, exhibit a comb back of spokes, which are reminiscent of wheels. It was only in the middle of the eighteenth century that bent elements were introduced into these designs.

This particular example with its bent hoop back and arm support illustrates the reductivist manner of construction evident in most pieces employing the bending methodology. The use of bent wood used in the crest rail and the arm support reduced the number of elements that would have been required in chairs employing traditional joinery by merging the stiles and crest rail into one component and the pair of arms into a single unit. With its seat hewn from a single block of wood, unlike other chairs employing four joined side rails and therefore requiring upholstery, the Windsor chair was economical to produce. The wedged construction by which the spoke elements were secured into the seat also eliminated the need for elaborate joinery.

These constructional factors reduced costs, and the Windsor chair eventually gained acceptance in increasingly more humble environments. However, in its earliest days, the Windsor was used almost exclusively in the establishments of the well-to-do.

Figure 1A
Jacques Rigaud. *Stowe Garden, Buckinghamshire* **(detail). Engraving, ca. 1739. The Metropolitan Museum of Art, New York (Harris Brisbane Dick Fund, 1942).**

1

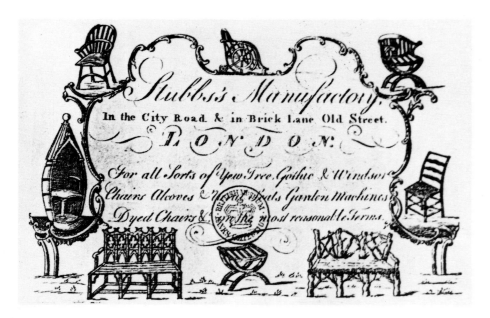

Figure 1B

Trade card of Stubbs' Manufactory, London. Late eighteenth century. Collection Dr. Geoffrey Beard, Bath, England.

Despite this, although eighteenth-century examples are known from inventory accounts to have been Japanned or executed in mahogany, they were never fully integrated into the truly high-style English interiors designed by such architects as William Kent or Robert Adam. Rather, by the end of the eighteenth century, the Windsor chair had become a popular fixture in middle-class interiors, rural dwellings, and inns, establishing an association that lingers to this day.

2

Armchair

Bent laminated wood, solid wood (painted), metal (left leg replaced)
33⅞ x 21¾ x 22 in.
86 x 55.5 x 56 cm

Made ca. 1805 by Jean-Joseph Chapuis (born Brussels 1765, died Brussels 1864)

Anderson House Museum, The Society of the Cincinnati, Washington, D.C.

THE profound reverence for the classical world in enlightened circles in early nineteenth-century Europe and the United States often resulted in the archaeological resurrection of the art, architecture, and design of ancient Greece and Rome. No chair employing the innovative technique of

2

bending wood more boldly expresses this allegiance to the past than this armchair painted in *le style antique* and based on the ancient Roman *sella curulis* (folding stool). This merger of technological innovation with fashionable aesthetics parallels the work of the American Samuel Gragg who used a bent-wood methodology to produce his body of chairs based on the ancient Greek klismos chair (cat. no. 3).

Chapuis's use of bent wood straddles the innovations devised by Samuel Gragg and Michael Thonet for the bending of wood in the production of furniture. Rather than bend single strips of solid wood as had Gragg, or use bundles of long strips of thin veneers as would Thonet, Chapuis glued together four strips of wood, each a quarter-inch thick, and bent them into designated configurations. These bentwood elements were used to execute the continuous pieces constituting the side rails and stiles, as well as the bold arc of the leg systems, which were shaped by sanding to their tapered forms. However, the longitudinal elements of this chair, its front and rear seat rails, were executed from solid wood. Due to the painted finish of the chair, it is impossible to determine whether the crest rail was fashioned from a bent laminate.

Unlike the Windsor chairs of the same period, which were intended for less sophisticated settings, identical models of this chair were among the furnishings of the Royal Palace at Laeken, near Brussels, during the early years of the Napoleonic occupation. As a result, the maker of this chair was thought to have been the Parisian *ébéniste* Claude Chapuis, but Denise Ledoux-Lebard (pp. 118–21) has proved that Jean-Joseph Chapuis of Brussels was in fact responsible for this design.

3

Side chair

Bent ash and hickory (painted)
32 x 17¼ x 16½ in.
81 x 44 x 42 cm

Made after 1808 by Samuel Gragg (born Peterborough, New Hampshire, 1772, died Boston 1855?)
Museum of Fine Arts, Boston (Gift of Mrs. Ralph Lowell, in memory of her godmother, Mrs. Arthur L. Williston [Mary DeForest Denny])

A fire in the U.S. Patent Office destroyed the documents explaining Samuel Gragg's technique for bending wood, patented in 1808, and as a result, his innovative process remains a mystery. Despite the loss of these papers, Gragg is recognized as a gifted chairmaker whose aesthetic contribution was almost as distinguished as the technological innovations he introduced in his designs. Like so many other craftsmen working with bent wood in the late eighteenth and early nineteenth centuries, Gragg subordinated his technological genius to his own subdued expression of the classicist mode of design, then at the height of fashion in Europe, England, and the United States. In his two most important chairs employing bent wood, Gragg was inspired by the ancient Greek klismos chair.

The first of these two chairs required a lesser degree of technical proficiency for their production. The stiles and rails on each side have been incorporated into a single rectangular-sectioned rod of bent solid wood. The five additional rods, bent to comprise the back and seat splats, are secured to the back seat rails in lap joints and to the front seat rail in dovetails. The front and back seat rails are made from cut solid wood. This fluid yet austere design is set on four turned legs that have been doweled into the front and rear seat rails. In an armchair version (figure 3A), the bend of the back and seat is enhanced by the graceful curve of the bent-wood arms.

3

Figure 3A
Samuel Gragg. Armchair, after 1808. Oak, ash, maple, beech, painted decoration. Museum of Art, Rhode Island School of Design, Providence (Gift of Wunsch Americana Foundation, New York).

The second side chair represents a simplification of the previous design in that a continuous stile and side-rail component has been extended and bent to incorporate the front legs as well (figure 3B). Rather than use thinner, and therefore more pliable, strips of wood glued into a laminate, Gragg constructed his chairs from pieces of solid wood bent to conform to the desired shape of the chair. This masterful use of bent solid wood, with its obvious time-, labor-, and cost-saving advantages over laminated wood, was a methodology that would elude Michael Thonet during nearly a quarter of a century of experi-

Figure 3B
Samuel Gragg. Side chair, after 1808. Bent ash and hickory (painted). Museum of Fine Arts, Boston (Charles Hitchcock Tyler Residuary Fund).

mentation. Also, by eliminating the individual stiles, side rails, and front legs used in chairs constructed along traditional lines, Gragg dramatically simplified the manufacturing process while introducing a more structurally substantial frame. Later in the nineteenth century these innovations would figure prominently as essential considerations of mass production.

In the Boston newspaper *Columbian Centinel*, Gragg advertised his designs as possessing "elastic backs and bottoms," an indication that his remarkable process of production was a move not just toward

constructional and material economy, but also toward greater comfort as well. That Gragg employed the word *elastic* in his advertisement suggests that he was seeking a clientele who would have understood and appreciated this quality. The original painted finish of this chair also reflects fashionable taste of the time.

4

Armchair

Bent laminated wood, solid wood, veneer (walnut?), cane (front stretcher and carved splat replaced)
35½ x 20⅝ x 21¼ in.
90.5 x 52.5 x 54 cm

Designed and made ca. 1836 by Michael Thonet (born Boppard am Rhein, Prussia, 1796, died Bistritz, Moravia, 1871)
Collection Rudolf Schöneberger, Boppard am Rhein, West Germany

DURING the second half of the eighteenth century, Germans dominated the cabinetmaking trade in Paris, the epicenter of luxury consumption allied with fashionable taste. During that period, the technical and aesthetic virtuosity of cabinetmakers earned them a reputation unrivaled for quality. However, the French Revolution and the Napoleonic Wars made considerable inroads into the ranks of princely clients who had once patronized them. By the time European peace was concluded at the Congress of Vienna in 1815, many German cabinetmakers were turning their attention to a marketplace defined by middle-class circumstances.

Through this atmosphere of general impoverishment, many traditional practices in the furniture-making trades gradually disappeared while a new era of technological development began. Cabinetmakers increasingly used machinery to reduce costs. The power-driven saw, for example, not only transformed techniques of pro-

duction but indirectly affected aesthetics as well. The saw could extract thinner, longer, and ultimately less expensive sheets of veneer from logs. As a result an increasing portion of the furniture for the lower end of the market was veneered, a technique formerly reserved for more deluxe furnishings.

The increased availability of inexpensive veneer, especially from indigenous woods, allowed Michael Thonet to experiment with the production of a chair made almost completely from machine-made parts. Veneers were used in both the decoration and construction of the frame. In particular, the chair's outer skin of veneer replicated the appearance of the more expensive chair fabricated from richly figured (grained) sections of solid cut wood. Because of these factors, Thonet's so-called Boppard chair (named for its designer's origins) stands at the crossroads of conventional Biedermeier aesthetics and innovative construction. However, nearly a quarter of a century earlier, during the Federal period in the United States, Bostonian Samuel Gragg produced a similar design fabricated from sections of bent solid wood (figure 4A).

Thonet's own later methodology required more labor-intensive steps to execute. After cutting long strips of wood from thick sheets of inexpensive veneer, Thonet soaked them in boiling glue and then bent and bound them into a mold shaped to the configuration of the side elements of the chair and its scrolled armrests (figure 4B). After the pieces had dried, they were joined by the crest rail, front and back seat rails, and stretchers. The lateral elements of the chair provided additional support in the form of sled runners. The construction of major elements of this chair from secondary woods eliminated the need for the more expensive, solid pieces of wood that Thonet's con-

4

Figure 4A
**Samuel Gragg. Armchair, 1808.
Bent ash and hickory (re-
painted). Smithsonian Institu-
tion, Washington, D.C. (Gift of
Richard H. Howland).**

temporaries used for chair construction.
Although no comparative figures are available, it is assumed that these early chairs,
including a similar side chair (figure 4C),
ultimately cost less to produce than those
made from traditional joinery, despite the
seemingly laborious process required to
bend the elements. In addition, while delicate looking, the chairs are remarkably
strong and lightweight.

Thonet's experimentation with bent laminated wood during the 1830s is apparent
in a comparison of the different constructional techniques employed in two different models of this armchair. In the example
shown here, the stiles are not integrated
with the side rails and front legs. Rather,
they are independent elements, made from
a bundle of rectangular-sectioned rods of
veneer, executed as independent elements
of the design, which were spliced into the
chair at the intersection of the side and
rear seat rails. This join was then covered
with veneer. In another example, in the
Bayerisches Nationalmuseum, Munich
(Himmelheber, fig. 115), the stiles, side rails,
and front legs were executed from one
continuous bundle of these laminates. In
both examples, these bundles of laminated
wood were backed on their inner sides,
beneath the seats, with cut sections of solid
wood that were most likely added for stability and served as seat frames for the caning. Splicing the stile into the frame of the
chair produced a structural flaw that even

Figure 4B
Detail of armrest.

Figure 4C
Michael Thonet. Side chair, ca. 1836–39. Bent laminated wood, solid wood, veneer, upholstery (front stretcher missing).

traditional cabinetmakers avoided. It is therefore possible that the example shown here is an earlier version of the armchair and that Thonet later eliminated this flaw from his design.

By standardizing the construction of the chair's parts and the method of production, Michael Thonet moved from the traditions and techniques of the craftsman's shop toward a mechanized production that he would perfect within a quarter century's time.

5

Side chair, for the Palais Liechtenstein
Cut laminated wood, solid wood, upholstery (modern), gessoed and gilded
36 x 17½ x 17½ in.
91.5 x 44.5 x 44.5 cm

Designed and made ca. 1843 by Michael Thonet (Born Boppard am Rhein, Prussia, 1796, died Bistritz, Moravia, 1871)
Bundes-Mobilien-Verwaltung, Vienna

FOR the first quarter of the nineteenth century, Western European design was dominated by a strident classicism. By the 1820s, many tastemakers began to interpret historic styles of the past more freely. The revival of mid-eighteenth-century Rococo was one of the first, and ultimately most enduring, of these alternative design strains to emerge and spread from Paris to London to the more reactionary courts of

Russia, the German states, and the Austro-Hungarian Empire.

Known as Zweites (second) Rokoko (Rococo Revival) in German-speaking circles, this revivalist style is evident in the gilded side chair made for the Palais Leichtenstein. The extensive use of gilding and the delicate cabriole posture of the front legs are reminiscent of mid-eighteenth-century taste. However, the chair is transitional in nature, for the complexities of its back align it with contemporary Biedermeier taste as well. With this synthesis of stylistic mannerisms, the Liechtenstein chair lent its graceful stance, form, and proportions to the body of mass-produced designs that Michael Thonet developed over the next twenty years. He produced three other side-chair models for the Palais Liechtenstein (figure 5A) and several small tables with cabriole legs.

6

Side chair, for the Palais Liechtenstein
Cut laminated wood, solid wood, molded laminated-wood seat (later), traces of gesso
35½ x 17⅛ x 18 in.
90 x 43.5 x 46 cm

Designed and made ca. 1843 by Michael Thonet (Born Boppard am Rhein, Prussia, 1796, died Bistritz, Moravia, 1871)
Bundes-Mobilien-Verwaltung, Vienna

A recent examination of this chair by Christian Witt-Dörring, Alexander von Vegesack, and the author has revealed aspects of its construction that permit a re-evaluation of the history and importance of the Palais Liechtenstein side chair. This example, which is in the former imperial collections of the Hapsburg family, was once coated with white sizing but does not appear ever to have been gilded. Nevertheless it is identical in design, proportions, and size to the gilded Palais Liechtenstein side chairs (cat. no. 5 and figure 6A).

The profound similarity of this chair's rounded form to those of its direct descendants made by Thonet from bent laminated and solid wood led many historians to presume that beneath the gilding of the Liechtenstein chair lay a frame of bent wood. However, this ungilded chair was not constructed from bent sections of wood as previously thought; instead elements of traditional joinery were employed. Sections of solid wood were cut

Figure 5A
Michael Thonet and sons. Side chairs, made for the Palais Liechtenstein, Vienna, ca. 1843–45.

5

6

Figure 6A

Michael Thonet and sons. Side chairs, gold (left) and white (right), made for the Palais Liechtenstein, Vienna. ca. 1843–45. Laminated veneer. Bundes-Mobilien-Verwaltung, Vienna.
SEE CAT. NO. 5

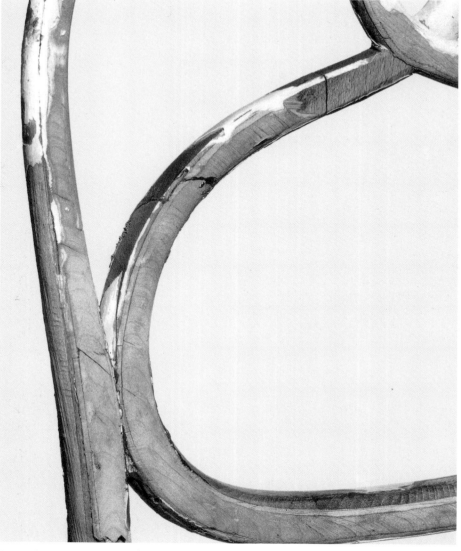

Figure 6B

Detail of intersection of back splat and stile.

into the requisite curves and then encased on both sides with three and sometimes four layers of thickly cut veneers. The pieces were then joined and further shaped by a rasp to the appropriate rounded forms of the frame (figure 6B).

When viewed beside its predecessor from the 1830s—the Boppard chair (cat. no. 4)—this method of construction seems anachronistic. It is possible, however, that in the early 1840s, Thonet still lacked the confidence in his evolving bent wood technology to use it for an important commission, where its liabilities might be exposed to a disgruntled and influential client. In addition, the application of expensive gilding to a fragile, bent laminate, a potentially unstable foundation, may have prompted Thonet to execute these designs from traditional materials and joinery.

7

Side chair, Model No. 4

*Bent solid beechwood, bent laminated wood,
upholstery (modern), painted*

36⅛ x 16¾ x 21¼ in.
91.5 x 42.5 x 54 cm

*Designed ca. 1850 by Michael Thonet (born
Boppard am Rhein, Prussia, 1796, died
Bistritz, Moravia, 1871)*
*Manufactured ca. 1859 by Gebrüder Thonet,
Vienna*

8

Armchair, Model No. 4

*Bent solid beechwood, bent laminated wood,
upholstery (modern), painted*

37½ x 21½ x 26 in.
95.5 x 52 x 66 cm

*Designed ca. 1850 by Michael Thonet (born
Boppard am Rhein, Prussia, 1796, died
Bistritz, Moravia, 1871)*
*Manufactured ca. 1859 by Gebrüder Thonet,
Vienna*

9

Settee, Model No. 4

*Bent solid beechwood, bent laminated wood,
upholstery (modern), painted*

37½ x 55½ x 26 in.
95.5 x 141 x 66 cm

*Designed ca. 1850 by Michael Thonet (born
Boppard am Rhein, Prussia, 1796, died
Bistritz, Moravia, 1871)*
*Manufactured ca. 1859 by Gebrüder Thonet,
Vienna*

10

Table, Model No. 5

*Bent solid beechwood, bent laminated wood,
veneer*

31½ x 49¾ x 33¼ in.
78 x 126.5 x 84.5 cm

*Designed ca. 1859 by Michael Thonet (born
Boppard am Rhein, Prussia, 1796, died
Bistritz, Moravia, 1871)*
*Manufactured 2nd half of 19th century by
Gebrüder Thonet, Vienna*

Alexander von Vegesack, Düsseldorf

7

FOR nearly thirty-five years after the reactionary Congress of Vienna (1814–15), the middle class of the Austro-Hungarian Empire was effectively eliminated from participation in the governing of the country. In response, they created their own microcosm of society, with interests primarily in education, the arts, and commerce. As a result, when the Revolution of 1848 overthrew the repressive administration of Prince Metternich, the middle class emerged from its isolation ready to participate in the cultural, social, and political matrix of imperial Vienna. Evidence of this was apparent in the public places of the capital. Coffeehouses, once viewed by reactionary governing circles as hotbeds of political dissent, appeared all over the city. Michael Thonet, then in his early years of experimentation with mass production, provided these establishments with his well-made furniture, which was produced at a price that made it competitive with furniture fabricated from solid wood and assembled with conventional joinery.

The Café Daum was located on the Kohlmarket near the Hofburg, the Imperial Palace. An economic and political center of Vienna, this location retained its status even after the city was transformed by the development of the Ringstrasse during the second half of the nineteenth century. As a gathering spot for government and military officials who worked at the Hofburg, the café came to be frequented by a fashionable crowd, predicating a need for a fashionable environment. The selection of Michael Thonet's designs to service this need reflects his rapid acceptance by an affluent, consumer society in the middle of the nineteenth century.

The furnishings first used in the Café Daum were constructed from a mahogany laminate. Although more fragile than the later designs constructed from solid bent wood, these original examples are said to have withstood more than twenty-five years

Figure 7A
Side chair, variation of Thonet Model No. 4, after 1875. Bent solid wood and cane. Manufactured by Sächsische Holzindustrie-Gesellschaft, Rabenau, near Dresden. Collection Dr. Klaus-Peter Arnold, Dresden.

wood parts from solid wood—a labor- and cost-saving device considerably more amenable to mass production than elements fashioned from laminates.

Two unusual components of this set indicate that it was intended for a particularly fine setting. The painted rosewood striations on the exposed wood and the use of an upholstered seat rather than the caned one that appears in some variations (figure 7A) identify the set as one of the finest of the series. Made from only seven major bent-wood parts, the side chair of the set illustrates Thonet's ability to produce a design of aesthetic merit allied with manufacturing ease. The ambitious use of scrolling on the back of the settee was very much in keeping with Zweites Rokoko (Rococo Revival) taste, which was fashionable in Vienna in the middle of the century.

The No. 5 table used to complete this ensemble was illustrated in Thonet's 1859 broadsheet-catalogue, which did not contain a table identified as a No. 4 model. A table listed as No. 4 model finally appeared in Thonet's 1866 catalogue.

of public use. Soon after completing this order, Thonet was commissioned to produce a large number of the same models, to be made from an ash laminate for the Hotel zur Königin von England in Budapest.

Eventually these models were altered for mass production, becoming known as the No. 4 series in Thonet's catalogue. The set shown here is constructed almost exclusively from a solid wood rather than a laminate, indicating that it was made after the late 1850s. Only the scrollwork in the backs of these pieces has been executed from a laminate. By then, Thonet had resolved many of the technical problems of bent wood construction and could manufacture most of his prefabricated bent-

8

9

10

11

Rocking chair

Wrought iron, metal, solid wood, upholstery (later)
40½ 1 x 25 x 44½ in.
103 x 64 x 113 cm

Designer unknown, 2nd quarter of 19th century
Manufactured mid-19th century, possibly by R. W. Winfield & Co., Birmingham, England
Collection Mr. and Mrs. Al Luckett, Jr., Boulder, Colorado

Fᴜʀɴɪᴛᴜʀᴇ constructed of metal dates almost as far back as the use of wrought iron. By the late eighteenth century, society witnessed a dramatic increase in the use of metal furniture. Even Thomas Sheraton, that English publicist of fashionable furnishings executed by means of traditonal joinery, acknowledged the hygienic importance of patent beds constructed of metal.

Experimentation continued throughout the nineteenth century, with the first major public display of metal furniture occuring at the Great Exhibition of 1851 held at the London Crystal Palace. Shown at that time, the Winfield rocker apparently did not score a critical success, probably because it was barely embellished with the decorative motifs so much in favor at the time. Examples of furniture constructed from metal tubing were received with considerable approval, not for the innovative concepts they conveyed, but for their rich encrustation of ornament. However, the tepid reception accorded the Winfield rocker may also have been due to the fact that the design was a familiar one, having been in use for over a decade by the time of the exhibition (figure 11ᴀ).

Apparently later production examples of the Winfield rocker were executed in bands of flat metal, which was an easier material to work than metal tubing. Although Michael Thonet does not appear to have attended the Great Exhibition of 1851, and although the chair was not illustrated in

any accounts of the event, he must have been made aware of the design. Perhaps his patron, the English architect P. H. Desvignes, who was in England at the time, sent him a drawing of the Winfield design; in any event, Thonet's No. 1 rocker, introduced in the company's first catalogue in 1859, owes a strong aesthetic debt to the Winfield piece.

*Figure 11*A
Advertisement for John Porter park and garden furniture (detail), London, ca. 1839. Collection Dr. Geoffrey Beard, Bath, England.

12

Side chair, Model No. 1

Bent solid beechwood, bent laminated beech-wood, cane
37 x 16½ x 19½ in.
94 x 42 x 49.5 cm

Designed ca. 1850 by Michael Thonet (born Boppard am Rhein, Prussia, 1796, died Bistritz, Moravia, 1871)
Manufactured ca. 1859 by Gebrüder Thonet, Vienna

Alexander von Vegesack, Düsseldorf

THE so-called Schwarzenberg chair was designed just prior to Michael Thonet's success at the Great Exhibition of 1851 in London's Crystal Palace. The model shown here, a slightly later example merchandized by Thonet as the No. 1 chair, illustrates Thonet's rapidly evolving grasp of manufacturing techniques appropriate for mass production. Laminated wood, expensive and time consuming to produce, has almost been entirely eliminated from the production of this later chair. Here it is used only in the elaborate configuration of the back, where the arc of the curves is extreme. Laminates were more pliable but constructionally less reliable than solid wood. Recognizing this, Thonet employed bent solid wood in the critical portions of the chair: the front legs and rear element comprising legs, stiles, and crest rail.

The design of these chairs, which were for the Palais Schwarzenberg, was itself a modification of the Palais Liechtenstein side chair (cat. nos. 5 and 6). The patronage of Michael Thonet by the princely families of the Austro-Hungarian Empire indicates that despite a quarter of a century of Metternich's repressive, autocratic rule, an enlightened attitude persisted in certain court circles. Watercolors of several interiors of the Hofburg, the city palace of the emperor, reveal that bent-wood furnishings later became part of those settings as well, including Emperor Franz Joseph's personal study (figure 6–8).

13

Chair, Model No. 13

Bent solid beechwood, cane
37 x 16½ x 19½ in.
94 x 42 x 49.5 cm

Designed ca. 1855 by Michael Thonet (born Boppard am Rhein, Prussia, 1796, died Bistritz, Moravia, 1871)

Manufactured ca. 1862 by Gebrüder Thonet, Vienna

Museum der Stadt Boppard, West Germany

THONET'S use of bent wood attained a confident and early maturity in this design, which appeared in the first catalogue in 1859. Between that catalogue and the second, some seven years later, circular stretchers were inserted under the seats of many models to provide added structural security.

The example of the No. 13 chair shown here was made around 1862, indicated by a drawing of the model that appears in an illustrated catalogue of the International Exhibition of 1862 in London. Seen in the background at the right (figure 13A), the chair has neither the ring stretcher beneath the seat nor the side braces between the stiles and seat rails that are used in later examples. It is likely that after several years of production and ensuing customer complaints, Thonet concluded that the frames of these rather fragile designs needed additional bracing.

However, it is apparent that the No. 13 chair was produced at least until 1873 without this element (Wilk 1980a, fig. 46, fifth row from top, at left) and that some time between that date and the appearance of Thonet's 1888 catalogue, the ring stretcher was incorporated into its design (figure 13B). It may have been that the company officials originally hesitated to add the stretcher, which detracted from the appearance of the chair, one of the most graceful in the company's line.

With its elaborately figured back and the decidedly ambitious treatment of the cab-

Figure 13B
Side chair, with stretcher, Thonet Model No. 13, ca. 1885. Bent solid wood and cane. Alexander von Vegesack, Düsseldorf.

riole legs, the chair displays the era's penchant for the revival of Rococo elements, here redefined by the use of bent wood, which was ideally suited to the execution of curvilinear forms. The tear-shaped insert at the knee provided extra stability at that critical joint, but as a technically time-consuming element to execute, it was used on only a few of the more expensive Thonet models, such as the No. 6 series.

Figure 13A
Bent-wood furniture exhibited by Gebrüder Thonet at the International Exhibition, London, 1862. (From *The Art-Journal Illustrated Catalogue*, 1862, p. 291).

THE INTERNATIONAL EXHIBITION.

We engrave a group of the BENT WOOD FURNITURE, the manufacture of Messrs. THONET, of Vienna, who have also an establishment in London. It has obtained large popularity in England as well as on the Continent, combining in a remarkable

degree lightness with strength, and being produced at singularly small cost. By a peculiar process in manufacture, the wood is bent to any shape. The designs are generally graceful and good, the great purpose of "use" being always kept in view.

12   13

14

Side chair, Model No. 14 [A]

Bent solid beechwood, bent laminated beechwood, solid beechwood, cane

35½ x 16⅛ x 20½ in.
90.5 x 41 x 52 cm

Designed ca. 1855 by Michael Thonet (born Boppard am Rhein, Prussia, 1796, died Bistritz, Moravia, 1871)

Manufactured ca. late 1850s by Gebrüder Thonet, Vienna

15

Side chair, Model No. 14 [B]

Bent laminated beechwood, bent solid beechwood, solid wood, cane, painted

36 x 16½ x 19½ in.
91.5 x 42 x 49.5 cm

Designed ca. 1855 by Michael Thonet (born Boppard am Rhein, Prussia, 1796, died Bistritz, Moravia, 1871)

Manufactured ca. late 1850s by Gebrüder Thonet, Vienna

16

Side chair, Model No. 14 [C]

Bent solid beechwood, solid wood, cane

35½ x 16 x 19½ in.
90 x 40.5 x 49.5 cm

Designed ca. 1855 by Michael Thonet (born Boppard am Rhein, Prussia, 1796, died Bistritz, Moravia, 1871)

Manufactured ca. late 1850s by Gebrüder Thonet, Vienna

17

Side chair, Model No. 14 [D]

Bent solid beechwood, solid wood, cane

37¼ x 15¾ x 18 in.
94.5 x 40 x 45.5 cm

Designed ca. 1855 by Michael Thonet (born Boppard am Rhein, Prussia, 1796, died Bistritz, Moravia, 1871

Manufactured ca. late 1850s by Gebrüder Thonet, Vienna

18

Side chair, Model No. 14 [E]

Bent solid beechwood, molded laminated wood, solid beechwood, solid wood, cane

34¾ x 16 x 21 in.
88.5 x 40.5 x 53.5 cm

Designed ca. 1855 by Michael Thonet (born Boppard am Rhein, Prussia, 1796, died Bistritz, Moravia, 1871)

Manufactured after 1860 by Gebrüder Thonet, Vienna

Collection Alessandro Alverà, Vienna

COMMERCIAL considerations were important to the ultimate shape of the No. 14 chair, an early design that eventually became Thonet's most popular model. By placing a high premium on the simplification of the manufacturing process, Michael Thonet was able to reduce costs per unit and thereby stimulate sales. An examination of the evolution of the No. 14 chair illustrates this reductivist process—achieved in part through increased technical proficiency —and its subtle impact on the aesthetic of the design.

The design of the No. 14 chair did not offer a major aesthetic alternative to the taste of the era. In fact, the design resembles a Biedermeier side chair in the collection of the Bundes-Mobilien-Verwaltung in Vienna (figure 14A), a design popular some thirty years earlier. The remarkable resemblance between these chairs is seen in the insertion of a C-shaped splat between the stiles of both chairs and the slightly flaired stance of the forelegs. However, the fluidity of the frame and the delicacy of the proportions of Thonet's chair reveal a shift in aesthetics.

An examination of five examples of the No. 14 chair suggests that No. 14 [A] was the earliest chair in this particular series. The flair of the front legs and the line of the rear legs and stiles reflect Thonet's abil-

Figure 14A
Biedermeier side chair, ca. 1825–35. Cut solid wood, veneer, upholstery. Bundes-Mobilien-Verwaltung, Vienna.

ity to introduce only a delicately controlled curve in solid wood through the bending process. Since Thonet was awarded a non-renewable patent for the bending of solid woods on July 10, 1856, this chair must date from some time around that period. The chair's curved crest rail is made of a laminated wood, indicating that this easier but more time-consuming process for bending wood was still the outer limit of technical innovation at that date. A compact curve increased the chance of breakage, but this chair has a cautious, broad curvature of the crest rail, which, with the chair's lack of stress-reducing capitals between the top of the front legs and the seat rail, is another indication of early manufacture. The closed form of the ring stretcher, made from a piece of bent solid wood, pre-dates the application of this methodology in the production of circular seat frames of later examples. It may be that the ring stretcher was a later addition, introduced to stabilize the frame. The seat rail of the chair has been manufactured from four pieces of solid wood secured in this form with interlocking finger joints (figure 14B).

In the second version, No. 14 [B] several labor-intensive manufacturing liabilities have been eliminated. Most importantly, the rear

Figure 14B
Detail.

Figure 15A
Back view.

support system—legs, stiles, and crest rail—has been produced from an economical single piece of bent solid wood strengthened with a single strip of veneer that braces the inner curvature of the crest rail (figure 15A). The inner splat, which is still spliced into the stiles, is made from two strips of wood instead of the four used in the earlier model. The support system beneath the seat reveals Thonet's attempt to reduce the number of parts of the chair by eliminating the ring stretcher. In its place he includes turned capitals that broadened the area of contact between the top of the leg and the underside of the seat rail, which is now constructed from three parallel rods of wood, each three-eighths of an inch (eight millimeters) thick, laminated togeth-

er, bent, and secured with a lapped scarf joint. The broad surface of this capital diffuses stress at an important junction of the chair, where breakage could be considerable. This piece has been painted in *faux* rosewood, indicating that it was a production piece and not an experimental model.

The third example, No. 14 [C], reveals a further simplification of the manufacturing process. Both the rear leg system and the inner splat are now constructed from single pieces of bent solid wood, and the proportions of the chair have begun to assume the appearance of the final production model. The seat has been greatly simplified; it has been constructed from a single piece of solid wood and secured into its saddle configuration by a lapped scarf joint. In addition, the chair's back is now executed in a complex curve, unlike the single curve of the earlier chairs. This new curvature, which made the chair more comfortable, was retained in later examples.

The fourth example, No. 14 [D], presents contradictions between its front and back portions. The rear element of the chair is still constructed from a single piece of bent solid wood, as is its inner brace. This time, however, the brace is no longer spliced into the rear stiles, a time-consuming and expensive process that, in addition, introduced a structural weakness by reducing the stile to accommodate the splat. Instead,

the C-shaped splat has been butt-jointed to the stiles and simply secured with screws. The seat has been executed from a single piece of bent wood that forms a circular, rather than a saddle, configuration. A circular form equally distributes the stress incurred in the grain of the wood when it is bent into a closed form, which would be selected for the final production model of the chair. However, the front legs of this particular version of the No. 14 chair appear to have taken a step backward in terms of technical development. Secured neither with a ring stretcher nor a turned capital, the join of the seat and these legs closely

Figure 16A
Detail.

resembles the earliest chair in this series. This may be a final attempt, albeit a failure, by Thonet not only to reduce the number of elements needed to produce a chair, but also to minimalize the chair's structure for aesthetic purposes.

The final version of the No. 14 chair, the production model that became Thonet's most popular design, looks heavier when compared with its antecedents. Through the process of experimentation, only necessary and minimal elements have been included in this design, all problematic ones eliminated. Through the subtle shaping of the components, Thonet retained a strong element of grace even in a design for general production. It was this chair—made of six pieces of bent wood, ten screws, and two washers—that achieved a resounding commercial success for Thonet and, later, for the numerous bent wood manufacturers who replicated its lines, proportions, and size after 1869, when Thonet's thirteen-year patent expired.

14

15

16

17

18

19

19

Table

Solid rosewood, bent rosewood, plywood, solid wood, rosewood, veneer, metal

28½ x 30¾ x 31⅛ in.
72.5 x 78.5 x 79 cm

Designed ca. 1855 by John Henry Belter (born Ulm, Germany, 1804, died New York 1863)

Made ca. 1855–63 by J. H. Belter & Co., New York

The Manney Collection

BELTER'S virtuosic use of bent laminates for the production of luxury furnishings has no parallel among furniture types developed by any single individual in the nineteenth and twentieth centuries. Even Michael Thonet's body of chairs (cat. nos. 5 and 6) and tables executed for the Palais Liechtenstein is ultimately not as extensive as the Belter designs produced in the 1850s and later.

The use of bent laminates permitted the fabrication of a frame far lighter and stronger than one constructed from solid wood by means of traditional joinery. One further advantage lay in the possible integration of structure and decoration, a cost- and time-saving procedure. Finally, the use of bent laminates precluded the use of expensive woods for the elements of the designs that were intended to be curved and carved: two essential components of Belter's aesthetic.

These final two factors figure most prominently in the construction of this table, which was designed to stand in the center of a room. Prior to the nineteenth century, large tables had rarely been given a central position in important interior spaces. With this new placement of the table, decoration was required for all four sides of the piece. Belter's extravagant Rococo Revival curves, encrusted with the rich carving

characteristic of the style, would have required an enormous amount of rosewood had they been made from solid materials by traditional methods. In addition substantial open-work carving would have weakened the solid wood, which was not as strong as a laminate. Through Belter's successful accommodation of these considerations, his work attained the flamboyant conclusions that placed it above contemporaneous work, according it the honor of being copied even during his lifetime. (Ingerman, p. 578). The use of bent laminates did not merely reflect his technical genius, but was also essential for the realization of his aesthetic. By the time of his death during the American Civil War, the Rococo Revival was losing its primary position among the numerous aesthetic possibilities becoming available to mid-nineteenth-century society.

20

Chest of drawers with mirror

Bent laminated rosewood, solid rosewood, silvered glass, marble, metal

94½ x 49 x 24½ in.
240 x 124.5 x 57 cm

Designed ca. 1855 by John Henry Belter (born Ulm, Germany, 1804, died New York 1863)

Made ca. 1855–63 by J. H. Belter & Co., New York

The Manney Collection

IN the course of his twenty-five-year career in the New York furniture-making trades, John Henry Belter received four patents from the United States government for the production of furniture employing innovative techniques. On the basis of these four patents Belter's oeuvre must be viewed as the most broadly based of all nineteenth-century cabinetmakers for two essential reasons. He attained a complex, dished curve for the production of chair backs, an achievement not rediscovered until the 1930s in the work of Alvar Aalto (cat. no.

20

Figure 20A
Interior of top drawer.

100), and he was responsible for producing the broadest body of furniture types in the nineteenth century. In addition to his masterful concept for the fabrication of a bed, which was patented in 1856, Belter received a patent four years later for the production of case pieces employing bentwood elements. Thonet did not introduce case pieces employing bent wood until forty years later.

Aesthetically, Belter's case pieces replicated all the effects achieved in similar, contemporary designs constructed from traditional joinery. However, the curved sides of Belter's drawers were produced through a dynamic bending of thick layers of veneers, shaped in a special mold known as a caul. Thickest at the front of each drawer, this continuous piece of laminated wood was progressively reduced at the sides of the drawers and was thinnest at the back. Belter also employed thin strips of bent laminated wood to divide the drawers into smaller compartments for storage (figure 20A).

21

Armchair

Bent rosewood, plywood, solid rosewood, upholstery (modern), metal
44 x 24 x 31½ in.
112 x 61 x 80 cm
Designed ca. 1855 by John Henry Belter (born Ulm, Germany, 1804, died New York 1863)
Made ca. 1855–63 by J. H. Belter & Co., New York
The Manney Collection

UNLIKE the contemporaneous work of Michael Thonet, which was often purchased for the hard-use settings of public spaces, the furniture of John Henry Belter was specifically conceived for the private parlors of America's East Coast plutocracy. Despite the rarefied, infrequently used environment of the carriage trade for which it was destined, the innovative construction of this furniture made it remarkably durable.

Dispensing with the use of the traditional cabinetmaker's joinery, which relied upon a structural system of rails and stiles for the chair's frame, Belter combined these elements into a single sheet of laminated wood (figure 21A). Acting as a base for both upholstery treatments and for carved and applied decoration, such a richly fig-

21

Figure 21A
Back view.

ured back also had inherent ornamental qualities unmatched by chairs constructed from traditional techniques. In addition, Belter's designs, although often of imposing size, were lighter than chairs constructed from solid wood, since laminated wood, in addition to being stronger than solid wood, could be used in thin sheets that reduced the bulk of these chairs.

This particular design—for which Belter's 1847 patent for "sawing arabesque chairs" and his laminating technique patented in 1856 were employed—reveals both his technical virtuosity and his aesthetic sensibilities. The elaborate treatment of the chair's crest rail, arms, and cabriole legs exhibits the taste of the era for forms and decorative devices inspired by Rococo design of the previous century. Frequently sold in suites with settees, side chairs, and tables displaying identical decorative patterns, such furniture was in the forefront of taste from the mid-1840s until several years after the American Civil War.

22

Side chair, Model No. 17

Bent solid beechwood, cane, solid wood
46 x 17½ x 21 in.
117 x 44.5 x 53.5 cm

Designed ca. 1862 by Michael Thonet (born Boppard am Rhein, Prussia, 1796, died Bistritz, Moravia, 1871)
Manufactured after 1862 by Gebrüder Thonet, Vienna
Collection Georg Thonet, Frankenberg, West Germany

IN both design and method of manufacture, this tall-back side chair pays homage to Sir Joseph Paxton's monumental Crystal Palace, constructed in London's Hyde Park for the Great Exhibition of 1851. Not only was the building erected in a remarkably short period of time, it was also designed to be disassembled after the close of the exhibition. These stipulations dictated that numerous elements of the structure be

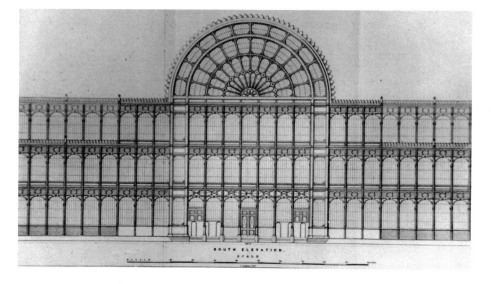

Figure 22A
Joseph Paxton. Elevation of south façade, detail of center, Crystal Palace, London, 1851. (From Cowper, *The Building Erected in Hyde Park . . . ,* pl. 41).

executed on a time-saving, prefabricated basis, one of the essential concepts behind Thonet's furnishings as well. Although there is no documentation to prove that there was a conscious effort on Thonet's part, the bond between this chair and the building is visually strengthened through the arrangement of geometric forms in the chair's back, which echo the glazing patterns of Paxton's building (figure 22A).

The impact of Japanese design on Western European art during the second half of the nineteenth century was monumental following the reopening of Japan in 1854. The truncated design of segmented circles in the back of this chair may be evidence of that influence.

23

Side chair

Wrought iron, sheet steel
31¼ x 15⅜ x 19 in.
79.5 x 39 x 48.5 cm

Designer unknown, ca. 1865
Manufactured after 1865, possibly by the Société Anonyme des Hauts-Fourneaux & Fonderies du Val d'Osne, France
Alexander von Vegesack, Düsseldorf

About the year 1800 English and American craftsmen had translated Windsor designs into wrought iron. By the middle of the century, when Thonet's designs were successfully integrated into European society, such emulation was duplicated. Mass-produced bent-wood furniture began to influence work in wrought iron, and its distinctive lines were copied by several foundries.

The Société Anonyme des Hauts-Four-

22

neaux & Fonderies was one of the firms that produced an extensive line of iron furnishings as well as architectural elements. The seat and back of the chair exhibited here are similar to that company's side chair model No. 6, which appears in a sales catalogue of about 1870 (figure 23A, second row from top, left), although that chair has an auxiliary system of stretchers for support. This method was probably less desirable because it required time-consuming welding (increasing the production costs) and was replaced by the arrangement seen here, which simply doubled the thickness of the legs and ran the stretcher up alongside the seat rail. This not only compensated for the inherent weakness of the material but also simplified the design. The clamped rings both secured the frame and added visual interest. The woven flat iron strips indicate that a seat cushion was intended. The design relates specifically to Thonet's well-known Café Daum chair (cat. no. 7), which was introduced just before the Great Exhibition of 1851 in London's Crystal Palace.

More durable than wood furnishings, but often less comfortable, these wrought iron

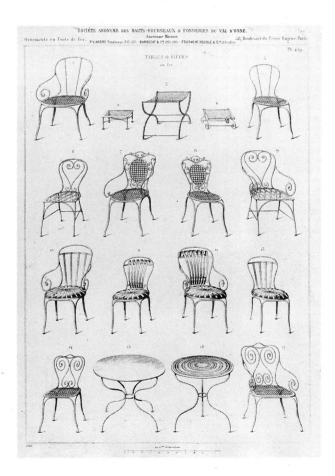

Figure 23A

Ironwork tables and chairs. Sales catalogue of Société Anonyme des Hauts-Fourneaux & Fonderies du Val d'Osne, Paris, ca. 1870. Henry Francis du Pont Winterthur Museum Library: Collection of Printed Books, Delaware.

23

designs were employed primarily in public and private garden settings. Their enduring popularity as outdoor seating is evidenced by the fact that Le Corbusier included such a chair in the garden court of his Pavillon de L'Esprit Nouveau at the 1925 Exposition Internationale des Arts Décoratifs in Paris. In 1936 the Salon des Arts Ménagers presented an installation at its annual salon in Paris entitled "L'Habitation d'Aujourd'hui" (Housing for Today), which included several similar anonymous garden seats whose designs originally dated to the nineteenth century (Herbst 1956, p. 41).

24

Table, Model No. 8

Bent solid beechwood, solid wood, marble (replacement)
29¾ x 30¼ x 19⅝ in.
75.5 x 77 x 50 cm

Designed ca. 1866 by Michael Thonet (born Boppard am Rhein, Prussia, 1796, died Bistritz, Moravia, 1871)
Manufactured ca. 1898–99 by Gebrüder Thonet, Vienna
Alexander von Vegesack, Düsseldorf

THE design of this table is frequently attributed to Adolf Loos, who used it in his Café Museum installation of 1898–99. However, the table first appeared in the 1866 Thonet catalogue, where it was offered with tops executed in a variety of shapes and materials, including the marble one chosen by Loos for the Café Museum (figure 37A). The paired stance of the legs and feet was a device originally used by Michael Thonet in his sewing table (figure 24A), which was exhibited at the London Great Exhibition of 1851. The feet of this table, like those of Loos's side chair for the Café Museum (cat. no. 37), are vaguely anthropomorphic in form, not unlike the pied-de-biche (hoof foot) used by early-eighteenth-century *menuisiers*.

24

25

Revolving desk-chair, Model No. 19

Cut solid wood, bent solid wood, turned wood, cane, metal

36½ x 21⅛ x 23 in.
92.5 x 53.5 x 58.5 cm

Designer unknown, ca. 1884
Manufactured after 1884 by Walter Heywood Chair Company, New York.
Collection Edward J Wormley, Weston, Connecticut

DEVELOPMENTS in the process of bending wood, as demonstrated by the Windsor chair and certain card tables, occurred in the United States in the eighteenth century. This evolution continued in the early nineteenth century in Boston with the work of Samuel Gragg (cat. no. 3) and later, in New York, in the virtuosic designs of John Henry Belter (cat. nos. 19–21). Thus the emergence of a bent-wood furniture industry in the United States in the second half of the nineteenth century was not so

*Figure 24*A
Michael Thonet. Sewing table, ca. 1851. Bent laminated wood, solid wood, veneer, mother-of-pearl. Collection Georg Thonet, Frankenberg, West Germany.

much a grafting of European circumstances on to American society, as it was a continuation of an extant tradition.

Walter Heywood Chair Company was very much a part of this tradition. Although it is not known precisely when the firm began to incorporate bent-wood elements into their designs, a member of the Heywood family was engaged in the production of chairs as early as 1826. At that time Windsor chairs were still very much a part of the middle-class domestic environment in the eastern United States. In this particular design, the one-piece bent-wood element that forms the continuous arrangement of stiles and crest rail replicates the same device used for the production of many Windsor chairs. The scrolled bent-wood arms, however, are more akin to those used on some of Gragg's chairs and on Thonet's early Boppard chairs dating from the 1830s (cat. no. 4). This reduction of elements, a concept so intimately associated with the repetitive craft production of Windsor chairs, was eminently suitable to mass production. Managers of the Heywood company were early advocates of mechanized production, and their sophisticated machinery is even said to have elicited the praise of Michael Thonet (Hanks, pp. 132–33).

According to a Heywood company catalogue of circa 1884, this office chair, the Continental Rotary, was available in a stationary model as well as one with four C-shaped steel springs that permitted a rocking motion. A rotating chair was in Thonet's catalogue as early as 1866 (Wilk 1980a, fig. 42, second row from bottom, third from left).

25

26

26

Folding deck-chair

Bent solid beechwood, solid beechwood, cane

37 x 22¼ x 31 in.
94 x 56.5 x 79 cm

Designer unknown, ca. 1873
Manufactured after 1873 by Gebrüder Thonet, Vienna
Collection Georg Thonet, Frankenberg, West Germany

THIS design was first introduced in a Thonet sales catalogue of 1866, three years before the expiration of the Austro-Hungarian patent that granted Thonet exclusive rights "to manufacture chair and table legs made of bent wood, the curvature of which is effected through the agency of steam or boiling liquids." In this deck chair, the designer, who may have been Michael Thonet himself, presaged several of the essential aspects of progressive furniture design of the 1920s: Low production costs, durability, light weight, and portability. It is possible that this type of collapsible design later inspired the famous camp chair, known as the "Indian" chair, produced by Maple & Co. (figure 75A), which lent its form to Le Corbusier's *sièges à dossier basculant* of 1928 (cat. no. 75).

27

Standing mirror, Model No. 9951

Bent solid beechwood, silvered glass, laminated wood, metal

76¼ x 41¾ x 23 in.
194 x 106 x 58.5 cm

Designer unknown, ca. 1875
Manufactured after 3d quarter of 19th century by Gebrüder Thonet, Vienna
Alexander von Vegesack, Düsseldorf

THE freestanding mirror was an invention of the early nineteenth century when larger sheets of glass became a technical reality. Even though smaller freestanding toilette

mirrors had been offered by Thonet as early as 1866, it was not until later in the century that full-sized frames for cheval or psyche glasses were made available by the firm, although at that time they were sold without the glass. The strength of bent wood made it an ideal support material for the weight of the glass, and the delicacy of the wooden frame provided a strong visual contrast to the commanding presence of the glass. The 1904 Gebrüder Thonet catalogue offers this model with glass for 110 Austrian kronen and without glass for 48 kronen, an indication of bent wood's low cost.

28

Side chair, Model No. 25

Bent solid beechwood, solid wood, cane
35½ x 16½ x 21 in.
90.5 x 42 x 53.5 cm

Designer unknown, ca. 1878
Manufactured after 3d quarter of 19th century by Gebrüder Thonet, Vienna
Alexander von Vegesack, Düsseldorf

PRIOR to the aesthetic revolution in bentwood furnishings in the early twentieth century, creativity at many of the firms had begun to wane—pure invention giving way to modification of existing models. Even this procedure, however, could produce designs of aesthetic merit. The No. 25 side chair, also available in an armchair version, consisted of a standard Thonet frame and a flamboyant back splat of three superimposed shapes. As a concession to the prolonged and rugged use these chairs received, Thonet began to furnish them with added reinforcements. The bentwood ring stretchers and turned capitals of the legs that had been developed nearly a quarter of a century earlier in the No. 14 chair (cat. nos. 14–18) were supplemented here by a seat rail that is thicker where it joins the legs. This gave the tenon of the leg maximum support but compromised the delicacy of the design evident in the earlier chairs.

27

28

Rocking chair, Model No. 1

Bent solid beechwood, solid beechwood,
cane

44 x 22½ x 44 in.
112 x 57 x 112 cm

Designed unknown, ca. 1862
Manufactured late 19th century by Gebrüder
Thonet, Vienna
Collection Georg Thonet, Frankenberg, West
Germany

IT is highly likely that Michael Thonet was influenced by the Winfield rocker (cat. no. 11), which was also exhibited at the Great Exhibition held in London's Crystal Palace in 1851, where he had first displayed his designs to an international market. This possibility is suggested by the marked similarity between Thonet's design and the Winfield model, one of the first rocking chairs to dispense with the differentiation between legs and runners. This consolidation of elements produced a radical design of sweeping simplicity, ideally suited to the enriching effect of bent wood, which could be easily contorted into fanciful shapes.

An Anglo-American invention of uncertain parentage, the rocking chair remained something of an alien concept in the environment of nineteenth-century Western European society. Nevertheless, Thonet, an innovator in the manipulation of materials and production methodology, apparently introduced his first rocking chair in the early 1860s, although the first published example, listed as the No. 1 rocking chair, does not appear until the firm's 1866 catalogue. It differed only slightly from the chair shown here, which was also marketed as model No. 1 when it was offered in Thonet's 1888 catalogue. The backswept scrolls of the runners, supports, and arms combine into a distinctive arrangement of details that suggests movement even when the piece is stationary.

29

30

Table

Engraved laminated wood, bent solid beech-wood, solid wood, turned wood (painted)
29¾ x 32½ x 32½ in.
75.5 x 82.5 x 82.5 cm

Designer unknown, ca. 1880
Manufactured last quarter of 19th century by Gebrüder Thonet, Vienna
Alexander von Vegesack, Düsseldorf

BY the third quarter of the nineteenth century, as bent-wood furniture became an accepted component of both public and private quarters, manufacturers introduced designs that were specifically historicist in nature. Often replicating the effects of many revivalist motifs and forms that had been produced through traditional means, these new bent-wood furniture designs were popular with a more conservative clientele.

The fluid bent-wood base of this table contrasts with its rectilinear top and applied decoration. The etched design, highlighted with paint, was meant to resemble the marquetry used on more expensive furniture.

30

31

Dolls' furniture

Bent solid beechwood, cane

Settee 11¾ x 14 x 9¼ in.
30 x 35.5 x 23.5 cm
Circular table 9 x 10½ x 10½ in.
23 x 26.5 x 26.5 cm.
Large armchair 12¾ x 6¾ x 8¾ in.
31.5 x 17 x 22 cm
Small armchair 9⅝ x 4⅝ x 6 in.
24.5 x 12 x 15.5 cm

Designer unknown, last quarter of 19th century

Manufacturer unknown, last quarter of 19th century

Barry Harwood Galleries, New York

As newly established entrepreneurs, the various manufacturers of bent-wood furnishings saw no reason to neglect any portion of the marketplace that might be serviced by their output. Even furnishings sized for dolls was an accepted avenue of production, as demonstrated by these diminutive versions of full-scale pieces in Thonet's regular line. Such miniature items were manufactured in the same manner as the regular-sized pieces, including the use of special molds for the setting of these delicate pieces.

The settee, large armchair, and table were retailed by Thonet in a *Puppenmöbel* (dolls' furniture) section, in which they are part of the No. 1 series (Wilk 1980b, p. 94); the small armchair is a modification of Thonet's full-size No. 14 armchair.

32

Music rack, Model No. 1

Bent solid beechwood, bent laminated wood, solid wood

23½ x 16¼ x 21⅞ in.
60 x 41.5 x 55.5 cm

Designer unknown, last quarter of 19th century

Manufactured last quarter of 19th century by Gebrüder Thonet, Vienna

Alexander von Vegesack, Düsseldorf

An examination of catalogues dating from the last quarter of the nineteenth century reveals that manufacturers of bent-wood furniture were servicing rapidly developing consumer needs. Unhampered by the restraints of tradition, they were able to introduce new types of furniture rapidly. As the leisure class grew, so did its pursuit of cultural pastimes. Music stands such as this one might have been fixtures in many a private residence.

Using a paired foot, which had been part of the Thonet vocabulary since the Great Exhibition of 1851 in London, the designer of this piece brilliantly exploited the curvilinear potential of bent wood.

32

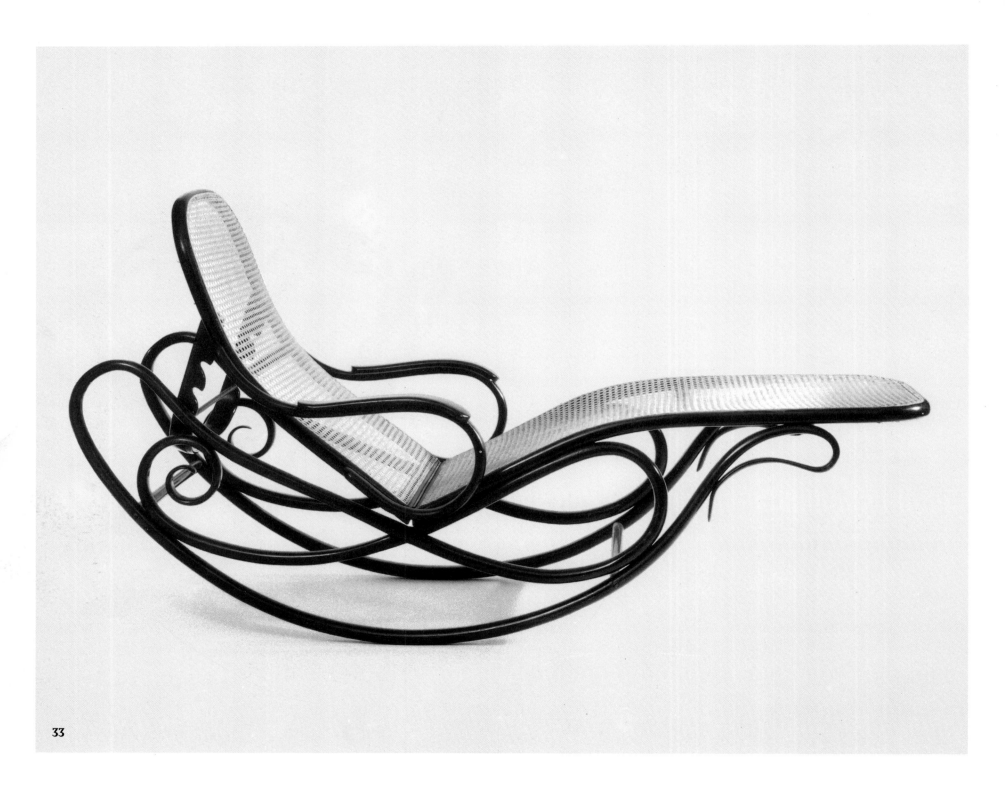

33

33

Rocking chaise, Model No. 7500

Bent solid beechwood, turned solid beechwood, solid wood, cane

32 x 26¼ x 68¾ in.
81.5 x 67 x 174.5 cm

Designer unknown, ca. 1880
Manufactured last quarter of 19th century by Gebrüder Thonet, Vienna

Alexander von Vegesack, Düsseldorf

MANY bent-wood furnishings formed part of an advantaged life style rather than an impoverished one in the nineteenth century. Few models illustrate this more vividly than this piece advertised as a *Schaukefauteuil* (rocking chaise). Only the most affluent could afford a reclining unit other than a sofa or bed; indeed, few people had the space in their homes to accommodate the luxurious sweep of this rocking chaise. Such a piece was never intended for the masses.

In the large body of rocking and stationary pieces, this particular model is one of the finest. The long rods of bent wood that form its sides appear to be single twenty-foot rods, but are in fact constructed from two separate pieces spliced near the intersection of the arms at the side rail. Borrowed from contemporary English morris chairs (named for their designer, William Morris), the adjustable back anticipates Josef Hoffmann's *Sitzmachine* (cat. no. 56) designed nearly a quarter of a century later.

34

Three-legged chair, Model No. 81

Bent solid beechwood, laminated wood, solid beechwood

31⅞ x 24½ x 23¼ in.
81 x 62 x 59 cm

Designer unknown, last quarter of 19th century
Manufactured ca. 1900 by Gebrüder Thonet, Vienna

Alexander von Vegesack, Düsseldorf

THIS chair was a harbinger of design developments after the turn of the century. With its simplification of elements and partial abstraction of the traditional chair form, the design anticipates the achievements of Gerrit Rietveld (cat. no. 73) and Marcel Breuer (cat. no. 72). By combining a broad front stance with a relatively shallow seat, the designer was able to produce a chair with more stability than that found in later three-legged models. The L-shaped iron brackets at the intersection of the seat rails and legs act as stabilizers for the minimal frame and replace the more common ring stretchers, which would have complicated the design. Soon after the turn of the century, Viennese Secessionist designers supplanted this functional structural element with spheres and ovals of turned wood that provided the same support but had overtones of an aesthetic doctrine.

34

35

Figure 35A
Dining room, Hotel Astor, New York, 1909.

35

Side chair, Model No. 51

Bent solid beechwood, solid wood, cane
36¼ x 15½ x 17½ in.
92 x 39.5 x 44.5 cm

Designer unknown ca. 1888
Manufactured after 1888 by Gebrüder
Thonet, Vienna
Alexander von Vegesack, Düsseldorf

IN its paradoxical design of structural lucidity and aesthetic exoticism, this chair represents a radical departure from traditional nineteenth-century seating forms, adding a distinctive note of the avant-garde to conventional public settings (figure 35A). By ingeniously splicing rods that had been bent in opposite directions above each foot, the designer created the impression of a chair constructed almost entirely from a single piece of bent wood. Even in the back, only the rectangular portion of the splat is the isolated element in the design. The geometric definition of its elements anticipate the progressive Viennese designs that were introduced after the turn of the century. The extension of the stiles

Figure 35B
Richard Riemerschmid. Side chair, 1899. Oak and leather. The Museum of Modern Art, New York (Gift of Liberty & Company Ltd.).

into the front feet would be explored by several Art Nouveau and Jugendstil designers, as, for example, Richard Riemerschmid (figure 35B), who used traditional joinery in the execution of his chairs displaying this device. The split leg, first used in 1851 in Thonet's sewing table (figure 24A), would eventually be used by Alvar Aalto in his 1946 stool (figure 48A).

36

Footstool, Model No. 2

Bent solid beechwood, cane
6¾ x 16 x 11⅝ in.
16 x 40.5 x 30 cm

Designer unknown, last quarter of 19th century
Manufactured last quarter of 19th century by Gebrüder Thonet, Vienna
Barry Harwood Galleries, New York

OF the four footstools offered in Thonet's 1888 catalogue, the No. 2 stool was the most expensive. Its cost can be attributed to the ambitious use of bent-wood scrolls that support the circular frame of the caned footrest. The fragile caning (actually unsuitable for a footrest) and delicate wooden scrolling of the legs have made these stools among the rarest of nineteenth-century bent-wood furnishings to survive.

36

37

Side chair

Bent solid beechwood, solid wood, cane
35½ x 16½ x 20¼ in.
90 x 42 x 51.5 cm

Designed ca. 1898 by Adolf Loos (born Brno, Moravia, 1870, died Kalkasburg, Austria, 1933)

Manufactured ca. 1899 by Jacob & Josef Kohn, Vienna

Alexander von Vegesack, Düsseldorf

THIS chair, designed by Adolf Loos for the Café Museum in Vienna (figure 37A) before the Secessionist vocabulary grew to dominate the Viennese design community after the turn of the century, gives no premonition of the aesthetic revolution that would radically transform style, including the appearance of a great many bent-wood furnishings. Originally attributed to Thonet production, the chair was actually manufactured by Jacob & Josef Kohn (Rukschcio and Schachel, pp. 418–19). It was the first of the architect-designed furnishings that would dominate the progressive sector of the bent-wood

furniture industry after 1900 and was also the first of such designs to be produced by Kohn, whose reputation after this time was built on this type of furniture. Such furnishings were often distinguished by their adherence to a grammar of geometric form, unlike the more flamboyant curvilinear bent wood designs that had characterized the work of the nineteenth century. However, in its appropriation of several elements already in the design vocabulary of the bent wood industry, the Café Museum chair was in some respects a summation of the earlier period.

By reworking the basic design of Thonet's No. 14 chair (cat. nos. 14–18) in the Café Museum chair, Loos revealed his respect for established, successful design. By the end of the nineteenth century, the No. 14 model had become a generic type of chair whose sober, yet elegant form was determined by a minimal number of elements and whose ease of assembly made it the most inexpensive design produced by bent-wood furniture manufacturers until that time.

Rather than isolate the splat of the chair between the stiles as Michael Thonet had done in his No. 14 chair, Loos incorporated

Figure 37A
Adolf Loos. Café Museum, Vienna, after 1899.

37

this element into a single piece of bent wood, which also comprised the stiles and rear legs. By indenting the line of this inner splat and the crest rail, Loos infused new vitality into what had become the most anonymous design of the century. He also removed the functional, turned stump-leg of the No. 14 chair from his design and replaced it with a splayed leg and shaped foot, reminiscent of the graceful pied-de-biche (hoof foot) of the early eighteenth century.

The Café Museum chair now in the collection of the Österreichisches Museum für angewandte Kunst is believed to be one of the actual chairs from the café. The brilliant red stain of the chair was selected to complement the deep red mahogany paneling used in Loos's interior.

In his published attacks on such contemporary designers as Henry van de Velde, who were intent on devising their own stridently individualistic, decorative statements, Loos expressed his belief that such an expenditure of creative talent was a waste of time: an act he repeatedly vilifies in his vituperative essay "Ornament und Verbrechen" (Ornament and Crime) published in 1908 (Ulrich, pp. 19–24).

38

Armchair, Model No. 715/F

Bent solid beechwood, laminated wood, upholstery (later), metal

30½ x 22⅛ x 22 in.
77.5 x 56.5 x 56 cm

Designed 1899 by Gustav Siegel (born Vienna 1880, died Vienna 1970)

Manufactured ca. 1900 by Jacob & Josef Kohn, Vienna

Barry Friedman Ltd.

As head of the in-house design department of Jacob & Josef Kohn after 1899, Gustav Siegel was responsible for many of the aesthetically advanced bent-wood furnishings manufactured and retailed by the

*Figure 38*A
Gustav Siegel. Interior with applied bent-wood wall decoration and chair of bent solid wood, Jacob & Josef Kohn display at the Exposition Universelle, Paris, 1900. (From *L'Art Décoratif Revue International*, July 1900, p. 164).

firm between the turn of the century and World War I. In the course of this association, however, Siegel's own reputation was submerged by that of his employer, thus transforming him into an almost anonymous figure in the history of bent-wood furniture design. In addition, as neither architect nor artist—two ideal means to artistic recognition in fin-de-siècle Vienna —he is still perceived as a two-dimensional figure. His contemporaries Josef Hoffmann and Koloman Moser, both of whom also designed decorative pieces, achieved greater fame as architect and painter, respectively.

The son of a cabinetmaker, Siegel was nineteen when he was appointed director

38

of Kohn's design department in 1899 (see the essay by Graham Dry in this volume; also Schweiger in Vienna 1979, n.p.). He devoted his career to the design of bent-wood furniture and was one of the earliest contributors to the aesthetic revolution that transformed bent-wood furnishing in the early twentieth century. Unlike so many of the ambiguous attributions attached to bent wood designs of this period, the authorship of this chair as well as Kohn's award-winning exhibition at the 1900 Paris Exposition Universelle is indisputably Siegel's. In that virtuosic installation, the twenty-year-old designer used bent-wood elements to define the sweeping members of the wall partitions and panels (figure 38A) and of an elaborate program of furnishings as well. (Wilk 1980a, fig. 69).

39

Tub chair, Model No. 720/F

Bent solid beechwood, bent laminated wood, solid wood, upholstery, metal

30⅛ x 24¾ x 24 in.
76.5 x 63 x 61 cm

Design of ca. 1902 attributed to Josef Hoffmann (born Pirnitz, Moravia, 1870, died Vienna 1956)
Manufactured ca. 1902–16 by Jacob & Josef Kohn, Vienna

Alexander von Vegesack, Düsseldorf, Courtesy Galerie Wolfgang Richter, Munich

IN its bold simplicity of form and lack of decorative embellishments, this chair reflects the reform mentality of the nine-

teenth century that rejected the historicist revivals. This attitude, which emerged as a reaction to the ornamental excesses of the 1851 Great Exhibition in London, was the conceptual base of the English Arts and Crafts movement. This philosophy dominated the enlightened European and American progressive design community for the remainder of the nineteenth century and into the decade following World War I. Many Anglophile Austrian architects and designers absorbed many of the principles of this movement at the turn of the century.

This chair, complete with metal sabots (shoes), appeared in a Jacob & Josef Kohn advertisement (figure 39A) in the catalogue of the fifteenth Secessionist exhibition, held in Vienna in 1902, in which it is described as being "in modernem Stil." It is one of the earliest of the large upholstered seating pieces marketed by Kohn in the wake of its highly acclaimed installation at the 1900 Paris Exposition Universelle (figure 38A). In an effort to

Figure 39A
Advertisement of Jacob & Josef Kohn, Vienna, in the catalogue of *XV. Ausstellung der Vereinigung bildender Künstler Österreichs Sezession*, Vienna, 1902.

39

238

capture a larger portion of the increasingly competitive bent-wood furniture market, Kohn included upholstered seating forms as part of its already extensive line. The complex matrix of secondary upholstery elements is disguised here behind the broad sheet of bent laminated wood that encases the chair. Plywood was also used in the construction of bent-wood case pieces, which were new to bent-wood furniture production.

The model for this tub chair, which was part of the installation, was not the first of the Kohn-produced designs to use square-sectioned bent-wood members for the definition of its frame. However, it did point the way to a greater use of an angular-edged wooden rod that better suited the geometric Secessionist aesthetic than the round-sectioned rods used extensively in nineteenth-century bent-wood production. The design of Otto Wagner's later Postsparkasse chair (cat. no. 46) and its numerous variations was based on the Siegel armchair.

This chair, as well as the armchair model No. 330/F, was shown in Kohn's sales catalogue of 1906, which included a drawing of the firm's installation at the Louisiana Purchase Exhibition held in Saint Louis in 1904 (see Massobrio and Portoghesi 1976, p. 74).

40

Desk chair, Model No. 725/BF

Bent solid beechwood, bent laminated wood, turned wood, upholstery (later)

34¼ x 22 x 22 in.
87 x 56 x 56 cm

Designer unknown, ca. 1902

Manufactured ca. 1902–16 by Jacob & Josef Kohn, Vienna

Alexander von Vegesack, Düsseldorf, Courtesy Galerie Wolfgang Richter, Munich

Figure 40A

"A Dining Room in Modern Style Carried Out in a New York Apartment," 1922. Designed by Edward H. Aschermann. (From Holloway, *The Practical Book of Furnishing the Small House & Apartment*, pl. 3).

DESPITE several recent claims that identify this chair as a design by Koloman Moser (see Müller, p. 48, pl. 1), no documentation from the era survives to support this assignment. A close examination of the chair suggests that, like many attributions formulated in the last decade, this, too, must be set aside. That the designer of this chair was well schooled in the technical complexities of bending wood is evident in the single rod of bent wood that defines the chair's forelegs, arms, and crest rail. This piece of solid wood was carefully shaped at critical junctions to counteract the considerable strain placed on the grain of the wood. Moser, an artist consumed by pursuit of the aesthetic, probably did not possess the training necessary to create a design of this subtle nature. The illusionary tautness of the lines of the chair is unequaled in other works of this scale. It is possible that the design may be the work of Gustav Siegel, the director of design at Jacob & Josef Kohn at the time.

The perception of this chair's modernity was so long-lived that it was included almost twenty years later in a design of a progressive interior (figure 40A).

40

41

Armchair, Model No. 330/F

Bent solid beechwood, bent laminated wood,
upholstery (later), metal
39⅜ x 22½ x 21¼ in.
100 x 57 x 54 cm

Designed ca. 1902 by Josef Hoffmann (born
Pirnitz, Moravia, 1870, died Vienna 1956)
Manufactured ca. 1902–16 by Jacob & Josef
Kohn, Vienna
Alexander von Vegesack, Düsseldorf, Courtesy
Galerie Wolfgang Richter, Munich

IN part because this armchair appeared on
the cover of a 1909 Jacob & Josef Kohn
catalogue, it can be attributed to Josef
Hoffmann. It was retailed by Kohn in its
line of upholstered furniture, as part of a
salon suite that also included a center table
by Hoffmann (cat. no. 59) and a matching
settee and side chair (figure 41A). In 1906,
the side chair was shown in a dining room
credited to Josef Hoffmann (figure 41B)
in a volume devoted to recent design in
Austria.

The upholstery of the chair and the metal
sabots (shoes) that sheathe its feet indicate
that it was not intended for either the
general market or public environments.

Figure 41B
Josef Hoffmann. Dining room
furniture, 1904. Manufactured
by Jacob & Josef Kohn, Vi-
enna. (from Holme, *Art Re-*
***vival in Austria*, pl. C14).**

Rather it was part of a higher-priced line of
furnishings directed toward private offices
and domestic settings. The sheet of bent
plywood enclosing the sides and back of
this chair and the lengthy rod of solid bent
wood defining the chair's continuous fore-
leg and crest-rail system display a masterful
handling of the bending process.

Figure 41A
Cover of Jacob & Josef Kohn
sales catalogue, ca. 1908.

42

Figure 42A
**Le Corbusier and Pierre Jean-
neret. Living room, Pavillon de
L'Esprit Nouveau, Exposition
Internationale des Art Décoratifs, Paris, 1925. (From *Le Corbusier et Pierre Jeanneret:
Oeuvre complète de 1910–1929*,
p. 107).**

42

Armchair, Model No. 9

Bent solid beechwood, solid wood, cane
30 x 23 x 19⅝ in.
76 x 58.5 x 50 cm

Designer unknown, ca. 1904
*Manufactured after 1904 by Gebrüder
Thonet, Vienna*
Alexander von Vegesack, Düsseldorf

THE predecessor of this design, the No. 8
chair, had been part of Thonet's line since
1866. However, it was not until after the
turn of the century that the No. 9 first
appeared in Thonet catalogues. During the
decade following its introduction, it was
ignored in modernist circles, eclipsed by
other bent wood designs that stridently
proclaimed their modernity via a Secessionist aesthetic.

At the end of World War I, however, this
chair was briefly accorded a singular status

Figure 42B
Mart Stam. Living room, Mart Stam House, Deutsche Werkbund exhibition *Die Wohnung* at Weissenhofsiedlung, Stuttgart, 1927. (From Gräff, *Innenraüme*, fig. 98).

when it achieved a delayed maturity in the vanguard of design. The No. 9 chair, regarded by many as the essence of machine production, was inexpensive, ahistoricist, and comfortable. As a result it was used in many of the most heavily publicized modernist installations of the 1920s, among them the Pavillon de L'Esprit Nouveau designed by Le Corbusier and Pierre Jeanneret for the 1925 Exposition Internationale des Arts Décoratifs in Paris (figure 42A) and several of the houses built for the Weissenhofsiedlung in Stuttgart in 1927 (figure 42B). Le Corbusier in particular was a proponent of this design, and he extolled its virtues in his avant-garde review *L'Esprit Nouveau* in the early 1920s. By the end of the decade, however, as bent tubular steel usurped bent wood in modernist furniture design, the No. 9 model was used with less frequency.

43

43

Side chair, for Purkersdorf Sanatorium, Model No. 322

Bent solid beechwood, laminated wood, turned wood, upholstery (later)

38½ x 17½ x 17 in.
98 x 44.5 x 43 cm

Designed ca. 1904 by Josef Hoffmann (born Pirnitz, Moravia, 1870, died Vienna 1956)
Manufactured ca. 1904 probably by Jacob & Josef Kohn, Vienna

Private collection, Ohio

A component of a specific architectural commission, the chair was used in the dining room of the Purkersdorf Sanatorium (figure 43A), a fashionable spa outside Vienna that catered to individuals suffering from nervous disorders. The chair, which appeared in Kohn's 1906 catalogue as model No. 322, was sold as part of a suite that included an armchair, settee, and table (see Massobrio and Portoghesi 1976, p. 75).

The rectilinear mass of the chair responds to the interior appointments of the dining room, in which a deeply coffered, gridwork ceiling exposed the building's reinforced-concrete structure. Despite having designed this chair for a specific setting, Hoffmann countered the tyranny of the *Gesamtkunstwerk* approach to the room by producing a chair whose virtues remained intact even after it was removed from its original environment. Through a careful manipulation of the chair's components, Hoffmann achieved a stable balance between the functional and decorative aspects of the design.

Hoffmann merged these two qualities in his use of geometry which, by the time the sanatorium was built, had become the leitmotif of his work. The circular perforations of the back, which offered visual interest and relief to the solid panel, also provided ventilation for the sitter's back. The use of turned wooden spheres at the junction of legs and seat rails not only aesthetically reiterated Hoffmann's use of this motif, but also added essential structural stability to this portion of the design, which had formerly been supplied by ring stretchers or L-shaped metal brackets.

It is in the single section of bent wood used for the entire rear portion of the chair that Hoffmann reveals the brilliant interplay between aesthetics and function. This continuous rod undergoes a geometric transformation: square-sectioned at the feet, the rod becomes circular-sectioned in its upper portion, particularly at the stiles and crest rail. This treatment is not merely decorative, for the section of wood had to be reduced to prevent a buckling of the inner surface of this curvature and a tearing of its outer face when the vertical line of the stile made the transition to the horizontal line of the crest rail.

The Purkersdorf chairs were originally upholstered in red oilcloth; the color of the wood was golden brown, unlike the deeper shades of red and brown that characterized pieces for the general market at

that time and the ebonized finish used on many of the more progressive designs.

Many of the furnishings in the Purkersdorf Sanatorium were dispersed some time in the mid-1960s, and chairs from the dining room are now in the collections of the Österreichisches Museum für angewandte Kunst in Vienna; the Bädisches Landesmuseum in Karlsruhe, West Germany; the Cleveland Museum of Art; and the Cooper-Hewitt Museum in New York.

Figure 43A
Josef Hoffmann. Dining room, Purkersdorf Sanitorium, near Vienna, ca. 1904. Furniture manufactured by Jacob & Josef Kohn, Vienna.

44

Clothing rack with umbrella stand, Model No. W675

Bent solid beechwood, solid beechwood, laminated wood

81 x 26 x 26 in.
206 x 66 x 66 cm

Designer unknown, ca. 1904

Manufactured ca. 1904–16 by Jacob & Josef Kohn, Vienna

Alexander von Vegesack, Düsseldorf

AFTER the turn of the century, the influence of progressive architects on design became evident even in the production of secondary furnishings. Clothing racks sold through the catalogues of bent-wood furniture manufacturers during the late nineteenth century consisted of single poles or pedestals supported by tripod and quatrepod bases. Eschewing the earlier format for a clothes stand, the designer of this piece multiplied the single-pole format by four to define a three-dimensional space, an architectonic device. In plan, this enclosure reveals a geometric transformation from its base to its crest. Rising from a rectangular base, the four bent-wood poles merge at the top in a configuration that is circular in section, revealing the subtle play of form evident in so many designs of the period. This conversion from square to circle is similar to the transformation of the piece of bent wood used in the rear portion of the Purkersdorf Sanatorium chair (cat. no. 43).

The panel secured above the bottom pan was meant to provide a support for umbrellas. Its functional gridlike plan reinforces the geometric aesthetic, as do the square-sectioned wooden rods that were used with increasing frequency after the turn of the century.

This clothes stand has been attributed to Josef Hoffmann (Gebhard, 59; New York 1981a, p. 35), but in fact, it has never appeared in any published interior ascribed to him, nor was it ever published as his work in any journal of the period.

45

Theater seating

Bent solid beechwood, bent laminated wood, solid wood, metal

37 x 88½ x 21¼ in.
94 x 225 x 54 cm

Designer unknown, ca. 1905

Manufactured after 1905 by Gebrüder Thonet, Vienna

Alexander von Vegesack, Düsseldorf

THE commercial success of bent-wood furnishings depended on the use of interchangeable, standardized parts. Such repetition is vividly apparent in the designs for theater seating, where identical elements are contained in each unit. Although a late-nineteenth-century innovation, these multiple seating groups quickly assimilated the decorative vocabulary of Secessionist Vienna—seen in the starkly geometric perforations that provide aesthetic relief in the broad expanse of the back panels. Despite their artistic treatment, which was available in historicist designs as well, these decorations also had a functional value by providing ventilation for uncushioned seats. The durability, ease of installation, and low cost of bent-wood furnishings in relation to traditionally constructed theater seating recommended these innovative units to the builders of less expensive auditoriums where seat cushions were not provided.

46

Armchair, for the Board Room, Österreichische Postsparkasse

Bent solid beechwood, laminated wood, upholstery, aluminum

30⅝ x 21¾ x 22 in.
78 x 55.5 x 56 cm

Designed ca. 1905–6 by Otto Wagner (born Vienna 1841, died Vienna 1918)

Manufactured after 1905–6 by Jacob & Josef Kohn, Vienna

Österreichische Postsparkasse, Vienna

FOR more than a decade following the publication of his *Moderne Architektur* in 1895, Otto Wagner dominated progressive architectural thought in Europe. His rationalist theories, propagated by his teaching, as a professor at the Akademie der bildenden Künste (Academy of Fine Arts) in Vienna, and in his writings, were tangibly realized in one of his most important buildings: the Österreichische Postsparkasse (Imperial Austrian Postal Savings Bank), constructed in Vienna from 1904 to 1906. This project may in fact be looked upon as a *Gesamtkunstwerk*, for Wagner was also responsible for the bank's furnishings. Many of these were constructed from bent wood, an indication of his respect for that material and its aesthetic possibilities.

It is remarkable that the armchairs designed for the bank's board room (figure

44

45

46

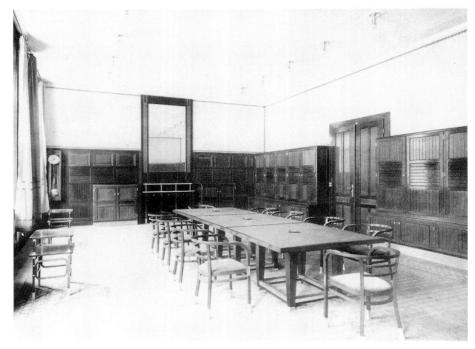

46A), the most conservative bastion within the organization, were constructed from bent wood, a material that had never been used in this type of environment. Wagner borrowed the form of the chair from Gustav Siegel's design shown at the 1900 Paris Exposition Universelle (cat. no. 38). However, he transformed the earlier design through a judicious use of aluminum accessories: extended sabots (shoes) sheathed the feet, and flat strips protected the sides of the chair. Wagner used the metal for both decorative and protective purposes, just as eighteenth-century cabinetmakers had used gilt bronze. The circular aluminum bolt heads echoed the bank's interior and exterior architectural fittings. Aluminum bolts were used throughout the building, most notably on the façade, where they gave the impression of securing the sheets of marble cladding to the reinforced concrete frame of the building.

Figure 46A
Board Room, Österreichische Postsparkasse (Imperial Austrian Postal Savings Bank), Vienna, 1904–6. (From *Das Interieur*, 1907, pl. 48).
SEE CAT. NO. 53.

Modified versions of the board-room chair were used in other private offices of the bank (figure 46B). Through a subtle varying of the amount of aluminum or brass hardware, the chairs reflected the importance of the office in which they were placed. These chairs, including variations made for the general market, were manufactured by both Gebrüder Thonet and Jacob & Josef Kohn.

Figure 46B
Otto Wagner. Variations of armchair designed for the Österreichische Postsparkasse (Imperial Austrian Postal Savings Bank), Vienna, ca. 1906. Left: bent solid wood, perforated laminated wood; right: bent solid wood, laminated wood, upholstery, bent flat aluminum, cast aluminum. Alternately manufactured by Jacob & Josef Kohn and Gebrüder Thonet, Vienna.

47

Etagère, for the Österreichische Postsparkasse

Bent solid beechwood, laminated wood, aluminum
54 x 47¾ x 14½ in.
137 x 102.5 x 37 cm

Designed ca. 1906 by Otto Wagner (born Vienna 1841, died Vienna 1918)
Manufactured ca. 1906 possibly by Jacob & Josef Kohn, Vienna
Österreichische Postsparkasse, Vienna

By 1904, Otto Wagner had attained full maturity as an architect. In his designs for the Österreichische Postsparkasse (Imperial Austrian Postal Savings Bank) in Vienna, he demonstrated his virtuosity by underscoring the institution's hierarchical arrangement through his manipulation of the building's spatial flow, his choice of ornamental motifs and materials, and the wealth of furnishings he designed.

Although not the first of the Viennese architects to turn his attention to bent wood as a means of expression, Wagner produced several of the most accomplished designs of the period. In his bold articulation of form in this bent-wood étagère, Wagner made no attempt to disguise an inexpensive material and a technique usually reserved for mass-produced objects: a particularly remarkable gesture for a piece designed to be used in one of the more luxurious, private areas of the bank. The use of aluminum bolts, an expensive and unusual material at the turn of the century, justifies this interpretation.

This particular design was apparently not merchandised as part of either Gebrüder Thonet's or Jacob & Josef Kohn's standard lines.

47

48

48

Stool, for the Main Banking Room, Österreichische Postsparkasse

Bent solid beechwood, molded laminated wood, aluminum
18½ x 16½ x 16½ in.
47 x 42 x 42 cm

Designed ca. 1906 by Otto Wagner (born Vienna 1841, died Vienna 1918)
Manufactured ca. 1906 by Jacob & Josef Kohn, Vienna
Österreichische Postsparkasse, Vienna

THE stool for the main banking room of the Österreichische Postsparkasse (Imperial Austrian Postal Savings Bank) illustrates Wagner's distillation and translation of an object's essential function into a tangible design. The combination of molded laminated and bent solid wood makes the stool lightweight and easily transportable, characteristics enhanced by the central handhold cut into the shaped seat. In addition, the four-square construction of the frame provides stability and gives the design a powerful linear outline. The ebonized finish contrasts with the lighter color of the tile and glass-brick floors of the main banking hall.

The complex curve of the shaped seat, bound into this configuration by the four bent-wood side rails, anticipates Charles and Ray Eameses' later chair seats, which retain their undulant forms without auxiliary braces. Alvar Aalto also used bent wood in this way to define the frame of his stool of about 1946–47 (figure 48A).

49

Side chair, Model No. 511

Bent solid beechwood, molded laminated wood, turned wood, solid wood
39⅛ x 16½ x 19⅝ in.
99.5 x 42 x 50 cm

Designer unknown, ca. 1905
Manufactured after 1905 by Gebrüder Thonet, Vienna
Alexander von Vegesack, Düsseldorf

THIS chair has often been associated with the Belgian architect Henry van de Velde, the foremost propagator of modernist principles in Germany immediately after the turn of the century (Candilis, p. 51), because the buttressed supports are similar to elements used on chairs designed by Van de Velde and produced by his own firm, Société Van de Velde, in Brussels

Figure 48A
Alvar Aalto. Stool, ca. 1946–47. Solid birch and bent birch. Marketed by Artek. Château Dufresne, Musée des Arts Décoratifs, Montreal (The Liliane Stewart Collection).

49

*Figure 49*A
Henry van de Velde. Side chair, ca. 1895. Ash and upholstery (modern). Manufactured by Société Van de Velde, Brussels. Barry Friedman Ltd., New York.

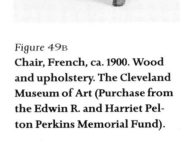

*Figure 49*B
Chair, French, ca. 1900. Wood and upholstery. The Cleveland Museum of Art (Purchase from the Edwin R. and Harriet Pelton Perkins Memorial Fund).

(figure 49A). In addition, the presence of Secessionist motifs has led to an attribution of this design to Josef Hoffmann and his circle (Müller, fig. 138). But neither architect was ever credited with the design in journals of the period.

However, the design can be traced to an earlier Thonet piece, the No. 51 chair (cat. no. 35). In both these chairs the extension of the stiles into the forelegs was not so

Figure 49C
Side chair, Model No. 511, Restaurant, New York City. Thonet Brothers Sales Catalogue, New York, 1910.

much an insight into the technical properties of bent wood as it was a stylistic device; other European designers at the turn of the century attained the same effect by means of traditional joinery and solid wood that had been cut and carved into the desired shape (figure 49B). This extension was thought by many progressive architects to provide the chair with a greater sense of visual cohesiveness. That the chair was used in a fashionable New York restaurant before World War I (figure 49C) indicates the extent of its geographic and social appeal.

50

Tall case clock, Model No. 1

Bent solid beechwood, laminated wood, oak veneer, glass, metal
86 x 17½ x 8¼ in.
208.5 x 44.5 x 21 cm

Designer unknown, ca. 1905
Manufactured after 1905 by Gebrüder Thonet, Vienna
Collection Georg Thonet, Frankenberg, West Germany

IN the final quarter of the nineteenth century, case pieces—desks, chests, cabinets—were added to the lines of bent wood manufacturers. Until then, these firms supplied only smaller furnishings—tables, chairs, étagères, pedestals, mirrors. Case pieces displaying the Viennese Secessionist aesthetic first appeared publicly in Jacob & Josef Kohn's remarkable modernist installation designed by Gustav Siegel for the Turin Exposition of 1902 (Wilk 1980a, fig. 69). Siegel included a tall case clock manufactured from circular-sectioned pieces of bent wood, a vestige of a nineteenth-century aesthetic in bent wood production. The use of square-sectioned bent-wood rods would increase dramatically after the turn of the century.

Thonet's tall case clock, with its Secessionist form and motifs, represents the firm's capitulation to the aesthetic lead that Jacob & Josef Kohn, its chief rival, had established with its installation at the Paris Exposition. In addition, there are remarkable similarities between the Thonet clock and a cabinet made in 1900 by Koloman

Figure 50A
Koloman Moser. Cabinet, 1900. Palisander, nickel-plated copper, silver-plated copper. Courtesy Sotheby's, New York.

Figure 50B
Detail.

Moser (figure 50A), even though the two case pieces were produced under entirely different circumstances. The Moser piece is a one-of-a-kind commission, produced in a cabinetry shop by traditional methods of construction. The clock is one of many, manufactured in a factory by a production-line bending process. Despite the radically different origins, the pieces share certain aesthetic elements. Attenuated in their proportions, both boxlike designs present thinly profiled legs capped with extended sabots (shoes), an indication of the increasing tendency on the part of the factory to replicate the effects of custom work.

The imbricated (scale-like) pattern of the parquetry on the interior of the clock (figure 50B) is a feature not usually found in standard bent-wood furnishings.

51

51

Wall mirror, Model No. 40/8
*Bent solid beechwood, silvered glass, laminated
wood*
22⅞ x 34½ x 1½ in.
58 x 87.5 x 4 cm

Designer unknown, ca. 1905
*Manufactured after 1905 by Jacob & Josef
Kohn, Vienna*

*Alexander von Vegesack, Düsseldorf, Courtesy
Galerie Wolfgang Richter, Munich*

Perhaps the most austere bent wood design produced at the turn of the century, this mirror evokes the same qualities of simplicity of form allied with the manufacturing process that Michael Thonet had incorporated into his most successful design, the No. 14 chair (cat. nos. 14–18). The mirror expressed the geometric vocabulary of the Secessionist movement more succinctly than any other model advertised at the turn of the century. The setting of one rectilinear form within another was a bold gesture in the face of embellished historicist designs that dominated mainstream taste at the time. The designer softened the austerity of the large expanse of glass and the mirror's linear definition by introducing a subtle shallow fluting to the bent-wood members.

52

Nesting tables, Model No. 988

*Bent solid wood, laminated wood, turned
wood*

*A. 29 x 24¾ x 17½ in.
74 x 62 x 44.5 cm*

*B. 26¾ x 18⅞ x 14½ in.
68 x 48 x 37 cm*

*C. 26⅛ x 16¼ x 12¾ in.
66 x 40.5 x 33 cm*

*D. 25⅜ x 13⅝ x 10⅝ in.
64.5 x 34.5 x 27 cm*

Design of ca. 1905 attributed to Josef Hoffmann (born Pirnitz, Moravia, 1870, died Vienna 1956)

Manufactured ca. 1905–16 by Jacob & Josef Kohn, Vienna

Alexander von Vegesack, Düsseldorf, Courtesy Galerie Wolfgang Richter, Munich

ALTHOUGH nesting tables had been an element of early-nineteenth-century furnishings, this group of tables presages the space-saving furniture developed after World War I by architects and designers who were trying to cope with housing shortages and minimal living space.

The designer, thought to be Josef Hoffmann, played on two of the most important decorative motifs of the Secessionist vocabulary—the circle and the square, which became the leitmotif in much of Hoffmann's work before World War I. Like the spherical stays used on chairs in which the junction of the seat and chair rail needed strengthening, the circular forms attached to the outer apron of the largest table are not purely decorative, for they provide a convenient handhold.

These nesting tables were intended to be stored in a closed arrangement, the inner tables being brought out when needed. As a result, the trellis pattern was not repeated on the smaller units, for such an addition would have complicated the design.

52

53

Table, Model No. 40

Bent solid beechwood, laminated wood, metal, brass feet (later)

30⅜ x 20⅝ x 20¼ in.

77 x 52.5 x 51.5 cm

Design of ca. 1904 attributed to Marcel Kammerer (born Vienna 1878, died Quebec 1969)

Manufactured after 1907 by Gebrüder Thonet, Vienna

Alexander von Vegesack, Düsseldorf, Courtesy Galerie Wolfgang Richter, Munich

THIS mass-produced design is clearly related to a similar table that was published in 1905 in the German design periodical *Das Interieur* (figure 53A), where it is identified as the work of Marcel Kammerer. That table has lavish metal mounts and an additional wooden ring stretcher, elements not included in the table shown here. However, a plant stand shown in the same illustration has stretchers made of solid metal rods resembling the pair used on this table. Despite the similarities, precise designer attribution cannot be established. In order to serve a general market that often had limited financial resources, Kohn may have had an in-house designer, such as Gustav Siegel, retool Kammerer's original design by deleting most of its cost-generating features. By the turn of the century, such borrowing of design elements, as well as entire designs, had become commonplace in the highly competitive bent-wood furnishings market (see the essay in this volume by Graham Dry).

Figure 53A

Marcel Kammerer. Furniture, designed ca. 1904. Manufactured by Gebrüder Thonet, Vienna. (From *Das Interieur*, 1905, p. 82).

54

54

Side chair

*Bent solid beechwood, molded laminated
wood, turned wood*

43 x 17¾ x 17¼ in.
109 x 45 x 44 cm

*Designed ca. 1906 by Josef Hoffmann (born
Pirnitz, Moravia, 1870, died Vienna 1956)*

*Manufactured after 1906, probably by Jacob
& Josef Kohn, Vienna*

*Alexander von Vegesack, Düsseldorf, Courtesy
Galerie Wolfgang Richter, Munich*

AT the 1908 *Kunstschau* in Vienna, Josef
Hoffmann presented a model country
house for which he designed bent-wood
furnishings fabricated by Jacob & Josef
Kohn. On the porch of this model Secessionist villa (figure 54A) was a small bent-
wood settee with two sets of a paired crest
rail and central splat delineated with turned
wooden balls. This distinctive treatment is
virtually identical to the single unit of this
side chair. An armchair version of the
chair appeared in a Kohn catalogue of
1906 (figure 54B), but apparently neither
the *Kunstschau* settee nor this side chair
was ever offered for sale in Kohn catalogues. This situation was true of Loos's
Café Museum side chair of circa 1899 (cat.
no. 37), which also was never retailed to
the public through sales catalogues.

Despite its omission from the general
market, the 1906 chair has come to be
viewed as one of the most powerful evoca-
tions of the geometric vocabulary employed by progressive designers in Vienna
at the turn of the century. The bold ar-

Figure 54A

**Josef Hoffmann. Settee, on
porch of small country house,
Jacob & Josef Kohn display at
the *Kunstschau*, Vienna, 1908.
(From *Deutsche Kunst und
Dekoration*, October 1908,
p. 37).**

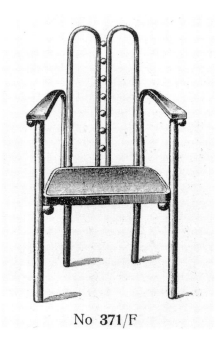

No 371/F

Figure 54B
Chair, Model No. 371/F. Sales catalogue of Jacob & Josef Kohn, Vienna, ca. 1906.

rangement of the back, designed for aesthetic impact and not for comfort, imbues this chair with a power that exceeds its diminutive size. In order to prevent the remarkably tight curvature of the paired crest rails from breaking, the diameter of the wooden rods was considerably reduced. The shaped saddle seat anticipates similar innovations developed by Charles and Ray Eames nearly forty years later in the complexly molded seats of their chairs (cat. nos. 117 and 118). However, the Eameses dispensed with seat rails and instead cantilevered the single sheets of plywood that form the seats over the legs.

55

Variation of the Cabaret Fledermaus chair

Bent solid beechwood, molded laminated wood, turned beechwood

28½ x 22¼ x 18⅛ in.
72.5 x 56.5 x 46 cm

Designed ca. 1907 by Josef Hoffmann (born Pirnitz, Moravia, 1870, died Vienna 1956)
Manufactured after 1907 by Jacob & Josef Kohn, Vienna
Alexander von Vegesack, Düsseldorf, Courtesy Galerie Wolfgang Richter, Munich

DESPITE limited floor space, Josef Hoffmann created an interior of great decorative ingenuity with his design for the Cabaret Fledermaus (Sekler, pp. 318–19). In his highly original scheme of decoration in the Cabaret's bar, Hoffmann played off brilliantly colored walls of decorative tiles against a boldly patterned black-and-white floor and a white ceiling and walls that had been stuccoed above the picture rail (figure 3–6). There must have been no hesitation by Hoffmann in his selection of furnishings, which had to be small, lightweight, durable, and schematically consistent with the decor. Bent-wood chairs had long been accepted as vital components of public spaces, and were easily adapted to the progressive aesthetic that defined the appearance of the Secessionist Fledermaus Cabaret.

The chair Hoffmann designed for the Cabaret (figure 55A) appears to be the only bent-wood furniture used there. Recent

55

traditions group this design with a tub chair and a settee variation that have inherited the appellation "Fledermaus" (Munich 1981a, p. 56), when in fact they were merely retailed as a suite in sales catalogues of the period (figure 55B). The Fledermaus tables were square in shape, serving as an appropriate foil for the curvature of the chair's arms, seat, and sled runners, which appear to end abruptly at the apron of the table. The chairs conformed to the dominant black-and-white color scheme: black-painted chairs were accented with white balls, and white-painted chairs had black ones. These spherical elements, an integral part of the geometric form language of the Secessionists,

serve a functional purpose as well. Formerly, conventional ring stretchers or L-shaped metal brackets had been used to provide additional bracing for the frames of bent-wood chairs. Here these turned balls, which became a leitmotif of Secessionist bent-wood furnishings, are screwed into the legs and seat rails for structural support.

The Cabaret Fledermaus chair is one of the few designs that can be documented to Josef Hoffmann. Soon after the Cabaret opened, the prominent critic Ludwig Hevesi praised the "new shape" of these chairs as "genuine Hoffmann" (Hevesi 1909, p. 243). When similar chairs were used by Hoffmann in the small country house

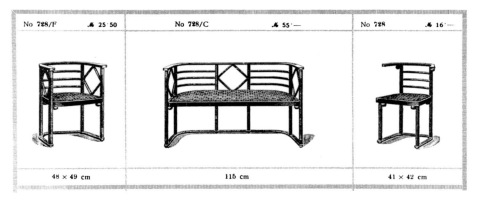

shown in the 1908 *Kunstschau*, critic Joseph Lux found much to admire in the furnishings of the model home manufactured by Jacob & Josef Kohn from "new ideas" by Josef Hoffmann (Lux 1909, p. 52).

This particular chair is not one of the original models from the Cabaret, but a slightly different version; like other models displaying variations in their seats and backs, it appeared in later Kohn catalogues. In this case, the pressed pattern on the laminated wood of the seat was not used on the original Cabaret Fledermaus model. One of the more popular bent wood designs of the era, the Fledermaus model became a generic type produced by numerous European manufacturers.

*Figure 55*B
Armchair, settee, and side chair, Suite No. 728. Sales catalogue of Jacob & Josef Kohn, Vienna, 1916.

56

Sitzmachine, Model No. 670
Laminated wood, bent solid beechwood, turned wood, metal
22⅛ x 26¼ x 44 in.
56 x 66 x 112 cm

Designed ca. 1908 by Josef Hoffmann (born Pirnitz, Moravia 1870, died Vienna 1956)
Manufactured after 1908 by Jacob & Josef Kohn, Vienna
Collection Mr. and Mrs. Al Luckett, Jr., Boulder, Colorado

ALTHOUGH chairs with adjustable backs were made as early as the second half of the seventeenth century (Thornton and Tomlin, p. 150), this type of chair was thrust into the vanguard of progressive thought during the second half of the nineteenth

*Figure 55*A
Josef Hoffmann. Café chair, Jacob & Josef Kohn Model No. 728, Theater of Cabaret Fledermaus, Vienna, 1907. (From *Deutsche Kunst und Dekoration*, December 1908, p. 158).

Figure 56A
Josef Hoffmann. Hall of small country house, Jacob & Josef Kohn display at the *Kunstschau*, Vienna, 1908. (From *Moderne Bauformen*, 1908, p. 370).

century when its operative design was adapted and retailed by the firm of William Morris in England. In fact, the chair came to be known as the morris chair after this foremost polemicist of the English Arts and Crafts movement. The Thonet company produced numerous variations on this adjustable form after 1880 (cat. no. 33). By the turn of the century, Vienna's progressive design community was still heavily under the influence of the British reformers, and not surprisingly, Josef Hoffmann applied bent-wood furniture construction to the morris chair.

Hoffmann brilliantly transformed what had become a generic seating form into one of the most memorable objects of Secessionist Vienna by using bent wood to express his geometric form language. He underscored the essential elements of the chair—a series of joined rectilinear planes—by enclosing bent-wood frames within bent-wood frames. Only with the segmental sweep of the back legs, which

indicated the arc attained by the adjustable back, did Hoffmann dramatically exploit the curvilinear potential of this material. Finally, the balanced interplay between the curvilinear and rectilinear was resolved in the chair's details: the square and rectilinear perforations in the sides and back of the chair were offset by solid structural spheres at the front of the chair and functional domes on the back legs.

Published for the first time in 1908 (figure 56A), the chair was carried in the sales catalogues of Jacob & Josef Kohn until at least 1916 as model No. 670.

57

Settee, Model No. 728/C

Bent solid beechwood, laminated wood, turned beechwood

28⅞ x 46¼ x 20½ in.
73.5 x 117 x 52 cm

Design of ca. 1908 attributed to Josef Hoffmann (born Pirnitz, Moravia, 1870, died Vienna 1956)

Manufactured after 1908 by Jacob & Josef Kohn, Vienna

58

Armchair, Model No. 728/3F

Bent solid beechwood, molded laminated wood, turned beechwood

30⅜ x 22 x 19¼ in.
77 x 56 x 49 cm

Design of ca. 1908 attributed to Josef Hoffmann (born Pirnitz, Moravia, 1870, died Vienna 1956)

Manufactured after 1908 by Jacob & Josef Kohn, Vienna

Alexander von Vegesack, Düsseldorf, Courtesy Galerie Wolfgang Richter, Munich

ALTHOUGH often referred to as the Fledermaus armchair and settee, neither was ever used in the famous Viennese cabaret (figures 3–6 and 55A). Rather, they were marketed by Kohn in conjunction with the famous Fledermaus chair (cat. no. 55), which was sold from the firm's regular stock. Numerous variations of the ensemble were offered by Kohn, with most modifications available in the decorative bent-wood elements used in the sides and backs of the pieces (figure 57A). The shaped crest rail of the armchair indicates that this piece was part of yet another variation of the 728/F line of side chair, armchair, and

57

58

Figure 57A

Armchair, settee, and side chair, Suite No. 728a. Sales catalogue of Jacob & Josef Kohn, Vienna, 1916.

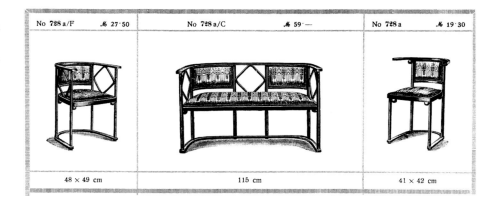

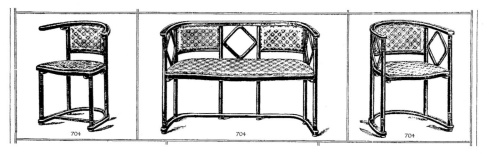

Figure 57B

Side chair, settee, and armchair, Suite No. 704. Sales catalogue of M. Carton Meubles, Ath, Belgium, ca. 1910–14.

settee retailed by Kohn (Dry 1980, p. 38). In addition, numerous other manufacturers of bent-wood furniture produced their own versions of these popular models (figure 57B).

The relationship established in these catalogues between the Fledermaus chair and the settee and armchair strengthens the supposition that Hoffmann was the chair's designer. Although there is no substantial evidence to support this position, similar armchairs and settees with backs articulated by turned vertical rods appeared in Hoffmann's small country house shown at the 1908 *Kunstschau* (figure 59A), where they were credited to this Viennese architect.

59

Table

Laminated wood, turned beechwood, bent solid beechwood, metal
28¼ x 25 x 25 in.
71.5 x 63.5 x 63.5 cm

Designed ca. 1908 by Josef Hoffmann (born Pirnitz, Moravia, 1870, died Vienna 1956)
Manufactured after 1908 by Jacob & Josef Kohn, Vienna

Alexander von Vegesack, Düsseldorf, Courtesy Galerie Wolfgang Richter, Munich

THE Apollonian imagery that captured the attention of many progressive European architects and designers in the early years of the twentieth century culminated in the triumph of stripped classicism before World War I. The Viennese—and Josef Hoffmann in particular—were especially attracted to this reductivist means of expression, which was based on the application of only the essential elements of classical form. Hoffmann's design for the Austrian Pavilion at the 1914 Deutsche Werkbund exhibition in Cologne was the summation of this movement, whose pre-eminent position in the design world would not survive the war.

This table represents one of the purest examples of distilled classicism in furniture design. The components of a column —base, shaft, and capital—have been translated into the table's design. The turned uprights supporting the tabletop complete this image with their reference to classical fluting. The metal that sheathes the base of the table serves the same purpose as ormolu does in traditional furniture designs —providing protection for one of the most vulnerable portions of the table.

At the 1908 *Kunstschau* in Vienna, Josef Hoffmann presented a full-scale model of a small country house, which contained his Secessionist designs for a total modernist environment. The furnishings of this temporary pavilion, including numerous bent wood designs executed by Jacob & Josef Kohn, were credited to Hoffmann in contemporary reviews (for example, Lux 1909, p. 52). Included among this furniture was an identical model of the table shown here, painted white and installed in the drawing room of the house (figure 59A) along with variations of the Hoffmann's Cabaret Fledermaus chair (see cat. no. 55).

The skirt of the table is constructed from a single piece of bent wood, secured into its circular configuration by a diagonally lapped scarf joint.

Figure 59A
Josef Hoffmann. Drawing room of small country house, Jacob & Josef Kohn display at the *Kunstschau*, Vienna, 1908. (From *Moderne Bauformen*, 1908, p. 374).

59

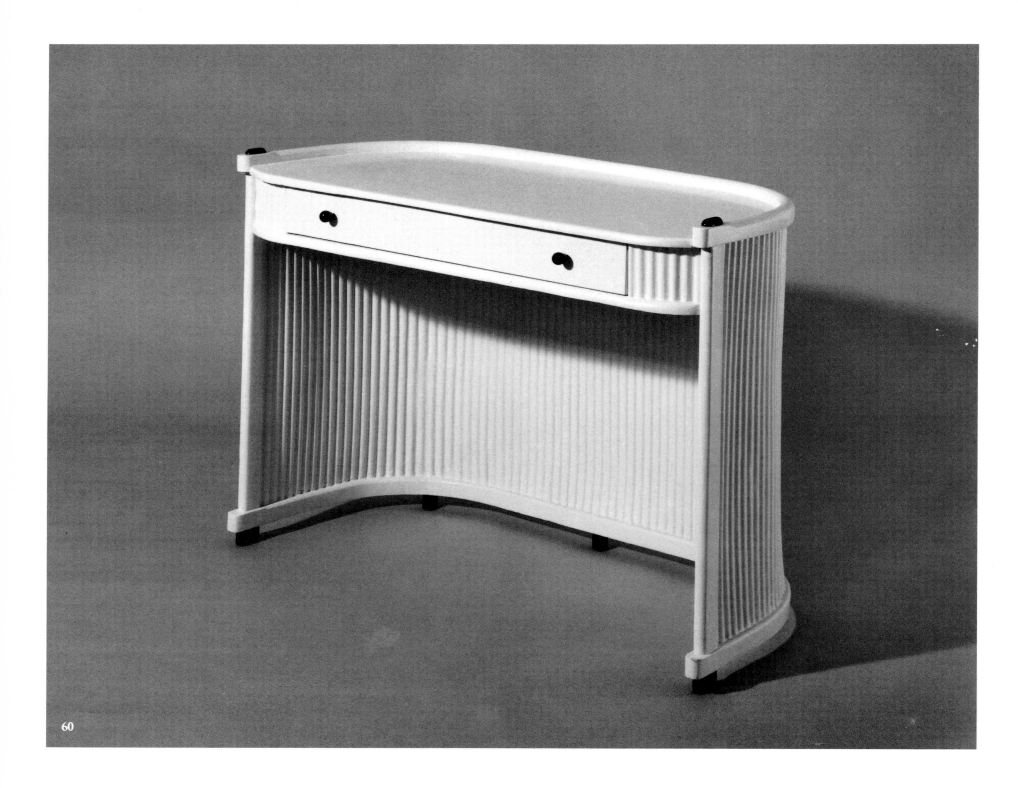

60

60

Dressing table

*Corrugated cardboard, bent solid wood,
laminated wood, solid wood (repainted)*

30⅜ x 42½ x 19¾ in.
77 x 108 x 50.5 cm

*Designed 1908 by Hans Günther Reinstein
(1880–?)*

*Manufactured after 1908 by Vereinigte
Möbelfabriken Germania, Bad Lauterberg,
Germany; or after 1911 by Press-Stoff-
Möbel-Gesellschaft, Vienna*

*Alexander von Vegesack, Düsseldorf, Courtesy
Galerie Wolfgang Richter, Munich*

I N the decade after the turn of the century,
the progressive architects reacted to the
stylistic mannerisms of Jugendstil design
and the uninspired plurality of historicist
eclecticism by pursuing the *Gesamtkunstwerk* (total work of art) based on classical
motifs. This search for unity is exemplified
stylistically and functionally by this small
vanity table, part of a larger line of furnishings designed by Hans Günther Reinstein.
Aesthetically, all the pieces in the line
(figure 60A) responded to the least common denominator of stripped classicism.
The outer shell of the vanity is made from
a thick cardboard, which was corrugated
for added strength. The fluted form attained through the corrugation coincided
with Reinstein's selection of the column
as the source of inspiration. Functionally,
the furniture achieved unity through Reinstein's application of the concept of *typen-

möbel (standardized furniture), whereby
different types of furniture could be constructed from interchangeable parts. The
cross-referencing of elements can be seen
in the outer shell of the vanity, which is
virtually identical to the outer case of
Reinstein's settee (cat. no. 61). The idea of
interchangeable parts had been employed

most brilliantly in the nineteenth-century
designs for bent-wood chairs; in the early
twentieth century, the practice was followed in the production of case furniture
by such noted German architects as Bruno
Paul and Richard Riemerschmid.

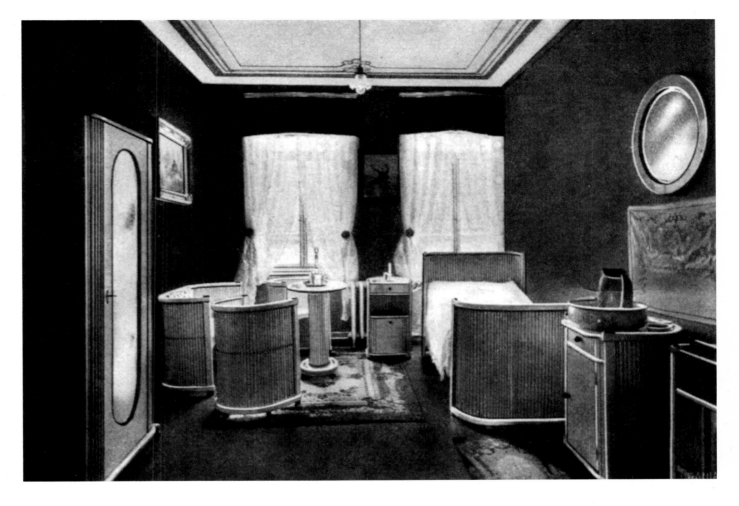

Figure 60A
**Hans Günther Reinstein. Fur-
nishings, ca. 1909. Manufactured
by Vereinigte Möbelfabriken
Germania, Bad Lauterberg, Germany. Bedroom, Kurhaus, Bad
Lauterberg, Germany.**

61

Settee

Corrugated cardboard, laminated wood, bent solid wood (repainted)

30 x 41½ x 18¾ in.
76 x 105.5 x 47.5 cm

Designed 1908 by Hans Günther Reinstein (1880–?)

Manufactured after 1908 by Vereinigte Möbelfabriken Germania, Bad Lauterberg, Germany; or after 1911 by Press-Stoff-Möbel-Gesellschaft, Vienna

62

Tub chair

Corrugated cardboard, laminated wood, bent solid wood, solid wood (repainted)

30 x 20⅜ x 18⅝ in.
76 x 52 x 47.5 cm

Designed 1908 by Hans Günther Reinstein (1880–?)

Manufactured after 1908 by Vereinigte Möbelfabriken Germania, Bad Lauterberg; or after 1911 by Press-Stoff-Möbel-Gesellschaft, Vienna

63

Table

Corrugated cardboard, laminated wood, bent solid wood (repainted)

29⅝ x 29½ x 19⅜ in.
75.5 x 75 x 49 cm

Designed 1908 by Hans Günther Reinstein (1880–?)

Manufactured after 1908 by Vereinigte Möbelfabriken Germania, Bad Lauterberg, Germany; or after 1911 by Press-Stoff-Möbel-Gesellschaft, Vienna

Alexander von Vegesack, Düsseldorf, Courtesy Galerie Wolfgang Richter, Munich

THIS set (figure 61A), often attributed to the Viennese architect Robert Oerley (see Müller, pp. 142–46), was actually designed by the German architect Hans Günther Reinstein, who developed a process whereby corrugated cardboard, made from waste products, could be molded under extreme pressure and used as the shell of

61

62

63

Figure 62A
Hans Günther Reinstein. Armchairs and table. Manufactured by Press-Stoff-Möbel Gesellschaft, Vienna. Garden Hall designed by Robert Oerley, *Wiener Fruhjahrsausstellung,* **Vienna, 1912.**

different types of furniture. Paper products had been used in furniture-making since the second quarter of the nineteenth century, when inexpensive mass-produced pressed ornament and papier-mâché furniture (usually constructed on a wooden core) were introduced. However, the intrinsic strength of Reinstein's shaped paper shell set it far above its nineteenth-century predecessors. Reinstein received patents for his process in Germany in 1908 and in Austria in 1910, and a factory in each country produced his designs. Neither factory appears to have labeled its furniture.

The form of the furnishings in this group is derived from popular bent-wood furnishings sold by most major bent-wood furniture manufacturers before World War I (figures 57A and 57B). However, Reinstein's selection of a powerful Neoclassical motif, the reeded column, for the outer surface of his furnishings places them in the vanguard of design at that time. As a student of the architect Peter Behrens after the turn of the century, Reinstein would have been deeply influenced by Behrens's own evolving classicism, which attained a mature expression in the decade before World War I. However, the use of stripped classicism by other contemporary European architects, such as Auguste (Gustav) Perret and Josef Hoffmann, was widespread at that time and continued until World War II.

64

Sitzmachine, Model No. 503
Bent solid beechwood, laminated wood, solid wood, cane
28¾ x 26⅜ x 37½ in.
73 x 67 x 95.5 cm

Designer unknown, ca. 1910
Manufactured after 1910 by D. G. Fischel Söhne, Vienna
Barry Friedman Ltd., New York

THE firm of D. G. Fischel Söhne, a large manufacturer headquartered in Vienna from 1878 onward, aggressively sought to service pan-European markets more economically by securing its own factories in Niemes, Bohemia, Weissenburg (Wissembourg) in Alsace, and Valisoara, Romania. Like so many other bent wood manufacturers at the turn of the century, Fischel produced a body of designs that vacillated

between individual creativity and outright replication of competitor's designs. In an effort to capture a large portion of the commercial market, even such industry giants as Jacob & Josef Kohn and Gebrüder Thonet often duplicated designs not protected by strict patent laws.

This Fischel design was borrowed from Kohn's No. 669 *Sitzmachine* (Dry 1980, p. 68) and its model No. 670 by Josef Hoffmann (cat. no. 56). In so borrowing, Fischel's designer inadvertently paid homage to one of the icons of the Arts and Crafts movement, the morris chair, and the strong aesthetic lead supplied by the Viennese Secessionists. Subtle variations between the Fischel design and the Kohn examples indicate that the Fischel designer was perhaps trying to accommodate the manufacturing process and improve upon Hoffmann's original design.

Each side element of the earlier Kohn chairs is constructed from a single piece of shaped wood, bent into the desired closed configuration. It was considerably more difficult to produce this than the side elements of the Fischel chair, which were each made from one piece of bent wood bound by one straight section of wood. In addition, the designer of the Fischel chair

extended the arms of the chair in a balanced arrangement with the extended feet of the sled runners, a device not found in the Kohn examples. This insistence on equalizing all parts of the chair is revealed by the manner in which a non-functional rod at the base mirrors the essential rod that supports the back.

In the contrast of color found in the unrestored wood and its planar simplicity, this chair is a remarkable symbol of the broad dissemination of progressive Viennese design principles at the eve of World War I. The model's number, 503, appears in a 1914 Fischel catalogue (Šimoniková, p. 248).

65

Armchair
Bent solid beechwood, laminated wood, solid wood
60 x 26⅜ x 30½ in.
152.5 x 67 x 77.5 cm

Designer unknown, ca. 1910
Manufacturer unknown, after 1910
Alexander von Vegesack, Düsseldorf, Courtesy Galerie Wolfgang Richter, Munich

THIS armchair was found in a psychiatric hospital outside Vienna. The only published designs that the chair resembles are the upholstered No. 666 chair manufactured by Jacob & Josef Kohn (Dry 1980, p. 68) and the fauteuil No. 6541 that first appeared in the Thonet 1907 catalogue. Despite the absence of this particular design from the catalogues of the period, it is unlikely that this was a special commission designed for the hospital, given the array of seating designs already available in the standard lines offered by the major bent wood manufacturing firms of the period.

64

65

Rather, this design is probably the product of one of the smaller firms, whose catalogues from the period have so far eluded scholars.

The design is a distinguished one, despite its anonymity. The rectangular depressions in the arms may have been designed to hold either trays or restraints for patients. The extensive use of plywood, braced for heavy use through the means of a medial brace bisecting the back of the chair, would have permitted easy cleaning, something not possible with upholstery.

66

Child's rocker

Bent solid beechwood, solid beechwood, cane (later)

29½ x 15¼ x 31⅜ in.
75 x 38.5 x 79.5 cm

Designer unknown, ca. 1914

Manufactured after 1914, possibly by Società Anonima "Antonio Volpe," Udine, Italy

Barry Harwood Galleries, New York

THE coordination of function and aesthetics with materials and manufacturing methodology is revealed in this small rocker. The stiles, diagonal stretchers, side rails, arms, front legs, sled runners, and back legs appears to have been executed from a single piece of bent wood in a frugal manner that does not preclude such decorative touches as the balanced, sinuous lines. This masterful handling of bent wood bridges the gap between rocker designs of the nineteenth and twentieth centuries.

The earliest bent-wood rocking chairs,

66

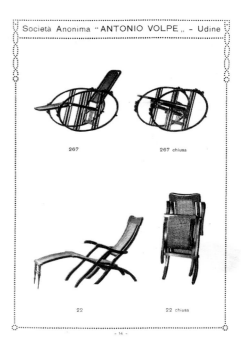

which appeared in the mid-nineteenth century, provided opportunities for the designer to test the limits of his material's pliability and its decorative possibilities (cat. no. 29). The wood was often contorted into extravagant shapes that threatened to overwhelm the rocking form with ornamental but rarely functional scrollwork (figure 66A). By the 1880s, these florid designs were augmented by a group of fixed and rocking chaises whose frames appeared to be constructed from a single piece of wood (cat. no. 33). The dramatic revision of taste in Vienna effected by the Secessionists at the turn of the century furthered this move toward simplification in the appearance of bent-wood furnishings. This small rocker is one product of this avant-garde mentality, which carried with it the premium of geometric simplification. The final stage of this development was the transformation of the side elements of these rocking chairs into closed forms, as evidenced by the design retailed in 1922 by the Italian firm Società Anonima "Antonio Volpe" (figure 66B).

Figure 66A
Rocking chair, Model No. 10.
Jacob & Josef Kohn advertise-
ment in *Cabinet Maker and Art*
Furnisher, **June 1, 1883.**

Figure 66B
Rocking chaise, Model No. 267.
Sales catalogue of Società
Anonima "Antonio Volpe,"
Udine, Italy, 1922.

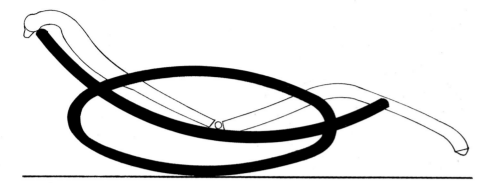

The concept of a closed form was most
likely devised just before World War I and
appeared in Jacob & Josef Kohn's 1916
catalogue in the form of a single, somewhat
ungainly design, the No. 827 rocking chair
(Dry 1980, p. 67). The Volpe chair has
generally been accepted as a design by
Josef Hoffmann manufactured by Kohn
(see Ostergard, no. 29; Gebhard, p. 20),
but these attributions have been negated
by this recent discovery (see the essay in
this volume by Graham Dry). The Volpe

chair was the conclusion of this simplification of form in bent wood. With its side
elements made from single rods of solid
wood bent into elliptical shapes and secured with a lapped scarf joint, this "egg"
chair projected an aesthetic appeal for the
1920s, not Secessionist Vienna. About 1930
Thonet offered model No. B306-0 (figure
66C), a variation of the Le Corbusier-
Jeanneret-Perriand chaise (cat. no. 76) with
an elliptical side frame that enabled the
chair to rock.

The red stain of this child's rocker is
original.

67

Club chair, Model No. B3

*Bent nickeled tubular steel, nickeled tubular
steel, fabric*

29¼ x 30⅝ x 26¾ in.
74.5 x 77.5 x 68 cm

*Designed 1925 by Marcel Breuer (born
Pécs, Hungary, 1902, died New York 1981)*

*Manufactured after ca. 1928 by Gebrüder
Thonet, Frankenberg, Germany*

*Collection Mr. and Mrs. Al Luckett, Jr.,
Boulder, Colorado*

67

AESTHETICALLY, model No. B3, Breuer's first revolutionary essay in tubular steel, was a direct outgrowth of earlier designs he had made of joined sections of cut wood in the cabinetry shops of the Bauhaus in Weimar. In those chairs, whose planar qualities were emphasized by sticklike frames and tightly bound canvas seats and backs, Breuer paid homage to the work of Gerrit Rietveld, the Dutch architect and furniture designer who was a member of the revolutionary group De Stijl. Immediately after World War I, De Stijl had a brief but powerful effect on the Bauhaus, primarily through Theo van Doesburg, who taught at the school in an unofficial capacity from 1922 to 1923.

A young student at that time, Breuer was deeply affected by the movement's advocacy of the principles of abstraction. He drew on these in 1925 when he began work on the chair that became model No. B3 and that would be named "Wassily" nearly thirty years later for the painter Wassily Kandinsky, who had taught at the Bauhaus and praised the chair generously. Impressed by the form, materials, and resiliency of a new bicycle, Breuer reputedly translated those qualities into a chair, pro-ducing a model whose aesthetic and technical components irrevocably transformed the language of chair design.

Breuer constructed the early prototypes of the chair with the assistance of a plumber, the only professional equipped to handle the joining of metal tubing (Wilk 1981, p. 37). A probable prototype is in the collection of the Bauhaus in Dessau, East Germany (figure 67A). The tubes of pipe steel in that example were welded rather than joined with nuts and bolts, making it constructionally the most complicated version of the chair known to exist and certainly not suited to mass production. Later production models exhibit variations in the arrangement of the elements of the frame (figure 67B)—evidence of Breuer's search for the most successful fusion of aesthetics and structural strength and ease of fabrication. The resiliency of steel tubing, when allied with leather and fabric, dispensed with traditional upholstery without sacrificing comfort.

In addition to the canvas and leather that were offered as upholstery material, *Eisengarn* (iron cloth) was also available in a variety of colors. This hard, durable fabric, which was relatively impervious to rot, made it possible for the chair to be used out-of-doors. Early production models were executed in nickeled steel, which was less expensive and less durable than the chrome-plated tubes of steel offered in later catalogues.

Figure 67A

Marcel Breuer. Club chair ("Wassily"), prototype, 1925. Bent nickeled tubular steel, nickeled tubular steel, *Eisengarn*. Wissenschaftlich-kulturelles Zentrum, Bauhaus, Dessau, East Germany.

Figure 67B

Marcel Breuer. Club chair ("Wassily"), Thonet Model No. B3, 1928–29. Bent tubular steel, tubular steel, *Eisengarn*. Collection Mr. and Mrs. Al Luckett, Jr., Boulder, Colorado.

68

Nesting tables, Model No. B9

Bent nickeled tubular steel, laminated wood
A. 19⅞ x 20 x 15¼ in.
50.5 x 51 x 38.5 cm
B. 17¾ x 18 x 15¼ in.
45 x 45.5 x 38.5 cm

Designed ca. 1925–26 by Marcel Breuer (born Pécs, Hungary, 1902, died New York 1981)
Manufactured after ca. 1927, probably by Gebrüder Thonet, Frankenberg, Germany
Stedelijk Museum, Amsterdam

Tʜɪs design, Breuer's favorite, was originally planned as a stool and later was modified into a group of graduated tables (Wilk 1981, p. 43). Reduced to a minimum number of elements, the stool was constructed from a single board of laminated wood and two pieces of steel tubing bent and joined into a single piece. The use of a continuous frame introduced sled runners into Breuer's growing repertoire of forms,

which align this design with later chairs in which he employed this feature. Although not a new concept, these floor runners came to be regarded as a leitmotif of the new designs executed in tubular steel. With them, the chairs acquired a degree of mobility impossible to achieve with the traditional arrangement of four individual legs. It was hoped that many households, particularly those with limited means, would find this feature attractive, for it permitted a chair or stool to be moved around at will to serve a variety of needs. The stool was in fact used in many of Breuer's early interiors, including the canteen of the new Bauhaus building in Dessau (figure 68A) which had been designed by Walter Gropius.

Figure 68A
Marcel Breuer. Stools, 1925–26, in Bauhaus canteen, Dessau.

68

This design may have added historical significance: Breuer claimed (Wilk 1980b, pp. 70–73) that by turning the stool on its side, he devised the concept of the cantilever independently of Mart Stam, the Dutch architect who has been accorded this honor by most historians. The tensile strength of tubular steel is considerably greater than that of solid wood and permitted this revolutionary cantilever, which was unattainable in bent solid wood.

69

Side chair, Model No. B5

Bent chromed tubular steel (replated), fabric (later)

33¾ x 17¾ x 21½ in.
85.5 x 45 x 54.5 cm

Designed ca. 1926–27 by Marcel Breuer (born Pécs, Hungary, 1902, died New York 1981)
Manufactured ca. 1929–31 by Gebrüder Thonet, Frankenberg, Germany
The Brooklyn Museum, New York (Gift of Mr. and Mrs. Alexis Zalstem-Zalessky)

THE B5 side chair, one of Breuer's earliest designs employing tubular steel, is also one of his most overlooked designs. It has been overshadowed by its predecessor, the Wassily chair infused with De Stijl precepts (cat. no. 67), which became the first successfully produced tubular steel chair. In addition, the revolutionary engineering principles of Breuer's later cantilevered chairs have also contributed to the languishing of this side chair's reputation.

In spite of the conventional design, Breuer avoided banality by extending the continuous line of the front legs, side rails, and

Figure 69A
Marcel Breuer. Dining room, Piscator Apartment, Berlin, 1927.

sled runners around the stiles and rear legs in a taut composition. This particular treatment of the seat anticipates his later cantilevered designs, for were the seat of the B5 not secured to the stiles with bolts, it would have been Breuer's first use of the cantilever principle. However, he incorporated the B5's cubic arrangement of mass in his more radical cantilever designs (cat. no. 72), which were introduced in late 1927 or early 1928 (Wilk 1981, p. 72).

This understated essay in tubular steel was perhaps more acceptable to those timid in their pursuit of modernity. On the basis of its conventional four-legged stance, the B5 retained traditional elements and was subdued in its propagation of the new aesthetic. Breuer himself chose the B5 for many of his public and private interiors (figure 69A) dating from the late 1920s.

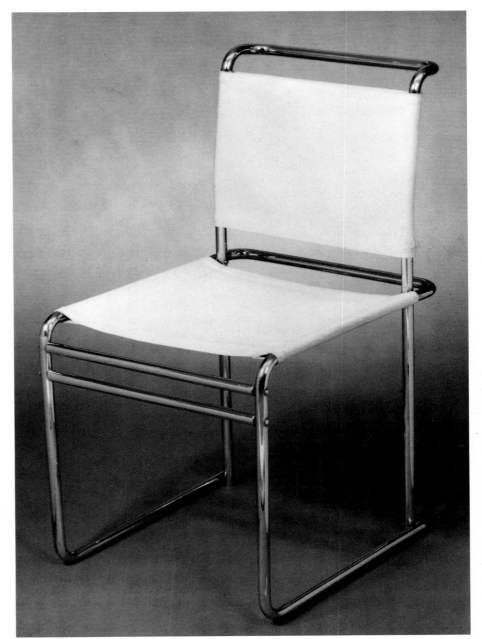

69

70

Side chair, Model No. MR10

Bent nickeled tubular steel, cane, bent solid steel, wood

31 x 19 x 27½ in.
78.5 x 48 x 70 cm

Designed 1927 by Ludwig Mies van der Rohe (born Aachen, Germany, 1886, died Chicago 1969)

Manufactured probably by Bamberg Metall-werkstätten, Berlin-Neukölln, 1931

Collection Mr. and Mrs. Al Luckett, Jr., Boulder, Colorado

THIS chair, one of the earliest of the revolutionary cantilevered designs, was first shown at the exhibition Die Wohnung (The Dwelling) at Weissenhofsiedlung, a massive exhibition of model, standardized public housing held in Stuttgart in 1927 (figure 70A). Sponsored by the Deutsche Werkbund under the artistic direction of its vice-president, Mies van der Rohe, the exhibition was a showcase for sixteen German and European progressive architects who presented their respective solutions to the international housing crisis. Included in the thirty-three structures erected on the exhibition grounds were meticulously detailed interiors that addressed the needs of a clientele with limited budgets.

This chair and its armchair variation (cat. no. 71) were the only cantilevered chairs shown at the exhibition other than two designed by Mart Stam, the originator of the concept. Stam's designs (figure 70B) lacked the aesthetic refinement of Mies van der Rohe's designs and reflected Stam's lack of confidence in the strength of the cantilever. Unlike Mies van der Rohe, Stam used rigid reinforced tubing, which had none of the resiliency of lightweight tubular steel. Furthermore, the lighter weight of Mies van der Rohe's chair made it easy to move in the minimal living areas intended for low-income people. The ease of mobility was enhanced by the addition of sled runners, which compensated for the elimination of the back legs and the subsequent loss of stability. Stability and visual unity were increased by a rear floor stretcher that imparted the impression of a chair constructed from a single, continuous piece of metal. The powerful arc of the

Figure 70A
Aerial view of Weissen-hofsiedlung, site of the Deutsche Werkbund exhibition *Die Wohnung,* **Stuttgart, 1927.**

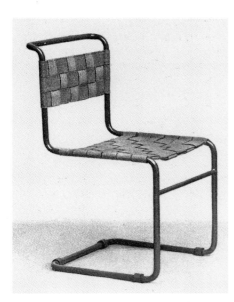

Figure 70B
Mart Stam. Side chair, 1926–27.

chair's legs differed from many later examples, which often proclaimed their minimal composition in a cubic arrangement of mass (cat. no. 72).

From the time of its introduction at *Die Wohnung* exhibition in 1927 until the middle of the 1930s, the MR10 side chair was manufactured by three firms. The Berliner Metallgewerbe Joseph Müller in Berlin produced the design from 1927 until 1930. In 1931, Bamberg Metallwerkstätten, another Berlin firm, manufactured this chair as well as an extensive line of Mies van der Rohe's furniture. In the following year, Thonet took over the production of several of Mies van der Rohe's designs, including the MR10, which was thereafter referred to as the MR533, and as MR533g when offered with woven cane. Metz & Co. of Holland also retailed this design in the 1930s, crediting it to Mies van der Rohe.

71

Armchair, Model No. MR20

Bent nickeled tubular steel, cane, bent solid steel, wood
31¾ x 22 x 33 in.
80.5 x 56 x 84 cm

Designed 1927 by Ludwig Mies van der Rohe (born Aachen, Germany, 1886, died Chicago 1969)
Manufactured probably by Bamberg Metallwerkstätten, Berlin-Neukölln, 1931
Collection Mr. and Mrs. Al Luckett, Jr., Boulder, Colorado

By the end of the 1920s Mies van der Rohe had reworked this design to produce lounge chairs and chaise longues. The tubular-steel frames of these chairs were available in a variety of decorative finishes: colored synthetic lacquer was an alternative to the nickel-plated coating. These finishes were less popular than the more durable and expensive chrome-

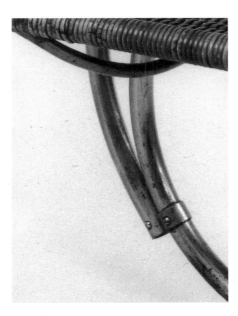

Figure 71A
Cuff joint at intersection of arm and leg.

71

plating that was also available. Additional options included leather and caned seats and backs of *Eisengarn* (iron cloth) in a variety of colors.

Rather than taper the ends of the arms into the front legs in a subtle conclusion, or splice them into the legs, thereby weakening the construction, Mies van der Rohe proclaimed in this chair the independence of these two elements with a bold cuff joint (figure 71A) that binds them together in a clearly utilitarian manner. Any attempt to resolve this junction with a more subtly integrated solution would have diminished the seemingly effortless quality of this design.

Figure 71B
Ludwig Mies van der Rohe. Interior, Mies van der Rohe House, Deutsche Werkbund exhibition *Die Wohnung* at Weissenhofsiedlung, Stuttgart, 1927. (From Gräff, *Innenräume*, fig. 107).

First shown in the apartment block designed by Mies van der Rohe for the 1927 exhibition *Die Wohnung* (The Dwelling) at the Weissenhofsiedlung in Stuttgart (figure 71B), the armchair, with its bold frame and simple upholstery, reiterated the lucid austerity of the building's interiors. Unlike many furnishings by other architects and designers shown at the three-month exhibition of low-income public housing, this design and its side chair variation achieved a highly successful rate of production during the succeeding decade as well as a lasting critical appeal.

Although considered by many to be the most graceful of all cantilevered chairs, the MR20 could be awkward in use, for the robust protrusion of the arms made it impossible to place the chair close to a dining table, desk, or other piece of furniture.

72

Side chair, Model No. B32

Bent chromed tubular steel, bent solid beechwood, cane

32 x 18¼ x 22½ in.
81.5 x 46.5 x 57 cm

Designed 1928 by Marcel Breuer (born Pécs, Hungary, 1902, died New York 1981)

Manufactured ca. 1931 by Gebrüder Thonet, Frankenberg, Germany

Barry Friedman Ltd., New York.

THE freestanding cantilevered chair is one of the most significant developments in twentieth-century design. Its radical elimination of the traditional four-legged form was a revolutionary step begun in 1925 with Marcel Breuer's tubular-steel club

72

chair, the B3 (cat. no. 67) later known as the Wassily chair. However, despite the superior body of designs Breuer produced in which he employed the cantilever principle, he was not the originator of the concept; this distinction belongs to the Dutch architect Mart Stam (Wilk 1981, p. 71). According to the German architect Heinz Rasch, at a 1926 planning meeting for the exhibition *Die Wohnung* (The Dwelling) to be held the next year at the Weissenhofsiedlung in Stuttgart, Stam showed Mies van der Rohe a drawing of his concept of a chair in which mass was firmly balanced on two legs. Breuer later claimed that he had devised his own cantilevered chair independently by simply turning one of his own B9 stools (figure 68A) on its side (Wilk 1981, pp. 70–78). It was after the appearance of the Stam and Mies van der Rohe cantilevered chairs at the exhibition that Breuer introduced his chair,

which came to be known after 1960 as the Cesca (the diminutive of Francesca, his daughter's name).

Although this was not Breuer's first essay in a cantilever form, it proved to be one of his most successful designs commercially. His debt to earlier bent-wood furnishings is evident in the seat and back constructed of bent wood and cane, which countered the clinical appearance of the chair's tubular-steel frame. This allegiance to the bent wood tradition is particularly evident in the seat. The side and rear seat rails are fabricated from a rod of solid wood bent into a C-shaped configuration and secured by a front rail made from a straight section of bent wood. This construction of the seat differs from that of models produced after World War II in which the seats have been made from four pieces of wood joined by mitered saw-tooth finger joints at the junctions of the four seat rails (figure 72A).

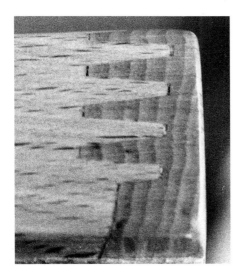

Figure 72A
Mitered sawtooth finger joint at intersection of front and side seat rail, detail of Marcel Breuer armchair variation of Thonet Model No. B32. Produced in Italy, manufacturer unknown, ca. 1983.

73

Armchair

Bent laminated wood, bent solid steel rod (painted), solid wood
36⅛ x 24¼ x 34 in.
92 x 61.5 x 86.5 cm

Designed after ca. 1927 by Gerrit Rietveld (born Utrecht 1888, died Utrecht 1965)
Possibly made ca. 1928 by G. van de Groenekan, Utrecht
Collection Mr. and Mrs. Al Luckett, Jr., Boulder, Colorado

BORN in Utrecht during a particularly stable period in Holland's history, Gerrit Rietveld was an early member of De Stijl, the revolutionary movement formed in Holland in 1917. Complete abstraction as defined by primary colors and a dominant use of horizontal and vertical lines constituted part of the founders' aesthetic philosophy. These principles materialized in an eloquent statement in Rietveld's Red/Blue chair of 1917–18. (figure 73A).

73

Figure 73A
Gerrit Rietveld. Armchair, 1917–18. Plywood and solid wood (painted). The Brooklyn Museum, New York.

Figure 73B
Alvar Aalto. Stacking side chair, 1930. Bent plywood and bent chrome-plated tubular steel. The Museum of Modern Art, New York (Lord & Taylor Fund).

In many respects, the small chair shown here is a direct descendant of the Red/Blue chair, fathered by infusions of contemporary European work in tubular steel. The intersecting planes of the seat and back, as well as the low cant, resemble the Red/Blue chair, but the fluid one-piece construction of the seat and back, as well as the closed form of the metal frame, look to the work of contemporary German designers and their quest for visually cohesive design. The use of metal—a material previously absent from the work of Rietveld, who was a cabinetmaker—further reflects the influence of progressive German designers of the period. Eschewing tubular steel, however, Rietveld selected a fine-gauge solid steel rod, a much less expensive material. The attenuated line defined by this rod contrasts dramatically with the generous sweep of the bent laminated wood. Such use of this material presaged Aalto's "hybrid" chair of 1930 (figure 5–49), which employed a continuous piece of bent plywood in a similar manner. As a founding member of the C.I.A.M. (Congrès Internationaux d'Architecture Moderne), Rietveld many have had some contact with Aalto when each attended the organiza-tion's conference in Frankfurt am Main in 1929.

In the bold use of standard-grade nuts and bolts to secure the wood to its metal frame, this chair differs from similar mod-els known to have been mass produced by Metz & Co., which display a much finer finish. This suggests that this chair may be a prototype in which the resolution of the overall design was more important than its final detailing.

74

Revolving chair (siège tournant), Model No. B302

Bent nickeled tubular steel, flat steel, solid steel, upholstery (altered)
29¾ x 23⅜ x 19½ in.
75.5 x 59.3 x 49.5 cm

Designed 1928 by Charlotte Perriand (born Paris 1903), possibly in collaboration with Le Corbusier (born La Chaux-de-Fonds, Switzerland, 1887, died Roquebrunne, France, 1965) and Pierre Jeanneret (born Geneva 1896, died Paris 1967)
Manufactured after 1929 by Gebrüder Thonet, Frankenberg, Germany
Collection Mr. and Mrs. Al Luckett, Jr., Boulder, Colorado

In 1925, Charlotte Perriand graduated from the Ecole de L'Union Centrale des Arts Décoratifs, a school for women in Paris (Stritzler, pp. 28–30). Within three years she emerged as a leading pro-gressive designer of international repute. Much of Perriand's exposure during this brief period came through two major trade fairs held annually in Paris—the Salon des Artistes Décorateurs and the Salon d'Automne—where leading architects, designers, artists, craftsmen, and manufacturers exhibited their work to the public.

At the 1926 Salon d'Automne, Perriand presented *Un Coin de salon* (Corner of a Salon), an intimate re-creation of an elitist, modernist interior constructed of luxuri-ous woods and textiles by means of tradi-tional joinery. The following year she displayed a private bar constructed in part from tubular and flat steel, which she entitled *Bar sur le toit* (Rooftop Bar). The selection of this "au courant" theme, alien

to mainstream contemporary Parisian taste, indicates her radical shift from traditional materials to those in keeping with the machine age. It was perhaps on the basis of this installation that Perriand gained the confidence of Le Corbusier, and she joined his atelier on the rue de Sèvres in October 1927.

In 1928, while working on the develop-ment of Le Corbusier's standardized plan, with which he proposed to transform the traditional arrangement of the interior, Perriand again exhibited on her own at the Salon des Artistes Décorateurs. In a dining room ensemble (figure 74A) she presented for the first time her revolving chair (*siège tournant*). Unlike the later installations that are credited jointly to Le Corbusier-Jeanneret-Perriand, this one was credited solely to Perriand, indicating that the de-sign of this chair was the work of Perriand alone.

Charlotte Perriand. Dining room, Salon des Artistes Décorateurs, Paris, 1928. (From Prou, *Interieurs au Salon des Artistes Decorateurs*, pl. 38).

Nonetheless, the revolving chair was a radical departure from Perriand's earlier designs and reveals her debt to Le Corbusier's respect for the virtues inherent in bent-wood furniture. The austere frame of the *siège tournant* bears a remarkable similarity to Thonet's model No. 9 armchair (cat. no. 42), particularly when this model was modified and placed upon a swivel base, an option available through Thonet since 1866 (Wilk 1980a, fig. 42, second row from bottom, third from left). Far from making an overwhelmingly radical statement, as her German contemporaries had done with their cantilevered chairs, Perriand reinterpreted the past and compensated for the coldness of steel with heavily padded elements.

This particular chair differs slightly from the earliest published examples of the *siège tournant* (figure 74A), for here the arms curve beneath the padded seat to join the chair rail rather than break sharply in a cut and welded joint. The leather upholstery and the seat cushion appear to be original; however, the arm roll of the back has been modified.

75

Armchair with tilting back (siège à dossier basculant), Model No. B301

Bent chromed tubular steel, chromed tubular steel, metal, fabric

25 x 23¼ x 24¾ in.
63.5 x 59 x 63 cm

Designed ca. 1929 by Le Corbusier (born La Chaux-de-Fonds, Switzerland, 1887, died Roquebrunne, France, 1965), Pierre Jeanneret (born Geneva 1896, died Paris 1967), and Charlotte Perriand (born Paris 1903)

Manufactured ca. 1929 by Gebrüder Thonet, Frankenberg, Germany

Collection Mr. and Mrs. Al Luckett, Jr., Boulder, Colorado

Unlike the Wassily chair (cat. no. 67), which attained its form in part through Breuer's exposure to the tenets of the progressive Dutch movement De Stijl, the *siège basculant* was inspired by a humble campaign chair retailed by Maples & Co. of London, an enormous interior-decorating enterprise with regional offices in Buenos Aires, Montevideo, and Paris. During the mid-1920s, Le Corbusier admired the firm's ahistoricist, well-constructed, and inexpensive furnishings, and he even included two specially made Maples club chairs in the living room of his standardized housing unit, in the Pavillon de L'Esprit Nouveau (figure 5–2) at the 1925 Exposition Internationale des Arts Décoratifs in Paris.

One design retailed through the firm's large catalogue, which catered to almost every taste, was a portable chair marketed as an "Indian" chair (figure 75A), apparently because it was used on traveling expeditions through India. It was this easily disassembled chair, with its canvas seat and a back that pivoted, that was transformed with new materials by Le Corbusier's atelier. Although not made to be dismantled, the *siège basculant*, along with its larger version, the *fauteuil basculant*, was an adaptation of a nineteenth-century prototype (Hanks, fig. 140, Electro No. 561 and No. 562) which was eminently suitable to the exigencies of modern life. Diminutive, durable, easy to clean, and light enough to be moved with ease, the *siège basculant* was one component of Le Corbusier's monumental plan for a global reformation of society that would emerge from a wholesale adoption of his own designs for reorganizing urban planning, architecture, and interior design.

Because of its large number of welded and finely finished joints (figure 75B), this chair cost considerably more to produce than many contemporary designs in tubular steel, such as Mies van der Rohe's MR10 (cat. no. 70), which was relatively inexpensive because of its simple design. As a result the *siège basculant* found limited commercial appeal and could be purchased only by the economically privileged.

Unlike the current examples of the *siège basculant* marketed by Atelier International, which have welded stretchers, this earlier example has stretchers joined to the legs with octagonal bolts.

Figure 75B
Butt joint at intersection of front stretcher and leg.

76

Chaise longue with continuous frame (chaise longue à reglage continue), Model No. B306

Bent chromed tubular steel, chromed tubular steel, sheet steel (painted), animal hide, reinforced rubber

33 x 21 x 61 in.
84 x 53.5 x 155 cm

Designed ca. 1929 by Le Corbusier (born La Chaux-de-Fonds, Switzerland, 1887, died Roquebrunne, France, 1965), Pierre Jeanneret (born Geneva 1896, died Paris 1967), and Charlotte Perriand (born Paris 1903)

Manufactured ca. 1929 by Gebrüder Thonet, Frankenberg, Germany

Collection Mr. and Mrs. Al Luckett, Jr., Boulder, Colorado

AN examination of the furnishings used by Le Corbusier in his 1925 Pavillon de L'Esprit Nouveau at the Paris Exposition Internationale des Arts Décoratifs reveals that his architectural language at the time was far in advance of his interior design program, for which he relied heavily on existent pieces. Along with Thonet's No. 9 armchair (cat. no. 42) and a pair of specially made upholstered chairs by Maples & Co. of London, he used custom-made cabinets that divided interior space while providing storage. Two years later, in the exhibition *Die Wohnung* (The Dwelling) at the Weissenhofsiedlung in Stuttgart, Le Corbusier and his partner, Pierre Jeanneret, employed many of the same furnishings as well as their own unremarkable design for two tubular-steel beds (figure 76A) that were fabricated by the L. & C. Arnold Company of Schorndorf, Germany.

76

Figure 76A
**Le Corbusier and Pierre Jean-
neret. Bedroom, Le Corbusier
and Pierre Jeanneret House,
Deutsche Werkbund exhibition
Die Wohnung at Weissen-
hofsiedlung, Stuttgart, 1927.
Beds manufactured by L. & C.
Arnold GmbH, Schorndorf,
Germany.**

By 1928 the first tubular steel designs for systematized furnishings—known as *équipment de l'habitation*—emerged from Le Corbusier's atelier. Intended for mass production, these designs required complicated constructional techniques, making them too costly for the popular market.

The chaise longue, a bold and carefully orchestrated arrangement of color, texture, materials, and form, is technically and visually the most complicated design in the series. The balanced interplay of geometric forms aligns with Le Corbusier's formulation of the doctrines of Purism, a theory of painting that asserted the importance of clarity and objectivity in composition. The seminal publication of the movement, *Après le cubisme*, published in 1918 and written

by Amédée Ozenfant and Le Corbusier, was a fervent call for a return to order after the breakdown of formal values initiated by the Cubism of Pablo Picasso and Georges Braque.

Le Corbusier's fascination with the iconography of the machine appears in this design in his use of movable elements: a concept not actively explored in the furniture designs of contemporary German designers. The airplane, the revered symbol of movement and speed during the 1920s, provided a substantial source of inspiration for the components of this design. The H-shaped stretcher system, elliptical in section, was reminiscent of the aerodynamically designed wing struts of a

Farman airplane (figure 76B), and on some production models the tubular-steel frames of these chaises were tightly bound with *Eisengarn* (iron cloth), another reference to the cloth-encased airplane fuselages of the immediate post–World War I era.

Perhaps more than any other design by Le Corbusier's atelier, the form of the chaise was determined by ergonomic considerations, predicated on supposed universal specifications. The neck-roll, secured with a strap, could be adjusted to fit an individual of any size, as could the angle of the chaise. The introduction of the ergonomic factor into furniture design was pioneered in Western European circles during World War I by the Danish designer Kaare Klint.

Unlike early-nineteenth-century chaises, which were completely immobile, or the later bent-wood rocking chaises (cat. no. 33), which moved when occupied, Le Corbusier's chaise longue merged elements of both types and could be easily set in a variety of positions without the need for usurping immediate space by its rocking motion. The earliest published example of the chaise (figure 76C) reveals that the design did not yet possess the continuous tubular-steel frame of the slightly later models produced by Thonet in the late 1920s and early 1930s. Instead, two substantial bars broke the fluid continuity of the frame at the head and foot of the reclining element. In the mid-1930s, Embru-Werke of Switzerland produced its own version of the chaise (figure 76D) under a licensing agreement with Le Corbusier. This model differs from its predecessors in that its H-shaped stretcher system was square-sectioned.

Figure 76B
Detail of wing struts, Farman airplane, ca. 1923. (From Le Corbusier, *Vers une architecture*, p. 99).

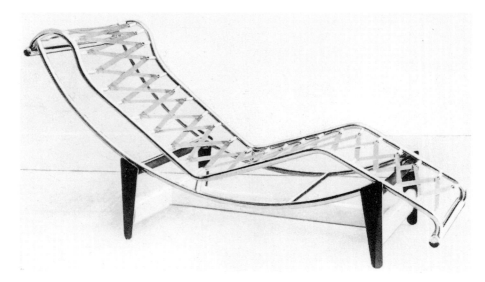

Figure 76C
Le Corbusier-Jeanneret-Perriand. Frame of chaise longue, prototype, 1928. (From *Le Corbusier et Pierre Jeanneret: Oeuvre complète de 1910–1929*, p. 157).

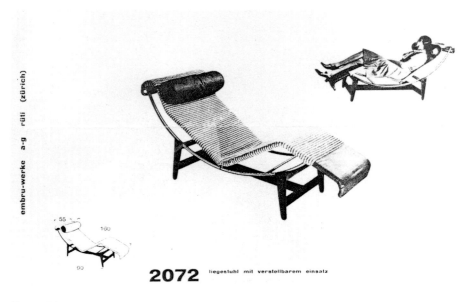

embru-werke a-g rüti (zürich)

2072 liegestuhl mit verstellbarem einsatz

Figure 76D
Le Corbusier-Jeanneret-Perriand. Chaise longue with adjustable section, Model No. 2072, manufactured by Embru-Werke AG, Rüti, Zurich.

77

Table, Model No. B19

Bent chromed tubular steel (replated), glass, rubber

26 x 40½ x 21 in.
66 x 103 x 21 cm

Designed 1928 by Marcel Breuer (born Pécs, Hungary, 1902, died New York 1981)
Manufactured after ca. 1928 by Gebrüder Thonet, Frankenberg, Germany
The Brooklyn Museum, New York (Gift of Mr. and Mrs. Alexis Zalstem-Zalessky)

THE socially conscious, progressive architect of the 1920s was preoccupied with the creation of enormous housing developments to cope with the shortage of dwellings that plagued nearly every major European urban center after World War I. In the designs for these projects, which were intended primarily for the financially disadvantaged, the architects pursued universal goals based upon common perceptions of the workers' needs, which included a radical restructuring of the interiors. It was intended that this metamorphosis of workers' dwellings would improve the inhabitants' mental as well as physical well-being. Furnishings that were aesthetically consistent with the new interiors, inexpensive to produce, durable, and hygienic became the rallying point of furniture design. Marcel Breuer, as one of the most versatile designers of furnishings for these new interiors, incorporated those qualities into his remarkable design of this table.

A variation of Breuer's earlier table (cat. no. 68), this table illustrates his pursuit of the structurally and visually cohesive frame in the seemingly continuous piece of bent tubular steel that forms the outer structure of the piece. This type of frame challenged the structure of a traditional table, in which the four legs are connected by four aprons that are secured to a tabletop. In his reworking of that formula, Breuer separated these elements and redistributed their stabilizing effect throughout the table: one pair of aprons remains in place at the top of the table, while the other pair is transformed into sled runners (along the floor), providing essential support there. The inner cavity of this outer frame is further stabilized by a bent tubular-steel frame whose rectilinear configuration is mirrored by a slab of glass.

From the repository of existing materials, Breuer extracted gummed rubber rings (a plumber's supply) to stabilize the sheet of glass without disfiguring the smooth material with metal bolts. Constructed almost exclusively from metal and glass, the table is a union of brilliant reflective and transparent surfaces, which produces a delicacy that cannot help but reduce the cluttered look of any interior in which it stands.

With the planar forms that confront one another at right angles, Breuer effectively reiterated here one of the aesthetic cornerstones of the Dutch De Stijl philosophy that he had acquired during his early years as a student at the Bauhaus.

77

78

Lounge chair, Model No. B35

*Bent chromed tubular steel, solid wood
(painted), fabric*

32⅞ x 22⅛ x 31½ in.
83 x 56 x 80 cm

*Designed 1928–29 by Marcel Breuer (born
Pécs, Hungary, 1902, died New York 1981)*
*Manufactured after ca. 1928 by Gebrüder
Thonet, Frankenberg, Germany*
Barry Friedman Ltd., New York

IN this consummate design, Breuer
achieved two of the major objectives of
avant-garde furniture design of the late
1920s. Firstly, the frame of this armchair
conveys the impression that it has been
essentially constructed from a single continuous piece of bent tubular steel—a
gesture toward economy of material and
means of production. Secondly, the revo-

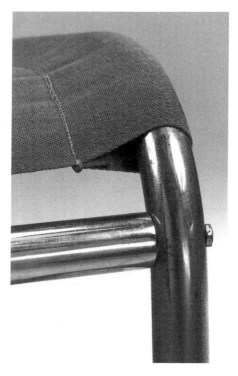

*Figure 78*A
Bolted butt joint.

lutionary principle of the cantilever is doubly realized here in the opposing directional dispositions of seat and arms, the dynamic placement of which has heightened the pliancy of this chair's frame.

Variations of this model are known to exist, with the most frequent alteration occurring in the type of stretcher used at the rear of the chair and its placement. The bold intersection of front stretcher and forelegs in the version shown here (figure 78A) indicates that this particular example may date from an early stage of production, prior to the introduction of refinements in the chair's details. In many other models, the ends of these stretchers taper subtly and partially lap the front legs in a smoothly finished joint, which, however, dilutes the impression of the constructional simplicity of the chair.

This design was used extensively in the Deutsche Werkbund installation at the 1930 Salon des Artistes Décorateurs in Paris, the first public display of German design in France since World War I. Breuer used several examples of the chair the following year in his Sportsman's House at the Berlin *Bau-Ausstellung* (Building Exhibition).

79

Armchair

Bent chromed tubular steel, flat steel, upholstery (later)
26 x 21¾ x 25½ in.
66 x 55 x 65 cm
Designed 1928 by René Herbst (born Paris 1891, died Paris 1983)
Made ca. 1928, possibly by Les Établissements Siegel et Stockman Réunis, Paris
Barry Friedman Ltd., New York

RENÉ Herbst was one of the leading members of the progressive Parisian design community during the two decades following World War I. He was responsible for the propagation of modernist ideals through publications and by means of installations shown at the annual design salons. With Raymond Templier, Jean Puiforcat, Le Corbusier, and Robert Mallet-Stevens, he was a co-founder of the U.A.M. (Union des Artistes Modernes), a highly visable design coalition formed in 1929.

Whether working for an elitist clientele who demanded modernist statements executed in luxurious materials by traditional means, or fabricating his more austere designs from tubular steel and synthetic materials, Herbst was a particularly adept designer. He began to incorporate metal elements in his furniture designs as early as 1925, but these furnishings were viewed by the conservative French press as aberrations, not as serious manifestations of a new direction to be pursued by French designers. By 1927, however, several contributions to the Salon d'Automne, such as Charlotte Perriand's *Bar sur le toit* (cat. no. 74) and Louis Sognot's installation (figure 89A), proved that increasing numbers of French designers were exploring the possibilities of using bent tubular steel for the production of furniture. In the following year, at the Salon des Artistes Décorateurs,

79

Figure 79A
René Herbst. Armchair, ca. 1928. Salon des Artistes Décorateurs, Paris, 1928. (From *Art et Décoration*, June 1928, p. 172).

Herbst exhibited this chair as part of his installation (figure 79A). By using four of these chairs, as well as numerous other furnishings executed in bent tubular steel with a nickel coating, Herbst indicated that his commitment to this particular material had broadened. His installation was adjacent to one by Charlotte Perriand, and by means of open doorways both displays appeared to be part of a homogeneous ensemble. Herbst translated the traditional four-legged format into a relatively untried material, whereas Perriand's chairs, although also reminiscent of an earlier form (cat. no. 42), were more startlingly modernist in their design and use of movable elements.

Herbst's chairs in this installation were fabricated in limited numbers and were executed in tubular steel that had been nickel-plated, a plating less durable than chrome, which had only recently become available. The elaborate components of this design required a considerable amount of handwork to attain the exquisite finish of the numerous joints, which placed this particular chair outside the realm of mass production.

80

Chair
Bent chromed tubular steel, chromed tubular steel, upholstery
28¼ x 20⅛ x 22⅛ in.
72 x 50.5 x 56 cm
Designed 1928 by Louis Sognot (born Paris 1892, died Paris 1970)
Made 1928 by unknown workshop, probably commissioned by the department store Au Printemps, Paris
Gallery Primavera, New York

Like many of the younger designers who emerged after World War I, Sognot was little hampered by a traditionalist approach to design and rapidly rose to maturity in the annual design salons held in Paris. Only four years after his first contribution to the Salon d'Automne in 1923, Sognot displayed his first grouping of furniture executed from tubular steel (see cat. no. 89). This model was first exhibited at the 1928 Salon d'Automne as part of an installation sponsored by Primavera, the art department of Au Printemps, a large Parisian department store (figure 80A), and in the following year at the Salon des Artistes Décorateurs as part of Primavera's modernist tearoom installation. The chair was undoubtedly fabricated by a metalworking shop commissioned by the store and was probably made in limited numbers.

The complicated and superbly finished joinery of the Sognot chairs reveals that this piece was custom-made. The mitered angles where the front and rear legs meet the floor stretcher indicate that these elements were cut, welded, and then polished, a laborious process requiring dexterous handwork.

80

Despite this adherence to the French tradition of luxury production, the antithesis of progressive furniture production at the time, this chair was regarded by contemporary French critics as being in the forefront of modern design. The sled runners on the bottom of the chair allowed it to be moved easily, unlike traditional four-legged chairs.

81

Lounge chair, Model No. B251
Bent chromed tubular steel, flat steel, uphostery (later)
29¼ x 28 x 37¼ in.
74 x 71 x 94.5 cm

Designed ca. 1929 by R. C. Coquery (French, dates unknown)
Manufactured after 1929 by Gebrüder Thonet, Frankenberg, Germany
Alexander von Vegesack, Düsseldorf

81

Figure 81A

Le Corbusier-Jeanneret-Perriand. *Grand Confort,* **large version, 1928.**

THE opulent cushions of this design recalled traditional concepts of comfort and challenged contemporary prejudices that tubular steel was cold to the touch, antiseptic, and uncomfortable. Coquery reduced much of the impression of heaviness of these cushions by streamlining their mass. As a result, this chair, with its backward cant, has a sweeping grace that other heavily upholstered chairs of the period do not have. The model's predecessor in the body of cushioned club chairs, *the Grand Confort* by Le Corbusier-Jeanneret-Perriand (figure 81A) eschewed the dynamic stance of Coquery's chair and instead displayed a cubic arrangement of mass. In addition, the frame of the earlier club

Figure 81C

Emile Guillot. Design of office and library. From left, chairs are by André Lurçat, Charlotte Perriand, R. C. Coquery.

chair encloses the cushions in a cagelike form, whereas the frame of the Coquery chair simply provides support for the cushions, which cover and engulf the steel tubing.

The wide appeal of this type of chair prompted numerous imitations; the Herman Miller Furniture Company of Grand Rapids, Michigan, produced a similar design by Gilbert Rohde (figure 81B). It is possible that Rohde may have seen the original in a Thonet catalogue or in an advertisement that grouped the Coquery chair with a *siège tournant* by Charlotte Perriand (cat. no. 74) and a armchair by the French architect André Lurçat (figure 81C).

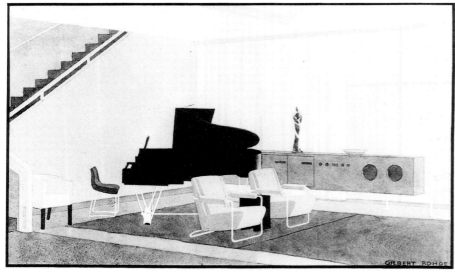

Figure 81B

Gilbert Rohde. "A 'Modern' Interior designed especially for *Fortune* **by Mr. Rohde." Watercolor, 1935. (From** *Fortune Magazine,* **November 1935, p. 99). The chairs are Rohde's design, manufactured by the Herman Miller Furniture Company, Grand Rapids, Michigan.**

82

Armchair

Bent chromed tubular steel, bent chromed
steel, plywood, bent solid wood, upholstery
32⅞ x 21⅛ x 24 in.
83.5 x 53.5 x 61 cm

Designed after ca. 1929 by W. H. Gispen
(1890–?)
Manufactured by Fabriek voor Metaalbewerking
N.V., Rotterdam
Collection Marty de Jong, Amsterdam

ATHOUGH Gispen's body of tubular steel designs responded to a technological and aesthetic lead established by others, he was instrumental in introducing tubular-steel furnishings into Holland during a highly critical period of acceptance between the two world wars. The configuration of the frame of this chair is remarkably similar to an earlier design by fellow Dutchman Gerrit Rietveld (cat. no. 73). By uniting the front and rear sections of the chair through a diagonal lateral stretcher, Gispen employed the same aesthetic device that had been used on Thonet's No. 51 chair in the nineteenth century (cat. no. 35). In addition, in this design Gispen also used the continuous frame, which others, such as Marcel Breuer and Mies van der Rohe, had pioneered in the late 1920s.

This model carries the particular distinction of having been used in the acclaimed Van Nelle factory in Rotterdam, which was built between 1928 and 1931 after the designs of L. C. van der Vlugt and Mart Stam. This building, the expression of the Neue Sachlichkeit (New Objectivity) mentality in architecture, which called for practicality, sobriety, and objectivity in design, could only have been furnished with pieces executed in tubular steel, a material that was preferred over wood by the progressive architects of the 1920s.

Gispen's own firm was reponsible for the production of these chairs.

82

83

Chair, Model No. MR90

Bent chromed flat steel, chromed flat steel,
leather, upholstery
29¾ x 29¾ x 29¾ in.
75.5 x 75.5 x 75.5 cm

Designed 1929 by Ludwig Mies van der
Rohe (born Aachen, Germany, 1886, died
Chicago 1969)
Manufactured probably by Bamberg
Metallwerkstätten, Berlin-Neukölln, 1931
Collection Mr. and Mrs. Al Luckett, Jr.,
Boulder, Colorado

THE classicist training of Mies van der Rohe's youth was not accomplished by formal academic training, but occurred in the Berlin architectural offices of Bruno Paul and Peter Behrens before World War I. This classical background is revealed in his designs for the furnishings of the German pavilion at the 1929 Exposición Internacional in Barcelona (figure 83A). Basing his designs for the pavilion's chairs, stools, and tables on the ancient folding stool called the *sella curulis*, Mies van der Rohe created an ensemble of great harmony, which wedded ancient form and modern material. This chair, which has since has been known as the Barcelona chair, was the most powerful design in the ensemble. By inverting classical principles of harmony, Mies van der Rohe drew one element of the curule form out of the traditional balanced arrangement to create the back of this chair, and thereby produced one of the icons of the modern movement.

*Figure 83*A
Ludwig Mies van der Rohe. Interior, German pavilion, Exposición Internacional, Barcelona, 1929.

The chair was crafted in limited numbers for a brief period in the late 1920s and early 1930s first by the Berliner Metallgewerbe Joseph Müller, Berlin, and, slightly later, by the Bamberg Metallwerkstätten in Neukölln, a suburb of Berlin. The model produced by the Bamberg Metallwerkstätten is rare, due to its high cost in the midst of a worldwide recession. Whereas a cantilevered tubular-steel chair (cat no. 70) sold by the Bamberg Metallwerkstätten retailed for 64 reichsmarks around 1931, the Barcelona chair in flat steel sold for 540. To a great degree, the complexity of construction dictated the high costs. Unlike the frame of the Knoll model of the Barcelona chair, introduced in 194, which is made of sections of stainless steel that have been cut and welded, these early models were made from separate elements that were chromed and then joined by lap or half joints and secured with chrome-headed bolts (figure 83B), techniques more aligned with traditional joinery than mass production. In addition, unlike most other metal-frame chairs of the period, the joined flat steel sections of the Barcelona chair were not resilient (figure 83C). The designer compensated for this liability by using leather straps as secondary support elements whose pliable qualities provided the cushions with a degree of suppleness they might not have had otherwise.

The imperial scale of these chairs dictated a need for large, padded cushions. The models installed in the German pavilion were upholstered in white kidskin. Rather than upholster these chairs with broad, featureless hides, Mies van der Rohe tufted them in a pattern reminiscent of the grid used in the plan of the pavilion. The leather cushions used on subsequent models added considerably to the cost of each piece.

Figure 83B
Bolted lap joints at intersection of stile and crest rail.

Figure 83C
Frame.

At the close of the exhibition, the pavilion was dismantled, and its opulent materials and furnishings were sold to recoup expenses. A year later, Mies van der Rohe would use several models of the Barcelona chair in the Tugendhat House in Brno, Czechoslovakia (cat. no. 84).

84
Armchair, Model No. MR50

Bent chromed flat steel, wood, upholstery (later)
31¼ x 23 x 22½ in.
79.5 x 58.5 x 57 cm

Designed ca. 1929–30 by Ludwig Mies van der Rohe (born Aachen, Germany, 1886, died Chicago 1969)
Manufactured probably by Bamberg Metallwerkstätten, Berlin-Neukölln, 1931
Collection Mr. and Mrs. Al Luckett, Jr., Boulder, Colorado

In 1928 Mies van der Rohe was commissioned by Grete and Fritz Tugendhat to design a home for them overlooking the city of Brno, Czechoslovakia. When completed two years later, the house and its furnishings (figure 84A) received considerable attention in the press, including an enthusiatic article by the Tugendhats themselves. In addition to using some of the models already shown in the German pavilion of the 1929 Barcelona Exposición Internacional (figure 83A), Mies van der Rohe introduced several new designs, among them this chair, which came to be known as the Brno chair.

The chair's flat steel frame reinforces the visual effect of the thin profile of the upholstered seat and back, which appear to float beyond the frame with a minimum of support. The heavy grade of steel used for the Brno chair enabled the designer to achieve a cantilever. Several years later Breuer experimented with a considerably lighter and therefore cheaper grade of flat steel (cat. no. 90), which prevented him from attaining a cantilever.

84

Figure 84A
Ludwig Mies van der Rohe. Brno chair, designed 1930. Bedroom, Tugendhat House, Brno, Czechoslovakia.

Part of Mies van der Rohe's last of body designs based on the cantilever principle, the Brno chair was available in either tubular or flat steel. This version was executed in nickeled steel; the Knoll version —introduced in 1960—has been made of chromed steel. The reflective quality of chromed steel would have been in concert with the luster of the polished metal, onyx, and glass used extensively throughout the Tugendhat House. In addition, steel columns, cruciform in section and finished in chrome, were used in the interior.

85

85

Side chair, Model No. ST14
Bent chromed tubular steel, plywood
34½ x 21 x 24 in.
87.5 x 53.5 x 61 cm

Designed 1929 by Wassili Luckhardt (born Berlin 1889, died Berlin 1972) and Hans Luckhardt (born Berlin 1890, died Berlin 1954)
Manufactured 1929–33 by Desta Stahlmöbel, Berlin

Alexander von Vegesack, Düsseldorf

FOLLOWING the hardships of World War I, minimal use of materials was the goal of many progressive architects and designers. The ideal was achieved in this remarkable side chair by Hans and Wassili Luckhardt. The Luckhardt brothers had been influential members of the postwar Expressionist movement in German architecture. However, by the middle of the 1920s, they came to believe that their visionary, individualistic buildings were unable to serve the needs of a society impoverished by war, war reparations, and severe inflation (Willett). As a result, they turned to a new architectural language based on a rationalized system of standardization and a use of new materials.

This chair, part of the ideological shift, appeared several years after the first cantilever designs by Mies van der Rohe (cat. nos. 70 and 71) and Breuer (cat. nos. 72 and 78). It was also available in a model in which the seat could pivot into a vertical

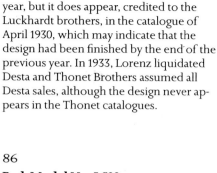

position when not in use, which reduced the bulk of the design, as did the thin, molded planes of bent plywood that form the seat and back.

A wheeled bar cart, designed by Alfred Zeffner (figure 85A), was constructed as a variation of the chair's tubular steel frame. This use of interchangeable, standardized components had been pioneered in the bent-wood furniture industry in the late nineteenth century. Both designs were used by the Luckhardt brothers in a model home, the Desta House shown at the *Bau-Ausstellung* (Building Exhibition) held in Berlin in 1931 (figure 85B), and both appeared in a Desta sales catalogue of the early 1930s.

The Desta firm was founded by Anton Lorenz in September 1929 (Wilk 1981, p. 76). The chair was not offered in the catalogue the firm issued in November of that year, but it does appear, credited to the Luckhardt brothers, in the catalogue of April 1930, which may indicate that the design had been finished by the end of the previous year. In 1933, Lorenz liquidated Desta and Thonet Brothers assumed all Desta sales, although the design never appears in the Thonet catalogues.

86

Bed, Model No. LS22

Bent tubular steel (repainted), Eisengarn (modern)

17 x 29½ x 81⅞ in.
43 x 75 x 208 cm

Designed ca. 1930 by Anton Lorenz (born Budapest 1891, died Boynton Beach, Florida, 1964)

Manufactured after 1930 by Gebrüder Thonet, Frankenberg, Germany

Collection Georg Thonet, Frankenberg, West Germany

ANTON LORENZ's fluid design represents the culmination of the pursuit of the continuous frame by Marcel Breuer, Mies van der Rohe, the Luckhardt brothers, and other progressive architects. This minimal design, however, added fuel to the pejorative criticism that tubular-steel furniture, despite numerous innovations, was reminiscent of a hospital environment.

This particular bed differs slightly from the design published in a Thonet catalogue of the early 1930s. There, an unobtrusive tubular-steel understretcher is more integrated into the design and is set closer to the *Eisengarn* webbing than is the brace used here. This difference may indicate that after the model entered the commercial market, it was found that the weight of the human body brought it into contact with the brace, which led to the introduction of a lower stretcher. This system of trial, error, and correction is responsible for the numerous subtle differences in many models of bent-wood and bent-metal furniture produced in the many factories across Eastern, Central, and Western Europe.

Anton Lorenz, the designer of this bed, was more of an entrepreneur and businessman than a creative talent. As founder and director of Deutsche Stahlmöbel (Desta) he was involved in numerous lawsuits with Marcel Breuer and Mies van der Rohe over the patent rights for many of their designs. In the late thirties Lorenz settled in the United States, where, after World War II, he introduced his highly popular reclining chair, the Barca Lounger.

This bed was shown in Lorenz's installation, Desta House, at the *Bau-Ausstellung* (Building Exhibition) in Berlin in 1931.

86

Desk, Model No. B65

*Bent chromed tubular steel, wood
(painted), metal*

31¼ x 58 x 30¼ in.
77 x 147.5 x 77 cm

Designer unknown, ca. 1930
*Manufactured after 1930 by Gebrüder
Thonet, Frankenberg, Germany*
*Collection Dr. William Greenspon, New
York*

In a 1930 Thonet catalogue, Marcel Breuer was credited with the design of the desk listed as model No. B65. Neither royalty statements nor conversations with Breuer (Wilk 1981, p. 184) have verified this attribution. The revision of this provenance is supported by the fact that the desk does not appear in any of the installations provided by Breuer during 1930–31, including his contributions to the Deutsche Werkbund section at the 1930 Salon des Artistes Décorateurs in Paris and his various interior schemes at the Berlin *Bau-Ausstellung* (Building Exhibition) the following year.

It is possible that the overall composition of the desk was borrowed from one of Breuer's earlier designs, the No. B21 typing stand of 1928 (Wilk 1981, p. 79), made from painted wood, glass, and tubular steel. The desk betrays a debt to this smaller work table in its use of an asymmetrical arrangement of elements and a continuous outline constructed from tubular steel. Nevertheless, the retooling of the earlier design produced what was aesthetically the most successful of all the desks made by Thonet at that time.

87

88

Armoire

Wood (repainted), bent chromed tubular steel, tubular steel, metal

72¾ x 51 x 23¾ in.
184.5 x 129.5 x 60.5 cm

Designer unknown, after 1930
Manufacturer unknown
Collection Dr. William Greenspon, New York

ATHOUGH the manufacturer and designer of this armoire are as yet unknown, the piece bears some resemblance to Thonet's model No. B101 designed by the architect J. Hagemann. However, both the design and construction reveal that it was not intended for the general market served by Thonet. Its meticulous construction suggests that the armoire may have been fabricated in a workshop environment rather than on the assembly line of a large factory. The smoothly finished, welded joints at the intersection of the sled runners and structural uprights require considerable finishing by hand. This manner of fabrication would have been unnecessary had this junction been fashioned from a single piece of bent tubular steel. Equally indicative of a costly methodology is the integration of door hinges, requiring special hardware, into the profile of the tubular-steel frame. Here the designer subjugated ease of construction to the primacy of aesthetics. Nevertheless, its luxurious austerity ranks the armoire as a suitable complement to other tubular steel designs of the era.

89

Armchair

Bent chromed tubular steel, plywood, upholstery

31½ x 20⅞ x 23 in.
77 x 53 x 58.5 cm

Designed ca. 1931 by Gilbert Rohde (born New York 1894, died New York 1944)
Manufactured after 1931 by Troy Sunshade Company, Troy, Ohio
The Baltimore Museum of Art, Maryland (Friends of Art Fund)

THIS armchair, Gilbert Rohde's earliest design in tubular steel, reveals the debt owed by many American designers to their European counterparts during the period between the two world wars. During Rohde's first visit to Paris in 1927, he may have seen Louis Sognot's radical smoking parlor shown at the annual Salon d'Automne (figure 89A). Sognot included four armchairs in this installation, which was one of the early public displays of tubular-steel furnishings in France. According to Joseph Roberto and Elizabeth Kaufer, his assistants at the time, Rohde, as did many American designers, subscribed to progressive European publications (Ostergard and Hanks, p. 101), several of which published Sognot's design.

Although Rohde derived the aesthetic of his chair from a Frenchman, he owed much to contemporaneous German fur-

88

89

Figure 89A
Louis Sognot. Smoking room, "Primavera" display at the Salon d'Automne, Paris, 1927. (*From Art et Décoration*, 1927, p. 177).

nishings in tubular steel that were designed specifically to be mass produced. Unlike Sognot's chair, which required elaborate welding and handwork, Rohde's design uses a frame made of a single length of bent tubular steel, which makes it suitable for mass production. Despite its European antecedents, Rohde's chair reflects an emerging modernist consciousness in America during the 1930s. Following World War II, several American designers, such as Eero Saarinen and Charles and Ray Eames (cat. nos. 112–118), would acquire a far more influential role in international design circles.

The Troy Sunshade Company, the manufacturer of this chair, marketed its products through offices in Amsterdam and Rotterdam, an indication that this design may have been sold in Europe at that time.

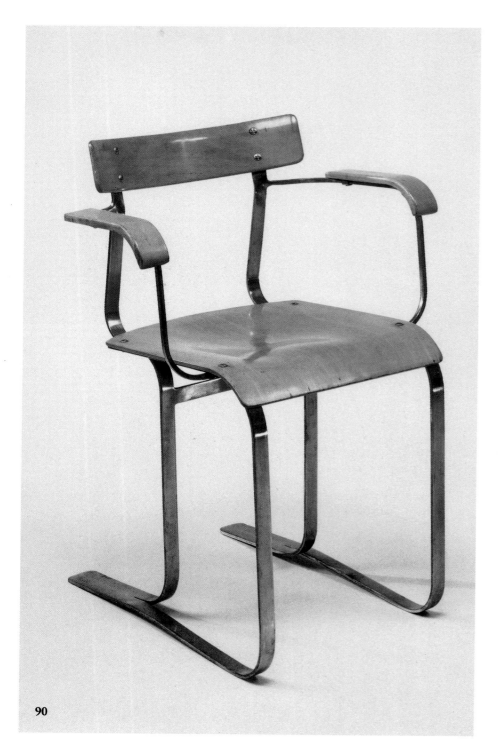

90

Armchair, Model No. 301

Bent brushed flat steel, bent plywood
28¾ x 22½ x 19¾ in.
73 x 57 x 50 cm

*Designed ca. 1932–33 by Marcel Breuer
(born Pécs, Hungary, 1902, died New York
1981)*

*Made after ca. 1932–33 by Meubles Stylclair,
Lyons*

Barry Friedman Ltd., New York

In the early 1930s, Breuer stopped working with tubular steel and turned instead to designing furnishings in flat steel. Although it lacks the resiliency and strength of tubular steel, flat steel has the advantage of being a less expensive material. However, some years earlier, Mies van der Rohe had produced expensive exceptions to this rule in the body of designs he made for the German pavilion of the 1929 Exposición Internacional in Barcelona (cat. no. 83) and shortly thereafter in the Tugendhat House in Brno, Czechoslovakia (cat. no. 84). The cost of carrying out these designs was high specifically because of the heavy-gauge steel used in their fabrication, but it was this very material that enabled Mies van der Rohe to achieve the cantilevered Tugendhat and Brno chairs (cat. no. 84).

Because Breuer's 1932 designs for the Wohnbedarf stores in Switzerland were intended for a general market rather than the luxury trade, he was forced to use a less expensive and therefore more delicate grade of steel. This eliminated the possibility of a cantilevered seat. To compensate for the technical liability of the metal, Breuer introduced resilient rear legs, away from the position traditionally occupied directly beneath the stiles. With this technical solution he added the necessary support and also paid homage to his earlier designs employing the cantilever principle (cat. nos. 72 and 78). The slight bow to the sled runners gives a degree of buoyancy to the frame.

The molded plywood seat and back anticipate his later designs in wood (cat. no. 109).

Meubles Stylclair, a French licensee of the Swiss Wohnbedarf stores, made the example shown here for the branch store in Lyons. In the mid-1930s, the furniture company L. & C. Arnold of Schorndorf, Germany, advertised that it was producing a model in aluminum designed by Breuer, which was nearly identical to this Wohnbedarf model No. 301. Wohnbedarf, too, produced an aluminum version of this design.

90

91

Armchair, for zeppelin *Hindenburg*

Bent tubular aluminum, solid wood,
upholstery, steel
34 x 23⅛ x 29⅛ in.
86.5 x 59 x 74 cm

Designed ca. 1935 by Fritz August Breuhaus
(born Solingen, Germany, 1883, died
Rodenkirchen, West Germany, 1960)

Manufactured ca. 1935 by L. & C. Arnold,
Schorndorf, Germany

Bodenseemuseum, Friedrichshafen, West
Germany

Eminently suitable for mass production, steel furniture was usually more durable and less expensive to produce than furniture constructed in a traditional manner from conventional materials. It was precisely these factors that attracted those avant-garde architects and designers who called for sweeping social reform to alleviate the conditions of the poor. Aluminum, however, was considerably more costly than steel, and its use for the mass production of furniture would seem inappropriate to the pursuit of any humanist cause.

However unsuited aluminum may have been for the general purposes, it was eminently satisfactory for use in "lighter-than-air" crafts: airships. The interiors of LZ129, the zeppelin *Hindenburg*, had been specially designed in 1935 by Fritz August Breuhaus, who had earned considerable distinction in the twenties for his modernist interiors aboard the Hansa-Lloyd ocean liner *Bremen*. Illustrations of the interiors of the *Hindenburg* reveal an extensive use of this armchair in the smoking parlors, dining room, and observation lounges (figure 91A).

Figure 91A
Fritz August Breuhaus. Lounge of "A" Deck, LZ 129, the "Hindenburg" zeppelin, 1936. (From *Innen-Dekoration*, April 1936, p. 272).

A 1936 catalogue of the L. & C. Arnold company includes promotional photographs of the *Hindenburg's* interiors with furnishings manufactured by the firm. Although seen in the photographs, this particular model was not available to the general public; it appears to have been made exclusively for the zeppelin firm. The research of Dr. Lutz Tittel, of the Bodenseemuseum in Friedrichshafen (communication to Alexander von Vegesack, Düsseldorf), suggests that the chair shown here, although an example of the model used throughout the *Hindenburg* and its successor ship, the *Graf Zeppelin II*, was most likely a prototype for production pieces.

Although unremarkable in terms of aesthetics, the design of this chair, with its broad, stable stance, sled runners, and minimal weight, was engineered for the special conditions of airship travel. This elitist means of conveyance, a revolutionary alternative to other means of passenger travel in the late 1920s, had no established traditions of interior design. The austerity of these interiors, although in the forefront of modernist taste, were largely the result of pragmatic considerations.

91

92

92

Dressing vanity, Model No. 3323

Bent plywood veneered with white holly and red ash, bent chromed tubular steel, flat steel, silvered glass, turned solid wood
66 x 51½ x 16 in.
167.5 x 131 x 40.5 cm

Designed 1935 by Gilbert Rohde (born New York 1894, died New York 1944)
Manufactured after 1935 by the Herman Miller Furniture Company, Grand Rapids, Michigan
Fifty-50 Gallery, New York

UNTIL 1930, the Herman Miller Furniture company was engaged in the production of inexpensive and highly interpretive historicist furnishings. In that year, under the design stewardship of Gilbert Rohde, the firm inaugurated an extensive program of modernist furnishings whose appearance was predicated on more than just superficial style changes. Evidence of this is seen in the bent-wood and bent-metal elements that were increasingly used to fabricate many of Rohde's modernist designs for this large manufacturing firm. Prior to 1930, these bent components did not constitute any part of Herman Miller's repertoire of constructional devices. However, throughout the decade preceding World War II, bent tubular steel was used by the Herman Miller company with increasing frequency. This vanity was retailed in a 1935 catalogue as part of the company's modernist line of bedroom furniture designed by Rohde. Here he chose to manipulate the bent steel in a manner similar to the work of contemporary French designers (cat. nos. 79 and 80), who were more concerned with aesthetic effects than with problems of mass production. The drum-like elements that contain the drawers were constructed from thick sections of plywood, bent into cylindrical forms, and veneered. By cutting, welding, and polishing the angles of the base rather than

bending them, Rohde simultaneously introduced higher costs and a more compact line to his design. By dropping the mirror to the floor, he merged two furniture forms, the dressing table and the standing mirror.

93

Stacking chairs

Bent chromed tubular steel, chromed tubular steel, plywood, upholstery, flat steel
32¾ x 15¾ x 19¾ in.
83.5 x 40 x 50 cm

Designer unknown, ca. 1935
Manufacturer unknown, possibly French
Alexander von Vegesack, Düsseldorf

THE design of these chairs incorporates modifications that enable several chairs to be stacked in a small space. This inventive design was ideally suited to large public spaces where furnishings had to be durable, easily cleaned, and lightweight. Stackability was an added premium. By the 1920s, several designers in England, as well as Otto Korhonen and Alvar Aalto in Finland (cat. no. 103), developed chairs and tables that accommodated the stacking principle. During the 1930s, this concept was explored by designers and architects throughout Europe.

It is believed that this chair was designed by the French architect Robert Mallet-Stevens. Although closely involved with the modern movement in France in his capacity as an architect, Mallet-Stevens is not remembered as a particularly gifted designer of furniture. The few pieces that he is known to have designed were usually produced for specific installations; many

A 739/L 4
(41 × 40 cm)

the Mallet-Stevens provenance. The appropriation of one another's designs had been a common occurrence among the various companies in the furniture industry since the third quarter of the nineteenth century. The simple lines of this chair are strongly reminiscent of Viennese bent-wood furniture of the early twentieth century, in particular the side chair model No. A739/L4 (figure 93A) in a Thonet catalogue of circa 1928–30. If the tubular-steel chairs shown here were indeed designed by Mallet-Stevens, this Viennese source of inspiration would not be remarkable. The influence of Viennese Secessionist design, and of Hoffmann in particular, is evident throughout much of Mallet-Stevens's career. For his own atelier in Paris (*Mallet-Stevens*, p. 283), Mallet-Stevens designed a tubular-steel transcription of Josef Hoffmann's Cabaret Fledermaus design (cat. no. 55), which was executed in bent solid wood. Josef Hoffmann's most opulent residential commission, the Palais Stoclet in Brussels (1905–11), had been built for Mallet-Stevens's uncle Adolphe Stoclet (Sekler, pp. 299–304).

were for his own residence in the rue Mallet-Stevens in Paris (*Mallet-Stevens*, pp. 279–81). However, even for the dining room there he selected Breuer's B5 chair (cat. no. 69) and in other rooms used furniture designed by his colleague Pierre Chareau (see figure 5–35).

These small chairs have been ascribed to Mallet-Stevens on the basis of their similarity to the tubular-steel side chairs he installed in a large restaurant he designed for the 1935 Salon des Arts Ménagers, in Paris (*Mallet-Stevens*, p. 344). However, the variations in detailing between those chairs and the pair shown here do not sustain

93

94

Armchair

Bent solid wood, bent laminated wood, solid wood, cane, metal

31½ x 21⅞ x 20¾ in.
80 x 55.5 x 53 cm

Designed ca. 1930 by Erich Dieckmann (born Kauernik, Prussia, 1896, died 1944)

Probably made after 1930 by Weimar Bau-und-Wohnungskunst, Weimar

Stattliche Museen, Preussischer Kulturbesitz, Kunstgewerbe Museum, Berlin

As a young student at the Bauhaus in Weimar, Erich Dieckmann distinguished himself at the school's 1923 exhibition with his hand-crafted furnishings for the Haus-am-Horn, an experimental single-family dwelling based on standardized requirements. This exhibition marked the school's shift from a craft orientation to an industrial one. By the mid-1920s the school attained a closer rapport with industry in order to service the needs of the impoverished element of society. In many respects, Dieckmann's own career as a designer of furniture reflects the shift in the school's ideological base.

Although in the early 1930s Dieckmann produced a series of flamboyant designs in tubular steel (figure 94A) which were labeled "spaghetti monsters" by Mart Stam, a vigorous proponent of a Neue Sachlichkeit (New Objectivity) philosophy, he was also capable of producing work of an entirely different aesthetic quality in bent wood. These austere and basically rectilinear designs, probably manufactured by his own firm in Weimar, included furnishings of all sorts executed in a variety of materials, frequently bent laminates. The chair shown here, one of the earliest designs produced by his firm, exhibits an inexplicable mix of materials. Despite the superior pliability of laminated wood, Dieckmann chose to bend solid wood to execute the most compressed curve of the chair's design—the

Figure 94A
Erich Dieckmann. Armchairs, 1931. (From Dieckmann, fig. 108).

Figure 94B
Josef Albers. Armchair, 1929. Bent laminated wood, tubular steel, and upholstery. Model No. ti 244. The Museum of Modern Art, New York.

parabolic leg system. Yet, for the more gentle curves of the design, such as the splats and one-piece stiles and side rails, Dieckmann used a laminate. With the added cost of assembling a laminate and the ready availability of inexpensive solid wood that could be bent, it remains a mystery as to why Dieckmann chose to mix the two techniques in a single design.

This chair, when viewed beside Josef Albers's 1929 ti244 armchair (figure 94B) and Gerrit Rietveld's armchair (cat. no. 73) and their bent-wood support systems, illustrates the persistent appeal of bent wood prior to its brilliant exploitation in Finland in the late 1920s and 1930s by Alvar Aalto. The explosion of interest in tubular-steel furnishings in Germany during the 1920s has overshadowed the continued development of progressive furnishings using bent-wood elements during that period.

95

Armchair

Bent solid wood, bent plywood, upholstery (modern)
27¼ x 20½ x 25¼ in.
69 x 52 x 64 cm
Designer unknown, ca. 1929
Manufactured after 1929 by D. G. Fischel Söhne, Vienna
Collection Theo Stachels, Munich

THE cantilever principle—the aesthetic transformation of the seating form brought about by a symbiosis of materials and manufacturing methodology—galvanized progressive thought during the second half of the 1920s. Initially, the principle was limited to the support system of chairs, but such designers as Kalman Lengyel, Jacques Adnet, and the Luckhardt brothers, as well as the anonymous designer of this chair, applied it to the back of the chair. Although tubular steel remained the primary metal for this radical concept, flat steel, aluminum, and laminated and solid wood were eventually added to the roster of materials used. In this design, the manufacturer took a nineteenth-century material—bent solid wood—and updated it with this treatment of the back. It would not be until Alvar Aalto's experiments in 1931–32 that a cantilevered system of bent laminated wood was developed (cat. nos. 98, 100, 101), which was capable of supporting the weight of the sitter.

95

96

96

Armchair

*Molded plywood, bent solid beechwood,
solid beechwood (repainted)*

31½ x 19¾ x 17¼ in.
80 x 50 x 44 cm

*Design of 1929, attributed to Josef Frank
(born Baden bei Wien 1885, died Stockholm
1967); also to Josef Hoffmann (born Pirnitz,
Moravia, 1870, died Vienna 1956) with
Oswald Haerdtl (born Vienna 1899, died
Vienna 1959)*

*Manufactured 1929, probably by Thonet-
Mundus, Vienna*

*Alexander von Vegesack, Düsseldorf, Courtesy
Galerie Wolfgang Richter, Munich*

WITH the exeception of its laminated seat
and back, this chair is identical to Thonet's
model No. A811/1F (figures 96A and 5–42),
which has been identified as the design of
Josef Frank (*Die Form*, 1932, p. 88). However, Frank's work with bent wood was
limited, and he is known for his exclusive
Viennese decorating firm, Haus und Garten,
which during the 1920s produced his modernist designs utilizing deluxe materials to
achieve exotic aesthetic effects for the luxury trade.

 This variation of the Thonet design has
also been attributed to Josef Hoffmann
and his associate Oswald Haerdtl. Dr. Christian Witt-Dörring, of the Österreichisches

Figure 96A
**Josef Frank. Armchair, Thonet
Model No. A811/1F. Bent solid
wood, solid wood, cane, metal.
Alexander von Vegesack,
Düsseldorf.**

Figure 96B
**Josef Hoffman and Oswald Haerdtl. Terrace of a
café, Österreichische Werkbund exhibition, Vienna, 1930. (From *Die Form*, July 1, 1930, cover).**

Museum für angewandte Kunst, supports this attribution by linking the perforations of this chair to those in the Purkersdorf Sanitorium chair (cat. no. 43), which was designed by Hoffmann a quarter of a century earlier. However, there is no documentation that might verify this proposal.

However, Hoffmann and Haerdtl used a side-chair version of this chair in their café terrace that was part of the 1930 Österreichische Werkbund exhibition in Vienna (figure 96B). As this was a temporary installation, they may have retained the frame of Thonet model No. A811/1F chair but had the firm retool the back to make the café's furnishings aesthetically consistent with their design scheme.

The use of a continuous piece of bent wood for the rear legs, stiles, and crest rail and the treatment of the arms was first seen in bent wood designs of the nineteenth century. Although the paint is modern, the brilliant color of the chair replicates that of the original. Thonet's 1930 centenary catalogue, in which the firm introduced painted bent wood, included several colorplates indicating the available colors of their painted models. The use of such inexpensive decorative treatments expanded customer selection during the Depression of the 1930s.

97

Etagère

Bent solid wood, solid wood, bent plywood, plywood (repainted)

17¾ x 36 x 14¼ in.
44.5 x 91.5 x 36 cm

Designer unknown, ca. 1930
Manufactured after 1930 by Thonet-Mundus-J. & J. Kohn, Vienna
Stedelijk Museum, Amsterdam

MADE of both bent laminated and bent solid wood, this étagère displays a fascinating manipulation of forms and materials. All the square-sectioned wooden ele-

97

ments have been bent, while those of circular section have not. Following World War I, the use of brilliantly colored bent-wood furnishings became popular, particularly in commercial establishments where decorating budgets were limited by the economic difficulties of the 1920s and 1930s. The popularity of painted furnishings was such that Thonet's hundredth-anniversary catalogue of 1930, where this table was advertised, contained colorplates of various models displaying this treatment.

The gently flared top seen in this table is a decorative device that was frequently seen in the more exotic, elitist designs of such modernists as Austrian Fritz Gross and the Germans Emile Fahrenkemp and Fritz August Breuhaus.

98

Child's chair, Model No. 103

Bent plywood, bent laminated birch
23 x 12⅞ x 16¾ in.
58.5 x 32.5 x 42.5 cm

Designed ca. 1931 by Alvar Aalto (born Kuortane, Finland, 1898, died Helsinki 1976)
Manufactured after 1931 by Oy. Huonekalu-ja Rakennustyötehdas AB, Turku, Finland
Alexander von Vegesack, Düsseldorf

ALVAR Aalto's concept of a chair with proportions suited to a child appeared in his work for the first time in 1930 (figure 98A), when he created a diminutive version of his "hybrid" chair (figure 5–49), in which a bent plywood seat and back were grafted

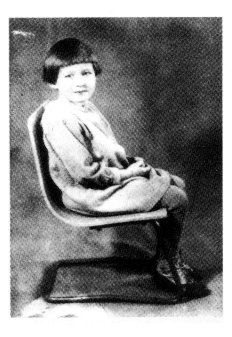

to a tubular-steel cantilevered base. Aalto found this mix of materials unsatisfactory. In addition, the bolts used to secure the plywood sheet to its base also marred the wood, a disfigurement he would avoid in his all-wood cantilevered designs (cat. nos. 100 and 101).

As part of his attempt to prove that wood could be an integral part of a modernist aesthetic, Aalto eliminated tubular steel from his repertoire of materials. Instead, he developed a cantilevered leg system constructed of laminated wood, a considerably stronger and more resilient material than bent solid wood, which cannot support the weight sustained by a cantilevered seat. With this solution Aalto inaugurated his series of furnishings (cat. nos. 99–101, 103, 104) that displayed a cohesiveness absent from the hybrid chair.

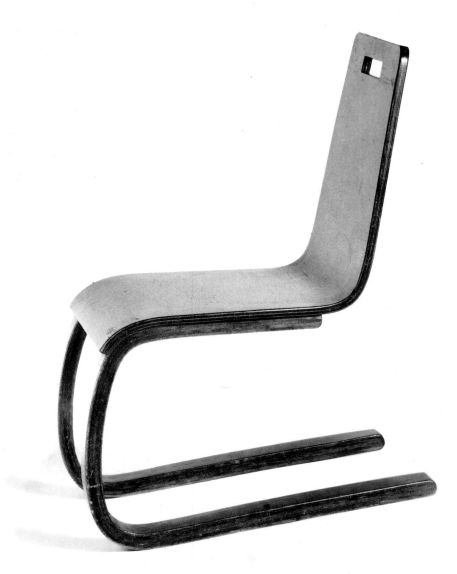

Figure 98A
Alvar Aalto. Children's version of "hybrid" chair, 1930.

98

99

99

Lounge chair, Model No. 41
Bent plywood (repainted), bent laminated birch, solid birch
25⅝ x 23¾ x 34½ in.
65 x 60 x 87 cm

Designed 1931–32 by Alvar Aalto (born Kuortane, Finland, 1898, died Helsinki 1976)
Manufactured after 1932 by Oy. Huonekalu-ja Rakennustyötehdas AB, Turku, Finland
Museum of *Applied Arts, Helsinki*

ALTHOUGH identified as the Paimio chair, this particular model did not constitute part of the original group of furnishings designed for the Paimio Sanitorium, Aalto's most famous essay in the International Style. However, the development of the chair was concurrent with the final stages of the construction of the building late in 1932, and the two have consistently been coupled in the literature.

Figure 99A
Isaac Cole. Patent Model for Plywood Chair, 1873. Two lengths of molded plywood, 7⅞″ high. The Museum of Modern Art, New York (Purchase).

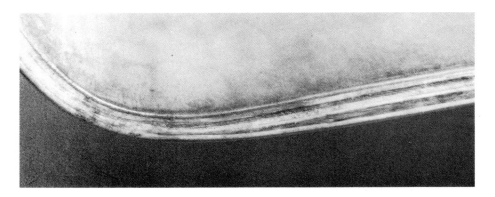

Aalto's quest for a design that lent itself to mass production was realized in this chair constructed from a minimal number of elements. Its closed frame is fabricated from a single piece of laminated wood bent into the appropriate form and joined across a single bias seam in a scarf joint. The seat and back are made from a single piece of plywood whose undulant configuration eliminates any need for upholstery. Although the one-piece construction of this portion of the chair was a nineteenth-century invention (figure 99A), Aalto transformed it by manipulating the sheets of veneer contained in the plywood matrix. He thinned the sheet of plywood at the obtuse angle of the seat where it rose into the back and the need for pliancy was the greatest (figure 99B); he retained the full thickness of the sheet in the scrolls of the front seat rail and at the crest rail, where the curvature of the wood is the most dynamic. By distributing stress throughout crucial points of the seat, Aalto sought to increase the pliancy of the seat. However, Aalto's quest for a resilient, all-wood chair was not fully realized in this design. It remained essentially rigid, unlike a slightly later armchair that was technically more advanced (cat. no. 100).

The critical and commercial reception of these two designs, as well as others by Aalto, helped reinstate wood as an alternative material in the progressive design community. Although other designers of the era, such as Erich Dieckmann (cat. no. 94) and Gerrit Rietveld (cat. no. 73), produced chairs in which they employed bent solid and bent laminated wood, Aalto's designs were the most technically advanced. In part, his work prompted Marcel Breuer to incorporate bent wood in his furniture of the 1930s. As a result, critics have accused

Figure 99B

Alvar Aalto. Detail of plywood seat, Paimio chair, 1931–32. Barry Friedman Ltd., New York.

Breuer of plagiarizing Aalto's technical innovations in the use of bent wood (Pallasmaa, p. 77), but have lost sight of the fact that Breuer's designs in tubular steel had helped to inaugurate several of Aalto's most important furniture innovations. Late in 1928, in his own apartment in Turku (see figure 5–54), Aalto had installed Breuer's "Wassily" club chair (cat. no. 67) and his B33 side chair and had also used Breuer's furniture in a restaurant there. The impact of these designs on Aalto's work was almost instantaneous. In 1929, he introduced the "hybrid" chair, a cantilevered tubular-steel and plywood side chair, clearly based on Breuer's revolutionary B33 model, a radical departure from Aalto's earlier designs. Until then, Aalto's furniture, which was constructed from solid elements of cut wood joined by traditional means, had been inspired by historicist prototypes.

Figure 99D

Marcel Breuer. Lounge chair, designed ca. 1929. Bent chromed tubular steel, solid wood (painted), *Eisengarn* (iron cloth). Model No. B35 in Thonet Sales catalogue, ca. 1930. Barry Friedman Ltd., New York

In addition, a drawing of an alternate conception of the Paimio chair (figure 99C) reveals a profile startlingly similar to Breuer's B35 chair (figure 99D) of 1928. Even the production model of the Paimio chair strongly evokes Breuer's earlier model, which was certainly well known by the late 1920s. Nevertheless, the Paimio chair, which relied on wood and organic shapes for its aesthetic and conceptual statement, became the touchstone of Aalto's distinctive design program of the 1930s.

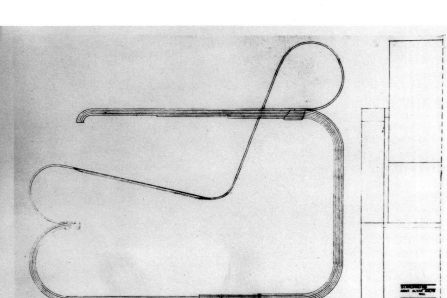

Figure 99C

Alvar Aalto. Design for alternate version of Paimio chair, 1931–32. Alvar Aalto Architects Ltd., lsinki.

100

Armchair, Model No. 31

Bent plywood (repainted) bent laminated birch, solid birch

27¼ x 23¾ x 31½ in.
69 x 59.5 x 80 cm

Designed ca. 1931–32 by Alvar Aalto (born Kuortane, Finland, 1898, died Helsinki 1976)

Manufactured after 1932 by Oy. Huonekalu- ja Rakennustyotehdas AB, Turku, Finland

Museum of Applied Arts, Helsinki

THIS armchair, in its numerous variations, was the most revolutionary of Alvar Aalto's seating designs. Although the use of a cantilever element had been pioneered in the previous decade by several German and one Dutch designer, Aalto transformed this remarkable innovation by executing it solely in wood. Unlike the designs of Mies van der Rohe (cat. nos. 70, 71, 84) and Marcel Breuer (cat. nos. 72 and 78) whose cantilevered chairs were executed in tubular or flat metals in combination with canvas, cane, leather, and wood used for the seat and back elements, Aalto produced a design whose materials were aesthetically cohesive and tactilely complimentary. The cold touch of metal had alienated many potential clients, who found Aalto's use of wood a far more humanist approach to modern design. In addition, Aalto's designs for cantilevered seating forms differed from much of the work in tubular steel in that he allowed the sled runners of the legs to end independently of one another, instead of connecting them with a rear stretcher, as was done in most work in metal. The concept of the continuous frame was no longer an ideal. Aalto used bent laminates for the cantilevered support and a bent plywood for the one-piece seat and back system.

To a great degree, advances in technology enabled Aalto to achieve his masterful designs of the late 1920s and early 1930s. The use of laminates, an essential component of Aalto's designs, had languished in the furniture-making trades in the latter half of the nineteenth century. During that period, laminates had been bonded with organic glues, such as those made with casein, a milk-based substance that lacked adhesive stability under conditions of extreme stress, heat, and humidity. This handicap had prompted Michael Thonet and most other early manufacturers of bentwood furniture to forsake the use of laminates. However, chemical glues with far greater stability were developed during World War I. During the 1920s these glues were introduced into the production of laminates, which were then used in the furniture-making trades.

Aalto's experiments with laminated wood began in the late 1920s when he formed a working association with Otto Korhonen, the technical director of Oy. Huonekalu- ja Rakennustyötehdas, a well-known furniture-making firm in Turku, Finland. Their collaboration began with the stackable side chair of 1929 (Pallasmaa, fig. 75), in gently bent sheets of thin plywood form the individual seat and back elements. This was followed by Aalto's first cantilevered designs for side chairs and armchairs constructed from single sheets of bent plywood bolted to tubular-steel bases. This incongruous combination of materials led Aalto to further experimentation with laminates, culminating in his all-wood, cantilevered chairs of 1931–32.

100

101

101

Armchair

Molded plywood (painted), laminated birch, solid birch

39¼ x 22⅞ x 36¼ in.
99.5 x 58 x 92 cm

Designed ca. 1931–32 by Alvar Aalto (born Kuortane, Finland, 1898, died Helsinki 1976)

Manufactured after 1932 by Oy. Huonekalu-ja Rakennustyötehdas AB, Turku, Finland

Alexander von Vegesack, Düsseldorf

THE complex curve in the headrest of this armchair represents a substantial achievement in terms of technical prowess, yet the chair has never been mentioned or illustrated in any monograph of Aalto's work. A simple curve executed in plywood had been used in the seats and backs of Aalto's other revolutionary designs of the period, most notably the so-called Paimio chair (cat. no. 99) and the cantilevered armchair (cat. no. 100). However, it is with the chair shown here that Aalto further explored the bending of plywood in order to achieve a compound curve. This difficult maneuver had been accomplished successfully by only one earlier designer —John Henry Belter (cat. no. 21). In the course of the execution of such a curve the complexity involved all too often places unnatural stress on the plywood, causing it to tear and buckle. However, the advantage of the compound curve is that it provides a shell form that is far more amenable to the human body than the flat

Figure 101A
Alvar Aalto. Furniture, shown at the Building Congress for the Nordic Countries, Helsinki, 1932.

Figure 101B
Alvar Aalto. Armchair, ca. 1931–32. Molded plywood, laminated birch, solid birch, leather straps. Philadelphia Museum of Art (Funds contributed by COLLAB in honor of Cynthia W. Drayton and the Fiske Kimball Fund).

curvature used in the so-called Paimio chair (cat. no. 99).

An armchair nearly identical to the example shown here was apparently first displayed at the Building Congress for the Nordic Countries held in Helsinki in 1932 (figure 101A). That model is identical to one now in the Philadelphia Museum of Art (figure 101B). The rectangular perforations in the headrest of these two chairs were used to secure pliable leather straps that cradled the sitter's head and kept it from touching the hard back of the chair. The circular perforations in the model shown here suggest that this example may be a prototype for the Helsinki and Philadelphia models. The design was first published in 1932 in an advertisement for the

firm, Oy. Huonekalu- ja Rakennustyötehdas (figure 101C), which produced all of Aalto's designs during this period. By calling it a "soft wood chair," the advertisement emphasized the chair's resilient qualities and the firm's dedication to providing this quality in their designs. It would appear that none of the chairs discussed here were ever retailed by Artek, Aalto's firm founded in 1935.

The stepped arrangement of the sled runners of the chair shown here, as well as the chairs exhibited in Helsinki and illustrated in the advertisement, is also evident in

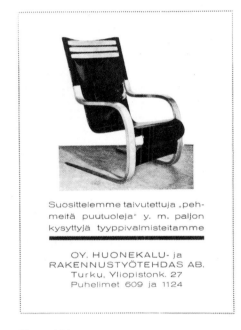

Figure 101C
Advertisement of Oy. Huonekalu-ja Rakennustyötehdas AB, Turku, Finland, for Alvar Aalto furniture. "We recommend 'bent-wood chairs' and our other much requested standardized products." (From *Domus* [Finland], April 1932).

Figure 101D
Alvar Aalto. Armchair, Model No. 401. Exhibited at the Milan Triennale, 1933. (From *Domus*, July 1933, p. 000).

the drawing of an alternative version of the so-called Paimio chair (figure 99C). Although this stepped device is disconcerting aesthetically, it may originally have been intended to dissipate the stress in the open-ended laminated wood cantilever used to support the chair. It is also possible that Aalto was trying to reduce the thick sections of laminated wood used in the legs, which lacked the delicate proportions of the tubular-steel frames of the earlier cantilevered chairs.

Perhaps the stepped runners proved to be technically unnecessary, as they were eliminated from Aalto's repertoire of designs. The examples of his furniture shown at the landmark exhibition of his work at Fortnum & Mason in London in 1933 (see figure 5–62) do not have this feature. The design shown here was apparently used

only in one other public commission, the Women's Hospital in Helsinki around 1934, indicating that the design was produced in small quantities.

The limited appearance of this model in the first half of the 1930s may be attributable in part to the fact that the complex curve was difficult and expensive to execute at that time. In addition, Aalto may have been dissatisfied with the awkward intersection of the thick laminated arm and the delicate plywood back, for he eliminated this junction entirely in his design for an upholstered armchair, model No. 401, that was exhibited at the Triennale di Milano (Milan Triennial) in 1933 (figure 101D). In that chair he also obscured the technical achievement of a compound curve by covering the shell of the seating element with upholstery.

Not until 1946, when Charles and Ray Eames exhibited their designs at the Museum of Modern Art in New York, would the compound curve become a fully integrated component of mass-produced furnishings (cat nos. 116 and 117).

102

102

Side chair

Bent solid wood, solid wood, upholstery
31¾ x 15 x 21 in.
80.5 x 38 x 53.5 cm

Designed ca. 1931 by Gilbert Rohde (born New York 1894, died New York 1944)

Manufactured after 1931 by the Heywood-Wakefield Furniture Company, Wakefield, Massachusetts

Collection Nancy Moore, Pound Ridge, New York

UNLIKE many other American designers who diversified their output by experimenting with various products during the 1930s, Rohde remained essentially a designer of furniture. Although he never aligned his work with a specific social program, as many of his European colleagues had, and never defined an aesthetic that was unique to him, Rohde was highly influential in the promotion of modernist taste in the United States in the decade before World War II. In the course of his short career, he worked for many of the major manufacturers of modern furniture. Although his association with the Herman Miller Furniture Company was the longest and most productive, he produced the most successful design of his career for the Heywood-Wakefield Company. Eight years after its introduction in 1931, this design had sold 250,000 copies. This may seem small in comparison with earlier Thonet production figures, but it was considerable for a chair that was viewed as distinctly modern and somewhat alien by a basically conservative American clientele. In addition, the chair was introduced during the Depression years and had to contend with nearly identical models designed by Rohde for both the Kroehler Manufacturing Company (figure 102A) and the Herman Miller Furniture Company (figure 102B). One reason for the chair's success lay in its low price. Since only a wrench was required to assemble the chair, it was shipped "knocked down," which

Figure 102A
Gilbert Rohde. Side chairs, ca. 1933. Manufactured by Kroehler Manufacturing Company, Grand Rapids, Michigan.

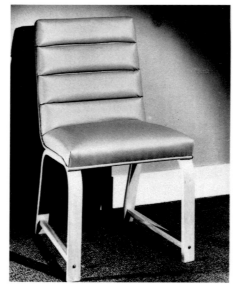 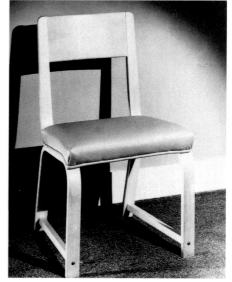

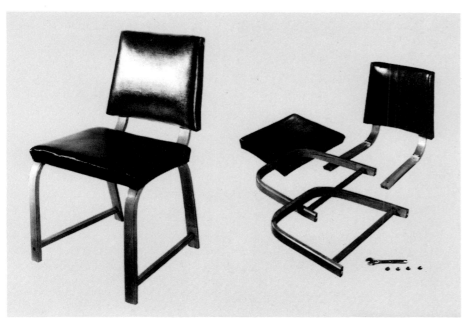

Figure 102B
Gilbert Rohde. Side chair (assembled and disassembled), ca. 1933. Manufactured by Herman Miller Furniture Company, Grand Rapids, Michigan.

reduced costs. The Herman Miller example sold for $9.00 in 1934.

Throughout the 1930s Rohde used the various models of this design in department store installations, where they received favorable critical reviews and strong sales.

103

Stacking stools, Model No. 60
Solid birch (bent portion laminated), birch veneer
17¼ x 13¾ x 13¾ in.
44 x 35 x 35 cm
Designed ca. 1932–33 by Alvar Aalto (born Kuortane, Finland, 1898, died Helsinki 1976)
Manufactured after 1975 by Artek, Helsinki
Museum of Applied Arts, Helsinki

MORE than any other designer of his time, Alvar Aalto was dedicated to the development of furniture that could be stacked efficiently in as small a space as possible. This theme first appeared in his work in 1929, in a design for a stacking side chair which he developed with Otto Korhonen, the technical director of Oy. Huonekalu-ja Rakennustyötehdas, a furniture firm in Turku. Within a decade of that collaboration, Aalto's repertoire of stacking forms had broadened to include tables, chairs, and stools.

103

His most efficient and ultimately most successful design in this body of stacking furniture was the so-called Tower of Babel stool. The design earned this appellation for its resemblance when stacked to the biblical tower that was intended to reach heaven. Aalto's design was such that within a space no greater than the diameter of a single stool, numerous stools could be stacked (figure 103A). A meticulous balance between the lift produced by the seat of each stool when placed upon another and the distance between each of the three legs, produces a triple-helix pattern which, theoretically, could be repeated endlessly.

The curvature of the leg, now known as the "bent knee," was executed by a process that made its first appearance in this stool. The result of a partial laminate, this curvature was created from a board of solid birch. A series of parallel channels were cut into the end of the board that was to be bent in which thin blades of wood were glued. With the ensuing dramatic increase of pliability, the board was then bent into a ninety-degree angle and secured until dry. This simplified means of construction resulted in a leg that was cheaper to produce than one made by traditional joinery or a leg assembled from a complete laminate. This bent-knee leg was eventually applied to numerous seating forms, tables, and platforms for case pieces.

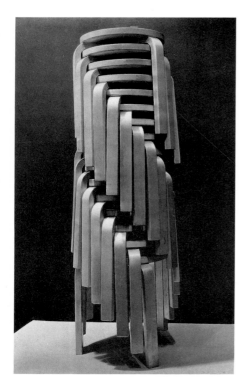

Figure 103A
Alvar Aalto. Stacking stools, ca. 1932–33, shown at the exhibition *Alvar Aalto: Architecture and Furniture*, The Museum of Modern Art, New York, 1938.

104

104

Table, Model No. 915

Laminated wood, plywood (repainted)
24¼ x 23½ x 20⅛ in.
59.5 x 59.5 x 51 cm

Designed ca. 1931–32 by Alvar Aalto (born Kuortane, Finland, 1898, died Helsinki 1976)
Manufactured after 1932 by Oy. Huonekalu-ja Rakennustyötehdas AB, Turku, Finland
Museum of Applied Arts, Helsinki

ALVAR Aalto's earliest furniture designs, which date from the mid-1920s, were only hesitantly modernist; their inspiration was predominantly historicist. Constructed by means of traditional joinery and from conventional materials, this furniture for the most part displayed classicist components stripped to their essential forms. Through his exposure to the work of other progressive architects working in Europe in the late 1920s, Aalto rid himself of these *retardataire* mannerisms in order to design furniture suited for mass production.

Many of these furnishings were developed in the early 1930s while Aalto was completing what would become his most important essay in the International Style, the Paimio Sanitorium. Several of these designs, including this table, were developed specifically for that building. The pair of closed structures that comprise the legs are constructed from laminated wood and the tabletop and shelf are made from bent plywood. The table exhibits an identical use of material to that seen in the so-called Paimio armchair (cat. no. 99), designed during the same year.

105

105

Armchair

Bent plywood, plywood, solid wood, upholstery (modern)
35¼ x 22⅛ x 18 in.
89.5 x 56 x 45.5 cm

Designed ca. 1933–34 by Gerald Summers (born England 1899, died England 1967)
Made after 1934 by Makers of Simple Furniture Ltd., London
The Mitchell Wolfson Jr. Collection of Decorative and Propaganda Arts, Miami

THIS armchair, reportedly once installed in the Richmond Theatre in Kew, England, may have been designed slightly earlier than the technically superior armchair Gerald Summers executed from a single sheet of plywood (cat. no. 106). The chair shown here, though essentially defined by a single sheet of plywood bent into a conical form, is actually constructed from several addi-

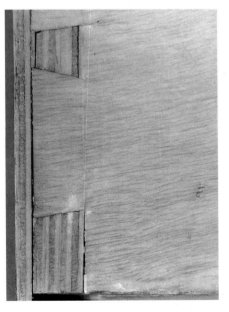

Figure 105A
Dovetails at intersection of front seat rail and side of chair, figure 105B.

Figure 105B
Gerald Summers. Side chair, designed before 1938. Bent laminated birch and upholstery. Manufactured by Makers of Simple Furniture Ltd., London. Barry Friedman Ltd., New York.

106

Armchair
Bent plywood
30⅛ x 24 x 34 in.
76.5 x 61 x 86.5 cm
Designed ca. 1934 by Gerald Summers (born England 1899, died England 1967)
Made after 1934 by Makers of Simple Furniture Ltd., London
The Mitchell Wolfson Jr. Collection of Decorative and Propaganda Arts, Miami

106

tional pieces of wood. The plywood shell of this chair is bound into its curvature by a board of plywood secured by means of dovetails (figure 105A). Unlike the permanently bent form of Summers's one-piece armchair (cat. no. 106), the curve of this chair is dependent upon an auxiliary brace.

The applied arms of solid wood indicate that Summers had to compensate for the basically vertical alignment of the narrow sheet of plywood that was unable to provide the sitter with a comfortable armrest. This flaw would be resolved in the one-piece armchair in which the plywood sheet is disposed horizontally.

A side chair variation of the armchair shown here was also produced by Summers's firm (figure 105B). These designs appeared on the market at the same time that Aalto's bent-wood furniture (cat. nos. 99 and 100) was exhibited in London at Fortnum & Mason in 1933 (figure 5–62).

No design better exemplifies the designer's search for a form that unified materials and manufacturing methods than this masterful armchair by Gerald Summers. Executed from a single sheet of plywood that was dexterously cut in carefully selected places, the design of this chair eliminated the need for any expense-generating, time-consuming joinery or disfiguring hardware. Further, its fluid form, shaped to receive the human body, dispensed with the need for upholstery.

Considering this simplification of elements, it is surprising to note that this chair was advertised in the *Architectural Review* (December 1935, p. 194) for £3 15s, five pence more than the upholstered, more complicated cantilevered chair by Alvar Aalto (cat. no. 100). It is possible that lower labor costs in Finland or the currency exchange rate eliminated Summers's financial edge in the English marketplace, even though his design was the easier of the two chairs to fabricate. In economically depressed England of the 1930s, five pence would have mattered considerably

to many potential buyers. The further popularity of Aalto's work in England may have been due to the fact that his designs were introduced to the British public at the prestigious British store, Fortnum & Mason, which may have enhanced his appeal over that of Summers, a native designer.

Summers's designs were probably executed in small numbers, for examples of his work are rare. However, these chairs were sold in 1934 in New York at James Pendleton (*Art and Decoration*, November 1934, p. 59), where they cost $40.00, and in Chicago they were retailed through Marshall Field.

Summers's design was not part of a larger aesthetic and ideological position, as were Alvar Aalto's furnishing of the early 1930s. According to Marjorie Summers, the de-

signer's widow, this model was the result of a commission that required him to produce a chair suitable for use in the tropics (Deese). Made without joinery, such a chair was less likely to weaken under conditions of extreme heat and humidity, and without upholstery, it was not subject to rot, nor could it become a breeding ground for insects.

Following World War II, the Dutch designer Hans Pieck produced a similar chair constructed from a single sheet of plywood (figure 106A). This design, unlike that of Summers, had a resilient back, which required a metal bar to stabilize this portion of the chair.

107

Tea trolley

Bent plywood, plywood, metal, rubber
26¾ x 37½ x 17 in.
68.5 x 95 x 43 cm

*Designed ca. 1935 by Gerald Summers
(born England 1899, died England 1967)*
*Made after 1935 by Makers of Simple
Furniture Ltd., London*
*Collection Sandy and Sherwin Schreier,
Southfield, Michigan*

Gerald Summers's firm, Makers of Simple Furniture Ltd. in Charlotte Street, London, was founded in 1929. The most gifted of all British furniture designers working in the 1930s, Summers slipped into obscurity during World War II. However, his legacy remains in the body of designs in which he used bent plywood. Like other designers working in England, such as Betty Joel and Marcel Breuer, who were using plywood, Summers may have imported the material from Estonia. With the invasion of the Baltic states by the Germans in the fall of 1939, supplies of this essential material were cut off, preventing further production of Summers's designs. Summers retooled his firm to manufacture ball bearings during the war, and the company never resumed the production of furniture.

107

This tea trolley displays one of the most supple forms created from plywood during the thirties. With a single sheet of plywood bent into a dynamic S-shaped configuration, Summers partially disguised that form by incorporating three parallel boards into the cart to serve as shelves. Made predominantly from four pieces of wood, the cart displays Summers's reductivist approach to materials and form that characterizes his armchair constructed from a single piece of plywood (cat. no. 106). The cart also reflects changing social conditions in Britain during the economically depressed 1930s. The years of World War I saw the drastic reduction in domestic staffs in many households, predicating a need for pieces such as this cart in dining rooms or elsewhere in the house.

108

Tea cart

Bent laminated birch, plywood, solid birch
22 x 18⅛ x 35½ in.
56 x 46 x 90 cm

Designed ca. 1935–36 by Alvar Aalto (born Kuortane, Finland, 1898, died Helsinki, Finland, 1976)
Manufactured after 1936 by Oy. Huonekalu-ja Rakennustyötehdas AB, Turku, Finland
Alexander von Vegesack, Düsseldorf

THIS tea cart was apparently first exhibited at the Triannale di Milano (Milan Triennial) of 1936, where it was included in an installation of Aalto's work. With side elements fashioned from single pieces of bent laminated wood, as was the so-called Paimio chair (cat. no. 99), the tea trolley was neither a technological nor aesthetic advance over Aalto's earlier designs, which had captured the attention of the progressive design community during the first half of the 1930s. In his use of the continuous side elements that incorporated sled runners, Aalto paid homage to earlier chairs in tubular steel by Marcel Breuer (cat. nos. 72 and 78) and Mies van der Rohe (cat. nos. 70 and 71).

108

109

Chaise longue

Bent plywood, laminated wood, solid wood
30¾ x 24¼ x 56 in.
78 x 61.5 x 142 cm

Designed ca. 1935 by Marcel Breuer (born Pécs, Hungary, 1902, died New York 1981)

Manufactured after 1936 by Isokon Furniture Company, London

Château Dufresne, Musée des Arts Décoratifs de Montréal, Canada (Collection Liliane & David M. Stewart)

MARCEL Breuer arrived in England in 1935, following the lead of Walter Gropius, who had emigrated the previous year. Gropius, Breuer's mentor at the Bauhaus more than a decade earlier, secured employment for his colleague by introducing him to Jack Pritchard, who had founded the Isokon Furniture Company in 1935. Pritchard had a thorough knowledge of furniture technology acquired through years of employment with the Venestra Plywood Company, and he now sought to capitalize on the growing appreciation for modern furniture in England by producing furnishings made of plywood. The success of Alvar Aalto's all-wood furniture shown in London in 1933 (cat. nos. 99 and 100) had been instrumental in creating a market for such designs. With this introduction to Breuer, Pritchard came into contact with an individual whose experience with progressive furniture was unmatched for its breadth. Breuer's experimentation during the 1920s and early 1930s with a variety of new materials, techniques of production, and innovative forms had placed him in the forefront of modernist design.

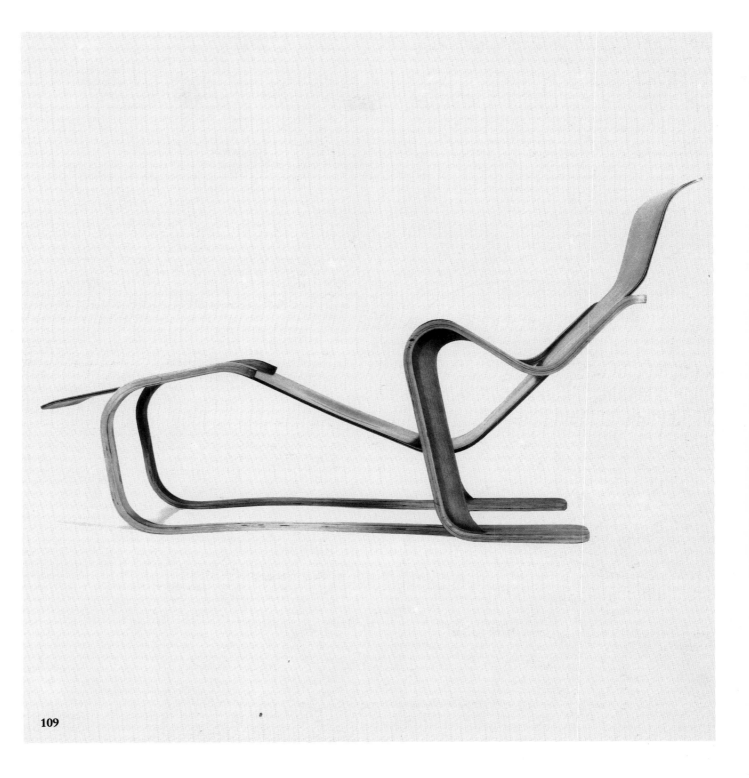

109

Although all-wood elements had been incorporated into some of Breuer's designs prior to his emigration to England, none had relied solely on that material as a means of expression. This chaise longue is part of Breuer's first body of designs for Isokon. Breuer translated into wood a bent aluminum and wood design he had produced in Switzerland several years earlier (figure 109B). Unfortunately, this transformation of materials produced a design seriously flawed in the resolution of the join between the bed of the chaise and its structural support system. A tenon extending from the plywood sheet of the back and the seat into a mortise cut into the laminated frame resulted in a join that had a tendency to loosen through continued use. In his designs of the early 1930s, Alvar Aalto was faced with a similar problem: how to retain structural stability without compromising the simplicity of the design. Ultimately, Aalto used auxiliary braces of solid wood in his so-called Paimio table and chair (cat. nos. 104 and 99) and in the numerous variations of his cantilevered armchair (cat. no. 100), all of which were constructed from sheets of plywood attached to laminated frames. It would not be until the 1950s that Jack Pritchard attained a degree of success with Breuer's design through the use of similar subsidiary braces.

Figure 109A
Alternate view.

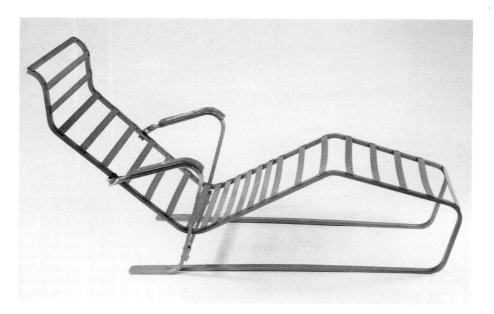

Figure 109B
Marcel Breuer. Frame of chaise longue, ca. 1935. Bent aluminum, aluminum, wood (painted). Manufactured by Embru-Werke AG, Rüti, Zurich. Barry Friedman Ltd., New York.

110

Club chair, Model No. B1001

Bent solid wood, solid wood, cane, upholstery
25 x 26¼ x 26 in.
63.5 x 67 x 66 cm

Designer unknown, ca. 1936
Manufactured after 1936 by Thonet-Mundus-J. & J. Kohn, Vienna
Morton Abromson, New York

THE bold use of a massive continuous piece of bent wood to define the structure of this club chair is reminiscent of designs produced by Otto Wagner (cat. no. 46) and Gustav Siegel (cat. no. 38) over three decades earlier. Unlike the piece of bent wood used in those designs, this robust element could not be incorporated into various models produced by the Kohn firm, as was the practice with the standardized elements of other bent wood designs. Unlike the interchangeable pieces of bent wood used in the earlier work, the massive piece of bent wood used in this chair was difficult to execute, expensive to produce, and impossible to incorporate in any other of the firm's models. By denying the irre-

ducible virtues of bent-wood furniture—substitution of standardized elements, ease of manufacture, and low cost—the manufacturer of this design was apparently intending it less for the general market than for the luxury trade. This richly upholstered chair would have been particularly suitable in the lounges of fine hotels and similar commercial establishments.

Although often described as one of Josef Hoffmann's late works (Munich 1981a, p. 50), this piece was most likely the creation of an in-house designer—perhaps Gustav Siegel, who was working for the Thonet-Mundus-J. & J. Kohn combine following the merger of these industry giants in 1922 (Wilk 1980a, p. 78).

The absence of Hoffmann's name in connection with this chair in any of the firm's catalogues or any trade publications of the period further weakens the Hoffmann attribution. The chair was produced at a time when designers of bent-wood and tubular-steel furniture were customarily credited with their output, and it would have been unusual for the firm to market this design without mentioning Josef Hoffmann, whose name still carried considerable prestige in the 1930s.

110

111

Chaise longue with book rest

Solid birch, laminated birch, plywood, metal, fabric

32½ x 21½ x 57⅞ in.
81.5 x 54.5 x 147 cm

Designed ca. 1940 by Bruno Mathsson (born Värnamo, Sweden, 1907)
Manufactured after 1940 by Firma Karl Mathsson, Värnamo, Sweden
Alexander von Vegesack, Düsseldorf

SWEDEN had dominated progressive design circles in Scandanavia in the 1920s with its elitist modernist essays executed in luxurious materials. However, Sweden abdicated that position at the 1930 Stockhomlsuställningen (Stockholm Fair). Organized by the distinguished architect Gunnar Asplund, the fair attempted to show that Sweden was deeply committed to the functionalist Neue Sachlichkeit (New Objectivity) mentality of many of its German compatriots. The grafting of this massive, ideological "about-face" to Swedish circumstances was considered by many to be unnatural, and the progressive edge in Scandanavia was determined in the 1930s by a Finn, Alvar Aalto.

By the end of the thirties, one Swedish designer, Bruno Mathsson, displayed a virtuosity that differed in part from Aalto's.

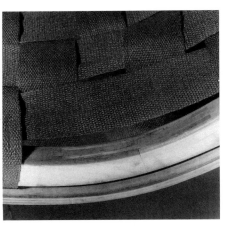

Figure 111A
Bruno Mathsson. Finger (box) joint of frame of chaise longue. Barry Friedman Ltd., New York.

Adopting a more luxurious aesthetic still determined by undulant lines and the use of wood, Mathsson became a leading figure in Swedish design circles.

Only the base of this chaise is constructed from laminated wood that has been bent. The upper frame, which supports the canvas webbing, is constructed from sections of solid wood cut into curves and joined by finger (box) joints (figure 111A).

The son of a cabinetmaker, Mathsson had his designs executed by his father's firm.

111

112

112

Traction leg splint
Molded plywood
4 x 8 x 41¾ in.
10 x 20.5 x 106 cm

Designed 1942 by Charles Eames (born Saint Louis 1907, died Venice, California, 1978) and Ray Kaiser Eames (dates not provided)
Manufactured ca. 1942 by the Evans Products Company, Los Angeles
Collection Catherine Kurland, New York

Developed by Charles and Ray Eames for wartime use by the U.S. Navy, this leg splint is included here because it straddles the technologies of the 1930s and the following decade. Flat curves, as seen in Aalto's so-called Paimio chairs and his cantilevered chairs (cat. nos. 98, 99, 100), defined the general tenor of avant-garde furniture design in the 1930s. Within a decade of the introduction of those designs, technological developments involving the molding of laminates permitted cusped or shaped complex curves, allowing for an expansion of the formal repertoire of progressive furniture designs. Although Alvar Aalto experimented with this concept in the early 1930s (cat. no. 101), it would appear that he did not apply it to mass production, and in fact he discarded the idea from later experiments.

Although the leg splint was successfully produced in large numbers, it nevertheless reflects the limitations of the Eameses' technical capability in 1941. To prevent tearing of the outer veneers when the flat sheets of plywood were molded, incisions were cut across the outer layer of the plywood splint. These cuts separated when the form was molded and reduced stress in the layers that were stretched the most (figure 112A). Three years later, in a design for a child's chair, the Eameses solved the problem of tearing without resorting to this device (cat. no. 113).

According to Ray Eames (communication to author), the metal splints in use at the beginning of World War II were secured directly to the leg. The pressure created by this contact failed to provide adequate support, and also often induced gangrene. The molded form of the Eameses' splint protected the leg and provided traction for broken bones. Lightweight and stackable (figure 5–76), these splints were readily transportable.

The original model of the splint was molded to Charles Eames's leg and then altered to more universal specifications.

Figure 112A
Detail.

113

Child's chair

Molded birch plywood (stained)
13¾ x 13¼ x 11 in.
35 x 33.5 x 28 cm

*Designed ca. 1944 by Charles Eames (born
Saint Louis 1907, died Venice, California,
1978) and Ray Kaiser Eames (dates not
provided)*
*Manufactured after 1944 by the Evans
Products Company, Los Angeles*
*Château Dufresne, Musée des Arts Décoratifs
de Montréal, Canada (Collection Liliane &
David M. Stewart)*

THE child's chair represents a significant
step in the development of the shell aesthetic that was inaugurated in the late 1920s
and early 1930s in the chairs of such designers as Gerrit Rietveld (cat. no. 73) and
Alvar Aalto (cat. nos. 98–101), which was
characterized by flat curves executed from
bent laminated wood. By the early 1940s,
complex curves determined the appearance of progressive seating forms. In the
designs of chairs, the shaped curve of the
plywood, which cradled the human body,
eliminated the need for upholstery without affecting the comfort of the design.
Omission of upholstery reduced production costs as well.

The shape of the perforation in the back
of the chair, actually a handhold for children, was felt by many to be a sentimental
gesture out of keeping with the progressive aesthetic and technical innovations of
the design. According to Ray Eames (communication to author), approximately five
thousand of these chairs were produced
in red, blue, yellow, and green stains as
well as in a natural finish.

113

114

Child's table

Molded birch plywood
16¼ x 26½ x 15½ in.
41.5 x 67.5 x 39.5 cm

Designed ca. 1944 by Charles Eames (born Saint Louis 1907, died Venice, California, 1978) and Ray Kaiser Eames (dates not provided)
Manufactured after 1944 by Evans Products Company, Los Angeles
Fifty-50 Gallery, New York

IN terms of form, materials, and technology, this small table is among the most simple of all the designs included here. Like the armchair by Gerald Summers (cat. no. 106), this table, made more than a decade later, was constructed from a single sheet of plywood. And like the genesis of Marcel Breuer's nesting tables (cat. no. 68), it is closely linked to a seating form, the Eameses' child's chair (cat. no. 113).

The simplicity of the design is deceptive. The subtle swelling of the plywood at the legs reveals the emerging technological innovations that would be brilliantly realized in the Eameses' chairs shown in 1946 at the Museum of Modern Art in New York (cat. nos. 116 and 117). In those designs the complex molding of the materials would be handled in a confident, dynamic manner; here the treatment is more hesitant. Rather than fully resolve the transition of the table's legs into the front and back skirts, the Eameses chose to cut into the skirts at this intersection, thus reducing the stress at crucial points. Nevertheless, the Eameses molded the plywood in this design for reasons other than the purely aesthetic. The work surface of this child's table, sometimes identified as a desk, has been molded with a functional rectilinear depression whose outer lip helps contain spilled liquids, crayons, and toys.

114

Coffee table

Molded plywood, bent plywood, rubber, metal

15½ x 34⅛ x 34⅛ in.
39.5 x 87 x 87 cm

Designed 1946 by Charles Eames (born Saint Louis 1907, died Venice, California, 1978) and Ray Kaiser Eames (dates not provided)
Manufactured after 1946 by the Herman Miller Furniture Company, Grand Rapids, Michigan

Barry Friedman Ltd., New York

INTRODUCED at the same time as the 1946 exhibition of the Eameses' work at the Museum of Modern Art in New York, this table was perhaps the most subtle of their designs in bent wood produced at the time. The impact of the shallow impression in the center of the table is lessened, to a degree, by the fact that the outer line of the table mirrors this form. In addition, the run of the wood grain obscures this masterful, compound curve. Originally mass produced by the Evans Products Company of Los Angeles, the table, like all the Eameses' furniture designs, was later produced by the Herman Miller Furniture Company.

115

116

Side chair, Model DCM

Molded ash plywood, bent steel rod, rubber, metal

29¼ x 20¼ x 21½ in.
74.5 x 51.5 x 54.5 cm

Designed 1946 by Charles Eames (born Saint Louis 1907, died Venice, California, 1978) and Ray Kaiser Eames (dates not provided)
Manufactured after 1946 by the Herman Miller Furniture Company, Grand Rapids, Michigan

Museum of Fine Arts, Boston (Gift of Edward J Wormley)

ALTHOUGH not the first design to combine bent wood and bent metal (see cat. no. 73), the DCM (Dining Chair Metal) side chair was the first mass-produced chair to use complexly molded plywood with a steel structure. By means of a much thinner gauge of steel rod than had been used by earlier furniture designers, the Eameses combined a delicate structural support system with sweeping panels of plywood to create a design of strong contrasts. Emphasis on the dichotomy between the "support" and "supported" was part of the unwritten functionalist code that had pervaded much of architecture and design since World War I. Here, minimal contact between the chair's metal frame (support) and the wooden elements of seat and back (supported) provided by shock mounts electronically bonded to the wood introduces a remarkable degree of resiliency to

the design. The small, metal pad feet, known as glides (and within the furniture-making trades as "domes of silence"), made it possible to move the chair around with ease.

The chair shown here appeared in the 1946 exhibition of the Eameses' work at the Museum of Modern Art in New York. After the show closed, Charles Eames presented this chair to designer Edward Wormley, who gave it to the Museum of Fine Arts, Boston, nearly a quarter of a century later.

116

Side chair, Model DCW

Molded walnut plywood, bent walnut plywood, rubber, metal
28¾ x 19¼ x 20½ in.
73 x 49 x 52 cm

Designed 1946 by Charles Eames (born Saint Louis 1907, died Venice, California, 1978) and Ray Kaiser Eames (dates not provided)
Manufactured 1946 by the Evans Products Company, Los Angeles
Museum of Fine Arts, Boston (Gift of Edward J Wormley)

THE abbreviation DCW was employed by the Herman Miller Furniture Company for "Dining Chair Wood," which differentiated this example from the metal version (cat. no. 116). Neither chair bore such appellations when they were first manufactured after World War II by the Evans Products Company of Los Angeles, which had also made the Eameses' traction leg splint (cat. no. 112) for the U.S. Navy. In 1946, the Evans Products Company sold its production rights to the Eameses' designs to the Herman Miller Furniture Company prior to the exhibition of this work at the Museum of Modern Art in New York in 1946 (communication of Ray Eames to the author).

The complex, dished curve the Eameses had introduced in the leg splint was brilliantly realized in their series of seating designs in which the shaped shell of the seats and backs offered the optimum in comfort in low-cost seating produced immediately following the war. This concept eliminated the need for labor-intensive upholstery and therefore reduced costs and made these designs available to a large public. The flat, unshaped curves used by such earlier designers as Gerrit Rietveld (cat. no. 73), Alvar Aalto (cat. nos. 98–100), and Gerald Summers (cat. no. 106) failed to provide this innovation.

The exclusive use of wood in this design presented the Eameses with a further challenge: how to secure these elements with-

out marring the appearance of the chair with unsightly bolts, like those used in Rietveld's work (cat. no. 73) and several of Aalto's designs, including his child's chair (cat. no. 98). Using a welding system developed by the Chrysler Corporation just prior to World War II (Drexler, p. 12), the Eameses electrostatically secured large rubber disks to the undersides of these molded pieces of wood. These pliable rings not only provided a means of secure, hidden joinery, but also introduced a degree of resiliency to the seats and backs of these chairs.

Unlike the earlier bent-wood furnishings developed by Aalto, which were intended to be consistent with his architectural doctrine, these designs by the Eameses carried no such programmatic overtones. By 1950 (Herman Miller Catalogue, 1950), these molded forms had been translated into fiberglass and wire shells for seating forms (Drexler, pp. 34–36), which supplanted bent and molded wood at the forefront of progressive furniture design.

117

118

Folding screen

Bent birch plywood (stained), canvas
68 x ¼ x 60 in.
174 x .6 x 152.5 cm

Designed 1946 by Charles Eames (born Saint Louis 1907, died Venice, California, 1978) and Ray Kaiser Eames (dates not provided)
Manufactured after 1946 by the Herman Miller Furniture Company, Grand Rapids, Michigan
Château Dufresne, Musée des Arts Décoratifs de Montréal, Canada

(Collection Liliane & David M. Stewart)

DURING the 1930s, Finnish design provided a radical alternative to the modernist design aesthetic that had been shaped a decade earlier by German, French, and Dutch designers. The Finns' masterful use of biomorphic forms and natural materials contrasted vividly with the modernist reli-

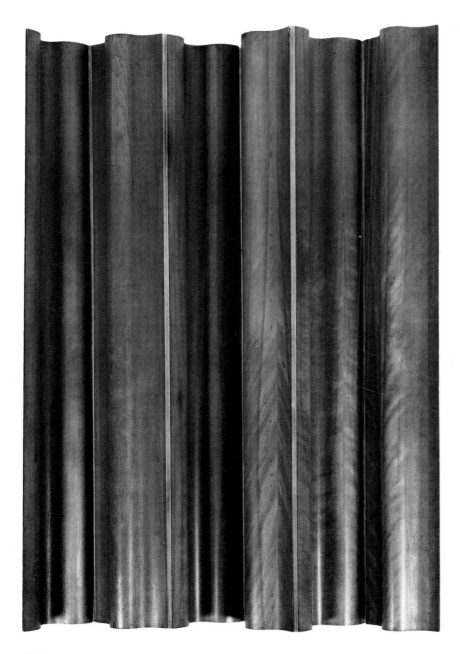

**Arthur Mack. Flexible screens,
ca. 1937–39. Marketed by Artek.**

ance on geometric forms, reinforced concrete, and tubular steel. The Finnish Pavilion at the 1939 New York World's Fair was critically acclaimed. This enormous showcase of Finnish artistry was designed by Alvar Aalto, whose work was already known in the United States. Through the merchandising efforts of his firm, Artek, Aalto's furniture had been seen in America before 1939. Included in the Artek line was a remarkable screen designed by Arthur Mack (figure 118A). Constructed of flat strips of wood connected by pliable canvas hinges, this fluid essay was in the forefront of the Finnish aesthetic in the years before the war.

Although the screen by Charles and Ray Eames resonates with the spirit of the earlier Artek design, it has greater stability and exploits brilliantly the technique of bending materials, which its predecessor had not. When the screen was moved, the ingenious configuration of its elements permitted each leaf to act as the receptacle for the adjacent blade of bent wood. This compact arrangement made the screen easily transportable, but it has also proved to be one of the most fragile of the Eameses' designs, as the canvas strips have a tendency to disintegrate.

The screen was available in a variety of lengths, heights, and finishes.

119

Desk

Molded plywood, bent laminated wood
30 x 44 x 23 in.
76 x 112 x 58.5 cm

Designed ca. 1946 by Paul R. Goldman
(born Boston 1912)
Manufactured after 1946 by Plymold
Corporation, Lawrence, Massachusetts
Museum of Fine Arts, Boston (Axelrod
Collection)

Like so many innovations in the decorative arts during the late 1940s, this desk benefited from the technological advancements brought about by the American war effort. According to the designer of this desk, his firm had been engaged during the war in the production of radio antenna masts constructed from molded plywood tubing for the U.S. Army Air Corps and Signal Corps. Following the armistice in 1945, his firm sought to retain production and employment levels by diversifying its products, and, this desk was one result.

Figure 119A
Detail of drawer.

The bent conformation of the outer shell of this case piece recalls the technique employed by Charles and Ray Eames in the production of their leg splint for the U.S. Navy (cat. no. 112). Sections of plywood were removed at the corners of the desk in order to achieve the compound curve without tearing the outer layers of the wood. Bent laminates were used for the secondary elements of the desk—the curved sides and backs. This made it possible to construct the drawers (figure 119A) from three pieces of wood rather than the five that are common with traditional joinery techniques. This methodology theoretically reduced production costs.

In its sleek, balanced proportions, the desk reflects the streamlined forms characteristic of the 1930s American design community. However, unlike the earlier designs, the streamlining was a result of the constructional components—the pieces of bent plywood—and not simply an applied effect.

According to the designer and manufacturer of this desk, the model was produced only from the end of World War II until 1947, when the Plymold Corporation went out of business. During those few years, it manufactured bedroom furniture and desks from molded plywood.

119

APPENDIX

Bent-wood furniture manufacturers

1849–1914

GRAHAM DRY

The third edition of W. F. Exner, *Das Biegen des Holzes*, published in 1893, was edited and enlarged by Georg Lauboeck. It contains a list (pages 30–31) of fifty-two firms known to be manufacturers of bent-wood furniture. Lauboeck had intended to present a complete list of firms, but his aim was thwarted because only a "few" companies responded to his request for information. The list presented here includes those firms cited by Lauboeck, but adds many whose names have since come to light; however, it is still by no means complete. In 1893 Lauboeck had hoped to "present a faithful picture of the bent-wood furniture industry, which has developed at a colossal speed," but even today this wish cannot be fulfilled.

The manufacturers are listed alphabetically, by country, according to nineteenth-century political divisions. The map of Europe has changed dramatically since 1840, and as borders have shifted the spelling of place names has changed accordingly. Those given after the manufacturers' names are the versions that applied until 1918; names in parentheses are the modern forms of both cities and countries. The Austro-Hungarian Empire, until its dissolution in 1918, encompassed parts of modern-day Czechoslovakia, Italy, Poland, Romania, and other countries. Firms that were originally located within the empire's borders are listed under the general heading for the Austro-Hungarian Empire.

Austro-Hungarian Empire

Altman és Huber/Máramarossziget, Hungary (Sighetul Marmației, Romania)

Furniture produced by this firm bears a paper label with, on the left, the illustration of a bent-wood rocking chair and, on the right, the words *Első máramarosi hajlitott butor és faárugyár / ALTMAN és HUBER / MÁRAMAROSSZIGET* (First Maramaros Bentwood Furniture Factory, Máramarossziget). See below, Sighet Co., Romania.

Altman ès Huber. Trademark label, ca. 1900. Private collection, Munich.

R. A. Bernkopf, Frenstat (Czechoslovakia)

Founded in 1883.

Reference: Jaromíra Šimoniková, letter to the author, April 26, 1986.

Florijan Bobič, Warasdin (Varaždin, Yugoslavia)

Founded in 1892, the firm was a member of the Mundus group (see below) until World War II.

Reference: Bang, pp. 111–12.

Ladislaus Dobrovits & Komp., Turócz Szt. Martón (Martin, Czechoslovakia)

Founded in 1889, the company had two branch factories by 1893.

Reference: Exner and Lauboeck 1893, p. 30.

Josias Eissler & Söhne, Kaschau (Košice, Czechoslovakia)

This company may be identical to the firm of J. Eisler & Söhne, lumber merchant at Nibelungengasse 7, Vienna, which exhibited "flagpoles" at the 1873 Vienna World Exhibition.

References: Vienna 1873c, p. 277, No. 64; Exner and Lauboeck 1893, p. 301; Massobrio and Portoghesi 1976, p. 60.

Jos. Farsky, Marburg (Maribor) and Windischgraz (Slovenj Gradec, Yugoslavia)

Reference: Exner and Lauboeck 1893, p. 30.

D. G. Fischel Söhne, Erste Böhmische Fabrik von Möbeln aus Massiv Gebogenem Holze, Niemes, Böhmen (Mimoň, Czechoslovakia)

Founded in January 1870 by the brothers Alexander and Gustav Fischel, the firm had representatives in Berlin, Cologne, Hamburg, Pest, Prague, and Rotterdam by 1873. In 1878 a head office was opened in Vienna, at Kohlmarkt 6; after several changes of address, a permanent headquarters was finally established in 1907 at Tuchlauben 11. By 1893 four branch factories were in operation. Some time before 1904 the firm was taken over by Ernst Hirsch, Vienna; in 1927 it passed to his son Richard. During these years Fischel won various awards, such as a Gold Medal at the Allgemeine Hygienische Ausstellung (Hygiene Exhibition) at Vienna in 1906, a Gold Medal the next year again in Vienna at the exhibition *Das Kind* (The Child), and a Gold Medal at the Exposition Universelle in Paris in 1925.

In 1930, main factories existed in Niemes, Wissembourg (Weissenburg), Alsace, and Valisoara (Romania). The company was expropriated in 1938; the Wissembourg factory continued production under the management of August Meder with the assistance of the former Czechoslovakian manager, Richter. Until 1945 Meder, proprietor of the Erste Acherner Stuhl-Fabrik August Klar, in Achern, Germany (see below), was head of the combined undertaking known as the August Meder Stuhl-Fabriken, vormals August Klar, Achern-Baden und Weissenburg-Elsass (August Meder Chair Factories, formerly August Klar, Achern-Baden and Weissenburg-Alsace).

References: Vienna 1873d, p. 277; Vienna 1906, p. 72, No. 288 (patent school benches); Vienna 1907; Paris 1925, p. 473; *Fischel 1870–1930*; Handelsgericht Wien, Handelsregister, Abt. A, No. 24/52; Abt. B, No. 38/225; Massobrio and Portoghesi 1976, ill. p. 60; Šimoníková.

Fiumaner Möbelfabrik-Aktiengesellschaft, Fiume (Rijeka, Yugoslavia)

Reference: Exner and Lauboeck 1893, p. 30.

Friedrich Flaschner, Bodenbach (Děčín, Czechoslovakia)

Reference: Exner and Lauboeck 1893, p. 30.

Ignaz Fuchs, Krakau (Cracow, Poland)

The firm exhibited bent-wood furniture at the Galizische Landesausstellung (Galician National Exhibition) held in Krakau in 1887 and was commended in a contemporary magazine for the "extremely neat workmanship of its products," although the pieces displayed old-fashioned constructive elements.

Reference: Neužil, p. 183.

Brüder Gross & Komp., Windisch-Feistritz (Slovenska Bistrica, Yugoslavia)

Reference: Exner and Lauboeck 1893, p. 30.

S. Gruber, Kamnitz (Kamenice, Czechoslovakia)

Reference: Exner and Lauboeck 1893, p. 30.

Oswald Hafenrichter & Komp., Pöltschach (Poljcane, Yugoslavia)

Reference: Exner and Lauboeck 1893, p. 30.

Harnisch & Komp., Neusohl (Banská Býstrica, Czechoslovakia)

Reference: Exner and Lauboeck 1893, p. 30.

Jos. Hoffmann, Bielitz (Bielsko-Biała, Poland)

Reference: Exner and Lauboeck 1893, p. 30.

Holzindustrie-Aktiengesellschaft, Borosjenő (Ineu, Romania)

Reference: Exner and Lauboeck 1893, p. 31.

Brüder Hornung, Kronstadt (Braşov, Romania)

Reference: Exner and Lauboeck 1893, p. 31.

Josef Jaworek, Teschen (Cieszyn, Poland)

In 1907 Josef Jaworek became one of the directors of Mundus (see below).

References: Exner and Lauboeck 1893, p. 30; Handelsgericht Wien, Handelsregister, Abt. B, No. 24/52.

Konrad Keller, Klagenfurt (Austria)

The name of Bonifac Keller, a carpenter, first appears in Klagenfurt guild records in 1812. His son Konrad took over the family business in 1845; parquet flooring, veneers, and furniture were produced in the following years. Konrad Keller died in 1876, and the business was carried on by his widow and two sons, Julius, who had studied furniture-making in Germany and France, and Josef. The production of solid bent-wood

furniture began in 1880/81 at Waagplatz No. 5–5a, and the 1880s were a period of great expansion for the firm. Various patents were applied for, and two hundred chairs a day were produced, with sales to Cairo, Alexandria, and the Levant. By 1895 the firm was called Julius Keller. By 1910 additional factories, not only for bent-wood furniture, were in operation at Welzenegg No. 2 and An der Walk No. 5–6. A branch factory was established in Marburg (Maribor, Yugoslavia) shortly before 1900.

References: Exner and Lauboeck 1893, p. 30; Kleinmayer; Julius Keller Centenary album 1912; Invoice letterhead 1910–19; Documentation in the Kärntner Landesarchiv, Klagenfurt (Director Hofrat Universitäts-Dozent Dr. Alfred Ogis).

Mihály Keszey, Stuhlweissenburg (Székesfehérvár, Hungary)

Reference: Exner and Lauboeck 1893, p. 31.

Jacob & Josef Kohn, Vienna (Austria)

The Kohn family firm was founded in 1850, probably in Wsetin, Moravia (Vsetín, Czechoslovakia), as a producer of lumber. Jacob Kohn went into partnership with his son Josef (1814–1884) on November 8, 1867. Their factory in Wsetin was built toward the end of 1869. Other factories were situated in Litsch, Moravia, 1869; Krakau (Cracow, Poland), 1871; Teschen (Cieszyn, Poland), 1871; Keltsch (Kelč, Czechoslovakia), Gross-Poremba, and Radomsk (Radomsko, Poland), 1885; and Holleschau (Holešov, Czechoslovakia), 1890.

At the expiration of Thonet Brothers's patent in 1869, Jacob & Josef Kohn immediately became Thonet's most serious rival. In the 1870s and 1880s, the firm imitated and varied successful Thonet models, often adopting the Thonet model numbers for identical chairs of their own production. Jacob & Josef Kohn's development was marked, as was that of Thonet Brothers, by a

persistent interest in the improvement of bent wood technology, and in 1878 the firm introduced a machine for the production of circular seat frames. In an attempt to widen the scope of bent-wood furniture during these years, the firm developed a range of furniture that combined conventional framed, carved, and joined seating with bent-wood elements. In 1887 examples were shown at the Galizische Landesausstellung (Galician National Exhibition), in Krakau, where Kohn exhibited in a pavilion of its own design, presumably made of bent wood, which a contemporary observer criticized as "peculiar." Shortly before this date, the firm had enlisted the services of the Viennese architect N. Hofmann (dates unknown), teacher of architectural drawing at the Technologisches Gewerbe-Museum (Technological Trade Museum) in Vienna. Kohn exhibited a "smoking-room" designed by Hofmann at the 1885 Antwerp World Exhibition, which demonstrated very successfully, in the words of a contemporary report, "that the technique of bent wood could also be made serviceable to artistic requirements." This is the earliest reference found so far to an association between a bent wood firm and an outside designer, and it anticipates by almost fifteen years Jacob & Josef Kohn's first steps toward a permanent collaboration with architects and designers of the modern Viennese school.

The fame of the Jacob & Josef Kohn company derives from this association with architects and designers from the turn of the century onward. It introduced a new concept of bent-wood furniture that allowed seating and other elements of interior decoration to reflect the most modern and indeed avant-garde features of contemporary Viennese design. This development was furthered around 1907 when the firm succeeded in bending rods of square cross section at sharp angles. This technical improvement enabled the production of furniture, such as Josef Hoffmann's adjustable arm chair No. 670 (cat. no. 56), which

Jacob & Josef Kohn. Trademark label, ca. 1907.

could take its place as an element of a uniform scheme of interior decoration that relied on the use of squares and cubic forms. In 1899, the firm produced chairs designed by Adolf Loos for the billiard room of the Café Museum in Vienna, and in the same year, Felix Kohn, the firm's proprietor, appointed Gustav Siegel, a pupil of Josef Hoffmann at the Wiener Kunstgewerbeschule (Vienna School of Applied Arts), as head of the firm's design department. Siegel was probably responsible for a majority of the designs produced between 1899 and 1914, the year in which Jacob & Josef Kohn merged with the Mundus company (see below). During this period, the golden age of bent wood design, Siegel supervised the production of furniture by such leading figures as Otto Wagner, Josef Hoffmann, Koloman Moser, and Hans (brother of Otto) Prutscher.

In 1907, the Kohn factories employed about 6,000 workers and were producing about 7,000 pieces of furniture daily. The firm was awarded a Grand Prix at the 1900 Paris Exposition Universelle. In 1901, Jacob & Josef Kohn built the Hall of Honour (*Ehrenhalle*) after Gustav Siegel's design for the Austrian section at the Glasgow International Exhibition. The firm participated in the 1901 Winter Exhibition at the Österreichisches Museum für Kunst und Industrie in Vienna, the International Exhibition of Modern Decorative Arts in Turin in 1902, and the Louisiana Purchase Exhibition in Saint Louis in 1904. Kohn also showed at exhibitions in Milan, London, and Bucharest in 1906, at the Kunstschau in Vienna in 1908, and in Buenos Aires and Munich in 1910. The firm's final exhibition as an autonomous company was at the Cologne Werkbundausstellung of 1914, at which bent wood furniture by Josef Hoffmann and his pupils at the Wiener Kunstgewerbeschule was displayed.

References: Vienna 1873c, p. 278; Philadelphia 1876, pp. 41–42; Antwerp 1885a, *Autriche*, Group 2, p. 8, No. 58; Antwerp 1885b; Neužil, p. 183; Exner and Lauboeck 1893, pp. 25–26; Paris 1900b, Vol. 8; Vienna 1900, Groups 12 and 15, p. 182; *Kunst und Handwerk* Vol. 50, no. 5 (February 1900), p. 168, pl. 293; Glasgow 1901, p. 194; "Bugholzmöbel als Stilmöbel"; Vienna 1908b, p. 114; Vienna 1908d; Munich 1910, p. 54; Cologne 1914a, pl. 621; Eisler, ill. p. 30; Munich 1979, nos. 25–27, 32, 35–46, 48, 52, 55, 57, 60, 64–82, 87, 93; Dry 1979b; Candilis, pp. 25–45, 68–69, 78–83; Müller, pp. 159–66; Dry 1980; Wilk 1980a, pp. 60–70; Behal, pp. 61–62, 139–42, 176–78; Vienna 1981, pp. 294–99; Munich 1981b; Ruckshcio and Schachel 1982, pp. 418–19; Asenbaum et al., pp. 87, 200, 210–11, 302.

Rudolf Lazar, Niemes (Mimoň, Czechoslovakia)

Founded in 1896 by Rudolf Lazar and Emil Kreher. Catalogues were published between 1901 and 1911. The company exported about ninety percent of its production.

Reference: Šimoniková.

Jakob Löbl, Hustopetsch (Hustopeče near Hranice, Czechoslovakia)

Reference: Exner and Lauboeck 1893, p. 30.

Ferdinand Meézas Komp., Windisch-Feistritz (Slovenska Bistrica, Yugoslavia)

Reference: Exner and Lauboeck 1893, p. 30.

Josef Meisels, Krakau (Cracow, Poland)

Exhibitor at the Galizische Landesausstellung (Galician National Exhibition) held in Krakau in 1887.

Reference: Neužil, p. 183.

Mundus, Vienna (Austria)

Mundus, a group of sixteen minor Austro-Hungarian bent-wood furniture companies, was founded on August 20, 1907, in Vienna, on the initiative of Leopold Pilzer. The company's capital amounted to four million kronen. Rudolf Weill & Co. (see below), Florijan Bobič (see above), and Josef Jaworek (see above) in Teschen (Cieszyn, Poland) are known to have been members; others probably were Harnisch & Komp. (see above), Holzindustrie-Aktiengesellschaft (see above), J. Sommer (see below), and Ungvárer Möbelfabriks-Aktiengesellschaft (see below). On August 16, 1914, Mundus merged with J. & J. Kohn; Kohn-Mundus in turn merged with Thonet AG in 1922 to form the Thonet-Mundus-J. & J. Kohn company. Mundus was dissolved on June 22, 1928, and deleted from the Handelsgericht Wien (Vienna Company Register) on December 28 of that year.

References: Sales catalogue, excerpt, 1913; Handelsgericht Wien, Handelsregister, Abt. B, No. 1/190; Massobrio and Portoghesi 1976, pp. 79–80; Bang, p. 111; Wilk, 1980a, pp. 77–78, 82–83, 118–119; Massobrio and Portoghesi 1980, p. 68.

Mundus. Trademark. Sales catalogue of Mundus, ca. 1908. (From Massobrio and Portoghesi 1976, p. 79).

E. Neuss, Pöltschach (Poljčane, Yugoslavia)

Reference: Exner and Lauboek 1893, p. 30.

Josef Neyger, Hernals near Vienna (Austria)

In 1873 Neyger's establishment was at Mittenbergstrasse 19, where bent-wood furniture was manufactured by the early Thonet method of glued laminated veneers; Neyger was still using this technique in 1876.

References: Vienna 1873c, p. 279, no. 143; Vienna 1873a, p. 497; *Kunst und Gewerbe* 1873, p. 353; Exner 1876, p. 24.

The Original Austrian Bent Wood Furniture Co., London

The company's address in 1882 was 3 Newgate Street, London E.C. It may have been an importer rather than a manufacturer.

References: *Cabinet Maker and Art Furnisher*, June 1882 (advertisement); Wilk 1980a, pp. 44–45.

E. M. Schlosser, Drholetz (Drnholec) Moravia, Czechoslovakia

E. M. Schlosser exhibited a new method of bent-wood chair construction at an exhibition held in Vienna in 1882, at which were shown the results of a competition organized by the Technologisches Gewerbe-Museum (Technological Trade Museum) for technical improvements in chair construction. Schlosser had developed a reliable and practical method of affixing the seat to the back element and to the front legs without the use of screws or tenons. His improvement consisted of forming the backrest and front legs from a single length of bent wood, thereby increasing stability. The inner part of the backrest and the back legs were also made from a single length of bent wood, which meant that the chair consisted of only three pieces of bent wood. This made it eminently suitable for export. Instead of caning, Schlosser used a perforated seat or bent beechwood strips, which formed both seat and backrest. Schlosser's new method of construction was especially commended by the Jury, which awarded him a Silver Medal.

Reference: Lauboeck 1882, p. 66.

J. Sommer, Mährisch-Weisskirchen (Hranice, Czechoslovakia)

Founded in 1886, with a branch factory in Keltsch (Kelč, Czechoslovakia), the firm is likely to be identical to J. Sommer & Co., bent-wood wholesalers in Dusseldorf and Mannheim, for whom Mundus, Vienna (see above), published a seventeen-page catalogue in 1913.

References: Exner and Lauboeck 1893, p. 30; Mundus sales catalogue, excerpt, 1913.

Karl Swobodas Nachfolger, Altsohl (Zvolen) and N.-Enyed (Ened, Czechoslovakia)

Founded in 1875.

Reference: Exner and Lauboeck 1893, p. 30.

Teibler & Seemann, Oberleutensdorf, Böhmen (Litvínov, Czechoslovakia)

Teibler & Seemann, Fabrik massiv gebogenem Möbel (Solid Bent-wood Furniture Factory), exhibited at the 1873 Vienna World Exhibition; the firm had representatives in London and Hamburg.

References: Vienna 1873c, p. 281, no. 214; Vienna 1873a, p. 496; Exner and Lauboeck 1893, p. 30.

Gebrüder Thonet. Medal commemorating 25 years of service to Gebrüder Thonet. Designed by Peter Breithut, Vienna, ca. 1908. Silver. Collection Leonhard Gmür, Lucerne.

Gebrüder Thonet, Vienna (Austria)

Michael Thonet (1796–1871) set up business as a cabinetmaker in Boppard am Rhein (Prussia) in 1819. In 1842, after experimenting with the technique of bending wood, he went to Vienna and obtained a patent for "bending even the most brittle types of wood by chemico-mechanical means into any shapes and curves desired." In 1849 Thonet began to manufacture bent-wood furniture in his workshop in Gumpendorferstrasse 396. The firm Gebrüder Thonet (Thonet Brothers) was founded on November 1, 1853. On July 10, 1856, the firm was granted a new patent for "manufacturing chairs and table legs made of bent wood, the curvature of which is effected

Gebrüder Thonet. Stamp (left) and trademark label (right), ca. 1905.

through the agency of steam or boiling liquids." The first factory was built in Koritschan, Moravia (Koryčany, Czechoslovakia), in 1856. Additional factories were erected in Bistritz am Hostein (Bystřice pod Hostýnem, Czechoslovakia) in 1862; Gross-Ugrócz (Hungary) in 1866; Hallenkau (Halenkov, Czechoslovakia) in 1867, with a branch in Wsetin (Vsetín, Czechoslovakia) in 1871; Nowo-Radomsk (Radomsko, Poland) in 1880; and in Frankenburg, Germany, in 1889. By 1900, Thonet Brothers employed some 6,000 workers and were producing about 4,000 pieces of furniture a day.

Selected References: Hamburg 1869, p. 24, Nos. 479–88, and advertising section, n.p.; Exner 1876, pp. 6–25; Sales catalogue 1888 (reprint, Dry 1979a); Exner and Lauboeck 1893, pp. 6–33, 67–69, 75–80; Sales catalogue 1895 (reprint, Frankenberg 1980); Thonet 1896; Heller; Culetto; Bang; Bangert; Mang 1969; Mang 1979, pp. 36, 38, 46–55, 59, 91, 99–100, 112–113, 115, 120–22, 126, 133, 142–43, 155; Massobrio and Portoghesi 1980; Wilk 1980 and 1980a (with full bibliography); Behal, pp. 51, 62, 67–69, 74, 141, 234, 239–46, 297; Mang 1982.

Ungvárer Möbelfabriks-Aktiengesellschaft, Ungvár (Užhorod, U.S.S.R.)

The firm probably shared exhibition space with Thonet Brothers and J. & J. Kohn at the 1900 Paris World Exhibition and probably was one of the Mundus group (see above). The firm's trademark incorporated a picture of a galloping horse and jockey.

References: Exner and Lauboeck 1893, p. 31; Malkowsky, p. 417; Dry 1983.

Rudolf Wagner & Co., Bielitz (Bielsko-Biala, Poland)

The firm exhibited a bent-wood chair at an exhibition held in Vienna in 1882 at which the results of a competition organized by the Technologisches Gewerbe-Museum (Technological Trade Museum) for technical improvements in chair construction were shown. In order to achieve a greater stability between backrest and front legs, the brace connecting the back legs to the lower side of the seat ring was extended and lengthened to connect to the front legs as well.

A further novelty of the firm was the use of wood-pulp board as seating instead of the usual caning. Rudolf Wagner & Co. was awarded a Bronze Medal for these improvements.

Reference: Lauboeck 1882, pp. 66, 69.

Rudolf Weill & Co. (location unknown)

Dr. Rudolf Weill was one of the two chief clerks when Mundus was formed in 1907; Leopold Pilzer (b. 1871), the man later responsible for the formation of the Mundus group (see above), had become a partner in Weill & Co. in 1893.

References: Handelsgericht Wien, Handelsregister (1907) Abt. B, No. 1/190; Wilk 1980a, pp. 77, 78.

Brüder Zartl, Miskólcz-Hámor (Miskolc, Hungary)

Reference: Exner and Lauboeck 1893, p. 31.

Identity Unknown

Factory in Cormons (Italy)

According to Exner, bent-wood furniture was being made in Cormons.

Reference: Exner 1876, p. 24.

Factory in Görz (Gorizia, Italy)

According to Exner, bent-wood furniture was being made in Görz.

Reference: Exner 1876, p. 24.

BELGIUM

L. & H. Cambier Frères, Ath

The firm was founded by Emmanuel Cambier, who had served his apprenticeship in cabinetmaking in Paris. In 1842 he employed two workmen in his workshop in the rue Basse-Boulogne. By 1856 he had twenty to twenty-five workmen and was producing armchairs, folding chairs, and "bed-couches," all after his own design. In 1855 he was awarded a Second Class Medal at the Paris World Exhibition. The firm expanded under his two sons, Léon and Henri, and by 1868 some one hundred workmen were employed, for the most part in the production of cane chairs, three-quarters of which were exported. A new factory was built 1880–82 and production of bent-wood furniture was perfected, at extremely competitive prices. At the turn of the century, the work force numbered 700, and a major part of the company's production was being exported to France and the United States. The firm's trademark consisted of a cross on a pedestal, with a

coat-of-arms showing a double-headed eagle and rampant lion in a smaller shield. Below the cross are laurel and oak branches with the motto, "Goliath & David."

On June 21, 1892, Léon Cambier was granted a German patent (Deutsches Reichs Patent 68602) for his invention of double diagonal bars of bent wood connecting the front and back legs of bentwood chairs, thereby giving them greater stability. The Dresdner Fabrik für Möbel aus gebogenem Holz, A. Türpe, Jr. (see below) was one firm to adopt Cambier's method of construction.

After World War I, the firm was taken over by Emile Cambier (see below, under France) and was known as Emile Cambier Successeur de L. & H. Cambier Frères, Léon A. Cambier. Cambier had showrooms in Brussels at 7, rue des Bogards, and later at 24, rue de la Braie. In Ath, furniture

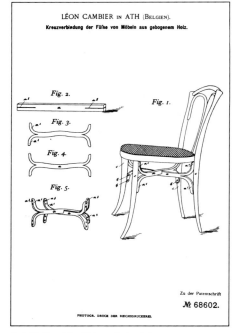

L. & H. Cambier Frères. Patent drawing No. 68602, showing double diagonal bars of bent wood. Berlin Patent Office, June 21, 1892.

Georg July Advertisement illustrating a chair with double diagonal bar construction. *Adressbuch von München,* July 24, 1905.

was sold from a store at 22 (later 18), rue de Pintamont. The firm went out of existence some time after 1945.

References: Exner and Lauboeck 1893, p. 31; A. Türpe Sales catalogue ca. 1906, p. III; Sales catalogue ca. 1914 (with trademark but no mention of firm by name); Sales catalogues, Emile Cambier (see below), ca. 1920, ca. 1925, and ca. 1936; Ducastelle, pp. 248–53.

François Carton-Herman. *See* Herman Frères & Carton.

Léon Delmée & Cie., Manufacture de Sièges et Meubles, Ath

Founded in 1901, the firm had showrooms at 10 rue du Rempart and factories situated on the same street.

References: Sales catalogue 1925; Ducastelle, p.253.

Emile Gignez, Ath

Founded around 1892, in the 1920s the firm was called Frères Gignez. A successor, the Anciens Établissements Pierre Gignez, was making bent-wood furniture in the 1950s, but the company no longer exists.

References: Sales catalogue 1952–53; Ducastelle, p. 253.

Herman Frères & Carton, Ath

The firm was founded in 1872 by François Carton and his brother-in-law Myrtild Herman. Both had learned their trades in Paris, Carton as cabinetmaker, Herman as coachmaker. On their return to Ath, they formed an association with two other Herman brothers and built a factory in the Boulevard des Glacis. Showrooms were at 5 rue du Moulin (now the Cinéma Eden). Myrtild Herman died in 1874 at the age of twenty-six, but the association continued for another twenty years. After 1893, when Joseph Herman left the business to become a piano manufacturer, François Carton assumed sole control of the company, which was renamed François Carton-Herman. In 1896 Carton employed over two hundred workers. The firm's trademark was a shield bearing the monogram *HC*, with the figure of a snarling lion, an oak branch, and the motto "Labor." A catalogue issued around 1912 shows various pieces of bent-wood furniture closely based on architect-designed furniture produced by J. & J. Kohn, Vienna (see above). Among these, the Carton-Herman suite No. 704, based on Kohn suite No. 728 is particularly noteworthy (see cat. nos. 57, 58). The firm went out of existence after 1945.

References: Antwerp 1885a, vol 1, *Belgique*, Groupe 2, p. 36, no. 464; *Mittheilungen* November 1885, pp. 163–64; Exner and Lauboeck 1893, p. 31; Sales catalogues, ca. 1912 and ca. 1920; Ducastelle, pp. 248–53.

Verlinden (location unknown)

According to Lehnert (1907), this was a "large manufacturer of bent-wood furniture."

Reference: Lehnert, vol. 2, p. 484.

Herman Frères & Carton Advertisement, ca. 1893. Private collection, Ath, Belgium.

Denmark

Svendborg Bent-Wood Furniture Factory, Svendborg

The factory exhibited bent-wood furniture in the Thonet style at the Nordische Austellung (Northern Exhibition) in Copenhagen in 1888.

Reference: Wesseley, p. 180 (firm cited as Wiener Möbelfabrik).

France

Hyppolite Bondeaux et Cie., Souppleville near Verdun

The factory was probably founded in 1878 and existed until 1914.

References: *Annuaires du département de la Meuse 1878–1914; Annuaire de Lorraine, guide illustré,* 1900, p. 928; ibid., 1914, p. 214; Exner and Lauboeck 1893, p. 31; G. Mauduech, director of Services d'Archives, Département de la Meuse, Bar-le-Duc, letters to the author, April 3 and 30, 1986.

Emile Cambier et Cie., Berlaimont

The firm was founded in the late nineteenth century by relatives of the Cambier family of Ath, Belgium (see above). At the death of the Cambiers who had founded the Berlaimont firm, the company was taken over by the heirs in Ath. Bent-wood furniture was produced until the company's closing in February 1935.

References: Dr. C. Decavel, mayor of Berlaimont, letter to the author, February 6, 1986; Sales catalogue 1906.

Auguste Couturier, Magny-en-Vexin (Seine et Oise)

The firm was founded as a chair factory in 1840 by Hilaire Clément Auguste Couturier (1817–1892). Bent-wood furniture was probably produced at the factory from the early 1870s onward and Hilaire's son Auguste Prosper Couturier (1841–1900) was granted a patent (*brevet d'invention*) in 1874 by the Minister of Agriculture and Commerce for the invention of a type of bent-wood chair *à assemblage direct invisible* (with construction concealed) in which the flat rear side of the chair seat was attached to a crossbar between the two sides of the chair back by means of two hidden screws.

The firm was awarded an Honorable Mention at the 1878 Paris World Exhibition. Some fifty men were employed at this time, and as many women were engaged in the production of caning. The firm supplied all the leading Paris stores and many churches throughout France. Bent-wood furniture was also exported. Léon Paul Couturier (1876–1959), whose wife Elise Blanche Couturier Guibert ran the firm during World War I, sold the business to M. Collet in 1920. The firm existed until 1940.

References: Exner and Lauboeck 1893, p. 31; Pierre Couturier, letter to the author, April 8, 1986, and private papers on the history of the firm; Conseiller Général G. Picard, mayor of Magny-en-Vexin, letter to the author, April 8, 1986 (the author is indebted to MM Couturier and Picard for their kind assistance).

Établissements Japy Frères, Beaucourt near Belfort, and Paris.

The company's factories were situated in Beaucourt and Fesches-le-Châtel (Doubs). In 1938, outlets were maintained in Paris, Nantes, Bordeaux, Toulouse, and Lyon.

References: Sales catalogues ca. 1938.

Frédéric Lebrun et Fils, Saint-Loup-sur-Semouse

Reference: Exner and Lauboeck 1893, p. 31.

Van Veersen et Cie., Sommedieu

Reference: Exner and Lauboeck 1893, p. 31.

Germany

Alsfelder Möbelfabrik, Alsfeld, Hesse

The Hammonia Möbelfabrik of Hamburg (see below) built a branch factory in Alsfeld in 1890/91. In 1893, after the firm's bankruptcy during the previous year, production was carried on in the Alsfeld factory under new, local ownership, under the name Alsfelder Möbelfabrik. In 1904, a branch factory was built in Angenrod. Between 1893 and 1914, the number of models rose from 125 to 510. In 1893/94, 21,803 pieces of furniture were manufactured; a maximum annual total was reached in 1906/7 with 87,868 pieces, In 1908, the firm exhibited "Viennese-style" bent-wood furniture at the Hessische Landausstellung für frie und angewandte Kunst (Hesse State Exhibition of Fine and Applied Art) in Darmstadt. By the end of 1918, 1,461,593 pieces of furniture had been produced. During the latter part of World War I, when the rubber shortage made the manufacture of tires impossible, the factory also produced wooden bicycle wheels. In 1934, the firm was merged with the Dresdner Fabrik für Möbel aus massiv gebogenem Holz, A. Türpe, Jr. (see below) when the latter was forced to give up its business in Dresden; the new company, now based in Alsfeld, was called Stuhlfabrik Alsfeld-Türpe GmbH, Alsfeld.

References: Alsfeld 1895, p. 37, no. 78; "Alsfelder Möbelfabrik"; Darmstadt 1908, p. 50; the author is grateful for information supplied by Kurt Reichel (Stuhlfabrik Alsfeld-Türpe), Dr. Herbert Jäkel (Geschichts- und Museumsverein Alsfeld), and Herr Klaube (Stadtarchiv, Kassel).

Andrecht & Bingel. *See* **Andrecht & Krüger.**

Andrecht & Krüger, Kassel

The firm Andrecht & Krüger, Fabrik von Möbeln und Holzwaren aus massiv gebogenem Holz, was founded in 1867. The factory was situated at the Wesertor, Fussweg nach Wolfsanger 7. In 1869 Carl Andrecht took Adolph Bingel as a partner, and the firm became known as Andrecht & Bingel. The partnership ended in 1873. Adolph Bingel (see below) was probably still producing bentwood furniture in the early 1890s.

References: *Adressbuch von Cassel*, 1868, 1869; *Kunst und Gewerbe* 1870, p. 250; Exner 1873, p. 402; Exner and Lauboeck 1893, p. 31.

Christian Becher, Stuhlfabrik, Aue, Saxony

Founded in 1875.

Reference: Broadsheet sales catalogue, ca. 1925.

Bieler & Co., Leipzig

Founded in 1870, the firm exhibited at the 1873 Vienna World Exhibition. In that year, one hundred thirty workers were employed, about eighty of whom worked at home, making caning.

References: Vienna 1873d, p. 347, No. 75; Vienna 1873a, p. 519.

Adolph Bingel, Kassel. *See* **Andrecht & Krüger.**

Reference: Exner and Lauboeck 1893, p. 31 (erroneously as "C. Bingel").

Franz Bubenhofer. *See* **Mechanische Stuhlfabrik Franz Bubenhofer.**

F. C. Deig & Co., Lauterberg, Sankt Andreasberg, and Oderfeld, Harz

Founded in the early 1850s, the firm possibly exhibited bent-wood furniture at the 1854 Allgemeine deutsche Industrie-Ausstellung (German Industrial Exhibition) in Munich. The factory in Oderfeld was later known as the Oderfelder Fabrik (see below) and exhibited bent-wood furniture at the Allgemeine Industrie-Ausstellung (German Industrial Exhibition) held in Kassel in 1870.

References: Steinbeis, in Munich 1854d, p. 85; *Kunst und Gewerbe* 1870, p. 250; Hannover 1878b, p. 201; Röger.

Dresdner Fabrik für Möbel aus massiv gebogenem Holz, A. Türpe, Jr., Dresden

The Dresden Solid Bent-wood Furniture Factory, A. Türpe, Jr. was founded in 1867, probably for the production of bent-wood furniture. By 1906 the firm had representatives in Amsterdam, Alexandria, Barmen, Berlin, Cairo, Frankfurt, Hamburg, Königsberg, Leipzig, Lübeck, Paris, Posen, and Seville. In 1934, the firm removed to Alsfeld in Hesse and merged with the Alsfelder Möbelfabrik (see above). The firm's trademark, found on furniture labels, was a crowned *T*.

References: Exner and Lauboeck 1893, p. 31; Sales catalogues, ca. 1904 and ca. 1906.

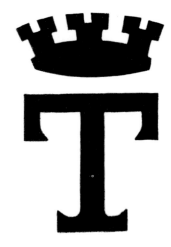

Dresdner Fabrik für Möbel aus massiv gebogenem Holz, A. Türpe, Jr. Trademark label, ca. 1900. Private collection, Munich.

Erste Acherner Stuhl-Fabrik August Klar, Achern, Baden

Founded as August Klar in 1795, the firm was registered as the Erste Acherner Stuhl-Fabrik August Klar on August 2, 1906. Bent-wood furniture production had begun around 1900, and the firm had representatives in Hamburg, Elberfeld, and Posen. In 1938, the firm's proprietor, August Meder, took over the Weissenburg (Wissembourg) factory of D. G. Fischel Söhne (see above) and until 1945 supervised production of both firms under the name August Meder

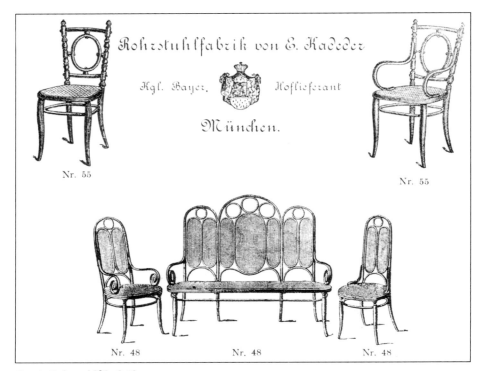

Page in Rohrstuhlfabrik Eleonore Kadeder sales catalogue, Munich, ca. 1893.

Stuhl-Fabriken, vormals August Klar, Achern-Baden und Weissenburg-Elsass.

References: Sales catalogues and broadsheets, 1900–40; Meder Sitzmöbel.

"Germania." *See* **Vereinigte Möbelfabriken "Germania."**

Haltenhoff & Zeidler, Bad Lauterberg

Founded in 1874. *See* Vereinigte Möbelfabriken "Germania."

Reference: Sales catalogue, July 1903.

Hammonia-Möbelfabrik, Hamburg

Founded in 1890 by a group of businessmen, mostly resident in Hamburg. The main factory was in Winterhude near Hamburg at Barmbeckerstrasse 255; in 1890/91 a branch factory was built in Alsfeld, Hesse. Mismanagement in Hamburg led to the firm's bankruptcy in 1893, and the Alsfeld factory was bought at auction on December 2, 1893, for 118,000 marks by a group of ten

partners, mostly resident in Alsfeld. The partnership was officially registered on March 17, 1894, as the Alsfelder Möbelfabrik (see above), with a capital of 125,000 marks.

References: *Adressbuch von Hamburg* 1890–93; Exner and Lauboeck 1893, p. 31 (firm listed as Hammonia-Aktiengesellschaft); "Alsfelder Möbelfabrik."

A. H. Hillegeist & Co., Möbelfabrik, Bad Lauterberg

Founded in 1876, by 1900 the firm had representatives in Berlin, Frankfurt, Karlsruhe, Elberfeld, Kirchheim, Zurich, and Rotterdam. In 1908, Hillegeist was one of the factories that formed the Vereinigte Möbelfabriken "Germania" AG (see below). In 1912, the firm left the "Germania" and carried on as Karl Hillegeist & Co. until 1914.

References: Sales catalogue ca. 1912; Dry 1982, p. 133; Röger.

Wenzel Hurt, Stuhlfabrik, Neuhausen near Dresden, Saxony

Around 1913, the chair factory listed fourteen bent-wood models in its price lists, including armchairs, rocking chairs, and stools.

Reference: Sales catalogue and price lists [ca. 1913].

Eleonore Kadeder. Trademark label, ca. 1890. Collection R. Barberics, Diessen, Bavaria.

Eleonore Kadeder, Munich

Founded in 1886 in Reichenbachstrasse 1b by Eleonore Kaderer and her husband Hans, a painter. Eleonore was the daughter of Georg July, proprietor of a Munich furniture store that included bent-wood furniture among its merchandise. About 1893 the Kadeder firm published a catalogue that showed bent-wood and conventional furniture in historicist and Biedermeier styles. In 1906, a new factory was opened in Freibadstrasse 14. At the München 1908 exhibition, bent-wood chairs designed by the Munich architect Emanuel von Seidl and made by Hans Kadeder, as the firm was by then known, were shown. Other Kadeder bent-wood chairs included in the same exhibition were probably designed by the Munich architect Richard Riemerschmid. Furniture production ceased in 1909 when the firm, which still exists, was sold to new owners.

References: Adressbuch von Munchen 1885; Sales catalogue ca. 1893; Munich 1908a, pp. 169 and 94 (advertisement section): *Die Kunst* 1908, pp. 463–65; Munich 1982, p. 246, no. 209.

August Klar. *See* **Erste Acherner Stuhl-Fabrik August Klar.**

H. N. Koste & Co., Hamburg

H. N. Koste opened a workshop in Hamburg in 1859. In 1862, as H. N. Koste & Co., he exhibited bent-wood furniture at the International Exhibition in London, showing chairs, a sofa, table, and piano stool "in curved wood." The Jury awarded the firm an Honorable Mention "for excellence of workmanship." Koste's bent-wood furniture at this time was of the laminated and glued variety, a technique that Thonet Brothers had given up as soon as the technology of solid bent-wood furniture had been perfected in 1859. Koste also exhibited bent-wood furniture at the Industrie- und Gewerbe-Ausstellung (Industry and Trade Exhibition) in Hamburg in 1869. He later sold his business to A. H. Fock and L. F. Bull.

References: London 1862c, Hamburg Section, No. 94; London 1862b, p. 333; London 1862e, p. 592 ("Honourable Mention for Thonet's imitator"); Meier-Oberist 1925, p. 104; Hamburg 1977, p. 64.

W. Kümmel Möbelfabrik, Berlin

Dining chairs designed for this firm in 1904 by Rudolf and Fia Wille incorporated a bent-wood arch-shaped element in the back.

Reference: Bruning, p. 36, pl. 54.

Mechanische Stuhlfabrik Franz Bubenhofer, Brumath, Alsace

A broadsheet sales catalogue issued around 1910 illustrates Thonet's Model No. 14 bent-wood chair (see cat. nos. 14–18).

Reference: Broadsheet sales catalogue [ca. 1910].

Oderfelder Fabrik, Oderfeld near Barbis

Founded by F. C. Deig in the early 1850s the firm exhibited bent-wood furniture at the 1870 Kassel Allgemeine Industrie-Ausstellung (Exhibition of Industry). At the 1873 Vienna World Exhibition, the firm (proprietor, Christian Hostmann) showed only conventional furniture. At some time after 1878 the firm was trading as Oderfelder Möbelfabrik Fechter & Kaltwasser and exhibited as such at the World's Columbian Exposition of 1893 at Chicago where their bent-wood furniture was displayed in a bent-wood pavilion six meters tall, the roof of which was supported by spiral bent-wood columns. The firm employed 250 workers that year and exported its products to numerous countries. The firm described itself inaccurately in letterhead used in the late 1890s as the "Erste deutsche Fabrik massiv gebogener Möbel (First German Factory for the Manufacture of Solid Bent-wood Furniture). In 1898, the firm went bankrupt, but production was carried on as the Oderfelder Möbelfabrik by a group of five Lauterberg factories. This association of furniture manufacturers anticipated the later affiliation of the Vereinigte Möbelfabriken "Germania" AG (see below) in 1908.

References: Kunst und Gewerbe 1870, p. 250; Vienna 1873d, p. 347, No. 72; Hannover 1878b, p. 201; Chicago 1893, p. 65 and advertisement section, p. 63; letterhead, 1895; Dry 1982, p. 133; Röger.

Georg Benedikt von Poschinger, Oberfrauenau

G. B. von Poschinger began to manufacture bent-wood furniture in 1875; production was carried on until von Poschinger's death in 1900.

Reference: Exner and Lauboeck 1893, p. 31.

Adolf Rose, Beuthen (Bytom, Poland)

Reference: Exner and Lauboeck 1893, p. 31.

Sächsische Holzindustrie-Gesellschaft, Rabenau

Founded in 1869, by 1871 the firm employed 639 workers. The company exhibited bent-wood furniture in Dresden (1871); Paris, Lyons, and Moscow (1872); the Vienna World Exhibition (1873); Dresden (1877); Leipzig (1879); Sydney (1879); Melbourne (1880); London (1891); and Leipzig (1897). Bent-wood furniture production probably ceased about 1912. The firm exhibited only conventional furniture at the Internationale Baufach Ausstellung (International Architecture Exhibition) held in Leipzig in 1913.

References: Vienna 1873d, p. 347, no. 74; Exner and Lauboeck 1893, p. 31; Sales catalogue, ca. 1900; Hamburg 1977, p. 33, No. 46; Dresden 1906, p. 199 and advertisement section, n.p.; Leipzig 1913, p. 228.

Friedrich Schäfer. *See* **Stuhl- und Tischfabrik Friedrich Schäfer.**

W. Schmidt & Sohn, Hamburg

Founded in 1867.

References: Meier-Oberist 1925, p. 104; Hamburg 1977, p. 64.

Viktor Schwarzhaupt, Munich

Schwarzhaupt took over factory space from Eleonore Kadeder (see above) in Reichenbachstrasse 1b in 1904; by 1906 the firm employed fifteen workers. After several changes of address, the firm closed in 1916.

References: Adressbuch von München, 1904–16; *Die Bayerische Holzindustrie,* p. 59; München, Stadt und Land, advertisement, n.p.

Gebrüder Seitz, Munich

Otto and Heinrich Seitz were probably making bent-wood furniture in their Munich factory at Geierstrasse 11½ in 1868. The Seitz firm exhibited bent-wood furniture at the 1869 Munich Lokal-Industrie-Ausstellung (Exhibition of Local Industry). In 1871, Otto Seitz and Friedrich Schwab founded a new firm, Otto Seitz & Co. A new factory was built that same year at Theresienwiese 2 for the manufacture of bent-wood furniture; production began in 1872, with 105 employees. The firm exhibited at the 1873 Vienna World Exhibition. Production probably ceased in the late 1870s.

References: Munich 1869, p. 62, No. 482; Vienna 1873d, p. 347, No. 73; *Kunst und Gewerbe* 1873, p. 369; Vienna 1873a, p. 519.

Albert Stoll, Waldshut

Founded in 1870 for the manufacture of bent-wood furniture; branch factories were erected the same year in Koblenz and Klingnau, both in Switzerland. Production of bent-wood furniture ceased in 1918.

Reference: Exner and Lauboeck 1893, p. 31.

Stuhl- und Tischfabrik Friedrich Schäfer, Tübingen

Founded in 1882; besides making bent-wood furniture, the firm specialized in the manufacture of "Tübingen" chairs, a local type of solid café and restaurant seating.

Reference: Sales catalogue, July 1931.

A. Türpe, Jr. *See* **Dresdner Fabrik für Möbel aus massiv gebogenem Holz, A. Türpe, Jr.**

Vereinigte Möbelfabriken "Germania," Bad Lauterberg

The "Germania," as it was popularly known, was formed on October 6, 1908. It consisted of a group of furniture factories located in Bad Lauterberg, Barbis, Oderfeld, and Sankt Andreasberg: Gustav Mennecke; Haltenhoff & Zeidler; F. G. Haltenhoff; Brune & Weiss (later Weiss & Hildebrandt); C. Jahns; Gebrüder Angerstein; A. H. Hillegeist; Oderfelder Möbelfabrik Fechter & Kaltwasser; Rojahn & Meyer; and the Harzer Möbelfabrik. The company was dissolved in 1915. H. G. Reinstein's "Press-stoff-möbel" (combined bent-wood and paperboard furniture) was made under the "Germania" name by the Oderfelder Möbelfabrik Fechter & Kaltwasser. "Press-stoff-möbel" was exhibited at the 1911 Dresden

International Hygiene Ausstellung (Hygiene Exhibition) by the Dresden retailing firm Raumkunst, Vereinigte Werkstätten für Kunstgewerbe. The furniture was advertised as the "Furniture of the Future" and as being ideal for use in sanatoriums and hotels. Raumkunst also claimed that "Press-stoff-möbel" was the only type of furniture that fulfilled all the requirements of hygiene.

References: Dresden 1911, p. 232, No. 689, and advertisement section, p. 255; *Innen Dekoration* 22 (1911), pp. 186–87 (where place name is erroneously given as Bad Lauterbach); company report, 1912; Dry 1982, p. 133; Röger.

Vereinigte Werkstätten für Kunst im Handwerk, Munich

Founded in 1897 by a group of Munich artists and designers, the firm manufactured or supplied bent-wood chairs designed by Bruno Paul (1874–1968) for the Café Kerkau in Berlin in 1910.

Reference: *Innen Dekoration* 1910, pp. 370–72.

J. H. C. Wipper, Hamburg

Wipper, the earliest recorded manufacturer of bent-wood furniture after Michael Thonet, exhibited his furniture in the Patriotische Gesellschaft (Patriotic Society) in Hamburg in 1857.

Reference: Meier-Oberist 1925, p. 104.

Identities Unknown

Factory in Lower Bavaria

Built in 1917.

Reference: Andés 1925, pp. 48–52, with description of the factory and an illustration of the ground plan and frontage.

Factories in the Bavarian Forest

Reference: Thurneyssen, p. 48, n. 1: "Important chair factories of this type [i.e., manufacturers of bent-wood furniture] are situated in the Bavarian Forest."

Italy

Giacomo Canepa, fu Giovanni Battista, Chiavari

Giacomo Canepa, successor to Giovanni Battista, had thirty-three employees in 1870 and was one of the largest chair factories in Chiavari at the time, producing one-eighth of the total number of chairs made by the twenty-four local factories. Chiavari, a town halfway between Genoa and La Spezia, was famous around the middle of the nineteenth century for the production of "Chiavari" chairs, which were formally derived from a French chair brought in 1807 from Paris. At its best, the "Chiavari" chair was a light but solid affair, made usually of either sycamore or cherrywood. Treated successively with sulphur fumes and white French polish, the finished product had the appearance of ivory. The seating was made of willow cane, sometimes woven in intricate patterns.

The Chiavari chair industry fell into a decline towards the end of the 1860s, in spite of the high taxes levied on similar, cheaper Austrian imports. In 1878 the Chiavari Società Economica (Chamber of Commerce) began to investigate the reasons for the decline of the town's chair industry. As a result of its findings, two local manufacturers, Giacomo Massa and Giacomo Canepa, were invited by August Thonet to Bistritz am Hostein to study the technology of bent-wood furniture production.

Canepa had produced "Chiavari" chairs exclusively before expanding production in around 1881 to include bent-wood chairs, at first on a very small scale. The pilot workshop made a maximum of six chairs a day, some in imitation of Thonet models, some in a combined style incorporating bent-wood and Chiavari chair elements: both types had already been exhibited in Milan.

That same year, the Società Economica was planning to build a bent-wood furniture factory in Chiavari which was to employ all those who had up to now worked for the chair-industry only at home. A second bent-wood furniture factory was planned to open on April 1, 1882, for the production of 450 chairs a day, a figure that was to be increased gradually to 1,400 chairs. These two factories have yet to be identified by name, but Fratelli Canepa (Canepa Brothers) exhibited bent-wood furniture made of chestnut and chairs of the mixed type (*di tipo misto*) at the 1885 World Exhibition in Antwerp.

References: Vienna 1873a, p. 421; Riby; Antwerp 1885b, vol. 2, *Italie*, Groupe 2, p. 12, no. 115; *Mittheilungen* November 1885, p. 163; Exner and Lauboeck 1893, p. 31 (firm erroneously listed as G. Canepa fu G. B. Chiavari).

Kopl, Trieste

Reference: Massobrio and Portoghesi 1976, p. 65.

Fratelli Sardella, Acireale

References: Exner and Lauboeck 1893, p. 31; Massobrio and Portoghesi 1976, pp. 81–82; Massobrio and Portoghesi 1980, pp. 74–75.

SL. Trademark label, n.d. Collection R. Barberics, Diessen, Bavaria.

SL (location unknown)

Furniture from this firm bears a label printed in blue, showing a seated lion with paws placed on a bent-wood chair; the letters *SL*, the "L" perhaps signifying the word *Leone* (lion), to left and right; and the words *Mobili . . . depositato*, indicating that the furniture is registered or patented and that this firm was more than simply a distributor.

Società Anonima Antonio Volpe, Udine

In 1883, Antonio Volpe, a local businessman in Udine, decided to build a factory for the manufacture of bent-wood furniture. Production began in 1884, with a work force of about twenty men, fifteen women, seven boys, and four apprentices. The Società Anonima Antonio Volpe, Udine, Fabbrica Italiana di Mobili in Legno Curvato imported its raw material (beechwood) partly from Austria. By the end of the century the firm was producing twenty to forty thousand chairs annually. The factory supplied only the Italian market, where its main competitors were companies in Cormons, Italy, and Marburg (Maribor, Yugoslavia; see above, Austro-Hungarian Empire). The company was awarded medals at exhibitions in Verona (1889), Milan (1894), Udine (1895), Turin (1898), Udine (1903), Milan (1906), and at Friuli's local industry exhibitions in 1911 and 1921. In 1907 the company received special recognition from King Victor Emmanuel III.

The Udine factory was destroyed in World War I but was rebuilt after 1918. About 1922 the company issued a catalogue with thirty-four pages of illustrations showing a selection of the firm's production. The cover has an illustration of a rocking chair, on which a fox (*volpe*) is sitting, with one paw raised. Production of bent-wood furniture came to an end in 1940.

References: Exner and Lauboeck 1893, p. 31; Occioni-Bonaffons, pp. 317–18; Sales catalogues, ca. 1922 and ca. 1938 (price list, 1939); Massobrio and Portoghesi 1976, p. 65; Vienna 1979, No. 70 (Volpe rocking chair No. 267, erroneously described as designed by Josef Hoffmann and manufactured by J. & J. Kohn); Massobrio and Portoghesi 1980, pp. 146–47, pls. 5–7 (Volpe rocking chair No. 267, as "J. & J. Kohn"); Wichmann, p. 197 (Volpe rocking chair No. 267, erroneously described as designed by Josef Hoffmann, 1905).

Wäckerlin & Co., Catania

Furniture made by this firm bears a label with an illustration of a bent-wood chair and Wäckerlin & C.[1] in a horizontal band surrounded by floral ornament.

References: Massobrio and Portoghesi 1976, pp. 83–86; Massobrio and Portoghesi 1980, pp. 69–73.

Wäckerlin & Co. Trademark label, ca. 1890. Collection R. Barberics, Diessen, Bavaria.

Zappalà, Raciti & Scavo, Naples

Reference: Massobrio and Portoghesi 1976, p. 62.

Poland

Wilhelm Gebetner, Warsaw

Reference: Exner and Lauboeck 1893, p. 31

Hellin, Ginsberg & Komp., Warsaw

Reference: Exner and Lauboeck 1893, p. 31

H. Gruman & Cie. (location unknown)

The firm's factories were called "Ksylos," but their location in Poland has so far not been traced. Their showrooms in Brussels were at 85 Boulevard Chavis.

Reference: Sales catalogue ca. 1920.

Gebrüder Lessel, Zwierzynie (Zwierzyniec)

Reference: Exner and Lauboeck 1893, p. 31.

Reicher, Zakrszow (Zakrzów)

Reference: Exner and Lauboeck 1893, p. 31.

Rubinstein & Sreneswski, Warsaw

Reference: Exner and Lauboeck 1893, p. 31.

Johann Stern, Warsaw

Reference: Exner and Lauboeck 1893, p. 31.

Romania

Jassy Furniture Factory "Fortuna," Jassy (Iași)

Reference: Exner and Lauboeck 1893, p. 31.

Sighet Co., Sighetul Marmației

A catalogue issued during the 1920s includes variations of well-known J. & J. Kohn designs. The firm was probably the successor to Altman és Huber, Máramarossziget, Hungary (see above).

Reference: Wilk 1980a, p. 69, fig. 78.

Russia

A. Bärenstamm, Petersburg

Reference: Exner and Lauboeck 1893, p. 31.

Kahan, Moscow

Reference: Exner and Lauboeck 1893, p. 31.

Woiciechow Joint-Stock Company, Woice-chow (Woijcieszow, Poland)

Founded in 1871 in Woicechow. The firm's headquarters and main stores were in Warsaw, in the building that housed the Europa Hotel; factories were in Warsaw and Prague. The company exhibited various pieces of bent-wood furniture at the 1889 Paris World Exhibition.

Reference: Paris 1889, Groupe III, p. 22, No. 7; Exner and Lauboeck 1893, p. 31.

Identity Unknown

Exner mentions "many failed attempts to establish bent-wood furniture factories in Russia and in other countries."

Reference: Exner 1876, p. 24.

Spain

Identity Unknown

Exner reports the "recent" establishment of a bent-wood furniture industry in Spain.

Reference: Exner 1876, p. 24.

Sweden

Identity Unknown

Carl Bergsten (1879–1935) designed a bent-wood chair for a Swedish factory in 1906, which may have been inspired by J. & J. Kohn chair Model No. 728A, the so-called Fledermaus chair (see cat. no. 55).

Reference: New York 1982, p. 83.

Switzerland

Emil Baumann, Horgen

Founded in 1880, by 1900 the company employed two hundred workers and called itself "the largest furniture factory in Switzerland." The firm exists today as Horgen-Glarus AG, Möbelfabrik, Glarus.

Reference: Culetto, p. 42.

Heinrich Robmann, Turbenthal, Zurich

Founded in 1862, the firm exhibited bent-wood furniture at the 1873 Vienna World Exhibition and showed "various pieces of furniture, impregnated and wormproof" at the 1883 Landesausstellung (National Exhibition) in Zurich.

References: Vienna 1873a, p. 479; Zurich 1883, p. 68, No. 803.

Albert Stoll, Koblenz

Albert Stoll, bent-wood manufacturer in Waldshut, Germany (see above), built branch factories in Koblenz and Klingnau in 1870. The Klingnau factory was soon sold to a Stoll employee; it exists today as Tütsch AG, Klingnau. Albert Stoll, Koblenz, exhibited bent-wood furniture (chairs, armchairs, and sofas) at the 1883 Landesausstellung (National Exhibition) in Zurich.

Reference: Zurich 1883, p. 70, No. 832.

Location Unknown

Arx

Furniture bears a label with ARX in a central panel between Renaissance-style balusters and the words "... [illegible] Vienna style furniture" below. On each side of the panel is a fortress-like edifice with the legend "Trademark."

Reference: Massobrio and Portoghesi 1976, p. 60.

Arx. Trademark label, ca. 1895. Collection R. Barberics, Diessen, Bavaria.

Brief

Reference: Solbad Hall, n.p.

Eibl

Reference: Solbad Hall, n.p.

Mazowia

The furniture label bears the word MAZOWIA and two circular devices with the motto SEMPER SURSUM, in imitation of a label used by J. & J. Kohn.

Glossary

Art Nouveau. The term *Art Nouveau* describes a movement in progressive French and Belgian architecture, interior decoration, and the decorative arts of the late nineteenth century, remaining somewhat fashionable until the First World War. It is characterized by the surface application of naturalistic motifs and rhythmic lines.

Arts and Crafts Movement. A late nineteenth-, early twentieth-century reform movement initiated in reaction to the effects of industrialization on the decorative arts in England. William Morris and other members of this movement were inspired by the writings of John Ruskin and believed in the promotion of craft ideals as the solution to the disintegration of aesthetic values in the decorative arts. The Arts and Crafts Movement, in its acknowledgment of the vital role of the designer in the creation of unified domestic environments, was a significant harbinger of twentieth-century modernism.

Biedermeier. A manner of design based on classicist principles and popular in Germany and Austria after the Napoleonic wars until the 1840s. By the early twentieth century, the term *Biedermeier* came to symbolize the German-speaking bourgeoisie of the early nineteenth century as well as the period's manner of design in the decorative arts. Biedermeier furniture is characterized by an allegiance to classical forms and ornament, a frequent use of indigenous woods (often inexpensive and light-colored), and a delicacy that contrasts with contemporary French Empire and English Regency design.

boarded construction. A primitive technique for constructing furniture, based on the structure of a four-sided box. The vocabulary of forms with a boxlike structure includes six-plank chests, boxes, five-plank stools, benches, and armchairs. Boarded construction has been known since the Middle Ages; in the late nineteenth century, the technique was revived in Austria and in England in Arts and Crafts designs.

butt joint. The simplest of joints in which two sections of wood are joined without any overlapping of parts.

burl. An abnormal or diseased growth on a tree, often resulting from an injury to the bark. When sliced into fine cross sections for veneer, burls produce beautifully figured or mottled patterns.

cabriole. A furniture leg, shaped in a double curve, the upper portion swelling outward, the lower portion inward, toward the foot which flares out again. This signature leg of high-style furniture design during the first half of the eighteenth century was superseded by the rectilinear mannerisms of neoclassicism in the second half of the eighteenth century.

caning. The process of weaving long, narrow strips of rattan bark to construct seats and backs. Cane was originally imported to Europe from the Orient by the Dutch East India Company and first appeared in English furniture in the late seventeenth century about the time of the Restoration. It was also frequently used in eighteenth-century French furniture.

cantilever construction. Specifically in terms of seating, the term *cantilever* refers to a chair in which the seat is supported only at one end, unlike traditionally made chairs, which are supported at both front and back.

case piece. In cabinetry, a case piece is a type of furniture with a boxlike structure that forms a chest of drawers, cabinet, or desk.

caul. A kind of mold that is heated and used to secure veneers to secondary woods during the drying process. Its heat keeps the glue from hardening until all excess glue has been pressed out at the edges.

chaise longue. A French term meaning literally "long chair," a chaise longue is an extended lounge chair with a support at one end so that a person can recline upon it.

cheval glass. A full-length standing mirror that was popular during the French Empire period when it was known as a Psyche.

clamped construction. A clamped-front chest, for example, consists of wide vertical members with one or more horizontal boards clamped between them secured with fixed joints. Recognized as the earliest kind of joined construction, clamped construction was used throughout the fourteenth century, when clamped-front chests with richly carved decoration were introduced.

crest rail. The horizontal top rail at the back of a chair or other type of seat furniture, mounted at a right angle to the stiles.

cuff joint. A kind of joint in which two elements are bound together by a third known as the cuff.

cutwork. See **fretwork**.

Deutsche Werkbund. Established in 1907, an organization of artists, architects, craftsmen, and industrialists dedicated to promoting the quality of German goods by combining art, craft, and industry. The Werkbund sponsored exhibitions, educational programs, and publications intended to heighten public awareness of design and to promote German industrial production on an international scale.

dovetailing. A cabinetmakers' technique in which two pieces of wood are joined by means of wedge-shaped tenons inserted into receptacles called mortises. This refinement became popular in the seventeenth century.

dowel. A rounded wooden pin.

ébéniste. A French cabinetmaker specializing in making veneered furniture known as ébénisterie (originating from ebony which was used in veneered furniture in the seventeenth century).

Eisengarn (ironcloth). A canvaslike material formerly used only in military belts and boot laces. It is unclear whether Eisengarn was made from horsehair or was a reinforced canvas.

finger joints. A series of even, square-cut projections and indentations executed at the end of one board and inserted into a mirror image in another board.

fretwork, cutwork, lattice-work. In furniture-making these are practically interchangeable terms used to describe wood cut into patterns, more or less intricate, and used as a decorative device.

gallery. In furniture, the miniature railing, made of metal or wood and used along the edge of a shelf, tabletop, or case piece.

Gesamtkunstwerk. A German term used to refer to the total or consummate work of art, especially popular in progressive, German-speaking circles in the late nineteenth and early twentieth centuries when architects sought to design buildings with fully integrated interiors and furnishings.

japanning. Any of various methods for imitating oriental "lacquer." The essential ingredient of true lacquer, the resin of *Rhus vernicifera*, was not available in Europe; imitations were made of gum-lac or seed-lac, different preparations of the substance deposited on trees by an insect and dissolved in spirits of wine. Numerous coats were applied for the decoration of furniture.

joinery. The technique of assembling furniture and woodwork; literally, the joining together of pieces of wood.

Jugendstil. The German manifestation of Art Nouveau; the term derives from the German periodical *Jugend* (Youth).

kerf. A slit or notch made by a saw.

Kunstfrühling. The German word for the Sacred Spring Movement, which centered around a group of Secessionist artists in Vienna, and was named for *Ver Sacrum*, the deluxe, visionary Secessionist publication.

kunstreform. (Art Reform Movement). A movement that sought to create new forms expressive of such values as honesty and functionality in design, thereby facilitating the aesthetic renewal of society. It was inspired by the English Arts and Crafts Movement.

laminate. To build up wood in layers, each layer being glued to the next and being also called a laminate. The grains of the layers may run in the same direction or criss cross. See also **veneer, plywood.**

lap joint. Any of several joints in which one piece of wood overlaps the other, usually at the end and at a right angle. In a full lap joint, one piece is notched to accept the full dimension of the second piece; in a half lap joint, both pieces are notched to fit into each other and form a flush joint. In a cross lap joint, the two pieces overlap at a point other than at the ends.

lattice-work. See **fretwork**.

lipp-work. A kind of basketwork in which a straw shell is woven around an inner support system of pliable wood, such as ash.

marquetry. A patterned use of wood, formed from two or more contrasting veneers, sometimes with the addition of other materials such as tortoiseshell, mother-of-pearl, and horn. Unlike parquetry, which is geometric in design, marquetry patterns are composed of floral, arabesque, and figurative motifs. The technique was practiced in Renaissance Italy and in eighteenth-century France and England. Traditional marquetry was cut horizontally while the veneers were secured with a simple foot-operated clamp.

menuisier. A French joiner, as distinct from a cabinetmaker or ébéniste. The menuisier specialized in small objects (*menus*), such as chairs and other pieces constructed from solid wood. Guild restrictions in France during the eighteenth century prohibited members of this profession from veneering their work.

mortise and tenon. A technique used to join two pieces of wood. A mortise (hole or groove) is cut into the side of one piece, and a tenon (a small projecting member) is cut from the end of the other. The tenon is placed into the mortise and a wooden peg is driven through the joint to secure the two pieces of wood.

papier-mâché. Papier-mâché was originally used in Persia and the Orient and was introduced in France and England in the seventeenth century. The material consisted of paper pulp from specifically prepared paper mixed with glue, chalk, and sometimes sand. After being pressed, molded, and baked, the substance became so hard that it could be sawed and was capable of taking a very high polish by a process resembling japanning.

parquetry. Wood work, usually flooring, in which veneers are arranged in geometric repeat patterns.

pied-de-biche. A type of foot used mostly on a cabriole leg and resembling the cloven hoof of a doe or stag. It became popular in the early eighteenth century.

plywood. A wood product consisting of sheets of veneer, lued together, with the grain of each sheet running at a right angle to the adjacent sheets. Plywood is considerably stronger than a basic laminate and because of its alternating grains counteracts the stress incurred in the wood when it is bent.

Psyche. See **cheval glass**.

rasp. A type of coarse file with raised points.

ring stretcher. A continuous piece of wood, bent into a circular configuration, which, when secured to each of a chair's four legs beneath the seat, increases the structural stability of the chair.

rush. A long grass that is twisted and woven to make seats; rush-bottomed seats have been made by chairmakers since the Middle Ages, but were especially popular in England during the late seventeenth and eighteenth centuries.

sabot. A French term for the metal shoe (usually gilt bronze) enclosing the foot of a furniture leg.

Sacred Spring. See **Kunstfrühling**.

scarf joint. A joint made by chamfering, halving, or notching two pieces of wood to correspond and lapping and bolting or otherwise joining them longitudinally into a single piece.

seat rail. The horizontal element of a seating piece uniting the four legs and acting as a support for the seat.

sled runner. A continuation of the front and/or rear legs into a stretcher that rests on the floor, enhancing the mobility of the object, as well as its structural strength.

splat. The central, vertical member of a chair back framed by the stiles, crest rail, and rear seat rail.

splay. The outward spread or slant of a furniture leg.

stile. The vertical member of the frame of a chest, wood panel, or window. The term also designates the two vertical rear elements of a chair including the extension of the rear legs above the seat rails.

stretcher. Structural cross-pieces or rings connecting the legs of chairs, tables, and other furniture forms. Particularly related to seat furniture, the stretcher enhances the stability of the chair imparted by the seat rails. See also **ring stretcher**.

turned capital. In bent-wood chairs, the turned capital is the top bulbous portion of a leg that forms a transition beneath the seat rails.

turnery. A process consisting essentially of shaping a piece of wood with chisels while the wood revolves around the fan axis between the jaws of a lathe. The use of the turner's lathe, as with the potter's wheel, represents the earliest form of shaping machinery employed by man.

veneer. A thin sheet of wood. Veneers of rare, expensive woods are often applied to the surface of a coarser wood. Veneering was widely used from the second half of the seventeenth century, specifically to extend the precious supplies of rare woods.

Vienna Secession (Wiener Sezession). An organization whose members, including artists and architects, seceded from the Kunstlerhaus, the conservative Viennese Creative Artists' Association, and established a new association. Though concerned primarily with the fine arts, the Secessionists also played an important role in the development of modern Viennese decorative arts; several members were designers of furniture, metalwork, ceramics, and textiles.

Vienna Workshop (Wiener Werkstätte). A collaborative commercial workshop for architects, designers, and artists who sought to bring quality design and craft into the marketplace. It was founded in 1903 by leading members of the Viennese avant-garde including Josef Hoffmann and Koloman Moser, and it closed in 1932.

Bibliography

Authors' note: Hundreds of primary and secondary sources, from the correspondence and records of manufacturers to modern texts, have been consulted in the preparation of *Bent Wood and Metal Furniture: 1850–1946*. This material is presented below in four sections: periodicals and directories; books and articles; exhibition catalogues and related publications; and manufacturers' sales catalogues and other company-related material. The reference notes throughout the book have been keyed to this arrangement: for example, citations by author's name (or article or book title when the author is unknown) and the year of publication, in the event that more than one work by the author is cited, will be found in section 2; sources cited by city and date relate to exhibitions and are found in section 3; references to company literature such as sales catalogues will be found in section 4. The periodicals and directories that are listed in section 1 are cited in the text by name, volume, and issue or date, with the city of publication given below.

1 Periodicals and directories

Adressbuch von Cassel (Kassel)

Adressbuch von Hamburg (Hamburg)

Adressbuch von München (Munich)

Annuaires du Département de la Meuse

Annuaires de Lorraine, guide illustré

Antiques (New York)

Der Arbeiterfreund Zeitschrift des Centralvereins in Preussen für das Wohl der arbeitenden Classen (Berlin)

Architectural Review (London)

Art and Decoration (New York)

Art et Décoration (Paris)

Berliner Architekturwelt (Berlin)

Bulletin de l'Effort Moderne (Paris)

The Burlington Magazine (London)

Dekorative Kunst (Munich)

Deutsche Kunst und Dekoration (Darmstadt)

Domus (Helsinki and Italy)

Die Form (Berlin)

Form Svenska Slojdforeningens Tidskrift (Stockholm)

Fremdenblatt (Vienna)

Handelsgericht Wien, Handelsregister (Vienna)

Hohe Warte (Vienna and Leipzig)

Illustrirtes Familien-Journal (Leipzig)

Innen-Dekoration (Darmstadt)

Das Interieur (Vienna)

Jahrbuch der Gesellschaft Osterreichischer Architekten (Vienna)

Die Kunst (Munich)

Kunst in Hessen und am Mittelrhein (Darmstadt and Kassel)

Kunst und Gewerbe (Nürnberg)

Kunst und Handwerk (Vienna)

Kunst und Kunsthandwerk (Munich)

Kunstgewerbeblatt (Leipzig)

Mitteilungen des Vereins für Dekorative Kunst und Kunstgewerbe (Stuttgart)

Mittheilungen des Technologischen Gewerbe-Museums, Section für Holzindustrie (Vienna)

Mittheilungen über Gegenstände des Artillerie- und Genie-Wesens (Vienna)

Moderne Bauformen (Stuttgart)

Das Neue Frankfurt (Frankfurt)

Die Rheinlande (Düsseldorf)

The Studio (London)

The Studio Year Book of Decorative Art (London)

Süddeutsche Bauzeitung (Munich)

Umeni (Prague)

Ver Sacrum (Vienna)

Die Weltkunst (Munich)

2 Books and articles

Aldred, Cyril. 1954. "Fine Wood-work." In *A History of Technology*, edited by C. Singer, E. J. Holmyard, and A. R. Hall, vol. 1, pp. 684–703. Oxford: Clarenden Press.

"Alsfelder Möbelfabrik." *See* Alsfelder Möbelfabrik, below, section 4.

Amherst, Alicia [Baroness Cecil Rockley]. 1896. *A History of Gardening in England*. 2d ed. London: B. Quaritch.

"Ancient Greek Furniture Authentically Reproduced Today." *Hellenic-American Chamber of Commerce: 16th Annual Dinner*, April 17, 1964.

Andés, Louis Edgar. 1903. *Die Holzbiegerei und die Herstellung der Möbel aus gebogenem Holz*. Vienna and Leipzig: A. Hartleben's Verlag. 2d ed. rev., 1925.

Asenbaum, Paul, Peter Haiko, Herbert Lachmayer, Rainer Zettl. 1984. *Otto Wagner: Möbel und Innenräume*. Salzburg and Vienna: Residenz Verlag.

Baker, C. H. Collins. 1912. *Lely and the Stuart Portrait Painters: A Study of English Portraiture before and after Van Dyke*. 2 vols. London: Philip Lee Warner, Publisher to the Medici Society.

Bang, Ole. 1979. *Thonet: Geschichte eines Stuhls*. Stuttgart: Verlag Gerd Hatje.

Bangert, Albrecht. 1979. *Thonet-Möbel*. Munich: Heyne Bücher.

Banham, Reyner. 1960. *Theory and Design in the First Machine Age*. London: Architectural Press. 2d ed. New York: Praeger, 1967.

Baroni, Daniele. 1978. *The Furniture of Gerrit Thomas Rietveld*. Woodbury, N.Y.: Barron's.

Die Bayerische Holzindustrie. Adressbuch der Holzindustrie Bayerns und der Pfalz. Munich: Verlag E. Bosenberg, [1906].

Behal, Vera. 1981. *Möbel des Jugendstils*. Munich: Prestel-Verlag.

Benedikt, H. 1958. *Die wirtschaftliche Entwicklung in der Franz-Josef-Zeit*. Wiener Historische Studien, vol. 4. Vienna: Verlag Herold.

Benton, Charlotte. n.d. "'L'Aventure du mobilier': Le Corbusier's Furniture Designs of the 1920s." *Journal of the Decorative Arts Society 1890–1940*, no. 6.

Benton, Tim, Charlotte Benton, and Aaron Sharp. 1975a. *Design 1920s*. Milton Keynes (Bucks.), Eng.: The Open University Press.

———, Charlotte Benton, John Milner, and Aaron Sharp. 1975b. *The New Objectivity*. Milton Keynes (Bucks.), Eng.: The Open University Press.

———, Charlotte Benton, and Dennis Sharp, eds. 1975c. *Architecture and Design: 1890–1939. An International Anthology of Original Articles*. New York: Whitney Library of Design. [First published as *Form and Function: A Source Book for the History of Architecture and Design 1890–1939*. London: Crosby Lockwood Staples, in assoc. with the Open University Press, 1975.]

——— and Charlotte Benton. 1977. *The International Style*. Milton Keynes (Bucks.), Eng.: The Open University Press.

Bramwell, Martyn, ed. 1976. *International Book of Wood*. London: Mitchell Beazley Publishers Ltd./New York: Simon and Schuster.

Brandstätter, Christian. 1978. *Das Wiener Kaffeehaus*. Vienna: Molden.

Brüning, A. 1905. "Neue Arbeiten von Rudolf und Fia Wille." *Berliner Architekturwelt* 7, no. 3: 102–13.

Bobek, Hans, and Elisabeth Lichtenberger. 1966. *Wiens bauliche Gestalt und Entwicklung seit der Mitte des 19. Jahrhunderts*. Vienna and Graz: H. Böhlaus Nachf.

Boll, A. 1933. "René Herbst." *Art et Décoration* 62 (June): 161–70.

Breuer, Marcel. 1928. "Metallmöbel und moderne Räumlichkeit." *Das neue Frankfurt* 2, no. 1 (January): 11–12.

———. Marcel Breuer papers. Marcel Breuer Collection. George Arents Research Library for Special Collections, Syracuse University, New York.

Bromberg, Paul. 1931. *Het Hollandsche Interieur*. Amsterdam: Moderne Schoonheid N.V. Uitgevers-Maatschappij Kosmos, 1931.

Brown, Theodore M. 1958. *The Work of G. Rietveld, Architect*. Utrecht: A. W. Bruna & Zoon.

Buddensieg, Tillman, ed. 1979. *Industriekultur: Peter Behrens und die AEG, 1907–14*. Berlin: Mann. English edition. Cambridge, Mass.: M.I.T. Press, 1984.

"Bugholzmöbel als Stilmöbel im Rahmen moderner Architektur und Interieurs." Vienna *Jahrbuch der Gesellschaft Österreichischer Architekten* (1908): 69–72.

Campbell, Joan. 1978. *The German Werkbund*. Princeton: Princeton University Press.

Campbell-Cole, Barbie, and Tim Benton. 1979. *Tubular Steel Furniture*. London: The Art Book Company.

Candilis, G., A. Blomstedt, T. Frangoulis, and M. I. Amorin. l980. *Bugholzmöbel/Meubles en bois courbé/Bent Wood Furniture*. Stuttgart: Karl Krämer Verlag.

Caplan, Ralph. 1976. *The Design of Herman Miller*. New York: Whitney Library of Design.

Chinnery, Victor. 1979. *Oak Furniture: The British Tradition. A History of Early Furniture in the British Isles and New England*. Woodbridge, Eng.: Antique Collectors' Club.

Cowper, C. 1852. *The Building Erected in Hyde Park for the Great Exhibition of the Works of Industry of All Nations, 1851*. London.

Culetto, Kurt. 1970. *Bugholzstühle: Das Werk Michael Thonets*. Schriften des Gewerbemuseums, no. 9. Basel: Gewerbemuseum.

Davis, Alec. 1937. "Design in England 1936." *Form Svenska Slöjdföreningens Tidskrift* 33: 35–38.

Deese, Martha. Forthcoming. "Gerald Summers and Makers of Simple Furniture Ltd." Master's thesis, Parsons School of Design/ Cooper-Hewitt Museum.

Defoe, Daniel. 1962. *A Tour through the Whole Island of Great Britain (1724–26)*. Reprint. London: Dent, Everyman's Library.

De Fusco, Renato. 1977. *Le Corbusier, Designer Furniture, 1929*. Woodbury, N. Y.: Barron's.

del Marle, A. F. 1927. "Metal." *Bulletin de l'Effort Moderne*, no. 39 (November).

Dennison, Baird. 1933. "From Angles to Body Curves." *Architectural Review* 74, no. 441 (August; supplement): 71–72, 78.

Denscher, B. 1985. *Kunst und Kommerz*. Vienna: Österreichischer Bundesverlag.

Deutsch, Davida. 1975. "Samuel Gragg's Boston Bentwood Chairs, 1809." *Antiques* 107, no. 5 (May): 939.

Dieckmann, Erich. 1931. *Möbelbau in Holz, Rohr und Stahl*. Stuttgart: Julius Hoffman Verlag.

Dorotheum Auction House. 1983. *Auction Catalogue—November 15*. Vienna: Dorotheum Auction House.

Drexler, Arthur. 1973. *Charles Eames. Furniture from the Design Collection*. New York: Museum of Modern Art.

Dry, Graham, ed. 1979a. *Thonet Brothers: The 1888 Catalogue*. Munich: Verlag Dry.

———. 1979b. "Triumphzug eines zeitlosen Möbels." *Die Weltkunst* 49, no. 21 (November): 2684–85.

———, ed. 1980. *Jacob & Josef Kohn. Bugholzmöbel/Bent-wood Furniture/Meubles en bois courbé. Der Katalog von 1916*. Munich: Verlag Dry.

———. 1982. "Hans Günther Reinstein und seine 'Möbel aus Pappe.'" *Kunst in Hessen und am Mittelrhein* 22: 131-35.

———, ed. 1983. *Ungarische Bugholzmöbel um 1900. Katalog der Ungvárer Möbelfabriks-Aktiengesellschaft*. Munich: Verlag Dry.

Ducastelle, Jean Pierre. 1980. "L'Archéologie Industrielle, in, Le Patrimoine du Pays d'Ath. Un premier bilan. Catalogue de l'exposition Ath et sa région." *Etudes et documents du Cercle Royal d'Histoire et d'Archéologie d'Ath et de la Région*, vol. 2, pp. 248–53. Ath.

Dufrène, Maurice. 193l. "A Survey of Modern Tendencies in Decorative Art." In *Decorative Art: The Studio Yearbook*, edited by C. G. Holme. London: The Studio.

Eames, Penelope. 1977. *Furniture in England, France, and the Netherlands from the Twelfth Century to the Fifteenth*. Furniture History, vol. 12. London: Journal of the Furniture History Society.

Eckstein, Hans. 1977. *Der Stuhl*. Munich: Keysersche Verlagsbuchhandlung.

Edwards, Ralph. 1954. *Dictionary of English Furniture*. London: Hamlyn Publishing Corp.

Eggert, K. 1976. *Der Wohnbau der Wiener Ringstrasse im Historismus*. Die Wiener Ringstrasse, edited by R. Wagner-Rieger, vol. 7. Vienna: H. Böhlaus Nachf.

Ehmer, Joseph. 1980. *Familienstruktur und Arbeitsorganisation im frühindustriellen Wien*. Sozial- und Wirtschaftshistorische Studien, vol. 13. Vienna: Verlag für Geschichte und Politik.

Eisler, Max. 1916. *Österreichische Werkkultur*. Vienna: Kunstverlag Anton Schroll & Co.

Evans, Nancy Goyne. 1979. *A History and Background of English Windsor Furniture*. Furniture History, vol. 15. London: Journal of the Furniture History Society.

Exner, Wilhelm Franz. 1873. *Beiträge zur Geschichte der Gewerbe und Erfindungen Österreichs von der Mitte des XVIII Jahrhunderts bis zur Gegenwart*. Rohproduction und Industrie, vol. 1. Vienna: Herausgegeben von der General-Direction Wilhelm Braumüller. K. k. Hof-Buchhändler.

———. 1876. *Das Biegen des Holzes, ein für Möbel-, Wagen-, und Schiffbauer wichtiges Verfahren. Mit besonderer Rücksichtnahme auf die Thonet'sche Industrie*. Leipzig: Bernhard Friedrich Voigt.

——— and G. Lauboeck, ed. 1893. *Das Biegen des Holzes*. 3d ed. Weimar: Bernhard Friedrich Voigt. 4th ed. Leipzig: Bernhard Friedrich Voigt, 1922.

Falke, Jacob von. 1883. *Die Kunst im Hause*. 5th ed. Vienna: Druck und Verlag von Carl Gerold's Sohn. 6th ed., 1897.

Felice, Carlo A. 1933. "Le Sezioni straniere alla Triennale." *Domus* 11, no. 65 (May): 282–83.

Fenz, Werner. 1984. *Koloman Moser*. Salzburg: Residenz Verlag.

Frampton, Kenneth. 1985. *Modern Architecture, A Critical History*. Rev. ed. London: Thames & Hudson.

Frank, Edgar B. 1950. *Old French Ironwork: The Craftsman and His Art*. Cambridge: Harvard University Press.

Fünfundzwanzig Jahre Postsparkasse. 1908. Vienna: Verlag der K.K. Postsparkasse.

Galerie W. Ketterer. 1982. *Wiener Jugendstil: 60 Auktion*. (November 20). Munich: Galerie W. Ketterer.

Gebhard, David. 1983. *Josef Hoffmann: Design Classics*. Fort Worth, Tex.: The Fort Worth Art Museum.

Geest, Jan van, and Otakar Máčel. 1980. *Stühle aus Stahl. Metallmöbel 1925-1940*. Cologne: Verlag der Buchhandlung Walter König.

Giedion, Siegfried. 1948. *Mechanization Takes Command*. 1st ed. New York: Oxford University Press. 2d ed., 1975. Reprint. New York: W. W. Norton, 1969.

Goyne, Nancy A. 1964. "Francis Trumble of Philadelphia: Windsor Chair and Cabinetmaker." *Winterthur Portfolio* no. 1: 221–42.

Gräff, Werner, ed. 1928. *Innenräume*. Stuttgart: Akad. Verlag Dr. Fr. Wedekind.

———. 1933. *Jetzt wird Ihre Wohnung eingerichtet*. Potsdam: Müller & I. Kiepenheuer.

"Grafische Musterblätter." Supplement to *Die Freien Künste* (Vienna and Leipzig, ca. 1890).

Gropius, Walter, ed. 1925. *Neue Arbeiten der Bauhauswerkstätten*. Bauhaus book no. 7. Munich.

Die Groszindustrie Österreichs, Festgabe zum glorreichen 50-jährigen Regierungsjubiläum seiner Majestät des Kaisers Franz Josef I. 6 vols. Vienna: Leopold Weiss, 1898–1908.

Günther, Sonja. 1984. *Das deutsche Heim: Luxusinterieurs und Arbeitermöbel von der Gründerzeit bis zum "Dritten Reich."* Werkbundarchiv, vol. 12. Giessen: Anabas.

Hanks, David A. 1981. *Innovative Furniture in America from 1800 to the Present*. New York: Horizon Press.

Hardy, John. 1979. "The Garden Seat: 1650–1850." *Connoisseur* 201, (June): 118–23.

Heller, Hermann. [1926]. *Michael Thonet, der Erfinder und Begründer der Bugholzmöbel-Industrie*. Brünn.

Herbst, René. 1954. *Un inventeur, l'architect Pierre Chareau*. Paris: Editions du Salon des Arts Ménagers.

———. 1956. *25 années u. a. m.* Paris: Editions du Salon des Arts Ménagers.

Heskett, John. 1974. "Germany: The Industrial Applications of Tubular Steel." In *Tubular Steel Furniture*, edited by Barbie Campbell-Cole and Tim Benton, pp. 23–27. London: The Art Book Company.

Hevesi, Ludwig. 1899. "Kunst auf der Strasse." *Fremdenblatt* (May 30), Feuilleton.

———. 1902. "Die Winterausstellung im Österreichischen Museum." *Kunst und Kunsthandwerk* 2, no. 1: 1–19.

———. 1906. *Acht Jahre Secession*. Vienna: C. Konegan.

———. 1909. "Kabarett Fledermaus" (1907). In *Alktunst-Neukunst: Wien 1894–1908*, pp. 240–45. Vienna: Verlagsbuchhandlung Carl Konegan.

Himmelheber, Georg. 1973. *Biedermeiermöbel*. Düsseldorf: H. Vogel. English edition. *Biedermeier Furniture*. Translated and edited by Simon Jervis. London: Faber and Faber, 1974.

Hirth, Georg. 1882. *Das Deutsche Zimmer der Renaissance*. 2 vols. Munich and Leipzig: G. Hirth Verlag.

Hitchcock, Henry-Russell, and Philip Johnson. 1932. *The International Style: Architecture Since 1922*. New York: W. W. Norton. Reprint, with a foreword and appendix by Henry Russell Hitchcock. New York: W. W. Norton, 1966.

Hoeber, Fritz. 1913. *Peter Behrens*. Munich: Georg Müller und Eugen Rentsch.

Hoffmacher, K. n.d. *Wien und die Wiener*. Vienna.

Hoffmann, Herbert. 1930. *Modern Interiors*. London: The Studio.

Holloway, Edward Stratton. 1922. *The Practical Book of Furnishing the Small House and Apartment*. Philadelphia: J. B. Lippincott.

Holme, Charles, ed. 1906. *The Art Revival in Austria*. Special summer number. London: The Studio.

Hughes, Bernard G. 1962. "Windsor Chairs in Palace and Cottage." *Country Life* 131, no. 3403 (May): 1242–43.

Ingerman, Elizabeth A. 1963. "Personal Experiences of an Old New York Cabinetmaker." *Antiques* 84 (November): 576–80.

"IRA." 1931. *Das neue Frankfurt* 5, no. 11–12.

Johnson, Paul. 1983. *Modern Times: The World from the Twenties to the Eighties*. New York: Harper & Row.

Jourdan, Jochem. 1975. *Ferdinand Kramer. Werkkatalog 1923–1974*. Hessen: Architektenkammer Hessen.

Kane, Patricia. 1971. "Samuel Gragg: His Bentwood Fancy Chairs." *Yale University Art Gallery Bulletin* 33, no. 2 (autumn): 26–37.

Kassak, Ludwig, and László Moholy-Nagy. 1922. *Buch neue Künstler*. Vienna: Verlag I. Fischer.

Katz, Wilber, ed. 1964. *Grundfragen der Kommunikationsforschung*. Munich: Juventa.

Kiefer, Klaus. 1967. *Die Diffusion der Neuerungen. Kultursoziologie und kommunikationswissenschaftliche Aspekte der agrarsoziologischen Diffusionsforschung*. Tübingen: J. C. B. Mohr.

Killen, Geoffrey. 1980. *Ancient Egyptian Furniture*. Warminster, Eng.: Aris and Philips.

Kirk, John T. 1982. *American Furniture and the British Tradition to 1830*. New York: Alfred A. Knopf.

"Kleine Nachrichten: Die Thonet'schen gebogenen Möbel." *Kunst und Gewerbe* 18, no. 26 (1884): 223.

Kleinmayer, F. von. 1900. *Illustrierter Klagenfurter Haus- und Geschäftsadresskalender für das Gemeinjahr 1900*. Klagenfurt.

Koschler, Hans. 1982. "Möbel für Arbeiterwohnungen—Fragen der Geschmacksdiffusion im Österreich der Jahrhundertwende." Ph. D. dissertation. Vienna.

Kracauer, Siegfried. 1971. *Schriften*. 2 vols. Reprint. Frankfurt am Main: Suhrkamp Verlag.

Kraemer, Hans, ed. 1900. *Das XIX. Jahrhundert in Wort und Bild*. 4 vols. Berlin: Bong & Co.

Kramer, Ferdinand. 1929. "Die Thonetindustrie." *Die Form* 4, no. 8: 206–8.

Lachmayer, Herbert. 1984. In Asenbaum et al., pp. 65–71.

Lancaster, Osbert. 1939. *Home Sweet Homes*. London: John Murray.

Lang, L. 1965. *Das Bauhaus 1919–1933. Idee und Wirklichkeit*. Berlin: Zentralinstitut für Gestaltung.

Lauboeck, Georg. 1882. "Technische Neuheiten im Baue von Sitzmöbeln." *Mittheilungen des Technologischen Gewerbe-Museums, Section für Holzindustrie* 6, no. 29 (May 15): 65–71.

———. 1900. "Möbel aus gebogenem Holze." In *Weltausstellung Paris 1900. Katalog der Österreichischen Abtheilung* vol. 8, pp. 1–4. Vienna: Herausgegeben von dem K. K. Österreichischen General-Commissariate.

Le Corbusier. 1910–29. *Le Corbusier et Pierre Jeanneret. Oeuvre complète de 1910–1929*. Introduction and texts by Le Corbusier. Zurich: Les Editions d'Architecture (Artemis), 1964.

———. 1923. *Vers une architecture*. Paris: Editions G. Crès.

———. 1925. *Almanach d'architecture moderne. Documents, théorie, pronostics, histoire. . . .* Paris: Editions G. Crès.

———. 1926. *L'Art décoratif d'aujourd'hui*. Paris: Editions G. Crès.

———. 1927. *Towards a New Architecture*. Translation by Frederick Etchells of *Vers une architecture* (13th ed.). London: Architectural Press; New York: Payson & Clarke. Reprint. New York: Frederick A. Praeger, 1972.

Ledoux-Lebard, Denise. 1984. *Les ébénistes du XIXe siècle, 1795–1889; Leurs oeuvres et leurs marques*. Paris: Editions de l'Amateur.

Lehnert, Georg, ed. [1907–9]. *Illustrierte Geschichte des Kunstgewerbes*. 2 vols. Berlin: Verlag Martin Oldenbourg.

Leisching, Julius. 1901. "Die Zukunft des neuen Stils." *Mittheilungen des Vereins für dekorative Kunst und Kunstgewerbe*, no. 5 (January): 140–49.

Levetus, A. S. 1908. "Austrian Architecture and Decoration." *The Studio Year Book of Decorative Art* (1908): xlv–xlvi. London: Offices of The Studio.

Lodder, Christina. 1983. *Russian Constructivism*. New Haven: Yale University Press.

Logie, Gordon. 1947. *Furniture from Machines*. London: George Allen and Unwin.

The London Chair-Makers' and Carvers' Book of Prices, for Workmanship. London: Committee of Chair-Manufacturers and Journeymen, 1807.

Loos, Adolf. 1899a. "Ein Epilog zur Winterausstellung." *Die Zeit* (February 18).

———. 1899b. "Weihnachtsausstellung im Österreichischen Museum (December 18, 1899)." In Loos, *Sämtliche Schriften*, edited by Franz Glück, vol. 1. Vienna and Munich: Verlag Herold, 1962.

Lotz, Wilhelm. 1928. "Möbeleinrichtung und Typenmöbel." *Die Form* 3, no. 6: 161–69. Translated as "Suites of Furniture and Standard Furniture Designs," in Benton 1975c, pp. 229–30.

———. 1930. *Wie richte ich meine Wohnung ein?* Berlin: Verlag Hermann Reckendorf.

Loudon, John Claudius. [1846]. *Encyclopaedia of Cottage, Farm and Villa Architecture and Furniture*, revised and edited by Mrs. Loudon. London: Frederick Warne/New York: Scribner, Welford, and Armstrong.

Lux, Joseph August. 1904–5. "Der Jahresbericht der Niederösterreichischen Handels- und Gewerbekammer—Eine Entgegnung." *Hohe Warte* 1, no. 4: 75.

———. 1905. *Die Moderne Wohnung und ihre Ausstattung*. Vienna and Leipzig: Wiener Verlag.

Máčel, Otakar. 1983. "Avantgarde-Design und Justiz. Oder: Die Prozesse um den hinterbeinlosen Stuhl." In *Avant Garde und Industrie*, edited by Stanislaus von Moos and Chris Smeenk, pp. 150–62. Delft: Delft University Press.

Macquoid, Percy, and Ralph Edwards. 1924–27. *The Dictionary of English Furniture, from the Middle Ages to the Late Georgian Period*. 3 vols. London: Offices of "Country Life"; New York: Charles Scribner's. Reprint. New York: Barra Books, l983.

Rob Mallet-Stevens, Architecte. 1980. Compiled by Dominique Deshoulières and Hubert Jeanneau with the collaboration of Yvonne Brunhammer. Brussels: Editions des Archives d'Architecture Moderne.

Malkowsky, Georg, ed. 1900. *Die grossen Errungenschaften des XIX. Jahrhunderts auf den Gebieten der Industrie, Technik und des Kunstgewerbes*. Berlin.

Mang, Karl. 1969. *Das Haus Thonet*. Frankenberg: [Privately printed].

———. 1979. *History of Modern Furniture*. New York: Harry N. Abrams.

———. 1982. *Thonet Bugholzmöbel*. Vienna: Brandstätter.

Martinie, H. A. 1928. "Le XVIIe Salon des Artistes Décorateurs." *Art et Décoration* 53, no. 6 (June): 161–200.

Marzona, E. 198l. *Brüder Rasch*. Düsseldorf: Edition Marzona.

Massobrio, Giovanna, and Paolo Portoghesi. 1976. *La Seggiola di Vienna*. Turin: Martano.

———. 1980. *Casa Thonet*. Rome-Bari: Editori Laterza.

McCoy, Esther. 1985. "The Rationalist Period." In *High Styles*, pp. 130–57. New York: Whitney Museum of American Art/Summit Books.

Meier-Oberist, Edmund. 1925. *Das neuzeitliche hamburgische Kunstgewerbe in seinen Grundlagen*. Hamburg: Verlag W. Thormann.

———. 1956. *Kulturgeschichte des Wohnens*. Hamburg: Ferdinand Holzmann Verlag.

Meyer-Schönbrunn, F. 1913. *Peter Behrens*. Monographien deutscher Reklame-Künstler, 5. Hagen and Dortmund: Verlagsanstalt von Friedrich Wilhelm Ruhfus.

Miller, R. Craig. 1983. "Interior Design and Furniture." In *Design in America: The Cranbrook Vision 1925-1950*, pp. 91-143. New York: Harry N. Abrams in association with The Detroit Institute of Arts and The Metropolitan Museum.

Milner, John. 1983. *Vladimir Tatlin and the Russian Avant-Garde*. New Haven: Yale University Press.

Moholy-Nagy, László. 1947. *Vision in Motion*. Chicago: Paul Theobald.

Moos, Stanislaus von. 1979. *Le Corbusier: Elements of a Synthesis*. Cambridge, Mass.: M.I.T. Press.

Morris, William. 1893. Preface to *Arts and Crafts Essays* by members of the Arts and Crafts Exhibition Society. London: Rivington, Percival & Co.

———. 1901. "Die niederen Künste." In *Kunsthoffnungen und Kunstsorgen*. Leipzig: Seemann. Translated from the English. Morris, "The Lesser Arts." In *Hopes and Fears for Art*, pp. 1-37. London: Ellis & White/Boston: Robert Brothers, 1882.

Müller, Dorothée. 1980. *Klassiker des modernen Möbeldesign: Otto Wagner—Adolf Loos—Josef Hoffmann—Koloman Moser*. Munich: Keyser.

Müller-Wulckow, Walter. 1931. *Die deutsche Wohnung der Gegenwart*. Leipzig: Karl Robert Langewiesche Verlag.

München Stadt und Land. Munich: Herausgegeben vom Münchener Graphischen Verlag, ca. 1905.

Das Münchener Schauspielhaus. Denkschrift zur Feier der Eröffnung. Munich: Heilmann & Littmann, 1901.

"Das Münchener Schauspielhaus." *Süddeutsche Bauzeitung* 11, no. 20 (May 12, 1901): 187-89.

Muthesius, Hermann. 1905. "Das Maschinenmöbel." *Hohe Warte* 2: supplement, p.2.

"Nachruf Josef Thonet" [obituary]. *Mittheilungen des Technologischen Gewerbe-Museums, Section für Holzindustrie* 8, no. 93 (September 15): 134.

Neužil, Franz. 1887. "Die Holz-Industrie auf der galizischen Landesausstellung in Krakau 1887." *Mittheilungen des Technologischen Gewerbe-Museums, Section für Holzindustrie* 8, no. 96 (December 15): 181-86.

Newberry, Percy E. 1893. *Beni-Hasan*. Part 1. Archaeological Survey of Egypt. London: Published under the Auspices of the Egypt Exploration Fund; sold by Kean Paul, Trench, Tribner.

Occioni-Bonaffons, G., ed. [ca. 1900]. *Guida del Friuli*. Illustrazione del Comune di Udine, vol. 1. Udine: Dalla Sede della Società Alpina Friulana, Editrice.

Oerley, Robert. 1900. "Wie ein modernes Möbel ensteht." *Das Interieur* 1, no. 12 (December): 177-92.

Oberhuber, Oswald, and Julius Hummel. 1979. *Koloman Moser*. Vienna: Österreichisches Museum für angewandte Kunst.

Ostergard, Derek. 1984. *Mackintosh to Mollino*. New York: Barry Friedman.

———, and David A. Hanks. 1981. "Gilbert Rohde and the Evolution of Modern Design, 1927-1941." *Arts Magazine* 56, no. 2 (October): 98-107.

Otto, B. 1931. "Die Entwicklung der mitteleuropäischen Bugholzmöbelindustrie." Ph. D. dissertation, Erlangen.

Ozenfant, Amédée, and Charles-Edouard Jeanneret [Le Corbusier]. 1918. *Après le cubisme*. Commentaires sur l'art et la vie moderne, vol. 1. Paris: Editions des Commentaires.

Pagano, Giuseppi. 1936. *Tecnica dell'Abitazione*. Milan: Hoepli (Quaderni della Triennale).

Pallasmaa, Juhani, ed. 1984. *Alvar Aalto Furniture*. Helsinki: Museum of Finnish Architecture/Finnish Society of Crafts and Design, Artek.

Palmer. R. R. 1960. *A History of the Modern World*. 2d rev. ed. with Joel Colton. New York: Alfred A. Knopf.

Pearson, Paul David. 1978. *Alvar Aalto and the International Style*. New York: Whitney Library of Design.

Percier, Charles, and Pierre François Leonard Fontaine. 1812. *Recueil de décorations interieurs comprenant tout ce qui a rapport à l'ameublement comme vases trepieds, candélabras . . . etc*. Paris: P. Didot l'Aine.

[Perriand, Charlotte]. 1929. "Wood or Metal? A Reply to Mr. Gloag's Article in our January Issue by Charlotte Perriand Who, as Champion of New Ideas, Has Adopted an Original Style of Expressing Them." *The Studio* 4, no. 4 (April): 278-79.

Poschinger, Hyppolit Freiherr von. 1955. *350 Jahre Poschinger in Frauenau*. Passau: Passavia Verlag.

Posener, J. 1964. *Die Anfänge des Funktionalismus*. Berlin: Ullstein.

———. 1978. "Werkbund und Jugendstil." In *Der Werkbund in Deutschland, Österreich und der Schweiz*, edited by L. Burckhardt. Stuttgart: Deutsche Verlagsanstalt.

Preissecker, Rudolf von. 1910. "Kunst und Arbeiterstand." *Das Interieur* 11: 97-104.

Pritchard, Jack. 1984. *View from a Long Chair*. London: Routledge & Kegan Paul.

Pritchard Archive. University of Newcastle-upon-Tyne, England.

Prou, René. 1928. *Intérieurs au Salon des Artistes Décorateurs 1928*. Paris: Charles Moreau.

Pudor, Heinrich. 1913. *Heimbaukunst*. Wittenberg: A. Ziemsen.

Pugin, Augustus Welby Northmore. 1841. *The True Principles of Pointed or Christian Architecture*. London: J. Weale.

Rasch, Heinz. 1960. "Aus den zwanziger Jahren." *Werk und Zeit* 9, no. 11 (November): 1-3.

———, and Bodo Rasch. 1927. *Wie bauen? Bau- und Einrichtung der Werkbundsiedlung am Weissenhof in Stuttgart 1927.* Stuttgart: F. Wedekind.

Riby, Carl A. 1882. "Chiavari's Sessel-Erzeugung." *Mittheilungen des Technologischen Gewerbe-Museums, Section für Holzindustrie* 3, no. 25 (January): 1–5.

Richter, Gisela. 1966. *The Furniture of the Ancient Greeks, Etruscans and Romans.* London: Phaidon.

Röger, Eike. 1982. "Die Lauterberger Holzwirtschaft im Wandel der Zeiten." *Rund um den Hausberg. Heimatbeilage des Bad Lauterberger Tageblattes.* (Local supplement, April 24).

Rogge, Henning. "Ein Motor muss aussehen wie ein Geburtstagsgeschenk." In Buddensieg, pp. 91–126.

Rosner, Karl. 1898. "Das deutsche Zimmer im 19. Jahrhundert." Part 4 of Georg Hirth, *Das Deutsche Zimmer vom Mittelalter bis zur Gegenwart.* 2 vols. Munich and Leipzig: Georg Hirth Verlag.

Roubo, Jacques-Andre. 1771–74. *L'Art du menuisier* Part 2, *Le Menuisier Carrossier, le menuisier en meubles et le menuisier ébéniste.* Descriptions des arts et métiers . . . approuvées par MM. de l'Académie des Sciences, no. 8. Paris. Reprint. Geneva: Slatkine Reprints, 1984.

Rukschcio, Burkhardt, and Roland L. Schachel. 1982. *Adolf Loos: Leben und Werk.* Salzburg: Residenz Verlag.

[Saarinen, Eero]. 1962. *Eero Saarinen on His Work: A Selection of Buildings Dating from 1947 to 1964, With Statements by the Architect.* Edited by Aline Be. Saarinen. New Haven: Yale University Press; rev. ed. 1968.

Sandgruber, Roman. 1982. "Die Anfänge der Konsumgesellschaft— Konsumgüterverbrauch, Lebensstandard und Alltagskultur in Österreich im 18. und 19. Jahrhundert." In *Sozial- und Wirtschaftshistorische Studien* vol. 15. Vienna: Verlag für Geschichte und Politik.

Sax, Emil. 1869. *Die Wohnungszustände der arbeitenden Classen und ihre Reform.* Vienna: Druck und Verlag von M. Bichler Witwe & Sohn.

Schildt, Goran, ed. 1978. *Alvar Aalto Sketches.* Translated by Stuart Wrede. Cambridge, Mass.: M.I.T. Press.

———. 1984. "The Decisive Years." In Pallasmaa, pp. 62–89.

Schölermann, W. 1900. "In Wien wurde kürzlich ein neues Caféhaus eröffnet." *Kunst und Handwerk* 50, no. 5 (February): 168–69.

———. 1907. "Ludwig Paffendorf, Cöln: Sein Wollen und Werden." *Innen-Dekoration* 18 (September): 261–73.

Schuldt, Jr., Hermann. 1881. "Über amerikanische Holzfournier-Sitze." *Kunst und Gewerbe* 15, no. 6: 43–47.

Schweiger, Werner. 1979. "Die Architekten: Gustav Siegel." In Vienna 1979, *see* below, section 4.

Seeger, Mia. 1931. *Der neue Wohnbedarf.* Stuttgart: Julius Hoffmann.

Sekler, Eduard F. 1985. *Josef Hoffmann: The Architectural Work. Monograph and Catalogue of Works.* Translated by the author.

Catalogue translated by John Maass. Princeton: Princeton University Press.

Semper, Gottfried. 1878–79. *Der Stil in den technischen und tektonischen Künsten.* 2 vols. 2d ed. Munich: Friedrich Bruckmann.

Sheraton, Thomas. 1791–94. *The Cabinet-Maker and Upholsterer's Drawing Book.* Reprint. New York: Praeger, 1970.

Silbermann, Alphons, and Udo Krüger. 1973. *Soziologie der Massenkommunikation.* Stuttgart, Berlin, Cologne, and Mainz: Kohlhammer.

Šimoníková, Jaromíra. 1985. "Ohýbaný nábytek severočeskeho původu (Bent-wood furniture of Northern Bohemia)." *Umění* (Prague) 33, no. 3: 243–52.

Sparkes, Ivan. 1977. *The English Country Chair. An Illustrated History of Chairs and Chairmaking.* 2d ed. Edinburgh (Bucks.), Eng.: Spurbooks, Ltd.

Spemanns Goldenes Buch vom eignen Heim. Berlin and Stuttgart: Verlag von W. Spemann, 1905.

Stam, Mart. 1926. "ABC I." In Benton and Benton 1977.

———. 1935. "De Stoel gedurende de lartste 40 jaar." *De 8 en Opbouw* (Amsterdam).

Sternberger, D. 1939. *Panorama oder Ansichten vom 19. Jahrhundert.* Hamburg: Claussen Verlag. Reprint,1955.

Stritzler, Nina. 1985. "Charlotte Perriand and the Development of the Corbusian Program for *Equipement de l'Habitation.*" Master's thesis, Parsons School of Design/Cooper Hewitt Museum.

Switzer, Stephen. 1718. *Ichonographia Rustica, or, The Nobleman, Gentleman, and Gardener's Recreation.* 3 vols. London.

Symonds, R. W. 1955. *Furniture Making in Seventeenth and Eighteenth Century England. An Outline for Collectors.* London: The Connoisseur.

"Die thermoplastischen Erzeugnisse von Carl Wittkowsky in Berlin." *Mittheilungen des Technologischen Gewerbe-Museums, Section für Holzindustrie* 8, no. 85 (January 15, 1887): 1–7.

The Thirties. London: Victoria & Albert Museum, 1979.

Thonet, Michael. 1896. *Ein Gedenkblatt aus Anlass der hundertsten Wiederkehr seines Geburtstages. Von seinen Söhnen und Enkeln, 2 Juli 1896.* Vienna: [Privately printed].

Thornton, Peter K., and Maurice F. Tomlin. 1980. *The Furnishing and Decoration of Ham House.* Furniture History, vol. 16. London: Journal of the Furniture History Society.

Thurneyssen, Fritz. 1897. *Das Münchener Schreinergewerbe: Eine wirtschaftliche und sociale Studie.* Münchener Volkswirtschaftliche Studien, vol. 21. Stuttgart: Verlag der J. G. Cotta'schen Buchhandlung.

Ulrich, Conrad, ed. 1964. *Programs and Manifestoes on 20th Century Architecture.* Cambridge, Mass.: M.I.T. Press.

Vellay, Marc, and Kenneth Frampton. 1984. *Pierre Chareau.* Paris: Editions du Regard.

Verarbeitung der Faserstoffe. Das Buch der Erfindungen, Gewerbe und Industrien, vol. 8. 9th ed. Leipzig: Verlag von Otto Spamer, 1898.

["Die verschiedenen Zeichnungen der Möbel der Firma Jacob & Josef Kohn"]. In "Zu unseren Illustrationen," *Innen-Dekoration* 12 (June 1901): 102–3.

Viaux, Jacqueline. 1962. *Le Meuble en France.* Paris: Presses universitaires de France.

Wagner, Otto. 1895. *Moderne Architektur: Seinen Schülern ein Führer auf diesem Kunstgebiet.* Vienna. 4th ed. retitled *Die Baukunst unserer Zeit: Dem Baukunstjünger ein Führer auf diesem Gebiet.* Vienna: A. Schroll, 1914. Reprint. Vienna: Locker Verlag, 1979.

Warnke, M. 1979. "Zur Situation der Couchecke." In *Stichworte zur geistigen Situation der Zeit,* edited by Günther Busch, vol. 2. Frankfurt am Main: Suhrkamp Verlag.

Weber-Kellerman, I. 1979. "Die Gute Kinderstube." In *Wohnen im Wandel,* edited by L. Niethammer. Wuppertal: Peter Hammer.

Wessely, Emil. 1888. "Die Nordische Ausstellung in Kopenhagen." *Mittheilungen des Technologischen Gewerbe-Museums, Section für Holzindustrie* 9, no. 108 (December 15): 180.

Westheim, Paul. 1910. "Das Kerkau-Café von Bruno Paul." *Innen-Dekoration* 21 (October): 369–77.

Wichmann, Hans. 1985. *Industrial Design, Unikate, Serienerzeugnisse: Die Neue Sammlung; Ein neuer Museumstyp des 20. Jahrhunderts.* Munich: Prestel-Verlag.

Wilk, Christopher. 1980a. *Thonet: 150 Years of Furniture.* Woodbury, N. Y.: Barron's.

————. 1980b. *Thonet Bentwood & Other Furniture: The 1904 Illustrated Catalogue, with the 1905-6 and 1907 Supplements.* Introduction by Christopher Wilk. New York: Dover Publications.

————. 1981. See New York 1981b.

Willett, John. 1978. *The New Sobriety: Art and Politics in the Weimar Period 1917-1933.* London: Thames & Hudson.

Wingler, Hans M. 1976. *The Bauhaus.* Cambridge, Mass.: M.I.T. Press.

Witt-Dörring, Christian. 1979. "Die Wohnraumgestaltung des Biedermeier. Das Wiener Interieur 1815-1848." *Alte und Moderne Kunst* 165: 1–7.

Wood, Andrew Dick. 1963. *Plywoods of the World.* Edinburgh and London: W. & A. K. Johnson & G. W. Bacon.

Ypserle de Strihou, Anne van, and Paul. 1970. *Laken: Een Huis voor Keizer en Koning.* Brussels: Arcade.

Zweig, Marianne. 1924. *Zweites Rokoko. Innenräume und Hausrat in Wien 1830-1860.* Vienna: Kunstlerverlag Anton Schroll.

3 Exhibition catalogues and related publications

Entries listed here are arranged alphabetically by city and date of exhibition; unless otherwise indicated, the city and date of the publication are the same as those of the exhibition.

Alsfeld 1895
Catalog der oberhessischen Industrie- und Gewerbe-Ausstellung zu Alsfeld 1895.

Antwerp 1885a
Exposition universelle d'Anvers 1885. Catalogue officiel général vol. 2.

————— 1885b
"Die Holz-Industrie auf der Internationalen Ausstellung in Antwerpen." *Mittheilungen des Technologischen Gewerbe-Museums* 6, no. 71 (November 15, 1885): 162–64.

Barcelona 1929
Exposición Internacional de Barcelona. Guía oficial.

Basel 1929
Typenmöbel. Gewerbemuseum.

Berlin 1930
Bau-Ausstellung. Catalogue.

Brussels 1910a
Breuer, Robert. *Deutschlands Raumkunst und Kunstgewerbe auf der Weltausstellung Brüssel 1910.* Stuttgart: Julius Hoffmann.

————— 1910b
Stoffers, G. *Deutschland in Brüssel 1910: Die deutsche Abteilung der Weltausstellung Brüssel 1910.* Berlin: G. Stilke.

Chicago 1893
Columbische Weltausstellung in Chicago 1893. Amtlicher Katalog des deutschen Reiches. Berlin: Reichsdruckerei.

Cleveland 1971
Pillsbury, Edmund P. *Florence and the Arts: Five Centuries of Patronage. Florentine Art in Cleveland Collections.* Cleveland Museum of Art.

Cologne 1914a
Jahrbuch des Deutschen Werkbundes 1915. Deutsche Form im Kriegsjahr: Die Ausstellung Köln 1914. Text by Peter Jessen. Munich: F. Bruckmann, 1915.

————— 1914b
Offizieller Katalog der deutschen Werkbund-Ausstellung Cöln 1914. Cologne and Berlin: Rudolf Mosse.

Darmstadt 1908
Illustrierter Katalog der hessischen Landesausstellung für freie und angewandte Kunst. Herausgegeben von der Geschäftsleitung.

————— 1914a
Koch, Alexander. "Ausstellung der Darmstädter Künstler-Kolonie 1914." *Deutsche Kunst und Dekoration* 34, no. 10 (July 1914): 241–71.

————— 1914b
Offizieller Katalog. Die Darmstädter Künstlerkolonie Ausstellung 1914.

————— 1976
Ein Dokument deutscher Kunst: Darmstadt 1901-1976. 5 vols. Hessisches Landesmuseum/Kunsthalle/Mathildenhöhe.

Delft 1975
Metalen Buisstoelen 1925-1940. Stedelijk Museum 'Het Prinsenhof'.

Dresden 1906
Offizieller Katalog der III. deutschen Kunstgewerbeausstellung, Dresden, 1906. 3d ed. Verlag und Druck von Wilhelm Baensch.

——— 1911
Offizieller Katalog der Internationalen Hygiene Ausstellung. Berlin: Verlag von Rudolf Mosse [1911].

Glasgow 1901
Official Guide and Catalogue of the Glasgow International Exhibition.

Hamburg 1869a
Industrie- und Gewerbe-Ausstellung von Erzeugnissen des Hamburgischen Gewerbefleisses.

——— 1869b
Catalog der Internationalen Gartenbau-Ausstellung in Hamburg 1869.

——— 1977
Jedding, H., et al., eds. *Historismus in Hamburg und Norddeutschland.* Hamburg: Museum für Kunst und Gewerbe.

Hannover 1878a
Knoevenagel and Haarmann, eds. *Hannoversche Gewerbe-Ausstellungs-Zeitung*, nos. 1–27. Verlag Brandes.

——— 1878b
Officieller Katalog der allgemeinen Gewerbe-Ausstellung der Provinz Hannover für das Jahr 1878. Verlag Schmorl und von Seefeld.

Helsinki 1932
"Nordic Building Exhibition." *Domus* (April).

Karlsruhe 1982
Zum Beispiel Stühle: Ein Streifzug durch die Kulturgeschichte des Sitzens. Giessen: Anabas, 1982.

Kassel 1870a
"Allgemeine Industrie-Ausstellung für das Gesammtgebiet des Hauswesens in Kassel: I. Möbel." *Kunst und Gewerbe* 4, no. 32 (August 6), pp. 249–52.

——— 1870b
Catalog der Allgemeinen Industrie-Ausstellung für das Gesammtgebiet des Hauswesens in Cassel. Druck von Gebrüder Gotthelft.

——— 1870c
Führer durch die Allgemeine Industrie-Ausstellung. Druck und Verlag von Fr. Scheel.

Leipzig 1897
Kleinpaul, Dr. Johannes, ed. *Officieller Katalog der Sächsisch-Thüringischen Industrie- und Gewerbe- Ausstellung, Leipzig 1897.* Verlag von G. L. Daube.

——— 1913
Internationale Baufach Ausstellung, Leipzig 1913. Offizieller Katalog. 2d ed. C. F. Müller Verlag.

London 1851a
The Art-Journal Illustrated Catalogue. The Industry of All Nations. London: James S. Virtue.

——— 1851b
Exhibition of the Works of Industry of All Nations, 1851. Report by Juries. London: Royal Commission.

——— 1862a
The Art-Journal Illustrated Catalogue of the International Exhibition 1862. London: James S. Virtue.

——— 1862b
International Exhibition 1862. Medals and Honourable Mentions Awarded by the International Juries. 2d ed.

——— 1862c
International Exhibition 1862. Official Catalogue of the Industrial Department. 3d ed.

——— 1862d
Beeg, Dr. "30 Klasse. Hausgeräth und Tapezierer-Arbeiten. . . ." *Amtlicher Bericht über die Industrie- und Kunst-Ausstellung zu London im Jahre 1862. . . .* vol. 2, pp. 1–50. Berlin: Verlag der Königlichen Geheimen Ober-Hofbuchdruckerei (R. v. Decker), 1863.

——— 1862e
Markert, H. M. "Classe XXX. Möbel und Tapezierarbeiten. . . ." In *Österreichischer Bericht über die internationale Ausstellung in London 1862*, edited by Joseph Arenstein, pp. 590–95. Vienna: Aus der Kaiserlich-Königlichen Hof- und Staatsdruckerei, 1863.

——— 1884
International Health Exhibition London 1884. Official Catalogue. 2d ed.

——— 1968
50 Years Bauhaus. Royal Academy of Arts/Toronto: Art Gallery of Ontario, 1969.

——— 1970
Modern Chairs 1918–1970. Exhibition arranged by the Circulation Department of the Victoria & Albert Museum. Whitechapel Gallery/Boston: Boston Book and Art Publisher, 1971.

——— 1972
The Age of Neo-Classicism. The Fourteenth Exhibition of the Council of Europe. Arts Council of Great Britain.

——— 1979
Edger, Gerhart. *Vienna in the Age of Schubert: The Biedermeier Interior 1815–1848.* Elron Press Ltd. and The Victoria & Albert Museum.

Los Angeles 1976
Connections: The Work of Charles and Ray Eames. University of California, F. S. Wight Art Gallery.

Mainz 1842
Rössler, Hektor. *Ausführlicher Bericht über die von dem Gewerbeverein für das Grossherzogtum Hessen im Jahre 1842 veranstaltete Allgemeine deutsche Industrie-Ausstellung zu Mainz.* Darmstadt: Gedruckt bei C. W. Leske. In Commission bei Gustav Jonghans, 1843.

Melbourne 1880
Weltausstellung in Melbourne 1880. Deutsche Abtheilung. Verzeichniss der Aussteller. Berlin: Gedruckt in der Reichsdruckerei.

Milan 1933
Esposizione internazionale della Arti decorative ed industriali moderne, Triennale.

Munich 1854a
Katalog der Allgemeinen Deutschen Industrie-Ausstellung zu München im Jahre 1854. Gemeinschaftlich gedruckt von G. Franz, W. Pössenbacher, Wtw., J. Rösl, C. R. Schurich, J. G. Weiss, and Dr. Wild, Wtw.

——— 1854b
Bericht der Beurtheilungs-Commission bei der allgemeinen deutschen Industrie-Ausstellung zu München im Jahre 1854. Verlag von Georg Franz, 1855.

——— 1854c
Jonák, Eberhard A. *Bericht über die allgemeine deutsche Industrie-Ausstellung zu München im Jahre 1854.* Prague: J. G. Calve'sche Buchhandlung. F. Tempsky, 1855.

——— 1854d
Steinbeis, Dr. von. "Gruppe X, Holzwaaren." In Hermann, Fr. B. W. von, ed. *Bericht der Beurtheilungs-Commission bei der allgemeinen deutschen Industrie-Ausstellung zu München im Jahre 1854,* pp. 1–150. Verlag von Georg Franz, 1855.

——— 1869
Catalog der Lokal-Industrie-Ausstellung. Druck der G. Franz'schen Buchdruckerei.

——— 1898
Offizieller Katalog der Münchener Jahres-Ausstellung 1898 im kgl. Glaspalast. 3d ed. Verlag der Münchener Künstlergenossenschaft.

——— 1908a
Amtlicher Katalog der Ausstellung "München 1908." Verlag von Rudolf Mosse.

——— 1908b
Michel, Wilhelm. "Die Ausstellung München 1908." *Die Kunst* 18, no. 11, (July 10): 425–84; same as *Dekorative Kunst* 11, no. 10 (July 10): 425–84.

——— 1909
Katalog der deutschen Brauerei-Ausstellung, München. Verlag von Rudolf Mosse.

——— 1910
Katalog für die Ausstellung Bemalter Wohnräume, München, 1910. Herausgegeben von der Ausstellungsleitung.

——— 1979.
Gebogenes Holz. Museum Villa Stuck. *See* Vienna 1979.

——— 1981a
Richter, Wolfgang. *Josef Hoffmann und sein Kreis: Möbel 1900–1930.* Galerie Alt Wien.

——— 1981b
Dry, Graham. "Josef Hoffmann and His Circle. Furniture 1900–30." *The Burlington Magazine* (April 1981): 262, fig. 84.

——— 1982a
Hoh-Slodczyk, Christine. "'Kunststadt' und Künstlervilla." In *Franz Stuck 1863–1928,* pp. 21–36. Museum Villa Stuck.

——— 1982b
Richard Riemerschmid. Vom Jugendstil zum Werkbund: Werke und Dokumente. Edited by Winfried Nerdinger. Munich: Münchner Stadtmuseum/Nürnberg: Germanisches Nationalmuseum. Prestel-Verlag, 1982.

New Haven 1982
Hewitt, Benjamin A., Patricia E. Kane, and Gerald W. R. Ward. *The Work of Many Hands: Card Tables in Federal America 1790–1820.* Yale University Art Gallery.

New York 1938a
McAndrew, John. *Alvar Aalto.* Museum of Modern Art.

——— 1938b
Bauhaus 1919–1928. Edited by Herbert Bayer, Walter Gropius, Ise Gropius. Museum of Modern Art.

——— 1941
Noyes, Eliot F. *Organic Design in Home Furnishings.* Museum of Modern Art.

——— 1947
Johnson, Philip. *Ludwig Mies van der Rohe.* Museum of Modern Art.

——— 1977
Glaeser, Ludwig. *Ludwig Mies van der Rohe. Furniture and Furniture Drawings from the Design Collection and the Mies van der Rohe Archive.* Museum of Modern Art.

——— 1982
McFadden, David Revere, ed. *Scandinavian Modern Design 1880–1980.* Cooper-Hewitt Museum/Harry N. Abrams Inc.

——— 1981a
Josef Hoffmann: Architect and Designer. Galerie Metropol.

——— 1981b
Wilk, Christopher. *Marcel Breuer: Furniture and Interiors.* Introduction by J. Stewart Johnson. Museum of Modern Art.

——— 1984
Johnson, J. Stewart. *Alvar Aalto: Furniture and Glass.* Museum of Modern Art.

Nürnberg 1896
Offizieller Katalog. Bayerische Jubiläums-, Landes-, Industrie-, Gewerbe- und Kunstausstellung.

Paris 1855
Beeg, Dr. "26 Klasse. Möbel und Dekorations-Gegenstände." In *Amtlicher Bericht über die allgemeine Pariser Ausstellung . . . im Jahre 1855,* edited by Dr. G. von Viebahn and Dr. Schubarth, pp. 608–49. Berlin, 1856.

——— 1878a
Stockbauer, J. "Von der Pariser Ausstellung." *Kunst und Gewerbe* 13 (1879): 100.

——— 1878b
International Exhibition, Paris 1878: Catalogue of the Austrian Section. Vol. 3. Vienna: K. k. Central Commission in Vienna for the World Exhibition in Paris, 1878. Vienna: n.d.

——— 1878c
Katalog der Pariser Weltausstellung, Österreichische Abteilung. Vienna: n.d.

——— 1889
Exposition universelle internationale de 1889 à Paris. Catalogue général. Vol. 3. Lille: Imprimerie L. Danel.

——— 1900
Poppenberg, F. "Das Kunstgewerbe auf der Pariser Weltausstellung." In *Das XIX. Jahrhundert in Wort und Bild*, edited by Hans Kraemer, vol. 4, pp. 233–60. Berlin: Bong & Co.

——— 1900b
Weltausstellung Paris 1900. Katalog der Österreichischen Abtheilung. Ausschmückung der Wohnstätten, vol. 8. Vienna.

——— 1925
Exposition internationale des arts décoratifs et industriels modernes. Catalogue général officiel. Imprimerie de Vaugirard.

——— 1979
Paris-Moscou. Centre Georges Pompidou.

——— 1982
Léger et l'esprit moderne/Léger and the Modern Spirit. Musée d'Art Moderne de la Ville de Paris/Houston, Tex.: Museum of Fine Arts/Geneva: Musée Rath.

Philadelphia 1876a
Weltausstellung in Philadelphia, 1876: Katalog der Österreichischen Abtheilung. Vienna: Österreichischen Commission für die Weltausstellung in Philadelphia, [1876].

——— 1876b
Reifer, Felix and Franz Thonet. *Bericht über die Weltausstellung in Philadelphia 1876: Holzbearbeitungs-Maschinen, Die Holzindustrie*. Herausgegeben von der Österreichischen Commission für die Weltausstellung in Philadelphia, vol. 4. Vienna: Commissionsverlag von Faesy & Frick, 1877.

Solbad Hall, Switzerland, 1972
Quintern, Henry. *Thonet Stil*. Galerie St. Barbara.

Stuttgart 1928
Schneck, Adolf. *Katalog Ausstellung Der Stuhl*. Julius Hoffmann/ Städtische Ausstellungsgebäude.

Venice 1984
Le Arti a Vienna: Dalla Secessione alla caduta dell'Impero asburgico. Palazzo Grassi. Venice: Edizioni La Biennale/Milan: Realizzazione Massota Editore, [1984].

Vienna 1873a
"Die Kunstindustrie auf der Ausstellung in Wien 1873. Holzindustrie." *Kunst und Gewerbe* 7, no. 45 (1873): 353–56; no. 46: 361–63; no. 47: 369–72.

——— 1873b
Wiener Weltausstellung. Amtlicher Katalog der Ausstellung des deutschen Reiches. Berlin: Druck der königlichen geheimen Ober-Hofbuchdruckerei (R. v. Decker).

——— 1873c
Weltausstellung in Wien. Amtlicher Katalog der Aussteller . . . Österreichs. Verlag der General-Direction.

——— 1873d
Amtlicher Bericht uber die Wiener Weltausstellung im Jahre 1873. . . . Vol. 2, 2d section. Erstattet von der Centralcommission des Deutschen Reiches für die Wiener Weltausstellung. Group 8. Holzindustrie.

——— 1873e
Brinckmann, Justus. "Die Erzeugnisse der Möbeltischlerei . . ." In Vienna 1873d.

——— 1873f
France. Commission supérieure à l'Exposition universelle de Vienne, 1873 . . . Rapports. 5 vols. Paris: Imprimerie Nationale, 1875.

——— 1880
"Bericht über die niederösterreichische Gewerbe-Ausstellung in Wien 1880." *Beilage zu den Mittheilungen über Gegenstände des Artillerie- und Genie-Wesens*. Group 16. Möbel und Wohnungseinrichtungen, pp. 75–77. Verlag des Technischen und Administrativen Militär-Comités, 1881.

——— 1899
Katalog, Winter-Ausstellung, 1899/1900. K.k. Österreichisches Museum für Kunst und Industrie.

——— 1900
Wochenschrift des Niederösterreichischen Gewerbe-Vereins 61.

——— 1901
Katalog, Winter Ausstellung, 1901/02. K. k. Österreichisches Museum für Kunst und Industrie.

——— 1902
Katalog, XV. Ausstellung der Vereinigung bildender Künstler Österreichs, Secession Wien.

——— 1906
Offizieller Katalog der Allgemeinen Hygienischen Ausstellung in Wien. Verlag der Ausstellungsdirektion.

——— 1907
Katalog, Ausstellung "Das Kind." Allgemeine Ausstellung für Erziehung, Schutz und Gesamtwohl des Kindes.

——— 1908a
Kammerer, Marcel. "Die Architektur der 'Kunstschau.'" *Moderne Bauformen* 7, no. 9 (1908): 361–62, ills. pp. 363–408.

——— 1908b
Katalog der Kunstschau Wien.

——— 1908c.
Lux, Joseph August. "Kunstschau—Wien 1908." *Deutsche Kunst und Dekoration* 12, no. 5 (February 1909).

——— 1908d.
Kuzmany, Karl M. "Kunstschau Wien 1908." *Die Kunst* 18 (1908): 531, 538–4l.

——— 1909
Katalog, Internationale Kunstschau.

——— 1912a
Benotto. "Frühjahrsausstellung im Österreichischen Museum." *Das Interieur* 13, no. 8 (August): 57–63.

———— 1912b
Planer, Fritz. "Raumkunst auf der Wiener Frühjahrsausstellung des Österreichischen. Museums für Kunst und Industrie." *Deutsche Kunst und Dekoration* 16, no. 3 (December): 175–85.

———— 1913
Winter-Ausstellung, 1913/14. K. k. Österreichisches Museum für Kunst und Industrie.

———— 1979
Asenbaum, S. and J. Hummel, eds. *Gebogenes Holz: Konstruktive Entwürfe Wien 1840–1910*. Vienna: Künstlerhaus/Munich: Museum Villa Stuck. (See also Schweiger.)

———— 1981
Moderne Vergangenheit Wien 1800–1900. Künstlerhaus.

———— 1985
Edmund Moiret: Möbel und frühe Plastiken. Museum für angewandte Kunst.

Zurich 1883
Officieller Katalog der vierten Landesausstellung Zurich 1883. 3d ed. Verlag des Centralcomité der Schweiz. Landesausstellung.

4 Sales catalogues and related publications

The majority of publications below were offered by manufacturers and sellers of bent wood and metal furniture. Most are in private collections in Europe and thus unavailable to the reader. However, they are listed here for documentary purposes. They are arranged alphabetically by firm and listed chronologically; unless otherwise noted, the sales catalogue bore the same title as the name of the firm.

Alsfelder Möbelfabrik, Alsfeld
ca. 1906. *Musterbuch der Alsfelder Möbelfabrik, Gesellschaft mit beschränkter Haftung, Alsfeld*. 54 pp.
ca. 1908. Catalogue (incomplete).
1918. "Alsfelder Möbelfabrik, Gesellschaft mit beschränkter Haftung, 1893/94 bis einschliesslich 1918." Alsfeld, September 7. Typescript. Private collection.

Christian Becher, Aue, Germany
ca. 1925. Broadsheet catalogue, bent-wood and other furniture. Private collection, Munich.

Emile Cambier et Cie., Berlaimont (Nord), France
1906. Catalogue. *Fabrication française des sièges et meubles en bois courbé, Emile Cambier et Cie*. 56 pp.

L. & H. Cambier Frères, Ath, Belgium
ca. 1920. Catalogue. *Meubles de Style et Ordinaires, Emile Cambier*. 98 pp.
ca. 1925. Catalogue. *Meubles-Chaises: Emile Cambier*. 62 pp.
ca. 1936. Catalogue. *Meubles-Chaises: Usine Cambier*. 93 pp.

F. Carton-Herman, Ath, Belgium
ca. 1912. Catalogue. *Meubles en bois courbé, Articles de Café, F. Carton Herman, M. Carton Successeur*. 25 pp.
ca. 1920. Catalogue. *Album Special de Meubles en bois Courbé et Articles de café des manufactures F. Carton-Herman*. 59 pp.; price list, 4 pp.

Léon Delmée et Cie, Ath, Belgium
1925. Catalogue. Bent-Wood Furniture. 48 pp.

Dresdner Fabrik für Möbel aus massiv gebogenem Holz, A. Türpe Jr., Dresden, Germany
ca. 1904. Catalogue. VI pp. and 43 pp.
ca. 1906. Catalogue. IV pp. and 60 pp.

Erste Acherner Stuhl-Fabrik August Klar, Achern, Germany
1895–1940. Catalogues and other material relating to the production of bent-wood and other furniture. Private collection, Germany.
[1970]. *175 Jahre Meder Sitzmöbel*. Achern: [Privately printed for the firm's 175th anniversary].

Karl Fätsch, Kandel, Germany
ca. 1900. *Catalogue of Perforated and Laminated Seats*. Private collection, West Germany. 5 pp.

D. G. Fischel Sons, Niemes, Czechoslovakia
1930. *1870–1930*. Album issued on the occasion of the firm's 60th anniversary. In English, French, German, and Spanish. Private collection, West Germany.

Emile Gignez, Ath, Belgium
1952/53. "La Chaise Gignez, Anciens Ets. Pierre Gignez, 25 Rue d'Angleterre, Ath—Les Specialistes du Bois Courbé." Catalogue supplement.

H. Gruman & Cie., Poland
ca. 1920. Catalogue. *Meubles et [sic] Bois Courbés [sic]*. 17 pp.

Haltenhoff & Zeidler, Bad Lauterberg, Germany
1903. *Catalogue of bent wood and other furniture, July 1903*. Stadtarchiv Bad Lauterberg. 20 pp.

Walter Heywood Chair Company, New York
[1887]. *Catalogue of the Walter Heywood Chair Company*.

Karl Hillegeist & Co., Bad Lauterberg, Germany
ca. 1912. Catalogue of bent-wood and other furniture. Unpaged. Private collection, Göttingen.

Wenzel Hurt, Neuhausen near Dresden, Germany
[ca. 1913]. *Stuhl-Fabrik, Neuhausen, Bezirk Dresden*. Price lists, E6, 4 pp., and V6, 2 pp.

Japy Frères, Beaucourt, France
ca. 1938a. Catalogue no. 410. *Meubles en Bois Courbé Japy*. 26 pp.
ca. 1938b. Catalogue no. 701. *Meubles d'enfants*. 8 pp.

E. Kadeder, Munich, Germany
ca. 1893. Catalogue of bent-wood and other furniture. 27 pp. Private collection, Munich.

Julius Keller, K. K. Priv. Möbelfabrik, Klagenfurt, Austria
1912. *1812–1912*. Album issued on the occasion of the firm's centenary. 23 pp.

Jacob & Josef Kohn, Vienna, Austria
A list of the J. & J. Kohn catalogues in American and German company archives can be found in Wilk 1980a, pp. 140–41. Some additions to the titles listed there are:

1904. *Katalog der Firma J. u. J. Kohn* (special issue for France).

1906. Italian catalogue, 106 pp. (published in Massobrio and Portoghesi 1980, pp. 345–411).

ca. 1908. Undated catalogue, 40 pp. Private collection, Diessen, Germany.

n.d. [1909?]. *Katalog der Firma J. u. J. Kohn*. Vienna.

1911/12. *Lagersorten* (stock chairs), August. Broadsheet catalogue issued for the Cologne branch, Hohenstaufenring 27, with price list dated February 15, 1912.

1916. *Katalog der Firma J. u. J. Kohn*. Vienna. 120 pp.

Meder Sitzmöbel. *See* Erste Acherner Stuhl-Fabrik August Klar, [1970].

Mechanische Stuhlfabrik Franz Bubenhofer, Brumath, Alsace [ca. 1910]. *Mechanische Stuhlfabrik Franz Bubenhofer, Brumath i.E. Spezialität in Wirtsschaftsstühlen.* Broadsheet catalogue.

Herman Miller, Grand Rapids, Michigan
1950. Catalogue.

Mundus, Vienna, Austria
1913. *Echte Wiener Möbel, Wiener Musterbuch "S"*. September 1, excerpt distributed by J. Sommer & Co., Düsseldorf. 17 pp.

Sächsische Holzindustrie-Gesellschaft, Rabenau near Dresden, Germany
ca. 1900. *Möbel aus massiv gebogenem Holz*. Sales catalogue. 42 pp.

Fratelli Sardella, Acireale, Sicily, Italy
Pages from catalogue reproduced in Massobrio and Portoghesi 1976, p. 82, and idem 1980, pp. 74–75.

Stuhl- und Tischfabrik Friedrich Schäfer, Tübingen-Württemberg, Germany
1931. Sales catalogue. July. 16 pp. Stadtarchiv Tübingen.

J. Sommer & Co., Düsseldorf. *See* Mundus.

Albert Stoll, Waldshut, Germany
1914. *Record-Stühle Catalogue*. Unpaged. Collection Stoll AG, Waldshut.

Gebrüder Thonet, Vienna, Austria
See note at Kohn, above. Thonet catalogues are similarly found in Wilk 1980a with additions to those titles listed here:

1888. 31 pp. *See* Dry 1979a.

1895. *Gebrüder Thonet, Verkaufskatalog 1895*. 120 pp. Reprint. Frankenberg: Gebrüder Thonet, GmbH, 1980.

1904. *Gebrüder Thonet, Verkaufskatalog 1904*.

1904. *Katalog der Firma Gebrüder Thonet*.

1910. *Zentralanzieger der Firma Gebruder Thonet*, no. 27 (July 15).

1911. *Katalog der Firma Gebrüder Thonet* (Supplement III).

1911. Catalogue and 1915 Supplement. Reprinted in Candilis, pp. 169–206.

Ungvárer Möbelfabriks-Aktiengesellschaft, Ungvár, Hungary
ca. 1900. Catalogue. 77 pp. Reprint. *See* Dry 1983.

Vereinigte Möbelfabriken "Germania," Bad Lauterberg, Germany
1910–11. *Geschäftsbericht der Vereinigten Möbelfabriken "Germania" AG*. Company report, July 1, 1910–June 30, 1911.

Società Anonima "Antonio Volpe," Udine, Italy
ca. 1922. Catalogue of bent-wood furniture. 34 pp.

1936. *Listino Catalogo Generale*. 11 pp.
1938. *Catalogo Generale*. 41 pp.
1939. *Listino Catalogo Generale*. 11 pp.

Wäckerlin & Co., Catania, Sicily, Italy
Pages from catalogue reproduced in Massobrio and Portoghesi 1976, pp. 83–86, and idem 1980, pp. 69–73.

Wohnbedarf
1956. *1931–1956. 25 Jahre Wohnbedarf*. Zurich: Wohnbedarf AG.

Index

Included in this index are artists/designers, manufacturers, and furniture authorities. Numbers in superscript refer to footnotes appearing on the page indicated.

Photographic Credits

The numbers listed below refer to figures.

Arkkitehtitoimisto Alvar Aalto & Co., Helsinki: 5–56, 99C

Alessandro Alverà, Vienna: 2–5, 2–11

Dr. Paul Asenbaum, Vienna: 4–21, 4–43, 4–44, 4–45, 4–46, 4–47, 4–53

Baltimore Museum of Art: 89

Ole Bang, Lyngby, East Germany: 6–5, 6–8

R. Barberics, Diessen, West Germany: App–11, App–12, App–13, App–14

Germán Barrios, New York: 1–25, 1–26, 1–27, 1–28, 1–30

Wolfgang Bauer, Vienna: 3–12

Dr. Geoffrey Beard, Bath, England: 1B, 11A

Biblioteca Comunale "V. Joppi", Udine, Italy: 3–46

Michael Bleichfeld, Hialeah, Florida: 105, 106, 107, 5–65

British Museum, London: 1–2

Brooklyn Museum: 69, 73A, 77, 1–45, 1–46, 5–6

Bundes Denkmalant, Vienna: 6–1

Bundes-Mobilien-Verwaltung, Vienna: 2–8

Joan Burgasser Design/Marketing Associates, York, Pennsylvania: 4C, 35A, 49C, 81C, 66C, 5–17, 5–18, 5–19

Richard Cheek, Belmont, Massachusetts: 3A

Christie Manson Woods, London: 1–4

Christie Manson Woods, New York: 1–22

Cleveland Museum of Art: 43, 49B, 1–14, 1–15

Cooper-Hewitt Museum, The Smithsonian Institution's National Museum of Design, New York: 1–7

Maria Cornelius, Bad Lauterberg, West Germany: 3–38

Danske Kunstindustrimuseum, Copenhagen: 1–6

Gerhard Döring, Dresden, East Germany: 7A, 3–17

Dr. Beate Dry-von Zezschwitz, Munich: 62A, 3–1, 3–3, 3–4, 3–5, 3–6, 3–7, 3–8, 3–9, 3–10, 3–11, 3–15, 3–16, 3–20, 3–21, 3–22, 3–23, 3–24, 3–25, 3–26, 3–27, 3–28, 3–29, 3–30, 3–31, 3–32, 3–33, 3–34, 3–35, 3–36, 3–37, 3–39, 3–40, 3–41, 3–42, 3–43, 3–44, 3–45, 3–47, App-1, App-3, App-4, App-6, App-7, App-9, App-10

Jean-Pierre Ducastelle, Ath, Belgium: App–8

The Office of Charles and Ray Eames, Venice, California: 5–77

Penelope Eames, Chichester, West Sussex, England: 1–8, 1–9, 1–10, 1–11, 1–12

Barry Friedman, Ltd., New York (Stuart Friedman): 49A, 99B, 105A, 105B, 109B, 111A, 5–73

Gebrüder Thonet, Frankenberg, West Germany: 2–4, 2–21, 2–23, 6–2, 6–6, 6–7

Photoatelier Gerlach, Vienna: 6–10, 6–12

Sophie-Renate Gnamm, Munich: 4, 4B, 5, 6, 6A, 7, 8, 9, 10, 12, 13B, 14, 14A, 14B, 15, 15A, 16, 16A, 17, 18, 22, 23, 24A, 26, 27, 28, 29, 33, 35, 37, 39, 40, 41, 42, 44, 45, 46, 46B, 47, 48, 49, 50, 50B, 51, 52, 54, 55, 57, 59, 60, 61, 62, 63, 65, 81, 85, 86, 95, 96, 96A, 98, 101, 1–21, 1–42, 2–6, 2–9, 2–13, 2–19, 3–13, 5–21, 5–24, 5–71, App-2, App-5

Richard P. Goodbody, New York: 1, 2, 11, 25, 31, 38, 53, 56, 58, 64, 66, 67, 67B, 70, 71, 71A, 72, 72A, 73, 74, 75, 75B, 76, 78, 78A, 79, 80, 83, 83B, 83C, 84, 87, 88, 90, 92, 99D, 102, 106A, 110, 112, 112B, 114, 115, 1–20, 1–36, 1–43, 1–44, 5–13, 5–16, 5–20, 5–46, 5–76

Archiv Oswald Haerdtl, Vienna: 6–9

David A. Hanks & Associates, New York: 81B, 102A, 102B, 1–51

Helga Photo Studio, Upper Montclair, New Jersey: 19, 20, 20A

Robert Keil, Vienna: 6–4

Robert E. Kinnaman, New York: 1–41

Kunstgewerbemuseum Staatliche Museen Preussischer Kulturbesitz, West Berlin: 94

Kunsthandlung Ritthaler, Diessen, West Germany: 54B

Metropolitan Museum of Art, New York: 1A, 1–3, 1–5, 1–13, 1–16, 1–19, 1–23, 1–24, 1–32, 1–34, 1–37

Lucia Moholy, Zurich: 5–7

Müncher Stadtmuseum, Fotomuseum, Munich: 3–2

Musée des Arts Décoratifs de Montréal: 48A, 109, 113, 118

Museum of Applied Arts, Helsinki (Rauno Träskelin): 99, 100, 103, 104, 5–52

Museum of Fine Arts, Boston: 3, 3B, 116, 117, 119, 119A, 1–39, 1–40, 5–79, 5–80

Museum für Kunst und Kulturgeschichte der Hansestadt Lübeck, West Germany: 3–18, 3–19

Museum of Modern Art, New York: 35B (V. Parker), 68A, 69A, 70A, 70B, 73B (J. Welling), 76A, 83A, 84A, 85A, 99A (K. Keller), 103A, 5–2, 5–4, 5–10, 5–15, 5–26 (V. Parker), 5–31, 5–32, 5–33, 5–40, 5–47, 5–48, 5–49 (J. Welling), 5–51, 5–53, 5–55, 5–58, 5–59, 5–60, 5–61 (K. Keller), 5–68, 5–74, 5–75, 5–78

Old Sturbridge Village, Massachusetts (Henry E. Peach): 1–38

Österreichisches Museum für angewandte Kunst, Vienna: 4–2, 4–14, 4–25, 4–29, 4–30, 4–33, 4–41

Österreichisches Postsparkasse, Vienna: 4–49

Philadelphia Museum of Art: 101B

Aarne Pietinen: 101A

Private Collection, New York: 5–1, 5–8, 5–9, 5–14, 5–23, 5–27, 5–28, 5–29, 5–30, 5–34, 5–37, 5–38, 5–39, 5–42, 5–43, 5–50, 5–54, 5–57, 5–62, 5–63, 5–67, 5–69, 5–70

Toni Schneiders, Lindau, West Germany: 91

Smithsonian Institution, Washington, D.C.: 4A

Sotheby Parke Bernet, New York: 50A, 109A, 5–35

John Sparks Ltd., London: 1–52

Stedelijk Museum, Amsterdam: 68, 97

Stanek & True, Des Moines, Iowa: 21, 21A, 1–48, 1–49

Martin Stoll GmbH, Waldshut-Tiengen, West Germany: 3–48

Technisches Museum für Industrie und Gewerbe, Vienna: 2–20, 2–22

U.S. Department of Commerce, Patent and Trademark Office, Washington, D.C.: 1–46, 1–50

Alexander von Vegesack, Düsseldorf: 13, 24, 30, 32, 34, 57, 82, 93, 108, 111, 2–2, 2–11

Victoria & Albert Museum, South Kensington, London: 1–17, 5–41

Welsh Folk Museum, St. Fagans. National Museum of Wales: 1–18

Henry Francis du Pont Winterthur Museum, Winterthur, Delaware: 1–33; Museum Library, Collection of Printed Books: 23A, 75A

Wissenschaftlich-Kulturelles Zentrum, Bauhaus, Dessau, East Germany: 67A

Yale University Art Gallery, New Haven, Connecticut: 1–29, 1–31

The American Federation of Arts